Journalism

Who, What, When, Where, Why and How

James Glen Stovall

Emory and Henry College
Professor Emeritus, University of Alabama

PEARSON

Boston   New York   San Francisco
Mexico City   Montreal   Toronto   London   Madrid   Munich   Paris
Hong Kong   Singapore   Tokyo   Cape Town   Sydney

Executive Editor: Karon Bowers
Series Editor: Molly Taylor
Series Editorial Assistant: Michael Kish
Senior Marketing Manager: Mandee Eckersley
Editorial Production Administrator: Anna Socrates
Editorial-Production Service: Omegatype Typography, Inc.
Composition and Prepress Buyer: Linda Cox
Manufacturing Buyer: JoAnne Sweeney
Cover Administrator: Linda Knowles
Interior Design: Carol Somberg
Electronic Composition: Omegatype Typography, Inc.

For related titles and support materials, visit our online catalog at www.ablongman.com.

Between the time Web site information is gathered and then published, it is not unusual for some sites to have closed. Also, the transcription of URLs can result in unintended typographical errors. The publisher would appreciate notification where these errors occur so that they may be corrected in subsequent editions.

Library of Congress Cataloging-in-Publication Data

Stovall, James Glen.
    Journalism : who, what, when, where, why, and how / James Glen Stovall.
        p. cm.
    Includes bibliographical references and index.
    ISBN 0-205-37204-X (alk. paper)
    1. Journalism. I. Title.
PN4731.S697 2005
070.4—dc22

                                          2004054801

Printed in the United States of America

10   9   8   7   6   5   4   3   2   1   09   08   07   06   05   04

This book is dedicated to

Sally and Jeff

Contents

Section Two   **Where**

Chapter 4

Newspapers   **56**

Chapter 7

News Web Sites

116

Section *Three*   Who and How

Chapter 11

Style

195

Chapter 12

Editors   **210**

Chapter 13

Editing and Headline Writing   **222**

Chapter 14

Visual Journalists
246

Publication and Web Site Design

Section **Four**   **When**

Chapter 26

Journalism: Present and Future   **478**

Preface

Journalists tell us about ourselves.

In doing so, they perform a role that is not just important but vital for our society. The information they provide gives us context for our personal world and a connection to a larger environment. That information helps us make decisions, from the mundane (whether or not to carry an umbrella because of the threat of rain) to the cosmic (where to get an education, what career to choose). None of these parts of our lives could be complete if we lacked the information provided to us by journalists.

Certainly, we get information from many sources besides journalism—friends, family, books, movies, bulletin boards, and so on—but journalism reaches across these other sources to provide information that helps us weave what we hear and read together. Journalism, directly or indirectly, touches every part of our lives. Wherever you are and whatever you are doing at the moment has been influenced by the work of a journalist.

Not only does journalism affect us personally, but it also has a profound effect on the society that we live in. This effect takes form at many levels and in all aspects of society—political, social, economic, and so on. Journalism determines not only how we see ourselves within a larger environment, but it also determines how we share that environment with other people. Journalism is especially important to American society, in which there is a tradition of access to information and the exchange of facts, opinions, and ideas. That exchange cannot take place without journalism.

That's why it is important to learn about journalism, whether or not you view it as a potential profession. This book, an introduction to the field of journalism, has a variety of purposes:

- to make you a critical consumer of the mass media
- to help you understand how news is produced and delivered
- to provide you with information about how news organizations work
- to give you some understanding about how audiences react to and interact with the news media
- to teach you the traditions and conventions that govern the culture of journalism
- to explore the possibilities for the future of journalism

For those who do view journalism as a possible career, this book describes the range of job possibilities and media in which you might work. It also gives you an overview of the rich history of journalism in America.

Finally, this book is designed to offer some practical, basic instructions in some of the major functions of journalism: reporting, writing, editing, and designing. The conventions and concepts of journalism are described here in some detail, and the book provides a means of getting started.

Viewed either as a career or simply an area of study, journalism is an exciting and important field that everyone should know and understand. This book, I hope, will provide a basis for that understanding.

As with any work of this type, many people contributed information and ideas along the way. I have been involved with journalism in one form or another for nearly forty years (beginning with my work on my high school newspaper), and I have been fortunate in encountering people who were willing to share, teach, and train.

My colleagues and students at the University of Alabama, where I taught for twenty-five years, were always available with ideas and encouragement. In particular, they include Ed Mullins, Bailey Thomson, David Sloan, Kim Bissell, Pat Cotter, George Daniels, Cully Clark, Joe Phelps, Yorgo Pasadeos, and Charles Self (now at the University of Oklahoma). Carol Olive, Cecilia Hammond, and Cheryl Parker have always been generous with their help and support.

Jacy Douglas helped in putting together this manuscript by getting in touch with a number of professional journalists whose stories I was able to use. Among them are Greg Screws, Wendy Fontaine, and Nora Shoptaw.

My former student, David Mattingly, a CNN correspondent, generously provided me with the story of his September 11 adventure (see the beginning of Chapter 1). Other former students, Garrett Lane and Jennifer Ackerman Edwards, contributed essays for this book. John Taylor, yet another former student, got his brain picked for many ideas along the way.

My newspaper experience includes stints with the *Bristol (Tennessee-Virginia) Herald Courier,* the *Knoxville News-Sentinel,* the *Birmingham News,* the *Tuscaloosa News,* and most recently the *Chicago Tribune.* I have friends at all of those places, particularly at the *Tribune* where Stacy Sweat, Steven Layton, Tony Majeri, and Bill Parker taught me much. Former *Tribune* colleagues who were always helpful are Celeste Bernard (now with the *Seattle Post-Intelligencer*), Kevin Hand (*Newsweek*), and Gary Thatcher (International Broadcasting Bureau).

Three of the many news organizations I visited while putting together this book were the Voice of America in Washington, DC, MSNBC.com in Seattle, and the *Fort Worth Star-Telegram,* where many people shared their professional insights with me.

Matt Bunker, Teresa Keller, and Guy Hubbs were kind enough to read chapters in this book while it was in progress, and all of them made many helpful suggestions. Other chapters were reviewed by Jennifer E. Follis, University of Illinois; Don R. Gregory, Westchester Community Collge; Leland F. Ryan, University of Kentucky; and Daniel Ryder, Mt. Blue High School. The reviewers had many good ideas that I latched onto with enthusiasm. My colleague at both the University of Alabama and Emory and Henry College, Tracy Lauder, was generous with her ideas. Tim Jackson, a first-class freelance writer and former student, gave me ideas that were included in the parts of this book about magazines and magazine writing.

Molly Taylor, acquisitions editor at Allyn and Bacon, and Michael Kish, editorial assistant, were always kind and helpful and most of all patient, and I appreciate their encouragement very much.

These are just a few. There are many more. Those not mentioned will know, I hope, how much I appreciate their help and value their friendship.

My wife Sally and son Jeff have now suffered through another book manuscript with their usual patience and support. These things would not happen if they were not there.

J.G.S

What

News and information are the products of journalism. But news is not just information. It is a special kind of information developed by journalists and formulated to fit the needs of the audience and the requirements of the media of journalism.

News is a vital ingredient of the mix of an open society. For individuals, news tells us about ourselves, helps us make decisions, and gives us a common pool of knowledge. In the larger society, news helps to confirm the assumptions on which our society is based.

The acquisition and dissemination of news is a difficult and expensive task. Consequently, a discernable journalistic culture—with definite rules and expectations—has grown up within news organizations. Understanding this culture is helpful to all of us who are news consumers, and it is vital to those who would take on the profession of journalism.

Chapter One

News and Society

1. News is the major product of journalism; news is information that journalists believe is important or interesting for their audiences.

2. Open society: a society in which information is exchanged with no or relatively little interference from the government or other organizations that control the norms of society.

3. News values: characteristics of information that make an event or subject news; they include timeliness, conflict, impact, currency, prominence, proximity, and unusualness.

4. News is one of the main ways in which a society examines itself; that examination provides an important means by which the society can find solutions to its problems.

5. News helps individuals in society make decisions about their lives and actions.

6. Watchdog: the term given to the news media as an independent observer of other parts of society (government, business, educational institutions, etc.) to see that they are doing their jobs properly.

7. Bias: beliefs, attitudes, and points of view that prevent journalists from evaluating and presenting information in the fair and accurate manner expected by the audience.

8. News organizations have an obligation to present information to their audiences and to keep channels of communication in society open. They also have the added burden of maintaining their own economic health in a capitalist economic system.

Vignette

The morning of September 11, 2001, was cool and clear in western Pennsylvania where CNN reporter David Mattingly was vacationing. His wife's family lives in that part of the country and Mattingly, one of CNN's top environmental reporters, always likes to get a feel for the outdoors wherever he is. He and his brother-in-law were about to set out on a fishing trip to Canada when the news came.

His wife's aunt called and told them to turn on the television. Something was happening that was too significant to be ignored, even for a long-anticipated vacation. Planes had crashed into the World Trade Center towers in New York City. Another plane had crashed into the Pentagon in Washington, DC.

Then the local news broke in and said a fourth plane—United Airlines Flight 93—had crashed in Pennsylvania. It was not clear then if it was connected to the other crashes.

Mattingly called his editor in Atlanta but could not get through. The lines were jammed, and all the editors were trying to get people to New York and Washington. He then called a friend in another part of the building and had that person walk into the newsroom and tell his editors that he was trying to get in touch. Shortly after that, Mattingly was in his car driving toward Shanksville, the small town near the crash site.

"During times like this, it's hard to be a reporter first," he said. "I had been affected personally by what had happened in New York, as were many other people, and it was hard to separate my emotions."

Mattingly was one of the first national reporters on the scene. He was allowed into the media area that the police had set up, but he was still about 200 yards from the crash site. That site was over a ridge and not visible to the reporters.

Using his wife's cell phone, Mattingly called Atlanta and was soon on the air with live reports. CNN had dispatched a satellite truck and camera crew from Detroit, and it took several hours for them to arrive. Mattingly went on the air live that evening sometime between 7 and 8 P.M. By then he had ridden on in a police van to view the crash.

"I had seen airplane crashes before," he said, "but this was different. There was no identifiable part of the plane that you could see."

Mattingly continued to send live reports for the next eight hours, finally leaving the scene at about 3 A.M. He found the nearest motel and checked in, exhausted but unable to sleep. He then realized it was September 12, his birthday.

That event was not the first, nor the last, big story that Mattingly has covered for CNN. He was on the scene when the U.S. Supreme Court decided the presidential election in 2000, and he was in Houston covering the trial of Andrea Yates, the woman who killed her five children. In 2003 he was part of the CNN team that covered the investigation into the murder of Laci Peterson, a woman eight months pregnant when she disappeared just before Christmas. Her husband was later charged with the murder.

News is all around us, permeating our lives. Whether it is the extraordinary events of September 11, 2001, or everyday occurrences such as the weather (see Everybody Talks about the Weather, p. 9), news is an integral part of our modern existence.

News is the major function of journalism. News is information that helps us expand our lives and order the society in which we live. Our experience with the weather is something we can share with others, but it is made richer and more meaningful when it is supplemented by the information and experiences we have with journalism.

This chapter outlines and explains some of the aspects of news. As we explore the concept of news, keep in mind a few basic points:

- **News is a construct of journalism.** That is, news is what journalism and journalists say it is. News does not happen naturally. News is not just information. There is lots of information around us; some of it qualifies as news, but most does not.

- **News relies on the experiences of the audience to be effective.** Journalists assume that we can understand what they are telling us about because we can relate our own experience to what they are saying. Most people gather lots of experiences as they go through their daily routines. These experiences are important to the way in which we process and interpret the news that journalists produce for us.

- **The more open a society is, the better the news process works.** When information is freely available, journalists find it easier to obtain, interpret, and process. News consumers have more journalistic sources that they can go to for information. America has created a relatively open society, although the pressures to close off information are constant. The events of September 11, 2001, have renewed efforts, particularly by the U.S. government, to restrict information. Such efforts and restrictions should be viewed very skeptically, even when they are called for in the name of "national security."

News Values

What makes an event or topic news in the eyes of the journalist? The same thing could happen to two people in two different places, and one would be a news story and the other would not. For instance, if you were involved in a minor automobile accident in which there were no injuries, the incident probably would not appear in your local newspaper. If the president were involved in that same type of accident, it would probably be the first story on all the nightly newscasts.

FIGURE 1.1   All Kinds of Weather Even disastrous floods such as the Red River flood in 1997 (pictured here) affect relatively few people directly. Yet they become part of our shared experience through the process of journalism and the mechanism of news. (Photo credit: Federal Emergency Management Agency)

The separation of events into "news" and "not news" categories is a function of what we call news values. These are concepts that help us decide what a mass media audience is or should be interested in. There are millions of "events" that occur in our society every day. Those few events editors and news directors select as news have at least one of the characteristics discussed here.

Impact

Events that change people's lives are classified as news. Although the event itself might involve only a few people, the consequences may be wide-ranging. For example, if Congress passes a bill to raise taxes or if a researcher discovers a cure for a form of cancer, both actions will affect large numbers of people. They have impact, and they would be considered news.

Timeliness

Timeliness is a value common to almost all news stories. It refers to the recency of an event. Without the element of timeliness, most events cannot be considered news. For example, a trial that occurred last year is not news; a trial that is going on right now

may be news. How much time has to elapse before an event can no longer be considered news? No single answer to that question applies to every case. Most events
that are more than a day to a day-and-a-half old are not thought to be news. (Look
in today's newspaper and see if you can find a news story about an event that occurred more than two days ago.)

Prominence

Prominent people, sometimes even when they are doing trivial things, make news.
The president of the United States is a prime example. Whenever he takes a trip—
even for purely personal and private reasons—his movements are covered in great
detail by the news media. The president is a prominent and important person. Anything he does is likely to have an impact on the country, and people are very interested in his actions. The president is not the only example of a prominent person who
often makes news. Movie stars, famous politicians, advocates of social causes—all of
these people make news simply because they are very well known.

FIGURE 1.2   Prominence as a News Value The president of the United
States is the ultimate example of the news value of prominence. Just about
anything the president says or does is newsworthy, whether he is playing a game
of golf or making a major speech, as shown here just after the 2003 State of the
Union address. (Photo credit: White House photos)

Proximity

Events occurring close to home are more likely to be news than the same events that occur elsewhere. For example, a car wreck killing two people that happens on a road in your home county is more likely to be reported in the local news media than the same kind of wreck that occurs 1,000 miles away. We are interested in the things that happen around us. If we know a place where something goes on, we are more likely to have a feeling for it and for the people involved.

Conflict

When people disagree, when they fight, when they have arguments—that's news, particularly if one of the other news values, such as prominence, is involved. Conflict is one of the journalist's favorite news values because it generally ensures there is an interesting story to write. One of the reasons trial stories are so popular with newspaper readers and television viewers is that the central drama involves conflict—two competing forces, each vying to defeat the other.

The Bizarre or Unusual

A rare event is sometimes considered news. There is an adage in journalism that goes, "When a dog bites a man, that's not news; when a man bites a dog, now that's news." These events, though they may have relatively little importance or involve obscure people, are interesting to readers and enliven a publication. For example, it's not news when someone's driver's license is revoked (unless that someone is a prominent person); it is news, however, when a state department of transportation revokes the license of a person called "the worst driver in the state" because he had twenty-two accidents in the last two years.

Currency

Issues that have current interest often have news value, and events surrounding those issues can sometimes be considered news. For example, a panel discussion of doctors may be held in your community. Normally, such a discussion might not provoke much interest from journalists. If the discussion topic were the latest cancer-fighting drugs, the news value of the event would change, and there would likely be a number of newspaper, radio, and television journalists covering it. Issues that have the value of currency come and go, but there are always many such issues being discussed by the public.

Beyond these basic news values, however, are many other factors that affect the daily news menu that is presented to you as a news consumer. One is the limited ability of a news organization to gather, process, and present news. Every broadcast organization is limited by time. There is only so much time in which news can be aired. Even twenty-four-hour news operations, such as Cable News Network or MSNBC, are limited by the number of hours in a day.

And, of course, twenty-four hours is not devoted to news. Much of this time is given over to promotions and advertising. In fact, on local news broadcasts, the amount of time available for local news is very small; when the time for ads, weather, and sports is subtracted from a thirty-minute newscast, there is usually only about seven or eight minutes left for local news. Sometimes a significant portion of that time is used up by chatting among the anchors.

Newspapers and magazines are limited by the amount of pages or space they have in which to place the news. In newspaper jargon, this space is called the "news hole." Except for special and important news events, a newspaper will not automatically add pages just because there is more news than anticipated. The amount of space available for news depends on the amount of advertising the newspaper ad staff has been able to sell, and most newspapers determine how large they will be by some formula based on advertising. For many newspapers, the ratio is about 50 percent news and 50 percent advertising, but in some it can be 40:60 (news to advertising) or even 30:70.

News web sites go a long way toward overcoming the limits of time and space that bedevil print and broadcast news organizations. Time is not a factor in presentation of news on the Web, and space is virtually unlimited. Far more information can be presented on the Web than in newspapers or on a news broadcast.

But news web sites run into another limitation that plagues all news organizations—limited staff. Any news organization can employ only a certain number of people to remain economically viable, and those people can gather, write, and edit only a limited number of stories each day. Consequently, there are significant events or topics in a community that may not receive the coverage they deserve because news organizations simply do not have enough people.

Why News Matters

News, essentially, is what journalists say it is, as we have seen in the previous section. But why does it matter? What is so important about news, and why should anyone who is not involved with journalism care?

Quote 1.1

WILLIAM BERKELEY

On the absence of printing and free schools

I thank God we have no free schools or printing, and I hope that we shall not have these for a hundred years. For learning has brought disobediences and heresy and sects into the world; and printing has divulged them and libels against the government. God keep us from both.

Sir William Berkeley was governor of the colony of Virginia from 1642 to 1652 and from 1660 until his death in 1677.

News performs specific and important functions for society. The contributions that news makes to our society can be classified into three categories: information, entertainment, and persuasion. These are not mutually exclusive. Rather, they are intertwined and sometimes difficult to separate in real life.

The information function of news is the most obvious and most important. News tells a society or community about itself. It helps to define and explain ourselves to ourselves. At one level, it simply gives us an awareness that there are people, places, and events that are beyond our personal experience. One psychological tendency that we have is to define the world in relationship only to ourselves and our experiences. News helps us step beyond ourselves to broaden our outlook and experience. Beyond the psychological aspects, news gives us a daily set of information that tells us about the world in which we are living.

That awareness can help us make decisions about our lives. Take the example of the weather. Many of us have made decisions about what to wear or whether to carry an umbrella based on the morning weather report. Sometimes we have made decisions about travel because we knew a storm was coming or one had just passed, knocking down trees that might block roadways. We have changed our schedules because of the news, making sure that we arrived on time for a concert or located ourselves in front of a television at the time we wanted to watch a baseball game.

Sometimes the news media are given too much credit for helping us make decisions. Some people believe that they manipulate us into making decisions on how to act or whom to vote for because of news reports we see or read. Advertising, particularly, is thought to have this magical power: We see an ad for something, and we go out and buy it. Decisions about what to buy or whom to vote for are much more complex than that, and the news media are not the only factors that help people make these decisions.

EVERYBODY TALKS ABOUT THE WEATHER

Everybody talks about the weather. When we meet a stranger or when we don't know what else to talk about with a friend, we can talk about the weather.

The topic offers many points of discussion. It's been too wet or dry. It's been too hot or cold. A cold front is moving in. It's about to get really hot. We wonder when the next hurricane, tornado, flood, or snowstorm will hit, and in the area when seasons change, we wonder what the winter, summer, or fall foliage will be like.

The weather is a shared experience, something that we all have in common. It changes constantly, so there is always something to talk about.

But beyond limited personal experience, what do we know about the weather? Probably not much. We know that in most places it is hot in the summer and cold in the winter, but we don't know how hot or cold it is. We know that we have had a lot (or a little) rain this spring, but we don't know exactly how much or how this year compares to what is normal. We know what the sky looks like right now, but we don't know if it will rain this afternoon or tomorrow. And if a major weather-related event occurs in another part of the nation, we don't have a clue about that.

Except through journalism and the news process.

They do contribute to a person's decision-making process, however, and the extent of this contribution is a source of continuing and important debate in our society.

News and the news media help us to organize and prioritize the world around us. By giving us certain types of information, news helps us orient our thinking about the world. It tells us what others think is important, thereby allowing us to decide if we want to accept or reject those priorities. Politics, economics, religion, personal awareness, and social interaction are areas of our lives that mean a great deal to us. News gives us information in each of these areas that aids us in knowing what we should think about and how we should assess the things that happen to us and to those around us.

News also gives us information about the issues that provide continuing debate and discussion about our society. Because we are a modern society—and a relatively free and open one—we believe that there should be a public discussion about any number of issues. The news media help select those issues, a process that scholars have called "agenda setting," give us information about those issues, and even provide a forum in which people can be heard.

FIGURE 1.3   News in Times of National Crisis In times of national crisis, news becomes particularly important to people. Whether it is a world war (this photo shows people standing in Times Square watching a news ticker give information about the Allied invasion of Europe) or a terrorist attack, news allows us to share the same information and reach a common understanding about current events. (Photo credit: Library of Congress)

The second major function of news is entertainment. This function is not a frivolous one; it is meaningful to us personally and has important implications for society. Much of the news we receive does not affect us personally. We do not necessarily need to know it in terms of how we order our lives or because of the decisions we have to make. Rather, much of the news is merely interesting.

But it is also distracting in a very positive sense. News, as we have said earlier, takes us beyond ourselves. It allows us to experience many people and events vicariously—experiences we would not have if it weren't for the news media. Those experiences are valuable and enriching. They deepen our lives and our thinking. This kind of news also gives us information that we can use for relating and interacting with others.

The entertainment function of news has been a matter of debate among journalists for many years. Some journalists and news shows have taken this function beyond what is considered to be standard journalistic practices and have thereby—in the minds of some—distorted the information being presented. One of the words for this is *sensationalism* (another term more recently used has been *infotainment*), which means that lurid aspects of the news are emphasized merely because those aspects will appeal to people and build an audience for the news program or publication. Supermarket tabloids and slickly produced, celebrity-emphasizing news shows are constantly under fire from journalists in more traditional organizations for practicing this kind of journalism.

The persuasion function of the news is the most subtle of the three functions but its importance is enormous. As we discussed earlier, news helps us make decisions about our personal and civic lives. It helps us to understand the world in which we live and order the experiences and events that occur in our realm. News aids in shaping our outlook. News can also help us decide what is important, what we will think about, and what we will discuss.

As such, many social critics have argued, the information we get from the news media helps to maintain social order. Some have even gone so far as to argue that news helps to control society by letting us know what is proper to think about and what is not. A crude example of this was the reaction of the news media and the public in the days and weeks after the events of September 11, 2001. During that time, much was said about the goodness of America, and a good deal of information about the nation's problems and the shortcomings of its leadership went unreported. Much negative information about the Muslim religion and people who adhere to that faith was presented by the news media. For a time, it became appropriate for many Americans not of that faith to think and speak negatively about it. This was just one instance in which the news media reflected and reinforced the social order.

Some people tend to see this persuasive function of the news as a great conspiracy whereby the masses of people are knowingly and openly controlled. That would mean that a significant number of people inside the profession of journalism are there for motives other than the accurate presentation of news and information. That is not the case. Rather, journalists too are citizens of society and have internalized the values that all of us share. They have an interest in maintaining the social order. But, like others, they also have an interest in raising questions about that order when necessary.

News and the Social Order

News is an integral part of modern society. It is particularly important to the functioning of various aspects of society. The following is a review of how news covers and affects some of the most important parts of our public life. This review is not comprehensive in its view of all aspects of society, but it does provide some examples as to how news works.

Politics is probably 90 percent talk and 10 percent action, as it should be. Much of politics is about ideas, attitudes, and beliefs. It is about presenting points of view and arguing those points, with some people attacking and others defending. It is about persuasion, discussion, and compromise. True, many politicians and political operatives

FIGURE 1.4   The Last Laugh for Harry Truman Tensions are always near the surface between presidents and the press. In 1948 President Harry S Truman surprised just about everyone on Election Day by beating Republican Thomas Dewey. The *Chicago Tribune,* which had vociferously opposed Truman, printed an early edition based on some first returns and ran the headline "Dewey Defeats Truman." Later in November, when Truman was traveling from Independence, Missouri, to Washington, DC, he stopped in St. Louis, and someone handed him an edition of the paper. Truman held it up and produced one of the great presidential images of modern American politics. (Photo credit: Associated Press Wide World Photos)

hold rallies from place to place, shake hands, and appear in many attention-getting situations. As legislators, they also propose and enact laws. If they are in the executive branch of government, they are in charge of putting laws into effect. But the main job of politics is to select and mold the ideas that hold us together as a civic society.

Much of daily journalism is devoted to the coverage of politics and the political arena. How we govern ourselves says a great deal about our society and in many ways determines the kind of life that we will lead. News coverage of this area of our society allows us to survey and record the way in which our governing philosophy is operationalized on a day-to-day basis. Journalism gives us information about who is running for election, what ideas they are presenting, and how they are conducting their campaigns.

One of the main jobs of news and the news media in the realm of politics is to serve as a "watchdog" on government and governmental officials. This role evolved from the development of journalism in the nineteenth century (see Chapter 22) when newspapers and magazines launched crusades against corruption and mismanagement of public funds. Many of these crusades also revealed problems with society, such as child labor, which the government had ignored and needed to be addressed. Journalism acted as an independent voice in the political system that could bring such problems to light and suggest reforms. The news media maintain that role today, sometimes with dramatic results such as in the Watergate scandal of the early 1970s.

A related role for news in the political arena is that of a conduit of public opinion. News not only tells us what the government is doing but also informs governmental officials about the public's reactions and concerns. By their selection of issues to spotlight and their approach to the information concerning these issues, the media also help to mold public opinion.

The news media's participation in the political system is far from perfect and is under constant criticism even from within the profession of journalism. In today's era of twenty-four-hour television news and always-on Internet availability, one of the major complaints about the media is that there is more opinion than information. In other words, ironically, there is not enough news. News organizations find it easier and cheaper to produce talk shows and opinion forums than news programs that present substantive information. This condition has led to another criticism that many people level at the news media—fragmentation. With so many people expressing so many opinions, the political system is becoming increasingly fragmented. Many political organizations, political parties in particular, have lost their ability to gather and coalesce opinions into concrete plans of action. This fragmentation has led to a shortened attention span on the part of the politicians and the public that focuses on short-term problems rather than long-term issues.

Another area of society in which news plays an important role is the economic arena. News provides consumers with important information to use in making choices, from deciding what toothpaste to buy to selecting investments for their money. News helps young people decide where to go to college and what career they should pursue. Just about every economic decision we make is influenced by the information we receive from journalism.

TEDDY ROOSEVELT AND THE "BULLY PULPIT"

Teddy Roosevelt called it a "bully pulpit," and he made it so.

Roosevelt ascended to the presidency in 1901 after the assassination of William McKinley in Buffalo, New York. Roosevelt was just 42 years old, the youngest man ever to hold the office. He was unlike anyone who had ever occupied the White House, particularly the faceless personalities who had been in office for the previous 40 years since the death of Abraham Lincoln.

Roosevelt loved a good argument. He did not mind controversy. And he loved the press, particularly reporters. They, in turn, loved him.

Roosevelt was always "good copy" for journalists. Despite childhood ailments of bad eyesight and asthma, Roosevelt was an energetic outdoorsman. He rode horses, went camping, explored the wilderness, and hunted wild game. With Roosevelt, there was always something interesting to write about. He was an environmentalist and scientist. He was also a historian and author of more than thirty books.

His bear-hunting exploits attached his name to America's all-time favorite toy—the Teddy bear.

Roosevelt relished making speeches. He had a high-pitched voice that pierced the inattention of an audience and made them sit up and listen. He waved his arms and pounded his fist.

He had much to debate. During his presidency, he championed legislation that reigned in railroads, established federal government inspection of meat, provided great consumer protection, and built the Panama Canal. He set aside vast stretches of land as national forests, parks, and monuments.

One of his enduring legacies is the lasting effect he had on politics, particularly the presidency. The force of his personality turned it into the white-hot center of American politics. Everything that Roosevelt did called attention to himself, and that was just the way he liked it.

Journalism also performs something of the same watchdog role on the economic system that it does on the political system. Many news organizations, both print and broadcast, have people on staff whose job is to be a consumer advocate. They not only help solve individual problems for consumers, but they also uncover corruption and unfair business practices. As in the political arena, many people criticize the news media for not being aggressive enough in bringing these practices to light. These critics point to the fact that news organizations are dependent on the advertising revenue they receive from the businesses they are covering. Consequently, for instance, a small-town newspaper that runs two pages of advertising from a giant chain department store is unlikely to write about how the chain forces its employees to work extra hours for less than appropriate overtime pay. Some media organizations do fall victim to this kind of pressure, but many editors and publishers have fought against it, even when it has cost them advertising income.

The legal system is another area of society in which news plays an important role. Adherence to the law is one of the basic operating principles of people in a civil society. In many nations of the world, there is no tradition of trust in the law or faith in those in power to administer the laws fairly. Those societies are open to civil strife and even civil war. Americans do have a basic faith in the law and a tradition of respecting those who administer it, but this faith must be constantly tended and renewed. News coverage of the system is a major way in which the law and the legal system can be seen to be working properly.

Ours has become an increasingly litigious society. That is, more people are looking to the courts to solve their problems, and more organizations and individuals are asking the courts to protect their property and their rights. Part of this increase in legal activity stems from the growing number of lawyers graduating from law school and going into practice. But part of it also stems from the increasing attention the news media—in a variety of forms—are giving to the legal system. Several high-profile trials, such as the O. J. Simpson murder trial in the mid-1990s, have stimulated this attention. But the news media have also found that trials are relatively easy to cover. They are confined to a single location and the participants are often readily available for interviews. They also provide the drama of conflict, a major news value (see discussion earlier in this chapter), and they usually have a definite conclusion, such as a verdict. Consequently, news consumers are inundated with trial coverage not only by daily journalism but also by television programs on cable channels such as Arts and Entertainment, The Learning Channel, and the Discovery Channel. CourtTV, another cable channel, devotes itself entirely to coverage of trials and has a substantial web site that supplements this coverage (www.courttv.com).

Despite the many positive aspects of this massive attention to the court system by the news media, critics make some valid points. One is that the trials that receive the most coverage are those involving celebrities or those whom the media have made into celebrities. Another criticism is that news coverage of trials is more likely to be entertaining than educational. Yet another criticism is that news coverage of high-profile trials does not give the public an accurate picture of how the legal system really works. Finally, critics point out that the news media's emphasis on criminal trials ignores a vast and important part of the legal system—civil litigation. Civil trials often have more long-term impact on the public because they formulate and refine public policy in many areas but, compared to criminal proceedings, they are virtually ignored.

A final area of society in which news plays a particularly important role is sports. Some people dismiss sports as being unimportant and meaningless. Those sentiments pointedly ignore the massive amount of time, money, and interest humans the world over give to sports. Newspapers have sports sections that are often larger than news sections. Local television news broadcasts devote a substantial amount of time to sports coverage. A number of cable channels carry nothing but sports events and news and commentary about sports. Our educational system is involved with sports at every level and, at the collegiate level, sports creates a major revenue stream for any institution. Professional athletes are among the highest-paid individuals in the world.

What Do You Think?

THE JOURNALIST'S DILEMMA

Even in an age of increasing interactivity, journalists have an uncertain relationship with their audiences. One of the enduring questions, often unstated, in newsrooms every day is, "Should we give audiences what they need—hard news and information, what's important, what has long-term effects on their lives—or should we give them what they want—sensationalism, celebrity, rumor, and opinion?"

Serious critics of the profession in every journalistic generation conclude that journalism has an inclination toward the latter—sensationalism, celebrity, and rumor.

The current generation of journalism is no different. Consider this:

Tim Rutten, media critic for the *Los Angeles Times,* noted in a column at the end of 2003 that Slobodan Milosevic had been on trial for two years. Milosevic had been president of Yugoslavia and is the first head of state to stand trial for war

crimes. He has been charged with sixty-six counts of involvement in atrocities in Croatia, Bosnia, and Kosovo, and his trial was taking place at the World Court in the Netherlands.

From January 1, 2000, to the end of 2003, Rutten found, the *New York Times* had printed 120 stories on the case. The *Washington Post* had printed 41 reports, and his own newspaper, the *Los Angeles Times,* had carried 58 stories.

Compare that with the coverage given to basketball star Kobe Bryant, charged with rape, and pop superstar Michael Jackson, charged with child molestation.

During 2003, the *New York Times* ran 113 stories on the Kobe Bryant case, the *Washington Post* 107 stories, and the *Los Angeles Times* 450 stories. The charges against Michael Jackson, which did not surface until the fall of 2003, produced 58 stories in the *New York Times,* 58 stories in the *Washington Post,* and 87 stories in the *Los Angeles Times.*

The charges against Bryant and Jackson are serious, but do they compare with the vast atrocities attributed to Milosevic? Many people, unfortunately, are charged with rape and child molestation, but how many people get charged with crimes against humanity?

It might be an easy conclusion to draw that news organizations should pay more attention to Milosevic than Bryant or Jackson, but before doing that, ask yourself this:

Whose trial would you rather read about (or hear about on television)—Slobodan Milosevic or Kobe Bryant and Michael Jackson?

Many city and state budgets devote millions of dollars to building and maintaining sports facilities, from Little League baseball fields to major league sports stadiums. Interest in sports—and news coverage of sports—is so pervasive that even those who claim not to be interested in it have trouble ignoring it or knowing something about the people involved in it.

FIGURE 1.5   The Thrill of Victory Sports is of great interest to many people, and it takes a great deal of the news media's time and attention. That attention is heightened when a major sports events such as the Olympics takes place. (Pictured here, U.S. athletes march into Olympic Stadium in Sydney, Australia, for the opening of the 2000 games.) (Photo credit: Department of Defense)

Two generations ago, news coverage of sports concentrated on sports events and ignored most of the other aspects of sports. Today, however, more attention is devoted to the salaries of athletes and the financial health of sports franchises than to the performance of the team. Such coverage reveals that athletes are not the individual role models that we idealize and that colleges and universities are not the paragons of virtue that academicians would like to claim. To cover news of sports takes more than knowledge of the game. It demands a wide range of understanding the rules of operations, economics, and even psychology.

Critics of news coverage of sports point out that the news media confer celebrity status on those athletes who are not ready or able to handle it. Another telling criticism, especially at a local level, is that news coverage of local teams is often favorable and forgiving rather than accurate and revealing because the audience of local fans demands that kind of coverage. Finally, critics point to the fact that with sports the news media is part of a system that encourages spectatorship rather than participation in sports and, consequently, gives it the wrong priority within our society.

Pressures on Journalists

Journalists meet many challenges in gathering, processing, and distributing the news. The most daunting is the sheer difficulty in doing the job, as we discuss throughout this book. Finding information, conceptualizing news stories, writing and editing copy, and then broadcasting or getting words into print or posted on a web site—none of these is an easy task.

A PASSPORT, A KEYBOARD, AND A PAYCHECK

Garrett Lane

Why study journalism? There is a noble reply. A free press is among our most cherished rights and remains critical to our democratic way of life. But there is another implication in the question. What about the lives of those who practice journalism? In other words, why should you study journalism and become a journalist?

I love being a journalist. I love press passes and scoops and deadlines and proofreaders' marks. I've been a working journalist for nearly eight years, and I still get excited every time I see my byline. I think you should study journalism and become a journalist, too. Here's why.

A journalist's life is a good one. It's a passport to a career, awash in options, full of open doors. You will be hard-pressed to imagine a more portable or versatile job. Pick a spot on the globe. Something's happening there, and journalists are writing about it. And it's not just the daily news flash. Journalists cover everything—French cuisine, Spanish soap operas, Italian red wines, Caribbean fly-fishing, American rockabilly music. Some journalists even write about the work of other journalists. How's that for flexibility?

Journalism offers you the rarest of perks: getting paid to do whatever makes you happy. You want to live in Michigan and restore vintage automobiles? Follow the professional surfing tour from beach to beach? Trek through rain forests? Jour-

nalists I know get paid to do all of those things. A journalism degree is a blank check. You can live anywhere, do most anything—your personal interests will only make you a better journalist.

And this world needs better journalists. We need good information to conduct our daily doings. We need it to buy groceries, understand foreign policy, and go on vacation. In my observation, if three or more people take up an activity, it's probably a story. Other people will want to know about it, why it happened, and what it means. And that's what journalists do—they make information make sense.

Clear communication remains a commodity. Technology offers us an astonishing variety of outlets. We can speak across distances and cultures with increasing ease. But these fine channels are useless unless someone collects, analyzes, and organizes the messages we send. I encourage you to study journalism because it is noble and essential. And I encourage you to become a journalist because of the life you will lead.

Garrett Lane is online editor of Southern Accents magazine, a national shelter publication that embraces a regional lifestyle. His professional experience includes work in print and online journalism as a reporter, illustrator, editor, instructor, and designer.

But journalists face difficulties in addition to the routine procedures of their job. These difficulties often prevent them from doing the job that they would like to do in giving their audience information.

One difficulty is their own bias or point of view. Journalists are supposed to be fair in presenting information, and some use the word *objective* to describe how journalists are supposed to approach their job. But no matter how well trained or experienced journalists are, they remain human beings who have feelings and ways of interpreting experiences that are different from other people. Journalists can never be completely objective or unbiased in presenting the news, and both they and their audiences should acknowledge this.

Another difficulty that journalists face in presenting the news is the very human trait of making mistakes. Journalists get things wrong, no matter how careful they are and no matter how strict the editing procedures are. Sometimes sources give them incorrect information. Sometimes they do not understand the information they have. Sometimes information gets tangled up in the editing process. Sometimes the point of view they have prevents them from seeing or understanding the event or topic they are covering. Most journalists and news organizations work very hard to keep errors to a minimum, and most of the time both are successful. But errors do occur, and when they do, the credibility of journalists and news organizations is damaged.

Journalists are also constantly confronted with the possibility of a "blame the messenger" syndrome. Journalists must deliver bad or uncomfortable news. That's their job. But the audience to whom they give this news is not always appreciative of their efforts. During the Vietnam War in the late 1960s, a lone journalist, Seymour Hersh, uncovered information that indicated U.S. servicemen had killed a village full of old men, women, and children. Exactly what happened in My Lai is still a matter of dispute, but whatever it was, the facts did not reflect well on the United States. Many people did not want to know this and blamed Hersh and other journalists for bringing it to light. They were called unpatriotic and un-American because they told people things they would rather not hear.

The Job of the Journalist

Journalists decide what is news, and in doing so they make many important decisions about what a society says to itself, how it explains itself, what social order is established and maintained, and how the problems and shortcomings of that society are revealed. In addition to doing all of these things, journalists also have certain responsibilities to their own profession:

- They must maintain the standards of their profession as well as the customs and conventions of the journalistic culture (see Chapter 2). These conventions include gathering news and information, editing it for their medium, and distributing it in ways that meet standards of fairness and accuracy.

- Journalists have the responsibility of maintaining the economic health of their news organizations. Because these organizations are not government sponsored

FIGURE 1.6   Always the News No matter what the political or economic situation—war or peace, boom or bust—people will always need to know the news, and they will always depend on journalists and the news organizations for which they work to provide it to them. They are willing to pay for that news, but they want it to be accurate and fair. (Photo credit: Library of Congress)

or supported (except in very rare instances), they must make enough profit to continue operation and to have the resources to practice the kind of journalism that is expected and necessary for society.

■ Finally, journalists are charged with fostering and promoting the idea of an open society in which information flows freely, people can think and speak creatively, and a variety of points of view about all topics is tolerated.

The chief tool that the journalist uses to do all of these things is news.

QUESTIONS FOR DISCUSSION

1. How much do you use the news to make decisions about your life? What types of decisions do you make based on the news you read or hear?

2. The author makes a number of statements in this chapter and elsewhere about how important the news is to society. Do you agree?
3. The author talks about a "blame the messenger" syndrome that sometimes occurs when the news media have to deliver bad news. How often do you think that happens? Can you think of any specific instances of it happening?
4. Do you think the news media pay too much attention to sports? Is this the news media's fault, or are they just giving the audience what it wants?

RELATED WEB SITES

Civic Journalism Interest Group, www.has.vcu.edu/civic-journalism

Committee of Concerned Journalists, www.journalism.org

Community Journalism Project, www.rtndf.org/resources/cj.shtml

Newseum, www.newseum.org

Pew Center for Civic Journalism, www.pewcenter.org

PJNet: Public Journalism Network, www.pjnet.org

The Readership Institute, www.readership.org

Web Credibility Project (Stanford University), www.webcredibility.org

"With the People," www.pewcenter.org/doingcj/pubs/pubs_toolbox.html

READINGS AND REFERENCES

Clark, R. P. (1994). *The American conversation and the language of journalism.* Poynter Paper No. 5, St. Petersburg: Poynter Institute.

Cohn, V., Cope, L., & Winsten, J. (2001). *News & numbers.* Ames, IA: Iowa State University Press.

Dennis, E. E., & Pease, E. C. (Eds.). (1997). *The media in black and white.* Rutgers, NJ: Transaction Books.

Fallows, J. (1995). *Breaking the news: How the media undermine American democracy.* New York: Pantheon.

Fry, D. (Ed.). (1985). *Believing the news.* St. Petersburg: Poynter Institute for Media Studies.

Gutierrez, F., Wilson, C., & Chao, L. (2003). *Racism, sexism, and the media: The rise of class communication in multicultural America.* Thousand Oaks, CA: Sage Publications.

Hohenberg, J. (1995). *Foreign correspondence: The great reporters and their times* (2nd ed.). Syracuse, NY: Syracuse University Press.

Klaidman, S., & Beauchampn T. L. (1987). *The virtuous journalist.* New York: Oxford University Press.

McGowan, W. (2001). *Coloring the news.* San Francisco: Encounter Books.

Meyer, P. (2002). *Precision journalism* (4th ed.). Lanham, MD: Rowman & Littlefield Publishers.

Reeves, R. (1999). *What the people know: Freedom of the press.* Cambridge, MA: Harvard University Press.

2

The Culture of Journalism

Key Concepts and Terms

1. Journalism has a distinct culture with norms, conventions, and expectations of behavior from those who are part of the culture. Many of those expectations are fueled by the public service aspects of the profession—the feeling among journalists that they are working for the public good, not just for their private benefit.

2. The processes of journalism are ideally governed by journalists themselves; few rules or restraints are imposed on them from outside the profession.

3. Despite the fact that many inside journalism consider it a profession, no rules or barriers bar those who want to become journalists; there are no educational or professional requirements to becoming a journalist.

4. A basic cultural requirement of journalism is that those in the profession have a high level of skill in using the language.

5. News organizations: entities that gather news and disseminate it to an audience.

6. Accuracy: the chief goal of journalists in producing and presenting news and information.

7. Civic journalism: a controversial concept that says journalism should be concerned with more than just observing society; it also should be devoted to finding solutions to society's problems.

8. Dishonesty and plagiarism are two of the most unacceptable practices in journalism.

9. Many practices of journalism are governed by competition; journalists want to be the first to publish or broadcast information, and they want to do it better than other journalists.

Vignette

The third Saturday in July 1999 broke warm and sunny in Chicago. The people of that midwestern city were looking forward to a day of leisure—as were people across the country. In Chicago the Cubs were in town playing an interleague game with the Kansas City Royals—an event that would put 40,000 people into Wrigley Field and many thousands more in front of their television sets for the afternoon. And if you did not like baseball, there were biking trails, the lakeshore, parks, museums, shopping downtown or at one of the malls, or just hanging around the house.

Most of the news staff of the Chicago Tribune *had the day off, as they normally do. Much of the* Sunday Tribune *gets put together on Thursday and Friday, so only a skeleton staff of editors, reporters, designers, photographers, and copydesk editors is necessary to put the paper to bed on Saturday.*

Unless something happens.

That Saturday, something was happening. The early morning television shows gave the first bits of news. A small plane carrying John F. Kennedy Jr., his wife, and her sister was missing off the coast of Massachusetts. The plane had taken off late Friday night from New Jersey headed for Hyannisport. The three passengers were to attend a wedding of a family member on Saturday.

Kennedy, thirty-eight years old, had been a celebrity since before he was born. He was being carried by his mother Jacqueline Kennedy during the 1960 presidential campaign of his father. He was born less than four weeks after his father had been elected president of the United States. As a toddler, he was often seen and photographed romping through the west wing of the White House.

Just before his third birthday, his father was killed by an assassin in Dallas, Texas. Three days later, during the internationally televised funeral of the slain president, the young Kennedy provided one of the most poignant images of those dark days by stepping out and saluting his father's casket as it rolled by on its military caisson. Kennedy had grown up to be drop-dead handsome, and his face had appeared on thousands of magazine covers. He never shied from the limelight and carried his celebrity with much grace. He had an interest in politics, and many had predicted that he had a future in elective office.

As the news unfolded that morning, many on the news staff of the Chicago Tribune *gave up their Saturday plans and headed back toward the Michigan Avenue tower. Although there were few local angles to pursue in this story, the* Chicago Tribune *is a national newspaper, with a full Washington bureau and correspondents in different parts of the country and several scattered around the world. Any major international event is covered like a local story at the* Tribune.

FIGURE 2.1   Image Revived When President John F. Kennedy was assassinated in November 1963, one of the most poignant images that his death produced was that of three-year-old John F. Kennedy Jr. saluting his father's casket as it rolled by the church where the funeral mass was held. Almost thirty-six years later, that image of John F. Kennedy Jr. again appeared in many newspapers and on broadcasts and web sites as the news media reported on the plane crash that killed him. (Photo credit: AP Wide World Photos)

Inside the newsroom, activity increased as the afternoon wore on. Reporters and editors in various forms of Saturday attire buzzed around editors' desks, exchanging what information they had been able to gather. A Tribune *staffer, an expert on transportation issues, was on a plane to Massachusetts and would be filing reports from the headquarters of the rescue operations later that afternoon. Reporters in Washington and Chicago worked the phones and their sources to find out anything they could about what Kennedy had been doing on that Friday, when the plane had left, and the route of the flight. Graphics and photo editors searched their archives and debated what information should go into the graphics they were planning. Editors called friends in other news organizations near and around Boston to find out what they knew.*

Getting the words right in all of these reports would be tricky. The Coast Guard, which was coordinating the search for the plane, was still calling this a rescue mission. Although nothing had been said officially about the possibility that Kennedy and the other passengers of the plane were dead, inside the newsroom there was no doubt. A plane lost over the ocean could mean little else than that it had crashed and the passengers had died.

Some of the Tribune *staffers tried to find out what might have happened. One graphics journalist talked to three different small plane pilots that afternoon, and they all told him the same thing. Kennedy, a relatively inexperienced pilot, had tried to fly after dark and had become disoriented and had lost control of his plane. He had not been trained to use the instruments necessary for night flying. He had probably left New Jersey too late in the afternoon to make it to Hyannisport before night fell, the pilots said.*

All during the day, television sets were on throughout the newsroom. If the rescue operation spotted even one fragment of wreckage in the ocean, that would change the whole story. As darkness fell on the East Coast, the operation shut down for the night.

By 9 P.M. in Chicago, the work of the reporters, editors, copy editors, and graphics journalists had come together. The next morning Tribune *readers found more than three pages of information about Kennedy. The front page included two stories by* Tribune *staffers, one from Hyannisport and the other from New York, about the event, with a time line on the day's events and how the story had unfolded. A two-page spread inside the paper included several stories about the Kennedys, a time line of the life of JFK Jr., and a graphic that showed what might have happened to the plane, plus information about the plane itself. In addition, the newspaper's Sunday Perspective section was reworked to include commentary about the tragedy. More than two dozen people had contributed to putting all of that together. Most had begun the morning looking forward to a day of leisure. Instead, they ended it exhausted, doing what journalists do—covering the news.*

The World of the Journalist

The world of journalism is exciting, demanding, tiring, exhilarating, and ultimately fulfilling to many people. It requires extraordinary energy and intellectual accomplishment under the constant pressure of daily deadlines. Journalists have to perform in pressure-packed environments. They have to produce, and they have to find ways of producing.

They have to do this because it is important that people know what journalists have to tell them—every day, every week, every month. And the way in which journalists tell them is important, too.

As we explore the culture of journalists, it will be helpful to keep the following things in mind:

- **Journalism is viewed as a public trust by the people who practice it.**   Journalists do not get into the field to make money. They want to make a good living (and most do), and they hope to do well, but they do not expect to gain wealth through their own hard work or cleverness.

- **Journalism is protected from most outside restraints.**   Journalists operate in an environment in which they are generally free of outside restraints. They must observe the laws that are imposed on all citizens, but within the journalistic working environment; there are few laws that allow outside forces, including the government, to impose restrictions on what they do or how they operate.

- **Journalism organizations, despite the public trust they bear, must survive in a capitalist economy.**   They do not receive government grants to operate. Instead, they have to be profit-making businesses, and they have to find ways of avoiding bankruptcy and maintaining good economic health.

- **Journalistic practices require high levels of skill and intellectual training.**   Journalists must know the language and how to use it; they must master the equipment that it takes to produce and distribute their product. These are not easy skills to acquire; training is a must. How this training is acquired is not prescribed by the profession.

- **Journalism is an open field of endeavor.**   There is no professional gate, such as a bar exam or medical board exam. A person can be hired by a news organization and, without any training at all, begin the practice of journalism. (Not a good idea, but it can happen.) A person can even declare himself or herself a journalist without the benefit of having an employer.

Despite its openness and independence, a definite culture exists within journalism. Walk into any newsroom or editorial office where journalism is practiced, and the feeling you will get is different from anything else you have experienced. This culture of journalism stems from its traditions and its peculiar practices and imposes itself on anyone who undertakes to work in this field. This chapter will explore some of the aspects of that culture.

Character and Characteristics

Almost without exception, movies and television shows portray journalists as jackals—unconcerned about the immediate or long-term effects their actions have on the people with whom they deal. Journalists, according to these portrayals, will do anything to get a story; they will lie, steal, betray confidences, and invade a person's privacy. Journal-

Quote 2.1

MAHATMA GANDHI

On journalism

I have taken up journalism not for its sake but merely as an aid to what I have conceived to be my mission in life. My mission is to teach by example and precept under severe restraint the use of the matchless weapon of *satyagraha,** which is a direct corollary of non-violence and truth. To be true to my faith, therefore, I may not write in anger or malice. I may not write idly. I may not write merely to excite passion. The reader can have no idea of the restraint I have to exercise from week to week in the choice of topics and my vocabulary. It is a training for me. It enables me to peep into myself and to make discoveries of my weaknesses. Often my vanity dictates a smart expression or my anger a harsh adjective.

*Sanskrit for "truth and firmness"

Mahatma Gandhi, 1869–1948, a philosopher and activist, was a leader of the movement to free India from British rule. He was a major exponent of nonviolent activism.

ism ethics, for these characters, is an oxymoron. They have checked their normal human feelings at the newsroom door.

Editors and television news directors are no better. According to their movie and television characters, they will do anything at all to sell another newspaper or gain a ratings point. They will twist the information their reporters gather to fit a preferred notion of the facts or some political agenda.

Thus, the entertainment industry tells us over and over that journalists are not like everyone else.

It's true; they're not.

But movie and television portrayals do not give viewers an accurate version of what it is like to be a journalist. At best, they tell only a small part of the story.

Journalists do have feelings. They do empathize with the people who are in their stories. Journalists often think about whether or not they are doing harm or good, and all too often, their choices are simply between "more harm or less harm." But journalists also understand that they have a job to do, a job that is not always pleasant or popular, and they have a commitment to the ideal behind that job.

The ideal is one of public service. Every committed journalist has that ideal as a part of his or her psychological mix. Whatever other personal or professional characteristics they have, most journalists believe that what they are doing is important for society. Even when individuals are hurt or made unhappy by their actions, journalists justify their actions with the thought that many others are better off because of them.

That commitment to the public good, allied with a number of personal characteristics either natural or learned, makes a person a part of the culture of journalism. One of the most important of those characteristics is skill with the language. Journalists must have a facility with the language that exceeds the demands of most other fields. Journalists must communicate with thousands—sometimes millions—of people; their ability to think and write clearly, using simple, direct language and everyday terms, is a given. Even those within the field who may not be using their language skills to communicate to a wide audience are expected to be able to write clearly and articulate their thoughts and information well.

A great deal of time and effort within the industry of journalism is devoted to improving the language skills of individuals. This begins with collegiate journalism programs that emphasize writing and that require a number of writing courses from their majors. It continues in the professional world. Many professional development workshops are offered to help people improve their writing. Some newspapers hire independent writing coaches on a regular basis, and a few of the larger ones keep a writing coach on their staff. Language skills and the efforts to improve them are an integral part of the culture of journalism and something the individual journalist must take seriously.

Another personal characteristic important to the culture of journalism is the willingness to work hard. Any form of journalism, particularly daily journalism on web sites, newspapers, or television stations, can be a stressful, intense, and sometimes frustrating effort. Journalists often feel enormous pressure from their editors, from their colleagues, and from the knowledge that they are producing something that a large number of people will see. Their working situations mean that they will be the only ones who can perform their particular task; that is, if they don't do it, no one else will. Consequently, they need to be able to handle the pressure and produce their work under less than ideal conditions. Few newsrooms, especially when they approach a deadline, are places of quiet contemplation. Rather, they are noisy and disruptive. Journalists must have the ability to close out distractions and do their work.

Many journalists, particularly reporters, work many hours for which they are not compensated. Although most have standard working hours, reporters may receive phone calls from sources during off-hours, or they may choose to pursue a story outside the newsroom. These extra hours rarely turn into overtime pay, not because of the unwillingness of publishers to pay overtime but because journalists see this as part of their job and simply do not ask for compensation.

Some people thrive on these conditions. They enjoy the noise and the chaos of a newsroom at deadline. They come to work understanding the challenge of putting together a good news story, and they rise to it. They gain great satisfaction from spending long hours in work they consider interesting and important. But for others the pressures of the news environment lead to frustration and dissatisfaction. Ultimately, many young journalists burn out and seek other jobs in somewhat less stressful public relations positions or completely outside the field.

Journalists are better at their craft if they have a natural curiosity about many things. For a lot of people, most of the world passes by largely unnoticed and unquestioned. Journalists, however, ask questions that may not occur to others. They want to know who does things, how they work, how did things get to be the way they are, and who is responsible. When journalists research a story, they should not be satisfied with vague, pat, or standard answers to their questions, particularly when they do not seem to explain what is really happening. For honest news sources, a journalist's curiosity is not a problem. In fact, it is a blessing. People like to talk about what they do and what they know, and they like to believe that the people they talk to are interested in what they are saying. Journalists are paid to be interested, but they will do a better job if they also develop the habits of curiosity. Those habits include asking "how" and "why."

Persistence and assertiveness are also valued personal traits within the profession. Persistence is most productive when it is combined with intelligence and creativity, particularly in news reporting. If important information exists, it is probably known by more than one person or available from more than one source. Reporters have to "keep digging" until they find out what they need. In other cases, persistence simply means being patient. Jennifer Autrey, a reporter on the investigative team of the *Ft. Worth Star-Telegram,* says that many of her days are spent talking with potential sources about things other than information about the story she is pursuing. "I just want them to be comfortable with me," she says, so that they will decide to open up and tell her what she needs to know.

Assertiveness in the face of "authority" is also a trait that can help a journalist. A photojournalism student once witnessed a car wreck in which a small truck had flipped over several times. She began shooting pictures as the paramedics were trying to extract the passenger of the truck from the wreckage. The driver was the aging mayor of the small town they were in. After a few minutes, a policeman approached the student saying that she could not take any more pictures and that she would have to turn her film over to the police. The policeman, of course, had no right to do that; he was simply trying to protect the mayor from public humiliation. Fortunately, the student refused to give up her film, and then the policeman said she could not publish the photographs. This, too, was wrong on the policeman's part. The pictures were eventually printed in the local paper.

One final personal characteristic worth mentioning that is encouraged by the culture of journalism is attention to detail. Reporters and editors learn that information they do not verify is likely to come back to haunt them. Early in the reporting process, reporters learn to ask people to spell their names, never assuming that they are spelling them correctly. This habit is indicative of how journalists should work. The information they produce is read by many thousands of people. Someone among those thousands is going to know if a fact is wrong and is going to call or email an editor about it. Getting facts wrong is one of the worst things that can happen to a journalist. Attention to detail helps prevent that.

Skepticism and Cynicism

Another trait of the culture of journalism allied to curiosity is skepticism. Some people try to hide things with their words and actions. Journalists should develop ways in which they can question the things that most people accept. Questioning almost everything is a personal trait highly valued in the field of journalism.

FIGURE 2.2	**How Journalists See Themselves and Their Jobs**

The American Journalist Survey, conducted by researchers at Indiana University in 2002, found the following attitudes about journalists and their jobs:

JOB SATISFACTION

very satisfied   33%

fairly satisfied   51%

PERCEPTION OF VALUES HELD BY OWNERS OF THE NEWS ORGANIZATION THEY WORK FOR (percentages are of those journalists who said these values are "very important" to their employers)

keep the audience as large as possible   89%

earning high, above-average profits   77%

producing high-quality journalism   73%

maintaining high employee morale   32%

IMPORTANCE OF JOURNALISTIC PRACTICES (percentages are of those journalists who said these practices are "extremely important")

investigating government claims   71%

getting information to the public quickly   59%

producing news of interest to the widest possible audience   15%

providing entertainment and relaxation   15%

Source: American Journalist Survey, Indiana University (www.poynter.org)

A young journalist was once assigned to do a story on the homeless people in his city. It was a difficult story because many of the homeless people he met were mentally ill, unwilling to talk, or simply unable to articulate information about themselves or their condition. Finally, after much discouragement, the journalist met a homeless man who was willing to talk and tell his story. He had been a war veteran, he said, but now could not get medical treatment because his benefits had run out. He told the reporter many stories, some harrowing, about being on the street. He could not understand why his country had let him down after he had given it so much. The young reporter thought he had a great story, returned to his office, and began writing. His story, he thought, would do some good and wake up some sleeping bureaucrats in the Veteran's Administration. Once the story was finished, he proudly presented it to an editor, who read it and told the reporter to call the local veterans hospital for a comment. It turns out that none of the homeless man's story was true. They knew who he was but said they had no record of his being a veteran of any branch of service. Still, they had tried to direct him to some social service agencies and could never get him to stick to any program that would take him out of his present state. The young journalist learned a valuable lesson about skepticism. He wanted to believe the homeless man so much that he did not do all of the reporting he should have.

Healthy skepticism is a far cry from cynicism, where someone not only questions but also disbelieves anything he or she is told. Some journalists who are lied to about many important things become cynics, especially toward groups of people such as government bureaucrats and public relations practitioners. Cynicism does not help a person become a better journalist; skepticism does.

Working within the News Organization

Journalists must take the personal characteristics described in the previous sections into the news organization where they encounter a different level of the culture of journalism. Within the organization, they have to learn the rules of expected behavior, both personal and professional. They become familiar with the customs, conventions, and shared values of the organization. These values may be peculiar to the organization itself, they may be part of the larger corporate entity that owns the local news organization, or they may be part of an even larger culture of shared values that is the field of journalism. Journalists need to adjust their personal traits to fit comfortably into this larger set of values.

New journalists must be oriented to a news organization just as any new employee must learn the rules and operations of a company. These include general attitudes toward working hours (how important is it to be on time, for instance), acceptable working attire, and operational rules (such as when it is appropriate to go to lunch or dinner). As employees learn these things, they are also learning how tightly the organization is run and what the management believes to be important.

Any news organization will expect its journalists to work very hard and be productive. This will go beyond just completing the tasks that are assigned by an editor. Journalists are generally expected to be proactive, to do more than the strict completion of assignments. They are expected to make suggestions about the things they are working on—additional stories, better headlines, changes in layout and design. Some young journalists come into an organization wanting to change many things and may be frustrated by the status quo into which the organization seems to be locked. In those instances, they need to be patient. The organization will eventually be affected by the presence of a good young reporter.

As part of the orientation process, a news organization may ask new employees to read and sign the organization's code of ethics (see Chapter 23), and most will certainly have a drug and alcohol policy that employees must adhere to. The code of ethics is a major indication of what the organization feels is important in the practice of journalism. New employees should talk with editors or other journalists about how the organization enforces this code of ethics and what parts of it are of particular concern to the organization.

All news organizations expect all employees to accept accuracy in the presentation of information as a chief and overriding goal. All of the actions of all journalists—whether they are reporting, writing, editing, or designing—should be oriented to this goal. This attitude toward accuracy is not only a shared value of journalists but also of the news organization. It is both a moral and practical value. Morally, individuals and organizations do not want to engage in activities that have an underlying dishonesty to them. Practically, inaccurate information—or information that was sloppily gathered and edited—will damage the organization's credibility and may cost the organization money in terms of lost subscriptions or lawsuits. Most news organizations do not take the trouble to explain this to their employees; they expect them to have this orientation when they first walk through the door.

Another custom and value of the news organization is likely to be collaboration. The news business is a collaborative one; that is, news is produced by many hands, not just by individual journalists. It takes reporters, editors, photographers, graphics journalists, designers, and many others to work together to make the day's product. A young reporter cannot expect to have his or her work go through the organization's editing process without change. These changes are made to improve the article, headline, or design. The changes may or may not do that. Although the individual journalist can object to individual changes, he or she cannot object to the process itself. That must be accepted as part of the normal workings of journalism.

Part of these normal workings, too, is the authority of the editor. An editor has to take responsibility for the actions and the products of the individual journalist (see Chapter 12). Because that responsibility rests on the editor, the individual journalists need to respond positively to the suggestions, directions, and commands of the editor. Most news organizations are oriented toward debate and discussion, so that editors are not totalitarian dictators whose commands cannot be challenged. Good editors invite discussions and even challenges because they respect the people they work with and want to hear their ideas. When the discussions are finished, however, it is the editor who must make decisions (and the higher up the organizational ladder an editor goes, the more effect his or her decisions will have on the entire organization).

Reporters decide, often in consultation with their editors, what articles they will write and what sources they will use in gathering the information for those stories. They may even decide the approach that a story will take. An editor decides if the story is acceptable, when it will run, where it will be placed, and how the news organization will respond if there are consequences to the story. Editors make these decisions by weighing many factors, and individual journalists have to respect the responsibility of the editor to make these decisions.

Dealing with Sources

As a representative of the news organization, the reporter must build a relationship with his or her sources. Sometimes these sources will be dealt with only once for a single story, and in those instances, the source will know the reporter only as a representative of the organization. In other instances, however, the reporter–source relationship will be ongoing. That relationship can become personal, but the professional aspects of it must always take into consideration the news organization. Although most organizations do not have many formal rules about how reporters should deal with sources, most of them will have standards that have developed over time.

For instance, a news organization will want a reporter to deal honestly with a source; that is, reporters are generally expected to identify themselves as reporters working for the news organization before gathering any significant information from the source. Most news organizations will not allow sources to have any control over information once it is given to the reporter. A reporter cannot promise to let a source review material or quotations before they are published or broadcast.

Some news organizations do have specific rules about when a source can be offered confidentiality and when unnamed sources can be used in a news story. Usually, a source can be offered confidentiality only if the information is vital to an important story the organization is pursuing and if that source is the only foreseeable way in which the organization can obtain the information. The organization will also take into account the reason the source needs confidentiality. Many news organizations tell reporters not to offer confidentiality to a source unless they have first consulted with an editor about it, although certain circumstances sometimes make that impossible.

The reason for these rules about offers of confidentiality is that such offers are not simply agreements between the individual reporter and the source. They are agreements between the organization and the source. If legal trouble for the reporter results from the offer of confidentiality, a news organization has the obligation to back the reporter up, and that could result in significant monetary costs as well as costs with regard to the organization's reputation and relationships.

Objectivity and Fairness

Another expectation that news organizations have of their journalists is that they will gather and handle information objectively. Part of the culture of journalism is that journalists will not pursue a political or social agenda; rather, their professional agenda is one of gathering all relevant information from all relevant sources. That information should be presented accurately and fairly. Sometimes, this orientation is referred to as objectivity, and it is the subject of continuing debate within journalistic circles. Despite the debate, objectivity in some form is a shared value of journalists, and it is in operation in all parts of the journalistic process.

One of the ways in which this ideal of objectivity and fairness is pursued is by having journalists maintain a separation from sources and organizations that the journalists may cover or make news decisions about. For instance, some organizations have rules against reporters and editors joining political parties or contributing time and

Quote 2.2

JACK FULLER

On objectivity

Objectivity, along with certain other concepts journalists have used to describe their truth discipline, assumes an independence between the observer and the phenomenon observed that simply does not exist. Whether at the level of skittering sub-atomic particles or the clash of nations, the object may be transformed by the attention paid to it.

Jack Fuller is a former editor of the Chicago Tribune *and president of the Tribune Company. He is the author of* News Values: Ideas for an Information Age *and five novels.*

money to political efforts. If not rules, there are certainly understandings that journalists may not be part of organizations they cover. A sports reporter who is the newspaper's outdoors writer would not be able to join a hunting club or fishing organization, for example. But does this mean that the person who writes about religion for the newspaper would not be able to join a church? Few news organizations would go that far, but it does demonstrate the problem with this approach to journalism. The idea of separation from the community is, like objectivity, one that is hotly debated within the profession. Yet, separation is something in which the culture of journalism places some value.

ARE THE NEWS MEDIA LIBERAL OR CONSERVATIVE? (PART 1)

Do the news media have a political agenda?

Many people think they do, particularly when the media seem to be speaking against those people's own political leanings.

But to ask this simple question and expect a simple answer is to demonstrate a lack of understanding about the news media and the way they operate. So, let's back up and start with a few basics.

The concept of the "news media" or "media" as being a monolithic whole is false. The news media are many different organizations with different purposes, processes, and audiences. They do not act in concert. They certainly watch what other news organizations do, and they are sometimes influenced by the actions of another organization. But to speak of the media as an entity, particularly one that an individual can monitor, is simply incorrect.

Many different people are involved in the process of journalism. They are individuals with many different backgrounds and points of view. That they should share a single political point of view is not logical. Nor is it possible for one individual to have much influence over all of these people.

Generally, journalists subscribe to the professional standard of presenting information accurately and fairly. They know that their profession is constantly under fire for bias—both from the left and the right—and they try to avoid giving ammunition to their critics.

A person who wants to criticize the media for political bias should acknowledge these fundamental truths about the media first.

Do news organizations fall short in their efforts to achieve fair and accurate reporting? Do individual journalists have biases that sometimes show up in their presentation of the news? If so, is it deliberate?

The answer to all of these questions is yes, sometimes. Journalism is practiced by human beings, not by angels. Humans do not always achieve the highest standards that they set for themselves.

When journalists fail to adhere to these standards, are they more likely to fail toward a liberal or conservative point of view? That's where you can get a good argument. Bernard Goldberg, a former correspondent for CBS News, writes in his book *Bias: A CBS Insider Exposes How the Media Distort the News* that the problem of liberal bias in the news media goes much farther than party politics. It is pervasive, he says, in the way in which the news media handle all political and social stories.

On the other hand, Eric Alterman, in his book *What Liberal Media? The Truth about Bias in the News,* argues that there is more conservative bias in the presentation of news than liberal bias. The reality is that conservatives just complain about it more, he writes.

So, what do you think? Before answering that, spend a couple of weeks reading these and other books about the media and exposing yourself to as many media outlets as possible. Then you'll have some evidence, not just impressions, for your conclusions.

Finally, an important part of the culture of journalism for a journalist to discover within the news organization is what happens when mistakes are made. When mistakes go beyond minor learning miscalculations is when the policies and processes of the news organization come into play. Most news organizations have a procedure for acknowledging and correcting mistakes. On many newspapers, corrections are run in certain prominent parts of the newspaper. When such a correction is run, chances are those who are responsible had to follow some internal procedures—filling out a form, writing a memo to the editor, and so on—as a way of acknowledging the seriousness of the error without being humiliated.

Unacceptable Practices

Incidents involving dishonesty or double-dealing on the part of the journalist are likely to result in the suspension of the journalist from work or dismissal.

Plagiarism

Copying the words of another person and using them as one's own without proper credit is plagiarism. The journalist who does this is taking credit for the work of another person, and to be found doing this is a serious blight on a person's reputation as well as the news organization that employs this person. A number of local newspaper columnists have gotten into serious trouble and have been dismissed because they copied other people's work and did not give proper credit. Journalists who get caught doing this are likely to blame the pressure of producing on a deadline, but the culture of journalism simply does not tolerate plagiarism.

Fabricating Information

In 1980, Janet Cooke, a reporter for the *Washington Post,* wrote a compelling series on the world of "Little Jimmy," an eight-year-old heroin addict in the inner city of the nation's capital. The story was full of detail and direct quotations. It was so well written that it won a Pulitzer Prize. The problem was there was no little Jimmy, and although Cooke had done a good bit of research on the problem of drug addition in children, she had written about a prototype, not a real person. Because she had been using anonymous sources and her editors did not have much information on what she was doing, she was able to get her articles into the paper.

Just a few days after the prize was announced in April 1981, the *Post*'s editors began to realize there was a problem with the story. They conducted an intensive set of interviews with everyone involved. After satisfying themselves that the story had been fabricated, they announced the deception, dismissed Cooke, and returned the Pulitzer Prize. It was a most embarrassing moment for a newspaper that had prided itself on its careful and precise procedures.

No news organization wants to go through what the *Post* suffered during the Janet Cooke fiasco. That is why fabricating information—when discovered—usually results in the immediate dismissal of all who have participated in it.

Altering a Photograph

Photographs are always the subjects of detailed attention and deep concern from editors. Photographs have immediate impact with the public when words often do not.
They are perceived to show a truth, an image that any of us would see if we had shot
the picture ourselves.

Certain darkroom or digital enhancements to a photograph are acceptable within
the culture of journalism. For instance, a photo editor might darken or lighten a photograph to make the subject more visible or more understandable to the viewer. But
a photo editor cannot change the essential information in the picture or the basic nature of the photograph itself. During the Iraqi War in 2003, a *Los Angeles Times* photographer assigned to a British military unit operating near Basra combined the
elements of two photographs he had taken and sent them to the newspaper. The photo
was published on the first page of the *Times* as well as in the *Chicago Tribune* and
the *Hartford Courant.* The next day an employee of the newspaper in Hartford noticed that a part of the photo seemed to be duplicated in another part of the photo;
she informed the copy desk, which set off an investigation back in Los Angeles. When
the photographer confessed that he had put elements of two pictures together, he was
fired immediately.

Working for a Separate Publication without the Editor's Knowledge

Most news organizations expect to have the complete professional efforts of the people whom they employ. Consequently, it is usually a violation of the rules of the organization for a reporter to cover a news story for his or her primary employer and
then write something about the same event or subject for another publication.

One of the major reasons for such a rule is that editors do not want journalists
to be tempted into holding back information about stories they cover. A journalist
might withhold some details from a news story for the newspaper, thinking that he
or she could include them in a magazine piece about the same event.

Daily news reporters often do sell articles to magazines and other publications
that are not considered direct competition to their own organizations. They do so,
however, only with the approval of their editors and usually when the subject of the
magazine article is not about something they would be working on for the newspaper. What is important here is that journalists must fully disclose their activities to
their editors. Often these extra-employment activities will not cause a problem for
the editor, but when there is the potential for a problem, the journalist is obligated
to tell an editor.

News Organizations in the Larger Culture of Journalism

News organizations provide the main venues for the culture of journalism. They are
the environment in which professional journalists work, and the factors that come
together to make a news organization contribute heavily to the culture of journalism.
Three of those factors are (1) although news organizations are profit-making ventures,

ARE THE NEWS MEDIA LIBERAL OR CONSERVATIVE? (PART 2)

Much of the question revolves around the meanings of the terms *liberal* and *conservative*.

One of the common understandings of people who are "liberal" is that they believe society has many areas in which change or improvements are needed. They see the government as the appropriate vehicle to implement these changes.

Opposing this point of view are "conservatives," who believe that much about society and social structures is good and should not be changed. In fact, some conservatives believe that liberal reforms of the recent past should be undone. They do not believe that the government is the proper vehicle for changing society and generally argue for government to be as small as possible, intruding in the lives of individuals only when absolutely necessary.

Set in this context, journalism can be seen as a "liberal" profession. The commonly accepted definitions of news do not assume that society is good; that is, journalism often devotes itself to reporting the ills of society—the scandals, corruption, poverty, and shortcomings of society's institutions. This reporting sometimes upsets those with privilege and power because it is seen as an attack on their position.

Another argument that journalism is a "liberal" profession follows from this. People are often attracted to journalism because they want to change things in society; they want to expose society's faults and shortcomings. People do not become journalists, it is argued, because they like the way things are.

But these liberal tendencies are counterbalanced (some might say overwhelmed) by "conservative" forces within the news media. One of the forces is the fact that news organizations are profit-making businesses. They are multimillion dollar entities operated by conservative, rich, and privileged men and women. To maximize their profits, news organizations generally do not go out of their way to offend significant parts of society.

This fact leads news organizations to ignore or downplay stories that might disrupt the order of society or might give a voice to those who lack power and privilege. Instead of concentrating on exposing the ills of society, critics argue, news organizations pay an inordinate amount of attention to celebrities and to stories that have little importance to a broader society.

So, what do you think? Are the liberal tendencies of the profession held in check by the conservative nature of its structure and organization?

---

they retain an independence few other businesses have; (2) the major operational tool that news organizations use to manage their work is deadlines; and (3) news organizations foster a spirit of competition that affects how they operate.

With rare exceptions, news organizations are businesses that must make a profit to maintain operations. As such, they must adhere to the laws and regulations that govern other businesses. That is, they must pay at least minimum wage to all employees, and they must not ask hourly employees to work more than forty hours a week without extra compensation. They must conform to all of the workplace health and safety regulations set up by local, state, and national agencies. They must pay the same taxes that other businesses pay.

But news organizations are not like other businesses. Their product—the news—remains unregulated. No laws exist governing what newspapers may or must print (with the small exception of certain postal regulations) or what televisions news programs can air. There are no government regulations about how a newspaper must

| FIGURE 2.3 | **Public's Confidence in the News Media Less Than Overwhelming** |

A national survey conducted by the Pew Center for the People and the Press in July 2002 found that many people had serious reservations about the news media and the job they were doing.

NEWS ORGANIZATIONS . . .

Are politically biased	59%
Are careful not to be biased	26%
Neither/don't know	15%
Try to cover up mistakes	67%
Are willing to admit mistakes	23%
Neither/don't know	10%
Usually get facts straight	35%
Usually report inaccurately	56%
Don't know	9%
Stand up for America	49%
Are too critical of America	35%
Neither/don't know	20%
Are highly professional	49%
Are not professional	31%
Neither/don't know	20%
Are moral	39%
Are immoral	36%
Neither/don't know	25%
Care about the people they report on	30%
Don't care	55%
Neither/don't know	15%

NEWS MEDIA . . .

Help society solve its problems	31%
Get in the way	58%
Don't know	11%

These results are based on a national survey of 995 respondents conducted July 22–28, 2002.

Source: Pew Center for the People and the Press http://people-press.org/reports/display.php3?ReportID=159

look, how many copies it can print, how many pictures it can have, or the size of type it must use for its body copy and headlines. Likewise, television and radio stations can broadcast their news in any way they want to and at any time they desire.

Most importantly, no laws exist that allow any individual or agency to review the content of a newspaper or news broadcast before it is presented to the public. Certainly libel laws can visit dire consequences on news organizations that illegally damage a person's reputation. But an individual who believes that he or she is about to be libeled by a news organization has no power whatever to stop the publication of that libel. Nor does any government have any power of prior review over a news organization.

In reality, of course, news organizations cannot act with absolute impunity. They must certainly weigh the consequences of what they publish and broadcast. We have already mentioned libel laws, but there are other consequences that serve as a check on the actions of journalists. One of the most important is the one we mentioned first in this section: The organization is a business that must make a profit. It must take some care not to offend its readers and viewers or its advertisers. But it certainly can offend those constituents if it chooses to do so.

This independence from regulation of its content is the basic fact of the larger culture of journalism in which news organizations operate. It gives editors and journalists the freedom to make decisions about content solely on how important the content is and on how they believe that content should be presented.

The independence of news organizations is tempered by the fact that they must produce a complex product—the news—on a daily or even hourly basis. To do that, they must use deadlines. In many ways, news organizations are no different from other businesses that must also operate through a series of production deadlines. However, with news organizations, these deadlines take on additional meaning because they affect the actions and thinking of the journalists within the organization.

Deadlines are part of the lore and modern mind-set of the journalist and the news organization. Both work to meet deadlines and make many decisions based on the fact that deadlines exist. A news organization must establish reasonable and workable deadlines that make sense to both the production and editorial sides of the operation. They must buy equipment that will allow employees to meet those deadlines. And they must have some plan in place for stretching or bending a deadline when necessary.

Some argue that news on the Web is changing the whole notion of deadlines (see Chapter 7). Because news and information can be distributed instantly on the Web—with little time necessary for production—some news organizations that have previously worked with only one or a few deadlines each day are now operating on their Web sites with no deadlines at all. News is ready whenever it is ready, and that's when it is posted. We have yet to realize the full implications of this thinking on journalists and their organizations.

A third concept important to the culture of journalism in news organizations is that of competition. Although many newspapers and some television news organizations today operate as monopolies, competition is still an important part of the thinking of journalists and their organizations. Journalists want to discover important information that no one else has found. They want to be the first to post, print, or broadcast it. They sometimes take pains to hide information from competitors until they are ready to release it. In 1999 when

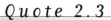

Quote 2.3

DUKE ELLINGTON

On deadlines

I don't need time. What I need is a deadline.

Duke Ellington was a jazz pianist, composer, and conductor who lived from 1899 to 1974.

the *St. Paul Pioneer-Press* investigated an academic cheating scandal in the University of Minnesota basketball program, reporters and editors kept what they were doing as quiet as possible for as long as they could because they did not want the *Minneapolis Star Tribune* to start its own investigation. The ploy worked. When the first story was printed by the *Pioneer-Press*, the *Star Tribune* had nothing on it. Stories such as these abound in the history of journalism, and they continue to appear today.

Getting a big story first—a "scoop" in the parlance of journalism—is a matter of great pride for a news organization. It affirms that the organization is practicing good journalism and brings a certain amount of praise to the organization from within the profession. Occasionally, that praise comes from those outside the profession, too. Even though it was thirty years ago, many people still remember that the *Washington Post* consistently beat the *New York Times* and all other news organizations in its reporting of the Watergate scandal that eventually toppled the presidency of Richard Nixon.

CIVIC JOURNALISM

In the 1990s an idea took hold in the field of journalism that challenged the assumption and practice of journalists separating themselves from their communities and playing the roll of independent observer.

Journalism should do more than observe, many journalists and professors said. It should participate. Civic life in America had become so fractured that journalists should lead an effort in local communities to find solutions to daunting problems.

Thus was born the civic journalism (sometimes called public journalism) movement.

In addition to the benefits of doing civic good, advocates maintained, this idea would help news organizations reconnect with their readers and viewers and would reestablish the relevance of journalism in the lives of people.

Many editors and news directors accepted this idea and devoted their news organizations to it. They did things such as taking surveys to find out what people saw as the real issues facing them. They held public meetings in which solutions to civic problems were discussed, and they participated in plans to implement those solutions. Newspapers such as the *Wichita (Kansas) Eagle* and the *Charlotte (North Carolina) Observer* took the lead in the civic journalism movement.

But not everyone believes that civic journalism is a good thing for the profession. Veteran journalist and educator Carl Sessions Stepp, for instance, says the civic journalism movement assumes that, first, civic life is broken, and second, journalism should fix it. Neither assumption may be correct, he writes.

Others, too, are bothered by journalists losing their ability to judge events independently. They cannot do so if they are participants in those events.

The civic journalism idea is still being debated. It continues to be adopted by some news organizations and resisted by others.

For more information and discussion about civic journalism, you should begin with the book *What Are Journalists For?* by Jay Rosen (Yale University Press, 1999) and you should visit the web site for the Pew Center for Civic Journalism (www.pewcenter.org).

A Dynamic Culture

The ways of journalists and news organizations are, in scriptural terms, wondrous to behold. Deadlines, competition, and "scoops" seem to work against the values of accuracy, meticulousness, and occasionally even honesty. Yet they are all part of the mix of what makes journalism a vital and exciting profession.

QUESTIONS FOR DISCUSSION

1. Compare the personal characteristics listed in this chapter to those listed for reporters in Chapter 8. Where is there overlap? What are the differences?
2. The beginning of the chapter describes the reaction of the *Chicago Tribune* to news that a plane flown by John F. Kennedy Jr. was missing. Should the *Tribune* have devoted so much time and effort to covering that story?
3. How do you react to the results of the survey presented in Figure 2.2? What would be your responses to these questions?
4. This chapter relates a story about the mayor of a small town who had wrecked his car. A student photojournalist took pictures at the scene but was told by a policeman that she should not be doing that. How would you have reacted in that situation? Should those pictures have been published?

RELATED WEB SITES

Best Practices: The Art of Leadership in News Organizations, www.freedomforum.org/templates/document.asp?documentID=16166

Committee of Concerned Journalists, www.journalism.org

The Pulitzer Prizes, www.pulitzer.org

Media Leaders Forum, www.manship.lsu.edu/forum/media_leaders_forum.htm

READINGS AND REFERENCES

Cappella, J. N., & Jamieson, K. H. (1997). *Spiral of cynicism: The press and the public good.* New York: Oxford University Press.

Fuller, J. (1996). *News values.* Chicago: University of Chicago Press.

Hachten, W. A. (1998). *The troubles of journalism.* Madison: University of Wisconsin Press.

Kovach, B., & Rosenstiel, T. (2001). *The elements of journalism.* New York: Crown Publishers.

Roberts, G. (Ed.). (2001). *Leaving readers behind: The age of corporate newspapering.* Fayetteville: University of Arkansas Press.

Chapter Three

Becoming a Journalist

Key Concepts and Terms

1. Becoming a professional journalist takes preparation and planning.

2. Journalism requires from its practitioners a wide range of knowledge and interests.

3. Potential journalists can begin their preparation by paying a lot of attention to news events and to the way they are reported in various media.

4. Becoming a journalist requires knowing a good bit about history.

5. Writing is the most important skill a potential journalist can develop.

6. Reading widely is the mark of a good journalist.

7. Internships: short-term jobs that college students get working for media organizations; traditionally, internships last for one semester and are often in the summer.

Vignette

Maybe it was September 11.

You sat in front of your television most of the day—except for the time you were on the Web trying to find out more news or messaging friends or on the phone talking about what happened. You watched the anchors and news reporters, live at the scene, bringing their audiences information under great pressure and emotion.

Or maybe it was something you read in a newspaper or magazine.

The writing or the photography planted the thought that this is something that would be fun and exciting and important. You could see your name as the byline for the article or in the photo credit for the picture.

Or maybe it was the Web.

You like surfing, but you have your favorite sites. You like to find things out and keep up with the latest that's happening. And you said to yourself, "If I could get somebody to pay me to do this, that would be great!"

Or maybe it was Sports Center.

You spend a good deal of time watching ESPN and sports on television. You think it would great to cover the big game for a live audience.

Or maybe you just like to write or take pictures or design pages and web sites. You like people to read and look at what you've done. You like to tell people things and enrich their lives. You're curious about the world, and you want to find a way to channel that curiosity.

Whatever sparked the interest—it doesn't really matter except to you—you're thinking about getting into some form of journalism.

The question to ask now is: How do I get there?

Prepare

Journalism, as we discuss elsewhere in this book, is a profession that requires no degree or special training to enter the field. A person may simply declare himself or herself a journalist and begin publishing and distributing a newsletter or posting a web site. In the eyes of the law and in the spirit of the First Amendment, that person is as much a journalist as a person who has an advanced degree and is an editor of a major daily newspaper.

Most people who want to enter the field of journalism go through a training process that may take years and that, in a very real sense, never stops. The field of journalism is so vast and dynamic that the people who work there are always journalists-in-training.

So how do you start? The first step is to develop a set of interests that may have nothing directly to do with journalism. These interests might include politics, sports, cooking, rock music, mystery novels, or rock climbing. Whatever it is that fascinates you should be pursued. Journalists are people who are interested in the world around them. They are genuinely curious—not about everything, of course, but about certain things. The interests you develop will likely have a direct bearing on your journalistic career. An interest, whether it is a hobby or an expertise, helps you get in touch with the world in the way that journalists need to be.

It also helps begin the process that all journalists should undertake of developing a wide range of knowledge about many different subjects. Journalists need not be historians, but they need to know enough history to understand the context in which events take place. America's war on terrorism, for instance, did not begin on September 11, 2001. It has roots that go back many decades. The breakup of the *Columbia* spacecraft in 2002 was not an isolated tragedy. It is connected to accidents that the space program has had dating back to the 1950s. Journalists have to understand and judge current events by what has happened in the past in order to draw intelligent conclusions about them.

This wide range of knowledge comes through reading. Nothing you can do to help you begin a journalism career will benefit you more than reading. You should also try to sample various media, particularly newspapers and magazines, even if you think they will not contain articles of interest to you. Not only will a wide range of reading help build a wide range of knowledge, but it will also help develop writing skills.

Survey after survey of media professionals, especially those who hire people for entry-level jobs, say that writing is the number-one skill that they look for in potential employees. Using the language well is an integral part of the profession. Journalists are expected to have knowledge of the rules of grammar, spelling, and punctuation. They should also have a wide vocabulary that includes the knowledge of the exact meanings of words and the common uses of those words. They should be confident in their use of the language, and they should understand journalistic forms.

All of this knowledge comes only through reading.

Learn about the Field

The field of journalism is in itself fascinating, and it is often in the news. The field is dynamic. New media organizations are being formed. Issues of journalism, such as news coverage, ethics, leaks, anonymous sources, plagiarism and misrepresentation, privacy, libel, and many others, are constantly under public discussion.

Quote 3.1

ANONYMOUS

On reading

The man who does not read good books has no advantage over the man who can't read them.

This quotation is often attributed to Mark Twain (it sounds very Twain-like), but there is no evidence that he said it.

People who want to get into journalism should learn as much about it as possible. A number of magazines pay a lot of attention to the media and the field of journalism, including *Time* and *Newsweek*. The field also has some excellent trade journals such as *Editor and Publisher*, the *Columbia Journalism Review*, *Presstime*, and the *American Journalism Review*. In addition, the Web offers some exceptional resources for people who want to keep up with what is going on in the field. Chief among them are the web site of the Poynter Institute in St. Petersburg, Florida (www.poynter.org), dedicated to journalism training; the web site of the coalition of the Project for Excellence in Journalism and the Committee of Concerned Journalists (www.journalism.org); Online Journalism Review (www.ojr.org), a product of the Annenburg School of Communication at the University of Southern California; and a web site dedicated to news about the media (www.IwantMedia.com). These are just a few of the sites you should visit on a regular basis.

In addition, there are numerous organizations that you can join. The Society of Professional Journalists (www.spj.org) is one of the major organizations for journalists. Its full membership is limited to working journalists, journalism educators, and college students majoring in journalism. The Quill and Scroll Society is an organization for high school journalists, which publishes *Quill and Scroll Magazine.* The American Society of Newspaper Editors has a special web site for high school journalists (www.high schooljournalism.org), and so does the Dow Jones Newspaper Fund (www.djnews paperfund.dowjones.com). Other journalism groups have been formed around ethnic identities, such as the National Association of Black Journalists (www.nabj.org) and the National Association of Hispanic Journalists (www.nahj.org), and around special journalists' interests and job categories (Investigative Reporters and Editors, National Conference of Editorial Writers, Society for News Design, Society for Environmental Journalists, etc.). Joining these groups not only gains you access to a lot of information, but also these organizations often gather up job and internship opportunities.

Another way of learning about the field is to read books by and about journalists. Sometimes these books are genuinely evocative about the field. Some are even highly critical of the state of the profession. One such book was Bernard Goldberg's memoir, *Bias: A CBS Insider Exposes How the Media Distort the News.* Much can be learned from these books, even if you may not agree with their conclusions. One classic book about reporting is *All the President's Men* by Bob Woodward and Carl Bernstein, the two *Washington Post* reporters who did the most to uncover the Watergate scandal in 1972 and 1973. (See the sidebar on Watergate in Chapter 23.) This book details the "legwork," the reporting methods that the authors used in getting information about the Nixon White House and reelection campaign. The methods they used are still applicable for reporters today.

Quote 3.2

GEORGE FOX MOTT

On the appeal of being a newspaperman

For one reason or another there has gathered about the newspaperman's job an atmosphere of mystery or romance, a sort of glamour that has an unfailing appeal for youth on the quest for a vocation.

George Fox Mott was a writer and educator in the first half of the twentieth century.

Finally, talking with journalists whenever you get the opportunity is a great way of getting connected to the field. Most reporters and editors are happy to talk about what they do and are complimented when asked. Any contacts you make at any stage of your career, even if it is just beginning, are bound to be helpful to you at some point.

Get Training

Most people who enter the field of journalism today have had some type of formal journalistic training. Most often this occurs in colleges and universities that offer degrees in journalism or mass communication. The nation has many fine and reputable journalism programs at colleges both large and small.

The decision to choose a college is usually not based on a single academic program alone. One thing to look for is the amount of nonjournalism courses required by the program. The general rule is that no more than 33 percent of the courses you take in college should be related to journalism or mass communication. You should have room in your schedule to take many other courses. If you have a nonjournalism interest that you want to pursue in college, such as business or criminal justice or political science, the requirements of the journalism program should allow you to do so.

Another thing to look at in choosing a college is the student media—the campus newspaper, the news web site, and the campus radio station. They will often reflect the quality of teaching that occurs at the college and the commitment the college has made to having a good program. At private schools particularly, you will want to check out how committed the college is to freedom of expression and to allowing the newspaper to be run without interference from the college's administration or the student government.

Go to Work

Journalism education is not just a matter of reading, going to class, and making good grades. It is also a matter of practice. You should start applying the skills of the journalist as soon as possible and in any way you can.

For some fortunate students, this means working on their high school newspaper or news web site if possible. Other students have to wait until they get to college before they are able to work with some kind of news organization.

But, within the first week on campus, you should make contact with one of the student media organizations. Most of these organizations do not require that you be a journalism major or that you have taken certain classes before beginning to work. All they want is to know that you are interested and are willing to show up when you say you can.

GETTING HELP

Journalists, whether they are just getting started or already in midcareer, have plenty of resources available to help them accomplish their goals. They have to know three words: *scholarships, internships,* and *fellowships.*

Someone who is just starting out will be most interested in scholarships, the financial aid that helps pay college tuition and expenses. If you are still in high school but have selected a college where you plan to study journalism, you will want to investigate the scholarships offered by the school. Most programs have some kind of a scholarship fund, but sometimes you have to ask about it and find out specifically what the requirements are.

Another place to look, whether or not you have selected a college, is the American Society of Newspaper Editor's web page for high school journalism. This site lists many scholarship opportunities by state and organization, as well as many scholarships for minorities: www.highschooljournalism.org/students/schl_index.cfm.

Many local and national organizations offer general scholarships and a few give money specifically for the student of journalism. Many journalism professional societies, both locally and nationally, offer scholarships (see the American Copyeditors Society, www.copydesk.org, for instance). Another good resource is the Youth and the Media Bibliography, which contains information on getting into journalism, including many sources of college scholarships (www.poynter.org/content/content_view.asp?id=6563).

You should note that many scholarships are awarded to college students already studying journalism rather than to high school students about to enter the field. If you are in high school, do not be discouraged by that—and do not forget it. Once you are in college, you will be eligible for many things that were not available to you before.

Many scholarships are available to students interested in pursuing broadcasting. You can begin at the Broadcasting Education Association (BEA) scholarships and grants page (www.beaweb.org/scholarships.html). There you will find links to many state broadcasting organizations that offer scholarships.

And while you are in high school and later in college, don't forget writing competitions sponsored by local and national groups. These can be a good source of money while you are in high school and also a source of college scholarships. For example, the Dow Jones Newspaper Fund foundation offers a national writing competition through the summer workshops that it sponsors. According to its web site, "Eight students chosen from the pool receive $1,000 college scholarships from the Fund. Incoming college freshmen at the time of the award receive their scholarships in the sophomore year. For graduating high school seniors, the award is payable for the freshman and sophomore years, provided the student maintains an average of 2.5 and an interest in journalism" (http://djnewspaperfund.dowjones.com/fund/hss_writing_competition.asp).

Once you are in college, gaining an internship in which you work for a professional news organization (and get paid) will be important. The place to start looking for an internship is with your college faculty, who are likely to have a good knowledge of where internships are offered locally. To search nationally, go to the ASNE web page on internships (www.asne.org/internships) for a long list of internships in every part of journalism, including graphics, photography, and design.

Another good source for internship information is the jobs page run by the *Detroit Free Press* (www.freep.com/jobspage/interns). That site lists internships plus tips on getting an internship and making the most of it.

If you are a working journalist and want to continue your education or do a special project, you may be able to get a fellowship for financial support. Many foundations and professional associations offer fellowships for investigative journalism, continued education, international travel, and the like. Start your search at www.journalismjobs.com/Fellowship_Listings.cfm. Fellowships are competitive, but the grants are often generous enough to support living expenses and travel.

March 21, 2004

Mr. Nicholas Stringfellow
City Editor, Woodridge Morning Call
1566 Main Street
Woodridge, Wisconsin

Dear Mr. Stringfellow:

I would like to apply for a summer internship with the Woodridge Morning Call. I understand from my journalism professors at Woodson State University that such positions are available.

I am a sophomore majoring in journalism at Woodson State University. My academic minor is history. Since beginning at Woodson, I have worked in various positions with the Woodson Gazette. I am currently the news editor of the paper and supervise a staff of about a dozen reporters.

Our university library receives copies of your newspaper, and I have had the opportunity to look at a number of current issues. I also look at your web site on a regular basis. I have noted that your paper gives a good deal of coverage to environmental issues affecting Woodridge and the surrounding area. The management of the environment is one of my major interests, and I believe that I could make a contribution to this coverage.

I am planning a career in journalism, but I have not settled on a specific goal. I enjoy reporting and feel like I am good at finding out information. An internship with your paper would help me hone my reporting and writing skills. I also believe that I could make a contribution to your newspaper if given an intern's position.

I have enclosed a resume to give you some more information. I trust that you will give it your full consideration, and I hope to hear from you soon.

Sincerely,

Tracy L. Jones

FIGURE 3.1   Letter of Application and Résumé Everyone should have an up-to-date résumé that can be sent out whenever the situation calls for one. Sometimes students worry that they have very little to put on their résumés. That's true, but potential employers do not expect that students will have a lot on their résumés. Résumés should be accurate and easy to read. They should contain information that the employer is interested in, such as the one shown here. Application letters are not easy to write. A letter should try to connect with the recipient on his or her terms—not on the terms of the writer of the letter. Here the writer is trying to show the recipient that she is really interested in a job and that she has taken some steps on her own to try to get one.

Tracy L. Jones

Campus address: Permanent address:
Box 8778   1227 East Elm Street
Woodson State University   Mount Moriah, Wisconsin 65888
Woodson, Wisconsin 65544
978-854-3211   978-567-8999
tjones04@woodsonst.edu

Education

Woodson State University
  Major in journalism; minor in history
  Current status: Sophomore
  Relevant courses: Introduction to Journalism, Newswriting, Editing
  Overall grade point average: 2.96; average in major courses: 3.30
  Scholarships: Freshman Alumni; Sophomore Scholarship of Merit

Mount Moriah High School
  Graduated June 2004, grade point average: 3.7
  Selected extracurricular activities: Editor, Eagle's Flight (student newspaper);
    Glee Club; Latin Club
  Honors: National Honor Society; First place, State Debate Tournament

Professional and work experience

News editor, Woodson Gazette. Duties: coordinate campus news coverage for
twice-weekly student newspaper; assign general assignment reporters, supervise
beat reporters; edit news stories. Previous positions: general assignment reporter,
student government beat reporter.

Clerk, Gaines Department Store, 2001–2004, part-time during the school year, full
time during the summers

Other activities

Volunteer, Habitat for Humanity, 2000–2004
Church mission trip, Cabrerra, Mexico, summer 2002

References

Dr. Morris Estes   Dr. Harry Coile   Dr. Mary Stephens
Principal   Professor   Professor
Mt. Moriah High   Department of Journalism   Department of History
1220 Eagle's Flight Drive Woodson State University   Woodson State University
Mt. Moriah, Wisconsin   Woodson, Wisconsin   Woodson, Wisconsin
65889   65544   65544
978-554-5545   978-654-6565   978-654-5505

FIGURE 3.1   Continued

As soon as you begin to work, save everything that you do (both in print and electronically if possible). You will want to build a "clip file," a scrapbook of your work that eventually you will be able to show to potential employers. Many students forget about doing this until they are trying to find a job, and then they have a difficult time finding their work. Get into the habit quickly of putting aside a copy of everything that you do.

During the first year of college, you should begin investigating the possibility of an internship. An internship is a job for a news organization that lasts a short amount of time. Many journalism programs will give a limited amount of academic credit for this work; some programs require that you have at least one internship before graduating. Normally, internships are completed during the summer. Many newspapers have come to count on having reporting, editing, and even photography interns during the summer.

Internships are highly valuable opportunities. Students get an inside view of a news organization, and they are expected to contribute in some way to the news product of the organization. Different organizations will have different ways of training and supervising interns. Most are genuinely interested in seeing that students have a good experience and that they learn a good deal about the profession during their time at the organization.

Having an internship can take a graduating student a long way toward getting his or her first job. Many editors and news directors in charge of hiring people straight out of college say the determining factor in offering a job to someone new to the field is whether or not that person has had an internship. These potential employers also place a high value on student media work on campus.

Some college graduates who want to get into journalism—particularly those who did not major in journalism as undergraduates—consider getting a graduate degree in journalism. Some journalism majors also feel the need to continue their education in a graduate program. Many of the major undergraduate journalism and mass communication programs offer graduate degrees. One type of degree is a traditional academic master's program that allows students to study the field of journalism and prepares students for entry into a doctoral program if they desire to teach at a college level. Another type of degree is the professional master's program that emphasizes practical training in reporting, editing, graphics journalism, web journalism, photojournalism, and other journalistic skills. In either type of program, students are usually advised to take whatever opportunities they have to get professional experience. Even for those who want to go into academia and teach, professional experience can be a valuable asset in gaining a job.

Get Started

Journalism is a highly competitive field. Getting a job is not an easy task. It takes a lot of preparation and motivation, as does working in the field itself. But nothing in life that is satisfying or truly valuable can be accomplished easily. The best time to start on the road to a journalism career is now.

JOINING UP

Journalists have many professional organizations and associations at the local, state, and national levels. They are devoted to advancing the interests of journalists by developing educational programs, holding seminars, conferences, and conventions, and in some cases protecting them from legal assaults. Mostly, however, these associations allow journalists to come together to share problems and solutions.

Even if you are a student, it is never too early to see what these associations have to offer. Web sites for these groups often have excellent information for the specialty area of journalism with which they are concerned. They are also likely to list scholarship, internship, and job possibilities.

Following is a list of some of the major organizations, but it is by no means complete. The names of the associations are usually indicative of their interests and purpose.

American Association of Sunday and Feature Editors,   **www.aasfe.org**
American Copy Editors Society,   **www.copydesk.org**
American Medical Writers Association (AMWA),   **www.amwa.org**
American Society of Newspaper Editors,   **www.asne.org**
Asian American Journalists Association,   **www.aaja.org**
Associated Press Managing Editors,   **www.apme.org**
Association for Women in Communications,   **www.womcom.org**
Association for Women in Sports Media,   **users.southeast.net/~awsm**
California Chicano News Media Association,   **www.ccnma.org**
Education Writers Association,   **www.ewa.org**
Foundation for American Communications (FACSNET),   **www.facsnet.org**
Garden Writers Association of America,   **www.gwwa.org**
Inland Press Association,   **www5.infi.net/inland**
International Federation of Journalists (IFJ),   **www.ifj.org**

International Science Writers Association,   **www.eurekalert.org**
Internet Press Guild,   **www.netpress.org**
Investigative Reporters & Editors,   **www.ire.org**
Journalism and Women Symposium,   **www.jaws.org**
National Association of Black Journalists,   **www.nabj.org**
National Association of Hispanic Journalists,   **www.nahj.org**
National Conference of Editorial Writers,   **www5.infi.net/ncew**
National Federation of Press Women (NFPW),   **www.nfpw.org**
National Institute for Computer-Assisted Reporting,   **www.nicar.org**
National Lesbian and Gay Journalists Association,   **www.nlgja.org**
National Press Club,   **www.npc.press.org**
National Press Photographers Association,   **www.sunsite.unc.edu/nppa**
National Society of Newspaper Columnists,   **www.columnists.com**
Native American Journalists Association,   **www.naja.com**
Newspaper Association of America,   **www.naa.org**
Organization of News Ombudsmen,   **www.infi.net/ono**
Religion Newswriters Association,   **www.intac.com/~caustin/rna1.htm**
Society of American Business Editors and Writers,   **www.missouri.edu/~sabew**
Reporters Committee for Freedom of the Press,   **www.rcfp.org**
Society for News Design,   **www.snd.org**
Society of Environmental Journalists,   **www.sej.org**
Society of Professional Journalists,   **www.spj.org**
Southern Newspaper Publishers Association,   **www.snpa.org**
South Asian Journalists Association,   **www.saja.org**

Quote 3.3

CARL HIASSEN

On why someone goes into the newspaper business

Nobody with a living brain cell goes into the newspaper business for the money. They're in it because digging up the truth is interesting and consequential work, and for sheer entertainment it beats the hell out of humping products for GE or Microsoft. Done well, journalism brings to light chicanery, oppression and injustice, though such concerns seldom weigh heavily on those who own newspapers.

Carl Hiassen is a reporter and columnist for the Miami Herald. *He is also a novelist, and his books include* Tourist Season *and* Double Whammy.

QUESTIONS FOR DISCUSSION

1. The author says that a knowledge of history is important for a journalist. Yet, many young people have little or no interest in history. What about you? How interested are you in history?

2. Do you know any media professionals—anyone who works for the local newspaper or radio or television station? Try to talk with that person to see how he or she got into the profession and report this to your class. If possible, have that person come and speak to the class.

3. Select a professional journalism association from one listed in this chapter. Take a thorough look at its web site. What impressions do you have of the organization? Is there anything about its purposes or activities that surprises you?

RELATED WEB SITES

Highschooljournalism.org, www.highschooljournalism.org

Journalism Rocks, www.freep.com/jobspage/high/index.htm

READINGS AND REFERENCES

Brooks, Brian S., Kennedy, G., Moen, D. R., & Ranly, D. (2001). *Telling the story: Writing for print, broadcast and online Media.* New York: Bedford/St. Martins.

Clark, R. P., & Campbell, C. C. (Eds.). (2002). *The value and craft of American journalism.* Gainesville, FL: University Press of Florida.

Fuller, J. (1996). *News values.* Chicago: University of Chicago Press.

Harrington, W. (1997). *Intimate journalism.* Thousand Oaks, CA: Sage Publications.

Itule, B. D., & Anderson, D. A. (2003). *News writing and reporting for today's media* (6th ed.). Boston: McGraw-Hill.

Klaidman, S., & Beauchamp, T. L. (1987). *The virtuous journalist.* New York: Oxford University Press.

Kovach, B., & Rosenstiel, T. (1999). *Warp speed: America in the age of mixed media.* New York: The Century Foundation.

Kovach, B., & Rosenstiel, T. (2001). *The elements of journalism.* New York: Crown Publishers.

Lambeth, E. B. (1992). *Committed journalism.* Bloomington: Indiana University Press.

Lewis, A. (Ed.). (2001). *Written into history: Pulitzer Prize reporting of the twentieth century from the New York Times.* New York: Times Books.

Reeves, R. (1999). *What the people know: Freedom of the press.* Cambridge, MA: Harvard University Press.

Roberts, G. (Ed.). (2001). *Leaving readers behind: The age of corporate newspapering.* Fayetteville: University of Arkansas Press.

Where

Society sanctions and supports several types of news organizations that practice journalism. These organizations are usually commercial and need to show a profit in order to survive. But they are more than businesses. They are quasi-public concerns that deliver a vital product to society.

News organizations come in a variety of forms, depending on how each disseminates the news. The method of dissemination will in some ways determine the organizational structure.

Each organization must fit with its method of dissemination, but it must also adhere to the rules and customs of the practice of journalism. Whether it is print, broadcast, or web, a news organization has to mold itself according to the standard practices and expectations of the field of journalism.

Chapter Four

Newspapers

Key Concepts and Terms

1. Newspapers are highly profitable businesses, but they are facing an uncertain future because fewer and fewer young people seem to be reading them regularly.

2. One of the major trends for newspapers during the last half of the twentieth century was concentration of ownership; that is, fewer and fewer companies are owning more and more newspapers.

3. Newspapers get revenue from two sources: 60 to 80 percent from advertising and 20 to 40 percent from sales and circulation.

4. Local news: news stories, photographs, charts, and other material that are produced by the newspaper's staff; most people consider the production of local news to be the most important function of a newspaper.

5. Managing editor: the person who is in charge of the day-to-day production of the newspaper.

6. In the United States today there are fewer than 1,500 daily newspapers; in 1910, there were more than 2,000.

7. The number of regular newspaper readers and the number of newspapers in circulation have remained about the same for many years, while the population has grown. Thus, newspapers have been circulating to a declining proportion of the population.

Frank Story reads a newspaper every day.

Frank works as a pilot for the Tennessee Valley Authority. He lives in Maryville, Tennessee, with his wife Jane and two sons. He subscribes

V i g n e t t e *to the* Maryville-Alcoa Daily Times, *a newspaper that circulates throughout Blount County. Occasionally, he reads the* Knoxville News-Sentinel, *a newspaper that is readily available since Knoxville is about 15 miles to the north.*

"My mom and dad subscribed to the Knoxville News-Sentinel," *Frank said. "They read it thoroughly. I guess it was through their example that I acquired the habit of reading a newspaper."*

When Frank travels, particularly to larger cities, he tries to find a local newspaper to read while he is waiting on his passengers. "I like the Washington Post *and the* New York Times," *he says. He enjoys looking at good photographs and reading international news and the editorial pages.*

"I think I read the editorial pages sometimes as much to disagree with what I am reading as anything else," he says.

Frank is a person who gives the newspaper industry comfort. But there is also a problem. Frank is fifty-four years old. People thirty years younger than Frank are less likely to have the newspaper reading habit. This fact weighs heavily on the newspaper industry today.

Initiators of Journalism

Newspapers today are the major practitioners of journalism. The practice of journalism occurs in many other media, of course, but when you think about journalism—what it is, where it happens, what it does—chances are you think about newspapers. It has always been so, because for centuries newspapers were the only news medium. Radio and television are less than a century old, and the Web has been around for less than a generation. Newspapers, however, have existed for centuries, even back to the Roman Empire.

The newspaper is part of the life, legend, and lore of modern society. Newspapers speak with an authority that few individuals can attain. They are a means of defining us as a community, something that all of us can share. They are a focus of information and opinion for a community. They may not always be loved—in fact, they rarely are—yet they almost always command attention.

But the newspaper's role is changing. During the middle part of the last century, most cities of any size had two or more "competing" newspapers; that is, the newspapers were owned by different companies, had a different set of readers, and competed not only for news but also for advertising dollars. But that situation has been changing since almost the beginning of the twentieth century. For the last fifty years now, the number of daily newspapers has been declining. Most cities that once had two or more newspapers have been left with just one.

That has been good news for the newspapers that have survived. They do not have to compete, and many have reduced their costs by hiring fewer people for the production of news. They have increased their profits further by charging whatever the market would bear for advertising. Those conditions made newspapers highly profitable organizations throughout the latter part of the twentieth century.

Despite their robust economic health, questions about the ultimate survivability of newspapers have always lurked in the background. Newspapers are expensive to produce, and they require the intense intellectual and physical labor of many people. In addition, newspapers have faced other challenges, as discussed next.

The Development of Broadcasting

In the 1920s and 1930s, radio offered the public an alternative to newspapers for both news and entertainment. As people spent more time listening to radio, they spent less time with the newspaper. That happened again when television entered households in the 1940s and 1950s.

Television not only captured the time and attention of the audience, but it also brought a different look and feel to the presentation of news and information. Television, it was found, could have a powerful and immediate impact on an audience, and the three major stories of the 1960s—the civil rights movement, the Kennedy assassination, and the Vietnam War—changed American society because they appeared on television rather than only in print. Newspapers had lost their grip on national news stories and became primarily a medium for local news (even though they still carried many national and international reports).

The challenge from broadcasting continued in the 1980s when cable systems offered audiences more channels, and news programs shifted from thirty minutes or an hour each day to twenty-four hours, seven days a week. When Atlanta entrepreneur Ted Turner launched the Cable News Network in 1980, he vowed that it would never cease its broadcasting. Many inside the world of journalism, particularly newspaper people, scoffed at Turner's bravado, but after more than twenty years, CNN has proved to be a staple of the news media, especially when major news stories break.

Declining Readership

Newspapers are attracting fewer and fewer readers. The number of newspapers circulated in the United States has remained flat for about forty years. In 1960, there were about 59 million newspapers printed in the United States every day; each Sunday, about 48 million newspapers were printed. In 2000 the number of daily newspapers was 56 million and the number of Sunday papers was slightly more than 59 million. During that same period, the United States experienced a 50 percent increase in population, from 180 million to about 275 million.

Another way of looking at the same thing is to examine the percentage of people who read a newspaper every day. In 1970, more than three-fourths (77 percent) of the population reported reading a newspaper each weekday. By 1990 that percentage had declined to 62 percent, and the decline continued over the next decade so that in 2001 it was 54 percent.

Readership surveys have indicated that older people were more likely to read a newspaper on a daily basis than younger adults (as exemplified by our discussion of Frank Story at the beginning of this chapter). People with more education and more income were also more likely to read a newspaper each day than those with less education and income.

Alternative Sources of Information

The disinclination of many young adults to read a newspaper on a regular basis has been worrisome for the industry for many years. As young people marry, put down roots in a community, and grow older, they are more likely to become newspaper readers. This tendency has offered some comfort to the newspaper industry,

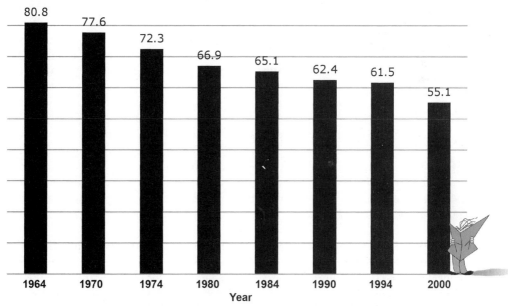

Daily Newspaper Readership as a Percentage of the Entire Population

Year	Percentage
1964	80.8
1970	77.6
1974	72.3
1980	66.9
1984	65.1
1990	62.4
1994	61.5
2000	55.1

Source: National Newspaper Association

FIGURE 4.1   Declining Readership Although the number of newspapers printed and in circulation every day has remained fairly constant over the last forty years, the percentage of readers among the entire population has declined significantly. The growth of other media and the increased distractions of daily life have been two of the reasons that may account for this decline.

but it may not hold for future generations. One of the reasons that people have grown into being regular newspaper readers is that there have been few alternatives to the newspaper. With the Internet and the growing number of sources of information on the World Wide Web, young people today may feel that they do not have to become newspaper readers. If a person were interested in international news, he or she would have the *New York Times* or dozens of other sources of information readily available on a computer screen. The multiplicity of sources strikes at the newspaper even at the local level, which has heretofore been the newspaper's strength. For instance, information about school systems—one of the chief concerns of young parents—may be more readily available on the school system's web site than in the local newspaper.

Concentration of Ownership

Fewer and fewer people and organizations own more and more newspapers. Whereas, just a few decades ago, most newspapers were "locally owned," that is, owned by a person, family, or group who lived in or near the area, now most newspapers are part of a group or chain. Gannett, the company that owns the nationally circulated *USA Today,* owns 96 daily newspapers with a total daily circulation of about 6 million, or more than 10 percent of all newspapers circulated in the nation. Gannett also owns more than 300 nondaily newspapers and operates 22 television stations. (In the United Kingdom, Gannett owns 15 daily newspapers.) The New York Times company also owns the *Boston Globe* and 16 other newspapers, as well as eight television stations and two New York City radio stations. The Tribune company, which publishes the *Chicago Tribune,* owns the *Los Angeles Times* and 10 other daily newspapers (including *Newsday* in New York, the *Hartford Courant,* and the *Orlando Sentinel*) and 23 major market television stations. The list of single companies that own dozens of newspapers and television and radio stations goes on and on.

Many who study the newspaper business are critical of this concentration of ownership. They believe that newspapers would better serve their communities if their owners were located in the communities and if the people who ran the newspapers were natives or long-term residents. The practice of most newspaper chains is to move publishers, editors, and even reporters from paper to paper. This practice means that staffs change often, and those in charge of covering a community never really get to know it.

Critics of ownership concentration also say that newspapers are acquired by large companies because they generate profits, and this will benefit the company's stockholders more than the community in which the paper is located. Chains, they say, are more likely to emphasize profits than good journalism, and decisions made at the corporate level are not always the best for a particular newspaper.

Others argue that concentration of ownership is not necessarily a bad thing. They believe that a strong chain or group can provide resources to the individual newspapers that the papers would not have if they were owned by a local group with no affiliation to other papers. They also say that chains offer journalists a chance for advancement that they would not have otherwise. In particular, they give people a chance to become editors and publishers that they would not have if a newspaper were owned by a family or a small, local group. Many chains, particularly Gannett, have taken the lead in hiring women and minorities—something that might not have happened under single, local ownership.

What neither chains nor single, local owners have done with any effectiveness is to increase the attractiveness of journalism for young people entering the profession. Starting salaries are perceived by many young people as being too low to make a good living, and although that perception is not entirely correct, beginning journalists often find themselves at a financial disadvantage compared to those who have entered other fields such as business or engineering.

Because of these and other challenges facing the industry, many people are prone to ask, "Will newspapers survive?"

The answer, of course, is unknown. Many who believe that they are likely to survive also say they are probably in for great changes, especially because the Web seems to be growing as a news medium and capturing young readers in ways the newspaper cannot. The newspaper is still the only organization in the community that has a large number of people devoted to gathering news and information about the community. It is still the only medium that is accessible to advertisers who need to reach a local audience. The newspaper continues to be a vital part of the communities in which it is located, and many people—even young people—feel that the local newspaper is "their" paper. They want it to survive even if they occasionally get put out with it. There is simply no substitute yet for the newspaper, and until that substitute is developed, the newspaper will exist.

FIGURE 4.2	Top 10 Newspaper Companies	
RANK	**REVENUE***	**TOP MEDIA PROPERTY**
1 Gannett Co.	$4,909	*USA Today*
2 Tribune Co.	3,844	*Los Angeles Times*
3 Knight Ridder	2,858	*Philadelphia Inquirer*
4 New York Times Co.	2,826	*New York Times*
5 Advance Publications	2,025	*Star-Ledger* (Newark, NJ)
6 Dow Jones & Co.	1,455	*Wall Street Journal*
7 Cox Enterprises	1,350	*Atlanta Journal & Constitution*
8 Hearst Corp.	1,323	*Houston Chronicle*
9 McClatchy Co.	1,040	*Star Tribune* (Minneapolis)
10 MediaNews Group	977	*Denver Post*

*Figures denote millions of dollars.

Source: Advertising Age, Top Media Companies, 2003. (www.adage.com)

Organizational Structure: The Business Side

Newspapers large and small have two main divisions: business and editorial.

The size and reach of the newspaper will determine how many people are employed on the business side and what they do. Some business functions are absolutely necessary to the life of the paper. These include advertising, circulation, and production.

Advertising accounts for between 60 and 80 percent of the revenue of the newspaper. Advertising is usually divided into two major divisions: classified and display advertising. Classified advertising pages are found in the back of the paper and consist of many ads in small type, usually with no pictures. These ads are the cheapest for customers to buy and the cheapest for the newspaper to produce, and they make up a very large percentage of the newspaper's income. They are also highly profitable. An advertising staff will have at least one person (or maybe several, depending on the size of the paper) who does nothing but handle classified ads. These ads come in by phone or by personal visits to the newspaper office, but they are rarely solicited by the staff, which is another reason why they are so inexpensive to produce. A newspaper might have standing agreements or contracts with local car dealers or real estate agents for classified ads for what they are trying to sell.

Display ads are the larger advertisements that are seen throughout the newspaper. This type of advertising is often solicited, or sold, by members of the advertising staff who visit local merchants and organizations. Newspaper advertising sales can be a lucrative business to get into because the salesperson usually receives a commission on each ad that he or she sells. A good salesperson who not only has selling skills but can also design effective, attention-getting ads can make a six-figure salary by working for a newspaper. The cost of the advertisement depends on the amount of space that it takes up on the page. The use of color in an advertisement can also add to the cost. Every newspaper sets its own advertising rates, and newspapers with more circulation can charge more for their space.

Producing and printing the newspaper is another major function of the business side of the newspaper. Newspapers are printed on large presses that are usually owned by the newspaper and located in the newspaper building itself. The pages may be produced by a variety of means, and the size of the newspaper's press will reflect the circulation size of the paper. The *Chicago Tribune,* which prints about 750,000 copies each day, has ten large presses located in a building about a mile from its Michigan Avenue office. On most evenings, the *Tribune* uses at least seven of these presses to print its edition.

Printing a newspaper is a highly technical job that requires many skilled people and sophisticated machinery. People in this side of the business are constantly trying to improve the efficiency of the machinery and the quality of the paper, ink, and other products used in the process.

Scheduling the production and printing of the paper is another major job of the production department. Most of the daily newspapers in the country today are morning papers; that is, they arrive at the reader's home or office early in the day, usually before most people are awake. The pages of the paper must be prepared in time for the presses to print them—a process that usually takes place through the evening and overnight. The newspapers have to be ready in time for the circulation department to distribute them.

The circulation department generates the other 20 to 40 percent of the revenue of a newspaper. Circulation departments are concerned with how the newspaper is distributed. Typically, newspapers are sold in two ways: by subscriptions delivered to a home or business, and by single-copy sales through newspaper racks or newspaper vendors. The number of single-copy sales depends on the location of the paper and the traffic patterns and the number of pedestrians in an area. Newspapers in small towns are less likely to depend on single-copy sales for their revenue than newspapers in large cities. One of the biggest problems that circulation departments have to solve is how to get the paper from the printing press into the hands of the readers. Even small newspapers have elaborate circulation systems that involve many people. Often large trucks or vans will carry bundles of newspapers away from the printing plant to distribution points around the city or the area. Then carriers will take the newspapers on individual routes to deliver the papers that land in the driveway or on the doorsteps.

In addition to the three major functions of advertising, production, and circulation, the business side of the newspaper takes care of other administrative duties, such as human resources, financial affairs, building security and maintenance, and promotion. Each of these functions is an important part of the ongoing operation of the newspaper. Most have to do with the internal workings of the company, but the promotions department is concerned about the public face of the newspaper. Many newspaper executives believe that their position in the community will be enhanced if the paper sponsors civic events, such as fairs, music festivals, and other recreational activities. Most newspapers also have some kind of Newspaper in Education program whereby copies of the newspaper are provided to local schoolteachers who use them as part of their classroom activities.

Organizational Structure: The Editorial Side

The other major division of the newspaper is the editorial side. The people on this side of the operation are concerned with producing the news, pictures, graphics, and entertainment information that you are most likely to associate with the newspaper. It is here that journalism is practiced.

The organization of the editorial side varies from paper to paper, just as the business side does, but most newspapers function in similar ways because of the practice of journalism itself. In this section, we will describe some of the major jobs within the organizational structure (see the organizational chart in Figure 4.3).

Editor

Sometimes called the editor-in-chief or the executive editor, this person is responsible for the entire news and editorial operation of the paper. The editor is really a manager more than an editor in the sense that he or she must make decisions about whom to hire and promote and what jobs people should have.

FIGURE 4.3   Newspaper Organizational Chart The organization of the editorial side of most newspapers will look something like this. The city editor (sometimes known as the metro editor) usually holds the most prominent place among the department editors because local news is usually thought to be the newspaper's most important product. There are more people working here than in any other department.

Editors rarely involve themselves in the day-to-day operations of the newsroom, but they must stay informed about what editors and reporters are doing. Anytime the newspaper undertakes a major project, such as a multipart series of stories or a major investigative piece, the editor is usually part of the planning process. This is particularly the case if the project is going to cost a significant amount of money. Editors must make sure that the editorial side stays within a budget that is usually set at the beginning of the budget year.

Editors are often the public face of the newspaper. They are the people who speak for the paper when necessary, and they often represent the paper at public meetings and forums.

A person rarely gets to be an editor unless he or she has worked in a number of journalistic jobs throughout the newsroom. That is, top people from other industries are almost never brought in to be the editor of a newspaper just because they are older and have managerial experience. An editor's position is a special one. The editor represents the standards that a newspaper has set for itself, and the editor must be thoroughly imbued with the culture of journalism (see Chapter 2).

Managing Editor

The second in command on the editorial side is the managing editor. This person is responsible for the day-to-day operation of the newspaper and making sure that all of the departments of the editorial side are functioning and contributing to the content of the paper in appropriate ways.

Unlike the editor, the managing editor is deeply involved in all aspects of the editorial operation, from planning large projects to editing the first or final drafts of important stories. A managing editor should be an experienced newsroom hand but should also have enough training and knowledge to deal with other parts of the newspaper's organization. A managing editor schedules the printing of special sections with the production department and often coordinates special projects with the advertising and promotions departments.

One of the main functions of the managing editor is to run the daily news meetings. In these meetings all of the section editors, or representatives from the departments, get together to discuss the day's news and how the newspaper will handle it. Morning newspapers often have two news meetings each day. The first, usually held early in the day, gives each of the sections an idea of what news is being processed for that day. That meeting also tells support sections, such as graphics and photography, what they need to be working on. The second meeting, held in the late afternoon, brings everyone up-to-date on the progress that has been made in developing stories. It is at that meeting when decisions are made about the stories that will appear on the front page.

Despite the need for news meetings being as brief as possible, they provide an excellent venue for a discussion of ethics and practices by the organization, and they are a means whereby the organization's values and priorities are formulated and communicated. A good managing editor can take these meetings beyond their operational purpose and make them valuable training sessions and forums for discussion. The views of a managing editor carry great weight, and the staff will look to the managing editor to set a high standard for their journalistic practices.

Section Editors

A newsroom is usually divided into sections. These sections go by different names, but almost all daily newspapers have separate sections that deal with the city (or metro) areas, national and international news, sports, features (sometimes called Lifestyles, Arts and Entertainment, etc.), and business. Although each of these may appear at the same level on the organizational chart, the first among these equals is the city or metro editor.

The city editor is responsible for managing the coverage of the local area. A city editor must decide how to distribute reporters so that they are aware of the important events that occur within the community. Two of the major areas are city government and education. How the city editor assigns reporters is a reflection of the role that the newspaper sees itself playing in the community. A city editor is usually at the center of the coverage of any breaking or sudden news events that occur in the area, and he or she must decide what resources to put into a story.

A good city editor is one who knows the city well and who knows where information can be found and who would be good sources for reporters. A city editor must understand the governmental, social, and economic structure of a city. He or she must also have a keen sense of the city's geography. Every bit of knowledge about the city helps the city editor make good editorial judgments about the paper's news coverage.

Daily newspapers usually subscribe to the Associated Press and other wire services for their national and international news. If they do, the national editor is the person who handles these stories. He or she will attend the news media and inform other editors what is happening in the nation and world that day. The national editor (sometimes called the wire editor) may also suggest that another editor "localize" a story; that means a reporter will take the wire story and find a local effect or angle for it. For instance, if the Centers for Disease Control in Atlanta issues an alert, a local reporter will take that information and check with local health authorities to see how they are responding to it.

The national editor must not only select and edit the national and international stories but also sometimes rewrites or revises stories, combining information from several different sources. This editor is responsible for making sure the latest information about national and international stories is in the newspaper.

At larger papers, the national editor may have a reporter in the state capital or in Washington, DC, and it then becomes the responsibility of this editor to make story assignments. Often such reporters are working for several papers at once, so the ability of the editor to make assignments is limited.

The largest newspapers, such as the *New York Times, Washington Post, Chicago Tribune,* and *USA Today,* have a far-flung network of correspondents throughout the nation and around the globe. At those papers there is both a national and an international editor, and there are assistant editors who select and edit stories from the wire services. These newspapers are expected by their readers to bring specialized coverage to many stories from many areas.

Another important section of the newspaper is sports, and the sports editor usually has an entire section (at least eight pages or more) to fill every day. No matter where it is located, a newspaper has to pay attention to local and national sports because a significant portion of the paper's readers is intensely interested in that subject. A sports editor must ensure that the major sports events in the area are covered, beginning at the high school level. If there are colleges and universities in the area, sports programs at those institutions must also get coverage. Larger cities are likely to have professional teams of one sort or another, and they will demand some specialized coverage. In addition, many sports departments have substantial travel budgets used for sending reporters to cover championship events, and a sports editor is responsible for allocating those budgets.

An additional feature of sports departments is the sports columnist. Sometimes a newspaper will have a single person dedicated to writing a sports column several times a week. Another approach is to have sports reporters contribute a column at least once a week. Occasionally, it is the sports editor who is also the sports columnist.

A newspaper must be sensitive to the sports interests of its readership, especially when that interest may not be part of regular sports coverage. For instance, golf might be popular even though a major golf tournament rarely occurs in that area. On the other hand, some sports may be considered major in one area but be of little interest in another area. Hockey, for instance, has little appeal in the southeastern United

States, and a newspaper there would not spend a great amount of its resources in covering it.

The business editor is in charge of another important section of the newspaper—news about the area's business and industries. On smaller newspapers, the business section may consist of one or two reporters who cover news of local businesses, but larger newspapers have many reporters and editors assigned to this task. One of the jobs of the business editor is to wade through all of the incoming public relations releases and try to find the important news of the business community.

As with other sections of the newspaper, knowledge of the local area is vital to the effectiveness of the business editor. If an area has a lot of heavy industries, much of the business coverage may concern issues such as labor unions and worker safety. If a university is the city's largest or chief employer, the news coverage often will be concerned with how businesses affect students and others associated with the institution. Understanding these conditions and relationships constitutes a large part of the business editor's job.

A final area of major concern for the newspaper's editorial organization is the features section. Newspapers use a variety of approaches handling all of the topics that might be included here. One of the most common names given to this section is "Lifestyles." The lifestyles editor handles a range of topics that might include personality profiles, arts and entertainment, food, gardening, hobbies, and society news. A set of assistant editors may be assigned to handle the topics that a newspaper believes is important to its readers. The lifestyles section is less attuned to the day's events that are being covered by other sections; instead, lifestyles editors must plan ahead and must think about their sections days or even weeks in advance. Some newspapers have weekly schedules so that on Wednesdays the main feature could be about food, on Thursdays about gardening, and on Fridays about entertainment events for the weekend. If that is the case, the lifestyles editor must manage the reporters in that section so this schedule can be met.

The lifestyles section has the most innovative page design in the newspaper. By thinking about a section several days ahead, designers may develop illustrations and other items that will give the lifestyles section a different look than the rest of the paper.

Supporting Sections

Each of the sections of the newspaper described previously is concerned with a particular area of news coverage. All are likely to have a section in the newspaper that they can point to as their own. But there are other groups of journalists on the editorial side of the paper that exist mainly to help those sections do their jobs. (The term *supporting sections* is not one that is usually used inside the newspaper, but it is a useful one in thinking about what these groups do.)

The copy desk is one of the most important parts of the newspaper. Copy editors read stories as they are written and check for technical, factual, and writing errors (see Chapters 12 and 13). A newspaper can have a central copy desk where most of the stories are sent and then distributed to individual copy editors, or it can be structured so that each section has a copy desk where copy editors can develop

Quote 4.1

STANLEY WALKER

On the characteristics of a good newspaperman

What makes a good newspaperman? The answer is easy. He knows everything. He is aware not only of what goes on in the world today, but his brain is a repository of the accumulated wisdom of the ages. He is not only handsome, but he has the physical strength which enables him to perform great feats of energy. He can go for nights on end without sleep. He dresses well and talks with charm. Men admire him; women adore him; tycoons and statesmen are willing to share their secrets with him. He hates lies and meanness and sham, but he keeps his temper. He is loyal to his paper and to what he looks upon as the profession; whether it is a profession, or merely a craft, he resents attempts to debase it. When he dies, a lot of people are sorry, and some of them remember him for several days. (1924)

Stanley Walker was a reporter and editor for the New York Herald-Tribune *in the 1920s and 1930s. He is the author of* City Editor.

specialized knowledge about that section. Either way, the copy editors are likely to answer to a chief copy editor, the person on the staff who is considered the expert on language and style.

Another supporting group that makes an important contribution to the operation of the newspaper is the photojournalists, and they usually work out of what is called the photo desk. The head of the photo desk is the photo editor, who attends news meetings and makes photo assignments based on what he or she hears at the meetings, requests that section editors make, and what the photographers on the desk may report themselves. On most newspapers there are far fewer photojournalists than reporters, so pictures are shot for the most important stories or ones that have obvious visual aspects. On larger newspapers, photographers may be assigned to the different sections and work exclusively for that section, but at most newspapers photographers are assigned out of a central desk.

The photo editor not only works with photographers, but he or she may also have picture editors—that is, people who process photographs. Most newspapers today either have photographers shoot with digital cameras, or they digitize prints or negatives. Picture editors are people who are skilled in using the computers and software that will enhance photographs and get them ready for printing. Photo editors go through pictures sent by wire services to select the best photos that will illustrate the national and international stories the newspaper is using.

The graphics desk is another group of journalists who contribute not only to how the newspaper looks but also to the informational content of the paper. A graphics editor (sometimes called an art director), like the photo editor, attends news meetings to hear what is going on and to decide what contributions the department can make to a story. Sometimes that story will need a map or a chart. At other times it may simply need a summary or bulleted list. Still other stories may require some annotated illustration to help readers understand what the story is about. The graphics department can provide these things.

On smaller newspapers, the graphics department may consist of only one person—someone who works on graphics for the most important local story of the day. Larger newspapers are able to devote more resources to graphics. The *Chicago Tribune,* for instance, divides its graphics staff into "artists" and "coordinators." A coordinator is a trained journalist who is an expert in conceptualizing a graphic and in gathering information for it. Assignments are given to coordinators who then work with the news reporters in gathering the information. Once the information is in, a coordinator will pair up with an artist to produce the graphic. These two will work together with one of the graphic assistant editors to complete the graphic. (For more on graphics journalism, see Chapters 14 and 15.)

Graphics journalists must work closely with another group that is essential to the operation and production of the newspaper—the design desk. All newspapers must have people who not only have good news judgment and understanding of what the newspaper is but who also can put headlines, pictures, and stories together on a page in a way that is easy to read and that reflects the graphic personality of the newspaper. They must also be experts in the page layout software that the newspaper uses. These people are called design editors or layout editors. It is at the design editor's desk that the various activities of all the desks previously mentioned come together in a newspaper.

There is no common way that the design functions of the newspaper are organized within the newsroom. Sometimes, particularly at smaller papers, a few design editors put together all of the pages of the paper from a central location within the newsroom. At larger papers, the various sections (news, sports, business, etc.) have design editors assigned to those sections, and the section editor is actually responsible for producing the pages in his or her section.

Whatever the organizational scheme, page designers must work, figuratively at least, from the same page. That is, they must all observe the same design rules in terms of typefaces for headlines and body copy, cutline and byline styles, and other design rules. At most newspapers there is a design editor who makes sure these rules are observed.

A senior design editor is usually the person in charge of putting together the front page of the newspaper, one of the final jobs of the editorial side each day. That person not only must have design skills but also must have the intelligence of a copy editor and the understanding of the newspaper's audience equal to that of any section editor. The design editor should be a skilled wordsmith so that he or she can write accurate, attention-getting headlines.

Finally, we should include in this list of supporting groups the newspaper's web site. On many newspapers, a small group of people is charged with uploading the newspaper's stories and pictures onto the paper's web site. This staff is also responsible for making sure the site is updated throughout the day and evening with the latest breaking news, both local and national. On a few newspapers, the web site has grown to be more of an independent entity with a staff that can produce its own content and that can use and supplement the content of the print edition. (At some newspapers, such as the *Tampa Tribune,* there is even a separate advertising staff that sells ads for the web site.) Most newspapers, however, have not progressed this far in the

THE BLACK PRESS: AN ALTERNATIVE VOICE IN AMERICAN JOURNALISM

The mainstream press, run for the most part by white males, has dominated journalism and its history, but significant voices have been raised from other corners of society. African American newspapers, the Black Press, have existed for many decades and continue to tell stories and raise issues that do not make it into the dominant newspapers.

The Black Press began in 1827 with the publication of *Freedom's Journal* in New York City. The publishers were Samuel Cornish and John Russwurm, two black men who believed that their readers needed a newspaper they could call their own. The *Journal* and black newspapers thereafter were committed to the education of their readers and expanding the freedoms and opportunities of blacks everywhere.

By the time the Civil War broke out in 1861, some forty black newspapers had been published at one time or another. They survived, if at all, through subscriptions, donations, and associations. They also had to weather the hostilities of whites who saw them as a threat to the social order.

The most famous journalist of them all—indeed, the most famous black man in America in the middle of the nineteenth century—was Frederick Douglass. Imposing with his personality and his voice, Douglass was born a slave in Maryland but escaped in 1838. He toured Great Britain speaking against slavery in the mid-1840s and came home to begin a newspaper called the *North Star.* Later the paper's name was changed to *Frederick Douglass's Paper.* Douglass's newspaper was a fearless voice in favor of emancipation. When southern states seceded in 1861, Douglass, unlike some abolitionistis who advocated letting the South go its own way, argued that they should be brought back into the Union.

Black newspapers continued through the nineteenth century and into the twentieth century giving a voice to black people and pointing out the evils of segregation. The *Chicago Defender* became one of the leading black newspapers in the early part of the twentieth century, in part because Chicago was the chief destination of blacks getting out of the South. At one point around the beginning of World War I, the *Defender's* circulation was 230,000.

The civil rights movement and the laws ending much of official segregation in the 1960s started the slow demise of the Black Press during the rest of the century. Black newspapers continue to be published, but they do not have the power or the constituency they once commanded. The tradition of the Black Press is being carried on, however, with some particularly strong web sites such as www.BlackAmericaWeb.com.

development of their sites. The news staffs remain oriented to the print edition, and web staffs often find it difficult to persuade reporters and editors to give them information about a breaking story before they have it ready for print.

The Editorial Page

Many people in journalism consider the news, business, sports, and features functions of the newspaper the heart of the business. The editorial page, however, is its soul. But the editorial section does not fit easily into the organizational structure of the newspaper.

One reason for this has to do with the culture of journalism (see Chapter 2) that puts a thick psychological wall between the news functions and the editorial functions. News reporters and editors do not want to have their activities and attitudes colored by the editorial stands that the newspaper takes. Some even go as far as not reading the newspaper's editorials, an extreme but understandable position.

To preserve this separation in structure and practice, the editorial section of the newspaper is sometimes located in a part of the building that is separate from the news and business functions of the paper. Editorial page editors rarely attend news meetings and are usually not part of the planning process for major projects. Some contact and coordination with the news sections must occur, particularly if the newspaper is going to take an editorial position on a subject that the news department is covering. Still, both the news side and the editorial side attempt to keep those contacts at a minimum.

The editorial section is headed by an editorial page editor who has a variety of people working with him or her. Chief among those are editorial writers who produce editorials each day. The section will also have its own copy editors and designers and possibly an assistant editor who handles letters to the editor and other communication with the public. An assistant editor will edit syndicated columns and might also coordinate the soliciting and production of op-ed articles, which are pieces written by experts or people with strong opinions about a topic. Most large papers

Quote 4.2

JAMES THURBER

On the drudgery of newspaper work

There is, of course, a certain amount of drudgery in newspaper work, just as there is in teaching classes, tunneling into a bank, or being President of the United States. I suppose that even the most pleasurable of imaginable occupations, that of batting baseballs through the windows of the RCA building, would pall a little as the days ran on. (1945)

James Thurber was a writer, cartoonist, humorist, and satirist who lived from 1894 to 1961.

will have an editorial cartoonist on the staff whose job it is to produce an editorial cartoon every day or several times a week.

Newspapers Today

The United States has fewer than 1,500 daily newspapers today. That number has been declining since 1910 when there were about 2,000 daily newspapers in circulation. The real change in the industry is not just the number of papers but also the environment in which they operate. As we stated earlier, about fifty years ago most cities of more than 100,000 people (and many smaller cities) had two competing newspapers that were owned by different people and published separately. In the 1960s the economics of the business forced many newspapers to consolidate with their rivals, and it was not uncommon to see a morning and afternoon newspaper published by the same company.

The Newspaper Preservation Act, which Congress passed in 1970, allowed newspapers with different owners to combine their advertising, printing, and business departments if they left their news and editorial departments to operate separately. This joint operating agreement (JOA) is credited with saving many newspapers from extinction, and it still exists in a number of cities (Birmingham, Alabama; and Seattle, Washington, for example). These agreements slowed but did not halt the declining number of newspapers, however.

Along with the declining number of newspapers has been a decline in readership. Surveys measuring readership have been conducted over many years, and they show a continuing drop in newspaper readership. Readership of Sunday newspapers has also declined, dropping from 73 percent in 1995 to 64 percent in 2001. Many in the industry have focused on the fact that young adults are far less likely to be readers than older adults, and they have said that newspapers should concentrate on persuading young adults to be readers. The readership decline has occurred through all demographic groups, however, not just young adults.

An additional aspect of newspaper readership is that more than 80 percent of all adults in the top fifty metropolitan markets say they have read a newspaper in the last week. Indications are that people have not given up reading a newspaper entirely; they are just doing it with less frequency.

The good news for the industry is that the newspaper remains an extremely strong advertising medium. Advertisers spent more than $44 billion in 2001 on newspapers, giving that medium about 20 percent of all of the money spent by the advertising industry. For many local advertisers, the newspaper is the only way to reach a significant portion of the community. Consumers seem to agree; about two-thirds of all adults say that newspaper advertising is their primary source of advertising and general shopping information.

Despite this mixed picture of declining readership and strong advertising revenue, newspapers are highly profitable organizations, and they remain the most likely source of jobs for those seeking entry into the field of journalism. Daily newspapers

FIGURE 4.4	**Top 25 Newspapers by Circulation**		
	Ranked by weekday averages for six months ending March 31, 2003		

RANK	NEWSPAPER	AVERAGE DAILY CIRCULATION	SUNDAY CIRCULATION
1	USA Today	2,162,454	No Sunday edition
2	Wall Street Journal	1,820,600	No Sunday edition
3	New York Times	1,130,740	1,672,965
4	Los Angeles Times	979,549	1,396,045
5	Washington Post	796,367	1,049,322
6	New York Daily News	737,030	810,533
7	Chicago Tribune	621,055	1,016,471
8	New York Post	620,080	420,179
9	Newsday	579,351	665,324
10	Houston Chronicle	548,508	739,389
11	Dallas Morning News	532,050	786,594
12	San Francisco Chronicle	514,265	553,703
13	Chicago Sun-Times	491,795	383,548
14	Arizona Republic	486,131	596,993
15	Boston Globe	448,817	680,115
16	Atlanta Constitution-Journal	419,568	658,581
17	Newark Star-Ledger	407,730	609,514
18	Philadelphia Inquirer	386,890	768,237
19	Minneapolis Star Tribune	375,505	669,358
20	Cleveland Plain Dealer	373,137	482,380
21	San Diego Union-Tribune	363,555	444,899
22	Detroit Free Press	363,490	719,885
23	St. Petersburg Times	354,869	442,348
24	Portland Oregonian	344,550	422,130
25	Miami Herald	328,124	444,119

Source: *Advertising Age,* Top Media Companies, 2003 (www.adage.com)

employ between 75,000 and 100,000 journalists at present, and the approximately 9,000 nondaily newspapers in the country employ many thousands more. Even though starting salaries are not as strong as they should be (rarely more than $25,000 a year), young people who want to begin a journalism career are most likely to start at a newspaper.

SMALL NEWSPAPER, BIG-TIME JOURNALISM

Most of the journalism practiced in America does not occur in the big cities or the major newspaper newsrooms that have been described elsewhere in this chapter. American journalism, by and large, is the product of thousands of reporters, editors, photographers, artists, and others who work for the small-town newspaper.

About 85 percent of all of the newspapers in the nation have circulations of less than 50,000. Consequently, if you are going into journalism, the small-town newspaper is probably where you are going to start—even if your goal is to get to the big city and the big time. That is where most of the entry-level jobs are, and few major city dailies are likely to hire you unless you have had some experience at a smaller paper.

But the small newspaper is not just a stepping-stone to a "big-time" job. For many journalists,

the small town and small newspaper is the big time. For starters, it gives you a wide range of experiences that you would probably not get in a larger organization. You are more likely to get experience as a photographer or a columnist or a page designer at a small paper than at the big-city daily.

Beyond your personal development as a journalist, the small-town experience helps you to learn what journalism is about and see the effect that good journalism can have on a community. You can meet a lot of interesting people and get a chance to tell their stories.

And when something big happens, you can be there—just like the staff of the *Grand Forks (North Dakota) Herald* when a devastating flood hit the town in 1997. Even though the *Herald's* staff members had to evacuate along with the rest of the town, they were determined to keep publishing. Eventually landing in Manvel, ten miles north of Grand Forks, the *Herald* never missed a day of providing news and information to its devastated readers. Staff members worked at the local school, sent the paper to Minneapolis for printing, flew the copies back to the area, and distributed them free at the evacuation centers. The *Herald* also kept an active and up-to-date web site during the crisis. That determination netted the *Herald* a Pulitzer Prize, journalism's highest award, for public service.

That's what small-town journalism can do. It's no small task.

Major Players in the Newspaper Industry

As with any industry, a few stand out as the best among newspapers. These organizations are some of the largest in terms of circulation, and they have many resources to devote to covering news. In using these resources, they not only set the standard for what is considered to be quality journalism, but they also show organizations with fewer resources what to strive for. These news organizations are widely influential among government and business leaders, not just because of their quality but also because of the perception that others are reading them and acting on their information.

New York Times

Because of its far-reaching news coverage and its location, size, and history, the *Times* is thought to be the leader of American journalism (daily circulation: 1,130,740; Sunday circulation: 1,672,965). It boasts of thorough, world-wide coverage of news events and important issues around the globe. The *Times* has many reporters stationed around the world, and it responds to major news stories with reporters, photographers, graphics journalists, and editors that few other papers can match. The *Times* maintains a large bureau of journalists in Washington, DC, where it is read avidly by ranking officials in all areas of government.

The ranking of the *Times* as the leader in journalism, its reputation for thoroughness of news coverage, and its moderate to liberal editorial stance have opened it to many critics. The newspaper, they say, is arrogant and riddled with mistakes and misinterpretations.

The *Times* has traditionally been a leader in the fight for a free press and a broad interpretation of the First Amendment. Two of the twentieth century's most important cases involving the First Amendment, *New York Times v. Sullivan* and the *Pentagon Papers* case (see Chapter 24), were fought by the *New York Times*.

The newspaper has also been a leader in developing the Web as a news medium. The *Times* web site (www.nytimes.com) pioneered many web innovations, including multimedia slide shows, graphics, and video reports as well as servicing individual web users with email alerts on topics of their choosing. The web site attracts one of the largest audiences of any news web site in the world.

Washington Post

The *Washington Post* is the major news source for the nation's capital (daily circulation: 796,367; Sunday circulation: 1,049,322). Its location and size put its influence, particularly with governmental officials, on a level with the *New York Times*.

The *Post* specializes in coverage of politics, not just in the capital but also around the nation. It has some of the most experienced and respected political reporters in the field. The *Post*, like the *Times*, has many critics, particularly because of its liberal editorial policies. These policies, critics say, show up all too often in the selection of news and in news reports themselves.

An indelible part of the *Post*'s history is the Watergate story in the early 1970s. Two young *Post* reporters, Robert Woodward and Carl Bernstein, spent months investigating a story that eventually resulted in the resignation of President Richard Nixon in 1974. *Post* editors allowed the reporters to work on the story even when it appeared that they would not be able to find the information they needed.

The *Post*, along with the *New York Times*, was one of the litigants in the *Pentagon Papers* case. And like the *Times*, the *Post* has been a leader in developing its web site (www.washingtonpost.com) as a news source for people around the world. Many of the newspaper's reporters and columnists are regularly scheduled for web chats with the public, and photojournalists believe that the *Post*'s picture galleries are among the best in the business.

USA Today

Some in the field of journalism do not consider *USA Today* to be among the best newspapers in the country, but it does have a larger and broader circulation than any other newspaper (daily circulation: 2,162,454; no Sunday circulation). Owned by the Gannett newspaper group, *USA Today* is edited and produced just outside Washington, DC, and printed at newspaper plants across the country.

One of *USA Today*'s targeted audiences is travelers. It is widely available in airports and is often distributed to hotel guests as part of the hotel service.

Most of the articles in the paper are shorter than those in other newspapers, and *USA Today* has come under fire from critics for its lack of depth. One of the derogatory names critics give it is "McPaper."

USA Today is relatively young by American newspaper standards. It was begun in 1982 as the brainchild of Allen Neuharth, a former reporter and editor and once chairman of the board of the Gannett corporation. Neuharth wanted something different and something national, and he put the considerable resources of Gannett behind that effort. Despite the criticism *USA Today* has received and its low standing in the minds of journalists, the paper has had a major impact on American journalism. Its use of color, graphics, and super-efficient writing has been imitated by many editors, even when they were dismissing the paper itself.

USA Today's web site has also been a leader in news web site development, especially in its use of animated news graphics.

Wall Street Journal

As the name implies, the *Wall Street Journal* covers the business of the nation, not just on Wall Street but also across the country (daily circulation: 1,820,600; no Sunday circulation). For several decades, it has marketed itself heavily as the newspaper that business men and women should read if they want to stay informed about issues that affect business. That marketing campaign has netted the newspaper the second largest daily circulation of any newspaper in the country.

The *Journal* has taken itself beyond business coverage, and its reputation for depth and analysis is unsurpassed. Each day the paper publishes a "leader" article in the left column of the front page and then continues on an inside page; these articles are often the result of months of research by reporters and editors. The *Journal* has an international circulation and publishes a variety of editions around the globe each day. The editorial voice of the newspaper is strongly conservative.

The *Wall Street Journal* is the first major newspaper to establish its web site as a subscription-only site; that is, very little of the content is free. A person must subscribe to the site, or subscribe to the newspaper and the site, to gain access to much of the site's content. The site has many thousands of subscribers because its content is thought to be valuable.

Chicago Tribune

The *Chicago Tribune* (daily circulation: 621,055; Sunday circulation: 1,016,471) is the crown jewel of the Tribune Company, which also owns the *Hartford Courant, Los Angeles Times,* and *Orlando Sentinel,* among other newspapers. The Tribune Company is a good example of the benefits and ills of media consolidation. It has enormous resources that it uses for journalistic endeavors, but its many critics say that its corporate culture is too bottom-line oriented.

The *Tribune* has a long and rich history of colorful publishers and lively reporting. It has maintained a worldwide outlook, especially during times of war, even though it is located in the center of the country.

The *Tribune* was one of the first newspapers to recognize the potential of the World Wide Web as a news media, and in the mid-1990s, it invested heavily in its web operation. When this investment did not result in expected profits, the company reduced its web presence. But the *Tribune* has taken some steps toward converging its reporting for print and broadcast. Because the company owns a number of television stations, *Tribune* reporters who work on major stories can expect to be interviewed by television reporters from other properties within the company or they may be asked to do stand-up reports for the cameras.

The Future of Newspapers

The newspaper industry faces an uncertain future. As we have seen earlier in this chapter, newspapers are strong, profit-generating businesses. Advertising revenue continues to pour in. But readership is still slipping steadily, and the presence of alternative sources of news and information, particularly advertising information, does not bode well for the industry.

A measure of the newspaper's decline as a journalistic force was seen in the first weeks of the Iraq war in March and April 2003. Much of the debate surrounding the media's coverage of the war centered around television and the Web; very little of it had to do with newspapers.

Still, newspapers remain strong and enduring sources of local information. They draw larger sustained audiences than any other news medium. Their history reinforces their role in the community, and even their most vocal critics do not call for their demise. In America, even when ownership resides elsewhere, the local newspaper is owned by the hearts of the community. As long as that is the case, the newspaper is likely to survive in some form.

FIGURE 4.5   Tribune Tower, Chicago The *Chicago Tribune* operates out of an impressive building on Michigan Avenue in downtown Chicago. The building was built by publisher Robert McCormick in the 1920s after McCormick had conducted a contest among architects for the best design. The façade of the building contains many Gothic features.

QUESTIONS FOR DISCUSSION

1. How often do you read a newspaper? Under what circumstances do you read a newspaper—when you are at home, when you are traveling, in order to learn what movies are playing in town, and so on? How often do your friends read newspapers?
2. Some people believe that newspapers are in for great changes during the next ten to twenty years. What do you think? How do you think newspapers will look in the next generation? Ultimately, do you think newspapers will survive?
3. The chapter talks about newspapers having a strict separation between the news and editorial departments. In the newspapers that you are familiar with, do you think this separation occurs? Is the idea of this separation a good one?
4. Of all the jobs on a newspaper described in this chapter, which appeals to you the most? Could you see yourself working for a newspaper in any capacity?

RELATED WEB SITES

American Society of Newspaper Editors, www.asne.org

NAA: Newspaper Association of America, www.naa.org

Project for Excellence in Journalism, www.journalism.org

Readership Institute, www.readership.org

SNPA: Southern Newspaper Publishers Association, www.snpa.org

"The State of the American Newspaper," www.ajr.org/state/index.html

Women in Newspapers: 2002, www.mediamanagementcenter.org/center/web/publications/data/WIN2002.pdf

READINGS AND REFERENCES

Itule, B. D., & Anderson, D. A. (2003). *News writing and reporting for today's media* (6th ed.). Boston: McGraw-Hill.

Lanson, J., & Fought, B. C. (1999). *News in the next century.* Thousand Oaks, CA: Pine Forge Press.

Picard, R., & Brody, J. (1996). *The newspaper publishing industry.* Boston: Allyn and Bacon.

Providence Journal-Bulletin Staff Writers. (1996). *How I wrote the story.* Providence, RI: Providence Journal Company.

Sloan, W. D., & Wray, C. S. (1997). *Masterpieces of Reporting,* vol. 1. Northport, AL: Vision Press.

Weaver, D., & Wilhoit, G. C. (1996). *The American journalist in the 1990s.* Mahwah, NJ: Lawrence Erlbaum Associates.

Woods, K., Scanlan, C., Brown, K., Fry, D., & Clark, R. P. (Eds.). *Best Newspaper Writing.* St. Petersburg, FL: Poynter Institute and Chicago: Bonus Books. Published annually since 1979.

Chapter Five

Magazines

Key Concepts and Terms

1. Magazines are different from newspapers not just in the frequency with which they are published but also because they deliver news and information with more depth and perspective.

2. Writing in magazines does not conform to all of the strictures for writing in daily newspapers; the requirements of accuracy and good writing are just as strict, however.

3. Most magazines are produced with relatively small editorial staffs.

4. Freelancing: writing articles for magazines on an assignment basis; freelance writers are paid for each assignment but are not part of the magazine's permanent staff.

5. Magazines are created because someone (or some group) has an editorial idea and can identify an audience that would be interested in the idea and a set of advertisers that would like to sell products to that audience.

6. Demassification: the process of appealing to audiences that might be widely scattered but that have a common interest.

Vignette

Magazine journalism conjures up a romantic picture for many people. They see a highly skilled and respected writer with time and space to develop important stories for a discerning audience. This writer has a paycheck and travel budget commensurate with the work he or she is doing. The writer also has the independence and confidence to develop a distinctive style and to present a unique view of the subject he or she is covering.

The realities of modern magazine journalism do not necessarily contradict this romanticized picture, but they are far more complex.

Magazine journalism is about news and information, but it distinguishes itself from newspaper journalism not just by the size, look, and feel of the publications in which it appears. Rather than being concerned with the coverage of daily news events, magazine journalism usually tries to take a longer view of events and their meaning. This journalism emphasizes the why and how of a topic, not just the who, what, when, and where.

Why Magazine Journalism?

The world of magazines is as diverse as U.S. society itself. For every topic and interest there seems to be a magazine—from artists and artisans to users of industrial zinc.

ON THE COVER OF *ROLLING STONE*

Jann Wenner didn't like the journalism he was reading and hearing in the 1960s.

Wenner did not think it was telling the story of the world in which he was living—the world of rock music and the counterculture. It wasn't just rock music and drugs and tie-dyed shirts. It was a whole way of life. Music was the key, "the glue," he said, "holding a generation together"—but it wasn't the only thing.

And mainstream journalism wasn't getting it.

So Wenner did what people sometimes do when they believe an important story is being missed. They find a way to tell it.

In 1967, in a second-floor loft in San Francisco, Wenner started *Rolling Stone* magazine. This publication, he was determined, would practice journalism on the edge. He told his writers to "report the hell out of (a story)." They were to get involved, be passionate, take chances, and tell their version of the truth.

The result was a remarkable string of writers and articles that broke new ground in journalism. Hunter S. Thompson made himself and his style (Gonzo Journalism) famous by reporting not just on his subjects but also on himself. Tom Wolfe took an assignment to write a series of articles on the *Apollo* space program. His reporting became the basis for his best-selling book (and later the movie), *The Right Stuff*. David Harris, the former husband of Joan Baez, wrote from his jail cell where he was serving two years for refusing to be drafted into the armed forces. Readers always had something to look forward to.

Of course, it didn't hurt that the magazine had named itself after one of the most popular rock groups of all time (Mick Jagger and the Rolling Stones). Nor did it hurt that a few years after the magazine began, the popular rock group Dr Hook and the Medicine Show had a top hit titled "The Cover of *Rolling Stone*," a lament about how a rock band could tell if it had made the big time.

A few weeks after the song became number one in 1973, the band was featured on the cover of *Rolling Stone*.

In 2002, the *National Directory of Magazines* listed more than 17,000 titles (nearly 500 of which were devoted to music and music trades, a popular subject with young people).

Most of us read some magazines on a regular basis. National surveys show that more than 90 percent of adults in the nation say they look at a magazine regularly. They do so because the magazine gives them information on topics in which they are genuinely interested. They do so, also, because the magazine is easy to handle and portable; in modern terms, it is "user friendly." Sitting down with a magazine that has interesting writing and information about important or timely topics is a pleasure many of us look forward to and enjoy.

To form a simple definition of magazine journalism, we could say that it is concerned with gathering and disseminating news and information in a nondaily publication. In addition, magazine journalism often probes the how and why of a subject, rather than the who, what, when, and where. It attempts to take a longer view of a subject rather than being bound by coverage of specific events. It also allows for a writing style that is free from the strictures of newspaper journalism, but that freer style does not lessen the burden on the writer to be accurate, clear, precise, and concise in his or her writing.

Many people are drawn to the thought of writing for magazines rather than newspapers for a number of reasons. These include the following.

- Magazine writing does not burden the writer with daily deadlines. Deadlines do certainly exist in magazine journalism, but it is generally true that magazine writers have more time to develop their stories and more space than is normally allotted even to a newspaper feature story.

- Magazine journalists get to write about more interesting topics. Some people view newspaper reporting as mundane and routine with too few opportunities to write interesting stories, particularly at the beginning of their careers. Magazines, however, seem to offer a way for writers to research and report information they do not see in newspapers.

- Articles receive more space and better display in magazines. The design of magazines is often livelier than that of newspapers. Because stories may not have to compete on the same page with other stories, many people feel their articles are more likely to be read in magazines than in newspapers.

- Magazines are more prestigious than newspapers. Consequently, people who write for magazines are more likely to be recognized for their work than those who write for newspapers. Part of the logic behind this thinking is that magazines are published less often than newspapers, that they take more time to edit and produce, and that their audience is more interested in the topic. There is more of a connection of interests between the writer and the magazine audience than the reporter and the newspaper audience.

- Magazine journalism allows a more creative and personal writing style than that found in newspapers. The inverted pyramid news story is still the standard form of writing for covering news events for the newspaper or the news web site, and many writers find this form dull and restrictive. Magazines, they feel, are a means of developing a personal style or experimenting with a variety of styles that eventually will help the writer find a voice.

■ Magazines are thought to have more impact on their audience than newspapers. Even though magazines may speak to a smaller or more widely dispersed audience, the readers are interested and educated, and they are reading because they look to the publication to add to their knowledge and opinions about a topic. Magazine journalism gets to the people who are truly engaged in a subject.

All of these ideas about magazines have much truth behind them. In many areas magazine journalism does accept a broader range of writing styles and does let writers have a chance to find their own voices. Audiences for magazines are more narrowly cast than are audiences for newspapers. These audiences do consist of those who are truly interested in a topic or subject area and who have already acquired some information about it. But there are many other aspects that those interested in magazine journalism must consider as they attempt to enter the field.

First and foremost is that the standard of journalism for magazine writers is very high—possibly higher than it is for newspaper journalism because of the extended amount of time the reporter has to put a story together. Reporting for any medium is hard work, but for magazine journalism it is especially hard. Facts must be checked and rechecked, and the amount of information necessary for the extended articles that magazine journalists write goes far beyond that of most newspaper journalists. Magazine journalists usually spend a great deal of time gathering information from their sources and doing background and follow-up research for their articles.

Another factor in considering a career in magazine journalism is that the magazine business is extremely competitive, both individually and structurally. A great many people are seeking to enter the field of magazine journalism, and there are relatively few writing positions on magazine staffs. These positions often require people with experience and expertise in a subject area—qualities that many students entering the market are unlikely to have. At the structural level, many magazines fail. One of the continuing conditions of the industry is that only a relatively few magazines are on solid financial ground, and although they may survive from year to year, that survival is perilous. A person determined to stay in magazine journalism may be forced to change jobs several times during his or her career.

Although much of the work in magazine journalism is interesting and occasionally glamorous, much of it is also routine and occasionally dull. Magazines may publish long articles on interesting topics, but also published are many lists and calendars and other information that simply need to be gathered and presented without a lot of creativity. People who begin as editorial assistants for a magazine are often put to work at this kind of a job and sometimes become discouraged because they do not have the opportunity to do other kinds of work.

Finally, magazine journalism is generally not a very lucrative field. Many people make a living in the field, and for some that living is very good. But the starting salaries for entry-level jobs in magazine journalism are often less than what a beginning newspaper reporter would make. Those who choose to do freelance work face a steep, uphill climb in putting together enough assignments to make a living without having to supplement it with a regular job.

Yet for those determined to do magazine work, the field is a worthy one with a great deal of tradition behind it. Those who can survive the initial jobs and low paychecks can find magazine journalism to be a satisfying and rewarding career.

Structure of the Magazine Industry

The diversity of the field of magazine and periodical publication makes magazines difficult to categorize discretely. Thousands of titles exist, and they have a variety of editorial operations, publication frequencies, purposes, structures, and circulation schemes. With that understanding, most industry analysts look at the content and see at least four major types.

Consumer Magazines

These magazines appeal to wide audiences over a large geographic area that have a special interest or point of view in mind, such as *Time, Newsweek, Good Housekeeping, TV Guide, Ebony, Harper's, Sports Illustrated, Rolling Stone, Money, Modern Maturity,* and *YM*. Consumer magazines are sold by subscription and also at newsstands, bookstores, and retail outlets. Most Americans subscribe to or read a consumer magazine on a regular basis.

The large category of consumer magazines can be subdivided by demographics, so that there are a number of magazines aimed at women, a different set for sports fans, another set for those interested in politics and public affairs, a group for teenagers (male and female), a growing group for geeks and computer nerds, and so on. Every major demographic group has a magazine or set of magazines published with it in mind. In fact, entrepreneurs in the magazine field spend a good bit of time trying to discover unserved or underserved groups that would be valuable for a set of advertisers. Sometimes a development within an industry or in society will create an interest strong enough to support a magazine publishing venture.

Business, Trade, and Professional Magazines

These magazines seek to serve people in an occupation or field of professional work. Occasionally, you may be able to find these magazines on newsstands, but they are mostly sold by subscription. This category includes well-known titles such as *Advertising Age* and *Editor and Publisher* to titles such as *Farm Futures Magazine* and *American Glass Review.*

The editorial product and approach of the publications vary widely. To be successful, editors and writers for such magazines must know the field thoroughly and must be on top of any changes that may occur. They must also have good sources among the leading industries or businesses in their field. Readers expect the magazine to be useful in telling them information about the industry they may not know from their own experience. Some magazines cover their industries and fields aggressively.

FIGURE 5.1 — Magazines by Circulation June 30, 2002

Top paid-circulation magazines for first half of 2002

RANK	PUBLICATION	AVERAGE PAID CIRCULATION
1	*Modern Maturity*	17,538,189
2	*Reader's Digest*	12,212,040
3	*TV Guide*	9,072,609
4	*Better Homes & Gardens*	7,602,575
5	*National Geographic*	6,890,852
6	*Good Housekeeping*	4,708,964
7	*Family Circle*	4,671,052
8	*Woman's Day*	4,167,933
9	*Time*	4,114,137
10	*Ladies' Home Journal*	4,101,280
11	*My Generation*	3,846,955
12	*People Weekly*	3,617,127
13	*Rosie*	3,503,993
14	*Medizine*	3,467,508
15	*Westways*	3,328,280
16	*Home & Away*	3,313,966
17	*Sports Illustrated*	3,252,896
18	*Newsweek*	3,248,097
19	*Playboy*	3,217,269
20	*Prevention*	3,131,814
21	*Cosmopolitan*	2,963,351
22	*Guideposts*	2,747,626
23	*Via Magazine*	2,655,203
24	*American Legion Magazine*	2,644,518
25	*Maxim*	2,569,172
26	*Southern Living*	2,546,471
27	*Glamour*	2,509,566
28	*NEA Today**	2,481,604
29	*Seventeen*	2,431,943
30	*Redbook*	2,380,410
31	*Martha Stewart Living*	2,323,129
32	*O, The Oprah Magazine*	2,275,599
33	*YM*	2,262,574
34	*AAA Going Places*	2,191,629
35	*Parents*	2,092,443
36	*Smithsonian*	2,040,294
37	*Parenting Magazine*	2,039,462
38	*U.S. News & World Report*	2,018,621
39	*Money*	1,945,265
40	*Ebony*	1,884,739
41	*National Enquirer*	1,801,598
42	*Country Living*	1,711,449
43	*Shape*	1,692,690
44	*Woman's World*	1,668,482
45	*In Style*	1,660,193
46	*Men's Health*	1,659,594
47	*Teen People*	1,651,723
48	*VFW Magazine*	1,645,944
49	*Entertainment Weekly*	1,635,623
50	*Cooking Light*	1,603,680

Source: Advertising Age, Top Media Companies, 2002 (www.adage.com)

Others, however, pull their punches with bad or embarrassing news about an industry or become a mouthpiece for the large companies of the industry; these magazines fear losing advertising revenue from within the industry if they are too aggressive in their coverage.

Sponsored, Association, or Company Magazines

These magazines are published by an organization involved with the readers in some way. A large company may publish a magazine for its employees that will include important company policies as well as lifestyle and feature articles that have nothing directly to do with the company. An association may publish a magazine for its members. (For example, *Modern Maturity*, published by the American Association of Retired Persons, falls into this category as well as the consumer magazine category listed previously.) Magazines that are published by the airlines fit into this category. They are written for people who fly on airlines and contain articles and advertising that would appeal to these readers.

These magazines have a variety of distribution schemes. Some support themselves well with both subscriptions and advertising, but most receive much of their revenue from the sponsoring organization. Some are distributed free or as part of association dues. Some industry-oriented publications are distributed free to certain types of professionals, who must periodically fill out questionnaires to demonstrate their interest.

Zines

A zine is a small, low-cost periodical that may have an erratic publication cycle and distribution system. Typically, zines are produced by one person or a small group of people committed to a particular topic or issue. The phenomenon of the zine has always been with us, but it exploded in the last two decades of the twentieth century when technology made desktop publishing possible. A person with a computer, a printer, and an idea could produce a publication at home, take it to a local copying service, and distribute it at will. Zines rarely sell enough advertising or subscriptions to sustain a long life, but they may continue to exist through donations. Hundreds, perhaps thousands, of zines are produced each year, often dying soon after they are born. Though zines do not have the financial impact that consumer publications have, they are an important part of the world of magazine journalism because they are a way of giving a voice to those who otherwise might have no access to the mass media.

A technological descendant of the zine is the online publication, that is, a set of articles, pictures, graphics, headlines, and other content that is never in printed form. Instead, it exists as a web site. A few online publications—*Slate* and *Salon* being the most prominent—have survived over a period of several years as online-only publications. These publications are updated daily, or at least often enough to make them interesting, but they do not try to cover the day's news as a news web site might. Rather, they attempt to provide perspective on events in the same way a printed magazine would.

SLATE.COM: OVERCOMING THE E-ZINE DOUBTERS

In 1996 Michael Kinsley was a well-known and well-respected writer and television personality as cohost of CNN's *Crossfire* and living life near the center of the political world in Washington, DC. When he announced that he was leaving town to (a) move to Seattle and (b) begin a web magazine, an e-zine, people were shocked. The World Wide Web was still new and relatively unused, and the concept of "publishing" on the Web seemed a pipe dream.

How could the talented, articulate, and influential Kinsley give up so much and move so far away to do something that few people had any concept of doing?

Kinsley had a couple of aces in hand as he headed west. One was the backing of Bill Gates and Microsoft, the giant software company that had made Gates the richest man in the world. Gates could see what others at the time could not—that the Web would continue to attract a larger and larger audience as speed and technology improved.

Kinsley had another ace: No one had done it before. There were, in fact, many other web magazines at the time, but no one had been given the time and resources to develop the concept that he had. It was his opportunity to have a real influence on the future of journalism, not just the politics of the present.

In its first years, Slate.com was many things, seeking to find itself and find an audience. Eventually, it settled into being an e-zine that emphasized news and information, particularly politics, art, and fashion. Rather than reporting the news, however, Slate.com chose commentary, often with an edge of irony and even sarcasm.

Finding the right editorial mix and the right business model has not been easy. Two years after it began, the editors decided to begin charging a subscription. That idea was dropped after only a few months when those editors discovered that readers were unwilling to pay directly for the content Slate.com was offering. Today the publication exists on advertising revenue and some residual activities. (For instance, Slate.com publishes a calendar that features "Bushisms," the fractured language of George W. Bush.)

Slate.com attracts more than 4 million "unique visitors" each month; that is, 4 million different people look at some of the content of the e-zine. That's a long way from 1996, when many of those same people were not sure what an e-zine was.

Creating a Magazine

The foregoing categories give us a limited view of the magazine field and are helpful in beginning to understand how magazine journalism works. Every magazine, no matter what its category, is a combination of three concepts: editorial idea, audience and circulation, and advertising or sponsorship. One way of expressing that combination is that a magazine is

1. an editorial idea, manifested by its content, which is
2. delivered to a target audience through some means of distribution (circulation)
3. for the benefit of both the audience and the advertisers (or sponsors) of the publication

The three parts of this magazine triad—editorial, circulation, and advertising—work together to make a successful publication. Magazine journalists, both writers and editors, need an intimate understanding of how this combination of factors works for any successful magazine.

The first of these is the editorial purpose of the magazine, which should be clearly defined so that writers and editors have an unmistakable understanding about what content to include and what to leave out. They might have an idea for a highly interesting article, but if it does not fit with the purpose of the publication, it should not be included.

Part of the process of defining the editorial purpose is defining the audience for the publication. An audience must not only be defined but it must also be accessible. It would be easy to say that you want to publish a magazine for people interested in growing azaleas and other flowering shrubbery, but finding those people might prove to be a problem. (If there was an organization to which such people belonged, that would be a place to start.) But the idea of audience and circulation must go beyond merely defining and finding an interested group of people. Because many magazines are increasingly dependent on circulation revenue, the audience must be maintained and developed. That is, an active circulation department has to find ways of getting people to subscribe and resubscribe to the publication.

The final part of the combination is advertising. In conceptualizing the editorial idea and the audience for a magazine, a magazine's creators must also take into account the likelihood that advertisers would exist and would want a vehicle (the publication) that would circulate to likely buyers of their products. Advertisers are not inclined to spend money advertising in publications whose content is not related to their product and, therefore, not drawing an audience that would be likely to buy their products.

None of the parts of the triad is easy to figure out, and none is easy to sustain. Editors and writers can get off track by misjudging what interests the audience. Circulation officials can waste time trying to develop audiences that are not interested in the content of the magazine or do not see that it is beneficial to them. Businesspeople and advertising sales staffs can misunderstand the purpose of the publication and waste time attempting to sell advertising to those who do not see that their advertising dollars will be well spent.

This model of magazine production is called specialization or demassification. It involves targeting a specific audience for an area of interest. It goes beyond saying that a magazine is published for sports fans; it calls for the editorial idea to be more specific in terms of a particular sport or approach to the coverage of that sport. This demassification is a far cry from the mid-twentieth century when many publications were produced with a mass market in mind. Many magazines were sold to as many people as possible, and advertising was sold more on the basis of circulation size than on a knowledge of what readers might be inclined to buy.

Another important aspect of the magazine field is the increasing concentration of ownership—a phenomenon that might seem to run counter to the demassification or increasing specialization of the market. It really does not, however. Concentration of ownership means that fewer and fewer companies are owning more and more magazines. (This trend is also evident in the newspaper business, which we discussed in the previous chapter.) These companies look for magazines that have good editorial ideas connected to well-defined and accessible audiences with advertising bases that can sustain them. They see such combinations as potentially profitable and try to acquire them if they are available. A large company can put considerable resources behind a magazine to sustain it until its triad combination becomes profitable. On the downside of ownership concentration, however, is the fear that corporate considerations will overcome the creativity and editorial independence that many magazines have traditionally exercised.

Staff Structure and Employment

Publishing a successful magazine is difficult and time-consuming work. It takes staff members with wide-ranging skills who understand and can execute the central idea behind the publication.

At the top of the organizational chart is the publisher, who is responsible for making sure all of the parts of the organization understand the mission of the publication and are informed about current goals and projects. The publisher is chiefly responsible for the financial health of the magazine and is often a person who acquires that position by working his or her way through the business side (advertising or circulation) of the magazine. In some cases, the publisher is the person who had the original idea for the magazine and may in fact be more oriented to the editorial parts of the organization.

Beneath the level of the publisher, magazines are usually organized into three or four major divisions: editorial, production, advertising, and circulation. Sometimes the editorial and production divisions are combined because the editorial division is responsible for the design of the publication. (Our focus here will be on the editorial division because that is where the journalism takes place.)

From a purely journalistic standpoint, the editor is by far the most important staff position on the magazine. The editor sets the direction of the magazine and interprets the mission by the decisions about content that he or she makes. The best editors are those who have a strong, clear idea about the editorial–audience–advertiser triad that we discussed in the previous section. Traditionally, the editor is the one who defines the magazine's personality, and good editors with a clear vision can leave a legacy that lasts long after they have left the publication. Harold Ross, the longtime editor of the *New Yorker* in the early part of the twentieth century, established a style and outlook that pervades the magazine even today. So did Hugh Hefner with *Playboy,* Helen Gurley Brown with *Cosmopolitan,* and Henry Luce with *Time.*

Not only does the editor make important decisions about content, but he or she also hires editorial staff members, and their competence and judgment are crucial to the editorial content of the publication. A magazine of any size is usually divided into departments, so that there might be an articles editor, a news editor, and even a fiction and poetry editor if the magazine carries that kind of content. Each of these editors might have assistant editors, depending on the size of the publication. They might also have positions such as copy editors, fact-checkers, staff writers, and editorial assistants. A copy editor is responsible for reading all copy carefully, making sure that

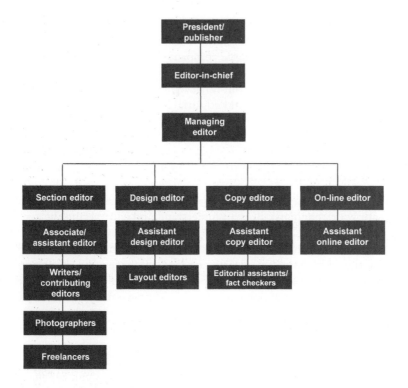

FIGURE 5.2   Magazine Organizational Chart The circulation of a magazine usually determines the size of the staff and the complexity of the organization. This organizational chart shows the most basic magazine staff. The section division could be duplicated depending on how many sections the magazine has.

it is clear, coherent, and grammatically correct and fits with the style of the publication. A fact-checker does exactly what the name implies; he or she checks all of the important facts of an article. Because magazines are published periodically (every week or every month) and because they are often printed on paper that is meant to last, they are considered to be more permanent than newspapers printed on cheap newsprint. Consequently, great care is taken to see that what is printed in a magazine is factually correct; mistakes can cause great and continuing embarrassment to the publication.

A staff writer can be assigned to write the standard or routine items that the magazine carries, or he or she may be asked to work on feature articles that the magazine will run. Editorial assistants have entry-level jobs and may be given any number of tasks from office work to helping a fact-checker or staff writer. The work can be dull, but it is a way of getting started at the publication.

Many magazines keep relatively few writers and reporters on their staffs as full-time employees; some magazines don't have any at all. Instead, editors commission freelance articles. That is, articles are written by people who have agreed to produce the article and be paid for it. Freelance writers may work on several articles for several different publications at the same time. A good freelance writer is someone the editor can depend on to deliver an article that is what the editor wanted and by the deadline that the editor has set. Such a person is likely to get other assignments from the editor.

The art department is another part of the editorial division. (Sometimes it is listed as a separate division.) Led by an art director, this department is responsible for the design of the magazine and must see the magazine through its design and production phases. An art director needs to understand the editorial–audience–advertising triad of the magazine just as much as anyone else. That person is in charge of the graphic personality of the publication. How the publication looks sends many messages to the reader about the publication itself. An art director may have a design staff, depending on how large the magazine is. An art director works with artists and photographers to produce material to support the articles in the publication. One of the art director's most important jobs is to commission the cover for each issue. A cover is often the focus of careful planning (and hot debate) among the magazine's staff.

A MONTH IN THE LIFE OF THE ART DIRECTOR OF A MONTHLY MAGAZINE

Jennifer Edwards
Sarasota Herald-Tribune

You would think that working for a monthly magazine would mean that you would have a lot of downtime. However, the opposite is true; every day brings new challenges and deadlines. Each month is divided into two distinct times—two weeks of preparation and two weeks of production.

During the preparation stage, the editor, freelance writers, freelance photographers, and I meet to brainstorm ideas for the next few issues. We discuss ways to illustrate stories, ideas for people to feature, and so on. I follow up with photographers who are working on their assignments, edit photos, and read stories. I also attend the major fashion photo shoot so I can share my ideas with the photographer, writer, fashion stylist, and models. When all the stories have arrived, I begin to sketch layouts so I can meet with the advertising layout coordinator to place the ads in the magazine.

One month before the issue comes out, the page dummies arrive with ads in place and the production stage begins. I will sometimes do two to three cover designs and every story is re-designed at least once. After I'm finished laying out the stories, proofs are printed and read by the editor. This stage is intense, as I only have a little more than a week to design the whole magazine before the proofs go to another copy editor to be read and corrected.

After the issue is corrected and double-checked, the pages are ready to be released to prepress. They place all of the ads and make PDFs of the pages so they can be sent out to the press. I check the files again for any technical issues. A week later (in early stages of preparation for the next issue), the editor and I go to the press to do one final check of the pages before they are printed. Ten days later, the magazine arrives, bound and trimmed, three days before they're inserted into the newspaper. When the current issue is finally released to the public, we're already in the midst of producing the next month's issue.

Jennifer Edwards is the art director of Style, *the magazine of the* Sarasota Herald-Tribune.

| FIGURE 5.3 | **Magazine Editorial Salaries** |

EDITORIAL DIRECTOR/EDITOR-IN-CHIEF

| 39 or younger | $70,945 |
| 40 or older | $86,739 |

MANAGING EDITOR

| 39 or younger | $50,482 |
| 40 or older | $60,276 |

EDITOR/EXECUTIVE EDITOR

| 39 or younger | $59,061 |
| 40 or older | $68,438 |

SENIOR EDITOR PROFILE

| 39 or younger | $57,658 |
| 40 or older | $63,028 |

AVERAGE SALARY BY REGION

	Editor-in-chief	Executive editor	Managing editor	Senior editor
Northeast	$98,668	$70,255	$63,934	$63,823
South	$78,048	$64,822	$49,162	$64,678
North Central	$92,968	$66,009	$54,807	N/A
West	$63,775	$61,383	$46,498	N/A

BIGGER MAGAZINE, LARGER SALARY

	Less Than $2M in Annual Revenue	$2M or more
Editor-in-chief	$83,100	$84,625
Executive editor	$61,018	$70,944
Managing editor	$54,042	$58,635
Senior editor	$58,048	$63,882

THE GENDER GAP

Editor-in-chief	Average	Managing editor	Average
Male	$82,494	Male	$56,970
Female	$84,833	Female	$54,684

Executive editor	Average	Senior editor	Average
Male	$66,119	Male	$66,472
Female	$65,123	Female	$55,602

Source: Folio Magazine, 2002 annual salary survey (http://foliomag.com/ar/marketing_editors_role_circa).

An art director's toughest job may be to work through all of the ideas and strong feelings that the staff has about the cover.

How much money do all of these people make? Earlier in the chapter we indicated that working on the editorial side of a magazine is not very lucrative. The table on editorial salaries (see page 92) shows that people who make it onto the staff of a successful publication and manage to stay there for some years can make a comfortable salary. Still, many people within the business report that magazine work is a twenty-four-hour, seven-day-a-week job that can be both rewarding and wearing.

Magazine Journalism

Magazines differ in size and structure from other print media, as we have mentioned. The most important difference, however, is their content. Journalism in magazines takes on a depth, tone, and approach that distinguish it from journalism in other media, particularly newspapers. Magazines are not worried about covering day-to-day events, although many magazines have "news" sections that will help readers catch up on the latest developments in the magazine's area of interest. The main job of the magazine is to give readers information and perspective.

Such journalism requires intelligence, understanding, and a considerable amount of hard work from reporters and editors. They must have a clear idea about the purpose and approach of their publication. They must maintain the highest standards of journalism, including a dedication to factual and accurate reporting and setting information within an accurate and understandable context. They must be like long-distance runners compared to the sprinters of the daily newspaper and web journalism worlds.

Beyond the basic requirements that information in magazine journalism needs to be accurate and fair, it must also be interesting. Part of the reason that people spend time with magazines is that they are interesting or entertaining to read. This was one of the basic ideas that Henry Luce and his friend Briton Hadden had when they began *Time* magazine in 1923. They wrote summaries of news events from newspaper clippings they had gathered, but they broke away from the bloodless presentation of information that characterized many of those stories. In its place, they developed a narrative style of writing that people came to enjoy.

The reporting, writing, and editing of a magazine make heavy demands on the skills and intelligence of a journalist. Following are some of the different types of writing and articles that journalists are normally asked to produce for magazines.

Extended Feature Stories

This type of article is one of the most common found in modern magazines. Like the newspaper feature story, the extended feature centers on a topic or idea rather than an event. Even when the feature story is about an event, there should be a larger idea behind the story than simply narrating the aspects of the event itself. Having a central idea—a single sentence or two summarizing what the story is about and why it is being written—is a vitally important aspect of writing this type of article and one that students often have difficulty with. (See the Chapter 10 on writing feature articles.)

The extended feature story is longer than most newspaper feature stories, usually beginning at a minimum of a thousand words and extending to several thousand. Such a story may develop more slowly than a newspaper feature. Extended features should contain a wealth of relevant detail and should add to the reader's understanding of the topic.

Details large and small should be accurate. Although accuracy has been mentioned before in this context, it cannot be overemphasized in journalism. A journalist should be meticulous about what he or she writes, confident that descriptions, names, identifications, sequences, and all other items in an article are correct.

An extended feature story has room for the writer's point of view or outright opinion, but writers should avoid including those opinions overtly or gratuitously. A writer's opinion is legitimate if it is a natural consequence of the information that he or she has presented in an article. Without evidence or information to back it up, opinions are not worth very much and, worse, are not very interesting.

Personality Profile

One of the staples of magazine writing is the personality profile. Readers love to read about other people—as long as those people are interesting and the writer can find an interesting aspect of their lives.

As with the extended feature, the writer should be governed by a central idea, not some vague notion such as the person is a celebrity or the mayor of the town. Articles about well-known people do make good reading and are popular with editors, but celebrities are not interesting merely because they are celebrities. The writer's responsibility is to find an innovative and interesting aspect of their lives to write about, and with celebrities that can be particularly difficult. The sex lives of various celebrities are probably not going to get much attention from an editor because that topic, as inherently interesting as it is, has already been written about so much.

In one sense, the term *personality profile* is a misnomer. Stories are rarely about someone's personality; rather they are about things the person does or ideas the person has. Writers often have to do a great deal of research about a person before they can come to a conclusion about a central idea or theme to the story. A personality profile will usually involve an interview with the subject of the profile, but ideally that interview should be conducted only after background research has been done. And that should not be the only interview conducted. The journalist should try to talk with as many people as possible to get a variety of points of view about the person and prepare questions to ask during the interview.

A variation on all of this is making the interview the central item of the article. The *"Playboy* interview," in which a reporter talks in depth with a subject and the interview is presented in a question-and-answer format, is the prime example of this technique. An article that follows this format does not call on the reporter to use many writing techniques, but the reporter does have to prepare good questions and does have to edit judiciously so that the personality and information the subject has will come through. The writer may also have to construct an introduction and conclusion to these types of articles.

Analysis and Interpretation

A magazine may want an article that takes an in-depth look at a person, event, or issue that will explain it thoroughly to the reader. For these articles, the reporter will need to develop an expertise about the topic and will need to know who and what the best sources of information are. Such articles can take months to report and develop, and they may involve investigative journalism techniques, that is, uncovering information that has been kept from public view.

What we now call investigative journalism was first developed by magazine journalists at the beginning of the twentieth century. That era spawned journalists who were concerned about the social ills created by massive immigration and industrialization. Lincoln Steffens, Ida Tarbell, and others wrote long series of articles about exploited workers, unsanitary food processing, and other social problems. They were tagged "muckrakers" by President Theodore Roosevelt, but their reports stirred social consciences and brought about changes in laws that improved society.

Although newspaper reporters have taken over much of the investigative reporting that occurs today, magazine journalists still produce these kinds of pieces. A journalist who undertakes the reporting and writing of an investigative piece should use commonly accepted journalistic reporting techniques and remember that fairness and accuracy are two indispensable qualities of writing. Conclusions in such journalistic pieces should be based on the information and evidence presented in the article.

Literary Journalism

This term refers both to a style of writing and an approach to the subject of the report. Some journalists feel that there are stories that can best be told if they go beyond the normal writing techniques that journalists usually employ. They believe they can better explain feelings, relationships, and events if they use dialogue, metaphor, point of view, and literary voice.

The problem is that in order to be considered journalism, such writing must adhere to the stricture of accuracy. A writer cannot make anything up—dialogue, for instance—nor can the writer squeeze facts into a form that distorts or makes them inaccurate just to satisfy a literary device. Using literary journalism techniques presents temptations even for the most experienced journalists, and those who practice this form of journalism have to constantly remind themselves of their obligations as journalists.

Another problem with literary journalism is the amount of time it takes to develop these kinds of articles. Writers often report that they have to spend many hours or days with their sources to gather the kind of information and understanding they need to write in this genre. A publication must be willing to invest the time of the writer and editor if it is going to produce worthy and successful literary journalism.

Travel Articles

One of the most romantic professional thoughts a young journalist can have is that of being sent by a publication to an exotic or exciting place and told to write about it—all expenses paid! Although that does not happen often, many magazines are very interested in travel articles.

Travel articles have a long history in journalism going back to Mark Twain, whose travel writing can be found in books such as *Innocents Abroad.* Twain had a unique viewpoint and brand of humor that he applied to the places he visited, and it is still this possibility that lures many young writers into the realm of traveling writing.

Travel writing often starts at home. Most of us live in a place, or near a place, that offers something interesting and unique. Discovering what that is and selling a magazine editor on it is one way that many young writers break into the field of freelancing (see the following section).

Good travel writing requires that the reporter give the reader a sense of time and place about a location. Finding out how people relate to a geographic location—how they use and enjoy the land—is one approach that travel writers use. Facts, descriptions, and details are more important to this kind of writing than vague feelings or opinions. Travel writers need to include supporting details.

Many other types of articles and many writing opportunities exist in the field of magazine journalism. Ralph Monti in his excellent monograph, "Career Opportunities in Magazine Publishing," advises those seeking entry into the field to look in the traditional places (beginning with *Writer's Market,* the major reference work for freelancers) and for what he calls "hidden opportunities" to write for money. These include corporation reports and even catalogs, which not only give descriptions of items for sale but also include articles about subjects and places related to those items.

Freelance Writing

Many people who want to get into the field of magazine journalism do so by accepting freelance assignments. Some people actually make a living at it.

Making freelance assignments is a common way for editors to generate articles for their publications. Or a writer will suggest an article to an editor, and if the editor likes the idea, he or she will make the assignment. Rather than keep writers on staff (and pay them wages and benefits), many magazines simply pay people to write one article at a time.

People who want to get into this business are likely to start with the subjects they are interested in and the magazine that they read. Knowing a publication and the kinds of articles that it publishes is the first step in the freelance process. An aspiring writer will contact an editor by writing a query letter. The letter will suggest an article for

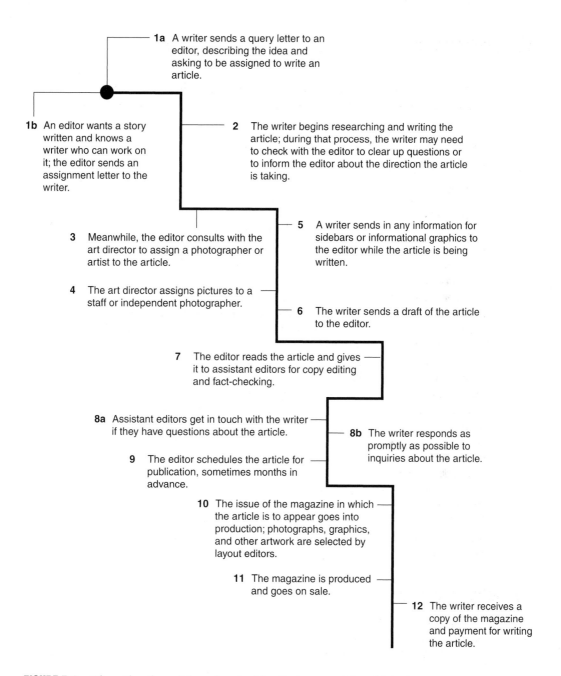

1a A writer sends a query letter to an editor, describing the idea and asking to be assigned to write an article.

1b An editor wants a story written and knows a writer who can work on it; the editor sends an assignment letter to the writer.

2 The writer begins researching and writing the article; during that process, the writer may need to check with the editor to clear up questions or to inform the editor about the direction the article is taking.

3 Meanwhile, the editor consults with the art director to assign a photographer or artist to the article.

4 The art director assigns pictures to a staff or independent photographer.

5 A writer sends in any information for sidebars or informational graphics to the editor while the article is being written.

6 The writer sends a draft of the article to the editor.

7 The editor reads the article and gives it to assistant editors for copy editing and fact-checking.

8a Assistant editors get in touch with the writer if they have questions about the article.

8b The writer responds as promptly as possible to inquiries about the article.

9 The editor schedules the article for publication, sometimes months in advance.

10 The issue of the magazine in which the article is to appear goes into production; photographs, graphics, and other artwork are selected by layout editors.

11 The magazine is produced and goes on sale.

12 The writer receives a copy of the magazine and payment for writing the article.

FIGURE 5.4 Time Line for a Magazine Article Getting an article published in a magazine is not a simple or straightforward process. The article usually begins as an idea from a writer who sends a query letter to an editor, or it can begin with an editor who sends an assignment letter to a writer. A writer who queries an editor must wait until the editor gives the writer the go-ahead to do the story. Even then, stories are done on speculation. That is, an editor is not obligated to accept the final story for publication. This time line shows most of the steps in the process, but depending on the article and the magazine, they might not all be necessary. (Thanks to Tim Jackson for information for this graphic.)

the publication, give some information on the writer, and may even make a case for why the assignment should go to the writer.

Editors usually respond to query letters fairly quickly. If they like an idea, they will offer an assignment to the writer, outlining what they want to see in the final article, the form in which it should be submitted, the deadline for submission, and terms of payment. A writer can then respond to that by saying whether or not all of the terms are acceptable.

Payments vary widely from magazine to magazine. *Writer's Market*, available at the reference desk of most libraries, lists hundreds of publications that buy freelance work and the standard payments they make for such work. The publishers of *Writer's Market* also publish a monthly magazine, *Writer's Digest*, that contains more current information about publications and many useful tips for writers.

Despite the fact that many people are trying to enter the freelance field, editors often complain that they cannot find writers who meet their deadlines with articles that are acceptable to the publication. Consequently, there is much opportunity in this field, particularly for young people.

The Future of Magazines

Few people doubt that magazines will continue to be a vital and viable medium for journalism in the future. Magazine readership shows signs of increasing, and magazine publishers have done better at accepting and integrating the Web into their operations. The field of magazine journalism, although highly competitive, is wide open for the young and the restless.

QUESTIONS FOR DISCUSSION

1. Does magazine journalism appeal to you as a career? Although some information in this chapter might discourage people from going into the magazine field, make a list of the some of the good things about a magazine career as well as some of the negative aspects.

2. This chapter mentions magazines published by airlines that are given to passengers to read on their flights. What kind of articles would appeal to this group of people? What advertisers would find this group a ready market for their products?

3. Do you have an idea for a magazine for an audience that is underserved? Try to state this idea in two or three sentences. Who is the audience? Where would you find these people? What advertisers do you think would be interested in this audience?

4. One of the basic forms of writing for a magazine is the personality profile. Think about the most interesting member of your family. List some of the facts that might be used to write a personality profile of this person.

RELATED WEB SITES

Folio Magazine, www.foliomag.com

Magazine Publishers Association, www.magazine.org

Mr. Magazine, www.mrmagazine.com

Periodical and Book Association of America, www.pbaa.net

READINGS AND REFERENCES

Gunderloy, M., & Janice, C. G. (1992). *The world of zines: A guide to the independent magazine revolution.* New York: Penguin.

Husni, S. (1998). *Launch your own magazine: A guide for succeeding.* Nashville, TN: Hamblett House.

Johnson, S., & Prijatel, P. (1998). *The magazine from cover to cover.* Chicago: NTC Publishing Group.

Tebbel, J. (1991). *The magazine in America, 1741–1990.* New York: Oxford University Press.

Woodward, C. (2002). *Starting & running a successful newsletter or magazine.* Berkeley, CA: Nolo Press.

Chapter Six

Television and Radio

1. Television is the news medium of impact and immediacy; when news of importance occurs, we are most likely to watch it on television first, and our impressions are formed by the pictures we see and the sounds we hear.

2. When it was developed in the early twentieth century, radio showed what impact broadcasting could have on its audience and how it had the potential to change journalism.

3. Format: the general type of programming that a radio station uses to fill up its day.

4. Ted Turner: the owner of an independent television station in Atlanta who pioneered the use of satellite and cable technology to expand the number of stations to which the audience had access.

5. Broadcast news is criticized because it often does not deliver explanation or depth for complex stories.

6. Although the business of broadcasting is regulated by the government, the government and courts have been very reluctant to get involved with program content.

Vignette

See It Now.

The title of the 1951 television news show hosted by Edward R. Murrow perfectly sums up television news. The name had been derived from Murrow's radio show, Hear It Now.

Many people consider Murrow the father of broadcast news. (See Chapter 23.) He first achieved fame at the beginning of World War II by broadcasting news reports from London during the time when Germans were bombing the city. Murrow began his reports with the signature line, "This is London."

He spoke clearly and precisely in a clipped midwestern tone. Every word was clear, and every sentence put the listener inside the British capital city with all of its danger and drama. Murrow directed the news coverage that the Columbia Broadcasting System (CBS) gave to the war in Europe. He boarded more than 20 air raids over Germany on Allied bombers, and his low-keyed descriptions added authenticity to his reports. When the Allied army crossed into Germany and discovered the Nazi death camps in which millions of Jews had died, Murrow was there, reporting the unbelievable in tones America had come to believe.

Broadcast news had been in existence for nearly 20 years by the time the war began, but Murrow developed a style of presentation that most newscasters tried to emulate. The "rules" of broadcast writing (some of which are found in Chapter 19) come from the practices that Murrow made popular.

After the war, CBS continued its tradition of presenting news over the air and asked Murrow to host a show called Hear It Now *in 1950. The next year, as more and more people were getting television sets in their homes, CBS asked its most famous newscaster to transfer the* Hear It Now *format to television. Murrow's show did for television what it had previously done for radio news; that is, it established a format and style of presentation that would become the standard of the profession.*

Viewers could see the pictures. They could hear the sound. And they could do it with an immediacy that no previous medium had offered them.

Impact and Immediacy

Broadcast news, when it occurred and developed in the twentieth century, was a remarkable divergence from the news in print that people had known. The inventions of photography and the telegraph had accelerated the presentation of news in the middle of the nineteenth century to a degree that would have seemed unbelievable in the 1820s. But that presentation was static, fixed in the medium of paper. The technology of broadcasting used sound and then sight to create a means of communication that few in the nineteenth century could envision.

Today, we depend on broadcasting to tell and show us what is going on in our world right now. We turn to broadcast news when anything of importance happens. We expect to see and hear what is happening, often as it happens. And, in general, we find what we see and hear to be believable.

Another characteristic of broadcast news is its ubiquity. Broadcasting is everywhere, literally, especially with radio. The portability of radio and its ability to pick up distant signals make it a medium that can be useful in almost any part of the globe. Television news has grown from a once-a-day phenomenon to all day, every day.

Broadcast news is fundamentally different from print. It begins in the same way with reporters gathering information, and many of the reporting techniques that broadcast journalists use are the same as those of print journalists. Broadcast journalists are working with a different medium, however, and it has different demands and expectations from the audience. The use of sounds and pictures demands little active participation from the audience; it can simply be seen and absorbed. The format of broadcast news shows offers viewers few options in terms of what they see and when they see it.

Also different is the environment in which we can absorb broadcast news. Print demands the individual's attention to the printed word. Broadcast news can be shared. Several people can watch a news show together, getting the same information and exchanging their interpretations of it. In some ways, this phenomenon takes us back to the colonial days of the tavern where people would come together to hear the latest news and be able to discuss it as they heard it. Consequently, some commentators have described broadcast news as creating a "global village" in which people in many parts of the world hear and share the same information.

The medium's lack of demand on the part of the viewer in taking in the news, joined with the emphasis on sound and pictures and the ability to deliver events and information instantly to the audience, gives broadcast news an impact that print cannot match. When anything newsworthy occurs, we turn on the television knowing that broadcast news organizations are geared to giving us the latest information and showing us the most recent pictures they have. In those moments, whether they are planned (such as Super Bowl parties) or unplanned (as with the morning of September 11, 2001), television brings us together in a way that no other medium can, gives us a common pool of information, and becomes part of our life experience.

But before television, there was radio.

Radio: News at a Different Level

During the latter half of the nineteenth century, scientists detected that the atmosphere was full of electronic waves. Harnessing these waves and making them useful became the goal of a number of dedicated innovators. Chief among them was Guglielmo Marconi who built a device that would send Morse code, the alphabet of dots and dashes used by the telegraph, through the air using these waves. Working independently, other scientists such as Lee De Forest and Reginald Fessenden figured out how to capture and send voices and music with these waves. They also constructed devices that would receive and project these sounds.

The electronic waves, or radio waves, traveled at the speed of light so that the transmission and reception of them, in effect, were instantaneous. None of the early radio pioneers conceived of the uses to which it could be put or the structure of twentieth-century communication they were building. The first inklings of this future came when radio was used as a supplement to the telegraph by extending the reach

FIGURE 6.1   Guglielmo Marconi

Guglielmo Marconi is often credited with the invention of radio, but he is only one of several people who made important contributions to its development. Marconi harnessed electromagnetic waves so that he could send Morse code signals over the air. Marconi was a visionary who saw great commercial possibilities in this new form of communication. (Photo credit: Library of Congress)

of the telegraph to places where telegraph lines could not be placed. Early in the twentieth century, the U.S. Navy realized the usefulness of being able to transmit messages from ship to ship and ship to shore. The sinking of the *Titanic* in 1912 was the first major news event in which radio communication played an important role. The speed with which news about the disaster was transmitted gave the general public an idea of the potential that this new medium had.

The concept of radio as a mass medium in which a single radio station would broadcast information that would be received by many listeners took several years to develop. And few in those early days had any notion that these radio stations located in various parts of the nation could be linked together to form a network that could transmit the same information to a vast audience. Finally, no one had an idea how all of this would be financed; broadcast advertising was not something that anyone had yet envisioned.

Yet all of this did happen, and by the middle of the twentieth century, radio was a mass medium that no other could match for speed and range. Radio, of course, was overtaken by television at that point, and while the technology of radio improved, its content and role changed completely.

Today, consumers in the United States have about 12,000 radio stations available to them, broadcast over AM (amplitude modulation) or FM (frequency modulation) waves. One estimate is that there are about 500 million radio receivers in the country, or two for every person in the nation. Radio stations and programs are identified by formats. The two major formats are music and news/talk. The music format can be subdivided in many ways, usually by genre of music (country, rock, jazz, classical, etc.). The news/talk format can be all news, in which information is continually updated throughout the day, or talk radio, in which listeners are allowed to call in to talk about topics relevant to a particular show, such as politics, health, or sports. Talk radio grew to exceeding popularity, particularly on AM radio stations, in the 1990s, and talk radio hosts such as Rush Limbaugh and Don Imus were nationally syndicated and became household names.

Another way of dividing up radio stations is by classifying them as commercial or noncommercial. The vast majority of stations are commercial. They receive most of their revenue through advertising sales. More than 500 stations, however, are noncommercial. They are owned by educational institutions and foundations, and they exist on a combination of government grants, money from their parent institutions, and private donations from listeners. Most of these stations are affiliated with

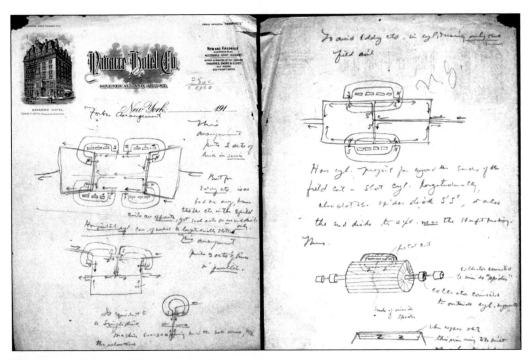

FIGURE 6.2   Lee De Forest Lee De Forest's schematic diagrams and notes are shown here scribbled onto hotel stationery around 1915. De Forest is one of several contenders for the title Father of Radio. De Forest experimented with receiving long-distance radio signals and in 1907 patented an electronic device named the audion. Until this time, radio was considered little more than "wireless telegraphy," since it sent Morse code (dots and dashes) instead of conveying actual sound like the telephone does. De Forest's new three-electrode (triode) vacuum tube boosted radio waves as they were received and made possible what was then called "wireless telephony." De Forest's invention allowed the human voice, music, or any broadcast signal to be heard loudly and clearly. (Photo credit: Library of Congress)

National Public Radio (NPR), which produces two major news programs each day: *Morning Edition* and *All Things Considered*. These two shows, as well as other news programming produced by NPR, have set a high standard for radio journalism.

Unfortunately, few commercial radio stations meet this high standard. Even though a news department might appear on the organizational charts of most radio stations, rarely will a commercial station invest much effort or money into gathering news. Most station managers believe that their audiences tune into their stations because of the nonnews programming, usually the music, that a station provides. They do not see news as something that will draw an audience. Consequently, the state of radio journalism outside of public radio is not a healthy one. Radio journalism on commercial stations is still vital in some of the country's largest cities where the stations are highly competitive. In midsize and smaller cities, however, stations often seem content with the segment of the audience they have, and they have little commitment to news and information.

The dominance of the current system—on-the-ground radio stations that use their format to appeal to certain segments of a local audience—is being challenged at the beginning of the twenty-first century by the advent of two technological breakthroughs. One is satellite radio, in which receivers capture radio waves directly from satellites. Satellite radio services offer listeners who pay a subscription fee a wide choice of formats, including some formats that commercial stations do not find profitable. These offerings are not confined to a specific geographic area. Consequently, although a single city might not have enough jazz aficionados to make a commercial station possible, there are certainly enough jazz fans across the country (or the world) to make stations devoted to the subgenres of jazz feasible. Satellite radio is still in its infancy, and its future is not certain.

Another challenge to the current system is Internet radio. The technology is now in place for a single Internet user, at a relatively low cost, to set up a web site over which he or she could broadcast news, commentary, or music. Some musical groups have actually done this, setting up stations that play nothing but their own music. The Internet has also been used to extend the reach of commercial and noncommercial stations in a variety of ways. Many stations have a web site that allows users to listen to their broadcasts. This means that a person far outside the range of the station can still hear what the station has to offer. Beyond this live streaming of the station's programming, there are other variations, such as the one pioneered by major league baseball. That site (www.mlb.com) offers visitors the live radio broadcasts of all major league baseball games for a small annual subscription fee. New York Yankees

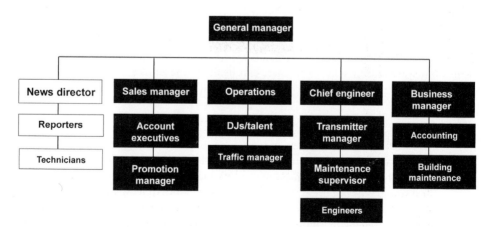

FIGURE 6.3   Radio Organizational Chart Most radio stations operate with relatively few people. This organizational chart shows more positions than are found at most stations in medium and small markets. The news department for a radio station might consist of only one or two people.

FIGURE 6.4   The Fireside Chats of Franklin Roosevelt President
Franklin Roosevelt used radio masterfully during his four terms in office.
Roosevelt had a distinctive voice and spoke with great confidence. He would
periodically take to the airwaves to explain the policies of his administration.
Because of the intimacy of these conversations—he sounded to many individuals
as if he were talking directly to them—they were called "fireside chats." (Photo
credit: Franklin Delano Roosevelt Library)

fans, no matter where they are, can listen to the Yankees games over WCBS as long
as they have an Internet connection that allows them to download the audio.

Local Television

Television evolved from radio in the first half of the twentieth century, and its early
prospects were uncertain. Receiver sets were expensive, and reception of the television signal was not great. Programming was limited. Many felt that radio was the su-
perior medium because it allowed people to continue with their activities while
listening. Television demanded people's attention.

That's exactly what it got after the end of World War II. With the war over and
prosperity returning to the nation, people seemed willing to put up with the limitations of this new form of entertainment. In fact, so many sets were sold and so many
television station licenses were granted in the early postwar era that the Federal Com-

munications Commission (FCC) stopped issuing licenses in 1948 while it considered how best to use the limited television spectrum. That freeze came to an end four years later, and the industry's growth was phenomenal. By 1955, two-thirds of the nation's homes had a television set; today that figure is at 98 percent.

The structure of the industry is built on local television stations. There are about 1,600 full-powered television stations in the country. These stations broadcast over a local geographic area on frequencies, or channels, assigned by the FCC. Another 1,600 low-powered stations are also in operation, broadcasting to a very limited area, such as a college campus and the surrounding neighborhoods. Television stations represent a major investment in equipment and personnel on the part of their owners (not to mention the time-consuming and sometimes expensive process of obtaining a license). Despite these initial and continued investments, owning a television station can be a highly profitable venture. Stations make almost all of their money by selling advertising, and their competition is usually limited to two or three other stations. They are usually free to set profitable advertising rates and often find many local merchants more than willing to pay them.

Local stations get most of their programming through their affiliations with national networks. An affiliated local station will get as much as 70 percent of its program content from a network. The remainder will be obtained from national syndicates that sell talk shows, games shows, and movies and from local production. The most common locally produced programming is news. Local news shows can draw large audiences, which in turn allows a station to charge high rates to advertisers. Local stations often compete with one another for the best newscast and the most up-to-date weather information. They will hire personalities as news anchors and commentators whom they believe will draw people into the newscast.

National networks not only provide entertainment programming for local stations, they also have a long history of providing national news shows. For the first six decades of television, these news shows were among the most important and influential journalism the field produced. The national news anchor, personified by Walter Cronkite, Dan Rather, Tom Brokaw, and others, is a famous and highly regarded individual. (Walter Cronkite, when he was the CBS News anchor in the 1960s and 1970s, was referred to as "the most trusted man in America.") With the advent of cable television during the last two decades and the creation of twenty-four-hour cable news networks, the audience and influence of these network news broadcasts have waned. Audiences have more choice and are not confined to the times at which these shows are aired.

The advent of cable television represents a major turn in the relatively brief history of television. Cable was first used to provide television to areas that over-the-air signals could not reach. A high tower would be placed in an advantageous location to capture the over-the-air signals, which would then be funneled through a cable and into the homes below. In the 1960s and early 1970s, some people began to see the possibilities of such a system. A satellite could beam signals to a tower just as an over-the-air station could. One of the first to try this was Ted Turner, owner of a struggling, nonaffiliated station in Atlanta. Turner's station specialized in showing old movies, something the networks did not offer. When Turner bought the Atlanta Braves

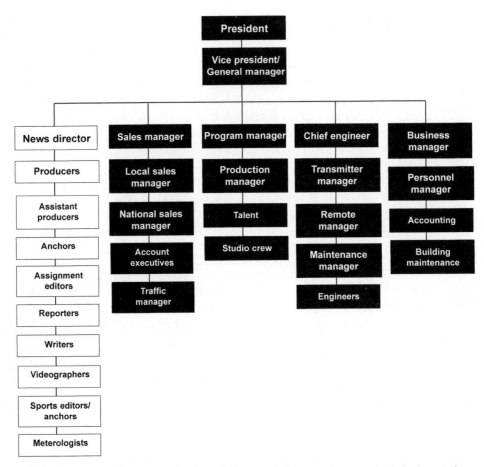

FIGURE 6.5   Television Organizational Chart Television stations, particularly those in large markets, can be complex operations. They need people who have a high degree of technical expertise and others who have a keen business sense. And they need people who understand news and information. This chart shows how the news division fits in with the other parts of the organization.

baseball team, he made the Braves the showcase of his station. Again, it was something the networks were not offering. People like Turner and Gerald Levin, the founder of Home Box Office and another pioneer of cable, demonstrated that the home television set could play more than just what the three networks and local channels were offering. Cable companies formed in just about every city in the nation, and the rush to cable by programming entrepreneurs was like the California gold rush of 1849. ESPN was established to give sports fans something to watch twenty-four hours a day. Religious channels sprang into existence. In 1980, Turner changed the face of television news by inaugurating Cable News Network, a twenty-four-hour news chan-

PUBLIC BROADCASTING

Educators in the 1950s and 1960s saw the value of television as possibly extending their reach and cutting costs. Many educational districts across the country applied for broadcasting licenses and prepared educational programs for their local audiences. These programs were often as dull as they sounded.

In the 1960s, the Carnegie Commission on Educational Television recommended that the federal government get involved, and Congress established the Corporation for Public Broadcasting, which set up the Public Broadcasting Service (PBS) as the center of a network of educational television stations and radio stations. With money it received from Congress and affiliated stations, PBS produced award-winning television shows, including news-oriented shows such as the *MacNeil/Lehrer News Hour,* a nightly news broadcast that emphasized depth coverage of major issues, and *Frontline,* a news documentary show.

The Corporation for Public Broadcasting may have had its greatest impact on journalism with the establishment of National Public Radio (NPR). NPR produces a number of shows for public radio stations around the country, but its two premier shows are *Morning Edition,* a two-hour morning news show, and *All Things Considered,* a show aired in the afternoons around rush hour in most areas.

These shows demonstrate the power of radio as a news medium. They contain innovative formatting and presentation styles. These shows, more than any other segment of broadcasting, have integrated the Web into their presentations, storing all of their audio on the Web as well as including additional information about the topics they are covering. NPR anchors and reporters often advise listeners at the end of their reports to visit the NPR web site for more information.

Public broadcasting does not sell advertising as commercial broadcasting stations do. Instead, it seeks local and national underwriters, people and organizations that will contribute money and services to a station or network. Stations may also receive support from state and local governments. A third source of income is direct donations from listeners.

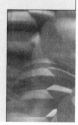

| FIGURE 6.6 | Top Ten Cable Television Companies, 2001 |

RANK	COMPANY	REVENUE*	TOP PROPERTY
1	AOL Time Warner	$13,542	Time Warner Cable (MSO)
2	AT&T Broadband	9,799	AT&T Broadband (MSO)
3	Comcast Corp.	5,131	Comcast (MSO)
4	Walt Disney Co.	4,303	ESPN
5	Viacom	4,282	Nickelodeon, Nick at Nite
6	Cox Enterprises	4,067	Cox Cable (MSO)
7	Charter Communications	3,953	Charter (MSO)
8	Cablevision Systems Corp.	3,064	Cablevision Systems (MSO)
9	Adelphia Comm. Corp.	3,060	Adelphia (MSO)
10	News Corp.	1,455	Fox Sports Networks

*Figures represent millions of dollars.

Source: Advertising Age, Top Media Companies, 2001 (www.adage.com)

nel with the ability to cover any story as it was beginning to break. No longer were CBS, NBC, and ABC the only national television journalists in town.

Television News

Television news today adheres largely to a structure developed by NBC News in the 1940s. Those first news shows used an anchor to introduce stories and relied heavily on visual images. The first shows, because they often lacked moving pictures, used many still photos with print identifications. By the late 1940s, CBS was also airing news shows, bringing the staccato cadence to the reporting that Edward R. Murrow used and emphasizing the dramatic voices of the reporters.

Television news directors realized that there was more than one way to present the news, and it was not long before newsmagazine shows appeared. These shows would have a more relaxed and entertaining format. Documentaries devoted to a sin-

THE JFK ASSASSINATION: TELEVISION'S FIRST BIG STORY

CBS news anchor Walter Cronkite interrupted his network's normal daytime programming on November 22, 1963 with the words:

"In Dallas, Texas, three shots were fired at President Kennedy's motorcade in downtown Dallas. The first reports say that President Kennedy has been seriously wounded by this shooting." The time was 1:40 P.M. Eastern Standard Time. Almost an hour later Cronkite, choking on his words, told his audience, "From Dallas, Texas, the flash, apparently official. President Kennedy died at 1:00 P.M. Central Standard Time, two o'clock Eastern Standard Time." He then looked over at the studio clock. "Some thirty-eight minutes ago," he said.

Lyndon Johnson takes the oath of office on *Air Force One* shortly after John F. Kennedy is pronounced dead on November 22, 1963. He is surrounded by his wife Lady Bird Johnson (on his right) and Jackie Kennedy (on his left). (Photo credit: National Archives)

For the next three and a half days, television turned its sole attention to this story. It was, in many ways, ill-prepared to do so. At the time television news was barely fifteen years old and

gle topic also began to appear. Interview shows with newsmakers were also developed in a variety of formats, from one-on-one journalist and newsmaker to a panel of journalists interviewing a newsmaker or celebrity.

All of these styles of news presentation are used today, but many of them are criticized because they deemphasize reporting information in a traditional journalistic fashion. Instead, they favor opinion and confrontation over the presentation of facts and information. They have given rise to what some have called the "babblerati," talking heads who have opinions but no real information.

Television news has always been subject to such criticism. The more basic and long-standing criticisms are these:

- ■ **It's too short and too shallow.**   The convention of writing broadcast news is so limiting that it doesn't allow writers enough time to give information and details that would enlighten listeners. Most broadcast news stories are twenty to thirty seconds long. That simply isn't enough time to do any view much good.

---

without satellites or many of the modern miracles of technology that we know today. Most television cameras, for instance, took a full two hours to warm up.

That lack of experience was evident on that Friday afternoon. On NBC Frank McGee and Chet Huntley anchored the network's coverage. Arms would extend into the picture handing them news bulletins. Telephone lines could not be connected to their sound system, so McGee wound up repeating the words of correspondent Robert McNeil to the audience as he listened over the phone. The men and women on the air were as confused as their audience.

But the story was there and turned out to be far more involved than the death of the president. Lyndon Johnson took the oath of office on board *Air Force One* (one of the few events of that story that was not broadcast), and the plane carrying the body of the dead president returned to Washington that evening. As it did, police in Dallas arrested a man they believed to be involved with the shooting.

Over the next four days, Americans stayed in front of their television sets. They saw images they would never forget:

- Jackie Kennedy, in her blood-stained pink suit, jumping off *Air Force One* after it returned to Washington with the body of her slain husband.
- A glimpse of Lee Harvey Oswald, the man police had arrested, being escorted through the Dallas City Police Station on Saturday.
- The shocking murder of Oswald by Jack Ruby on Sunday morning as Oswald was being transferred to the Dallas County Jail. NBC was broadcasting the transfer live when the shooting occurred.
- Jackie Kennedy and her daughter Caroline kneeling in front of the president's casket as it lay in state in the Capitol rotunda.
- The riderless black horse that led the funeral procession through Washington, DC, on Monday.
- Three-year-old John Kennedy Jr. saluting his father's casket as it passed in front of the church where his funeral mass had been held.

For four days, Americans watched and mourned. And in those four days, television news showed its capacity to inform and unite.

■ **Pictures or audio drive a story.**   One of the sayings in the profession is "If it bleeds, it leads." That means the bloodier or more horrific the pictures, the more likely it is that the story will lead the newscast. Another aspect of this criticism is that stories are broadcast because the station has film or audio, not because the stories themselves are newsworthy.

■ **Broadcast news emphasizes the superficial rather than the substantive.**   This criticism is related to the two preceding points. Critics say broadcast news reporters often pick out the sensational or the most unusual aspect of a story to emphasize rather than what is the most important.

■ **Broadcast news writers depend on clichés rather than information, particularly to end their stories.**   Many reporters find an ending that says, in effect, "Who knows?" or "We'll have to wait and see." For years, the reporter who covered the Supreme Court for National Public Radio would end her stories about cases before the Court by saying, "A decision is expected by next summer." That sentence tells us nothing because most Supreme Court cases are decided before the Court recesses for the summer.

Many of the criticisms spring from the fact that broadcasting has developed as an entertainment medium. Its purpose is not to transmit information but to distract in a variety of ways. Even serious journalism has to meet the sight and sound demands of broadcasting, and it does not always do so successfully.

FIGURE 6.7   **Top Ten Broadcast Television Companies, 2001**

RANK	COMPANY	REVENUE*	TOP PROPERTY
1	Viacom	$7,240	CBS-TV Network
2	NBC- TV (General Electric Co.)	5,360	NBC-TV Network
3	Walt Disney Co.	5,166	ABC-TV Network
4	News Corp.	3,464	Fox-TV Network
5	Tribune Co.	1,130	WPIX-TV (WB), New York
6	Univision Communications	872	Univision Network
7	Gannett Co.	663	WXIA-TV (NBC), Atlanta
8	Sinclair Broadcast Group	646	KOVR-TV (CBS), Sacramento
9	Hearst Corp.	643	WCVB-TV (ABC), Boston
10	Belo	598	WFAA-TV (ABC), Dallas/Fort Worth

*Figures represent millions of dollars.

Source: Advertising Age, Top Media Companies, 2001 (www.adage.com)

Regulation of Broadcasting

The First Amendment and other traditions of free speech and free press apply to broadcast journalism, as they do to other news media (see Chapter 24). Broadcast journalists do not carry the burdens of prior restraint or a greater susceptibility to libel and privacy laws than journalists for other media. They have the freedom to report, interpret, and criticize just as other journalists do. Certainly, on the many forms of talk radio and television that we have today, freedom of speech is on display.

Even so, broadcasting operates under more government regulation than do the print media. The initial reason for this regulation is the limited broadcast spectrum; there are only a finite number of radio and television channels available in any area. In order to keep signals from intruding on one another, the broadcast industry needs a traffic cop. That cop is the federal government, specifically the Federal Communications Commission (FCC). The law setting up the FCC mandated that broadcasting in America be conducted in the "public interest, convenience and necessity," and it gave the agency power to issue and revoke broadcast licenses. These licenses are issued for a limited time and must be renewed every eight years.

The FCC's power to revoke a license makes broadcasters extremely sensitive to any regulations the commission might impose. Revocations have occurred rarely in the history of the FCC, but when they occur, they are financially devastating. A broadcaster is left with a huge financial investment and no way to recover the losses.

Most of the regulations the FCC has imposed on broadcasts have had to do with technical, business, and operations matters. Both Congress and the FCC have been reluctant to intrude on the programming aspects of broadcasting and for the most part have tried to prevent their regulations from affecting journalistic practices. Still, the government has taken some action in these areas when legislators and regulators believed it was necessary to do so. For example, the Children's Television Act requires stations to carry educational and information programs for children and limits the amount of commercial time within programs directed at children. There are also laws and regulations mandating "equal time" for candidates running for political office; that is, if a station allows a candidate to appear on a nonnews show, it must offer the same opportunities for all candidates running for that office. Cable TV companies are also under obligation to carry local stations on their list of offerings.

Although certain television regulations may have some effect on broadcast journalism, most journalists do not view them as intrusive or as a hindrance to their work. Broadcast journalists can still operate with a great deal of freedom about what they cover and what they say.

The Future of Broadcasting

Broadcasters face an uncertain future; so do broadcast journalists. The field was relatively stable during most of the twentieth century, but in the 1980s, with the growth of cable television, the field changed drastically. Part of the change was to offer more opportunity for broadcast journalists to break into the field and ply their trade. With the growth of the Internet as a news medium, as we shall see in the next chapter of this book, broadcast journalism may again undergo profound changes.

QUESTIONS FOR DISCUSSION

1. Some people believe that the broadcast spectrum should be privatized; that is, the government should sell portions of the spectrum to broadcasters and get out of the business of licensing stations. One of the arguments is that broadcasters have to make such heavy investments in land and equipment that they should have the security of owning the channel over which they broadcast. What do you think?
2. With the advent of cable and now the Internet, what do you think is the future of over-the-air broadcasting?
3. What kind of radio stations do you listen to? When are you most likely to listen? What would you like to hear on radio that you are not hearing now—music, talk shows, information, others?

RELATED WEB SITES

Broadcasters: WWW Virtual Library, http://archive.museophile.sbu.ac.uk/broadcast

FCC: Federal Communications Commission, www.fcc.gov

Library of American Broadcasting, www.lib.umd.edu/UMCP/LAB

MIBTB—Broadcasting Training Program, www.webcom.com/mibtp

Museum of Broadcast Communications, www.museum.tv/index.shtml

Museum of Television and Radio, www.mtr.org

NAB: National Association of Broadcasters, www.nab.org

RTNDA: Radio and Television News Directors Association, www.rtnda.org

Shoptalk, www.tvspy.com/shoptalk.cfm

TV Rundown, www.tvrundown.com

READINGS AND REFERENCES

Albarran, A. B., & Pitts, G. G. (2001). *The radio broadcasting industry.* Boston: Allyn and Bacon.

Allen, C. M. (2001). *News is people: The rise of local TV news and the fall of news from New York.* Ames, IA: Iowa State University Press.

Brinkley, J. (1997). *Defining vision: The battle for the future of television.* New York: Harcourt Brace and Company.

Brown, J., & Ward, Q. (1998). *Radio-television-cable management.* New York: McGraw Hill.

Butler, J. G. (2002). *Television: Critical methods and applications.* Mahwah, NJ: Lawrence Erlbaum Associates.

Carr, F., Huffman, S., & Tuggle, C. A. (2001). *Broadcast news handbook*. Boston: McGraw Hill.

Carroll, V. (1997). *Writing news for television*. Ames, IA: Iowa State University Press.

Chantler, P., & Harris, S. (1997). *Local radio journalism*. Boston: Focal Press.

Covington, W. G. (1999). *Creativity in TV & cable managing & producing*. Lanham, MD: University Press of America.

Cremer, C., et al. (1995). *ENG: Television news*. New York: McGraw-Hill.

Day, J. (1995). *The vanishing vision: The inside story of public television*. Berkeley, CA: University of California Press.

Donald, R., & Spann, T. (2000). *Fundamentals of television production*. Ames, IA: Iowa State University Press.

Fleming, C. (2002). *The radio handbook*. New York: Routledge.

Foote, J. S. (Ed.). (1998). *Live from the trenches: The changing role of the television news correspondent*. Carbondale, IL: Southern Illinois University Press.

Frank, R. (1991). *Out of thin air: The brief wonderful life of network news*. New York: Simon & Schuster.

Freedman, W. (2002). *It takes more than good looks to succeed at TV news reporting*. Chicago: Bonus Books.

Goldenson, L. H. (1991). *Beating the odds: The untold story behind the rise of ABC*. New York: Scribners, Maxwell Macmillan.

Head, S. W., & Sterling, C. H. (1996). *Broadcasting in America*. Boston: Houghton Mifflin.

Howard, H. H., Kievman, M. S., & Moore, B. A. (1994). *Radio, TV, and cable programming* (2nd ed.). Ames, IA: Iowa State University Press.

Jankowski, G. F. (1995). *Television today and tomorrow: It won't be what you think*. New York: Oxford University Press.

Lindner, K. (1999). *Broadcasting realities*. Chicago: Bonus Books.

Looker, T. (1995). *The sound and the story: NPR and the art of radio*. Boston: Houghton Mifflin.

Murray, M. D. (1999). *Encyclopedia of television news*. Phoenix, AZ: Oryx Press.

Pease, E. C., & Dennis, E. E. (Eds.). (1995). *Radio: The forgotten medium*. New Brunswick, NJ: Transaction Publishers.

Postman, N., & Powers, S. (1992). *How to watch TV news*. New York: Penguin Books.

Pringle, P., et al. (1999). *Electronic media management* (4th ed.). Boston: Focal Press.

Sherman, B. (1995). *Telecommunications management*. New York: McGraw Hill.

Smith, D. (2002). *Power producer* (3rd ed.). Washington, DC: RTNDA.

Tompkins, A. (2002). *Write for the ear . . . shoot for the eye . . . aim for the heart*. Chicago: Bonus Books.

Utterback, A. S. (1997). *Broadcaster's survival guide*. Chicago: Bonus Books.

Wertheimer, L. (1995). *Listening to America*. Boston: Houghton Mifflin Company.

Chapter Seven

News Web Sites

1. The Web is an ideal news medium because it can handle information in most of the formats of the traditional media, such as text, pictures, graphs, audio, and video.

2. The Web has characteristics that allow it to go beyond traditional media in presenting information—capacity, flexibility, immediacy, permanence, and interactivity.

3. Of those characteristics listed previously, interactivity is most likely to have the greatest long-term effect on journalism; interactivity refers to the ways in which journalists and the medium connect with the audience.

4. Most news web sites today are operated as an arm of the traditional news organizations—newspapers, magazines, and broadcast stations.

5. Shovelware: content that was created for another medium and is placed on a web site with minimal or no changes.

6. Web log: a periodically (often continuously) updated web site that posts the thoughts and observations of a single writer and often the responses to those observations.

Vignette

The news of the capture of Saddam Hussein could not have come at a worse time for the nation's newspapers. The deposed Iraqi strongman, the subject of an intense manhunt for months, had been pulled out of a "spider hole" by American troops near his home town of Tikrit on Saturday evening, December 13, 2003.

FIGURE 7.1   "We Got Him!" This photo of a grungy Saddam Hussein appeared on news web sites shortly after the announcement of his capture on December 14, 2003. The story of the capture came too late for the Sunday print edition of newspapers, but the Web has allowed them to compete for the immediacy of news. (Photo credit: Department of Defense)

Word of his capture had remained a secret for about twelve hours while his identity had been confirmed. But by 5 A.M. (Eastern time) Sunday, the news had begun to spread. Television and the Web were delivering to their audiences what information they had.

At the same time newspapers were landing on doorsteps and on sale in newsracks across the country. Sunday is the biggest day of the week for newspapers. It is their largest circulation day. It is the day they showcase their best reporting, design, and photography.

Yet, no newspaper carried a word about the capture of Saddam Hussein that morning. It was too late. For most, it would be twenty-four hours before the newspapers had a shot at telling their audiences about the weekend's big news. By that time, however, the story could take on a new light.

A few newspapers brought in staffs that morning and produced special editions. The Clarksville Leaf-Chronicle, which served the Ft. Campbell, Kentucky, area, had an edition on the street by early that afternoon; so did the Tampa Tribune.

But most newspapers that felt the need to respond to the story turned away from their print products and instead concentrated on their electronic product—their web sites. Saddam's capture represents just another instance in which newspapers have the chance to compete in the world of breaking news. That chance did not exist a decade earlier. In today's world, however, the Web threatens to change just about everything in journalism.

The Difference of the Web

The essence of the Web is news, but the Web is not a newspaper on a computer screen. Nor is it a broadcast station that you can pick up through a browser. It is different from traditional media in some significant and profound ways.

Capacity

A newspaper reporter might be confined to writing 500 or 600 words for a story. A photographer might spend all day covering an event and expect to have only one picture in print. A graphics journalist might get a one- or two-column space. At a broadcast station, a reporter would have only forty seconds to tell a story, and a five-minute statement from a news source would have to be reduced to a seven-second sound bite. All of these journalists experience the two great frustrations of professional journalism—the lack of time and space.

The Web greatly mitigates, if not entirely eliminates, these limitations. A reporter can take as many words or as much time as necessary to tell the story. A photographer can post ten pictures of an event, not just one. A graphics journalist might be limited by screen width (around 10 inches or so), but even this limitation represents a vast expansion of the space that is normally allotted.

With the Web news reporters can include with their reports the full text of speeches they cover, biographical information on their sources, and maps, charts, and pictures that help expand the reader's understanding of the subject. They can include audio of the sources and video of the scenes where the story took place.

To be sure, there are limitations. Servers, the computers that store information for web sites, do have a finite capacity for holding information, but generally it takes a long time before those limits are reached. More practically, the limitations of the Web have to do with the size of the screen that visitors are using, the time it takes to load the information onto the visitor's screen, and the time and effort the reporter wants to spend (and the news organization is willing to support) in gathering the information.

The Web offers more possibilities for presenting more information in more ways than either print or broadcasting.

Flexibility

The Web can handle a wide variety of forms for the information it presents—words, pictures, audio, video, and graphics. In this regard, it is far more flexible than print or broadcast.

The relative newness of the Web as a medium means that many of these forms have not been fully explored and there is a great deal of room for imagination and creativity on the part of people who enter this field. For instance, the *New York Times,* like many other news organizations with substantial web sites, regularly produces picture galleries of photos that the paper's far-flung set of photographers have taken. On many of these galleries, not only can visitors see the pictures and read the cutline text, but also they can hear an audio of the photographer talking about his or her work.

The audio picture gallery is a new form of presenting information that the Web has spawned. There are many other forms waiting to be created and developed by imaginative journalists.

Immediacy

The Web can deliver information immediately, often as events are unfolding. Broadcasting, particularly television, can do the same thing and with great impact, as many of us experienced on September 11, 2001. But the Web's qualities offer an immediacy that broadcasting cannot match in four important ways.

VARIETY.　Most major breaking news events are multifaceted. That is, they involve a variety of people, places, and activities. The terrorist attacks of September 11 are a dramatic case in point. At the same time the towers in New York were collapsing, a plane was crashing into the Pentagon, and the government was shutting down air traffic across the country. Locally, school systems and government offices were deciding whether or not to remain open. A mother wondering if she would have to pick up her child at school that day would probably not have found that information on television. But a good local news organization could put that information on its web site so that it could be accessed immediately. Many sites did just that.

In a less dramatic vein, let's say you want to know the score of a sporting event. How likely are you to find that out immediately when you turn on the television or radio? Even if you are looking at ESPN's scores rolling across the bottom of the screen, you are probably not going to see the score you are interested in immediately. You can find that information far more quickly on ESPN's web site and other sports-oriented sites.

EXPANSION.　As noted earlier, the Web has a huge capacity to hold and display information. For instance, in any major disaster story the names of victims are important and of interest to many people. Yet those names rarely make it onto a televised news broadcast. Limited by a finite amount of time, television could not be expected to fill the information needs of the viewers about a major breaking news story. Television generally only shows us and tells us one thing at a time. It may or may not be what we are interested in or what we want to know.

The Web can often satisfy our need for information more immediately. It can provide a variety of information that viewers can select. One may want the names of victims; another may want background about the disaster; another may want the latest developments; and so on. A good news web site can provide all of these things so that readers can choose.

DEPTH.　As the third part of the immediacy characteristic of the Web, depth is closely akin to capacity, but what we are really talking about here is quality. Information can be posted immediately on a web site, but to get it ready, it must undergo at least minimal editing. The broadcasts of a breaking news event, though often done by people who are thoroughly professional, have no buffer between their creation and their distribution. Because the Web is essentially a word medium, web journalists have some opportunity to edit their work or to let others look at it before it is disseminated.

CONTEXT.　Finally, the Web can offer immediacy with context, something broadcasters find difficult to provide with their breaking news stories. The limitations of television to provide context are evident in the live coverage of many events. Take golf matches, for instance. The camera and announcers may concentrate on a single player or a single shot while a graphic overlays part of the screen showing the leader board. Still, those two things may not tell the whole story of the match because other important actions may be occurring in different parts of the course. Watching a golf match on television is undoubtedly dramatic for those interested in the sport, but television has difficulty giving a complete picture until the match is finished. The Web has the power to summarize and update, while adding information in various parts of the coverage.

GETTING THE NEWS: SEPTEMBER 11, 2001

When a hijacked airliner loaded with passengers flew into the north tower of the World Trade Center, the world hardly had time to react before a second airliner coming from the opposite direction slammed into the south tower. In an hour and half, both buildings—two of the tallest in the world—had collapsed.

Meanwhile, another airliner was flown into the west side of the Pentagon, headquarters of the U.S. Department of Defense, in Washington, DC. A fourth airliner, which passengers had struggled to regain control of from its hijackers, crashed into a rural area of Pennsylvania.

The devastation caused by the September 11, 2001, attacks, both at the Pentagon in Washington, DC (above) and the World Trade Center in New York City (right) set off a hurricane of activity on the World Wide Web.

Permanence

Although the Web can seem almost as ethereal as broadcasting, actually it is the most permanent medium because it does not deteriorate. Nothing *need* be lost. Properly archived and maintained, data on the web in its electronic form can exist far beyond any tangible medium we now have. This permanence is an often overlooked quality of the Web, but it is one that gives the medium great power. It has taken us some time to recognize the permanence of the Web and to put that permanence to good use.

The world turned to their television sets to find out what had happened and what it meant. Desperate for more news than what television could offer, they turned to the Web.

- From the time the second tower was hit (9:05 A.M.), the CNN web site got 9 million hits an hour; that number increased to 19 million an hour by the next day. At that time, CNN had been getting about 14 million hits a day.
- MSNBC reported that in the first twenty-four hours of the disaster, 12.5 million people logged onto its site; the previous record had been 6.5 million on November 8, 2000, the day after the disputed presidential election.
- Some 64 percent of those who used the Internet said they got some of their information about the events from the Web and that they got details that were not available from other sources.
- The web portal Yahoo! had forty times its usual amount of traffic during the first hour after the attack on the World Trade Center.
- To handle the increase in traffic many web sites, including the *New York Times* and CNN, stripped off advertising and graphics in order to increase the loading speed for visitors.
- People trying to check on friends in New York City and Washington, DC, found phone lines clogged and resorted to email and instant messaging.
- Yahoo! and other sites posted lists of victims and missing persons.

Web sites have been abandoned, addresses have changed, and data have been over-written without being properly saved. Much that has been created during the first decade of the Web has been lost, but those losses are not due to a failure of the medium. Rather, they are failures of the operators.

This permanence leads to two other qualities about the Web that render it so pow-erful: duplication and retrievability. Because the Web is such an open medium and because the technology that creates a web site is shared, any part of a web site can be duplicated and stored in a different location from where it originated.

Duplication renders information on the Web safe because it can be stored in var-ious places; retrievability renders it powerful, particularly in the area of web jour-nalism. A simple example of this characteristic is the murder that is thoroughly covered by the local press. Six months later, someone is arrested and accused. Six months after that the trial begins. A reporter covering the trial may be new to the news organiza-tion, but he or she can easily retrieve what has been written before to become informed about the background of the story. Stories about the trial will probably have at least a paragraph or two of background material, but they can also contain links to ear-lier stories that will allow readers to gain insight into the case. Journalism is some-times criticized because of its episodic coverage and lack of context. Retrieving previous stories for the reader is just one way that a single article can be shown to be part of a continuing story over days, months, and years.

Interactivity

Although all of the qualities of the Web listed previously (capacity, flexibility, imme-diacy, and permanence) have the potential of changing journalism as it is practiced on the Web, those qualities pale against the potential the Web has for interactivity. This quality portends a new relationship between journalist and reader/viewer/con-sumer, and that new relationship could mean a new form of journalism.

All news media are interactive to some extent, of course. Television viewers and radio listeners must turn their sets on and select channels. Remote controls allow users to switch channels at will. Beyond that, however, these media offer no opportunities to interact. They provide no choices and no feedback loops while programs are being broadcast.

Newspapers and magazines are more interactive in the sense that readers can choose what parts to read and what to ignore. Headlines, refers (text that directs read-ers to another part of the paper), layouts, and sectioning help readers make these choices. But print media offer no channel through which readers can immediately re-spond or interact with the journalists who have produced the publication.

Web journalism offers the same choices that print media offer, only more of them. Whereas the choices in newspapers are pages and headlines, the choices on the Web can be built into the articles and web pages with hyperlinks. These allow readers to veer off within a story to information that is most interesting or relevant to them. An array of choices gives readers more control over what they see and read, and it height-ens the nonlinearity of the Web itself.

Where the Web is really different, however, is with the immediate feedback channel that it offers to users and journalists alike. News web sites have only begun to explore the techniques for channeling this feedback, using techniques such as instant polls, email, forums, bulletin boards, discussion groups, and online chats with reporters, editors, and sources themselves. These channels can be immediate and active, and as web journalism develops, they will become an increasingly important part of the journalist's milieu.

This new relationship will have profound effects on the way journalists gather information and make decisions. Readers are likely to become sources of information and lead journalists to new inquiries and stories. They could provide valuable perspective to journalists who are new to a story or not part of the community they cover (two of the major criticisms of journalists today), offering points of view that journalists would not normally hear in talking with "official" sources about their stories (see Chapter 9). The public journalism movement (often called civic journalism), which seeks to involve the community in journalistic decision making, could be taken to a new level with the Web.

The other side of interactivity is that while the audience can reach toward the news organization, the news organization can find out more about the audience. An organization may ask or require that users register to see its site. (The *New York Times* does this and gains valuable data on who is looking at its site.) But the technology of the Web allows those who run web sites to be less intrusive in finding out information about their visitors. Data can be gathered on where hits are coming from—both from individual computers and the URLs immediately before the hit. The web site can also track a user's progress through the site even to the point of seeing how long the user spends looking at a particular page. Developing email lists, bulletin boards, and forums is yet another way of gathering information about users.

With these and other methods, it is very easy for an organization to see what the most popular parts (and least popular parts) of a web site are and to make editorial and advertising rate decisions accordingly. Few news organizations have gone that far yet, but they inevitably will do so. Such data will allow news organizations to develop content to better serve general and specialized audiences.

These characteristics—capacity, flexibility, immediacy, permanence, and interactivity—set the Web apart from traditional media. They will be the continuing themes that will be developed in the subsequent chapters of this book.

The News Web Site

News web sites of the early twenty-first century represent a curious hybrid. They contain the content of media that are from seventy-five (television and radio) to four hundred (newspapers) years old, presented with a technology that is still in its first generation. Where did news web sites come from? What are they now? What are they likely to be in both the near and distant future? None of these questions is easily answered, and maybe none is ultimately that important as the Web develops and changes. But the news web site—whatever it was and is and will be—is the major form of the practice of web journalism and will be for the foreseeable future.

News web sites will change substantially, if not radically, during the first decade of this century. No news web site is coming close to using the Web to its full potential yet. The Web's capacity, flexibility, immediacy, permanence, and interactivity have not been fully explored or exploited by any news organization. Newspapers, news-magazines, radio stations, and television stations, whose history and investments have been in other products, have been timid in approaching the Web. Yet, the strength of their acceptance by the public as credible sources of news and their financial commitment to the production of news make them the first and foremost players in this new field of web journalism.

A news web site is a site that is devoted to delivering timely news and information to its audience. Those producing the site observe the traditional customs and practices of journalism in gathering, writing, and presenting the news. A news web site is a means for a news organization to display and distribute its content. That content is directed at an audience that is defined either by interest or geography.

A news organization's web site can use one of the following four methods of populating the site with content.

Shovelware

This term, often used in a denigrating way by people interested in web development, refers to the practice of simply shifting the content produced by the organization for another medium (newspaper, radio, or television) to the web site with little or no change. What you see in the newspaper or hear on the television is what goes on the web site.

Most news organizations use shovelware for a variety of reasons. First and foremost, it's cheap and easy. The news stories and pictures are already there, having been produced for the traditional medium, and they can be easily transferred to the web site. Many newspapers have found software that will allow them to do this almost seamlessly from their editing systems. Consequently, it takes little time and effort (and little extra money) to get content onto the Web.

Another reason for shovelware is that it works. News stories written in an inverted pyramid form (see Chapter 10) are appropriate for the Web. They give the most important or interesting information first and then present information in descending order of importance. Ideally, they are written concisely and precisely, all qualities that good writing for the Web demands. News organizations that shovel their print content onto their web site come away with a well-populated site at little or no extra cost. They have extended their brand to the Web, they have reached people who might not be subscribers, and they have created new advertising opportunities. The information comes in a form readers are used to seeing—the news story.

Moderate Updating

Some news organizations have discovered the immediacy function of the Web. They have also discovered that a growing number of their audience turn to the Web when breaking news occurs or when that kind of information is anticipated.

For instance, a local college basketball hero is eligible to enter the National Basketball Association draft at the end of the season even though he had another year of eligibility left in his college career. Once the last game has been played, he calls a press conference for 1 P.M. the next day to announce his decision. The next newscast from the local television station is at 5 P.M., and the local newspaper will not be out until the next morning. The local television station has decided not to cover the press conference live (too expensive) and not to break into programming to announce the decision (too costly in other ways).

But thousands of people who are interested want to know the decision as soon as it is announced. The logical alternative is the news web site, which can be updated as soon as the information is known.

This process is not as easy as it sounds for some news organizations, however. Those that are using rigid content management system software may not have the ability or the technical expertise to move stories quickly onto a web site. Some news organizations have web sites managed by outside companies, and it may take some special arrangement with that company to break the normal cycles of when stories and pictures are posted.

Aggressive Updating

The owners of a news organization at some point may catch a vision of the possibilities of the Web—especially its quality of immediacy—and move toward an aggressively updated site. This type of site employs staff members who post new items on a site throughout the day, and the software the organization uses allows for this to happen easily and quickly.

This kind of updating begins with the shovelware that the organization has produced for its other product (print or broadcast). The web site staff will look at these stories and see which ones might involve breaking news. For instance, a newspaper might run a preview story in the morning edition about a meeting of the city council scheduled for that day. The council, the story says, is set to vote on a proposed increase in property taxes. The web site staff will make arrangements with the reporter who is covering the council meeting to find out how the council voted soon after it happens and will update the story accordingly. (This process of rewriting an existing story, or rewriting the top paragraphs of a story with new information, sometimes take on the old wire service term of a *writethru.*)

The web site staff may also look for ways to enhance content that does not need to be updated. For instance, a newspaper may have room to run just one picture along with a story. The capacity of the web site can accommodate many more than that, and the staff may want to set up a photo gallery if the photographer has other good

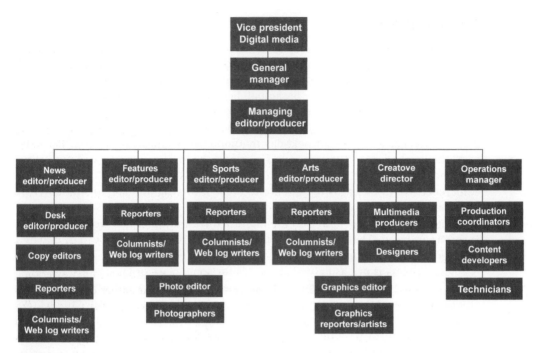

FIGURE 7.2   **News Web Site Organizational Chart**   Few news web sites are as fully developed as this chart indicates. As sites grow and as their value is recognized within the larger news organization, however, they will undoubtedly add more people and positions. In this organizational scheme, a key position is the desk editor/producer (far left column). This is the person who posts content to the site and makes decisions about how often the site should be updated.

shots that were not used. Likewise, a television reporter may have audio or video related to a story that could not be included in the regular newscast but may be suitable for the web site.

News organizations that subscribe to the Associated Press or some other news service may build in a feed for those services to the site. As stories are produced and sent by the wire service, they automatically appear on the site. A new story can show up every few minutes, and on the splash page of the site, headline links to these stories will be constantly changed.

Having the site change every few minutes or even every few hours is one of the hallmarks of aggressive updating. Those who work with the Web believe that a site should continually change and present new information. Some content management systems allow editors to mark more than one story or picture that should be placed at the top of the opening page or section page. These items will then "rotate"; that is, they change positions on the page as the page is refreshed. This rotation gives the site the appearance of having new information all the time.

Original Content

A few news organizations have gone a step beyond aggressive updating to more extensively developing original content for their sites. These organizations have developed staffs who are devoted to using the web site for original reporting. They work with software packages, often involving a variety of software programs that allow maximum flexibility in developing pages and forms of presentation.

Web sites with the original content philosophy use stories, pictures, graphics, and other information that have been put together for the traditional medium. They also work with the news staffs on important stories, so that the web presentation of those stories can use the advantages of the Web as a medium.

Because they are produced by news organizations, these original content web sites also incorporate the aggressive updating philosophy. Their first job is to try to stay on top of events, and the staffs feel like they can prove their worth most readily when breaking news occurs—particularly in their local areas—and they can provide information that no other organization is providing.

But much of the normal day-to-day activity of the staff is devoted to developing and managing content for the site. A big city web site might gather crime statistics for neighborhoods around the city to form an interactive map (as the *Chicago Tribune* web site did in the early days of news web sites) that readers could click on and find crime information for a single neighborhood. The web site staff might set up an interactive chat session with a reporter who had covered a big story, a columnist, or a local celebrity. The staff could help a photojournalist produce an audio photo gallery for a story the photographer has been shooting.

Original content sites are likely to have their own advertising staffs in addition to their editorial staffs. Advertising managers and salespersons are not only involved in selling ads for the site, but they also track site hits and try to keep up with the demographics of site users. To the extent that the leadership of the news organization demands it, these web ad staffs work with the advertising staffs for the traditional media to enhance the sales for both.

Owned and Operated

Who owns a news web site? As we alluded to in the previous section, most news web sites are owned by traditional news media companies, such as newspapers, television stations, radio stations, and newsmagazines. Most news organizations have web sites that are actively maintained and updated periodically.

The major news web sites that draw the largest audiences are the *New York Times* (www.nytimes.com), MSNBC (www.msnbc.com), CNN (www.cnn.com), the *Washington Post* (www.washingtonpost.com), the *Chicago Tribune* (www.chicagotribune.com), the *Los Angeles Times* (www.latimes.com), ABC News (www.abcnews.com), CBS News (www.cbsnews.com), and Fox News (www.foxnews.com). The *Wall Street Journal* (www.online.wsj.com/public/us) has a large web site that was an early leader in gaining paid subscriptions to most of its content.

FIGURE 7.3   Photo Galleries The capacity of the Web allows photojournalists or photo editors to show as many pictures as they would like. They are not confined by the space of print or the time of broadcasting. Some news organizations have even combined audio commentary with the photos they show on their galleries.

A somewhat different approach can be found with NBC News. That organization has joined with the computer giant Microsoft to produce an excellent and extensive news site, MSNBC (www.msnbc.com); this site also includes items from the *Washington Post* and *Newsweek*. CNN (www.cnn.com), one of the leading sites in drawing visitors, has done something similar by pairing with *Time* and *Sports Illustrated* magazines for some of its content.

All of these web sites use the name of the news organization and are active in extending the brand of the company. Each has enjoyed a measure of success in being innovative and in developing repeat visitors.

During the first decade of the World Wide Web, no one knew exactly what the Web would become or how people would view it. Inside the news organization, the Web was limited to those who had computers with connections to it, and the connections themselves were often slow or even inoperable.

The *News York Times* committed itself to a web site in the mid-1990s. From the time the site was launched in January 1996, it has been considered a leader in web site development. The *Times* (like the *Chicago Tribune* that developed a separate web staff in the mid-1990s) had a staff that could produce original content, but the newspaper itself was foremost in the thinking of the company. The *Times* sought to extend its brand to the web audience, so the web site at first looked very much like the distinctive appearance of the newspaper itself. It even carried headlines in a font that emulated the type font of the paper's headlines. The web site was rarely allowed to get ahead of the paper in covering the news, even though the Web was more immediate than the printing press. Fierce battles within the organization about the purpose and role of the site occurred, and stories are told that at one point information could not be posted on the web site until it had appeared in the newspaper. Still the site has developed steadily, adding features and building audiences, so that in mid-2004 it was attracting about 10 million viewers a month and is looked to as the top newspaper web site in the country.

Independently Owned

Some news web sites do not come from established news organizations but spring from the minds and efforts of individuals or small groups. They are produced for various reasons and with a variety of approaches but all with the assumption that on the Web, initially, a Matt Drudge can look as big as the *New York Times*.

Drudge publishes a one-man site and gained fame for first posting rumors of President Bill Clinton's affair with Monica Lewinsky. Independently owned and operated sites are hailed by those who see the Web as giving a forum to people who would otherwise not have a voice. In this way, the Web harkens back to the early days of the republic when a single printer could start a newspaper and espouse his or her faction's point of view. Indeed, producing and posting such a site are vastly less expensive and far easier than printing and distributing any sort of publication. A web site can be produced in less than half a day and can cost less than $100 in out-of-pocket expenses.

Quote 7.1

ARTHUR SULZBERGER

On the Web as a news medium

Newspapers cannot be defined by the second word—*paper*. They've got to be defined by the first—*news*. If we're going to define ourselves by our history, then we deserve to go out of business.

Arthur Sulzberger is the publisher of the New York Times.

Individual sites rarely generate enough income to sustain the producer on a full-time basis. In fact, they rarely produce income at all. But they do offer an opportunity for individuals to break the hold that traditional media organizations have had on communicating with wide audiences and on the definition of journalism itself. These sites can build small but significant followings, can engender lively discussions, and can give voice to points of view that would not normally appear in traditional media.

Swimming in more traditional channels, a few news-oriented, web-only publications are beginning to appear. These sites emulate the sites of local newspapers or broadcast entities with news and advertising staffs that post new information on a daily basis and are directed at serving a geographic region, such as a city or county. Examples of such sites are the *Oswego Daily News* (www.oswegodailynews.com) and the *Fulton Daily News* (www.fultondailynews.com). Sites such as these emphasize local news, or hyperlocal news, as web sites sometimes refer to it. They are born of a dissatisfaction with the local metropolitan daily newspaper that does not—and cannot—cover the news of local communities in any depth. They are sustained initially by local businesses who find advertising in larger newspapers too expensive and too inefficient in that the ads reach an audience that the advertiser finds unnecessary. These sites build a local audience by writing unpaid obituaries, covering the activities of local civic clubs and kids' soccer leagues, and posting pictures of newborn babies. These are items that larger newspapers and broadcast stations would ignore, but they are important to the lives of individuals.

Web-only publications are more likely to resemble traditional magazines than newspapers, however. Part of the reason for this is that news—information on breaking stories—is difficult and expensive to gather, and meeting daily deadlines can be a wearing process. A magazine is produced with longer deadlines, and the readership does not expect it to keep up with breaking news stories. One of the most successful of the early webzines was *Salon* (www.salon.com), which was begun in 1995 as an intelligent but middle-brow publication that commented on politics, news, people, and life in general. *Salon* was part of a series of original content publication sites and online communities. David Talbot, the founder, and his staff sought to explore how the Web could be used to deliver information and comment that people would want. They also attracted advertisers and eventually sectioned off part of the site as "premium" for which subscribers are charged a fee.

Salon was followed in 1996 by *Slate* (www.slate.com), a publication chiefly sponsored by Microsoft. The company managed to attract the high-profile Michael Kinsley, then a host of CNN's *Crossfire*, to move from Washington, DC, to Seattle to become its editor, and the site quickly won praise for its provocative commentary. *Slate* drew a large audience, but that audience dried up when *Slate* began charging a subscription price for most of its content. That plan was soon dropped, and the site has since tried to create revenue through advertising and sponsorships.

Some news web sites are devoted to a subject rather than a group of people. WebMD (www.webmd.com) tries to satisfy the needs of consumers for medical and health-related news. By concentrating all of its efforts and expertise in this one area, the site can produce news that, according to its own site description, is "more reliable. In a medium often accused of providing outdated and inaccurate information, WebMD stands out as a credible, authoritative source of health news." The site goes far beyond just providing massive amounts of news and information that include sections on hundreds of diseases and conditions. The site also attempts to build communities of people interested in a particular health-related topic. It sponsors live chats with experts and celebrities and sends out dozens of topic-specific newsletters. It allows a user to build a medical profile and to edit that profile as conditions change. The profile is used to provide the user with specific information about topics of interest. The site also helps consumers find doctors, treatments, and eligibility for programs and support. A part of the site even offers a management program to help physicians operate more efficiently. The site attracts more than 15 million visitors a

QUESTIONS OF CREDIBILITY PLAGUE THE WEB

"You can't believe anything you read on the Web."

You've heard it before, and it's true. Sometimes. But the *New York Times* is on the Web and so is Foxnews.com. And so is the Bible and the Koran. And Shakespeare and Milton and some of the most perceptive, knowledgeable, and thoughtful writers of our time. To dismiss the Web as completely lacking in credibility is ignorant and silly.

The Web—like print and broadcasting—contains a wide variety of content, some of which can be dismissed without a thought but some of which is profound. It's not the medium that should be in question. It's the messenger and the messages.

Yet questions of credibility continue to plague the Web and those who work in it, particularly in journalism. Those legitimate questions of credibility often revolve around one of the most important characteristics of the Web: speed.

Speed is one of the most dangerous tendencies of journalism, although it can also be a great strength. Journalists like to work fast and tell their stories quickly, especially when competing journalists are involved. Just about any journalist will tell you that getting an exclusive story—a "scoop"—is the best feeling in the world.

The Web allows for instant dissemination. No waiting for presses to run or hourly newscasts to roll around. But that can be a problem. During January 1998 when the press was swirling around the Bill Clinton–Monica Lewinsky story (and Clin-

ton was still denying the affair), the *Dallas Morning News* thought it had a story nailed down that said a Secret Service agent was going to testify that he had seen Clinton and Lewinsky in a compromising position.

Pressured by the thought that another news organization might break the story, editors of the newspaper put the story on their web site several hours before the newspaper went to press. The story was picked up by the Associated Press and quickly became the lead around the nation that evening.

Four hours later, however, the source the newspaper was using told them it was inaccurate. The *Dallas Morning News* withdrew the story, and that withdrawal became another major story. Had the newspaper's editors simply waited with the story until their normal press time, they probably would have saved themselves a great deal of embarrassment.

Traditional journalists cite this and similar incidents as evidence of the Web's credibility problem. Despite the dangers, however, journalists are unlikely to sacrifice the Web's warp speed for a slower, more deliberate editorial process. Good journalists, whatever medium they work for, will make sure they have verified, legitimate information before they publish it. And when they do, they will use the fastest means possible.

month, and its Medscape information portal, which is aimed at physicians and health care professionals, has more than a half million doctors registered.

Web Logs: A New Form of Journalism?

What if there was a newspaper in which readers contributed news items and essentially decided what was in the newspaper by their contributions, or a broadcast station in which viewers produced the stories that were seen by the rest of the audience? And the reporters could—in fact, were expected—to sprinkle their reports with a bit of attitude, at least to let their point of view show?

And no item could be longer than three paragraphs (in the newspaper) or one minute (broadcast)?

And everybody who read or watched was interested in the topic that was being reported?

FIGURE 7.4   Weblogs, a Form of Personal Journalism

Thousands of people, including some journalists, maintain active weblogs that allow them to present information and commentary on that information in ways that traditional journalistic practice would not readily accept. Here the writer (called a "blogger") uses an aspect of the Web—links—to enhance what he is saying to the reader. (The links are the bold type inside his paragraphs.)

And anyone listening or watching could respond by disagreeing with the reporter, correcting information, or just offering another point of view, either directly to the reporter or to the group as a whole?

And while some topics would die for lack of new information, interest, or responses, other topics might stay alive for days, weeks, or months?

To some this would not be much of a newspaper or news broadcast, and it certainly would not be journalism. After all, journalism should be practiced by trained journalists. Their work should go through the standard editing process, and it should be presented to the audience with little indication as to how the reporter feels about the information. And while members of the audience might want to respond, their responses would be confined to phone calls to reporters and letters to the editor, usually published several days after the original item appeared. Corrections, when absolutely necessary, would be placed obscurely on an inside page if it's a newspaper and broadcast rarely if it's a television station. Now, that's journalism.

Or is it?

What is described at the beginning of this section is neither a newspaper nor a news broadcast and would probably be completely unmanageable in either of those media. But on the Web, such "publications" are called weblogs, and they are growing in number and audience. The weblog is a powerful manifestation of the interactive qualities of the Web, and many people believe that this interactivity will spark a dramatic change in journalism itself. J. D. Lasica, senior editor of *Online Journalism Review,* says that the weblog is a grassroots phenomenon "that may sow the seeds for new forms of journalism, public discourse, interactivity and online community."

Weblogs have proliferated since 1997 and 1998, due in part to several sources of free software available to those who want to begin a weblog. There are literally thousands of weblogs, ranging from free-form journals in which comments about any topic are welcomed to tightly controlled discussions with a limited list of contributors. In this latter type of weblog, noncontributors can watch the discussion and can post comments on items in the log, but they cannot initiate their own items.

So, is this journalism?

Weblogs have some of the elements of traditional journalism in that they dispense information to an audience, but they lack the traditional editing process that should include some independent assessment of the accuracy of the information being presented. Some bloggers would disagree. *Blogger* is the term used for people who run weblogs. It comes from combining the final "b" in web with "log;" thus "blog" and "blogger." Bloggers argue that contributors to weblogs feel an obligation to their potential audience to present information that they think is correct. Furthermore, they say, a weblog is a self-correcting entity; inaccurate information can be corrected, or at least challenged, as discussion of a topic continues. In this sense, weblogs may be compared to talk radio—a comparison that many bloggers do not appreciate.

To be fair, contributors to weblogs are usually identified (unlike people who call in to talk radio shows), and many seem to take seriously their responsibility of contributing substantial information to the discussion. And, on some topics, weblogs are a source of up-to-date information that no media organization attempts to match. In addition, weblogs have an inherent respect for their audiences and take advantage of their wide-ranging knowledge and expertise. Although contributions may not come from trained journalists and may not be vetted through a traditional editing process, weblogs offer the possibility of presenting a much wider range of viewpoints about information than would be possible in the traditional media.

Consequently, those who are committed to weblogs believe they have seen the future, and they expound this belief with almost religious fervor. Rebecca Blood, who has operated a personal journal weblog called Rebecca's Pocket (www.rebecca-blood.net) has articulated those feelings eloquently in an essay about weblogs:

> Traditional weblogs perform a valuable filtering service and provide tools for more critical evaluation of the information available on the web. Free-style blogs are nothing less than an outbreak of self-expression. Each is evidence of a staggering shift from an age of carefully controlled information provided by sanctioned authorities (and artists), to an unprecedented opportunity for individual expression on a worldwide scale. Each kind of weblog empowers individuals on many levels.

Weblogs are a powerful demonstration of the interactive and personal qualities of the Web. They are likely to change journalism, but how profound that change will be depends neither on journalists nor on bloggers. It will depend on the readers themselves. Will news consumers continue to want their information filtered through the standard journalistic processes? Will they prefer it varnished with the overt point of view of the writer? Or will they find the information and presentation of a weblog more informative, more provocative, and ultimately more useful? If the answer to the last question is "yes"—and many bloggers believe that it will be—then journalism is in for a radical change. Certainly, journalists need to take note of weblogs now for their information value and for ideas about the ways in which they may use the Web to help readers become more fully informed.

Whither Web Sites?

A news web site presents news content—pictures, stories, graphics, video, and so on—to audiences over the Web. These sites not only show the content, but they also reflect the structure, appearance, and even values of the news organization itself. In short, they are an extension of the brand of the news organization.

As the Web travels through its second decade and develops in new and sometimes unexpected ways, news web sites are more difficult to define or even categorize. News web sites range from the "traditional," which uses the content, look, and feel of the news organization it represents, to the highly innovative that seeks to evolve the site into a different entity.

And, as we have seen, news web sites are not the exclusive purview of news organizations. Individuals, small groups of interested people, and corporations of every size have gotten into the news business by producing a web site. In fact, these non-news organizations have demonstrated the nature and power of the Web and the expectations that people have for finding new information. The Web has made them into news organizations, whether or not that was their original intention.

QUESTIONS FOR DISCUSSION

1. Are you persuaded by the chapter's assertion that the Web is the most permanent medium?

2. Most news web sites, particularly those run by newspapers, have taken on the same format used traditionally. How do you think they could change to take more advantage of the Web?

3. Just as radio had to change greatly with the advent of television (see Chapter 10), some people are predicting the same thing will happen to newspapers because of the Web. What do you think?

4. Most web sites are now free, but many would like to start charging a fee. What would you pay for on the Web? What are you paying for now?

RELATED WEB SITES

The Elements of Digital Storytelling, www.inms.umn.edu/Elements

ONA Digital Journalism Credibility Study, www.journalists.org/Programs/Research.htm

READINGS AND REFERENCES

Albarran, A. B., & Goff, D. H. (Eds.). (2000). *Understanding the Web.* Ames, IA: Iowa State University Press.

Alexander, J. E., & Tate, M. A. (1999). *Web wisdom: How to evaluate and create information quality on the Web.* Mahwah, NJ: Lawrence Erlbaum Associates.

Burke, C. B. (1994). *Information and secrecy: Vannevar Bush, Ultra, and the other Memex.* Metuchen, NJ: Scarecrow Press.

De Wolk, R. (2001). *Introduction to online journalism.* Boston: Allyn and Bacon.

Dizard, W. Jr. (1994). *Old media/new media: Mass communication in the information age.* New York: Longman Publishing.

Gilster, P. (1997). *Digital literacy.* New York: John Wiley & Sons.

Grossman, L. K. (1995). *The electronic republic: Reshaping democracy in the information age.* New York: Viking.

Hafner, K., & Lyon, M. (1996). *Where wizards stay up late: The origins of the Internet.* New York: Simon & Schuster.

Hall, J. (2001). *Online journalism: A critical primer.* Sterling, VA: Pluto Press.

Harper, C. (1997). *And that's the way it will be: News and information in a digital world.* New York: New York University Press.

Kaye, B. K., & Medoff, N. J. (1999). *The World Wide Web: A mass communication perspective.* Mountain View, CA: Mayfield Publishing Company.

Koch, T. (1996). *The message is the medium.* Westport, CT: Praeger.

Nielsen, J., & Tahir, M. (2001). *Jakob Nielsen's 50 web sites.* Indianapolis, IN: New Riders Publishing.

Reddick, R., & King, E. (1999). *The online journalist* (3rd ed.). Fort Worth, TX: Harcourt Brace.

Rich, C. (1998). *Creating online media: A guide to research, writing, and design on the Internet.* New York: McGraw-Hill.

Segaller, S. (1998). *Nerds 2.0.1: A brief history of the Internet.* New York: TV Books.

Stovall, J. G. (2004). *Web journalism: Practice and promise of a new medium.* Boston: Allyn and Bacon.

Ward, M. (2002). *Journalism online.* Woburn, MA: Focal Press.

Wendland, M. (1999). *Wired journalist: Newsroom guide to the Internet* (3rd ed.). Washington, DC: RTNDA.

Weinberger, D. (2002). *Small pieces loosely joined.* Cambridge, MA: Perseus Press.

Wickham, K. (Ed.). (1998). *Perspectives: Online journalism.* Boulder, CO: Coursewise Publishing.

Who and How

The people who make up the profession of journalism produce, process, and present the news every hour, every day, every week, every year. Their job never stops because the news never stops, and the audience that consumes the news never stops wanting it.

Journalism contains many different jobs, and many different kinds of people with a variety of skills work to fill those jobs. No one type of person or personality is a journalist. The field draws from all segments of society and requires many kinds of contributions. Their efforts make journalism, and that is where we will begin our study of the profession.

Learning to be a journalist is no easy or simple task. A number of skills must be mastered, particularly that of writing and using the language. But journalists must also understand the nature of the information they should gather and the appropriate methods of gathering that information.

In addition, they must process that information into a form that is appropriate to the medium for which they are working. They learn to do this quickly because news is a perishable product. News must be disseminated as quickly as the medium will allow and in a form that is palatable for the audience.

The skills required to do this take a great deal of effort to acquire. Chapters in this section outline those skills and give readers opportunities to begin acquiring them.

Chapter Eight

Reporters

Key Concepts and Terms

1. The essential act of journalism is gathering information. This is done by reporters.

2. Deadline: the time when a story is due.

3. Interview: the way in which much information for journalism is gathered; reporters talk with sources (people who have information) in person, by telephone, by email, or any number of other ways of communicating.

4. Beat: the area or subject that a reporter regularly covers and writes stories about, such as the police beat or education beat.

5. Editors oversee and direct the activities of reporters. Few people in journalism work alone. Many people are involved in the process of gathering and disseminating information.

6. Journalists must adhere to a personal standard of integrity; they must be able to deal honestly with their sources and they must be able to evaluate information honestly.

7. Journalists must pay attention to details—the exact spelling of someone's name, the exact time that something happened, and so on.

Vignette

James Fallows, in the epilogue of his book Breaking the News, *tells the story of James Wooten as a young reporter. Wooten had been a reporter for the* New York Times *with many front-page bylines. He had also been a writer for* Esquire *magazine and a correspondent for ABC News. In the last three decades of the twentieth century, he had covered many of the major news stories that had occurred around the world.*

But one of his most profound experiences had come in the 1960s when he was a young reporter for the Huntsville Times *in Huntsville, Alabama.*

Robert Kennedy, brother of the slain president and then a United States Senator from New York, had made a well-publicized tour of the South. He had been looking at the poverty-stricken conditions in which many people lived.

Wooten got the idea of looking at the same conditions in the Huntsville area and doing a series of stories about them. The five stories he produced all appeared on the front page, and the paper received many letters about them. One of those letters, Wooten told Fallows, he had been carrying in his wallet for thirty years. The letter commended the young reporter for "serving as the conscience for us all" and for his ability "to see and to hear and to feel for the rest of us and then . . . to tell us the reality that is beyond our reach. . . ."

Every news reporter wants to cover the big, breaking story. Every reporter wants to be on the scene first, wants the world to hear or read the information he or she has gathered. All reporters, just as David Mattingly of Cable News Network did on September 11 (see the beginning of Chapter 1), feel the call of news. When it happens they want to be at the center of the action and involved in the process of bringing information to the public.

But even when news, as in the Big Event, does not happen—even when everybody else is ignoring it, as in Wooten's case at the *Huntsville Times*—reporters still feel the need to tell the stories they believe their audiences need to hear. They want to, in the words of the letter writer, bring to the audience a reality that is beyond their reach.

It's what reporters do. They make journalism.

Reporters are the starting point of journalism. Without reporters, journalism could not be practiced. Although many other people, such as editors, photographers, videographers, graphics journalists, and designers, contribute to the news that we read and see every day, reporters are the ones who start the process.

Reporters gather the information that appears on news programs, newspapers, and web sites. They put that information into the form—the news story—that is acceptable for the medium for which they are reporting. They work with photographers, videographers, editors, and graphics journalists to make sure that the information is presented in a clear, complete, and—most importantly—accurate way.

Reporters are special people with special jobs. They must know how to get information and how to talk with people. They must recognize news and the value of the information they have. They must know how to use the language, both orally and in written form. They must be able to work and produce quickly. They must, above all, have a commitment to the practice of journalism that allows them to devote all of their energies to their task. They must have the drive that makes someone like David Mattingly abandon the peace of a fishing boat for the confusion and even danger of covering a big story.

FIGURE 8.1   A Change in the Action President Calvin Coolidge (top photo, center, standing) is photographed with the White House correspondents of his day in 1923. In the 1920s, Coolidge met regularly with reporters—on Tuesdays at 10 A.M. and Fridays at 4 P.M. The White House did not generate much news then, and covering the White House was a quiet beat. Fifty years later, the scene had changed drastically, as shown in this 1970 photo of President Richard Nixon meeting with reporters in the White House pressroom. The White House had become one of the world's chief news centers and a beat that many reporters aspired to. (Photo credits: Library of Congress (Coolidge); National Archives (Nixon))

What Reporters Do

A typical reporter comes into her newspaper office anxious to see what the news of the day is. She begins calling some of the sources on the regular beat that she is working. She checks in with her editor to see what he knows and what he wants her to work on. She tells him what she has found out about what is happening on her beat. They talk about what she will be working on that day and possibly for the rest of the week. She will be able to get something in by the newspaper's deadline on that day. At some point during the day, she may leave the office to go to an event or to interview a news source.

So, what is she doing?

To talk about that, let's discuss some of the terms that we used in that first paragraph.

News is not just information; it is information with certain qualities that lift it into the realm of news. (Those qualities are explained more fully in Chapter 1.) In order to be considered news, the information must be recent or timely. If the information is about the number of murders that occurred in the city, it should include any murders that occurred on that day or the day before. Information about murders that occurred last week or last year is not likely to be news. The information should also be interesting or have some importance to the lives of the people who read the newspaper. Each of these qualities about the information may make it newsworthy.

Reporters learn to judge information on these and other criteria and decide if it is news. They know what their newspaper, television station, or web site is interested in and what kind of news they normally run. They have an idea of what their readers want and need to know to make judgments about their lives and their community.

Not only do reporters make this judgment, but also they learn to "conceptualize" the news. They can take information and decide how it should be presented to the public. Editors certainly help in this process, but the task of deciding how information should be presented as news first falls on the reporter. Sometimes this conceptualization is easy. For instance, if a reporter is covering a trial and the jury renders a verdict, that verdict will be the focus of the reporter's story. At other times, however, it is not so obvious. If the reporter is covering a trial and there are witnesses and arguments all day long, where does the reporter focus the story? The reporter has to decide what is the most important thing that happened at the trial and build a story based on that.

Some reporters are general assignment reporters; that is, they come to work most days not always knowing what stories they will cover. For many journalists, this is an exciting aspect to the job. They end up meeting many people and covering stories on many different subjects. Their challenge is finding information and persuading people to talk with them.

Other reporters on a news staff are assigned to a beat. A beat is an area that the reporter covers on a regular basis. Some of the standard beats are police, government, business, education, and the arts. A reporter who spends time working on a beat will become an in-house expert on that area, and he or she will be assigned stories that fall into that area. Beat reporters are knowledgeable about what has happened on their beats and can be good judges of information and events that come to light concerning their areas. They also develop sources of information that they trust and can call on regularly to help them put together their stories.

Quote 8.1

H. L. MENCKEN

On being a newspaper reporter in 1899

My adventures in that character (a newspaper reporter) . . .
had their moments—in fact, they were made up, subjectively, of
one continuous, unrelenting, almost delirious moment—and when I revive them now it is mainly to remind myself and inform historians that
a newspaper reporter, in those remote days, had a grand and gaudy
time of it, and no call to envy any man. . . . I believed then and believe today, that it was the maddest, gladdest, damndest existence
ever enjoyed by mortal youth.

H. L. Mencken was a newspaper and magazine editor, critic of American letters,
and chief curmudgeon of the first half of the twentieth century. His sharp wit was
always at war with pomposity and hypocrisy and earned him the title "Sage of
Baltimore." The passage quoted here is from his memoir Newspaper Days.

Sources are an important part of the journalistic process, and a reporter, if nothing else, is an expert in sources. Information comes from three types of sources: stored
(anything written down, in a book, report, library, or on a web page), observational
(things that the reporters see for themselves, such as sports events), and personal (discussions with people). Ideally, reporters would prefer to use observational sources because they like to be on the scene of events to see for themselves what is happening.
Being present is not always possible, however, because of the unpredictable nature of
news; no one knows when a fire is going to break out or a serious traffic accident
will occur.

Most information for news stories comes from personal sources—reporters talking with people who have information. Much of the information that reporters seek
has not been recorded (thus precluding the use of stored sources) because it is so new,
such as the appointment of a new city revenue commissioner or the flooding of neighborhoods because of a heavy rainstorm. Reporters must know the people who have
new information and must know how to obtain it from them.

Getting information from people is no easy task. First, a reporter cannot compel
someone to talk. A reporter must persuade a source to spend the time and effort required to produce information. Although some people are quite happy to talk with
reporters, others are very reluctant for a variety of reasons. For example, people do
not trust reporters to tell the truth, they do not want the publicity, they do not like
the newspaper or television station the reporter represents, and so on. Another reason getting information is difficult is that sources may not know what reporters want,
or they simply may not have the information the reporter needs.

The act of a reporter talking with a source is called interviewing, and reporters
must be skilled in the art of efficient interviewing. Reporters can sometimes interview
their news sources in person, and a story may be a combination of observations and

interviews with people on the scene. Most often, however, interviews will be conducted by telephone, with reporters calling sources from the office of their news organization. (Television reporters must often include interviews in their video reports, and for those, of course, they must interview the source in person.) A print or web reporter is looking not just for information from the source but also for what the source says in the form of "direct quotations," which might be included in the story. (The art and techniques of interviewing are explained more fully in Chapter 9, and the use of direct quotations in writing is found in Chapter 10.)

A reporter's relationship with a source is one of the most important parts of a reporter's work. Usually, that relationship is straightforward: a source will give the reporter the information the reporter asks for. (No money will be exchanged for this information. A tenet of American journalism is that a journalist should not pay for information.) The source may cooperate with the reporter for a variety of reasons—simply because the reporter asks, because the source thinks the public should have the information, because the source will benefit if the information is made public, and so on. Implicitly, the reporter has agreed that he or she will try to present the information accurately and fairly. Sometimes, however, the relationship can become far more complicated and may even involve promises from the reporter that he or she will keep the name of the source confidential. (See Chapter 2.) A reporter has to understand how to handle sources and what the commonly accepted rules of journalistic procedure are to develop a professional relationship with a source.

Another relationship a reporter must develop is one with the editor (or news director in the case of television news). Editors control what goes on in the news organization. They make decisions about what reporters should cover and what is included in the newspaper, the web site, or the news show. In most news organizations, a reporter will work directly under the supervision of an editor. (See Chapters 4–7 for information about how different news media are organized.)

One of the jobs of an editor is to keep up with what reporters are doing and what stories they are working on. An editor can give advice to a reporter about how to cover a story, what kind of information to look for, where that information can be found, and what sources of information are most likely to be productive. Editors also advise reporters about how stories can be written. Reporters are responsible for following their editors' directions and for keeping the editors informed about what they are doing. Most reporters say that having a good editor working with them is their most valuable asset. A good editor can instill confidence in the reporter, can offer good ideas, and can be a soundingboard for complaints, problems, and ideas that a reporter has. A bad editor, on the other hand, can obstruct the reporter from doing the best job and can undercut the reporter's confidence. Editors and reporters need to trust each other and have confidence that each can do his or her job. If that does not happen, the news organization is likely to suffer.

Reporters and editors work together to meet the deadlines that the news organization has established. The deadline for a morning newspaper, such as the one our reporter, introduced at the beginning of this section, works for, is often early in the evening, possibly around 7 P.M. That means the reporter has to turn in a draft of the story by that time. Some stories can be turned in later but only if an editor approves

Quote 8.2

ANNA QUINDLEN

On the value of newspaper reporting

I learned in newspapers to make every word count. All those years of being given 1,200 words, of having the 1,200 pared to 900 at 3 o'clock, of having to take out another 100 to shoehorn it into the hole in the layout; it teaches you to make the distinction between what is necessary and what is simply you in love with the sound of your own voice.

Anna Quindlen is the author of several books and a columnist for Newsweek *magazine. She won a Pulitzer Prize in 1992 for her work as a columnist for the* New York Times.

it. Deadlines conform to the news organization's production schedule, so if a reporter misses a deadline, other people in the process will not be able to do their work. And whereas print deadlines are somewhat flexible (by a few minutes), broadcast deadlines are unyielding. A news broadcast airs at a certain time every day; stories must be turned in so that they can be edited and put on the air. Being late and missing a deadline means having no story at all.

Personal Characteristics

All types of people become reporters, so reporters are hard to characterize. Yet there are some personal traits that many reporters share and that seem necessary for success.

One is curiosity. Good reporters want to know things and want to find things out. The best reporters have what is called in the business a "nose for news." They can see or sense that something will make a good story. They recognize when something is a bit unusual or when things don't quite add up the way you might expect.

Another characteristic is at least a bit of boldness. Reporters must be somewhat assertive, even at the risk of making someone angry. Reporters occasionally have to ask the awkward, embarrassing, or even rude question and have to go where they may not be wanted. Reporters have to remember that they do not represent just themselves; they represent their news organizations and the people who watch or read what they produce.

Tenacity helps a person be a good reporter. Even if rebuffed, good reporters remain in pursuit of information that is necessary for a story. They may have to look for the same information in different places or may have to devise several means of getting that information. Reporters are always looking to expand their sources, so information can be complete and confirmed.

Reporters should have a retentive memory. They should remember where information is or from whom it can be obtained. Reporters should be able to connect disparate facts.

Reporters should develop the ability to listen. Much of a reporter's professional life is spent having to interview people. Reporters must be able to understand what a source is saying, even when the meaning is sometimes hidden rather than revealed by the words. They have to have the ability to connect personally with a source whenever possible.

Reporters must be persuasive. They have no subpeona power over their sources. People do not have to talk with them or give them information. Reporters sometimes have to convince their sources that it is worth their time and effort to help out.

Attentiveness to details is another part of the reporter psychic arsenal. Interviewing is not just another form of casual conversation. Reporters are after certain information, and they must be sure that information is obtained. It has to be right, and it has to be verified.

The willingness to work hard is undeniably a characteristic that every successful reporter must have. Reporting is difficult and sometimes frustrating. Reporters who get turned away from a story too easily don't become good reporters. The hours can be long and the work tiring and not immediately rewarding. Reporters develop the ability to sustain themselves through periods of difficult, tedious labor.

Reporters must also have an element of competitiveness to their character. Whatever the competition, whether it is another news organization or just within themselves, reporters need to display a drive to be the best. Their organizations usually have a competitive corporate spirit, and this spirit is expected on an individual basis.

Another important characteristic is integrity. Reporters have to study their own moral framework in terms of what they believe is acceptable and unacceptable behavior. If they do not have a high standard of personal honesty and devotion to the truth, they will find it hard to take on such professional standards. In practice reporters need to examine the assumptions or prejudices they bring to the analysis of information. How does the reporter feel about the general subject and about the particular information he or she has? Does the reporter like or dislike the people who are the principle sources for the story? Is that going to affect how the reporter handles the information?

PROFILE OF THE AMERICAN JOURNALIST

Age (median): 41
Education: College graduate, 89 percent
Gender: Male, 67 percent; Female, 33 percent
Race: White, 90.5 percent; Non-white, 9.5 percent
Income: $43,588 (median)
Political affiliation: Democrat, 37 percent; Republican, 19 percent; Independent, 33 percent; Other, 11 percent

Source: American Journalist Survey, *Indiana University (2002).*

Most professional journalists believe that reporters can be accurate and fair even though they may dislike the information they are reporting or the people who are giving it to them. But to do this, reporters must acknowledge their own feelings and make sure they do not get in the way of the journalistic process. Sometimes a reporter simply cannot overcome those feelings and may need to request that an editor assign someone else to cover a story. While that is unusual, it is not unheard of, and it shows a great deal of honesty on the part of the reporter.

Quote 8.3

GAY TALESE

On the view journalists take of the world

Most journalists are restless voyeurs who see the warts on the world, the imperfections in people and places. Gloom is their game, the spectacle their passion, normality their nemesis.

Gay Talese was a reporter for the New York Times *and one of the pioneers of the New Journalism movement of the 1960s. He is the author of a number of books, including* The Kingdom and the Power *(an inside view of the* Times*) and* Honor Thy Father *(an inside view of the mob).*

Becoming a Professional

Most reporters develop an obsession with accuracy—getting the latest, most up-to-date information and presenting it in a manner that can be understood by a mass audience. They want to write truthful reports, but they also understand how important this practice is to their professional lives and reputations. To achieve this level of accuracy, they develop techniques of gathering and checking the information they have that few outside the field of journalism would attempt.

Good reporters try to understand information from various points of view. They talk with as many people as possible who have some knowledge of the subject to see what they can add and how they interpret an event, situation, or issue. Often their own point of view, particularly when they do not feel personally involved in a news story, is a consensus of these bits of information, opinions, and perspectives. They develop judgments about whom they can trust and whether or not information or perspectives make sense to them. Getting different people to talk about the same situation helps immeasurably in gaining an understanding of that situation.

Reporters do not mind asking questions and will sometimes ask questions even when they think they know the answers. More difficult is to ask questions when everyone around seems to understand a situation except the reporter. Again, good reporters will risk looking as if they are slow or plodding by asking questions about what everyone else seems to know.

Good reporters are also unafraid to question commonly held assumptions. They do not mind looking like the "oddball," the guy or gal who does not quite get it. They will ask "why" and "how" even when it seems obvious. Or they will question someone who appears to be an authority when that person says things that do not make sense or that seem to violate common sense.

The best reporters will check and recheck their information, often from different sources if possible. They will look for contradictions in what different people tell them and they will try to resolve those contradictions. Experienced reporters always check the spelling of names they are using, especially if they are using them for the first time and there is any possibility that a name may vary from a common spelling.

For instance, many people have the last name of "Brown." A few are named "Browne," however, and a reporter never makes an assumption about a name such as that one. Good reporters will know the sources (directories, web sites, etc.) they can use efficiently to check small facts such as these.

In addition to accuracy, the reporter is also obsessed with speed. A reporter has to meet a deadline, as we have discussed earlier in this chapter, which necessitates that reporters work speedily and efficiently. But there are reasons for speed and efficiency that go beyond meeting a deadline. Reporters usually have an enormous amount of work to do. They have to learn how to work efficiently; that is, they must understand from the very beginning of an assignment what information they will need to complete that assignment.

Reporters also have to be available when their sources want to talk and when certain information will become available. For instance, a reporter may put in calls to several people early in the day and wait for most of the day for those calls to be returned. A reporter then has to ask questions efficiently that quickly elicit the information necessary to put together a story.

Earlier in this chapter, we mentioned the personal quality of competitiveness that reporters need. They should have the drive to make themselves better and to some extent prove that they are as good as or better than others who are doing the same job. This quality also takes on a professional and corporate aspect in the world of journalism. It becomes a great part of what the reporter thinks about and why the reporter acts as he or she does.

One of the most exciting aspects of being a reporter is knowing something interesting or important that few other people know. If the reporter is the only journalist who has this information, the excitement is increased. That knowledge, and the exclusive possession of it, makes the reporter feel that he or she has done a good job. When a reporter can "own" a story, it means that the reporter will take special pride in reporting and presenting it to the public. The reporter, in journalistic terms, has a "scoop."

A scoop for a reporter is especially sweet when there are other reporters who are after the same information. Bob Woodward and Carl Bernstein, the two young *Washington Post* reporters who broke the Watergate scandal in the early 1970s, consistently built their stories around information that no one else had. (Find out more about Watergate in Chapter 23.) They gained that information through a bit of luck and a great deal of "legwork," that is, talking with many people, checking records, even staking out people to watch what they did and where they went. They persisted in asking sources for information even when they were refused, and eventually many of the sources who initially refused relented. These reporters simply did more to get their information than others working on the same story.

Scoops are not just personal, however. They are corporate. They enhance the reputation of the news organization, and they are encouraged and sometimes rewarded by management. News organizations enjoy the recognition that comes from being the first to print, post, or broadcast an important story. As with the individual reporter, a scoop can enhance the standing of a news organization among its peers in the journalistic world, and this means a lot. It can sometimes be a financial boon

THE MOST GRATIFYING MOMENT

Wendy Fontaine
The Newport Daily News

I once wrote a profile about a woman who has the most bizarre job I've ever heard of: she styles hair for dead people at a local funeral home. And by that I mean she washes, blow dries and curls it, just as if the person were alive. The woman, whose name is Georgie, had been doing this job for about 40 years when I met her.

I interviewed Georgie and went to the funeral home to see where she does her work. It was such a weird experience. During one of our interviews, there was a man laid out for his wake on the other side of the room.

The woman had an amazing perspective about her job. She considered her work a gift that she gives to her "clients," as she calls them. Styling their hair and making them beautiful would be the last nice thing that anyone would ever do for them, she said. She considered it her privilege to prepare them for their funerals. I thought that was the most wonderful sentiment.

The story ran on the front page a few days later, and I got a lot of calls about it. I was even asked to speak about the story to a journalism class at a local private school.

But the most amazing comments I got came from Georgie's adult daughter, who called me from several states away to thank me for the story. The daughter recalled tagging along to the funeral home with her mother, but said Georgie had never really talked about what she did. She said the story showed her things she never knew about her mother and prompted her to look at Georgie in a different light. She said she felt closer to her mother after reading my article.

That was the most gratifying moment of my career.

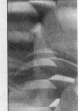

Wendy M. Fontaine is a freelance writer and former reporter for The Newport Daily News *in Newport, Rhode Island. She grew up in Livermore Falls, Maine, and graduated from the University of Maine at Orono. She lives near Bar Harbor, Maine.*

to an organization, but more often, it is simply a matter of polishing the organization's reputation. The more a news organization can be the first to report important stories, the better its reputation becomes among professionals and eventually with the public.

Getting There: Becoming a Reporter

In previous generations, most people who entered the field of journalism did so as reporters. Because reporters did the basic job of journalism, people within the profession believed that those coming into the field had to prove themselves in that position before moving on. Although this feeling has changed somewhat throughout the profession, many journalists still feel that no matter what kind of journalist you wind up being, a reporter's position is where you should begin.

But being a reporter is not a good job choice for everyone and certainly not a good career choice for most people. Being a reporter is a demanding and difficult task. A reporter has to work hard day after day under difficult conditions, and the money that a reporter makes is not as much as could be made in many other professions.

Quote 8.4

Still, some people have a drive and determination to do the job of a reporter. They find the reporter's life exciting and gain a satisfaction from seeing their work printed and read by many people or broadcast and seen by thousands of viewers. Good reporters gain a certain amount of local fame for the work they do, and that fame—if their work is good—can eventually turn into respect. A reporter is an independent voice in a community and a representative of an organization (a newspaper, television station, or web site) to which people pay a great deal of attention. Whether people like a news organization or not, they understand the power that it has to inform the community and shape how the community views the issues of the day.

What does it take to be a reporter?

An aspiring reporter must develop the ability to write and handle the language with ease and confidence. A reporter must also have an interest in public affairs and should have a keen sense of public service; that is, a reporter should be interested in making a community a better place to live by making information about the community available. Reporters should be naturally curious and should be bold enough to meet new people and ask questions. All of these interests and qualities are ones that a potential reporter will be developing from childhood.

One common characteristic of almost all young reporter wannabes is the desire to practice the craft; that is, most try to begin writing and publishing as soon as they can. People who want to become reporters find ways of doing it before they take their first journalism class or get their first real job interview. The opportunity to find out information, write it, and publish it is a powerfully seductive idea, and many young people get involved with it by working on the church newsletter, joining the high school newspaper or yearbook staff, covering high school football games for the local newspapers, and many other activities.

QUESTIONS FOR DISCUSSION

1. The author lists a number of characteristics of a good reporter. How many of those characteristics do you have? Do you think you would be a good news reporter? Do you think anyone you know would be a good reporter?

2. What do you think are the major differences between newspaper and television reporters? (Chapter 19 discusses reporting for television and radio more

thoroughly.) At this point in your reading, what do you perceive as the most important differences?

3. What opportunities are available to you now to practice the craft of reporting?
4. Have you ever thought of starting a newspaper or newsletter for a group with which you are associated? What kind of news would this publication contain? What could you tell people that they do not know already?

RELATED WEB SITES

American Society of Journalists and Authors, www.asja.org

Education Writer's Association, www.ewa.org

National Association of Black Journalists, www.nabj.org

National Association of Hispanic Journalists, www.nahj.org

National Association of Science Writers, www.nasw.org

Religion Newswriters Association, www.religionwriters.com

Society of Professional Journalists, www.spj.org

READINGS AND REFERENCES

Adams, S. (2001). *Interviewing for journalists.* New York: Routledge.

Baker, B. (2001). *Newsthinking: The secret of making your facts fall into place.* Boston: Allyn and Bacon.

Brooks, B. S., Kennedy, G., Moen, D. R., & Ranly, D. (2001). *Telling the story: Writing for print, broadcast and online media.* New York: Bedford/St. Martins.

Brooks, B. S., Kennedy, G., Moen, D. R., & Ranly, D. (2002). *News reporting and writing* (7th ed.). New York: Bedford/St. Martins.

Clark, R. P., & Campbell, C. C. (Eds.). (2002). *The value and craft of American journalism.* Gainesville, FL: University Press of Florida.

Clark, R. P., & Scanlan, C. (Eds.). (2000). *America's best newspaper writing.* New York: Bedford/St. Martins.

Fallows, J. (1996). *Breaking the news: How the media undermine American democracy.* New York: Pantheon Books.

Fedler, F. (2000). *Reporting for the print media* (7th ed.). New York: Oxford University Press.

Harrington, W. (1997). *Intimate journalism: The art and craft of reporting everyday life.* Thousand Oaks, CA: Sage Publications.

Itule, B. D., & Anderson, D. A. (2003). *News writing and reporting for today's media* (6th ed.). Boston: McGraw-Hill.

Killenberg, G. M. (1989). *Before the story.* New York: St. Martin's Press.

Killenberg, G. M. (1992). *Public affairs reporting: Covering the news in the information age.* New York: St. Martin's Press.

Lewis, A. (Ed.). (2001). *Written into history: Pulitzer Prize reporting of the twentieth century from the* New York Times. New York: Times Books.

Rich, C. (2003). *Writing and reporting news: A coaching method* (4th ed.). Belmont: Wadsworth.

Ross, L. (2002). *Reporting back: Notes on journalism.* Washington, DC: Counterpoint.

Sloan, W. D., & Wray, C. S. (1997). *Masterpieces of reporting, vol. 1.* Northport, AL: Vision Press.

Stewart, J. B. (1998). *Follow the story: How to write successful nonfiction.* New York: Simon & Schuster.

Wolfe, T. (1973). *The new journalism.* New York: Harper & Row.

Chapter Nine

Reporting

Key Concepts and Terms

1. Who, what, when, where, why, and how: the key questions that journalists must answer when they are gathering their information and writing their stories.

2. Stored sources: information that is contained in written or electronic files.

3. Accuracy: the main goal of reporting; journalists go to great lengths to make sure their information is correct and presented in an accurate context so that readers and viewers will have the same understanding of that information that the journalist does.

4. Personal sources: the people who give journalists information; in daily journalism, personal sources are most important because they have information that is not stored yet.

5. Almost all good journalists are good interviewers; they know how to talk with people, and they know how to listen.

6. Observational sources: information that the journalist sees in the course of reporting; stories about sports events, for instance, are written mainly with observational sources.

7. Quotation: what a source says; a direct quotation is the exact words that a source uses whereas an indirect quotation uses different words that mean the same thing as the words the source used.

This chapter has been adapted, in part, from material in James Glen Stovall, *Writing for the Mass Media*, 5/e. Published by Allyn and Bacon, Boston, MA. Copyright © 2002 by Pearson Education. Adapted by permission of the publisher.

The process of journalism begins with gathering information. Reporting is a talent that some people have; it is a skill that anyone can acquire. But takes a great deal of thought, preparation, and practice. Reporters have to understand information and where it comes from. They must be persuasive in dealing with sources of information. They must also be honest and forthright.

None of this is easy. This chapter introduces you to some of the basics of gathering information for a news story.

Five Ws and One H

Basic to all writing is having the information that you will use in the writing process. Writing for the mass media requires that certain information be gathered at the beginning of the writing process. A journalist gathering information or writing a story tries to answer six basic questions for the reader:

Who.   Who are the important people related to the story? Is everyone included so that the story can be accurately and adequately told? Is everyone properly identified?

What.   What is the major action or event of the story? What are the actions or events of lesser importance? A journalist ought to be able to state the major action of the story in one sentence, and this should be the theme of the story.

When.   When did the event occur? Readers of news stories should have a clear idea of when the story takes place. The when element is rarely the best way to begin a story because it is not often the most important piece of information a journalist has to tell a reader, but it should come early in the story and should be clearly stated.

Where.   Where did the event occur? Journalists cannot assume readers will know or be able to figure out where an event takes place. The location or locations of the event or action should be clearly written.

Why and how.   The reader deserves an explanation about the events. If a story is about something bizarre or unusual, the writer should offer some explanation, so the questions the event raises in the reader's mind are answered. The writer also needs to set the events or actions in a story in the proper context. Reference should be made to previous events or actions if they help to explain things to the reader.

Acquiring the information needed to write anything for the mass media is an essential part of the writing process. Information is not always self-evident or readily available. The process of "reporting"—gathering the information—takes considerable skill, creativity, and tenacity. What the writer needs, of course, depends on what he or she is writing about, but essentially a writer has three fundamental sources of information: people, records (any information written or stored so others may find it), and personal observation.

Types of Sources

Reporters have three types of sources: stored (information in books, reports, libraries, and so on, in print or electronic forms); personal (people); and observational (events, places, and so on, that a reporter can see). Most of the information that a reporter uses comes from personal sources, that is, people whom the reporter talks to. People have more current information than can usually be found in stored sources, and reporters can rarely be on the scene when news events actually occur. Consequently, the main job of the reporter is to find the people who have information or whose point of view is relevant to the reporter's story.

Stored Sources

"You can look it up!" Casey Stengel used to tell reporters who gathered around him in the manager's office of the New York Yankees baseball team. Stengel, who led the Yankees to a record string of championships in the 1940s and 1950s, was known for his long, involved answers to the simplest questions. He would often end his circumlocutions by saying, "You can look it up!" as a challenge to those who might not believe what he had just said.

What Stengel told reporters is what most of us already know: a vast amount of information is available to be "looked up." This stored information includes any books, reports, articles, press releases, documents, and computer-stored information to which a reporter has access. Here are some examples of reporters using stored sources:

> Furillo, who died Sunday, played right field for the Brooklyn and Los Angeles Dodgers from 1946 through 1960. He won the NL batting title with a .344 average in 1953, when he missed the last few weeks of the season because of a broken hand he sustained during a fight with manager Leo Durocher.

> A City Social Services Department report estimated that more than 10,000 people were "without permanent or temporary shelter" in the city last year.

> A statement issued by the new administration said that foreign policy problems would be high on the president's agenda.

Stored sources are located in many places—government documents, company records, books, magazines, and so on. A news reporter should be familiar with the holdings of the local public library because that can be a major source of stored information.

Chances are, however, the modern journalist has a library as close as the keyboard of his or her computer. That "library," of course, is the World Wide Web, or the Internet. Most libaries and many businesses are connected to the Internet so that employees can "look it up" more easily than ever before.

Akin to the Internet is the stored information that is found in online or electronic information services. Such services provide subscribers with fingertip access to a wide range of information, such as newspapers, magazines, television transcripts, governmental reports, legal opinions, encyclopedias, library card catalogues, and many other sources. These services come through telephone lines from central data banks and tie in to personal computers. People who work with information, particularly those in the mass media, are relying more and more heavily on these online databases.

In most cases, information that comes from stored sources, like that which comes from personal sources, should be attributed. In two of the preceding examples, the attribution is clear. Occasionally, as in the first example, the information may either be common knowledge or be available in many references so that telling the reader the source is not that important.

Using stored information, whether it comes from a library or from the Internet, presents the reporter with two basic problems. The first problem is management—how do you find what you need? Sometimes just "looking it up" is not nearly as simple as it sounds, and when you are faced with the enormous amount of information that is available through the Internet, the problem is compounded. Most reporters develop strategies for exploring information sources mainly through experience. The more a reporter uses a library or an Internet search engine, the more he or she will understand what information is available and where it is more likely to reside.

The second problem is that of reliability. Is the information that you get correct? How do you know? Assessing the reliability of information has always been a problem for reporters, but it, too, has been compounded by the expansion of information that is available. Reporters should consider carefully the source of the information in assessing its reliability. They should also try to find the same information from another source, if possible and if there is some doubt about the original source. They should remember that just because something is in a book in the library or posted on a web page on the Internet does not make it accurate.

Personal Sources

Most information in most news stories comes from personal sources—that is, people. A news reporter is likely to spend most of his or her nonwriting time talking to people either face-to-face or over the telephone. In fact, many would argue the more people the reporter talks to, the better a story is likely to be because of the variety of information and views the reporter can obtain.

Here are some examples of paragraphs from news stories in which the information comes from personal sources:

> According to the theater owner, Martin Miller, about 340 attended the first-night showing of the controversial film.

> Although he attended the inauguration, the congressman said he disapproved of the amount of money spent on the event.

> "I'm against that proposal because it's unfair to the middle class," the senator said.

The first two examples are indirect quotations or paraphrases; the third is a direct quotation. The next chapter discusses more fully the handling of direct and indirect quotations.

Interviewing is when a reporter talks to a source. (Interviewing will be discussed in detail later in this chapter.) All writers who deal with information, whether they are newspaper reporters, magazine writers, or public relations practitioners, must master the art of interviewing. A reporter tries to determine what information the source has and would be willing to share. Then the reporter attempts to ask the kind of questions that would elicit this information. The techniques of interviewing are discussed more fully in the next section of this chapter.

Journalists develop sources among the people whom they contact regularly; that is, the reporters will find people who have information and are willing to talk with them about it. Reporters soon realize that many people can provide information and sometimes information can come from surprising sources. For instance, most reporters who are assigned to a regular beat learn that secretaries, rather than their bosses, are the best sources of information. Secretaries often know what is happening before their bosses do. Consequently, many reporters get to know the secretaries on their beats very well. As reporters and sources deal with each other, they should develop a relationship of mutual understanding. Reporters find out whom they can trust among their sources, and sources realize the information they give to reporters will be used wisely.

One general rule governs the relationships reporters have with their sources—reporters should always identify themselves clearly to their sources. Sources should know before they talk to reporters the information they give may be used in a news story. Sources should have the opportunity not to talk with news reporters if they do not want to.

Attribution in a news story means telling readers where information comes from. Attribution phrases are those such as "he said," "she said," and "according to officials." Most of the major information in a news story needs to have some attribution, particularly information that comes from personal sources.

Observation

The third major source of information for the news reporter is observation. Whenever possible, news reporters attend the events they are writing about. They like to see for themselves what happens, even though they rarely write from a first person point of view. Here are some examples of news reports that have used observational sources:

> The anti-abortion rally drew people from many areas of the Midwest. Cars in the parking lot bore license tags from Missouri to West Virginia.

> Bailey High's Sam Love kicked a 14-yard field goal in the first period, and Mateo Central's Jack Mayo had a 34-yarder in the second period to account for the second-lowest scoring first half in the history of the championship game.

> The packed courtroom listened, in a hushed silence, as the defendant took the witness stand and began to tell her story.

In each of these cases, it is clear that the reporters attended the events they described. One indication of this is the lack of attribution in each of these paragraphs.

Observing is more than just watching an event or being there. Good reporters are active observers. They often enter a situation knowing what they want to watch for and what information they need for an article. They also remain open to bizarre or unusual events, so that such events can be included in what they write.

Good observation requires the reporter to develop a sense of what is important and significant. The fact that two members of a city council confer before a vote is taken and then vote the same way may raise a question in the mind of a reporter—a question that he or she will want to find the answer to after the meeting has occurred. If the reporter had not seen the conference, no question would have been raised, and something significant might have been missed.

Good reporters also put themselves in a position to see what they need to see. Physical positioning is a key part of good reporting. A reporter who wants to do a story on what it is like to be on the sidelines at a football game would not stay in the press box during the game. Visiting a scene before an event takes place, if possible, is a good idea and usually allows a reporter to gain insight about an event.

News reporters are obligated to put what they see into their stories whether or not it makes the people they are writing about look "good" or "bad." Some actions or information may be embarrassing to people, even those in authority. A reporter must not make a judgment about what to include in a news report based on that. The reporter's obligation is to the readers who are expecting an accurate account of an event.

Generally, reporters do not participate in events. If the event is a demonstration, they do not carry signs and march with a group. At a city council meeting in which citizens are asking questions or making statements to the council, they do not join in by asking their own questions. At the same time, reporters should not leave their humanity behind. If they can prevent injury and help out in an emergency situation, they should certainly do so.

Interviewing

Interviewing is one of the most important skills that a reporter can acquire. Most reporters can tell you some funny stories about interviews they have conducted and the circumstances of those interviews. (I was interviewing a U.S. senator once in the Senate dining room. He had ordered coffee, and I had a cup of hot tea. I squeezed the lemon for my tea, and the juice went straight into the corner of my eye. I had to continue conducting the interview while trying to get my eye clear.)

Few reporters get through a day without interviewing someone. Following are some advice and instruction (Stovall, 2002):

> The first step in interviewing is deciding, sometimes simultaneously, what inf
> needed and who would be the best source for that information. A journ
> a clear idea of what information it will take to make a good article. D
> of clear idea takes some experience, but it is certainly within the gra
> reporter. The information that a reporter needs will often dictate v
> to provide that information, but the selection of the source may de
> as well. For instance, the best source for certain information mig

TEN TIPS FOR COVERING A BEAT

News reporters are often assigned to cover a beat—a place or topic of interest—on a regular basis. Some common beats on a local newspaper are education, city government, police, and business. On a campus or high school newspaper a beat might be academics, student organizations, faculty, student programs, and so on. Here are ten tips you can used to get started:

1. Find the place. Make sure you know and understand the physical location of the place (or places) of your beat. Sometimes that is a story in itself. What are the functions of your office or activity? What constituency does it serve?

2. Get the publications of the office or offices that you cover; find the web site. Anything that is written down about the organization should be in your possession. Get any brochures, pamphlets, and fliers the office has—even on events that have already occurred.

3. Find out who is in charge. Who makes the decisions? Who carries them out?

4. What public activities are planned by the organization? This is likely to be your first story, and certainly it would be a source of stories throughout the semester. Is there a seminar, speaker, exhibit, or something else that the organization would like to have publicized? When you are gathering information, don't forget about pictures or images.

5. Be sure to identify yourself fully. Make sure the people you talk with know that you are a reporter for a news organization. Make sure they have your phone numbers and email address.

6. Find out who has information. Often it is the secretaries; they are likely to know more than their bosses. Always, always be nice to secretaries, even if they appear abrupt or rude. Weathering a little rudeness can score you a lot of points with some people. Hang in there, and always be polite and businesslike.

7. Show up on a regular basis. Don't just email or call. Let people know that you are after information and that you need to produce stories. If you establish a relationship, they are likely to begin helping you out. Make a stop by your beat a part of the route you take every couple of days, if not every day.

8. Use the telephone and email, but do not rely solely on them.

9. Try to generate several story ideas at once, and work on them all at the same time. Some won't pan out; some won't pan out immediately but will eventually.

10. Think about covering your beat not just in terms of events but also in terms of people and ideas. Most places have interesting people who would be good subjects for profiles and interviews. For example, the student health center at a university may be offering flu shots; that's a good story. But how likely are students to get the flu? Are they more likely than other parts of the population? Why? Begin to ask questions like that and you've got the makings of a good story.

might be hesitant to talk with a journalist. These are situations in which journalists might have to find other sources of information.

The second step to a successful interview is preparing for the conversation. This preparation may include doing research on the topic of the interview or on the person to be involved. In general, the more the journalist knows about both, the more successful the interview is likely to be. In the world of daily journalism, time and deadline pressure may limit much preparation. In such instances, the journalist must draw upon his or her experience and the cooperation of the source.

Another part of the preparation phase of the interview is figuring out what questions to ask. The questions, of course, will depend on the information needed, but they will also depend on the willingness of the source to give information. Information that is simple and not necessarily controversial can usually be gained from clear, straightforward, and efficient questions, as in the following exchange:

Reporter: Can you tell me how the wreck occurred?

Police officer: Well, the witnesses said it wasn't raining but the roads were pretty wet from a thunderstorm that had just come through the area. The car traveling in the westbound lane put its brakes on for some reason and the car skidded out of control and into the eastbound lane.

Reporter: Why did the car brake?

Police officer: We're not sure. Maybe an animal ran across the road. Sometimes at night, especially in wet conditions, you think you see things that aren't there and you hit the brakes.

Reporter: What happened when the car skidded?

Police officer: It skidded about fifty feet and slammed into a car in the eastbound lane. A third car, also traveling eastbound, then crashed into those cars. Fortunately for everyone else, those were the only three cars involved in the wreck.

Reporter: Was anyone hurt?

Police officer: Yeah, two people were hurt pretty bad, and two others were injured. Everyone was alive when we got them to the hospital. You'll have to check with the hospital to see how they are doing.

This short exchange has given the reporter a lot of information (though certainly not everything) that can be included in a story. Chances are the reporter did not have much time to prepare for this interview. But the reporter understands news values and story construction well enough to ask relevant and productive questions.

Sometimes the information a reporter seeks is much more controversial and the source is not as adept or as willing to give the information. Journalists should be sensitive and empathetic with their sources, but they should also remember their professional responsibilities.

Interviewers have different methods of asking questions, and they will employ these methods when they are appropriate for the situation. Following are some of the various types of questions they can ask.

Closed-ended questions: These usually require very short answers or the question itself may contain a choice of answers from which the respondent will choose. *Examples:* How often do you travel out of town? Do you feel good or bad about the way things turned out?

Open-ended questions: Sometimes an interviewer will want to give a subject the chance to say anything he or she wants. Open-ended questions allow this to happen. *Examples:* What do you think is the most important issue facing the city council now? When you think about a person who is homeless, what picture comes into your mind?

Hypothetical questions: These are questions that set up a situation or condition and ask the interviewee to respond to it. They are sometimes known as "what if" questions. *Example:* If someone came to you and asked your help in finding a job, what would you tell that person?

Agree–disagree questions: As the name implies, these questions ask respondents to express agreement or disagreement with a statement or action. *Example:* Some people say congressmen should be prevented from serving more than two terms. Do you agree or disagree with that?

Probes: These are questions that follow up on something the interviewee has said. They can be neutral (Can you tell me more about that?), provocative (Are you saying you will never do that?), or challenging (I think a lot of people will find that difficult to believe.). The purpose of a probe is to get the interviewee to give more information about what he or she has just said.

Personal questions: These questions have to do with the personal life of a subject. They may be very relevant to the article the journalist must do, but these questions need to be approached carefully. Most experienced interviewers agree such questions should be left until the middle or end of the interview, giving the respondent a chance to establish some trust in the interviewer.

One of the most important products of planning an interview is for the journalist to have a list of questions that will be asked when the interview takes place. Because interviews are not always predictable, it may not be feasible or necessary to ask every question—and it may be that unplanned questions arise—but a journalist should always have a plan for the interview session.

The next step in the interview process is to establish contact with the source and to set up some mutually agreeable time and place to conduct the interview. When a reporter is working near a daily deadline, he or she may insist the interview be conducted immediately on the phone. In other instances, however, a source should be told who wants to conduct the interview, for what publication it will be conducted, and what information, in general, the reporter needs. The reporter should be flexible about the time and the place of the interview so that it is as convenient for the source as possible.

During the interview itself, a reporter should keep in mind the interview is taking place to obtain certain information but also remain open to possibilities that other, more interesting or important information may be obtained. If a source decides to offer some new or surprising information, the reporter should be able to evaluate the worth of the information and handle it appropriately. Most of the time, however, a reporter's planning will pay off with an efficient and productive interview. The following are a number of things that an interviewer should keep in mind about an interviewing situation.

- Control the situation. Keep the conversation on track by remembering what you came for and what information you need to get from the source. Refer to your notes or questions.

A DOZEN INTERVIEWING TIPS

1. Think of what your audience will want to know.
2. Prepare as much as possible; know as much as you can about the person you are interviewing.
3. Have questions ready to ask, but the interview may go in a different direction than what you planned. Be ready to respond to that.
4. Dress so that you represent yourself and your news organization well.
5. Introduce yourself, shake hands if appropriate, and tell why you are there, even if the interviewee knows the reason.
6. Try to make your questions as short as possible, and don't be afraid to wait for an answer.
7. Listen to what the interviewee has to say with all the concentration you can muster.

Listen for the substance of what he or she is saying, but also remember that you need words and sentences you can put into direct quotations.

8. Ask your interviewee how to spell his or her name, and also ask for the person's exact title.
9. Ask for permission to call back if there is information that you need.
10. Know the background of the person you are interviewing.
11. Ask the most difficult questions toward the end of the interview if possible.
12. Take note of the surroundings and of the characteristics of the interviewee.

- The first few questions will set the tone for the interview, so the reporter should think carefully about how the interview should be structured. If there are difficult questions the reporter needs to ask—questions that would make the source uncomfortable—they are usually not the questions that should be asked first. Those questions will be easier to ask and answer later in the interview when the reporter and source have established some rapport.

- Take notes. Do so as unobtrusively as possible, but if you are there as a journalist, the source will expect you to do this. Write down the key words and phrases that the source uses if you cannot get every word. Concentrate on what is being said so you can reconstruct an accurate quote later. Even during the interview session you should begin thinking about what information and direct quotations you will use in your article.

- If you don't understand what a source has said, ask that the quote be repeated. Read back what you have written to make sure that you have it right. If you don't understand a word or phrase the source has used, ask about it. It is better you show your ignorance to the source than to thousands of readers or viewers when you do your story.

- If a source attacks or criticizes you, try to respond as little as possible. Remember you are there to get information, not to defend yourself.

- Use a tape recorder only if you have the permission of the source. Ask the source's permission before you turn it on. If the source is reluctant, you might say, "This will help me make sure I get everything you say correctly." If the source will not permit the use of the tape recorder, do not use it.

- Even if you use a tape recorder, always take notes. A tape recorder may not work, or the tape may be bad. Any number of things can happen.

- Sometime during the interview, take note of something other than what is being said such as gestures or other physical details of the source, pictures or awards on the wall, or other objects in the room. You may see something you want to ask about or something you will want to use in your article.

- Always be courteous and professional.

As soon as possible after the interview, you should go over your notes and listen to your tape recording. Many reporters will listen to a tape and fill in their notes. If there is no tape, it is a good idea to read your notes carefully and fill in parts of the interview you may want to use in your article.

If possible, a reporter should check important information that the source has given with another source to verify it. Many reporters have been taken in by sources who sounded as if they knew exactly what they were talking about. These reporters have looked foolish in print or on the air when they used the information they had obtained.

Finally, a reporter should never hesitate to call a source back for more information or for clarification of information or discrepancies. These callbacks show that a reporter is serious about producing an accurate report, and sources who are honest will not mind helping the reporter in this effort.

A Note on Accuracy

The overriding goal of the writer for the mass media is accuracy. The attempt to be accurate must govern all of the actions of the writer, from the way he or she gathers information to the language that is used to convey that information. Previous chapters have discussed the necessity of using the language precisely and about the attention that a writer must give to the format, style, and usage in writing. These efforts are important because ultimately they help increase the accuracy of the writing that is produced.

This attention to precise writing should be preceded by an attention to the details of reporting. Developing good habits in gathering information will pay off for the reporter in many ways. The following are some of the areas of reporting that deserve the special effort of a reporter.

Spell names correctly. One of the most important possessions a person has is his or her name. The misspelling of a name is more likely to offend someone than almost any other mistake. Consequently, news reporters should take special care to make sure they have the correct spelling for the names they use in their stories. They should never assume they can spell a name correctly. For instance, "John Smith" may really be

John Smithe
John Smythe
John Smyth
Jon Smith

The person whose name you are using is the best source for the correct spelling, and you should never be afraid or embarrassed to ask. In fact, asking specifically often demonstrates that you are trying to be careful and increases the confidence that source has in you.

Checking with the person may not always be possible, however. In that case, telephone directories and city directories are generally reliable sources for correctly spelled names. The people who put these directories together are professionals and understand that they are creating a resource that will be checked by others. Police reports, printed programs, and other such material are not reliable sources, and they should not be used for name checking.

Quote your sources correctly. This chapter has already discussed gathering and using quoted material, and more discussion will follow in the next chapter. The point here is to make sure you get it right. Many people who are used as sources in news reports complain about being "misquoted" or "quoted out of context." Often that is a way for the source to back away from what he or she has said after it has been printed or broadcast. On the other hand, news reporters do make mistakes, and it is their responsibility—not that of the source—to make sure they have heard and understood what the source has said. The simplest solution to understanding correctly what the source has said is to ask. Make sure you know not only what words the source has used but also the meaning that the source has given to them.

Get information from more than one source if possible. As a general rule, news stories are better if reporters get information from more than one source. Different people know various things about a situation, or they may have differing viewpoints about it. The more people a news reporter talks to about a story, and the more records that he or she checks, the more likely he or she will be to understand the story fully.

Getting information from multiple sources sometimes will saddle the reporter with contradictory information. Where the contradictions are apparent and important, the reporter should attempt to resolve them among the sources; otherwise, the reporter will have to choose which source he or she feels is the most reliable. Either way, the process of resolving contradictions will usually deepen a reporter's understanding of the information.

Make sure that the numbers in a story add up correctly. Numbers don't have to throw journalists, but they often do. For instance, consider this paragraph about a student election that appeared in a college newspaper:

> Officials said a total of 5,865 ballots were cast, representing a 34.2 percent turnout. Smith defeated Jones by receiving 3,077 votes to Jones's 2,385, a margin of 393 votes.

The reporter should have done two things with this story. He or she should have added up the totals for the two candidates to make sure that totals matched the total number of ballots cast. If the numbers did not match, the news reporter should have found out why. Second, the story reports that "officials" said there was a 34.2 percent turnout. The reporter should have gotten the figures that these officials used and done his or her own calculations. It may be that the 34.2 percent figure is correct. The reporter should have made sure.

QUESTIONS FOR DISCUSSION

1. If you were going to interview someone for a news story, how important do you think your appearance—the way you are dressed and groomed—would be?
2. Why do journalists rely so heavily on personal sources?
3. Many journalists are relying more and more on email interviews in which the reporter emails questions to a source and the source emails the answers. Compared to telephone interviews, what are the advantages and disadvantages of this method of interviewing?
4. If a source is reluctant to talk with a reporter, what techniques can a reporter use to persuade the source to talk with the reporter?

RELATED WEB SITES

Investigative Reporters and Editors, www.ire.org
Society of Professional Journalists, www.spj.org

READINGS AND REFERENCES

Aamidor, A. (1999). *Real feature writing.* Hillsdale, NJ: Lawrence Erlbaum Associates.

Adams, P. (1997). *Writing right for today's media.* Chicago: Nelson-Hall.

Adams, S. (2001). *Interviewing for journalists.* New York: Routledge.

Brooks, B. S., Kennedy, G., Moen, D. R., & Ranly, D. (2001). *Telling the story: Writing for print, broadcast and online media.* New York: Bedford/St. Martins.

Brooks, B. S., Kennedy, G., Moen, D. R., & Ranly, D. (2002). *News reporting and writing* (7th ed.). New York: Bedford/St. Martins.

Fink, C. C. (2000). *Bottom line writing: Reporting the sense of dollars.* Ames, IA: Iowa State University Press.

Houston, B., Bruzzese, L., & Weinberg, S. (2002). *The investigative reporter's handbook.* (4th ed.). Boston: Bedford/St. Martin's.

Leiter, K., Harriss, J., & Johnson, S. (2000). *The complete reporter.* Boston: Allyn and Bacon.

Ross, L. (2002). *Reporting back: Notes on journalism.* Washington, DC: Counterpoint.

Snyder, L. L., & Morris, R. B. (Eds.). (1962). *A treasury of great reporting.* New York: Simon & Schuster.

Stephens, M., & Lanson, G. (1997). *Writing and reporting the news* (2nd ed.). Fort Worth: Harcourt Brace.

Stovall, J. G. (2002). *Writing for the mass media.* Boston: Allyn and Bacon.

Writing Exercises

EXERCISE 9.1

News values

Read the story and answer the following questions.

CHILLICOTHE, Mo. — A jury has recommended a 69-year-old woman be sentenced to death for the murders of four transient farm workers whose bodies were found buried in northwestern Missouri last year.

Jurors in Livingston County Circuit Court deliberated more than three hours before making the recommendation Tuesday night in the case of Faye Copeland, whom the jury had convicted Saturday of five counts of first-degree murder.

The jury of eight women and four men recommended Copeland be sentenced to life in prison without parole on the fifth murder conviction.

Circuit Judge E. Richard Webber must decide whether to accept the jury's recommendations or to sentence Copeland to life in prison. He ordered a pre-sentence investigation.

If sentenced to death, Copeland will become the oldest person on Missouri's death row.

Copeland's attorney, public defender David Miller, has said he will file a motion for a new trial. Miller said he would appeal the court's refusal to allow a psychologist to testify about "battered-wife syndrome."

Miller had argued Faye Copeland was dominated by her 74-year-old husband, Ray, who is awaiting trial on the same charges, and had only a minor role in the crimes.

Ray Copeland's trial is scheduled to begin Jan. 24 but the court first must determine whether he is mentally competent to assist in his own defense. His attorneys contend Ray Copeland suffers from senile dementia, including an organic brain disorder.

The bodies of the victims were found last year in shallow graves in barns or dumped in wells on farms in Livingston County where Ray Copeland had worked. Investigators said the victims had been shot to death. No bodies were found on the couple's farm near Mooresville, about 65 miles northeast of Kansas City.

The Copelands originally were arrested on charges of conspiracy in an alleged fraudulent cattle-buying conspiracy.

Authorities contended the couple hired the transients to work as cattle buyers, then killed and buried them. Prosecutors said the Copelands netted $32,000 by reselling the cattle. The fraud charges were dismissed after the murder charges were filed.

EXERCISE 9.2

News values—selecting news

You are the editor of your hometown newspaper, and you need to select the stories that will go on the front page for tomorrow's paper. Following are the first two paragraphs of the news stories from which you must make your selection. Which four of the following would you select? In what order? Be prepared to justify your answer. Check Chapter 1 for a description of news values if necessary.

DEARBORN, Mich.—Ford Motor Co. said Monday it is recalling more than 127,000 1987-model Ford Thunderbirds and Mercury Cougar cars with 3.8 liter V6 engines to correct unacceptable emissions levels.

Dealers will be asked to install free of charge a vacuum retard delay valve and change the ignition timing. Cars affected were built for sale in 49 states, with California and Canadian vehicles not affected.

A Bay Minette woman was uninjured after a fiery one-car accident on Alabama 225 early Monday morning.

The 1987 Chevrolet driven by Janice Singleton, 28, apparently caught fire in the wreck just north of Baldwin 40, a state trooper spokesman said Monday.

Ms. Singleton was able to escape the car and then abandoned it, the spokesman said. She later notified local police that she was unhurt.

MONTGOMERY, Ala.—An 8-month-old North Carolina boy was reunited with his mother, while the Iowa couple accused of abducting him were expected to be returned next week to North Carolina to face kidnapping charges.

The infant's mother, Susan Tarlton of Greensboro, N.C., offered advice to other parents when Larry Wayne Tarlton arrived at a North Carolina airport. The child was abducted three weeks ago.

CAPE HATTERAS, N.C.—The severed bridge that is the only link between Hatteras Island and the mainland could be repaired within 45 days, state officials say.

Previous estimates indicated repairs could take at least six months. A dredge battered the bridge during a Friday storm, causing a 370-foot section of the structure to collapse.

BELLEVUE, Wash.—Government health experts Wednesday launched a nationwide, federally funded program to detect hepatitis B among pregnant women and immunize their infants against the serious liver infection.

Doctors from the U.S. Centers for Disease Control and the National Foundation for Infectious Diseases told public health officials at the first of a series of regional conferences that efforts to stop hepatitis B have largely failed despite the availability since 1981 of safe and effective vaccines.

TORONTO—Union officials representing about 10,000 striking Canadian steelworkers said Monday's tentative settlement with Stelco Inc. that includes full pension-indexing was a major victory for its members.

Leo Gerard, the Ontario director of the United Steelworkers of America, said the union's negotiators had achieved its five major objectives.

1. What are the news values that are present in each of the stories? Refer to a description of news values in Chapter 1 if necessary.

2. List the who, what, when, where, why, and how elements of each story.

3. Which of the three major types of sources of information are used in these stories?

4. List the sources specifically mentioned in each story. How do you think that the reporters were able to get this information?

5. Based on your limited knowledge about the events, analyze each of the stories for accuracy. Are there points in the story that might not be accurate? If you were the editor, what would you question? What would you want the reporter to double-check?

Chapter Ten

Writing News and Features

Key Concepts and Terms

1. The ability to use the language efficiently, effectively, and confidently is the mark of a good journalist.

2. Although the journalist must learn certain writing techniques and structures to be successful, those requirements do not lessen the creativity of the writing process.

3. All journalistic writing should share four characteristics: accuracy, clarity, precision, and efficiency.

4. Precision: the ability to use the language correctly, following commonly accepted rules of grammar, punctuation, and spelling and using words for precisely what they mean.

5. Good journalistic writing uses the simplest words possible and a variety of sentence structures.

6. Attribution: giving credit to sources for their information; this is one of the most important journalistic writing conventions.

7. Inverted pyramid: the major structure of news stories; the most important information (often the latest information) is at the beginning of the story, not at the end; information is presented in order of its importance.

8. Lead: the first paragraph in a news story; pronounced LEED.

9. Feature writing often centers around people and their interests rather than events, but many of the same writing conventions of news writing (particularly a concern for accuracy) are also required for feature writing.

10. One of the most effective ways of learning to write is to read good writing and to try to model your writing on what you have read.

This chapter has been adapted, in part, from material in James Glen Stovall, *Writing for the Mass Media*, 5/e. Published by Allyn and Bacon, Boston, MA. Copyright © 2002 by Pearson Education. Adapted by permission of the publisher.

Writing and reporting are the central tasks of the journalist. These are very different tasks, and inevitably some journalists are better reporters—that is, gatherers of information—than writers. As we saw in the previous chapter, reporting requires a person to talk with people in certain ways and to look for information intelligently and creatively. Writing requires the reporter to sift through that information and mold it into the appropriate form for the medium he or she is using.

Having the proper information—all the relevant facts of a story, the proper identification for the people involved, the times and dates, accurate direct quotations, and so on—is vital to the writing process, but it is only the beginning. There comes a time when the information gathering must cease and the writing must begin.

The ability to write well requires that the writer have a thorough knowledge and understanding of the subject. In addition, the writer must understand the basic structure of the news story and the conventions or customs of news writing in order to complete the process.

Basic Writing Characteristics

All writing for the mass media shares four characteristics: accuracy, precision, efficiency, and clarity. These characteristics should be on display in any nonfiction writing for a large audience.

Accuracy has been a continuing theme throughout this book because so much of journalism and journalistic procedures are directed toward achieving it. Writers must learn to use the words and phrases that will convey the information they have in a way so that readers will not only understand it but also be able to form an appropriate interpretation of it. Writers must not only present facts, but they must also present them within a proper context.

Achieving accuracy is no easy task. Factual information has to be processed by the writer, and the result of that processing can come out in many different ways. A reader has an expectation in reading a news story that if he or she had seen and heard the same things that the reporter saw and heard, the reader would interpret them in the same way.

Precision is one of the basic means of achieving accuracy. Precision in this context means that the writer uses the language accurately and according to commonly accepted rules of grammar, spelling, punctuation, and diction. Some people argue that grammar, spelling, and punctuation are not important. The thoughts, the ideas, the information—now, that's what's important, they say. They are wrong on two levels. First, thoughts, ideas, and information take their shape in the words used to express them; if those words, phrases, and sentences are not correct, how can the thoughts, ideas, and information be correctly expressed?

But those who argue that grammar, spelling, and punctuation are not important are wrong on another, more practical level. The media professions simply do not tolerate misuse of the language. English is the basic tool of the profession, and those who do not use the language well cannot be taken seriously by other professionals or by the general public. To say otherwise is to be unrealistic. Simply put, write would work in journalism must know the language and use it precisely.

Efficiency is another highly valued characteristic of journalistic writing. Most us think, talk, and write inefficiently. Good journalists must learn how to write so that they can include as much information as possible in a small amount of time and space.

The practical reasons for this are that, except for the World Wide Web, space is limited in all media and readers also consider their time to be limited. They expect the media to give them information quickly and efficiently; they do not want their time wasted by irrelevant information or unnecessary words. Many of the writing conventions and procedures that we present in this book are aimed at helping students learn how to write efficiently.

Beginning writers sometimes confuse efficiency with brevity. Although the two characteristics of writing have some things in common, they are not the same. Achieving efficiency does not mean reducing the amount of information in a news story. Achieving efficiency has to do with the way in which information is presented rather than the amount of information. A long article may be more efficiently written than a shorter one. They key is how much information gets to the reader and how quickly.

Clarity is also a prized characteristic of journalistic writing. Clarity means that a reader can understand what the writer is saying without having to figure out what the words mean or what the writer has in mind. Clear writing does not have to be read a second time to discover its meaning.

As information becomes more detailed and complex, clear writing is harder to produce. Writers who work with complex information sometimes forget to ask themselves some basic questions about how their audience will react to the writing, such as, "Will a reader understand the words I am using?" and "Will the reader be able to picture the information I have if I say it this way or that way?" The first turn toward clarity is for the writer to try to put himself or herself in the place of the reader, asking, "What does the reader know about this information, and what can I do to add to the reader's knowledge and understanding?"

One road to clarity is through simplicity, a basic tenet of modern writing. Journalistic writers should try to write as simply as possible, using the most basic words and sentence structures that are appropriate for the information. This is not to say that every sentence should be a simple sentence or that every word should be a one- or two-syllable word. Variety in sentence structure makes for interesting and readable writing. But using long or unfamiliar words when short, simple words would do is not a sign of good writing and does not present information efficiently or clearly to the reader.

Most sentences that we write are too long, particularly those written on a first draft. Long sentences are often the result of a lack of clarity in the thinking of the writer. That is, a writer is trying to say too many things or the writer has not worked out what pieces of information he or she needs to present. Simply shortening a sentence or breaking one long sentence into two sentences will greatly increase the clarity of a piece of prose.

ADVICE

ectives or adverbs.
housand opinions.
han a long word; a
a long one; a short
paragraph better than a long one.

- Use words precisely. **Mark Twain:** The difference between the right word and the almost right word is the difference between lightning and the lightning bug.

- Mistakes in grammar, spelling, and punctuation obstruct your content.
- Unnecessary words drain the power from your writing.
- Summarize if necessary, but say something.
- Read, analyze, emulate.

Writing Conventions

Whereas some journalistic writing is narrative or chronological, much of it is not. That is, in presenting information about an event or a subject, journalists do not necessarily begin at the beginning or with the first thing that happened. Instead, they are likely to start with the last thing that occurred or, as we will see later in the chapter, the most important information. How, then, do writers make this kind of nonnarrative writing hang together?

Journalism has developed a number of writing conventions for presenting information. Those conventions, or ways of writing, tell us much about what journalists believe is important, and they deserve some attention from students who are beginning to learn this type of writing.

No two writers will approach any event or issue in exactly the same way, so there is no formula that a writer can always use. The information the writer has, the amount of time there is to write the story, and the amount of space available to print the story will be major factors in determining how the story is developed. Still, writers must be aware of the tools and conventions of writing in order to make the story acceptable for the publication for which they are writing. Following are some of those tools and conventions that writers of news stories must use and observe.

Attribution

A major convention of news stories is the use of attribution. Attribution simply means telling readers where the information in a story comes from. Attribution is important because it establishes the news report's credibility. Readers are more likely to believe that the publication is trying to be accurate in its reporting if they know clearly the source of the information. News reports in which the information is properly attributed reflect the professionalism of the publication and its reporters.

Another reason for attributing information in a story is to allow the reader to assess the information by assessing its source. Some sources are more credible than

Quote 10.1

JOSEPH PULITZER

On how to write for an audience

Put it before them briefly so they will read it, clearly so they will appreciate it, picturesquely so they will remember it and, above all, accurately so they will be guided by its light.

Joseph Pulitzer (1847–1911) was editor and publisher of the New York World *and one of the great men of journalism of the nineteenth century.*

others. By telling the reader where information comes from, the news reporter is letting the reader make up his or her mind whether the information can be believed.

In most cases the attribution can be included in a natural or unobtrusive way. Look at these examples:

The county executive said the county is facing a budget crisis.

According to the fire department report, the cause of the fire was faulty electrical wiring.

The jury has stopped deliberating and has retired for the evening, the judge said.

Most of the major facts in a news story should be attributed to some source (unless they come from an eyewitness account by the reporter), but information that is common knowledge to most readers usually does not have to be attributed. For instance, in the sentence, "A heavy cloud of smog hung over the city today, National Weather Service officials said," the attribution is unnecessary and even silly.

The most common verb of attribution is *said. Said* is a neutral word. It simply connotes that words have been spoken; it doesn't say anything about the way in which they were spoken. Consequently, it is the kind of word that journalists ought to be using. It is also unobtrusive in a news story. Even if used repeatedly, it does not jump out at the reader and get in the way of the information that is being transmitted.

Trying to find substitutes for the word *said* is a dangerous game for the journalist. Although there are many words that might be used in its place, writers should remember that they must use words for their exact meaning, not simply for variety's sake. Too often writers misuse these substitutes and create erroneous impressions about what was said. Another danger in the search for substitutes for *said* is that most substitutes are not neutral. If used, they make a statement about how the journalist feels about what was said. For instance, a person accused of a crime may "say" that he is innocent, or he may "claim" that he is innocent. *Claim* carries a negative or doubtful connotation, one which the journalist should not be implying.

Other Writing Conventions

In addition to attribution, journalists must observe a number of other writing conventions, such as:

Short Sentences, Short Paragraphs

News stories use short sentences and short paragraphs. The newswriter tries to get information to the reader as quickly as possible. That is accomplished more easily if the writer uses short sentences. They are easier for the reader to digest. Paragraph length usually should be kept to three sentences or less and to less than 100 words.

Third Person

News stories are usually written in the third person. A writer does not intrude into a story by using first-person pronouns (unless they are part of a direct quotation from one of the story's sources). Except for unusual cases when the writer witnesses a dramatic event or is somehow a participant in that event, he or she should not tell the story from the point of view of the first person.

By the same token, news stories rarely directly address the reader by using the second-person pronoun *you*. Occasionally, lead paragraphs are questions directed at the reader, but this device can be overused quickly, and it is best avoided when you are beginning to learn newswriting.

An Attitude for Accuracy

Accuracy forms the core of the writing process. Journalists expend much energy in making certain that all of the information they have is correct. Achieving accuracy is not just a matter of reporting and writing techniques but also a state of mind that journalists should foster. Journalists should never be satisfied with information about which they have doubts. Journalists have to make every effort to alleviate those doubts and to clear up any discrepancies.

This attitude extends not only to the major information that a journalist has but also to the smallest bits of a story. Making sure that dates and identifications are correct, that numbers in a story add up properly, that locations are correct—all of these things are part of a journalist's job. Journalists should take special care with the names of people to make sure they are spelled correctly.

Journalists strive for accuracy because they realize that their readers and viewers trust them and expect their reports to be accurate. If those reports are not accurate, journalists will lose that trust and eventually lose their readers.

The Inverted Pyramid

Once a writer has gathered the information necessary to begin a story, he or she must decide on the structure of the story. The goal of a proper structure is to get information to the reader quickly and to allow the reader to move through the story easily. The reader must be able to see the relationships between the various pieces of information that the reporter has gathered.

The most common structure for writing news stories is called the inverted pyramid. A daily newspaper or web site contains many stories. Most stories must be written so that readers can get the most information in the least amount of time. The inverted pyramid structure concentrates the most interesting and important information at the top of the story so that readers can get the information they need or want and then go on to another story if they choose. Headlines and lead paragraphs should be written to describe what the story contains as succinctly and as interestingly as possible.

The lead, or first paragraph, is the focal point of the basic news story. It is a simple statement of the point of the entire story. Lead paragraphs are discussed more fully in the next section of this chapter.

The inverted pyramid

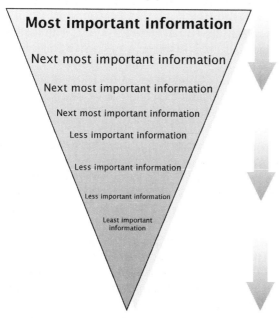

The second paragraph is almost as important as the lead. It takes some of the information and adds to it. A good second paragraph will put the readers into a story and will give them incentive to read on.

The body of the inverted pyramid story adds detail to information that has been introduced in the lead and the first two or three paragraphs. The body should provide more information, supporting evidence, context, and illumination in the form of more details, direct and indirect quotes, and other description.

The major concept of the inverted pyramid structure is to put the most important and latest information toward the top of the story. As the story continues, the writer should be using information of less importance. There are two reasons for writing a story this way. One is what we have already talked about: Putting the most important information at the top allows a reader to decide quickly whether or not to stick with the story.

The inverted pyramid also organizes the information in such a way that the reader can be efficient. Not every reader will read all of every story in a

FIGURE 10.1   The Inverted Pyramid The inverted pyramid is the writing structure used for news stories by most news organizations for print and web journalism. It demands that the writer put information in descending order of importance rather than in chronological order. Consequently, if a reporter were covering a football game, he or she would put the final score of the game in the first, or lead, paragraph.

newspaper. In fact, one of the strengths of a newspaper is that it offers a wide variety of information that will appeal to many people. The inverted pyramid structure for news stories allows the readers to get as much of the most important information in that story as quickly as possible; it also allows the readers to stop reading and go on to something else when they have satisfied themselves with that story.

The inverted pyramid structure demands that the writer make judgments about the importance of the information that he or she has gathered—judgments based on the news values discussed in the previous chapter.

The Lead Paragraph

The most important part of the news story is the first, or lead (pronounced LEED), paragraph. The lead should tell the reader the most important information in the story. It should be written so that the reader will be interested in going further into the story. A lead on a story might simply say:

> The Midville County Commission voted against raising property taxes last night.

An otherwise good story will not be read by many people if the lead is dull or confusing. The lead is the first part of the story a reader will come in contact with after the headline, and if the lead does not hold the reader's interest and attention, little else will.

In writing the lead, a reporter must make a judgment on what to put in a lead based on the news values discussed in the previous chapter. The writer must get information to the reader quickly but also accurately and interestingly. Accuracy, speed, and entertainment are finely balanced in a good lead paragraph.

Leads on news stories generally contain at least four of the five Ws and H that were discussed in the previous chapter. Those four elements are who, what, where, and when. A lead paragraph may emphasize any one of these elements, depending on the facts that are available to the reporter, but usually all four of these questions are answered in the lead. Sometimes the lead will contain or emphasize the why and the how of a story, but such stories are unusual.

Lead paragraphs should say neither too much nor too little. One of the mistakes that beginning news writers often make is that of trying to put too much in a lead. A lead should not be crowded with information; rather, it should tell enough to answer the reader's major questions about a story in an interesting and efficient way.

Leads can come in a wide variety of forms and styles. Although journalistic conventions restrict what writers can do in some ways, there is still plenty of room for creativity. The following types of leads and examples demonstrate some of the ways writers can approach a story.

The straight news lead is a just-the-facts approach. It delivers information quickly and concisely to the reader and does not try to dress up the information. For instance:

> Two people were killed and four were injured today when a truck collided with a passenger car on Interstate 59 near the Cottondale exit.

This straight news approach is the most common type of news lead and lends itself to most of the stories a reporter will have to cover. Because of this, a couple of technical rules have been developed for this kind of story. Such leads should be one sentence long, and they should contain about thirty words (a maximum of thirty-three words). It is particularly important for the beginning writer to master this one-sentence, thirty-word approach because of the discipline of thinking that it requires. A writer must learn that words cannot be wasted, particularly at the beginning of the story.

The summary lead is one in which there may be more than one major fact to be covered. Again, the one-sentence, thirty-word approach should be used even though such an approach may require even more effort on the part of the writer. For example:

> A tractor-trailer truck carrying dangerous chemicals crashed on Interstate 59 today, killing one person, injuring four others, and forcing the evacuation of several hundred people from their homes.

The emphasis in this kind of lead is on outlining the full story for the readers in a brief paragraph. Writers using summary leads need to take care that they do not crowd their leads with too much detail but also that they do not generalize too much. A balance should be achieved between including enough detail to make the story interesting and enough general material to avoid confusing the reader.

Up to this point, we have been dealing with straight leads for the most part. Straight leads give the who, what, when, where, how, and why elements of the story to the reader in a straightforward, no-frills fashion. Other types of leads exist, however, and the good news writer should be aware of when they can be used most effectively.

The blind lead is a lead in which the people in the story are not named. The two previous examples are blind leads. This kind of lead is common when the people in the story are not well known. In the last lead about the accident, we assume that none of the people involved in the accident are well known. If one of the people hurt was the mayor of the city, we would not want to write a blind lead. We would want to mention his name in the lead.

The direct address lead is one in which the writer speaks directly to the reader. The main characteristic of this lead is the word *you*, present or implied.

> If you're a property owner in the city, the City Council is about to take at least $50 more from you each year.

The direct address lead is a good way of getting the reader's attention, but it should be used sparingly. It is also important to follow up a direct address lead quickly in the second and third paragraphs with information about the lead. By implication, the direct address lead promises the reader some immediate information.

The question lead attempts to draw the reader into the story by asking a question.

> Why doesn't the president tell Congress how he stands on the pay increase issue?

The question lead has some of the same advantages and disadvantages as the direct address lead. It is a good way of getting the attention of the reader. On the other

INVERTED PYRAMID CHECKLIST

When you write an inverted pyramid news story, use the following checklist to make sure that you have done it correctly.

Information should be presented in descending order of importance.

____ Leads
- One sentence
- 30–35 words maximum
- Lead tells the most important information in the story and gives specific facts.

____ Second paragraph
- Expand or develop some idea introduced in the lead.
- Should not drop the story into a chronological narrative.

____ Attribution
- All major information should be attributed unless it is commonly known or unless the information itself strongly implies the source.
- Don't dump a string of direct quotations on the reader.
- Direct quotations should be no more than two sentences long.
- Direct quotations and their attribution should be punctuated properly. Example: "John did not go with her," he said.
- Elements of a direct quotation should be in the proper sequence, as in the preceding example: **direct quote, speaker, verb.**

____ AP style
- Always check numbers, dates, locations, titles, and so on.

____ Check the following
- Pronoun–antecedent agreement
- it, its, it's
- Avoid these structures: "it is . . .", "there is . . .", "there are . . .". They are passive and vague.

- Use the **past tense,** not the present.
- Comma splices and run-on sentences are grammatically incorrect. For example,

   He picked up the ball, he ran down the field.

   Sally does not know where he is he is not here.

- Don't make plurals by adding 's.

____ Short paragraphs
- Any paragraph longer than three sentences is definitely too long; any paragraph that is three sentences is probably too long.

____ Wordiness
- Check for too much verbiage, redundancies, unnecessary repetitions, and so on.

____ Name, title
- When you put the title before a name, **do not** separate them with commas, such as

   (WRONG): **Game warden, Brad Fisher, arrested the trespassers.**

- When the name comes before the title, the title should be set off by commas.

   Brad Fisher, the game warden, arrested the trespassers.

____ Transitions
- Use them to tie your paragraphs together.
- Don't jump from one subject to another in a new paragraph without giving the reader some warning.

____ Names
- Check them once more to make sure they are spelled correctly.

hand, it can easily be overused. It, too, promises to give the reader some immediate information, and the writer should make good on that promise.

The direct address and the question lead also imply that the story has some compelling information for the reader. That's why writers should be careful to use them only when that is the case. Otherwise, the reader will likely be disappointed.

The direct quote lead uses a direct quotation to introduce the story and to gain the reader's attention. The direct quote, of course, should be something that one of the participants in the story said, and it should be compelling and informative enough to serve as the lead.

> "A city that cares!"
> That's what mayoral candidate George Bramble promised today as he hit the campaign trail in . . .

Developing the Story

The inverted pyramid requires that writers make judgments not only about what should be at the beginning of the story but also about the relative importance of all the information they present in the story. In other words, writers must not only decide what the most important information is for the lead, but they must also decide what the second and third most important pieces of information are. Developing the story in a logical and coherent way requires much skill and practice.

If the lead paragraph is the most important part of the news story, the second paragraph is the second most important part of the story. In some ways, it is almost as important as the lead but for different reasons.

A lead paragraph cannot contain all of the information in a news story. If it is written well, it will inform the reader, but it will also raise certain questions in the reader's mind about the story. Chief among the roles of the second (and succeeding) paragraphs is to answer these questions. The writer does this by providing additional information about the story. The writer must decide what information is most important and what will help the reader to understand the story.

One method that writers use to make these judgments is to put themselves in the place of the reader and ask, "If I were a reader of this story, what would I want to know next?" For instance, a lead might say

> Authorities are searching for a state prison inmate who escaped from a work crew at the Kidder Correctional Facility yesterday.

That lead gives some information about the story, but it also raises a number of questions, such as:

Who was the inmate?

Why was he in prison?

How long had he been there and how long was his sentence?

How did he escape?

Where is the search for him taking place?

Is the inmate dangerous?

What does he look like?

How have the prison officials explained his escape?

These are just a few of the questions that could be asked about this story. The writer must answer these questions in a logical and coherent manner that will result in a unified and interesting story. The order in which these questions are answered will depend on the specific information that the writer has to work with.

The writer will probably want to give the name of the inmate quickly and the circumstances of the escape. Beyond that, the type of information the writer has will dictate the order in which the questions are answered. For instance, the second paragraph might go something like this:

> Billy Wayne Hodge, 22, who was convicted two years ago of armed robbery, walked away from his work crew yesterday afternoon at about 3 P.M., according to prison officials. The crew was picking up trash along Highway 69 about four miles from the prison at the time of the escape.

This paragraph answers some of the questions but leaves others unanswered. Even though a second paragraph can be longer than the lead, it still cannot answer all of the questions a lead can raise. Now the writer will have to decide what questions he or she will answer in the third paragraph. Again, those decisions will be based on the kind of information the writer has. The writer might want to say something about the search for the prisoner. For instance:

> Sheriff Will Harper said last night that he thought the prisoner was still in the thick woods in the area of the escape. He said deputies would patrol the area tonight and a full-scale search would begin early today.

Or the writer may expand on the circumstances of the escape:

> "It appears that one of our guards wasn't watching the prisoners as closely as he should have been," Sam Mayer, the prison warden, said. "There were 15 men in the work crew and only two guards."

Either choice might be appropriate, depending on the circumstances of the story and the writer's preference. Still, the writer has not answered all of the questions raised by the lead, but the story is becoming more complete.

Quote 10.2

NATHANIEL HAWTHORNE

On the power of words

Words—so innocent and powerless as they are, as standing in a dictionary, how potent for good and evil they become in the hands of one who knows how to combine them.

Nathaniel Hawthorne (1804–1864) was an American novelist whose books include The House of Seven Gables *and* The Scarlet Letter.

Feature Styles

Dividing feature stories from news stories is misleading. The two actually have a great deal in common. The difference is in emphasis. The styles commonly used for feature stories assume that the reader has more time to read. They still require a central theme. The writer must be able to summarize the point of the story. But the writing may require that the reader go further in order to fully understand the point of the story. Of course, that means the writer must sustain interest for a longer period of time.

Feature writing is a way for both readers and writers to get away from the relevant facts-only approach of most news stories. Feature stories generally contain more detail and description. They go beyond most news stories by trying to discover the interesting or important side of an event that may not be covered by the six basic news values.

Feature stories are also a way of humanizing the news, of breathing life into a publication. Most features center around people and their activities and interests. A good way for a feature writer to approach the job is to believe that every person is worth at least one good feature story.

Feature stories not only vary in content but also vary in structure. The following is a brief discussion of some of the structures a feature writer may use. Feature stories have no single structure that is used most of the time. Feature writers are freer to adapt whatever structure is suitable to the story they are trying to tell.

Anecdotal Features

This style usually begins with a story of some kind and usually will follow with a statement of facts to support the point of the story. Quotations, anecdotes, and facts then weave in and out of one another throughout the story. The trick is to keep the quotes and the anecdotes relevant to the point of focus and to keep the story interesting without making it trite.

Suspended Interest Features

This style is often used for producing some special effect. Usually it is used for a short story with a punch line. But sometimes it is drawn out into a much longer story. In either case, the style requires the writer to lead readers through a series of paragraphs that may raise questions in the minds of the readers while at the same time keeping readers interested in solving the puzzle. At the end, the story is resolved in an unexpected way.

Question and Answer

This is a simple style used for a specific effect. An explanatory paragraph usually starts the story. Then the interviewer's questions are followed by the interviewee's answers word for word. Using this style requires articulate participants in the interview. Sometimes, however, it makes clear how inarticulate an interviewee is about a topic. In any case, it is effective for showing the reader an unfiltered view of the interviewee's use of language.

Characteristics of Feature Writing

To the reader, the feature story seems to exhibit a more relaxed style of writing than a news story. It may be easier to read than a news story, and because of its content it may be more entertaining. Feature writers, however, work just as hard and are just as disciplined as news writers. They may work under a slightly different set of rules than news writers, but the goals of a feature writer are essentially the same ones that a news writer has: to tell a story accurately and to write well.

The main thing that sets feature stories apart from news stories is the greater amount of detail and description features contain. This difference is the backbone of a good feature story. Whereas the news story writer wishes to transmit a basic set of facts to the reader as quickly as possible, the feature writer tries to enhance those facts with details and description so that the reader will be able to see a more complete picture of an event or a person. For instance, whereas the news writer might refer to "a desk" in a news story, the feature writer will want to go beyond that simple reference by telling the reader something more, such as "a mahogany desk" or "a dark mahogany desk." Or better yet, the writer might rely on verbs to enhance the descriptions of the subject: "A large, soft executive chair enveloped him as he sat behind a dark mahogany desk."

The three major kinds of descriptions that should be contained in a feature story are description of actions, description of people, and description of places. All of these are important to a good feature story, but the description that makes for the strongest writing is generally the description of actions. Telling about events, telling what has happened, telling what people are doing—these things make compelling reading. Descriptions of this type help readers to see a story, not just read about it. In addition, feature writers should make sure that readers see the people in their stories, just as the writers themselves have seen the people. Feature writers also need to describe adequately the places where the stories occur. Readers need an idea of the surroundings of a story to draw a complete picture in their minds.

A couple of tips will help writers attain more vivid descriptions in their stories. One is the reliance on nouns and verbs. Beginning writers sometimes feel that they should use as many adjectives and adverbs as possible to enhance their writing, and in doing so, they rely on dull and overused nouns and verbs. That approach is a wrong turn on the road to producing lively, descriptive writing. A second tip for writers is to remember the five senses. Often writers simply describe the way things look, and they forget about the way things sound, feel, taste, or smell. Incorporating the five senses into a story will help make a description come alive for a reader.

Feature stories often contain more quotations and dialogue than news stories. News writers use direct quotations to enhance and illuminate the facts they are trying to present. Feature writers go beyond this by using quotations to say something about the people who are in their stories. Quoted material is generally used much more freely in feature stories, although, as in news stories, dumping a load of quotes on a reader without a break often puts too heavy a burden on the reader. Dialogue and dialect are other devices a feature writer may use if the story calls for them.

Quote 10.3

THOMAS MANN

On writing

A writer is somebody for whom writing is more difficult than it is for other people.

Thomas Mann (1875–1955) was a novelist and winner of the Nobel Prize for Literature in 1929. His novels include Death in Venice *(1912) and* The Magic Mountain *(1924).*

One of the charms of feature writing for many writers is that they can put more of themselves into a story. Unlike news stories, in which writers stay out of sight as much as they can, feature writers are somewhat freer to inject themselves and their opinions into a story. Although feature writers have a little more latitude in this regard, they must use this latitude wisely and make sure that a feature story does not become a story about themselves rather than about the subject they are trying to cover.

Read, Analyze, Emulate

The following pages contain examples of various kinds of news stories and some writing exercises that will help in learning how to write in a journalistic fashion. You should pay close attention to the example stories. They demonstrate many of the basic tenants of writing that are discussed in this and other chapters in this book. Read them carefully and try to figure out why the writer put them together in that particular way.

Once you have done this, you should try to emulate the writing in these examples. This technique is called "modeling." Try to make the stories that you write look and read like the stories in the examples. You may even want to use some of the same wording if it is appropriate. By doing this, you can get a feel as to how news stories should be written. More importantly, you can gain some confidence in putting together your own stories.

QUESTIONS FOR DISCUSSION

1. How does writing news and features differ from what you have been taught about writing English themes?
2. Why is attribution so important in news writing?
3. The author says the most common and useful verb of attribution is "said." What are the reasons for that statement? Do you agree?

RELATED WEB SITES

Power of Words, www.projo.com/words

Poynter Online's Writing and Editing Tipsheets, http://poynteronline.org/content/content_view.asp?id=31907

Writers on Writing, www.nytimes.com/books/specials/writers.html

Writers Write: The Write Resource, www.writerswrite.com

READINGS AND REFERENCES

Baker, B. (2001). *Newsthinking: The secret of making your facts fall into place.* Boston: Allyn and Bacon.

Botts, J. (1994). *The language of news: A journalist's pocket reference.* Ames, IA: Iowa State University Press.

Clark, R. P. (1995). *Free to write: A journalist teaches young writers.* Portsmouth, NH: Heinemann Educational Books.

Franklin, J. (1994). *Writing for story: Craft secrets of dramatic nonfiction.* New York: Plume.

Hennessy, B. (1997). *Writing feature articles* (3rd ed.). Oxford: Heineman.

Knight, R. M. (1998). *The craft of clarity: A journalistic approach to good writing.* Ames, IA: Iowa State University Press.

Murray, D. M. (2000). *Writing to deadline: The journalist at work.* Portsmouth, NH: Heinemann.

Strunk, W., Jr., & White, E. B. (1999). *The elements of style* (4th ed.). New York: Macmillan.

Zinsser, W. (2001). *On writing well.* 25th anniversary edition. New York: Harper Resource.

EXAMPLE 10.1

Inverted pyramid news story

The following story demonstrates many of the qualities of writing and the inverted pyramid structure that are discussed in this chapter. Read the story carefully paying particular attention to the structure of the story (lead and second paragraphs) and the way in which information is attributed to its sources.

The Brown Middle School soccer team had a successful trip to the state tournament this weekend in Montgomery and a scare on the bus trip home.

The team bus skidded off Highway 59 near Risterville after a deer ran across the front of the bus. No one was seriously injured in the wreck, but some of the children suffered cuts and bruises.

Bus driver A. P. Hill said the deer dashed in front of the bus before he could stop.

"The thing just came up at us all of a sudden," he said.

The accident occurred about 8:15 P.M., according to state troopers who were called to the scene.

"All the kids were pretty good about it, and of course were glad nobody was hurt," Rose Midgelin, one of the troopers on the scene, said.

The team had been returning from a weekend soccer tournament in Montgomery where it had won three out of four games and finished second in its division.

That finish, according to team coach Randy Fowler, is the best that any middle school has ever done at a state level.

"They played with a lot of spirit and showed a lot of skill," Fowler said."Our doing this well will help us continue to build a solid soccer program for this area."

In its last game on Saturday, the team beat Dorchester Middle School 3–2 for a second place overall.

"I think we probably learned a lot, too. It's good to see how other teams from other areas play the game," Ray Johnson, one of the co-captains of the team, said.

After the accident, state troopers called a wrecker and pulled the bus out of the ditch. The team arrived in Tuscaloosa about midnight on Saturday.

EXAMPLE 10.2
Inverted pyramid news story

The following story demonstrates many of the qualities of writing and the inverted pyramid structure that are discussed in this chapter. Read the story carefully paying particular attention to the structure of the story (lead and second paragraphs) and the way in which information is attributed to its sources.

A teenager described as a "good guy" who "wouldn't hurt anybody" took a teacher and about 15 students hostage at gunpoint Monday in a local high school classroom, gradually releasing his captives until the standoff ended more than eight hours later.

The suspect, Eli Dean, 18, did not fire a shot during the siege at Central High School, and no injuries were reported.

By midafternoon, Dean, who recently was suspended from school for pranks, had released all but five students from a classroom, and early in the evening released four more hostages, state police Sgt. Martin Jenkins said.

The siege ended about 7:30 P.M. EST when Dean surrendered and released the last student, he said.

The youth was armed with a pistol, believed to be a .44-caliber revolver taken from his stepfather's room, Jenkins said, but no shots were fired throughout the ordeal.

Dean, twice suspended from the school in the last two weeks for setting off a fire alarm and breaking a window, went to the school to speak to Melody Money, 43, a teacher who had counseled him about previous trouble at the school, the state police sergeant said.

Dean walked into Money's classroom about 11:10 A.M. and brandished the revolver in front of her and about 15 students, Jenkins said.

The suspect was persuaded to release most of his captives soon after the siege began, but state police could not give an exact count of the number of hostages freed.

Dean continued holding six students and Money until about 2 P.M., when a freshman, Stacy Medelli, was allowed to leave, followed soon by the teacher, Jenkins said.

Dean made no demands throughout the standoff.

A fellow student, Amanda Garr, said she believed the young gunman was "upset" at the recent suspensions but expressed astonishment at his reaction.

"Eli, to me, is the best guy anybody could ever ask for," Garr said. "Something got in him and he's gone crazy about it. He's a very good guy. He wouldn't hurt anybody."

Garr said she and other students at first thought there had been a bomb threat when the school was evacuated and a police SWAT team moved into place, but later "we found out it was Eli and everybody started crying."

The youth's parents and stepfather, Rocky Williams, were called to the school to help police negotiators. Williams said he believes Dean took his .44-caliber revolver from their home.

EXAMPLE 10.3

Preview story

This story is a typical preview story—one that announces an upcoming event. It is one of the simplest news stories to report and write. The basic information about the event is contained in the lead paragraph. The reporter has also talked with someone about the event and included direct quotes in the story.

The Emory and Henry Canoe Club will hold its organizational meeting for the 2003–2004 year on Thursday, June 5 at 7 P.M. in 314 Ferguson Center.

The major items of business will be to elect officers for the year and plan trips and other activities, according to Merrill Lynch, president of the club.

"We are looking forward to an exciting year," Lynch, a junior in rocket science, said. "We hope to attract several new members this year."

Lynch said the club is open to any student, staff or faculty member who is interested in canoeing. Lynch emphasized that members do not have to be experienced in canoeing to join the club.

Last year, the club had 12 active members. Several of those have graduated, but Lynch said he hopes more than half of them will be returning to participate in the club's activities.

Lynch said the club's members usually take at least one major white-water canoe trip each semester.

"There are a number of great locations for canoeing within just a short drive from Emory," he said. "One of the things we will want to do at the meeting is to decide where we will go this summer." Lynch mentioned the possibility of going somewhere near the Great Smoky Mountains National Park.

Lynch said the club will be conducting some instructional classes in canoeing before going on the trip.

"We usually go to one of the local creeks and make sure everybody knows the basics," he said.

EXAMPLE 10.4

Event story

This story is about an event that the reporter attended. Notice that some of the information is not attributed to a source, indicating that the reporter was there. As with the other examples, notice that the basic conventions of journalistic writing are observed. (In case you think you recognize this story, it was used in one of the exercises in the previous chapter.)

> CHILLICOTHE, Mo.—A jury has recommended a 69-year-old woman be sentenced to death for the murders of four transient farm workers whose bodies were found buried in northwestern Missouri last year.
>
> Jurors in Livingston County Circuit Court deliberated more than three hours before making the recommendation Tuesday night in the case of Faye Copeland, whom the jury had convicted Saturday of five counts of first-degree murder.
>
> The jury of eight women and four men recommended Copeland be sentenced to life in prison without parole on the fifth murder conviction.
>
> Circuit Judge E. Richard Webber must decide whether to accept the jury's recommendations or to sentence Copeland to life in prison. He ordered a pre-sentence investigation.
>
> If sentenced to death, Copeland will become the oldest person on Missouri's death row.
>
> Copeland's attorney, public defender David Miller, has said he will file a motion for a new trial. Miller said he would appeal the court's refusal to allow a psychologist to testify about "battered-wife syndrome."
>
> Miller had argued Faye Copeland was dominated by her 74-year-old husband, Ray, who is awaiting trial on the same charges, and had only a minor role in the crimes.
>
> Ray Copeland's trial is scheduled to begin Jan. 24 but the court first must determine whether he is mentally competent to assist in his own defense. His attorneys contend Ray Copeland suffers from senile dementia, including an organic brain disorder.
>
> The bodies of the victims were found last year in shallow graves in barns or dumped in wells on farms in Livingston County where Ray Copeland had worked. Investigators said the victims had been shot to death. No bodies were found on the couple's farm near Mooresville, about 65 miles northeast of Kansas City.
>
> The Copelands originally were arrested on charges of conspiracy in an alleged fraudulent cattle-buying conspiracy.
>
> Authorities contended the couple hired the transients to work as cattle buyers, then killed and buried them. Prosecutors said the Copelands netted $32,000 by reselling the cattle. The fraud charges were dismissed after the murder charges were filed.

EXAMPLE 10.5

Speech story

Covering speeches is one of the standard jobs of a journalist. Pay particular attention to the lead paragraph. Note that it includes something specific that the speaker has said, not just the fact that he spoke. Also notice how the direct quotations are handled. They usually follow an indirect quotation that explains or introduces what the speaker has said. Then the writer has punctuated this introduction with a pithy direct quotation.

A former official of the National Aeronautic and Space Administration told a campus audience Wednesday that it was time for America to "turn its head back toward the earth" and abandon manned space flight.

Jack Cotter, who recently retired after working for more than 30 years at the space agency, said the manned space program was too costly and Americans are not getting any benefits from it.

"I would like to think otherwise," he said to an audience of more than 150 students, faculty and members of the community. "After all, I spent most of my career helping us get into space."

Cotter was the third speaker in this semester's "Science in Daily Life" series. Joseph Edison, professor of biology at Spring Hill University in Dayton, Tenn., will conclude the series on Monday at 7:30 P.M. in the Board of Visitors room of the Van Dyke Center.

Cotter pointed to the *Challenger* accident of 1986 and the *Columbia* accident of 2003 as evidence that the manned space program has become too costly. "Space is a very dangerous place," he said. "The folks at NASA don't really want to talk about that because they do not want people questioning what they do."

Cotter, who was an assistant program director on the NASA team that put the first man on the moon in 1969, said America got into the space program largely because the Russians were already there.

"It was a race, pure and simple," he said. "We had to beat the Russians."

He described how President John F. Kennedy pledged to America that it would land the first man on the moon in 1961. "Kennedy said that would happen before the decade was out," Cotter said. "Then it became our job to make it happen."

Cotter joined NASA in 1966 after a tour of duty in Vietnam. He had earned a degree in mechanical engineering from the University of Fargo before going to Vietnam.

"Those were exciting times," he said. "Just about everybody supported us, and we could get just about anything we wanted from Congress. Remember, we had to beat the Russians, and it was during the Cold War."

Cotter called what developed inside the agency a "cowboy atmosphere" where the tendency was to take undue chances with people's lives. That is when he began to have his doubts about the wisdom of what the agency was doing.

"I stayed with the agency because I believed that if we did it right, it would be worth doing," he said. "I believed that a lot of people would benefit from it."

Cotter said the *Challenger* and *Columbia* accidents convinced him that it was simply too dangerous.

"We got to the moon," he said, "but we are never going to get to Mars. It's just too far away."

EXAMPLE 10.6

Obituary story

The obituary is another basic form of journalistic writing. This story begins with the details of the death and the funeral arrangements—the news that readers are likely to want first. The story goes on to give details of the person's life, quoting someone who knows the person and can speak about her. It ends with information about survivors and how the family would like for friends to respond. An obituary story sometimes uses more formal language than is found in other news stories. (Do you know why? Answer follows.)

> Mattie Harrison, longtime organist for the Forest Lake United Methodist Church, died at her home on Wednesday after a long illness. She was 84 years old.
>
> Harrison, a lifelong resident of Midville, had battled cancer in her last years but had managed to remain active until just a few months ago.
>
> "She never gave up," John Hall, senior minister at the church, said. "She always had such a wonderful spirit. She was such an inspiration. We used to love to see her coming through the door."
>
> A memorial service is planned for her on Saturday at 2 P.M. at the church.
>
> Harrison was born Mattie Chalmers and grew up on the west side of town and attended the old City High School, graduating in 1935. She attended Midville State University and in 1940 received a degree in elementary education. She also married Alexander Harrison, a local plumber, that year.
>
> She had played the piano and organ since childhood, and after she began married life, she gave private lessons.
>
> "I imagine that she taught hundreds, if not thousands, of Midville children how to read music and play the piano," Hall said.
>
> She began playing the organ at the church when it first acquired one in the 1950s, and she was the regular organist for the next 35 years. She was also a member of the Forest Lake Women's Book Club.
>
> Harrison's husband died in 1995, just after they had celebrated their 55th wedding anniversary.
>
> Harrison is survived by two daughters, Estelle Wilson of Abingdon, Va., and Hollice Wakefield of Midville; one son, Alexander Harrison Jr., of Pleasant Ridge, Tennessee; ten grandchildren; and six great-grandchildren.
>
> In lieu of flowers, the family has requested that contributions be made to the Mattie Harrison Scholarship Fund at Midville State University of the organ fund at Forest Lake United Methodist Church.

Answer: Many people clip and save obituaries and expect them to be written more formally.

Writing Exercises

EXERCISE 10.1

Using verbs

Autobiography
Write a 150-word autobiography in the third person (do not use *I*, *me*, or any other first-person pronoun.)

DO NOT READ THESE INSTRUCTIONS UNTIL YOU HAVE FINISHED WRITING.

Count the number of linking verbs and multiply by –5; count the number of passive voice constructions and multiply by –10; add those together to get a negative score. Count the number of active, descriptive verbs used in the active voice and multiply by 5; give yourself an extra 5 points if your first verb was an active, descriptive verb. Add the two scores (positive and negative numbers). Do you have a positive or negative score?

EXERCISE 10.2

Information

Instructions—1
Tell step-by-step how to do something. For example, tell how to change the oil in a car, use a tape recorder, or build a fire. Use simple terms and simple sentences so that anyone who can read could understand it. The following is an example of such a set of directions.

In order to drive a nail into a piece of wood, follow these steps:

1. Be sure the wood is on a solid surface.
2. Check the nail you are using to make sure it is straight; if it is bent, discard it.
3. Hold the pointed end of the nail against the wood with the thumb and the first finger.
   And so on.

The activity that you describe should have at least seven steps.

EXERCISE 10.3

Wordiness

Rewriting
Rewrite the following letter using simpler language. Make sure that you include all of the information contained in the original letter.

Dear Stockholder:

In accordance with company policies and the federal law, this letter is to inform you of the general annual meeting of the stockholders of this company which will be held on the 30th day of March of this year. The place of the meeting will be in the ballroom of the Waldorf Hotel, which is located at 323 Lexington Avenue, in New York. The beginning time of the meeting will be at nine o'clock in the morning on the 30th of March.

The agenda for this meeting includes a number of items and actions of great import to the company and its stockholders. The election of officers for the company's board of directors will take place beginning at approximately half past ten o'clock. This election follows the annual reports on the company's activities and financial position which will be presented by the president of the company and the chairman of the board of directors. Other items on the agenda include discussions of the company's operations in the foreign arena and the possibilities for investments in new areas of technology. Time will also be appropriated for discussions of general concerns of stockholders and for the answering of questions from stockholders directed to the company's officers. It is the sincere wish of the company's board of directors and officers that you will be able to attend this most important and hopefully informative meeting. The input of the company's stockholders is an important part of this company's operation and planning for the future.

Sincerely,

The Company President

EXERCISE 10.4
Wordiness

Paraphrasing
Rewrite the following by paraphrasing the direct quotations. Make what you write no more than half the length of the original quotation. Try to include most of the information that is in the quotation. The first quotation has been paraphrased to give you an example of what is expected.

Example:

Tom Nelson, president of the citywide Parent Teachers Association: "Our major concern this year will be security in the schools, particularly in the high schools. We will be working with school officials on ways we can help create a safer environment for the education of our children. A number of incidents in the past year have been very disturbing to many parents. We are going to try to provide a way for those parents to make a real difference in their local schools."

Paraphrase

Tom Nelson, president of the city Parent Teachers Association, said the chief concern of the organization this year would be security, particularly in the high schools. Nelson said parents would be working with school officials to make the schools safer.

Martin Goldsmith, general manager of the local public radio station: "Our goal in this year's fundraising effort is to raise $100,000, which will be about 15 percent more than we raised last year. The money we are seeking—this $100,000—will go toward our programming efforts. We spend about $130,000 buying programs each year for the station, and those costs are going up each year. There is a lot that our audience would like to have on the station, and this is the way for them to help pay for it."

Marilyn Wall, president of the Walls Tire Co., a locally owned tire manufacturer: "The current year has been a good one for our company and its employees. Our orders were up about 20 percent over last year, and we were able to recall many of the employees that we had had to lay off during the past three years. In addition, we have expanded our workforce to add about 20 new jobs in various parts of the factory."

Marsha Moss, director of the local symphony orchestra: "The response of the audience to last night's concert was particularly gratifying. They seemed to enjoy everything that we put on the program. I can tell you that playing before an audience like that is a lot more fun than playing to a bunch of critics. It's good to know that people appreciate the many hours of hard work that this orchestra puts into each concert that we do."

EXERCISE 10.5

Wordiness

Phrases

Edit all unnecessary words from the following expressions.

wore a white goatee on his chin

throughout the length and width of the entire nation

was positively identified

appeared to be ill

a dead body was found

in the city of Los Angeles

cost the sum of ten dollars

broke an existing rule

for the month of May

for a short space of time

an old pioneer

the present incumbent

will draw to a close

at the corner of Sixth and Elm streets

for the purpose of shocking

EXERCISE 10.6

Wordiness

Sentences

The following sentences use too many words. Edit them carefully to reduce the number of words, but do not cut out important information. If necessary, rewrite them completely.

1. He was kind of a large man, heavy in weight, and not a very bright guy whose ability to think things through thoroughly was pretty limited.

2. The actual photograph was taken by John Smith and showed a room that was littered with paper and other items and furnished with furniture of a cheap quality.

3. Always confused by any kind of mathematical problem, Sally, for no reason that anyone could ever figure out, signed up for one of the hardest and most difficult math courses in the entire curriculum.

4. His past performance in not being able to win people over to his particular point of view certainly indicated to us that he was very likely to do poorly as a political candidate running for mayor.

5. My future plans include enrolling in a college or university where I can study the field of journalism and can improve my natural-born talent for writing.

6. The committee, meeting in executive session with no one else there, made the decision to cease and desist the practice of requiring members of the organization to pay money to attend all of the functions of the organization.

EXERCISE 10.7

Constructing an inverted pyramid news story

The following is a set of notes that a reporter has made about a local flood. Use these notes to construct an inverted pyramid news story.

Flooding
reporter's notes

Heavy rains for three days; flooding on several parts of the Cornish River near West Harperville; one bridge out along Highway 14
75 people evacuated from homes; 200 houses have received some damage
one church, Cornish United Methodist, had basement flooded

Kyle Render, Ticonderoga County Emergency Management Service
"Worst flooding in 15 years; all crew are out seeing if there are people or animals that we can pick up; don't know of anyone who is trapped, but we aren't sure about everybody."

Police chief Billy Herbert says one person reported missing; Carl Carter; reported missing by daughter; his is one of the houses that is under water up to the second story now.

Bridge along highway 27 okay, passable, according to police

Herbert: "We are urging people to stay away from the area. Don't go down there looking. We need to keep the roads clear in case we find someone that we need to get out quickly."

Keith Schneider, pastor of Cornish UMC, said church basement contained a lot of furniture that is ruined; church still under water; won't be able to go in until waters recede. "My heart is broken about this. These people just finished paying off the mortgage last year before I became pastor. Now they're going to have to face some pretty hefty repair bills."

Morley MacMann, farmer whose fields were flooded. "Fortunately the water didn't get to my house. I guess we can be thankful of that. But these are my best fields that are under water now. I was going to start planting in a day or two, but now I'll have to wait until the field is okay."

Police say people who need shelter can go to the First Presbyterian Church in West Harperville; a variety of assistance offices will be set up there.

Flooding occurred just after midnight when water began to flow over the banks at Niles Bend; just as that was happening came two hours of torrential rain; weather service said three inches fell in the area during that two hours; during the past three days there has been seven inches of rain in the area.

EXERCISE 10.8

Modeling a news story

Read the following story carefully taking note of how it is written. The story is a standard inverted pyramid news story and exhibits many of the writing conventions discussed in this chapter. On the next page is a set of notes about a trial that is very similar to the one in this story. Use those notes to write an inverted pyramid news story that reads very much like this one. The purpose of doing this modeling is to give you some practice and confidence in being able to handle the inverted pyramid structure of news writing.

> A Brownsville woman received a 20-year prison sentence Monday for her part in a robbery of the Trust National Bank last year.
>
> Anne Evenson, who lived with her mother on Mine Road before the robbery, wept softly as Circuit Court Judge John Sloan read the verdict to a packed courtroom. The 20-year sentence means that she could be eligible for parole in seven years.
>
> Evenson's attorney, Harriet Braden, said after the court recessed that she is planning to file an appeal.
>
> "I think that we will be able to demonstrate that Miss Evenson was an innocent victim and did not receive a fair trial," she said.
>
> Braden said the appeal will be filed sometime next week.
>
> District Attorney Ed Sims said, however, that he thought the trial had been a fair one and that Evenson had received the sentence she deserved.
>
> Evenson was convicted last week of first degree robbery for driving the get-away car for her boyfriend, Reggie Holder, after he robbed the bank of almost $29,000.

Holder was convicted last month for first-degree robbery and also received a 20-year sentence.

Evenson testified during her trial that she drove the car for Holder but that she thought she was simply taking him to the bank to make a deposit and pay some bills.

Having read the story on the previous page, you should use these notes to construct a similar story.

Hanging Jack

- Jack Carr; circuit court Judge in Tuscaloosa County; known far and wide as a tough judge; "Hanging Jack"; today he proved it.

- Six months ago Bubba Bowers murdered; found lying dead at his front door by a neighbor; Bubba had been sick for a while; had emphysema and was pretty much disabled by that, or so the neighbors said. He was 59 and looked 75.

- Police investigation: found Hattie, his wife wandering in the woods in back of their house; muttering to herself about how she "got rid of the old bastard." Hattie is nearly 60 now and has two kids and two grandkids.

- Everybody in neighborhood stayed away from Bowers; some said he beat her up pretty regular.

- District Attorney Norris Gray charges Hattie with Bubba's murder; first degree murder; has evidence that she was buying ammunition for Bubba's shotgun the week before he was killed.

- Three-day trial last week. Hattie testifies: "Yeah, I killed the old bastard. I's afraid of him." Her attorneys argue that Bubba was beating her up, and she suffered a lot of emotional distress and finally felt like she had no choice but to defend herself. Hattie's kids testified for her; said their dad was a violent man and had knocked her and them around for years. But Norris Gray forced a damning admission from them: they had no evidence that Bubba had touched her lately.

- Olis Milsaps; general practitioner in Coaling; he would treat Bubba sometimes when he got real sick; last time he saw him was six months ago. "The man could hardly stand up then. I don't see how he could be much of a threat to anyone."

- Jury finds her guilty of first-degree murder.

- Judge has a choice about sentencing: death penalty; life in prison without parole; twenty years to life, which means she could be paroled in seven years.

- Today he made his choice: life without parole. That's Hanging Jack for you.

- As soon as he announced his decision in court today, Hattie's daughter, Myrtle Price, wailed, "No, no, no!" Hattie herself sank down in her chair and sobbed uncontrollably; judge adjourns sentencing hearing and orders courtroom cleared; Hattie is still sobbing when bailiffs take her out.

- Norris Gray, clearly pleased with herself: "I think Mrs. Bowers got what she deserved. Mr. Bowers was a helpless old man, and she killed him."

- That's not how Dulcie Wannamaker felt. She's Hattie's lead attorney. "Last week we had an outrageous verdict. Now we have an outrageous sentence." She has already filed an appeal of the outrageous verdict.

- Mrytle Price: "Mamma is a good woman. She don't deserve this. She don't deserve none of this." Myrtle is more composed now. She and Dulcie talk to you just outside the courtroom.

Chapter Eleven

Style

Key Concepts and Terms

1. Style in journalism is not a way of forming phrases or sentences (as in literary style) but rather refers to the rules of usage and the discipline the writer imposes on the writing.

2. *The Associated Press Stylebook and Libel Manual* is the chief arbiter of style rules in print and web journalism.

3. Most news organizations have a local style-book, a publication that supplements the *AP Stylebook* and lays down the rules for local references.

4. According to the *AP Stylebook*, there is one and only one way to spell a word.

5. Adherence to style rules is one of the ways that a journalist has of maintaining the aura of the "impersonal reporter."

6. Journalists should make sure their words and phrases are not disparaging or insulting to any part of their audience.

The mark of any professional writer is the precision with which he or she uses the language. Not only should a writer's knowledge and application of the rules of grammar, spelling, punctuation, and diction be perfect, but also the professional writer

The material in this chapter has been adapted from James Glen Stovall and Edward Mullins, *The Complete Editor* (revised edition), 2000.

should understand and adhere to the rules of style that are commonly accepted for the field. For print journalists, the main source of those rules is the *Associated Press Stylebook and Libel Manual*. This chapter is a general introduction to the concept of style and the specific rules of that manual.

Style is a special case of English correctness that a publication adopts. It does so to promote consistency among its writers and to reduce confusion among its readers. Once a style is adopted, a writer won't have to wonder about the way to refer to such things as times of day or geographic locations.

Journalistic style may be divided into two types of style: professional conventions and rules of usage. Professional conventions have evolved during years of journalistic endeavor and are now taught through professional training in universities and on the job. The rules of usage have been collected into stylebooks published by wire services, news syndicates, universities, and individual print and broadcast news operations. Some of these stylebooks have had widespread acceptance and influence. Others have remained relatively local and result in unique style rules accepted by reporters and editors working for individual publications.

For example, a publication may follow the *Associated Press Stylebook* and say that AM and PM should be lowercase with periods: a.m. and p.m. The writer will know that a reference to the president of the United States is always simply "president," lowercased, except when referring to a specific person, such as President Clinton.

Likewise, the reader will not be confused by multiple references to the same item. Unconsciously, the reader will anticipate the style that the publication uses. Consequently, if the reader uses a college newspaper regularly and that paper always refers to its own institution as the "University," uppercased, the reader will know what that means.

Similarly, a reporter may follow the usual convention in newspaper writing and write the sequence of time, date, and place of a meeting despite the fact that it may seem more logical to report the date before reporting the time.

Having a logical, consistent style is like fine-tuning a television. Before the tuning, the colors may be there and the picture may be reasonably visible. Eventually, however, the off-colors and the blurry images will play on the viewer's mind so that he or she will become dissatisfied and disinterested. That could cause the viewer to stop watching altogether. In the same way, consistent style fine-tunes a publication so that reading is easier and offers the reader fewer distractions.

Beyond that, the question may still remain: Does style really matter? The answer is an emphatic "yes!" Many young writers think of consistent style as a repressive force hampering their creativity. It isn't. Style is not a rigid set of rules established to restrict the creative forces in the writer. Style imposes a discipline in writing that should run through all the activities of a journalist. It implies that the journalist is precise not only with writing but also with facts and with thoughts. Consistent style is the hallmark of a professional.

Editors are the governors of the style of a publication. It is their job to see that style rules are consistently and reasonably applied. If exceptions are allowed, they should be for specific and logical reasons and should not be at the whim of the writer.

Editors should remember that consistent style is one way of telling readers that every effort has been made to certify the accuracy of everything in the publication.

Wire Service Stylebooks

For many years, the Associated Press has published the stylebook used as the bible for style for newspapers around the United States. Most public relations departments and many magazines also use the sound advice in this manual as the foundation of their style rules. Since the Associated Press has published its stylebook in a form commonly available to students in universities around the country, we shall refer to that stylebook in this section of our discussion.

Here is some representative advice on style covered by the *Associated Press Stylebook and Libel Manual.*

Capitalization. Unnecessary capitalization, like unnecessary punctuation, should be avoided because uppercase letters are harder to read and make the sentence look uninviting. Some examples: Main Street, but Main and Market streets. Mayor John Smith, but John Smith, mayor of Jonesville. Felicia Mason, executive director of the Alabama Press Association. (Note lowercase title after name but uppercase for Alabama Press Association, a formal name and, therefore, a proper noun.)

Abbreviation. The trend is away from alphabet soup in body type and headlines. But some abbreviations help conserve space and help to simplify information. For example: West Main Street, but 20 W. Main St. The only titles for which abbreviations are used (all before the name) are Dr., Gov., Lt. Gov., Mr., Mrs., Rep., the Rev., Sen., and most military ranks. Standing alone, all of these are spelled out and are lowercased. Check the stylebook for others.

Punctuation. Especially helpful are the sections of the stylebook dealing with the comma, hyphen, period, colon, semicolon, dash, ellipsis, apostrophe, quotation marks, and restrictive and nonrestrictive elements.

Numerals. Spell out whole numbers below 10, and use figures for numbers 10 and above. This rule applies to numbers used in a series or individually. Don't begin sentences with numbers, as a rule, but if you must, spell them out. Use numbers for virtually all measurements and dimensions.

Spelling. In journalism a word has but one spelling. Alternate spellings and variants are incorrect (because of the requirement of style consistency). Make it *adviser,* not *advisor; employee,* not *employe; totaled,* not *totalled; traveled,* not *travelled; kidnapped,* not *kidnaped; judgment,* not *judgement; television,* not *TV,* when used as a noun; *percent,* not *per cent; afterward, toward, upward, forward* (no *s); vs.,* not *versus* or *v.; vice president,* not *vice-president.* Check the stylebook or a dictionary for others.

Usage. Comprise means "contain," not "make up": "The region comprises five states," not "five states comprise the region" and not "the region is comprised

TRADEMARKS

Did you know that you should not Xerox any of your papers, play Frisbee, or wipe your nose with a Kleenex?

It's not that we should not do any of these things. It's just that we need to state them correctly. In all of the activities listed in the previous paragraph, trademarked names were used as common words. Careful writers try to avoid doing that, and the *AP Stylebook* helps us with a long list of trademarks that we often hear used as common words. Following are ones that should always be capitalized and never used to refer to a group of products with different manufacturers:

Allen, a trademark for a type of wrenches
Astro-Turf, type of synthetic covering
Bisquick, baking mixes
Clorox, a type of bleach
Coke, a type of soft drink
Desk-Jet, electronic printer
Dictaphone, a voice processing product
Discman, portable compact disk player
Formica, laminated plastic
Frisbee, flying disk
Jacuzzi, therapeutic whirlpool bath
Jell-O, gelatin and pudding desserts
Karo, a type of syrup
Kitty Litter, cat box filler
Kleenex, facial tissues
Loafer, laceless shoe
Matchbox, die-cast toy vehicles
Ouija, a board game
Pampers, disposable diapers
Ping-Pong, table tennis equipment
Popsicle, flavored ice dessert
Pyrex, cooking dishes and glassware
Q-tips, cotton swabs

Ritz, a brand of toasted crackers
Rolodex, a rotary directory of file cards
Scotch, adhesive tape
Speedo, swimware, sunglasses
Styrofoam, plastic foam (Note: Cups and other serving items are not made of Styrofoam brand plastic foam.)
Twinkies, a brand of snack foods
Valium, a tranquilizer
Vaseline, a brand of petroleum jelly
Velcro, hook and loop fasteners
Vice-Grip, locking pliers and wrenches
Walkman, portable tape or disc player
Weejuns, footware
Xerox, photocopier
Zippo, cigarette lighter

The companies that hold these trademarks have spent much money acquiring them and promoting them into exclusive brand names. Consequently, they are very protective of how they are used, and they often ask journalists not to use them generically.

One might think that it would be good for a company to have its brand become a commonly used word. The problem is that if the word does slip into common usage, a company can lose the trademark and then cannot control how the word is used.

In addition to the stylebook, a good source of registered trademarks is the International Trademark Association (www.inta.org). The web site for this organization lists hundreds of words and phrases that are trademarked.

of five states," because it is passive and sounds stuffy. *Affect* means to "influence," not "carry out." *Effect* means a "result" when it's a noun and means to "carry out" when it's a verb. *Controller* and *comptroller* are both pronounced "controller" and mean virtually the same thing, though *comptroller* is generally the more accurate word for denoting government financial officers and *controller* is better for denoting private sector financial officers. *Hopefully* does not mean "it is hoped," "we hope," "maybe," or "perhaps." It means "in a hopeful manner": "Hopefully, editors will study the English language" is not acceptable usage of the word. Good editors may use some fad expressions because readers do, but they do not use them as crutches, and they should know when they are using them.

Ages.   Use numerals always: a 2-month-old baby; she was 80; the youth, 18, and the girl, 6, were rescued.

Dates.   Feb. 6 (current calendar year); in February 1978 (no comma); last February.

Dimensions.   She is 5 feet 9 inches tall; the 5-foot-9-inch woman; 5-foot-9 woman; a 7-footer; the car left a skid mark 8 inches wide and 17 feet long; the rug is 10 by 12. The storm brought 1 1/2 inches of rain (with space between the whole number and the fraction). In tabular material, convert fractions to decimals. For fractions without whole numbers it is 1/2, 2/3 and so on.

Journalistic Conventions

A strong sense of professionalism has developed in journalism during the more than three hundred years of journalism history in America. With this professionalism has come conventions in journalistic writing. As with rules of style, these conventions are known to trained journalists and used by them to communicate things about their stories to readers. Most readers do not notice these conventions when they read a publication, yet most regular readers know these conventions and what they indicate about the judgments made by editors and reporters.

The conventions include both the basic structures of the stories and the individual ordering of facts. They even include words within sentences that are regularly used in certain types of stories.

Inverted Pyramid

Though there is some argument about this structure among professional journalists, the inverted pyramid is the structure most commonly used for the modern American news story. For the editor, the inverted pyramid structure means two things: facts should be presented more or less in the order of their importance, with the most important facts coming at the beginning; and a story should be written so that if it needs to be cut, it may be cut from the end without loss of essential facts or coherence. The inverted pyramid is certainly not the only acceptable structure for the presentation of news, but its use is so widespread that, if it is not used, the nature of a story must dictate the alternate form used by the writer. For example, short features and long take-out stories do not follow this form. Although efforts to replace the form as the dominant one crop up now and then, it remains the most widely used. Now web journalism has come along to reinforce its usefulness.

Types of Stories

The news values discussed in Chapter 1 make it incumbent that editors cover and give importance to certain types of stories. These kinds of stories are handled so often that a set of standard practices governing how they are written has been established. For instance, the disaster story must always tell early in the story if anyone was killed or injured. Another example of this routinization of stories is the obituary. Newspapers develop their own styles for handling obituaries, and some even dictate the form in which the standard obituary is written. For instance, the *New York Times* has a set two-sentence lead for an obituary: "John Smith, a Brooklyn real estate dealer, died at a local hospital yesterday after a short illness. He was 55 years old."

Other types of routine stories are those concerning government actions, the courts, crime, holidays, and weather. Part of an editor's job is to make sure that the paper covers these kinds of stories fully and that it reports other stories that have become important to the community that the newspaper serves.

Balance and Fairness

One of the tenets of American journalism is fairness. Journalists should attempt to give all people involved in a news story a chance to tell their sides of it. If an accusation is made by a news source concerning another person, that person should be given a chance to answer in the same story. Journalists should not take sides in a controversy and should take care not even to appear to take sides.

Producing a balanced story means more than just making sure a controversial situation or issue is covered fairly. In a larger sense, balance means that journalists should understand the relative importance of the events they cover and should not write stories that overplay or underplay that importance. Journalists are often criticized for "blowing things out of proportion," and sometimes the charge is valid. They should make sure that they are not being used by news sources and being put in a position of creating news rather than letting it occur and then covering it and presenting it.

The Impersonal Reporter

Closely associated with the concepts of balance and fairness is the concept of the impersonal reporter. Reporters should be invisible in their writing. Not only should journalists not report their own views and opinions, but they should also avoid direct contact with the reader through the use of first-person (*I, we, me, our, my, us*) or second-person (*you, your*) pronouns outside of direct quotes.

Reporters and editors inherently state their opinions about the news in deciding what events they write about, how they write about them, and where they place those stories in the paper. No journalist can claim to be a completely unbiased and objective observer and deliverer of information. Yet stating opinions directly and plainly is an unacceptable practice. Even for a reporter to include himself with the readers is a poor idea. For example, the following lead is not acceptable because of its use of a first-person pronoun: "The Chief Justice of the Supreme Court said yesterday our legal system is in serious trouble." A foreign citizen—someone who makes no claim to the legal system of the United States—may read that story. The reporter should write for that person as well. For magazine audiences that are more tightly defined, personal writing is more common and *I* and *our* are frequently used. But in newspapers these approaches are limited to certain sections of the paper and to signed columns.

Sources

Much of the information printed in a newspaper comes from what we might call "official" sources. These sources are thought to have expertise on the subject being written about, not merely opinions about the subject. An example of this reliance might be found in a story about inflation. A journalist writing a story about inflation would probably use information from government reports and the studies and opinions of respected economists and influential politicians. These would be the "official" sources, and they would have a large amount of credibility with the reader. An "unofficial" source might be a homemaker, who would certainly have an opinion about the effects, causes, and cures of inflation but who would not have information that would be credible in the mass media.

Young journalists often make the mistake of relying too heavily on one or the other of these kinds of sources and especially on the convenient source. They interview people who have opinions about news events, such as their roommates, rather than those who can provide information to support an opinion about a news event. When a source is quoted in a story, it should be readily apparent why that source is used. Jill Johnson, a college student, is not going to have much credibility in a story about the use of child labor in Brazilian sewing factories, though she may have views worth reporting; however, Jill Johnson, the leader of the local chapter of the International Human Rights Coalition, will have high credibility in the story. Editors refer to a concept known as the "source ladder," with top officials, such as a university president, at the top rung, managers and technicians in the middle, and consumers and interested citizens at the bottom. For balanced journalism, all are important.

Attribution and Quotations

Journalists should make it clear to the readers where information has been obtained. All but the most obvious and commonly known facts in a story should be attributed. Editors should make sure that the attributions are helpful to the reader's understanding of the story and that they do not get in the way of the flow of the story.

Journalistic conventions have grown up around the use of indirect and direct quotes. First, except in the rarest instances, all quotes must be attributed. The exception is the case in which there is no doubt about the source of the quote. Even then, editors should be careful. Second, journalists disagree about whether a direct quote should be the exact words, and only the exact words, a person speaks or the exact meaning the quoted person intended. Most of the time, people's exact words will accurately express their meaning. If they don't, paraphrasing them and removing the quote marks is the best approach.

Sometimes, however, a journalist must choose between accuracy of words and accuracy of meaning. People misspeak. When we know they misspoke and know what they meant, should we crucify them on their own words? Generally, no.

Finally, direct quotes in news stories rarely include bad grammar even if the person quoted used bad grammar. Quoting someone who uses English incorrectly can make that person appear unnecessarily foolish and can distract from the real meaning of the story. In a news story, a journalist usually cleans up bad grammar in a direct quote. (Feature story writers may choose not to follow this practice.)

These conventions and others you will learn about as you continue your study of journalism are important ones for journalists to observe if they are to gain the respect of their readers and colleagues. They should not be looked upon as arbitrary rules that must be followed at the expense of accuracy and clarity. Rather, they are sound practices that are extremely useful to journalists in the process of deciding what to write and how to write it.

Language Sensitivity

Editors must understand that language has the ability to offend and demean. Readers and viewers of the mass media are a broad and diverse group, and those who would communicate with them should be aware of language sensitivities of some of the people within that group. While some people have gone to extremes in identifying supposedly offensive language, there are terms and attitudes in writing that should legitimately be questioned and changed. The current state of public discourse demands it.

Editors have not always paid attention to such sensitivities. Phrases such as "all men are created equal" and "these are the times that try men's souls" drew no criticism for their inherent sexism when they were first published, partly because women were not allowed to be a major part of public life. We may accept those phrases now because we understand the context in which they were written, but we would not approve of them if they were written in our age.

Editors should examine their copy closely to make sure that they have treated people fairly and equally, that they have not lapsed into stereotypes, that they have not used phrases or descriptions that demean, and that they have included everyone in their articles who is germane to the subject. Following are areas in which editors need to take special care.

Sexist Pronouns

It is no longer acceptable to use the pronoun *he* when the referent may be a man or woman. "A student should always do his homework" should be "A student should always do his or her homework." In some instances, rewriting the sentence using plurals is easier: "Students should always do their homework." Sometimes a sentence can be rewritten so that it does not require any pronoun. "A student should always do the assigned homework."

BASIC AP STYLE RULES

The *AP Stylebook* is full of rules, and journalists who use it throughout their careers learn many of them. The following are the most basic rules that journalists use again and again from the time they write their first stories.

- Spell out, do not abbreviate, names of organizations, firms, agencies, universities and colleges, groups, clubs, and governmental bodies the first time the name is used. (i.e., on first reference).

- In street addresses, spell out the name and designation when no number is used but abbreviate the designation when a number is used: 1234 Goober St., 3506 Loblolly Ave., 80 Crabtree Blvd. But the words *road, alley, circle, drive,* and so on are never abbreviated.

- Capitalize names of holidays, historic events, church feast days, and special events (e.g., Mother's Day, Labor Day) but not seasons (fall, autumn, summer, winter, spring).

- Capitalize the proper names of nationalities, peoples, races, and tribes: Indian, Arab, Caucasian, African American, Hispanic.

- As a general rule, spell out both cardinal and ordinal numbers from one through nine. Use Arabic figures for 10 and above.

- Use commas in numbers with four or more digits: 23,879 students.

- The words *billion* and *million* may be used with round numbers: $3 million. (Do not use the word *dollars* in this expression.)

- General rules for the hyphen: (1) The hyphen is used in phrasal adjectives: a 7-year-old boy, an off-the-cuff opinion. (2) The hyphen is not used in sequences in which the adverb has an *-ly* suffix: a gravely ill patient. (3) In combinations of a number plus a noun of measurement, use a hyphen: a 3-inch bug, a 6-foot man, a two-man team.

- Generally, identify people in the news by their first name, middle initial, and last name: David R. Rockefeller.

- Identify a person and use the full name in first reference, but in second reference, use the last name only.

- Do not use courtesy titles—Mr., Mrs., Miss, and so on—unless not using them would cause confusion. (For example, you might want to use them when both members of a married couple are quoted in a news article.)

- Time in newspaper usage is always a.m. or p.m. Don't use tonight with p.m. or this morning with a.m., because it is redundant. Don't use the terms *yesterday* and *tomorrow* to describe when an event occurred. It is acceptable, however, to say *today*.

- Never put both the day of the week and the date that an event will occur. *Right:* The fireman's ball will be on Jan. 3. *Wrong:* The fireman's ball will be on Monday, Jan. 3.

- Refer to time of day using lowercase letters and periods. When the time is on the hour, do not use ":00." *Right:* It's 7 p.m. *Wrong:* It's 7:00 p.m.

Titles

Many nouns that had sexist connotations are being phased out, often becoming not only gender neutral but also more descriptive. *Firefighter* and *mail carrier* for *fireman* and *mailman* are examples. Editors need to be watchful for gender-biased terms and pose alternatives.

Descriptions

Women have often been described in terms of their appearance and attire, whereas men are rarely described this way. Editors should be sensitive to what is relevant to the understanding of a story. Sometimes references to appearance and attire are important to an article, but often they are not. They are included gratuitously and as such are offensive.

Racial descriptions and references may not be necessary. John Kincaid is the mayor of Birmingham, Alabama. To describe him as "John Kincaid, the black mayor of Birmingham," is not necessary unless it is important to the understanding of a story to know his race. The test here is to ask the questions, "What if Mayor Kincaid were white? Would it be important to know that?"

Stereotypes

Our society abounds in stereotypes, and not all are based on race. We describe women who stay at home as women who "don't work." We refer to a "Jewish mother" as someone with certain hectoring characteristics, not allowing that not all Jewish mothers have those characteristics. We write about "Southern bigots," ignoring that bigots can live anywhere in the country. An older woman who has never married is called a "spinster," a reference many see as derogatory. We should constantly question these blanket references and phrases to see if they serve our journalistic purposes.

Illness and Disability

American society is taking some steps, by private initiative as well as by law, to open itself to people who have various handicaps, disabilities, or limitations. One of the things that Americans should learn as this happens is that identifying people by these limitations is in itself unfair and inaccurate. To say that a person "has a handicap" is different from saying that a person is "handicapped." The way in which these limitations are referred to can also be disabling. For instance, to describe someone as a "reformed alcoholic" is neither complimentary nor benign; "reformed" implies that the person did something wrong and now the problem is solved. A person who is an alcoholic but who no longer drinks is "recovering." To say that someone has a "defect," such as a "birth defect," is to demean by implication (i.e., the person is defective). It would be better to say a person "was born with a hearing loss." As with many situations, being specific makes using the general, and often offending, term unnecessary.

These are just some of the areas in which editors need to maintain great sensitivity and to continue close examination of their work. Constantly questioning what is in the copy you read and making reasonable changes is not just the mark of a good editor; it is also a sign of a sensitive editor.

QUESTIONS FOR DISCUSSION

1. Why do you think so much emphasis is put on adhering to style and style rules in journalism?
2. The chapter devotes a whole section to language sensitivity, but many people would dismiss this as simply political correctness. How do you feel about it? Are there words or expressions that offend you or members of your family?
3. How do style rules and the journalistic conventions described in this chapter help promote objectivity?
4. Journalists are under no legal obligation to use trademarks as the owners of the trademarks would wish. For instance, journalists (or anyone else for that matter) may use "xerox" as a verb if they want to. Should journalists do this, or should they be sensitive to what the trademark owners want?

RELATED WEB SITES

AP Stylebook, www.apstylebook.com (users can subscribe to the stylebook online)

No Train, No Gain, www.notrain-nogain.org

The Slot, www.theslot.com

READINGS AND REFERENCES

Bernstein, T. M. (1958). *Watch your language.* Manhasset, NY: Channel Press.

Bernstein, T. M. (1995). *The careful writer: A modern guide to English usage.* New York: Free Press.

The Chicago manual of style (14th ed.). (1993). Chicago: University of Chicago Press.

Copperud, R. (1964). *A dictionary of usage and style.* New York: Hawthorne Books.

Jordan, L., (Ed.). (1976). *The* New York Times *manual of style and usage* (Rev. ed.). Chicago: Quadrangle Books.

Lippman, T. W. (1989). *The* Washington Post *deskbook on style.* New York: McGraw Hill.

Strunk, W., & White, E. B. (1972). *The elements of style* (Rev. ed.). New York: Macmillan.

U.S. Government Printing Office Style Manual (Rev. ed.). (1973). Washington, DC: U.S. Government Printing Office.

Writing Exercises

EXERCISE 11.1

Make the following sentences, expressions, and words conform to AP style and correct grammar, usage, and spelling.

1. co-operate, preelection, pre-heat, preflight, pre-dawn, postmortem
2. The Reverend Johnny Milton led the Easter services at 4:30 A.M. this morning.
3. Flowers adorned either side of the altar at the Brown-Morris wedding.
4. Bronson's Co., Incorporated, is opening a new factory near Wilsonville next month.

5. 8:00, 8 o'clock in the morning, 12 noon, 12 p.m., 1:36 A.M.

6. Over 50,000 people attended the midsummer All-Star baseball game.

7. Bill Brody, the school's best runner, placed 22nd in the Regional Track Meet this year; Howard Wilson, a freshman, was 1st.

8. The French Army and the U.S. Army joined forces today in an effort to keep the peace in war-torn Lebanon.

9. Mix the ingredients in a ratio of 12–1.

10. A 12-to-one majority in the voice vote expressed the widespread approval of the bill.

11. Karl Teague, Dean of the College of Arts and Sciences, will address the graduating class at 11:15 in the morning.

12. freelancer, duffle bag, sister in laws (plural), t-shirt

13. The Gross National Product rose significantly in January, 1994.

14. The case in question is now in Federal District Court.

15. I found my material in the "Encyclopedia Britannica," in "The Autobiography of Lincoln Steffens," and in several magazine articles.

EXERCISE 11.2

Make the following sentences, expressions, and words conform to AP style and correct grammar, usage, and spelling.

1. Over 50,000 people attended the major league All-Star Game.

2. Jill Brody, normally the team's best runner, placed twenty-second in the 5,000 meter run; Janice Wilson, a freshmen walkon, was first.

3. 5,000-meter run. Janice Wilson, a freshman walk-on, was first.

4. By a 12 to 1 majority, the decision was to mix the ingredients in a ratio of 2 to 1.

5. A freelancer should always pack an extra T shirt before going deep sea fishing with a group of attorney-generals.

6. The Gross National Product rose a tenth of a percent in the first quarter.

7. The researcher took her material from the "Encyclopedia Britannica" and the "Autobiography of Lincoln Steffens".

8. The precious stone was 20 carrots.

9. The group fundamentally performed a fund raising function.

10. John Phelps served as his father's lawyer.

11. The mode is the middle score in a group.

12. The mean is the most frequent score.

13. The median is determined by adding the scores and dividing by the number of scores

14. dance troop, Boy Scout troupe

15. Texarkana, AR.

16. Harlingen, Tex.

17. Salt Lake City, Utah

18. Sioux, City, IA
19. Albany, NY
20. Honolulu, Hawaii

EXERCISE 11.3

Copy edit the following story to conform to AP style and correct grammar, usage, and spelling. Deal with other problems you may find.

> Three classes of second-graders at Midville Elementary School have made use pf 40 pounds of things most people would rather throw away; toilet paper cylinders, egg cartons and empty spools, and the products of the students's efforts are on display in the school's are gallery.
>
> Caterpillars, bunnies, Easter baskets, and puppets are included in the display along with more ambitious efforts such as Jo Anna Moore's model of a steamship made entirely of styrofoam.
>
> The art project was one component of an enviromental awareness program formulated by the state Enviromental Association in a booklet called "Recycling: Using the Unusable."
>
> The entire Woodvale school system has adopted the program, whih includes collection of aluminum, showing film strips, and a campus clean-sup day.
>
> "The purpose is to make children more aware of the potentail value of things we normally throw away, Woodvale Principal Donna Estill said.

EXERCISE 11.4

AP Style Test 1

This exam consists of twenty-five sentences and three choices for each. Select the one that conforms to AP style.

1. The kickoff is set for 11:45 _____.
   a. AM
   b. A.M.
   c. a.m.
2. The public address announcer asked, "Is there a _____ in the house?"
   a. doctor
   b. Dr.
   c. Doctor
3. He lives at 127 Elm _____.
   a. Street
   b. St.
   c. Str.
4. The philosopher was born in 360 _____.
   a. Before Christ
   b. B.C.
   c. BC

5. The operation was performed by _____ Louise Smith and Fred Jones.
   a. Doctors
   b. doctors
   c. Drs.
6. Early this _____ he opened his eyes for the first time in a week.
   a. a.m.
   b. A.M.
   c. morning
7. Tennessee became a state on _____ 1, 1796.
   a. June
   b. Jun.
   c. date should read "6-1-1796"
8. He became a _____ citizen only last year.
   a. United States
   b. U.S.
   c. US
9. _____ called for a summit meeting with European leaders.
   a. The President
   b. Pres. Bush
   c. President Bush
10. I looked for him somewhere along _____ Avenue.
    a. 5th
    b. Fifth
    c. fifth
11. The soldier had already gone through two _____.
    a. courts martial
    b. court martials
    c. court-martials
12. The Jefferson County _____ failed to indict anyone for the crime.
    a. Grand Jury
    b. grand jury
    c. grand Jury
13. Ken Griffey _____ is now on the same team with his father.
    a. junior
    b. Junior
    c. Jr.
14. He had to take the exam _____ times before he passed it.
    a. 2
    b. two
    c. twice
15. His October _____ deadline was drawing close.
    a. thirty-first
    b. 31
    c. 31st

16. The colors of the flag are red, white __ and blue.
    a. comma
    b. semicolon
    c. no punctuation
17. Exxon _____ announced it was raising its prices for oil.
    a. Corp.
    b. Corporation
    c. corporation
18. His inauguration took place on the steps of the _____.
    a. capital
    b. capitol
    c. Capitol
19. The neighborhood group decided to withdraw _____ lawsuit.
    a. its
    b. their
    c. they're
20. _____ Joseph Barlow appointed all of the members of the committee.
    a. Lieutenant governor.
    b. Lt. Gov.
    c. Lieutenant Governor
21. The _____ was a term used to describe conflicts between the United States and the former Soviet Union.
    a. Cold War
    b. cold war
    c. Cold war
22. His first thought was to get in touch with the _____.
    a. Federal Bureau of Investigation
    b. FBI
    c. U.S. FBI
23. The _____ comes on Wednesday this year.
    a. fourth of July
    b. Fourth of July
    c. 4th of July
24. The president summoned _____ Smith to the Oval Office.
    a. Sec. of State
    b. Secretary of State
    c. secretary of state
25. With _____ of the game left, the star player was injured.
    a. two-thirds
    b. two thirds
    c. 2/3

12

Editors

Key Concepts and Terms

1. Editor: a person who has some responsibility for the news organization and how it functions; editors are in charge of the process of journalism.

2. Copy editor: a person charged with checking the writing that reporters and other editors produce; these people must have a wide range of knowledge as well as an expertise in how the language is used.

3. Editors should develop relationships of trust and mutual purpose with reporters. A reporter should come to count on an editor's expertise and support.

4. Editors, in addition to their responsibility to their news organization, have a responsibility to the audience the organization serves; they must constantly consider how the organization can best deliver information to that audience.

5. Editors set and enforce the standards for a news organization; their sense of honesty and ethics will permeate the news organization.

Vignette

When the Pulitzer prizes, journalism's top professional awards, were announced in April 2002, Howell Raines, executive editor of the New York Times, *stood in the middle of the newsroom accepting and offering congratulations all around. The* Times *had just won seven Pulitzers, more than any newspaper had ever won at a single moment.*

Six of the prizes were for the newspaper's coverage of the September 11 terror-ist attacks. When that happened Raines had been on the job for just a few days. He rallied the Times *staff members out of the shock of that morning and led them to re-markable coverage of the day's events and their aftermath.*

His reward was the recognition by the journalistic world, in the form of Pulitzer prizes, of what he and his team had done.

Fourteen months later, in June 2003, Raines stood at virtually the same spot in the New York Times *newsroom where he had been when the Pulitzers were announced and informed the staff that he was resigning.*

For several weeks before then, the Times *had been humiliated by reporters who had been less than honest about what they had seen and heard and the people they had talked to about their stories. These scandals had opened the doors to criticism of Raines by the* Times *journalists themselves, many of whom believed that he was arrogant and vengeful in the way he ran the paper.*

The downfall of Howell Raines tells a sad, troubling, and instructive story. As a reporter, he was known to be hardworking, intuitive, and brilliant. He was also an excellent writer. He had authored several books and had won a Pulitzer prize him-self in 1992 for an article he did on his childhood in Birmingham, Alabama. As the top editor at the world's most prestigious newspaper, however, he developed a dif-ferent reputation. Despite the accolades Raines received for the coverage of Septem-ber 11, many of the Times' *reporters had grown to dislike him intensely. Some said that his political inclinations colored his news judgments. Others thought he ignored the advice and opinions of senior editors who had developed expertise in certain fields they covered. And many staff members complained that he had a few favorite reporters who received special treatment and plum assignments.*

One of those reporters was Jayson Blair, a 27-year-old national correspondent who had covered many important stories for the paper in the previous few months. Some editors had begun to question where Blair was getting the information for his stories, but Blair was thought to be a favorite of Raines (and managing editor Ger-ald Boyd, who also resigned along with Raines). No one wanted to confront Raines by insisting that Blair needed to be watched more closely. In April 2003, Blair sent a story to the Times *that used quotations that had appeared in a Texas newspaper a few days before. Blair had not talked to the person who had said the things in the story; he had simply copied the quotations from the newspaper story, which is some-thing any experienced reporter knows not to do.*

Blair resigned on May 1, and editors and reporters for the Times *began looking into the stories he had written for the paper. They found many instances where he had plagiarized information or simply made it up. The newspaper published the findings within two weeks of the resignation, but by this time, Blair was no longer the central issue. Howell Raines and has management style had taken over the debate.*

Ten days after the report appeared, the Times *suspended another reporter, Rick Bragg. Also a Pulitzer prize winner and best-selling author, Bragg often used the help of "stringers" in his reporting. Stringers are people who help a reporter gather information, and using them is a common practice at the* Times. *Some editors felt that Bragg had crossed the line, however, claiming to have described things in his reporting that he had not witnessed. Unapologetic about what he had done and disgusted with his treatment by the* Times, *Bragg resigned.*

Bragg is also from Alabama and known to be good friends with Howell Raines. Many at the Times *saw him as one of the reporters Raines favored with lenient treatment and lavish assignments, although Bragg had earned his stripes (and his Pulitzer) before Raines had become executive editor.*

The situation with Rick Bragg differed substantially from that of Jayson Blair. No one accused Bragg of manufacturing facts or direct quotes. Bragg may have relied too heavily on his stringers, but his basic journalistic integrity was not in question. Still, the perception that Bragg was getting favored treatment was simply additional evidence that Howell Raines should not be editor of the New York Times, *and more staff members began to say that publicly. Those public pronouncements made it difficult for Raines to recover or garner any support from the staff. Although he needed only the backing of the publisher (not the staff) to remain in his job, Raines could not be effective without the respect of the staff. So, during the week after Bragg quit, Raines announced that he too was leaving the newspaper.*

The story of Howell Raines's short tenure of nineteen months as head of the New York Times *is unique in many ways, not the least of which is that it happened at the* Times *itself. But there are also lessons to be learned from it for any journalist.*

One is that editors bear the responsibility for what happens in their news organizations. Another is that editors must respect the people who work with them. They must treat them fairly but also as individuals who have talents, strengths, and weaknesses. Editors must also make decisions openly and must have the confidence to allow themselves to be questioned and contradicted. But they must do this in a way that does not allow them to lose the respect of the staff. Despite his hard work, his many talents, and his stellar accomplishments, Raines was unable to carry out these lessons, and when difficulties arose, he could not maintain his position as editor.

The Most Important Job

No one has a more important job in today's media environment than the editor. Editors take on responsibilities far beyond those of a writer. Editors must not only be

FIGURE 12.1   Editors of the *New York Tribune,* before 1850 This odd-looking assortment of characters constituted the editorial staff of the *New York Herald Tribune* and one of the most influential groups of editors in the nineteenth century. They are seated, left to right: George M. Snow, financial editor; Bayard Taylor; Horace Greeley; George Ripley, literary editor; standing, left to right: William Henry Fry, music editor; Charles A. Dana; Henry J. Raymond. Greeley was the editor of the *Tribune* and remained a major force in American journalism until his death in 1870. Charles Dana was an assistant secretary of war during the Civil War and later owner and editor of the influential *New York Sun.* Raymond founded the *New York Times* in 1851. (Photo credit: Library of Congress)

responsible for the work of reporters and writers, but they must also have the whole publication in mind in going about their routines. They must understand the purpose and approach that the publication has in handling information and serving audiences. Editors must know the language and style rules of their publication. They must lead, cajole, and sometimes force their writers into doing their best work.

Editors must understand the context of the information presented by their news organizations. They must be sensitive to the nuances of how information fits together. They must have enough memory about recent and ancient events that they can judge the nature, credibility, and legitimacy of the information they present.

Editors must be deeply steeped in the culture of journalism. As a part of their nature, they must understand the importance of accurate information and the generally accepted procedures for assuring accuracy. They must value the faith, trust, and intelligence of their audience. They must know that hard work is the norm—something the profession assumes but also rewards.

And editors must lead. They must have the highest standards and expect others in their environments to meet those standards. Their very attitudes and approaches to the daily routine of editing should tell all those around them that honesty, integrity, hard work, devotion to accuracy, intelligence, and humanity are the norm.

The job of the editor is more than just fixing copy and designing a good page. The editor sets the standard and tone for the kind of journalism that is practiced at a publication. That is why the editor has the most important job.

Every place that handles information and puts it into some form for distribution needs an editor, a person who understands the information, the procedure by which it will be processed, and the medium through which it will be disseminated. We may traditionally think of editors as working for newspapers or magazines, but editors— no matter what their job titles—are everywhere. This information age cannot do without them.

Who Is the Editor?

Editor is a title thrust on many professionals in journalism. An editor may head the news organization or may simply have some small job that extends beyond a single position. Some publications even call their writers "contributing editors," although they do not edit anything except their own copy. For our discussion in this chapter, we will consider as editors those people who have wide responsibilities that extend over several people and have some broader effect on the news organization.

The head of the news organization may simply be referred to as the "editor" or the "editor-in-chief" (or, at the *New York Times,* the "executive editor"). For other editors, the words in front of the word *editor* (e.g., managing editor, sports editor, etc.) describe the duties of the person who holds that position.

Other editors head departments within the news organizations. These may be news editors, sports editors, business editors, lifestyle editors, graphics editors, and photo editors. They are responsible for a staff of reporters and editors within their departments or areas. They direct news coverage of their areas for the organization.

One of the most important and celebrated of all editorial positions is the copy editor. This is the person charged with reading the words produced by the reporter or writer and is central to the editorial process. Because the words the news organization distributes are so important, the copy editor can exercise a major influence over what the news organization says and how it appears to the public. Copyediting (see Chapter 13) is a specialized skill that is highly valued in quality news organizations. Many young journalists enter the profession hoping to attain the position of copy editor because of their interest and skill with the language.

A design or layout editor is responsible for how the publication (or web site) looks. On newspapers, these people make decisions about where stories are placed on a page, what pictures are used, and what graphics may be needed to supplement a story.

Traits of an Editor

Editors must have agile minds. They must have a wide assortment of facts and concepts they can call up for instant use. They must know history and literature. Their knowledge of grammar and punctuation must be thorough. They need not necessarily be expert spellers (although it certainly helps), but they must be able to spot and question possible misspellings. They should know their communities geographically and socially. They must know where to get information as well as a reporter does, and many editors spend a good deal of their time developing their own sources.

Editors must be able to find mistakes and to question what they do not understand. If an editor does not understand something in a story, there will be few readers who do. Editors must also be able to spot errors in logic or lapses in common sense. They should be wordsmiths, people who not only know how to use words precisely but also have a feel for the language and a love for good writing.

In addition to all of these traits, editors must have in their heads a clear idea of what kind of publication they are producing. They must know what is and what is not appropriate, what similar or opposing publications are doing, and the ins and outs of their own operation. Editors must edit with readers in mind, and to do that they need some information on who the readers are and what they expect from the publication.

It typically takes years of hard work and experience to acquire the tools of a good editor. And for all such editors, maintaining and adding to those tools is a matter of constant effort. Students who wish to become editors must begin now by sharpening their skills and expanding their knowledge and sensitivity.

The Editor–Writer Relationship

Editing is a partnership that an editor enters into with the writer. Professional writers understand that, in most situations, they will rarely be on their own. The editorial process demands that the writer's products come under the scrutiny of some other person. That person, or persons, must then take as much responsibility for the writing as the writer. At the reporting and writing stage of journalism, the writer is the senior partner in the relationship with the editor. At the editing stage, the editor becomes the senior partner. *Partner* is the key word.

A good way to operate in this relationship is for both the writer and editor to recognize the strengths that they bring to the process. The writer should be the expert on the subject and substance of the writing. The writer should know the sources of information about the subject and should have a means of assessing their completeness and credibility. Good reporting means that the writer knows far more about the subject than he or she is able to put in an article.

The writer should also be an expert in the approach the story takes. The writer should understand the material so thoroughly that he or she has considered a variety of tacks the writing could take. The approach that the writer has taken in putting the material together should be obvious and appropriate, and the writer should be able to defend it to the editor if necessary.

The editor's strength in this relationship lies both in ignorance and expertise. On first reading, an editor can simulate the position of a reader as someone who knows nothing or very little about the subject. An editor can ask the same questions about the copy that a reader would ask, the main question being, "Does this copy make sense?" Here the editor is acting as the reader's representative.

The editor should—must—recognize instances of lack of clarity. The editor must point out legitimate, unanswered questions that the writer has failed to address.

This "ignorance" is not the only strength that an editor brings to the editing partnership, of course. An editor should be an expert on the publication for whom both the writer and editor are working. The editor must know what the publication's standards are, what it will accept and not accept, who the audience is, and the possible effects any story will have on any member of the audience and on the publication's reputation.

The editor is the person held accountable for these awesome responsibilities.

Another area of strength that an editor is likely to have is a broader range of experience in the field of journalism than the writer. Editors usually get to their position through the reporting and writing process. At some point in their careers, they should have been doing what the writer has done, and that experience should have imbued them with some empathy for the difficulties of the writer. In addition, editors will probably have worked with a variety of writers. Having seen the approaches of different writers, they may be able to offer suggestions and approaches to a writer based on the experience of others.

In this same vein, a good editor will probably have a broader view of the field of journalism than the writer. The editor will have been able to see a greater variety of publications, will have studied other journalistic environments and situations, and will have discussed the care and feeding of writers with other editors. This broad view of the field should add a source of stability to the editor–writer relationship.

Finally, the editor should be a confident wordsmith. Editors should know and understand the applications of the standard rules of grammar, punctuation, and style. They should be aware of trends in the language, the changing meanings of words, and the development of jargon and clichés. Good editors maintain a keen interest in the language.

Ideally, the editing process works because both the writer and editor believe that they are trying to produce a good piece of writing. Both realize they have a stake in making the writing good. They should both be sensitive to the pressures of the other's job and sometimes even of their personal lives. Their relationship should be one of respect and good faith.

Ultimately, an editor is the senior partner in this relationship. The editor, or in many cases a team of editors, must decide on whether or not a story is to be published. And the writer, for better or worse, has to live with that decision.

EDITORS, WATCH OUT FOR THOSE WRITERS

Beginning copy editors, particularly students, are sometimes intimidated by the fact that something has been written. They do not believe that they should change it. Not so! Good editors always question what a writer has written on two grounds: Is it right? Is it written as well as it could be? Editors should have the confidence to change what they believe is wrong or not good enough.

The following is a list of some editing problems that student copy editors are most likely to run into in editing the work of other students.

Remember, you're the editor. If you don't like it, change it.

- Always correct for AP style errors.
- Always correct grammar, spelling, and punctuation errors.
- The best sequence for the elements of a direct quotation is direct quote, speaker, verb. If a writer has it another way, either change it or make sure there is a good reason for it to remain the way it is.

  Best: "The president will not support a tax increase," Smith said.

  Not good: Smith said, "The president will not support a tax increase."

  Terrible: "The president will not support a tax increase," said Smith.

- Make sure that direct quotations and their attributions are punctuated correctly.
- The writing should conform to the style and general customs of the publication. For instance, most newspapers require that lead paragraphs be one sentence and a maximum of thirty to thirty-five words. As an editor for that publication, you should enforce that rule.

- Eliminate conditional statements when possible. Take this sentence: "Many non-Greek students may have questions concerning the effects of Greek life on their academics." That could be true. It might also not be true. In either case, the writer has just put it out there with no attribution. It contains no information value. A good editor will eliminate it.
- Be careful about using *the* when you should use *a*. For instance, in the following sentence, "Rush Week officially begins with the hazing meeting at 3 p.m. on Friday in Wiley Hall." The implication of *the* is that all of us who read that sentence are familiar with "the hazing meeting." We're not. A good editor will change that sentence to read, "Rush Week begins with a meeting about hazing at 3 p.m. Friday in Wiley Hall." (Note the other changes as well.)
- In news stories, words should be used literally, not as figures of speech. "The Greek system is going to start opening its doors to outsiders very soon." Of course, the Greek system is not going to start opening its doors because it does not have any doors to open.
- Be alert to the oddball phrase. For instance, "Sophomore Amanda Parsons brought forth the petition to have class schedules published three semesters in advance." Amanda probably did not "bring forth" the petition as much as she "wrote" it. Don't let writers get away with that kind of palaver.

What the Editor Must Do

An editor should ensure that a story is accurate, complete, precise, and efficient.

Accuracy is the chief goal of the editing process. Presenting accurate information in an accurate context must be the priority for the editor and the writer. The editor

Quote 12.1

T. S. ELIOT

On the difficulty of being a good writer

Some editors are failed writers, but then so are most writers.

T. S. Eliot was one of the twentieth century's great writers and poets. He was also the founder and editor of Criterion *magazine, an influential literary journal. Eliot's poems include* The Waste Land *and* Ash Wednesday. *He also wrote the plays* Murder in the Cathedral *and* The Cocktail Party, *among others. He won the Nobel prize for literature in 1948.*

must raise questions about the facts in a story, and those questions must be answered to his or her satisfaction.

The editor must be concerned not only about the individual facts but also about their sum. Do all of the facts together present a correct and fair context for the reader and for those involved in the story? Thousands of discussions on this very point take place at all publications every week.

Completeness means that a story does not raise questions that it fails to answer; it also means that the writer and editor have included enough information in the story so that the reader can understand it. Editors must understand when a story is incomplete. They must demand that writers revisit their copy to answer all of the significant questions of a story. Few things are more frustrating to a reader than to be left wondering about a story or what it means. It is the editor's job to see that this does not happen. It bears repeating: The editor is the reader's representative regardless of the medium.

Precision is also the responsibility of the editor. Precision has to do with the use of the language and the proper style for the publication. Editors must guard against writers who use words with meanings and implications readers will not understand. The editor is the enforcer of the general and local style rules of the publication.

Efficiency is one of the most difficult characteristics for a writer to detect about his or her writing. That's where an editor comes in. An editor should be able to spot those words, phrases, and passages that do not add to the substance of an article. Every word should carry some weight. If it does not—if it is redundant or unduly repetitious or simply unnecessary—it should be cut.

All of these are duties to the copy that the editor deals with. The editor also has certain duties to the writer that engender an atmosphere of respect and trust. For instance:

Editors must be sensitive to a writer's style. To some degree, writers should be given license to present information in the style with which they are comfortable. This license is more limited in the world of daily journalism than it is in magazine or newsletter publication.

Still, editors in all publications should remember that writers take great pride in their work. Editors should not make arbitrary or needless changes when those changes do not improve the copy substantially.

Any major changes in the copy should be checked with the writer if possible. The editor often has the power to change anything he or she pleases, but that power should be exercised judiciously. Asking questions of a writer or making suggestions is generally a more effective way of handling problematic copy than simply making changes and letting the writer see them in print.

Most writers with any experience have stories about how an editor changed their copy and did not tell them—and the editor turned out to be wrong. Editors should remember that they can be wrong, too.

Editors should not change the wording of a direct quotation.   Again, checking with the writer on questionable quotations is the first duty of an editor. When a direct quotation appears that does not make sense or does not fit well into the story and the editor cannot reach the writer, the editor should either cut it out or paraphrase it unless he or she has independent knowledge about the quotation. An active editor might go so far as to telephone the source to ask for a clarification.

When serious disputes arise about a story between a writer and editor, a third person should be asked to consult.   Often a third person can see things about copy that neither the writer nor the initial editor can see. They may be able to suggest ways to satisfy both the writer and the editor.

Editors should remember that it is the writer's name that is going on the story, not their own. They may have more experience, responsibility, and power than the writer, but the writer has professional effort and pride invested in the copy. The editor must not only make sure the copy meets the standards of the publication but also must do so in a way that encourages the writer to do his or her best in the future.

It is a delicate dance.

Getting to Be an Editor

An editorship is not for everyone. Many people go into journalism because they want to report and write or because they like to take pictures or because they enjoy creating graphics. They are focused on the creative part of the craft and often want to work alone (as much as the profession will allow). They do not want the broader responsibility to an organization that an editorship entails, and they do not relish the thought of managing other people.

But many others are attracted to journalism because they want to contribute to the news organization more broadly and because they feel they can have an impact beyond an individual contribution. Their skills with the language (in the case of copy editors) or with managing people (as with section editors) give them incentive to take on an editorship. The fact that editors are likely to be paid more money than most reporters or writers is also an incentive to aspire to an editorship.

So how do you get there?

Most people begin as reporters or copy editors. Those who move into the ranks of higher editorships are those whose work and dependability are apparent at this beginning level. Future editors usually have to demonstrate that they can master the rudiments of reporting and writing, even though they may not have to excel at these skills.

Future editors must also demonstrate that they understand the culture of journalism and the demands that it makes both professionally and personally on them. Journalists must be fundamentally honest people and must adhere to the standards set forth by the news organization in particular and the profession in general.

Future editors must also show that they can work easily with other people, that they can make contributions to a group without necessarily getting individual credit, and that they take as well as give direction. Showing respect for colleagues while also upholding high journalistic standards is likely to indicate that a person is editor material. Editors must be able to raise questions without offense. They must be able to spot mistakes, discrepancies and contradictions in the work of others, and they should also be willing to have their own work put under scrutiny.

Finally, a good editor should understand the purpose, objectives, and operation of the news organization for which he or she wants to work as editor. An editor may have the power to change procedures and operations but should exercise that power with discretion.

A person who would be an editor should watch good editors at work and do what they do.

QUESTIONS FOR DISCUSSION

1. After reading this chapter, do you think you have what it takes to be an editor? What do you think are your strengths? What are your weaknesses?
2. This chapter makes much of the editor–writer relationship. Think about some of the ways that a strong relationship between an editor and writer would be able to produce better journalism.

RELATED WEB SITES

American Association of Sunday and Feature Editors, www.aasfe.org/index.html

American Copy Editors Society, www.copydesk.org

American Society of Newspaper Editors, www.asne.org

Associated Press Managing Editors, www.apme.com

National Conference of Editorial Writers, www.ncew.org

READINGS AND REFERENCES

Baskette, F. K., Sissors, J. Z., & Brooks, B. S. (2001). *The art of editing* (7th ed.). Boston: Allyn and Bacon.

Berg, A. S. (1978). *Max Perkins: Editor of genius.* New York: Dutton.

Bernstein, T. M. (1995). *The careful writer: A modern guide to English usage.* New York: Free Press.

Bowles, D. A., & Borden, D. L. (2000). *Creative editing* (3rd ed.). Belmont, CA: Wadsworth.

Davis, F., & Dunlap, K. F. (2000). *The effective editor: How to lead your staff to better writing and better teamwork*. St. Petersburg, FL: Poynter Institute.

Ellis, B. G. (2001). *The copy editing and headline handbook*. New York: Perseus Books Group.

Frazell, D. F., & Tuck, G. (1996). *Principles of editing: A comprehensive guide for students and journalists*. New York: McGraw-Hill Text.

Friend, C., Challenger, D., & McAdams, K. (2000). *Contemporary editing*. Lincolnwood, IL: NTC/Contemporary Publishing Group.

Harrigan, J. T., & Dunlap, K. B. (2003). *The editorial eye* (2nd ed.). Boston: Bedford/ St. Martin's.

LaRocque, P. (2003). *Concise guide to copy editing*. Oak Park, IL: Marion Street Press.

Rivers, W. L., & Rodriguez, A. W. (1995). *A journalist's guide to grammar and style*. Boston: Allyn and Bacon.

Ryan, B., O'Connell, M., & Ryan, L. B. (2001). *The editor's toolbox*. Ames, IA: Iowa State University Press.

Smith, R. F., et al. (1996). *Editing today*. Ames, IA: Iowa State University Press.

Stepp, C. S. (1989). *Editing for today's newsroom: New perspectives for a changing profession*. Hillsdale, NJ: Lawrence Erlbaum Associates.

Stovall, J. G., & Mullins, E. (2000). *The complete editor*. Dubuque: Kendall/Hunt.

Walsh, B. (2002). *Lapsing into a comma*. New York: McGraw-Hill.

Zinsser, W., et al. (1994). *Speaking of journalism: 12 writers and editors talk about their work*. New York: HarperCollins.

Chapter Thirteen

Editing and Headline Writing

Key Concepts and Terms

1. Good copyediting skills are a must for any editor.

2. Headlines: a few words used to describe a story or article; they appear in larger type than the body of the story, and they are what the reader uses to decide whether or not to read the story.

3. In copyediting editors should not only fix technical errors (grammar, punctuation, spelling, style, etc.), but they should also work to improve the writing.

4. Copy editors should always check the math in a story and make sure the numbers add up.

5. Good copyediting requires that editors have a wide range of knowledge and that they be skilled in finding information efficiently.

6. Jargon: specialized language used by a particular group but not understood by a general audience.

7. In the use of language, the simpler the better; simple words and phrases are more readily understandable, efficient, and memorable.

8. Redundancy: an expression that uses more words than necessary, for example, *Easter Sunday* or *old adage*.

9. Headline writing takes special skill and efficiency in using the language.

Editors, particularly copy editors, are best thought of as readers' advocates. They are supposed to read the copy created by reporters and others with a fresh, questioning eye. Not only are they to fix technical errors in grammar, spelling, and punctuation, but they are also supposed to call attention to errors in fact, unclear writing, wordiness, and other deficiencies of writing. And it is their responsibility to correct these deficiencies. They should approach their work not with an attitude of arrogance but with a confidence that they can improve the work that is before them. This chapter is designed to give beginning copy editors some of the tools to gain that confidence.

The second part of this chapter relates some of the principles of one of the hardest jobs the journalist has—writing headlines. Headlines are an extremely efficient use of the language, and because we can read them so quickly, we get the impression that they must be easy to write. They're not. People with great talent and intelligence struggle with writing headlines. Creating an accurate and clear statement with just a few words is mightily difficult as you will find out when you begin attempting to write headlines.

Copyediting and headline writing are often handled by the same people in a newsroom. Knowledge of the language is the basis on which these tasks can begin, but the work goes much further than that. The successful copy editor must understand the fundamental principles of journalism, beginning with accuracy.

Accuracy

Accuracy is the most important consideration of an editor. Accuracy is the central reason for much of what an editor does. In the pursuit of accuracy a word of doubtful spelling is checked, one last fact in the story is looked up, or a source is called close to deadline when parts of a story are in question.

A reputation for accuracy is a publication's most valuable resource. Not only does it inspire the confidence of readers, but also an obvious willingness on the part of editors to strive for accuracy opens up new sources of information for the newspaper and often gets the paper out of embarrassing and dangerous legal entanglements. This reputation for accuracy may be the best way to ensure the survival of the publication. One example of this is the reputation for reliability that the *New York Times* built during the "yellow journalism" era. While other papers, especially in New York City, were trying to outdo one another in their sensationalism and outrageousness, the *Times* remained a calm, thoughtful voice that readers found they could count on. Today, the one New York paper that survives from that era is the *New York Times*.

No substitute exists for accuracy. Readers are notoriously unwilling to accept the very reasonable excuses that reporters are inexperienced, that the publication is understaffed, or that the paper was having a busy news day. Few readers have any concept of what the pressure of deadlines can do to good reporting or editing. What they understand is that a headline did not accurately reflect the content of a story, that the capital city of their home state was misspelled, or that their child was misidentified in the cutline of a picture that included several other children. Readers won't easily forgive such mistakes, nor will they forget them. Just a few errors are enough to get a publication in trouble, damage its credibility, and demonstrate to readers that it is unworthy of their attention and money. Like weeds in a garden, a bad reputation needs no cultivation; all it needs is a start.

For an editor, the pursuit of accuracy is a state of mind. An editor must be willing to check everything in doubt and must be willing to doubt anything. An editor must cast a cold eye on the work of the reporters, even those with the most experience and best reputation; the editor must demand an accounting from them as much as from novices. The editor must even be willing to doubt his or her own knowledge and experience and must occasionally recheck what he or she knows to be true. Such editors may make life hard on themselves and those around them, but their efforts will pay dividends for the good reputation of the publication.

Checking Facts

Obviously, an editor cannot check every single fact in a story. Time pressures will not allow a daily newspaper editor to do this even if the resources were available. Instead, certain elements of stories should always raise some questions in editors' minds. The following is an explanation of some of those elements.

Names and Titles

There is no quicker way for a publication to lose readers than to misspell names. A name is a person's most valuable possession; to misspell it shows an inexcusable sloppiness on the part of the writer and editor. If there is any way possible, names should always be checked for proper spelling. Titles present another possible problem area for journalists. An editor should do his or her best to ensure that titles are correct. Titles, of course, should conform to AP style or the style used by the publication. They should also be technically correct and written as those who use them regularly would write them. For instance, most people probably think that a person who teaches at a college or university is a "professor." That title would suffice for most readers, but for those who know better, there is a vast difference between calling someone "professor" and "assistant professor." The journalist should seek technical as well as general accuracy in titles. An efficient and effective editor knows where to look or whom to call to double-check these important matters.

Numbers

Any time there are numbers in a story, bells should ring in the head of the editor—especially if those numbers are supposed to add up to something in a story. An inconsistency in numbers is easy to check if the answers are contained in the story, but it is often overlooked. Too often editors look at numbers and assume that they are correct. Editors cannot make such assumptions safely. They need to make sure that percentages add up to 100 and that all other numbers add up correctly.

Places

Editors should be extremely careful about describing places and place names. To say that something is happening in Nashville when it is really happening in Knoxville or to describe St. Louis as the capital of Missouri or to write that Holland is part of Scandinavia can make a publication look foolish.

The Story's Inner Logic

We have already said that the numbers in a story should add up correctly. So should the facts. Readers should get a good idea of the time sequence of a story even if the facts of the story are not presented in chronological order, as they almost never are. Questions raised in one part of the story should be answered in another part of the story. One example of raising such questions in a story would be to state, "This building is the third tallest in the state," and not mention the two taller buildings. All of the facts in a story should have a logical relationship to one another that the reader can easily discern. Throwing facts into a story without proper transitions or a logical sequence presents obstacles that can ultimately decrease readers' interest in a story and in the publication.

A DAY IN THE LIFE OF A COPY EDITOR

Nora Shoptaw
News & Record, Greensboro, N.C.

"And what do you do?" asks the well-meaning gentleman. Internally I groan because I know what's coming.

"I work at the newspaper," I reply.

"Oh, have I seen your byline? What's your beat?" he smiles, proud of his knowledge of newspaper hierarchy.

"No, I'm a copy editor." And his face twists in confusion.

The problem with being a copy editor is that your best work goes unseen. You don't get the same name recognition as the reporters. But I believe that copy editors have to be the best writers in the newsroom.

Copy editors must have a multitude of skills. First and foremost, you must have an eye for detail. You must relish the intricacies of the English language, the joy of a well-placed comma, the logic of abbreviations. You must be able to recall the hundreds of grammar and AP style rules at will and on deadline. You must be able to read and understand a 60-inch centerpiece story, spackle any holes in it, trim the fat, and write a thoughtful, concise headline. And don't forget to breathe.

Second, depending on where you work, you may be designing pages as well. In that role, you must take a blank page, 72 picas by 21.5 inches, and create something that lures readers who shuffle busily past the metal news rack, intent on their problems. It must catch their eye, using only a few words and pictures. It must present to them the world on a platter, or in this case, newsprint. And then you have to do it all over again the next day.

And you have to have something else: a thick skin. Because yours are the last hands that touch a page before it becomes public property, before thousands of eyes examine it over their morning coffee. You are the last line of defense in the fight for accuracy and eloquence. And when the system breaks down, it often falls in your lap. But whenever you make mistakes—and you will—you'll also be a better copy editor for it.

Nora Shoptaw is a special sections designer for the News & Record *in Greensboro, North Carolina.*

Brevity

"Brevity is the soul of wit," according to Polonius, Shakespeare's ill-fated character in *Hamlet*. Polonius was in reality one of Shakespeare's most verbose personalities. Words came tumbling out of his mouth. Not only was he verbose, but he was also boring. Polonius was one of those people everyone tried to avoid.

Publications can do the same thing. They can use too many words, piling phrase upon phrase and letting the sentences run on long after the thoughts have run out. They put too many words in the way of what really needs to be said.

Editors need to recognize when writers are being long-winded. They should remove the well-turned but unnecessary phrase and eliminate that which has already been stated. The process can go too far, of course. Accuracy and clarity should never be sacrificed for brevity's sake, but brevity should be another major goal in the mind of an editor.

Many editors approach editing a story thinking that it deserves to be a certain length and no longer. Sometimes a writer writes 300 words and an editor wants only 200. How does one go about paring such a story down? Here are some tips:

- **Get to the point.**   What is the story about? What happened? What does the story need to tell the reader? An editor needs to be able to answer those questions in the simplest terms possible. Answering those questions is sometimes the hardest part of writing or editing, but once that is done, the job can become much easier.

- **Watch for redundancies and repetitions.**   Redundancies show a lack of disciplined thinking. They slip into writing unnoticed, but their presence can make the most important stories seem silly. Repetition is also an indication that the editor was not concentrating on the story. Sometimes facts need to be repeated for clarity's sake, but this is not often the case.

- **Cut out unnecessary words.**   There may be words in a story that simply add nothing to the meaning. These words are hard to pin down, but a sharp-eyed editor can spot them. They are words such as "really," "very," and "actually." They're simply phrase-makers, but they don't tell the reader much.

Finally, when you have run out of things to write about, stop writing.

Clarity

After accuracy, clarity must be one of the chief goals of an editor. Facts that are unclear are of little use to the reader. The English language is extremely versatile, but that versatility can lead to confusion when the language is in the hands of amateurs. Editors must be experts in the language and in the proper and clear organization of a story. Editors must be on constant guard against writing or story structures that could be confusing to the reader.

Like the pursuit of accuracy, the pursuit of clarity is a state of mind for editors. They must make sure that everything they do in some way promotes the clarity of the copy before them. Like the reader, an editor must approach a story as someone who was not there and did not see it happen and who has probably not discussed it with anyone. This approach is doubly difficult for an editor who may in fact know a great deal about the story's subject. Editing for clarity demands a rare degree of mental discipline.

The opposite of clarity is confusion. Confusion can infiltrate a story in many ways, and it is the editor's responsibility to eliminate this confusion. A common source of confusion is the reporter who does not understand what he or she is writing about. If a writer does not understand his or her subject, it is highly unlikely that he or she will be able to write about it so that other people can understand it. Reporters rarely recognize this shortcoming, however, and it is up to the editor to point it out and to make any necessary changes, assisted by the reporter.

Clear writing is an art, but it is also a skill. Expressing thoughts, ideas, and facts in a clear way is one of the most difficult jobs writers have, even though the product may read as if the clarity were easily accomplished. The key to clear writing is understanding the subject you are writing about. When a writer can express his or her thoughts about a subject in clear terms, then that understanding has been achieved.

The following are some tips for helping writers and editors achieve clarity.

- **Keep it simple.**   Many people believe that they can demonstrate their intelligence by using complex terms. Their language, they feel, will show others that they have mastered a difficult subject or that they speak or write with authority. Consequently, they use big words and complex sentences to express the simplest ideas.

    The problem with this attitude is that people forget their original purpose for writing is to communicate ideas. Any writing that draws attention to itself and, thus, draws attention away from the content is ineffective. Writing, especially in the mass media, should be as simple and straightforward as possible. Reporters and editors should use simple terms and sentence structures. They should avoid piling adjectives and phrases on top of one another. They should use their talents and intellect not to talk down to their readers but to transmit ideas and facts as efficiently as possible.

- **Avoid jargon.**   Jargon is specialized language that almost all groups in society develop. Students, baseball managers, doctors, and gardeners use words that have special meaning for them and no one else. Journalists are not doing their jobs if they simply record jargon, however accurately, and give it back to the reader. Today's journalists must be translators. They must understand the jargon of different groups they cover but must be intelligent enough not to use it in their stories. Editors must make phrases such as "viable alternative," "optimum care," and "personnel costs" mean something to the reader. They cannot simply thrust such phrases on the reader and believe that they have done the job adequately.

- **Be specific.**   Journalists must set the stage of the story for their readers. They must make sure that the readers have a clear picture in their minds of what is going on, when it is happening, where it is happening, and how it is taking place. Reporters and editors cannot assume that readers know very much about the stories they write and edit.

Readers who have not seen what reporters have seen won't know what reporters are talking about. One aspect of this problem occurs with the use of *the*, especially by inexperienced reporters. For example, a lead may begin in the following way, "The City Council Tuesday approved funds for purchasing *the* new computer system for the finance department." A reader is likely to ask, "What new computer system?" While covering the story, the reporter kept hearing everyone talk about "the new computer system," so that's what appeared in the story. Editors particularly need to watch for this kind of assumption and to make sure that readers are not left out of the loop.

- **Check the time sequence.**   Most news stories will not be written in chronological order, but readers should have some idea of the narrative sequence of the events in a story. When the time sequence is not clear, readers may become confused and misunderstand the content of the story.

- **Use transitions.**   Transitions are necessary for smooth, graceful, and clear writing. Each sentence in a story should logically follow the previous sentence or should relate to it in some way. New information in a story should be connected to information already introduced. Readers who suddenly come upon new information or a new subject in a story without the proper transition will be jolted and confused.

Editing Procedure

An editor ideally should be able to read through any story at least three times. Sometimes, of course, there isn't time to do that, but in this section we'll assume that for any given story, the time is available. Here's how that time should be used.

The first reading of any story should be a fairly quick one. This reading allows the editor to get the "feel" of the story, to find out what it is about, and to spot any major problems that are readily identifiable. The editor should note the story content and structure. This first reading may be all an editor needs to realize the story should go back to the reporter for rewriting. As much as possible, editors should do first readings as if they knew little or nothing about the subjects. This, of course, is the position of the average reader on first reading the story.

If the editor deems the story good enough for the rest of the editing procedure, the second reading should take place much more slowly. It is on this reading that the major editing is done. Accuracy, clarity, and brevity are the major goals of the editor. With these goals in mind, editors should use the following guidelines in editing any story.

The Lead

The editor should pay particular attention to the lead or, in the case of a magazine article, the introduction. It is the most important part of a story. A good lead will get the reader into a story; a boring or confusing lead will send the reader somewhere else.

Story Structure

After the lead, the editor should deal with the organization of the story. Is the story put together in a logical manner, especially with regard to the lead? Facts should be given in a manner that will satisfy the reader. Not all of the facts can be given at once, nor should they be. The story should develop in a way that allows the reader to understand the information the story is attempting to convey. The editor's job is to make sure that happens.

Completeness

Every story should have all the facts necessary for the reader to understand the story. Although reporters and editors must make certain assumptions about the readers' prior knowledge, these assumptions cannot be carried too far. For instance, if an editor is dealing with a city council story, he or she cannot assume that the reader has read last week's city council story. If some action the council takes is a follow-up to action taken the previous week, the story must explain that.

Another area of completeness that is often overlooked involves the failure of a story to provide all of the facts the reader is led to expect. A story might talk about a new day care center about to open. The reader, particularly a parent who might want to use the center, would want to know what hours it plans to keep, what age children the center will accept, and how much it will cost. Stories without such facts are incomplete.

Style

Every publication should have a set style, and every editor should see that the story conforms to this style. Most newspapers use the *Associated Press Stylebook* and supplement this with a local stylebook. Style should not be a straitjacket into which an editor forces all copy; rather it should be a help to writers and editors in achieving accuracy and consistency.

Names and Titles

Journalists should be particularly careful in handling names and titles, and editors must make every effort to ensure their accuracy. Names that have unusual spellings should always be checked. Editors need to remember that even the most common names may have uncommon spellings (as in *Smith, Smyth,* and *Smythe*). Nothing should be taken for granted when dealing with a person's name. There is no quicker way for a publication to lose credibility than by misspelling a name.

Titles, too, need special care. Formal titles should be correctly stated; they are extremely important to the people who hold them. Titles should also be descriptive of the jobs people have. If they are not, editors may consider adding a line of job description in the story if this will clarify things to the reader.

Quotations and Attribution

Good editors understand how to use quoted material properly. A good news story usually has a mixture of direct and indirect quotations, and a news writer must have a good sense of when to use them.

Most news stories will use more indirect quotations than direct quotations. An indirect quotation may contain one or a few of the same words that a speaker has used but will also have words that the speaker did not use.

Indirect quotations should maintain the meaning of what the speaker said but use fewer words than the speaker used. Writers and editors can paraphrase what people say and be more efficient than the speakers themselves. Journalists can get more information into their stories if they use indirect quotes.

If that is the case, why worry about using direct quotations at all? Why not just use indirect quotations all of the time?

Direct quotations are used by the skillful writer and editor to bring a story to life, to show that the people in the story are real, and to enhance the story's readability. Occasionally, people will say something in a memorable or colorful way, and that should be preserved by the writer.

The following are some of the basic rules for using direct quotations in news stories:

- **Use the exact words of the speaker.**   Anything that is within quotation marks should be something the speaker actually said. The words should be the speaker's, not the writer's.

- **Use direct quotations sparingly.**   Good writers and editors will let people speak, but they won't let them ramble on. Most newswriters avoid putting one direct quote after another in a story.

- **Use direct quotations to supplement and clarify the information presented in the indirect quotes.**   In a news story, a direct quote is rarely used to present new or important information to the reader. It is most commonly used to follow up information that has already been put in the story.

Knowing how to deal with direct and indirect quotations is one of the most important skills that a newswriter or editor can acquire. It takes some practice to paraphrase accurately and to select the direct quotations that should be used in a story. The key to both is to listen carefully so that you understand what the speaker is saying and so that you remember the exact words that the speaker has used. For the editor, a sensitivity to a good quotation and to a reader's tolerance must be developed.

The correct sequence for a direct quote and its attribution is direct quote, speaker, verb. This sequence is generally used in news stories because it follows the inverted pyramid philosophy of putting the most important information first.

Triteness and Clichés

Even the most common news stories should have some freshness about them. Editors need to be sensitive to the fact that some words and phrases are overused. "Dead on arrival," "straight as an arrow," "very," "basically," "quite," "mainly," "really," and "actually" are all words and phrases that can easily show up too many times in a publication.

Wordiness

A story should not be one word longer than necessary in order to maintain accuracy and clarity. Most reporters, especially young ones, use too many words. Editors should be on the lookout for such expressions as "a total of," "in order to," "as a result of," and "at this point in time."

Repetition and Redundancy

Speakers who use the same words over and over quickly become boring, and so do writers. English is a language with a large variety of words easily understood by most people. Reporters and editors should take advantage of this variety and make sure they don't repeat major nouns, verbs, or adjectives in one sentence or paragraph.

A redundancy is a phrase or set of words in which the same meaning is transmitted twice. Some redundancies make writers and editors look foolish. "A dead corpse," "we should not forget to remember," "apathetic people who don't care" are phrases in need of editing.

Offensive Language

Different publications maintain different policies on printing offensive language. Not too many years ago, "hell" and "damn" were regularly expunged from a story. Today much stronger language finds its way into many publications. The editor's job to see that the policies of the publication are carried out. If no such policy exists, one should be developed that takes into account the goals of the publication and the sensibilities of its readers. As with most editorial decision making, it always helps to confer with others on sensitive matters.

Principles of Headline Writing

Headline writers must learn to catch the most important and interesting details of news stories as they edit them. They must discover what the reporter is trying to say about the topic and detect those angles and elements of the story that lie at its heart.

Style is important. A copy editor and headline writer must have a complete knowledge of style and an ability to apply that knowledge.

But for the good copy editor, style is only a part of the process. Far more important is shaping the story so that excess baggage is cut out and the remaining words clearly create those images and thoughts important to the story. This process of shaping the story and detecting its central elements leads directly to good headlines.

Words must be used precisely. Headlines are abbreviated news stories. Headline writers must create vivid impressions with only a few words. They must be vocabulary experts.

The headline must serve the dual function of informing and attracting the reader. Every word must create understanding and interest. This dual task requires that each word be carefully selected for its maximum impact on the reader.

Good headline writers must be knowledgeable about as many subjects as possible. They must quickly grasp relationships between pieces of information. They must be able to see what reporters are driving at in their copy or even perhaps to see things the reporter may have missed. This ability requires that headline writers read their own and other newspapers and tune in to as many radio and television broadcasts as possible. Following are some general principles that headline writers must follow.

Accuracy

Above all else, a headline must be accurate. Headlines that contain inaccurate information or leave false impressions are doing a disservice to the reader and to the publication. As in every other activity of the reporter or editor, accuracy is the main goal in writing headlines.

Sometimes inaccuracies are obvious and are the result of laziness on the part of the headline writer. For example, in the following headline and story, the headline writer simply read one thing and thought another.

> **Arson cause**
> **of school fire**
>
> Investigators are searching through the rubble of Joy School today trying to find the cause of the fire that destroyed the 50-year-old building on Friday.
>   Fire Marshal Benny Freeman said no concrete clues have been found but did not rule out arson as a possible cause of the blaze.

The headline makes a definite statement about the cause of the fire but the story does not. The writer of this headline simply did not read the story carefully enough and did not understand what it said.

Logic

Headlines should not only be accurate, but also they should make sense. Some headline writers assume that readers are going to read the story for which the head is being written. Consequently, they write headlines that can be understood only if the story is read. For example,

> **Senator wants Labor Secretary on leave**

was the headline on a story about a senator who called for the secretary of labor to take a leave of absence while being investigated. Readers who only read the headline would be confused; they might be able to figure it out, especially if they were to read the story, but the reader is not obligated to figure anything out.

The problem of logic in headlines occurs, as in the preceding example, when a headline tries to include several disparate ideas. If these ideas are not in logical order, the headline can be confusing. The following two examples demonstrate this kind of confusion.

> **Judge denies policy on Haitians biased**

> **'Serious case of vandalism,'**
> **as train derails, kills one**

Each of these headlines demonstrates that the headline writer did not have a clear idea about what the headline should say. Getting a good idea—one that will be easy for the readers to grasp—and sticking with that idea as the headline is being written is an important and difficult part of the headline writing process.

Another problem with logic in headlines is the attribution of feelings, characteristics, or actions to things that are not capable of such feelings, characteristics, or actions. In literature, we might call this "personification" or a "pathetic fallacy." It occurs in the following headline.

> **Martial law rules Bolivia**

When you read it closely, the headline does not make much sense. Martial law cannot rule anything; people rule and they may use martial law to rule. Keep in mind what people or things in your headlines can and cannot do.

Specificity

A headline should be as specific as possible in presenting information to the reader. Many beginning headline writers fall into the trap of writing general headlines or using words with general meanings, and their headlines don't say much. The reader ought to be able to get a good idea about what is going on in the story from the headline.

If this is not the case, the headline needs to be rewritten. Examples of this lack of specificity can be found in the following headlines.

Sex and drugs cause
for combined efforts

Governor waits to announce plan

Nuclear report cloudy

Another problem related to lack of specificity in headlines is that of attribution. Headline writers should not express their opinions in headlines; nor should they express the opinion of others without proper attribution. Remember that headlines are statements of fact, not opinion. To state opinion as fact is to mislead the reader, as in the following headlines.

Chances for budget passage good

Marine training builds character

The foregoing statements need some form of attribution. Sometimes headline writers can get around the problem of attribution by putting the expressions of opinion in quotation marks. Quotation marks indicate that the words used come from someone in the story, not from the headline writer. However, when quotation marks are used, the headline writer should make sure that the words within the marks appear within quotation marks inside the body of the story. For example, in the preceding headlines, if we were to put quotation marks around the words "good" and "builds character," we would need to make sure that the stories quoted someone saying these things.

Word Precision

Using words precisely is a must for the headline writer. Because headlines appear in larger type than body copy, they are more likely to be read and carry more authority than the smaller type. For that reason, it is imperative that the words in the headline are used for their exact and most common meanings. For example, in the following headline,

Lovers' quarrel named
cause of murder–suicide

the word *named* is misused. People might say that a lover's quarrel caused the murder–suicide, but a cause of this sort of thing is usually not "named."

Double Meanings

Double meanings, or double entendres, crop up in headlines all the time, and editors should keep a constant watch for them. They can be embarrassing for the newspaper and for the people involved in a story. Double meanings can range from the hilarious to the scatological:

Father of 10 shot;
mistaken for rabbit

Three states
hit by blizzard;
one missing

Mother of 12
kills husband
in self-defense

Editors should read headlines to try to discern every possible meaning that the words in the head could carry.

Guidelines

Headlines must conform to certain rules. These rules may vary according to the publication, but the following guidelines will help you in producing consistent, informative heads.

- Headlines should be based on the main idea of the story, which should be found in the lead or introduction.
- If facts are not in the story, do not use them in a headline.
- Avoid repetition. Don't repeat key words in the same headline; don't repeat the exact wording of the story in the headline.
- Avoid ambiguity, insinuations, and double meanings.
- If a story qualifies a statement, the headline should also. Headline writers should understand a story completely before they write the headline.
- Use present-tense verbs for headlines that refer to past or present events.
- For the future tense, use the infinitive form of the verb (such as *to go, to run*, etc.) rather than the verb *will*.
- *To be* verbs, such as *is, are, was,* and *were*, should be omitted.
- Alliteration, if used, should be deliberate and should not go against the general tone of the story.
- Do not use articles *a, an,* and *the*. These take up space that could be put to better use in informing the reader. In the following examples, the second headline gives readers more information than the first.

New police patrols help
make the streets safer

New patrols help make
westside streets safer

■ Do not use the conjunction *and*. It also uses space unnecessarily. Use a comma instead.

**Mayor and council
meet on budget for next year**

**Mayor, council agree
to cuts on new budget**

■ Avoid using unclear or little-known names, phrases, and abbreviations in headlines.

■ Use punctuation sparingly.

■ Never begin a headline with a verb.

■ Headlines should be complete sentences or should imply complete sentences. When a linking verb is used, it can be implied rather than spelled out.

■ Fill out most of the space allowed for headlines; do not leave gaping holes of white space. In most newspapers headlines should fill at least 90 percent of the maximum space allowed.

■ Avoid "headlinese"—that is, words such as *hit, flay, rap, hike, nix, nab, slate,* and so on. Use words for their precise meaning.

■ Do not use pronouns alone and unidentified.

■ A noun and its modifier should be on the same line in a multiline headline. So should a preposition and its object. Violating this rule is called splitting, and following are examples of split headlines. With the greater use of larger headlines, many publications are relaxing this rule, but following it is still good discipline for the headline writer.

**President withdraws support of
new welfare reform legislation**

**Council plans new
efforts to control dogs**

■ With a multiline head, try to put the verb in the top line.

■ Be accurate and specific.

Procedure

Having the most thorough knowledge of the story, the editor should be the one who writes the headline. Assuming that is the case, here are some tips on how to produce a headline.

■ Make sure you understand what the story is about.

■ Find the action verb and the most important noun. What is happening in the story? What are the people in the story doing?

■ Sum up the story with key words; build this summary around the verb you have chosen.

- Break the head into logical line units.

- Once the first draft of the headline is written, begin substitution as necessary. Most of the time the first draft of a headline will not fit, and it may not say what you want it to say. Don't be afraid to use a thesaurus. Remember the logical substitutions, using a name for a title and vice versa, such as "Clinton" and "President." Remember nicknames, too, such as "Say-hey Kid" for Willie Mays.

- If all else fails, begin again. Try a fresh approach using something different about the story to construct the headline.

Headlines on the Web

Headlines on news web sites follow the same general form as newspaper headlines. They are succinct, descriptive of the copy they are headlining, and specific enough to offer information to the reader. They usually have a complete sentence motif that contains a subject and a verb (stated or implied), and they emphasize nouns and verbs more than other parts of the language.

Given that, however, fewer rules govern the writing of headlines for the Web. Being a fairly new medium, the Web has not developed the rules and protocols that the established medium of newspapers has. And it probably won't. Many of the newspaper rules are designed to save space and to make headlines fit into a certain space.

On a web site, the issue of space is not as crucial, although it still exists. In a sense, the Web seems infinite because it can hold an enormous amount of information—far more than can be found in a daily newspaper. But the purpose of a headline on a web site is almost the same as it is in a printed publication. It must convey information about the copy to a reader quickly and succinctly, it must be accurate, and it must be specific enough to be interesting.

Consequently, although a headline writer on a web site has a little more leeway in the spacing requirements than a newspaper headline writer, the writer must be brief and clear. He or she may be able to use a few more articles, adjectives, and adverbs, but their use is restricted. Take a look at the examples of headlines on the Web sites listed at the end of the chapter. You will find many similarities to headlines on a newspaper page.

QUESTIONS FOR DISCUSSION

1. Why is accuracy so important for a publication? What does the editor have to do with ensuring accuracy?
2. Bring an example of unclear or confused writing to class. Why is it unclear? What could be done to make it clearer?
3. Look for an example of a headline in a newspaper or on a news web site that is too vague to be easily understood. Bring it to class and be prepared to discuss how it could be improved.

RELATED WEB SITES

American Copy Editors Society, http://copydesk.org

No Train, No Gain, www.notrain-nogain.org

Poynter Online's Writing and Editing Resources, http://poynteronline.org/subject.asp?id=2

Poynter Online's Writing and Editing Tipsheets, http://poynteronline.org/content/content_view.asp?id=31907

The Slot, www.theslot.com

READINGS AND REFERENCES

Baskette, F. K., Sissors, J. Z., & Brooks, B. S. (2001). *The art of editing* (7th ed.). Boston: Allyn and Bacon.

Davis, F., & Dunlap, K. F. (2000). *The effective editor: How to lead your staff to better writing and better teamwork.* St. Petersburg, FL: Poynter Institute.

Ellis, B. G. (2001). *The copy editing and headline handbook.* New York: Perseus Books Group.

Fellow, A. R., & Clanin, T. N. (2002). *Copy editor's handbook for newspapers* (2nd ed.). Englewood, CO: Morton Publishing.

Ryan, B., O'Connell, M., & Ryan, L. B. (2001). *The editor's toolbox.* Ames, IA: Iowa State University Press.

Smith, R. F., et al. (1996). *Editing today.* Ames, IA: Iowa State University Press.

Walsh, B. (2002). *Lapsing into a comma.* New York: McGraw-Hill.

Writing Exercises

EXERCISE 13.1

Wordiness

Each of these paragraphs or sentences contains far too many words. Edit them so that they use fewer words but still retain the same information and meaning.

1. Thorough knowledge of the academic regulations and policies of the University and its academic divisions is essential for all students. Each student is expected to become familiar with the University of Westmedia undergraduate catalog and to consult with the academic advisers provided by the student's division.

2. She donated $25,000 of her own money to the cause.

3. The company makes labels for a wide variety of products found in retail stores and outlets.

4. Revenue reductions for the state will amount to $500 million if the programs are eliminated.

5. People in Asian countries have been eating jellyfish as a delicacy for hundreds of years.

6. As you carefully read what you have written to improve your wording and catch small errors of spelling, punctuation, and so on, the thing to do before you do

anything else is to try to see where sequences of subjects and verbs could replace the same ideas expressed in nouns rather than verbs.

7. The committee made the decision to wait until they had more information that would help them in making a final determination.

8. They entered into an agreement to take all the necessary steps to complete the task in a timely manner.

EXERCISE 13.2
Wordiness

The following sentences use too many words. Edit them carefully to reduce the number of words, but do not cut out important information. If necessary, rewrite the complete sentence.

1. Owing to the fact that the prerequisite courses had not been taken by John, he was having a great deal of difficulty and had to spend a lot of time figuring out his schedule for the semester that is coming up.

2. There is little consideration given by our professors to the very real problem that our textbooks are often extremely costly and expensive.

3. Alex said that the thing to do if he wanted to improve his writing would be to read as many good books as he could possibly read in the time available to him.

4. Baseball has always been thought of as the national past-time, but for all intents and purposes, football has replaced baseball as the favorite sport for many people across this country.

5. During the period of time that included most of February, Laura stayed cooped up in her room and tried to fight off the effects of a very bad and debilitating cold.

6. Basically, I have a disinclination and a disinterest in helping people who are not willing to do some things such as show up for work on time and put forth the effort that it often takes to succeed in this life.

EXERCISE 13.3
Wordiness

The following sentences use too many words. Edit them carefully to reduce the number of words, but do not cut out important information. If necessary, rewrite the complete sentence.

1. He was kind of a large man, heavy in weight, and not a very bright guy whose ability to think things through thoroughly was pretty limited.

2. The actual photograph was taken by John Smith and showed a room that was littered with paper and other items and furnished with furniture of a cheap quality.

3. Always confused by any kind of mathematical problem, Sally, for no reason that anyone could ever figure out, signed up for one of the hardest and most difficult math courses in the entire curriculum.

4. His past performance in not being able to win people over to his particular point of view certainly indicated to us that he was very likely to do poorly as a political candidate running for mayor.

5. My future plans include enrolling in a college or university where I can study the field of journalism and can improve my natural-born talent for writing.

6. The committee, meeting in executive session with no one else there, made the decision to cease and desist the practice of requiring members of the organization to pay money to attend all of the functions of the organization.

EXERCISE 13.4

Redundancies

Correct for style, spelling, and grammatical errors. Also, tighten to remove redundancies but do not rewrite this story. Underline changes you make. You may use a dictionary and stylebook.

Zipping through the sky, like 7 irate super-charged bees, they dart and flit trying to cut off each other's tail. Its all part of combat. In attempting a kill, quite often one will plunge down to the ground.

If you've ever wished there was something different and exciting you could do on a Sunday afternoon, then mark the third Sunday of every month on your calendar. That's when the Azalea City Model Aero Club meets at its field on the old Irvington landfill site to do battle, get together and fly remote-controlled airplanes.

"Each plane trails a long colorful crepe paper tail," said President Richard Moore. "The goal is to cut off the other plane's tail. The pilot who registers the most cuts is the winner."

ACMA holds an open combat event every third Sunday of each month. Heat times are 3 p.m., 4 p.m. and 5 p.m. All pilots are welcome, however, they must be AMA members. "Open" means anything that is airworthy can be flown.

"Combat is where a number of people can fly any type plane," said Frits Jetten, the club's Vice President. "But you don't want to fly an expensive plane. The plane that most pilots fly is basically just a wing with a small fuselage. One that is fast and agile. You certainly don't want to fly your best plane. I've seen as many as eleven go up with no collisions, but sometimes there is a kill, and you might lose the entire plane."

All the planes go up into the air at once. Each pilot has a spotter who helps him keep an eye on his plane. Pilots and spotters stand more than 100 yards from the planes which are flying overhead. There might be other planes with similar colors, but with the aid of the spotter, the pilot can concentrate on their own flying skills, while the spotter keeps an eye on the entire field and tells the pilot when his plane is straying away.

Frits Jetten's present combate plane is a blue and white plane, Scat Cat, that has been crashed several times, but after each crash Jetten has been able to make repairs and continue to fly, and make cuts.

Gordon Barton's flying wing (the Spook) revealed pilot error in a recent heat race. Gordon was keeping too close to the ground and apparently lost concentration for a couple seconds, and the Spook fell down to the ground below.

"A few pilots do not think they are good enough, or are not ready to fly combat." Barton says. "If you have graduated past the high wing trainer and can do the standard aerobatic maneuvers rolls, loops, fly inverted, and land smoothly you can fly combat. Anyone wanting to fly can touch base with any of our combat pilots, and they will be willing to provide advice and insight to anyone wanting to get active into combat.'

You do not need to own a plane or be a member of the club to enjoy the flying activities. The events are free to spectators, and the public is invited at no charge.

EXERCISE 13.5

Errors, style, and clarity

The following story has a number of errors that need to be corrected. Read through it carefully and make any changes you believe are necessary so that it will be clear to a reader.

Flooding due to last nights rain storm, has damaged sevierely consturction work on the city's newest radio station.

WXXg, which was secheduled to go on the air next month, has had it's air date moved back at least a mont, according to station spokesman Linda Rival.

Miss Rival, who is also one of the station's co-owners and has been advertised as planning to be one of the station's diskjockeys, said the floods severely damaged the interiro of the station and knowked down the half-completed towar.

"We haven't detemined the full extent of the damage, said Miss Rival, but I's sure its going to be bad.

She said the station would be delayed at least a month in going on the air.

The flooding was caused by some heavy rains that feel throughout the state earlier in the weak. Several homs and businessses in the area of the station known as Flat plains was reported damaged.

EXERCISE 13.6

AP style

Edit the following story so that it conforms to AP style. Make sure you deal with other problems in the story. You should discuss with your instructor any additional information you need and incorporate it into the story.

A majority of people in the state favor the raising of Federal taxes on cigaretes and alcoholic beverages, according to the poll conducted by the state's lagest newspaper.

The propsed "sin taxes" were endorsed as a means of raisng tax revenues and to discourage smoking and drinking, according to the Oct. 25-26 telephone poll of 1,598 adults in a scientific random sample.

Fifty-two per cent said they think state taxes on cigarettes should be raised, while 41% said they should not.

The 52 per cent who said cigarettes taxes should be raised broke down this way: 5 percent said taxes should be reasied to increase revenues, 10 percent to discourage smoking and 33 percent both.

Fifty-five per cent said Federal taxes on alcoholic beverages should be raised broke down this way: 11 percent said taxes should be raised to increase revenues, 9 percent to discourage drinking and 35 percent both.

The state Senate Budget Committee recently drew up a number of proposals to raise taxes next year, including one which would double the excise taxes on cigarettes, liquor, wine and beer.

The proposed increases, which Senate leaders say will be considered next year, would raise the price of a pack of cigarettes by 8 cents, the price of a gallon of liquor by $10.50, a barrel of beer by $9 and a gallon of wine by 34 cents. These increases will riase the prices of cigaretts and alcohol significatly over the price in neighboring states.

Sixty-two percent of the poll respondents said they drink alcoholic beverages, while 32 percent said they smoke cigarettes.

the results of the polls can vary from the opinions of all Americans because of chance variations in the sample. For a poll based on about 1,600 interviews, the results are subject to an error margin of 3 percentage points either way because of chance variations.

EXERCISE 13.7

AP style

Edit the following story so that it conforms to AP style. Make sure you deal with other problems in the story.

The Green County Comission borrowed more than $500,000 from restricted accounts to meet current expenses. Thats according to a state audit released last Friday.

Much of the indebtitude remains in an unpaid condition, according to county officials.

Loans totaling at least $320,000 were made from the countys road fund to the gasoline tax fund according to the audit that covered the period from October. 1, 1990 through September 301994.

By law, the county's road fund — called the "RRR fund" — only can be used for resurfacing, restoring and the rehabilitation of county roads.

The other loan totaling $100,000 was made from proceeds of the county's 1998 general obligations warrant to the general fund to meet current expenditures. The money from the warrant can be used only for capitol outlay expenditures.

The county was notified at the end of July by the state and started a repayment plan then, officials said.

Examiners found the county did not follow the bid law on the purchase of cleaning supplies for 1998 and the minutes of county commission meetings was not indexed from June 1997 through Sept., 1998.

"Several county funds had deficit fund balances," the audit states.

County Commission Clerk Tony Sanks says that steps were taken to repay the loans, with about $175,000 of the road fund loan already repaid. "We're taking steps now to pay it off, he said.

EXERCISE 13.8

Editing a longer story

This may take some time. Read this story carefully and note any questions you have about it. You may want to discuss these with your instructor. Edit the story so that it conforms to AP style. Make sure you deal with other problems in the story.

A Midville policeman shot a criminal during a struggle early Tuesday, then had his weapon turned on him before the suspect fleed and was overpowered by two other officers, police said.

Officer David Stuart shot Anthony Douglas, 31 of Duval Street, in the left side as they grappled over Stuarts .357-caliber handgun pistol behind a house in the 1000 block of Cherokee Street early in the morning shortly after 2 a.m., police said.

After being shot, Douglas continued to fight and Stuart fired again but missed, police said. Douglas then managed to take Stuart's eapon and pointed it at the officer before running off, police say.

The suspect was found moments later hiding near apartments several blocks away on Murray Hill Court, said police spokesman Tom Regan. Two officers nabbed him, Regan said.

Douglas apparently discarded the deadly weapon after leaving Stuart, Regan said. Investigators found it in a yard near the scene of his altercation with the officer, he said.

Douglas a convicted felon who was released from the penitentiary in December and was listed in stable but guarded condition Tuesday evening at Springhill Memorial Hospital, a spokeswoman declared.

Stuart was scratched during the confrontation, but the spokeswoman said that between the suspect and he, neither was bad hurt. It was difficult to tell who's injury was worst.

Douglas will be charged with first-degree robery because he took Stuart's weapon by force, Regan said. He likely will face more additional charges, the spokesman insisted.

Stuart, a five-year veteran, will be assigned to administrative duties until the departments shooting examination team finishes its review, Regan said. The special group of officers investigates any use of deadly force by officers.

The reviews of any fatal police-involved shooting is routinely sent to the district attorney's office, Cashdollar said. He said a report on Tuesday's shooting must be sent to District Attorney John Johnson Jr.

No one is more interested than him in such shootings, Tyson said. Such inquiries have only one purpose getting at the truth, he added. The district attorney spoke like he would look into the matter personally.

Tuesday's chase-and-struggle began shortly after 2 a.m. when Stuart, patroling Duval Street noticed an older model Dodge 600 parked in Baumhauer Park, police said. When Stuart turned his marked cruiser around to check out the car, the vehicle drove off in a hurry with its lights off, police said.

Stuart confronted Douglas at gunpoint as he leaped out of the passengers side of his car, but Douglas grabbed the weapon, police said. Douglas broke away and ran around the side of a house, where Stuart again met him with his gun drawn from his holster, police said.

Douglas grabbed the gun and tried to move it toward Stuart's face, according to police. Stuart forced the gun down and fired a shot, hitting Douglas in the side, police said. The scuffle continued, however, and Stuart tripped over an air-conditioning unit, losing control of his gun, police said. Douglas picked up the weapon, pointed it at Stuart and ordered him to flee, police said. When Stuart slipped, Douglas ran off, police said.

Thompson and officer Tim McDonald spotted Douglas moments later near apartments in a cul-de-sac on Murray Hill Court, Regan said.

Reagan said he was "not aware" that investigators had found anything illegal in Douglas's vehicle. The investigation, however, is continuing. The spokesman added that he did not know what affect such a finding might have or whether a jury might be adverse to such evidemce.

EXERCISE 13.9

Headline critique

Critique the following headlines. If possible, suggest how you might rewrite them.

Earlier deadlines
and new nightmares
for some taxpayers

Senate panel questions HHS nominee

24 candidates say
they will run for
Los Angeles mayor

Iraq yields
to UN on
two points

New car from Ford
is a solid winner

EXERCISE 13.10

Headline critiques

Critique the following headlines. If possible, suggest how you might rewrite them.

Jackson mayor cites 3%
drop in crime last year

Bill may allow
residents to buy
vacant city land

Lawmakers dislike new system

Two children caught
in house fire die from smoke

Sergeant gets calls
offering aid to five
motherless children

EXERCISE 13.11

Headline writing

Write headlines for the three stories that follow. Your headline writing assignment will be supplied by the instructor.

SAN FRANCISCO, Calif.—Like Goldilocks and the bowls of porridge, many wine drinkers find standard 750-milliliter wine bottles too big and 350-milliliter "splits" too small.

The larger bottles are a bit much for a couple to share with dinner or lunch, and the splits are not quite enough. To make things worse, wine does not keep well, and many consumers feel obliged to finish off a bottle once it has been opened.

Last month a coalition of California winemakers won federal approval for a compromise size, the 500-milliliter bottle. Winemakers hope to begin selling the new size early next year.

"It's the perfect size for dinner," said Napa Valley winemaker George Vierra, who led a petition drive for the 500-ml bottles with the federal Bureau of Alcohol, Tobacco and Firearms.

Vierra was eager to find an alternative to the standard wine bottle because of his own experience.

KUALA LUMPUR, Malaysia—Malaysian and Indonesian leaders are wrestling with a double-edged sword—windfall profits from the rise in world oil prices but fears that a global recession will harm other carefully nurtured exports.

While both stand to gain the most among Asian nations from the petroleum boom triggered by Iraq's Aug. 2 invasion of Kuwait, the fate of other products designed to wean the two from overdependence on oil hangs in the balance.

Fresh from his huge re-election victory to a third, five-year term, Malaysian Prime Minister Mahathir Mohamad is expected to use the additional revenue to finance infrastructure projects and act to curb inflation, up from 2.8 percent to 4 percent this year due to higher oil prices.

BOSTON, Mass.—Hundreds of thousands of people skipped meals and even young schoolchildren forfeited snacks Thursday as Oxfam America held its annual nationwide fast to dramatize the plight of the hungry.

The Boston-based nonprofit organization also sponsored "hunger banquets" in five cities, hoping celebrity participants would focus more attention on the worldwide problem.

"We ask people to give up a meal or all meals for a day. They donate the money they would have spent on food to Oxfam America," said Ken White, a spokesman for the organization. He said the money is used to fund self-help, grass-roots efforts to combat hunger in 33 nations.

Chapter Fourteen

Visual Journalists

Key Concepts and Terms

1. Visual presentation of information can be as important as words; information and ideas are sometimes more understandable if they are visually presented or if they have a visual element.

2. Graphics journalist: a person who uses visual forms of presentation; the information the graphics journalist gathers should be suitable for these forms.

3. Visual journalism includes graphics, photojournalism, and layout and design.

4. Visual journalism developed during the latter part of the twentieth century in great part because computer technology made it easier to produce.

5. Design: the general rules that govern the appearance of a publication; these rules include general page format, type font and size, styles for bylines, cutlines, photographs, graphs, and so on.

6. Layout: the day-to-day use of design rules to produce the publication.

Vignette

Imagine journalism without many words.

That's what Celeste Bernard does every day. Bernard is the graphics editor of the Seattle Post-Intelligencer. Each day, she has her staff try to tell their stories with as few words as possible. Instead, they use photographs, drawings, maps, and charts. But doing that takes all the skills of a good reporter.

"Careful reporting is behind every respectable graphic," she says. "Diagrams can't be drawn unless the concepts or processes they illustrate are fully understood."

Bernard understands what all visual journalists know. Pictures, charts, and drawings are better at presenting some information than paragraphs of words. Still, the words—what few there are—are important.

"Visual journalists must craft together words that thread together concepts, pictures or trends," she says. "It is difficult work and usually means that a day's worth of reporting is boiled down to a few well-chosen words."

Even words and figures arranged in a visual way allow readers to discern a great deal of information that would be ponderous or impossible if the same thing was in paragraph form. For instance, look at the following table. It shows what grade averages high school students reported having as they took the Scholastic Aptitude Test for three different years:

GRADES REPORTED	1993	2002	2003
A+, A, A– grade averages	32%	41%	42%
B grade averages	51%	47%	47%
C grade averages	17%	11%	11%

Look at this table closely; what are the facts that you can discern from it? (What reported averages went up during this ten-year period? Which ones went down?) What do you make of these figures? With just a few words arranged visually, you can learn a great deal.

Now look at the table that follows—team standings for one of the divisions in major league baseball three days before the season ends—and see how much information is there:

TEAM	WINS	LOSSES	WINNING %	GAMES OUT
St. Louis	88	71	.543	—
Houston	87	72	.537	1.0
Chicago	85	74	.525	3.0

In this simple table, you can see how many games each team has played and how many each has won and lost. But you do not even have to read the numbers to get the main point of the table. The order in which the teams are listed tells you which team has done better than the others. Their records can be compared. And knowledgeable baseball fans can know, at a glance, how difficult it will be for the other teams to catch up to the first-place team.

Some forms of visual journalism are standardized and routine. Baseball standings, such as the preceding ones, have been around since the 1870s. Other forms, however, are not so standard, and that is one of the things that makes the work of Celeste Bernard and others in the area of visual journalism—especially graphics journalism—so exciting. Every day they come to work, they face the challenge of not only gathering information but also figuring out how to present it so that readers and viewers will understand it and be engaged by it.

Words and Pictures

Journalism is a craft dominated by words. Most people enter journalism because they are fascinated by the power of words and because they want to exercise that power themselves. But words are not the only tools of the journalist. Photographs, graphics, and design help journalists present information to the public. These tools that have been available for many decades are becoming increasingly important to the profession, and the journalists who use them well add to the power of their words.

For too long, the nonword tools of journalism, and the journalists who use them, have been treated as second-class citizens in the profession. Their work has been considered a lesser part of journalism, worthy but not as worthy as words. This attitude, which still prevails in some newsrooms, ignores the important human function of seeing or visualizing, and it ignores the duty that journalists have in helping their audiences understand fully the information they present.

Fortunately, this attitude is waning, and within the last two generations, there is an increasing respect for what visual journalists do. The reasons for this change are varied.

Audiences seem to demand more visual presentations and explanations from journalists.   We are now well into a third generation of people whose lives have been dominated by television. A great many young people have grown up with video games and other types of entertainment that rely on visual images in addition to words. Today, computer screens have taken their place beside books as the major source of stored information for many people, especially students, and those screens are likely to contain pictures and graphics as well as words. The power of pictures is becoming increasingly apparent, and audiences are more sophisticated than ever in interpreting visual explanations.

Technology allows us to produce more visuals more easily.   Not long ago, a picture had to go through a painstaking process to make it into print. The advent of computers and digitization has made the use of pictorial and graphic forms of presentation—and their integration with type—not only easy but also routine.

Many young people are now entering journalism with both training and determination to be visual journalists.   Fifty years ago, except for photojournalism, this was generally not the case. People inevitably began their lives as professional journalists by becoming news reporters. As careers progressed, some people developed interest in design and became layout editors. Beyond that, however, there were few openings for what we today know as graphics journalists. Few editors and managers had any sense that visual information was something they should pay any attention to.

The flexibility of the Web—a medium that can handle information in a wide variety of ways—is forcing many journalists to pay attention to the visual aspects of their stories. Journalists must learn more about how information can be presented visually. They are coming to understand that their words can be enhanced if they have visuals to go along with them. Consequently, more reporters are carrying cameras, gathering information that can be put into charts and graphs, and even making suggestions to page designers about how their information should be packaged.

Photojournalism—Journalism, Only Different

The photographer is possibly the most stereotyped of all journalists. That stereotype goes something like this: The photojournalist zooms around in his sports car and torn jeans, unworried about the alimony payments he owes his second wife. Editors don't want him in their meetings because he always looks lost and haggard. Most reporters think the guy is a little weird, mainly because he has spent his professional and leisure life breathing in smelly darkroom chemicals. He smokes so much, speculation among his colleagues is that he'll probably die of lung cancer at age 45. He's not stupid, but he can't write a complete sentence. That's why he's a photographer, of course.

Still, occasionally the guy will take a picture that makes a page pop.

As with many stereotypes, bits of truth can be found here and there in this picture, but it's mostly smoke (especially the "he" part, since many photojournalists today are women).

Photojournalism today is practiced by men and women highly skilled and deeply thoughtful about what they do and what they produce. Photographers understand the impact that their pictures can have.

Photojournalism is journalism, but with a far different method and outcome than the journalism practiced in other parts of the newsroom. The picture may indeed be worth a thousand words, as the ancient Chinese proverb goes, but to try to equate words and images may be a fool's errand. The picture is fundamentally apart from the word, and its production and effects are certainly different.

Philosophers, practitioners, and consumers have wondered at the power of the still image, particularly since the advent of photography in the 1830s. Before then, the unseen world was, for the most part, a matter of imagination, supplemented only by paintings and other artwork. (See Chapter 21.) Words, via books, magazines, and newspapers, helped people form an image of the greater world that they would probably never see. But that formation was slow—something like a slow horse and buggy. Photography brought the world into view at the speed of a lightly loaded freight train.

And the pictures carried with them an aura of accuracy that even the most skilled painter could not match. With photography, seeing was truly believing—and re-membering. Images were etched onto the brain with far greater ease than one could remember the shortest scriptures.

The power of the still image is still with us. We carry in our heads, clearly fo-cused, a picture of an airplane crashing into the World Trade Center, a firefighter car-rying the bloody child from the building explosion in Oklahoma City, streams of smoke from the exploded *Challenger* spacecraft, a Vietnamese police chief firing a bullet into the head of a Viet Cong soldier, the wonder in the eyes of the Holocaust victim at his survival—and a hundred other images that we did not personally wit-ness. Most of us are living proof that the photojournalist is doing his or her job.

If journalism is the first rough draft of history, then photojournalism is our first impression, and it is often a lasting impression.

Life and Times of the Photojournalist

News organizations place great value on pictures. The modern reader expects to see news and information as well as read about them. The image is an indispensable part of the information mix that any news publication must offer to its audience. Not only

FIGURE 14.1   Shooting the Scene The most visible of visual journalists are photographers. No publication can do without them. They must have their equipment ready at a moment's notice to cover any kind of news story.

does photography add to the understanding of the words, but it also allows the publication to develop a more interesting graphic personality.

Newspapers and newsmagazines will have from one to dozens of people devoted to taking and editing pictures. These photography staffs usually operate as separate units within the organization, but they must cooperate with the other parts of the news department. For most of the twentieth century, photographers and photo editors had such different jobs, skills, and expectations that there was rarely any crossover with other parts of the newsroom; that is, a photographer was unlikely to become a news reporter or vice versa. Both could work a story together, and in an emergency they might be able to do each other's job, but this kind of interchange was rare.

The reasons for this lack of crossover are many and obvious. The photojournalist covering the same assignment as the reporter has many considerations that differ from the reporter. The photojournalist must know the physicality of the scene—the people, the topography, the architecture, the light, and so on. The photojournalist need not be as concerned about a sequence of events, understanding motives of those involved, gathering detailed information, or getting quotes as the reporter. Instead, the photojournalist must understand the camera and other equipment being used. The photojournalist must certainly know a good deal about the scene that he or she is shooting and must get names and information about the pictures that are shot, but that knowledge does not have to be turned into a linear news story.

The photojournalist generally brings two things to a news story: illustration and visual context. Pictures are used to give a variety to the printed page that will make it interesting to look at and will draw readers into the page and into the stories. More importantly, pictures help expand the reader's understanding of a story by giving the reader a visual cue. Even a single picture of a newsmaker's head and shoulders (a "mugshot" in journalistic parlance) can give a context to a story that words cannot match.

To provide illustration and context, the photojournalist seeks at least one of three qualities in the pictures he or she takes: setting, expression, or action. Setting gives the viewer an idea of the general area in which a story takes place—a street, a football field, a room, and so on. Even when the setting is described or implied in a story, a picture showing the scene can be a valuable supplement to the reader.

Most photojournalists attempt to go beyond setting to the qualities they consider more interesting to themselves and to their readers: expression and action. Facial expressions can be subtle or overt. Either way, they are powerful reminders of our humanity and interaction. Facial expressions can indicate to us how someone is feeling and what their reaction is to a particular moment or situation. They can be both interesting and revealing. One of the reasons that pictures of children are so appealing is that people believe their expressions to be more honest than those of adults. They are not sophisticated in hiding or altering their expressions as some adults are.

Expression can be found in more than just the face, however. Hands can be expressive, as can other parts of the body and the body as a whole. In fact, the way two people are pictured together can say much about their relationship at that moment. In the late 1980s, when official statements from Buckingham Palace insisted that

FIGURE 14.2 Scene-Setting Photos Some photographs are valuable in giving views of the scene in which the action occurs. In this photo, a U.S. Army medic takes time out to examine an Iraqi baby during the 2003 invasion of Iraq. The bright sunlight and bare, sandy surroundings tell us much about the environment where U.S. forces were operating during that war. (Photo credit: Department of Defense)

FIGURE 14.3 Expressive Moments People's faces are likely to tell important stories about the events journalists cover. Photojournalists look for those expressions, as in this photo of a young woman at the 1963 March on Washington during which Martin Luther King, Jr. gave his famous "I Have a Dream" speech. (Photo credit: National Archives)

FIGURE 14.4   Capturing the Action Photojournalists try to capture the action of an event, even at the risk of their lives. One of the most dangerous jobs during a war is that of the combat photographer. This Department of Defense photograph shows soldiers during the war in Iraq firing on a building suspected of housing the sons of Saddam Hussein. (Photo credit: Department of Defense)

Prince Charles and Princess Diana were happily married, one had only to look at a picture of them in public to realize they were hardly speaking to one another.

Action is a far different quality of photographs but no less revealing and interesting for readers. Photographs that capture movement show not only expression, but they also put readers into a moment with the subjects of the photographs. Action shots allow readers to build the context around the frozen moment—to think about what came immediately before and after the moment of the shot and to experience in some way what the subjects in the photograph are experiencing. Often this experience of imagining is more powerful than a video that shows the action but does not let the viewer add his or her own experience to it.

The Digital Revolution

Print publications underwent a revolutionary, two-stage change beginning in the 1960s when writing and editing moved from a manual to an electronic operation. Reporters scanned and later "entered" their stories onto computers rather than typing them on typewriters. Copy editors retired their copy pencils and pastepots and "called up" on their computer screens the stories the reporters had entered in order to correct them.

By the early 1980s, that change had settled in, and the revolution migrated to its second stage, transforming the production operation of the publication. Computers were built (the Macintosh being foremost among them) that could show a page on a computer screen and could allow the operator to manipulate the objects (text, lines, and pictures) on the page without ever having them in a tangible paper form.

The process of journalism changed enormously because of this new technology. Editors took over the functions that were normally reserved for the "composing" or "paste-up" room of the publication, giving them more control over the publication but placing on them a much heavier production burden than they had ever known.

Through these three decades, photojournalism changed relatively little. Cameras became more sophisticated and easier to operate, film became more sensitive and development became faster, but the essential process of photojournalism stayed the same. What photographers had been doing for more than 150 years, they continued to do—exposing light to film and developing film and prints with chemicals. Many predicted that photography would always be that way.

But the electronic revolution was not finished.

By the 1990s, the adjective *digital* was appearing in front of *camera* more often, and *scanning*—converting a print to a digital file—was becoming a common practice. Digital cameras did not need the space or the chemicals that film cameras required, and scanning negatives (if a photographer insisted on using a film camera or the publication could not afford to convert) eliminated expensive photographic paper. Many photographers resisted these changes. Some argued, with good reason, that digital cameras could not deliver the quality of photograph that film cameras could. Others simply did not want to change the way they and their professional ancestors had operated.

Neither of those attitudes could stand up to publishers and editors who viewed the digital revolution in photography as a chance to save large amounts of money and time. Change, they told their employees. Quality will follow, and process is just process.

Now in the early twenty-first century, the revolution is almost complete. Even though great technical improvements have been made in digital cameras, many photographers are dissatisfied with the quality of the pictures they produce. A few even miss the hours in the darkroom with their hands in developing chemicals, believing they have lost a valuable part of the process of photography. But a new generation of photojournalists, who never touched a film roller or turned on a safe light, is coming of age, and they are completely comfortable with digital photography.

The digital revolution not only changed the economics of photojournalism, essentially making it less expensive, but it changed the process as well. Photojournalists always need to adjust to their equipment, and digital cameras have presented them a set of options. What kind of storage media (in the place of film) does the camera use? How are pictures to be downloaded and transmitted? What size settings does the camera have, and what is appropriate for a particular shooting assignment?

The major change the digital revolution has brought in the process of photo-journalism is speed. With digital cameras, pictures are produced instantly, and the only delay is getting them from the camera to a computer. This means that photographers can take more pictures and stay on the scene longer. They can transmit photographs from the scene of the action. They can even edit what they shoot at the scene before transmitting the photos. Consequently, a working photojournalist may be called on to do many more tasks than were once expected.

Another major change has come with editing photographs. The dodging and burning techniques that went into developing a print in the darkroom are now about as useful as the nineteenth-century skills of chiseling line drawings into wood blocks. Enhancing a photo now means calling a file up with Adobe Photoshop, the premier software program for this purpose, and performing an almost automatic set of tasks such as lightening, sharpening, and adjusting the color.

Photoshop and other software programs allow the editor to go beyond working with the internal content of the photo. An editor can combine two or more photos into a collage or lay type over a photo or cast a shadow under it. Operations that once took years of practice and hours of work can now be completed in just a few seconds.

Not only has the digital revolution changed photo editing, but it has also changed photo editors. In the film and chemical days, photographers kept control of the process because they were the ones who had learned the darkroom techniques. Few nonphotographer editors or reporters could go into a darkroom and operate with any skill or efficiency. In this digital age, picture taking and photo editing have become two separate skills that are not necessarily connected. People who have never picked up a camera professionally can learn Photoshop and become highly skilled photo editors.

And not only has photo editing slipped away from the exclusive grip of the photojournalist, but also photography itself has become more egalitarian. As digital cameras become lighter and easier to operate, more reporters are taking cameras on their assignments. Freed from many of the technical considerations of camera operation, they are having to learn about lighting, value, focus, composition, and the decisive moment. They, too, are having to gather the information necessary to write appropriate cutlines.

The digital revolution has made photojournalism more economic and more democratic. It has sparked a mini-convergence in the newsroom, so that while photojournalism remains very different from the journalism of the written word, journalists themselves are finding it easier to practice both forms.

Designers

People who do not understand publication design or who are not interested in it, even those inside the field of journalism, sometimes believe that the pages of a publication come together more or less automatically. Maybe there is a computer program somewhere that makes decisions about what will go onto a page, how big the pictures will be, and how large the headlines will be. Although such programs have been conceived,

FIGURE 14.5   The Impact of an Image A photo can have such impact that it represents far
more than the scene it pictures. Such was the case with this 1968 photograph taken by Eddie
Adams of the Associated Press. South Vietnamese National Police Chief Brig. Gen. Nguyen Ngoc
Loan is shown executing a Viet Cong officer with a single pistol shot in the head in Saigon,
Vietnam, on February 1, 1968. The Viet Cong officer had just murdered a South Vietnamese
colonel, his wife, and their six children. The police chief considered his action just. The photo
came to symbolize for many people much that was wrong with America's involvement in South
Vietnam in the 1960s. It won that year's Pulitzer prize for spot news photography. (Photo credit:
Associated Press Wide World Photos)

developed, and tested, they have generally proved to be inadequate. Good page design requires the brain of a human being, not the artificial intelligence of a computer.
Everything that appears on a page of any publication is the product of a decision that
someone has made. Most of those decisions are made by page designers.

Page designers are the people who work for newspapers and magazines who take
the material produced by reporters, editors, photographers, and graphics journalists
and put it together on the page of the publication. Often they have or share in the responsibility of writing much of what people first see on the page—the headlines.

Page designers must be highly skilled in many ways. First, they must be good journalists. They have to understand news and news values, and their commitment to accuracy and the journalism culture (see Chapter 2) must be as strong as any reporter

or editor. They must also have a good visual sense, and they must understand visual language, or how the look of something communicates to the viewer. They must be able to use the page design software of the publication so that they can put into effect the design decisions they make. They must also know how to handle pictures—selecting, cropping, enhancing, and sizing them to fit into the publication. They must be good with the language. Although they are not called on to write a great deal, they must understand words and how they are used.

And they have to perform all of these tasks at the same time. A good page designer, to use modern jargon, is a multitasker. Designers have to keep many things in their heads at one time. They have to be able to make decisions based on a number of factors that the news of the day will present to them. They have to think ahead as they are designing their pages, understanding that what they do at the moment will affect the decisions they make an hour or two later. Finally, they have to be able to finish their pages in the pressure cooker atmosphere of a publication on deadline. The designer who cannot meet deadlines costs the publication a great deal of money and eventually will not have that position.

Every publication has a graphic personality. This personality has developed over the life of the publication and is the product of many and continuing decisions that editors have made about the content and visual aspects of the publication. Some publications, particularly smaller publications such as weekly newspapers, do not pay a lot of attention to their graphic personality and may not be very consistent in their appearance. Even this inconsistency is part of the graphic personality. Other publications pay a great deal of attention to how they look, and they are highly consistent in the way in which they appear to readers. The *New York Times*, for instance, has evolved its graphic personality over many decades so that there is no doubt in the minds of its regular readers as to how the *New York Times* should look.

The graphic personality of a publication tells its readers much about what kind of publication it is—how serious it is, how good it aspires to be, how it views the content it presents, and so on. Just as the way you dress and groom yourself tells the world something about you and your personality, the way a publication looks tells its readers much the same thing.

Designers play a vital role in maintaining and developing the graphic design of the publication. They understand not just the design rules and procedures that the staff uses to produce the publication but also the reasons that lie behind those rules. For instance, some newspapers emphasize having large pictures on their section front pages. They may do so for any number of reasons: the editors feel their readers like large pictures; or the newspaper has a good photo staff that produces good pictures; or the newspaper's printing presses give the paper good reproduction on such pictures; or any of a number of other reasons. The page designer has to understand this inclination to use large pictures and the reason behind it. That understanding must be factored into the decisions the designer makes about the pages as they are being put together.

Designers exert a great deal of power within a publication. Although they often work under the direction of an editor, they must make many decisions on their own. Often it is left to them where a story is placed on a page or how large a headline it gets or whether or not a picture or graphic is run with the story. Because their work takes them right up to the publication's deadline, many of their decisions will not be checked or changed before the presses roll.

They will be second-guessed after publication, however. Many newspapers have daily critiques that focus on design decisions. Designers sometimes have to explain or defend their decisions. These critiques are part of the ongoing process of the publication and demonstrate how dynamic a field journalism is. For designers confident about what they know and what they do, this is an enjoyable process. They have the immediate satisfaction of seeing their work produced and of knowing that it is important and that other people are paying attention.

For those interested in getting into design, training should begin early. Students should look at as many publications as they can and should begin to notice the differences and similarities in format, pictures, headline sizes, and the way in which stories fit together on the page. These kinds of comparisons will give them an idea of the variety of design tools and elements and how they can be used. Students should begin to understand what gives a publication a consistent look and helps evolve a consistent graphic personality. Developing this kind of understanding will go hand-in-hand with working on their own publication designs. They will soon discover that they are doing more than simply placing publication elements on a page. They are being creative and communicating in an important way with their readers.

Graphics Journalists

Graphics journalism combines words and images to present ideas and information in ways that cannot be accomplished by text or illustration alone. The best graphics journalism helps viewers understand and picture the information. It gives insights into the topic. And it opens up the possibility that viewers will find meanings and interpretations beyond those intended by the journalists.

To date, graphics journalism has not fulfilled its promise in print journalism. Much good work is being done, to be sure. Newspapers such as the *New York Times, Chicago Tribune,* and *Washington Post,* among many others, produce excellent, informative graphics under the pressure of daily deadlines. Newsmagazines such as *Time* and *Newsweek* fill their graphics staffs with excellent artists and journalists. But graphics journalism is expensive. It takes time and consumes valuable and always scarce space in the publication. The difficulties of producing good graphics are not always understood or appreciated by a news organization's management. A graphics reporter must have a special orientation to both information and design that is often ignored by journalism schools and misunderstood by top-level editors. These editors do not understand informational graphics the way they understand reporting, writing, and editing.

Graphics journalism is simply very hard to do. The research that goes into building a good graphic demands concentration and special talents of the journalist. Conceptualizing a good graphic takes not only good information but also a thorough understanding of visual forms of presentation. In addition to the visual forms, graph-

FIGURE 14.6   Alfred Waud, Civil War Artist Alfred Waud was the professional ancestor of many of today's artists and visual journalists. During the Civil War, Waud roamed about the Union armies as an artist for *Harper's Weekly.* Although Matthew Brady and others took many photographs of the war, those pictures could not yet be mass produced. Waud and a few other artists allowed the home front to see the battlefield and the soldiers through their drawings. (Photo credit: Library of Congress)

ics journalists must be experts in the language because they have so little space and, consequently, so few words to use. They have to make every word count. Graphics journalists are required to perform intellectual multitasking that rarely occurs anywhere else in the newsroom. A good informational graphic is easy to look at. It should present its information in a way that is easy to understand. But there is nothing easy or quick about graphics journalism.

Graphics journalists sometime describe what they do as narrow and deep, comparing it to news reporters who write stories that are wide and shallow (though not in a pejorative sense). That is, graphics journalists will hone in on a part of the larger story and explore that part in depth. In print, exploring or extending a part of the story with graphics is usually all that can be done given the limitations of time and space.

The World Wide Web greatly extends the possibilities of graphics journalism. As in no other area of the profession, graphics journalism holds the promise of discovering new storytelling forms. The graphics journalist has more room to be creative and yet remain within the traditional bounds of journalistic accuracy than any other type of journalist. The graphics journalist can both tell and show in powerful and enlightening ways.

The Importance of the Visual

Many people in journalism, especially some reporters and editors, underestimate the importance of visual journalism. They believe that their words carry more value than pictures, graphics, or page design. What they are sometimes not willing to concede is that there are other ways of presenting information to the readers, and these forms of presentation have great impact. All of us remember certain pictures of dramatic and emotion-filled events. All of us have been drawn into reading stories because of a clever or interesting graphic or illustration or because the design has made it easy for us to look at it.

Visual journalists not only convey valuable information, but they also control the graphic personality of the news organization. How a publication looks is more than simply appearance. It is an integral part of what the publication is. Consequently, visual journalists do important work that has great value for both the reader and the news organization they serve.

QUESTIONS FOR DISCUSSION

1. Stereotypical assumptions about photojournalists are given at the beginning of the chapter. Based on your knowledge of photojournalists (including what you may have seen on television or in the movies), do you think any of these characterizations are fair?

2. Think about some of the big news events that you remember. Do you remember pictures associated with them?

3. Someone has theorized that the reason that many people are so interested in the Civil War is that it was the first major event in American history to be photographed. The photographs are black and white and often very dramatic. Do you agree or disagree with that? (You might be interested in viewing the Library of Congress's Civil War photo collection. It can be found at www.loc.gov.)

4. Find a large informational graphic in a newspaper or newsmagazine. Think about all of the information you see in the graphic, including the drawing or visual in the graphic itself. Where did that information come from? What did the graphic journalist have to do to gather it? How many people do you think it took to put the graphic together?

RELATED WEB SITES

American Institute of Graphic Arts, www.aiga.org

Design Management Institute, www.dmi.org/dmi/html/index.htm

Design with Reason, www.ronreason.com

National Press Photographers Association, www.nppa.org

News Page Designer, www.newspagedesigner.com

Society for News Design, www.snd.org

Society of Illustrators, www.societyillustrators.org

Society of Publication Designers, www.spd.org

University and College Designers Association, www.ucda.com

READINGS AND REFERENCES

Ames, S. E. (1989). *Elements of newspaper design.* New York: Praeger.

Ang, T. (2000). *Picture editing.* Oxford: Focal Press.

Arnold, E. C. (1981). *Designing the total newspaper.* New York: Harper and Row.

Bohle, R. H. (1990). *Publication design for editors.* Englewood Cliffs, NJ: Prentice Hall.

Denton, C. (1996). *Graphics for visual communication.* Dubuque, IA: William C. Brown.

Finberg, H., & Itule, B. D. (1990). *Visual editing: A graphic guide for journalists.* Belmont, CA: Wadsworth.

Garcia, M. R. (1993). *Contemporary newspaper design.* Englewood Cliffs, NJ: Prentice-Hall.

Garcia, M. R. (1996). *Newspaper evolutions.* St. Petersburg, FL: Poynter Institute.

Garcia, M. R. (1997). *Redesigning print for the Web.* Indianapolis, IN: Hayden Books.

Garcia, M. R. (2002). *Pure design.* St. Petersburg, FL: Miller Media.

Garcia, M. R., & Stark, P. (1991). *Eyes on the news.* St. Petersburg, FL: Poynter Institute.

Harris, C. R., & Lester, P. M. (2001). *Visual journalism: A guide for new media professionals.* Boston: Allyn and Bacon.

Harris, R. L. (2000). *Information graphics.* New York: Oxford University Press.

Harrower, T. (2001). *The newspaper designer's handbook.* Boston: McGraw-Hill.

Holland, D. K. (2001). *Design issues: How graphic design informs society.* New York: Allworth Press.

Holmes, N. (1984). *Designer's guide to creating charts and diagrams.* New York: Watson-Guptill.

Holmes, N. (1991). *Pictorial maps.* New York: Watson-Guptill.

Lester, P. M. (Ed.). (1995). *Visual communication: Images with messages.* New York: Wadsworth Publishing Company.

Lockwood, R. (1992). *News by design: Survival guide for newspapers.* Denver: Quark Press.

Lupton, E. (1999). *Design, writing, research: Writing on graphic design.* New York: Kiosk.

Meggs, P. B. (1998). *A history of graphic design.* New York: Van Nostrand Reinhold.

Meyer, E. K. (1997). *Designing infographics.* Indianapolis, IN: Hayden Books.

Moen, D. R. (2000). *Newspaper layout and design: A team approach.* Ames, IA: Iowa State University Press.

Monmonier, M. (1989). *Maps with the news: The development of American journalistic cartography.* Chicago: University of Chicago Press.

Newton, J. H. (2001). *The burden of visual truth: The role of photojournalism in mediating reality.* Hillsdale, NJ: Lawrence Erlbaum.

Society for News Design. *Best of newspaper design.* Baltimore: SND, Annual.

Stephens, M. (1998). *The rise of the image, the fall of the word.* New York: Oxford University Press.

Stovall, J. G. (1997). *Infographics: A journalist's guide.* Boston: Allyn and Bacon.

Tufte, E. R. (2001). *Visual display of quantitative information.* Cheshire, CT: Graphics Press.

Wilbur, P., & Burke, M. (1998). *Information graphics.* New York: Thames and Hudson.

Chapter Fifteen

Graphics Journalism

Key Concepts and Terms

1. All journalists should have knowledge of visual and graphic principles and how they work in the presentation of information.

2. Purpose and content should be the chief considerations in the design of a graphic, not the ability of a computer program to design a fancy or pleasing picture; design should always give way to function.

3. Accurate presentation of information is the chief goal of a graphics journalist.

4. Depth: making a two-dimensional graph appear three-dimensional; adding this quality to a graph may distort its meaning and should be done with care.

5. Just as good journalistic writing often takes the simplest form possible, good graphics should also be as simple as possible.

6. The most commonly used graphic forms in journalism are the pie chart, the bar chart, the line chart, and the map; each has a set of conventions for its use that journalists must understand and observe.

7. Journalists should look for ways to use graphic forms to present information, particularly with regard to location, numbers, process, and content.

This chapter was adapted from material in James Glen Stovall, *Infographics: A Journalist's Guide* and *Writing for the Mass Media*, 5/e. Published by Allyn and Bacon, Boston, MA. Copyright © 1997 and 2002, respectively, by Pearson Education. Adapted by permission of the publisher.

Graphics journalism attracts many people into the field of journalism who have a good visual sense, who want an outlet for their creativity, and who also understand news and information. Graphics journalists need to understand the principles of design and the standard forms of visual presentation. This chapter will introduce you to some of those concepts.

Graphics presentation is an integral and necessary part of the information formats used by publications today. Graphics are neither decorations nor afterthoughts. For certain types of information, they are the best means of telling the reader information that the publication wants to transmit. For this reason, all journalists should have an understanding of what graphics are and how they should be used. This understanding begins with a knowledge of some of the basic principles of design.

The design principles discussed in this chapter specifically relate to informational graphics and their use in modern journalism. Much has been written about the many facets of visual design for both artistic and informational purposes, and students interested in this area have a wide variety of sources they can go to for additional information and discussion. In this chapter, we will confine our discussion to those principles that will be useful to the development of informational graphics and that will help in understanding other parts of this book.

Principles of Design

Certain design principles exist because of the structure of the language and the conventions that have been developed over many centuries about how ideas and information should be communicated. Others have developed because of the physical structure of the eye and the way we see and process information. Both types of principles are presented in this section.

Most people have some knowledge and understanding of these principles, even though they may not be specifically aware of them. The basic principles of design follow.

Reading normally occurs from left to right and from top to bottom.   This principle is obvious, but it is important for anyone involved in design to remember. The tendency of left-to-right, top-to-bottom reading and viewing is so prevalent that it seems natural. Viewers of the printed page will begin at the upper left corner of the page.

This tendency does not obligate the designer to start a design in the upper left corner of a section or page. Readers will begin their viewing elsewhere if given a reason to do so. That reason might be a brightly colored picture in the middle of a page or a strong, dark headline on the right side of the page. Designers need to be aware of the times when they violate this left-to-right, top-to-bottom principle.

There is nothing wrong with constructing a graph in this way as long as the graphics journalist is aware of what he or she is doing. Giving this kind of emphasis to the headline or any other element of the graph may be perfectly appropriate, but it should be what the journalist means to do. It should not happen accidentally.

Focus and contrast are particularly important design elements for the graphics journalist.   In this instance, focus means a concentration of ink or color so that the eye of the reader is drawn to that point. Those who design graphics are aware of this visual principle and are likely to make use of it. Focus works because of contrast. Contrast means that a dark element is surrounded by white space, thus giving more emphasis to the dark element. Contrast is one way for the graphics journalist to make sure that readers see what the journalist wants them to see.

The graphic should achieve a balance among its elements that invites the reader into the graphic and guides the reader through it.   The design principle of balance means that the size of elements should not be out of proportion to their importance to the graphic itself. The elements should be clearly delineated. If elements overlap, they should do so for a purpose and should not obscure important information. While the placement of elements might guide a reader through the graphic, the reader should also be able to browse or scan.

The best way for anyone to develop a sense of balance for graphic forms is to study closely informational graphics wherever they appear. This examination should be accompanied by questions about the size and placement of elements and a judgment about what works and what does not work. It would be a disservice to the profession to reduce balance to a set of "correct" formulas that are most pleasing to the author. The possibilities of graphics journalism are too broad for that to be useful. Individual graphics journalists should use their imagination and creativity within the discipline of generally accepted forms and customs that are discussed later in this chapter.

Graphics should have a unity that draws attention to the information they are presenting and away from their design.   Elements in a graphic should work together rather than compete with one another. What this usually means is that a graphic should have a small number of type fonts (only one, if possible) and contrasting shades or colors.

Purpose and content, rather than form, should drive the creation of the graphic. Today's graphics journalist has many powerful tools at his or her disposal. Combined with some talent and imagination, these tools enable the journalist to create slick, eye-catching graphics that can dazzle editors and readers alike.

But how far should the graphics journalist go in using these tools? The journalist should always ask the questions, "What is the purpose of what I am doing?" and "What is necessary to accomplish that purpose?"

Consider the graphics in Figure 15.1. The paragraph states rather simply what the information is. The table gives this same information in a nonparagraph form. The pie chart, which in the hands of an experienced graphics journalist took about five minutes to create, presents this information in a straightforward but graphic way.

TABLE

Popular Vote Presidential Election 1992	
Bill Clinton	43%
George Bush	38
Ross Perot	19

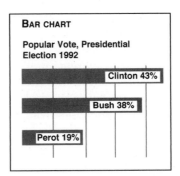

BAR CHART

Popular Vote, Presidential Election 1992

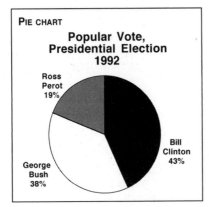

PIE CHART

Popular Vote, Presidential Election 1992

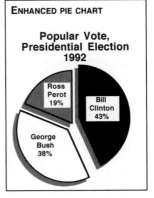

ENHANCED PIE CHART

Popular Vote, Presidential Election 1992

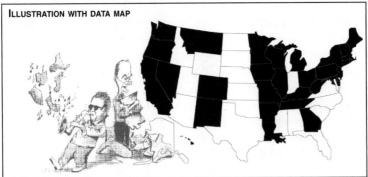

ILLUSTRATION WITH DATA MAP

FIGURE 15.1   Same Information, Different Forms Information can often be represented in a variety of ways. It is up to the graphics journalist to choose the form that best fits the data and allows the journalist to make a point with it.

The enhanced pie chart took more time to create—about fifteen minutes—and is more likely to capture the attention of the reader. Finally, the illustration using the outline of the United States and the drawings of the candidates took a good part of the working day for a talented illustrator to produce, and it certainly gives the reader some entertainment as well as some information.

In each case, the purpose of the graphic is different, even though the information is the same. Editors and journalists need to have a good idea of why they are presenting information. The purpose and content of the information should combine to help the journalist decide what is the best form for the information.

Conventions of Graphics

Graphic forms have been in use since the times that cave dwellers drew pictures on their walls to tell stories. In modern times, the graphic forms that we are most familiar with have been developed over several centuries. These forms are used within certain conventions or customs that are generally accepted by those who create informational graphics. The purpose of these graphic conventions is to establish some understandings between the developer of the graphic and the reader on what the graphic represents. Just as journalistic writers and editors have style rules, graphics journalists have expectations that are not all that different from the general rules of writing.

The first and most important convention is the adherence to accuracy. The information in a graphic should be accurate to whatever standard is acceptable to the publication. Information should be correct, up-to-date, and presented in a proper context. Grammar and spelling should be correct. All of the other normal procedures for ensuring accuracy of information should be followed by the graphics journalist.

Another convention that must be strictly observed is that the form of the graphic should be appropriate for the data or information that is being presented. This convention is particularly important in working with numerical data. Certain graphic forms are appropriate for certain types of data and are most inappropriate for other types of data. These forms and their appropriateness will be discussed later in this chapter. Understanding these forms and their appropriateness for data is essential.

When graphic forms are used to represent numerical data, the presentation should be physically proportional. This convention is violated with surprising regularity in graphs presented in magazines and newspapers. Many times the violations occur because the graphics journalists do not understand the data they are trying to represent. Sometimes graphics journalists violate this convention because they want to emphasize a larger point than the individual items of data that are in a graph.

The idea of proportionality is sometimes subtle and difficult to understand. Proportionality is easiest to achieve when there is only one dimension involved in the objects that must be proportional. The graph of population figures shown in Figure 15.2 is a simple bar chart, so representing the populations of the various states with different sizes of bars is a seemingly simple matter. If the area of the bar represented the population, the bar representing Florida would have to be approximately twice as big as the bar representing Georgia, as in the example on the left. Generally, we do not construct charts in this way because they are not particularly pleasing to the eye. Rather, on the right, we have two bars whose heights represent the populations of the states.

Whenever a third dimension is introduced or when objects are taken off a flat plane, the problem of achieving proportionality becomes more difficult. Here we encounter both depth and perspective, two elements that make an object appear to be three-dimensional. Depth means adding a side or two to the objects in a graph to make them appear as if they are coming off the page. (Computer graphing programs contain a function that will add depth automatically to most objects that it creates.) Depth does nothing to make a graph more accurate because the elements in a graph rarely represent actual objects. Depth often diminishes the true proportionality of the objects in a graph because it moves them away from a background scale that readers use to measure them. On the other hand, depth can make a graph more attention-getting and more interesting to look at.

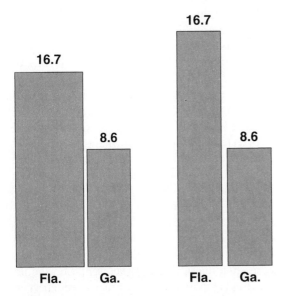

FIGURE 15.2   Proportionality In most graphics that represent numerical data, proportionality is achieved by using only one dimension of the figure that represents the data. In the graph on the left, both dimensions are used to achieve proportionality. In the other, only one—the length along the imaginary y-axis—is used. The second graph displays the more conventional use. Problems with proportionality often occur when the designer of the graphic is working with two-dimensional figures.

The element of depth also means that graphics journalists must deal with perspective. Perspective is an artistic technique that controls the viewpoint of the viewer toward the graphic. Perspective is based on the observation that the closer something is to us, the larger it is. As an object gets farther away, its actual size does not diminish but our perception of it does. It will diminish to a vanishing point, where we cannot see it at all. The vanishing point is located along a horizon line.

Perspective also can diminish the proportionality of the elements of a graph, so that the objects of the graph do not actually represent numerically the values that the graph is trying to show. Consequently, many who have studied this field believe that depth and perspective should not be used. There are others, however, who argue that the use of depth and perspective makes the elements of a graph appear more realistic. As humans, they say, we do not view objects in the real world with exact proportionality. Consequently, graphs should be good representations of the information they are showing but should not be held to a high standard of proportionality.

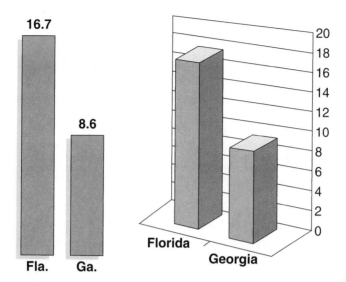

FIGURE 15.3 **Depth** The subject of depth in infographics can be controversial. Computer applications make depth easy to achieve when building graphics. Depth can easily distort or obscure data when that is not the intention of the journalist. The major reason for adding a depth function to a graphic is to gain the attention of the reader and to make a visual impression. This reason may not be strong enough to offset the dangers that are inherent in using it, however. Graphics journalists should use extreme caution when considering whether or not to add a third dimension to their graphics. The illusion of depth can be created in two ways, either by shadowing (left) or a 3-D perspective (right).

The Good Graphic

So far, this chapter has discussed some of the conventions and techniques that have come into use with modern informational graphics. We will end this chapter with a discussion of the development of the attitude or philosophy of the graphics journalist. Not only should the graphics journalist have a good grasp of the tools and techniques of the field, but he or she should also have some depth of understanding about what is to be accomplished with graphics.

We can begin by talking about the relationship of the graphics journalist to the audience. A good journalist of any stripe has a healthy respect for the audience. This respect is particularly important in this age of graphics. Many people view graphics as a way of imparting information to people who could not understand it otherwise or are too lazy to read text. For journalists to take this view of their audience would be demeaning to the audience and the work that they do.

Graphics should be produced because they are the best way of gaining the attention of readers and helping them understand the information that is being presented. The fact that they may make the publication look better or that they are interesting for the journalists themselves to produce may also be considerations, but they are clearly secondary.

This respect for the audience should do away with the old bromide: "Graphics must be simple; otherwise, people won't read or understand them." Informational graphics should be understandable, but that does not mean they should be simple. A graphic is often the best means of presenting complex information to the reader. As Edward Tufte writes in his book *Envisioning Information,* "Clutter and confusion are failures of design, not attributes of information. Often the less complex and less subtle the line, the more ambiguous and less interesting is the reading. Stripping the detail out of data is a style based on personal preference and fashion, considerations utterly indifferent to substantive content" (p. 51).

Tufte, who is one of the leading thinkers about informational graphics, argues that graphics should be "data rich." That is, graphics should have enough information in them and should be designed in such a way that readers can browse through them. The ideal graphic is one that allows the reader to make discoveries about the information that are not pointed out by the graphics journalist and not immediately apparent.

It is simply not true that readers glance at informational graphics and then look away any more than it is true that readers glance at and then look away from headlines or pictures. Readers will take time to look at, read, and study what is interesting to them. Interesting information that is attractively presented will find an audience.

Types of Graphics

Most people think informational graphics are charts and graphs. For our purposes, we should expand our definition to say that an informational graphic is anything that is not clearly a headline, body copy, picture, or cutline. That is, informational graphics make use of type in special ways as well as use graphs or chart forms.

The two major content principles of informational graphics are accuracy and clarity. Above everything else, an informational graphic should present information accurately. This is important to remember because graphics are easy to distort. Graphics often present relationships, and the basis of those relationships should be clear to the reader.

Clarity is the second major principle. Clarity begins in the mind of the editor. He or she should have a clear idea of what information is being presented and of how it is best presented. Although a single graph may show different things, it should be governed by a central idea, much as a good story should have a central theme or idea behind it.

Three general types of informational graphics are used in newspapers: type-based graphics, chart-based graphics, and illustration-based graphics. Each may use elements of the others, but this classification is a good way to begin to understand what they are.

Type-Based Graphics

Type-based graphics are those in which text, or type, is the major graphic element. Sometimes it is the only graphic element. These graphics use type to draw attention to themselves in addition to providing informational content. Following are some common types of text-based graphics.

LISTS.   Some of the best graphics are nothing more than lists, and lists are readable and popular with readers. They are clean and easy to produce, and they give readers interesting information quickly. A list might be a simple listing of items, such as a movie reviewer's five favorite movies of the year, or it may contain some additional information about the items.

REFERS.   A *refer* (pronounced REE-fer) is short for *reference* in newspaper jargon. It is a way of telling the reader that there is another story on the same subject elsewhere in the paper. It is also a good graphic device that breaks up body type. A refer may include only the page number, or it may have other information about the item.

PULL QUOTES.   A pull quote is part of an article that is set off in larger type. It generally serves two purposes: It is a good way of breaking up large amounts of body copy type; it also gives the reader some interesting point or flavor of a story.

SUMMARIES.   One of the best graphic devices for getting information quickly to the reader is the summary box. A summary box can be used on almost any story. It is best used when a story has several parts or important points. For instance, a city council might take a number of actions in one meeting. A summary box can list these actions so that the reader can quickly know what they are.

CHRONOLOGIES.   Events rarely occur without some significant historical context. That context may be very recent, but it also may be important in explaining to the reader what has happened and why. Chronologies take a good deal of time and care to produce, but they can help heighten reader interest in a story.

ORGANIZATIONAL CHARTS.   These charts (also called tree charts) demonstrate relationships within an organization. The most common are those that show the relative positions of jobs within a corporation. A standard way of presenting this kind of chart is to have the names of positions within boxes with lines connecting the boxes that represent reporting channels and responsibilities.

Another type of organizational chart is most often found on the sports page. This chart will show the match-up of teams or individuals playing in a tournament and how they will proceed to a championship. Still another type of organizational chart is the genealogical chart that traces a family's history through several generations (thus, the term *family tree*). All of these charts make it easy for the reader to see some relationship of a part of the chart to a larger entity such as an organization or a family.

Refer

Court orders club to comply with new law

The state supreme court has order a Midville bar to cease and desist allowing dancers to perform completely nude dances on their premises.

The court ordered the Flesh Mill, located at 213 Broad Street, on the corner of Broad and Main Streets, not to permit certain kinds of floor shows, dances and performances which have been outlawed by a recent state law

See related court stories, page 3

while the constitutionality of that law is being tested in the courts.

The court ordered the proprietors and owners of the shop to remove various acts, performances and demonstrations from the stage, tabletops and floors of

the business.

The Flesh Mill owners, Heavy Heat and Bob Beatle, have sued the state and taken it to court, saying the state law which the state legislature passed last session unduly restricts and limits their rights as businessmen.

In the initial court battle which was initiated four months ago, state attorneys argued that the shop and all others like it in

Pull quote

Court orders club to comply with new law

The state supreme court has order a Midville bar to cease and desist allowing dancers to perform completely nude dances on their premises.

The court ordered the Flesh Mill, located at 213 Broad Street, on the corner of Broad and Main Streets, not to permit certain kinds of floor shows, dances and performances which have been outlawed by a recent state law

"This is not at all what we wanted to happen," said Bob Beatle, one of the bar's co-owners.

while the constitutionality of that law is being tested in the courts.

The court ordered the proprietors and owners of the shop to

remove various acts, performances and demonstrations from the stage, tabletops and floors of the business.

The Flesh Mill owners, Heavy Heat and Bob Beatle, have sued the state and taken it to court, saying the state law which the state legislature passed last session unduly restricts and limits their rights as businessmen.

In the initial court battle

Drop cap

Court orders club to comply with new law

The state supreme court has order a Midville bar to cease and desist allowing dancers to perform completely nude dances on their premises.

The court ordered the Flesh Mill, located at 213 Broad Street, on the corner of Broad and Main Streets, not to permit certain kinds of floor shows, dances and performances which have been outlawed by a recent state law

while the constitutionality of that law is being tested in the courts.

The court ordered the proprietors and owners of the shop to remove various acts, performances and demonstrations from the stage, tabletops and floors of the business.

The Flesh Mill owners, Heavy Heat and Bob Beatle, have

sued the state and taken it to court, saying the state law which the state legislature passed last session unduly restricts and limits their rights as businessmen.

In the initial court battle which was initiated four months ago, state attorneys argued that the shop and all others like it in the state should have to abide by the law until the court had ruled on the law. Today the state

FIGURE 15.4 Type-Based Graphics Type-based graphics come in a wide variety of forms. In the middle column of each story are three types: refer (pronounced ree-fer,) pull quote, and drop cap.

Chart-Based Graphics

Chart-based graphics are graphics that present numerical information in a nontext form. These forms are likely to be proportional representations of the numbers themselves. These are what many people refer to when they talk about informational graphics.

Chart-based graphics have become highly popular in today's newspapers. Computer software has made them relatively easy to produce. Many journalists today spend a great deal of time gathering information that can be presented in charts.

In addition to the principles of accuracy and clarity discussed earlier, informational graphics should share a number of other characteristics. The following are some of those characteristics.

SIMPLICITY.   Graphics can be complex, but their appearance should be uncluttered. One of the criticisms of many graphics is that they are "chartoons." That is, they have too many little figures and drawings that do not add to the reader's understanding of the information in the graphic. A graphic should contain the minimum items necessary for understanding the information and the maximum items for good appearance.

CONSISTENCY.   Publications often develop a graphics style just as they adopt a writing style. This style includes rules about what kind of type is used, when color is appropriate, how information is attributed, and a variety of other matters. Like style rules for writing, these rules help both the staff in producing graphics and the reader in understanding them.

ATTRIBUTION.   Information in graphics should be attributed, just as information in news stories should be attributed. As with other information in a publication, sometimes the source is obvious and does not need to be specified. In other cases, attribution is vital to the understanding of a graphic.

USE OF COLOR.   Charts lend themselves to color, and many publications use charts to showcase their ability to handle color. Color helps emphasize certain parts of the graphic; it also contributes to a pleasing appearance. Color is easy to overuse, however, and editors should be careful that the use of color does not get in the way of the information in the chart.

HEADLINES.   Oddly enough, one of the most difficult things about producing an informational graphic is writing its headline. Headlines for graphics do not have to follow the rules of headlines for articles; in most publications, they can simply be labels. They need to identify the central idea of the graphic, however, and this is difficult to do in just a few words. One approach many graphics journalists use is to write the headline before the graphic is built. Doing that gives them the central idea to keep in mind while producing the graphic.

Most mass media publications use three types of chart-based graphics: the bar chart, the line chart, and the pie chart. Each type of chart is best used for presenting

Bar chart

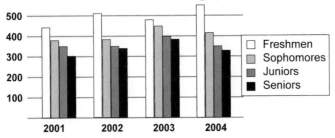

Students at Lenoir College, 2001-2004

- Freshmen
- Sophomores
- Juniors
- Seniors

Line chart

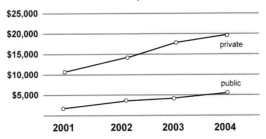

Tuition at public and private colleges in the state, 2001-2004

private

public

Pie chart

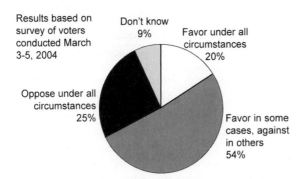

Attitudes toward abortion

Results based on survey of voters conducted March 3-5, 2004

Don't know 9%

Favor under all circumstances 20%

Oppose under all circumstances 25%

Favor in some cases, against in others 54%

FIGURE 15.5   Chart-Based Graphics These charts typify the three basic charts that are used to present numerical data. Graphics journalists have to understand the purposes and conventions of their use.

certain types of information and is inappropriate for other types of information. Editors need to understand what charts are appropriate for what types of information.

BAR CHARTS.   The bar chart is the most popular type of chart because it is easy to set up and it can be used in many ways. The bar chart uses thick lines or rectangles to present information. These rectangles represent the amounts or values in the data presented in the chart. (There are technically two types of bar charts. One uses the name *bar chart* and refers to charts in which the bars run horizontally. The *column chart* refers to bar charts in which the bars run vertically. Column charts are more commonly used when time is an element in the data. For the purposes of this text, however, we will not make a distinction between the bar chart and column chart.)

The two major lines in a bar chart are the horizontal axis, known as the *x*-axis, and the vertical axis, known as the *y*-axis. Both should have clearly defined starting points so that the information in the chart is not distorted, particularly the axis that represents the amounts in the graph.

One of the reasons a bar chart is so popular is that it can show both amounts and relationships. The bar chart can also be used to demonstrate changes in relationships over time. The relationships shown in the "Size of Classes at Lenoir College, 2001–2004" in Figure 15.5 tell the reader that the college changed a good deal during the period shown. Studying this chart might suggest some possible reasons for the changes.

LINE CHARTS.   Whereas the bar chart may show change over time, the line chart must show change over time. It can also show a change in relationships over time. In some instances, it is preferable to the bar chart because it is cleaner and easier to decipher.

One of the standard conventions of the line chart is that the *x*-axis represents the time element and the *y*-axis represents the amounts or quantities being represented.

Line charts can use more than one line to show not only how one item has changed but also the relationship of changes in several items. Data points can be represented by different shapes for each item. The danger with multiple-line charts is that too many lines can be confusing to the reader. Graphics journalists should avoid putting more than three lines in a line chart. A variation on the line chart is the area chart. This type of chart is good for showing how the division of something changes over time.

PIE CHARTS.   The pie chart is another popular means of showing data, but its use is specialized. A pie chart should show how an entity or item is divided up, and the divisions are most commonly expressed in percentages that add up to 100 percent. Figures also may be used to identify the parts of a pie chart, but it is important that the creator of a pie chart keep the concept of percentages in mind.

Despite the strict limits of the kind of data that can be shown in a pie chart, this type of chart can be used in a variety of ways. A pie chart can show only one set of data at a time, but several charts can be used together to help compare sets of data.

Graphics journalists have found some unusual ways to use the pie chart form. Taking shapes that are not circles and dividing them up as pie charts is something readers will occasionally see. This technique can be artful and attention-getting, but care must be taken that the data are not distorted.

MAPS.   One of the most common and useful graphic devices in today's mass media is the map. Maps are quick and easy to use. They provide readers with important information that can be used to help explain events and put them in physical context. In addition, they help to educate a public that many have tagged as geographically illiterate.

Certain conventions should be followed in using maps. First and foremost, a map should always be proportional to the geographic area that it represents; that is, it should be "to scale." Let's say that a country is 2,000 miles long from north to south and 1,000 miles long from east to west. The longitude (north to south) to latitude (east to west) scale is 2 to 1. Any map that represents that area should have the north–south line twice the distance of the east–west line.

Another important convention of maps is that the northern part of the area represented is always at the top of the map. This northern orientation dates from ancient times and is one of the assumptions that most people make when they look at a map.

A third convention of maps is that they include a distance scale, usually somewhere close to the bottom of the map. Not every map needs a distance scale because sometimes such a scale is irrelevant. On those maps in which the area is likely to be unfamiliar to the reader, distance scales are extremely helpful. A distance scale usu-

FIGURE 15.6   Maps Maps can be extremely useful tools for conveying information. They can help readers locate events or, as shown here, they can add a dimension to information that text is unable to do.

ally consists of two parts: a line that is marked off to indicate units of distance on the map and text that tells what the scale is, such as "1 inch = 5 miles."

Many maps in newspapers or magazines appear with insets, which are smaller maps that show a larger area that includes the area shown in the map. For instance, a map of Great Britain might include an inset of Western Europe to show where or how large Great Britain is in relation to other countries.

The print media put maps to three basic uses: symbols, location, and data.

SYMBOLS.   The shapes of many states and countries are well known and are excellent graphic devices. They are particularly useful when an article is divided up as a series of reports on different counties, states, or countries. Although such use does not require that these maps have a distance scale, they should follow the conventions of being proportionally scaled and having the north at the top.

LOCATION.   Using maps to indicate the location of events is what we think of as the most common and logical use of maps. Here all of the conventions of map usage should come into consideration.

These maps may be enhanced by a number of devices. Cities, towns, and other locations can be identified. A map may also include buildings or other sites that would help the reader get the point of the map. Hills, valleys, mountains, rivers, forests, and other topographical factors can be included on a map with drawings or shadings.

Maps may serve as backgrounds for other information that journalists want to convey to their readers. For instance, to give readers a better sense of the story about a trip by the pope, a publication might include a map with text and arrows pointing to the different locations the pope will visit and the dates on his schedule.

Location maps may not always be of areas that we think of as geographic locations. For instance, the floor plan of a house or other building can be treated as a map if it helps readers understand something about an article. In the general sense, maps are a way of looking down on something and seeing it as a whole rather than seeing part of it from the limits of ground level. Such a bird's-eye view can be revealing and insightful.

DATA.   In 1854, central London experienced an outbreak of cholera. In searching for a way to arrest the spread of the sickness, John Snow, a local physician, took a map of the area where the deaths occurred and plotted with dots the residence of everyone who had died of cholera. He also marked the location of the public water pumps in the area. His map indicated that many of the deaths were clustered around the Broad Street water pump. Upon discovering this, he had the handle of the pump removed and, thus, ended the cholera that had claimed more than 500 lives in that area.

Snow used what we refer to as a data map as a lifesaving device. A data map places numerical data on geographic locations in a way that will produce relevant information about the data. Data maps can aid in our understanding of the data and the areas in which data occur. Data maps also allow readers to view large amounts of information at a single sighting in an orderly and logical way.

Data maps take time and effort to produce, and they should be created with great care. Data maps that are not carefully thought out can allow viewers to reach superficial or incorrect conclusions. Creators of data maps should be particularly careful that the data they have are, in fact, related to geographic location rather than being distributed randomly.

Illustration-Based Graphics

Newspaper illustration has a long and rich history dating back to the 1700s. Many nineteenth-century American artists, such as Winslow Homer and Frederick Remington, began their careers in journalism. For much of the twentieth century, illustrators on newspapers were confined to the sports pages and to editorial cartooning, but in those places readers could find top-notch artists. With the current emphasis in newspapers on graphics has come a renewed interest in newspaper illustration. Many newspapers are expanding their art staffs and looking for people who can combine artistic skills with a sense of news and information. They are also looking for people who are adept at using the computer.

As the name implies, illustration-based graphics use illustration rather than type or charts to form the basis of the graphic. An illustration may be drawn by hand or generated by computer, or it may be hand drawn and then enhanced by a computer.

Publications use illustrations for two purposes: to draw attention to a story and to make a point about the story. Usually, illustrations do not duplicate photographs. They go beyond the photograph in helping the editors emphasize something about the story or add to the reader's understanding of the information in an article.

DRAWINGS.   As mentioned earlier, a drawing may be generated by hand or with the aid of a computer. Even when a drawing is originated by hand, it is often entered into a computer system by means of a scanner. A scanner operates like a photocopying machine, but instead of transferring the image onto another piece of paper, it translates the image into a set of computer signals that can be recognized by a software program.

Many publications use clip art files as a basis for their illustrations. Clip art is a set of computer drawings in a format that can be accessed by a publication's computer system. These drawings are sold by the disk and cover a vast array of subjects. Publications buy the rights to use them when they purchase the disks. These drawings can be called up by a staff artist and changed in whatever way is necessary for the publication.

Drawings can illustrate things that cannot be photographed. One of the most common uses of drawings in this way is for courtroom pictures. Many courtrooms still do not allow the use of video or still cameras, but most will let illustrators do drawings of the participants.

Drawings may also be used to help explain why things happen. For instance, if a bridge collapses, a photograph can record the aftermath and effects of the event. A

Going for the title

Smith can clinch title with one hit tonight

By Rich Randell

Jim Smith needs just one hit tonight to bring the Bay City Bluebird something they haven't had in 20 years - a batting title.

Smith's average stands at a searing .335. He is currently tied with the first baseman of the Palatino Pirates, Rod Carney, for the batting lead in the Wine Valley League.

Because the Carney was called up to the Pittsburgh Pirates two weeks ago, he will not have another chance to raise his average.

Going into tonight's final game of the season, then, Smith needs only one hit in three or fewer times at bat to pass Carney and take the batting title.

"This is a big deal for me," Smith said.

"Maybe if I can grab the title, that will be something else for the Cardinals to evaluate. That could be another reason for calling me up."

The Bluebirds are a farm team of the St. Louis Cardinals, which has not finished filling out its 40-man roster for September. Smith is hoping to land one of the spots and finish this season in the major leagues.

Smith's manager, Biff Laritino, has vowed to do everything he can to help Smith out.

"As soon as Jim gets a hit tonight, I'm going to pull him out of the game," Laritino said.

"This kid is really something. He has hit consistently all year long. I'm glad that he is in a position to take the title. I am going to recommend to the Cardinals that they pick him up when our season is over," he said.

In addition to his average, Smith has pounded out 20 home runs this year and has knocked in 67 runs, helping the Bluebirds to the best season they have had in more than five years.

"Jim has been a team player all year long," Laritino said.

"He hasn't worried about his average. He just wants us to win. Tonight is his night, and the team is going to try to help him accomplish something."

The Bluebirds play the Brighton Braves tonight at historic Kelly Field in the last game of the season. Tonight is fan appreciation night, and tickets are half priced.

FIGURE 15.7   Illustration-Based Graphics A strong illustration, such as the one used with the story here, can be both attention-getting and content-laden. The illustrator definitely had something to say about this subject.

drawing can present the structure of the bridge and emphasize the points where the collapse occurred. Both photographs and drawings can help the reader understand the event.

One point should be emphasized about good newspaper illustration and especially drawings: they take time to produce, and generally the better the drawing, the more time it takes. Computers can speed the process along, but a good illustration still takes the time of a talented person.

Developing Infographics

Large newspapers have multiperson graphics departments devoted full time to producing infographics, particularly for breaking news. The *Chicago Tribune*, for instance, maintains a staff of graphics coordinators (or reporters) who work on information that will go into a news graphic and a set of artists who will design and execute the graphic.

What these coordinators find is that graphics reporting differs in some significant ways from news reporting. Graphics reporting demands that the journalist focus in on a part of the story and find specific, detailed information that a person writing a news story might not have to have. For instance, a news reporter might be able to quote a source saying the number of independently owned drugstores had decreased during the last ten years. A graphics reporter, if he or she were going to create a chart showing that, would have to have precise figures for each year of the period shown.

On the other hand, a news reporter would be concerned with quoting people and getting the quotations exactly right so they could be included in a story. A graphics reporter might talk to many sources of information, but he or she rarely worries about quoting those people.

One skill that a graphics reporter must develop is writing succinctly. Most infographics have an extremely limited amount of space for text, and a graphics reporter must learn to use words with exceptional efficiency (something we alluded to in Chapter 14). Such honing of language is hard work and takes time. Often it is done with a looming deadline, so the person who becomes a graphics reporter must have confidence in using the language.

A graphics reporter also deals in a specialized kind of information, and knowing the nature of this information is important for editors to understand how infographics should be developed. When a news story needs an infographic, graphics reporters and editors tend to think along the following lines:

Numbers.   Are there numbers that need to be shown with this story? Will showing the numbers add to the reader's understanding? A newswriter who must handle a substantial amount of numbers in a story will find that an infographic could be a great solution.

Location.   Are readers likely to know where a story is taking place? Even if they do, could a map show information more efficiently than a paragraph description? Should it be a simple locator or does it need to be married with some other information? Is a data map called for—does the geography relate to the numbers?

History and context.   How did the events of the story get to this point? Is there a history that the reader needs to know about? Time lines, as we mentioned earlier, are good ways of showing the events of a person's life or the history of an issue. Another form that this takes is the fact or profile box. Can we add to the reader's understanding of an organization or person that would not be included in a story?

Process.   Should we show the reader how something works? Sometimes we can do that with text or text married with pictures.

Procedure.   Is there a step-by-step procedure that shows how something happened? Somewhat akin to a time line, a procedural chart can show how an event occurred. (A *process* refers to something that is not unusual and happens periodically; a *procedure* refers to a single, often unique, event.)

Profile.   This might be thought of as "information-plus." An organization, company, person, or almost any element in a story can be outlined or explained with extra information in a variety of ways.

Good graphics demand the same kind of accuracy, completeness, precision, and efficiency that good newswriting demands. Editors must have an understanding of what it takes to make a good graphic and why they can be an efficient way of getting information to a reader.

QUESTIONS FOR DISCUSSION

1. The author says that simple is better in graphic presentation. Do you agree? Find some examples of "simple" and "fancy" graphics (*USA Today* might be a good source for both) and see what you think.

2. Select a news story from a newspaper or news web site and try to list as many graphics as possible that might be designed to accompany the story. The story may not have all of the information to do such graphics. If not, what information would have to be found to make these graphics work? Where would that information be located?

3. Are the qualities that make a good graphics journalist different from those that make a good news reporter?

RELATED WEB SITES

American Institute of Graphic Arts, www.aiga.org

News Page Designer, www.newspagedesigner.com

Nigel Holmes / Explanation Graphics, www.nigelholmes.com

Poynter Online's Design / Graphics Resources, http://poynteronline.org/subject.asp?id=11

Poynter Online's Design / Graphics Tipsheets, http://poynteronline.org/content/content_view.asp?id=31883

Society for News Design, www.snd.org

Society of Illustrators, www.societyillustrators.org

Visualjournalism.com, www.visualjournalism.com

READINGS AND REFERENCES

Denton, C. (1996). *Graphics for visual communication.* Dubuque, IA: William C. Brown.

Finberg, H., & Itule, B. D. (1990). *Visual editing: A graphic guide for journalists.* Belmont, CA: Wadsworth.

Harris, C. R., & Lester, P. M. (2001). *Visual journalism: A guide for new media professionals.* Boston: Allyn and Bacon.

Harris, R. L. (2000). *Information graphics.* New York: Oxford University Press.

Meggs, P. B. (1998). *A history of graphic design.* New York: Van Nostrand Reinhold.

Meyer, E. K. (1997). *Designing infographics.* Indianapolis, IN: Hayden Books.

Moen, D. R. (2000). *Newspaper layout and design: A team approach.* Ames, IA: Iowa State University Press.

Monmonier, M. (1989). *Maps with the news: The development of American journalistic cartography.* Chicago: University of Chicago Press.

Newton, J. H. (2001). *The burden of visual truth: The role of photojournalism in mediating reality.* Hillsdale, NJ: Lawrence Erlbaum.

Stovall, J. G. (1997). *Infographics: A journalist's guide.* Boston: Allyn and Bacon.

Tufte, E. R. (2001). *Visual display of quantitative information.* Cheshire, CT: Graphics Press.

Working with Graphics Exercises

EXERCISE 15.1

Information in a Chart

This exercise demonstrates how much information can be found in a simple, well-constructed chart. Look closely at the accompanying chart. Make a list of all of the information that this chart tells you about the ethnic populations of each city.

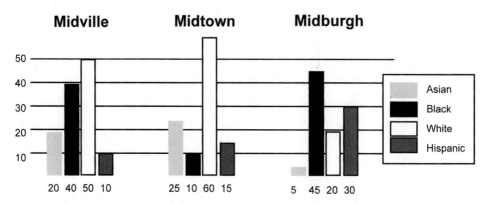

Ethnic populations of three area cities

| Midville | Midtown | Midburgh |

Legend: Asian, Black, White, Hispanic

Midville: 20 40 50 10
Midtown: 25 10 60 15
Midburgh: 5 45 20 30

Numbers represent percentage of each ethnic group in each city

EXERCISE 15.2

Time Line

Select a famous person and look up a biography of that person in an encyclopedia. Build a time line of that person's life. (Web sites devoted to this person are a good source of material, but you cannot publish an image from another's web site without permission unless that image is in the public domain.)

Specifications: Your time line should fit on an 8.5 × 11-inch page (horizontal or vertical); it should contain an introductory explainer box (fifty words maximum) and at least ten to fifteen entries. The entries will probably have a very limited word count (maybe twenty or fewer). You may use any graphic style of time line you choose. Be sure to give credit at the end of the chart to the sources of information you used. See the example that follows.

Purpose: This assignment will force you to make some choices about what to include about this man's life. It will also give you some practice in writing concise, meaningful entries.

Example

George Washington
George Washington is one of the chief figures in American history. Many people give him most of the credit for helping the nation secure its independence from Great Britain and for establishing the kind of government we have today. The following are the major events in his life:

1732—George Washington is born to Augustine and Mary (Ball) Washington at Wakefield Farm, Westmoreland County, Virginia.

1748—Washington begins career as surveyor in a venture to the Shenandoah Valley on behalf of prominent Virginia landowner, Lord Thomas Fairfax.

1752—Washington inherits rights to Mount Vernon plantation upon the death of brother Lawrence Washington.

EXERCISE 15.3

Building Charts

Assignment 1: Go to the College Board web site (www.collegeboard.com) and use the figures that you find there to produce three infographics. One should have a line chart, one a bar chart, and one a pie chart.

Assignment 2: Go to the Census Bureau web site (www.census.gov) and use the figures that you find there to produce three infographics. One should have a line chart, one a bar chart, and one a pie chart.

Assignment 3: Go to the Gallup Poll web site (www.gallup.com) and use the figures that you find there to produce three infographics. One should have a line chart, one a bar chart, and one a pie chart.

Specifications: Each of the three infographics you produce should have a headline, explainer box, chart, source, and credit line. Use the following basic form, although you may develop variations of it.

Explainer box: Use complete sentences. It should be fifty words or less. It should illuminate the information in your chart, add other information, emphasize some point about your chart, or help the reader to interpret the chart.

The purpose of this assignment is to give you experience in turning numerical data into a simple infographic.

The charts you produce (whether bar, line, or pie charts) follow this form. Remember, the simpler the better.

Headline headline

Your explainer box should illuminate the information you are presenting. It should add to the reader's understanding and help the reader interpret the data.

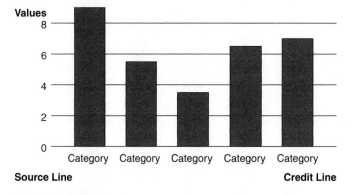

Source Line **Credit Line**

EXERCISE 15.4

Building Charts

Assignment 1: Go to the American Cancer Society web site (www.cancer.org) and use the figures that you find there to produce three infographics. One should have a line chart, one a bar chart, and one a pie chart.

Assignment 2: Go to the U.S. Department of Commerce business statistics web site (www.stat-usa.gov) and use the figures that you find there to produce three infographics. One should have a line chart, one a bar chart, and one a pie chart.

Assignment 3: Go to the Pew Research Center for the People and the Press web site (www.people-press.org) and use the figures that you find there to produce three infographics. One should have a line chart, one a bar chart, and one a pie chart.

Specifications: Each of the three infographics you produce should have a headline, explainer box, chart, source, and credit line. Use the following basic form, although you may develop variations of it.

Explainer box: Use complete sentences. It should be fifty words or less. It should illuminate the information in your chart, add other information, emphasize some point about your chart, or help the reader to interpret the chart.

Purpose: This assignment will give you experience in turning numerical data into a simple infographic.

The charts you produce (whether bar, line, or pie charts) follow this form. Remember, the simpler the better.

Headline headline

Your explainer box should illuminate the information you are presenting. It should add to the reader's understanding and help the reader interpret the data.

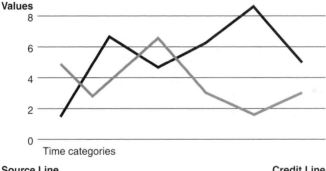

Source Line   **Credit Line**

Chapter Sixteen

Photojournalism

Key Concepts and Terms

1. Despite the ease of the technology, taking a good picture—one that is worthy of good journalism—is difficult; it takes both skill and planning.

2. Three types of photos dominate photojournalism: establishing shots, midrange shots, and close-ups.

3. Pictures can be inaccurate in that they can place information in an inaccurate context; photojournalists must have the same commitment to truth and accuracy that other journalists have.

4. A pen and notebook are as important to the photojournalist as a camera.

5. Three of the most important elements in making a good photograph are drama, emotion, and action.

6. Mug shot: journalistic slang for a picture of a person's head and shoulders.

7. Cropping: in the photo editing process, eliminating unnecessary parts of a photograph.

8. Scaling: changing the size of a picture to fit into a publication or web site.

9. Proportionality: maintaining the relationship between the width and depth of a photograph when it is being changed in size; the opposite of proportionality is distortion.

10. Cutline: the words that explain what is in a photograph.

This chapter has been adapted from material in James Glen Stovall and Edward Mullins, *The Complete Editor*, revised edition, 2000.

Pictures are one of the most important parts of a newspaper. Pictures help editors and reporters tell the stories they must tell. They inform and illustrate. They give the reader, who lives in a visual world and who expects visual messages from the print media as well as from the broadcast media, something to see as well as read.

Basics of Photojournalism

Taking pictures is easy. Taking good picture—pictures that people want to look at, that tell a story, that give viewers insight and understanding—is far more difficult than simply pointing the camera and snapping the shutter.

Working as a photojournalist is even harder. Not only do you have to take the picture, but you also have to carry equipment, juggle a pencil and notepad, stay alert for the next picture, worry about the next assignment, and work against a deadline. That takes talent, skill, practice, and persistence.

Much of the work of the photojournalist is going on assignment. That is, a photographer will get an assignment sheet from an editor or reporter and will have to go someplace to take a picture. Usually that picture will be used by the publication to illustrate a story. A photojournalist has to understand what the story is about and what will best illustrate the story. With specific assignments a photographer may be told exactly what the picture should be and who should be in it. On the other hand, assignments may be general, particularly when an event in which the action cannot be fully anticipated is being covered.

Whatever the case, a photographer must approach each assignment with some understanding of what the publication needs. Often that understanding is based on the photographer's experience and what the publication has required in the past. Ideally, however, a photographer can at least talk with the reporter covering the assignment to gain some background on what is likely to be happening and what would make the best shots.

When assignments do not call for specific shots, a photographer will often take three kinds of photographs: establishing shots, midrange shots, and close-ups.

Establishing shots seek to take a broad view of the scene where the action or event is taking place. They are designed to give viewers a good idea of the entire scene of the action and even beyond. Establishing shots, when done by amateurs, can be weak and tepid. They may tell us a lot, but they may not be very interesting or have much impact. Occasionally, however, an establishing shot will be a powerful statement about the subject itself. (See the example in Figure 16.1.)

Midrange shots bring the viewer closer to the subject. They are good for showing action because they often take in movement. Midrange shots put the subject within a context. They give the viewer some idea of the environment surrounding the subject but without showing too much that would draw attention away from the central idea of the photograph. They also give viewers an idea of how the subject relates to the surroundings.

FIGURE 16.1   Types of Photos Photojournalists often think in terms of three kinds of pictures: establishing shots (left), midrange shots (lower left), and close-ups (lower right). Each type has advantages for telling the viewer about the scene or event. (Photo credit: Library of Congress, Farm Security Administration photos. Photographers Dorothea Lange, top; Lee Russell, middle; Walker Evans, bottom)

Close-up shots are those that bring the viewer face-to-face with the subject. They are totally about the subject and not about the surroundings. In a close-up shot, for instance, the viewer has to concentrate on the expression on a person's face rather than having any clue as to why that expression occurred. Close-up shots deprive the subject of its context. In doing so, they can make the subject dramatic and compelling.

Beginning photographers have little trouble getting establishing shots or midrange shots. Close-ups, however, are often another matter. To get a good close-up shot, the photographer has to get physically close to the subject. A photographer has to overcome the discomfort of getting close and the self-consciousness that might occur when someone looks straight into the camera. Although these are not easy things to do, a professional attitude that allows photographers to do their job can be developed with time and practice.

Photographer's Commitment

Good photojournalists must be committed to the equipment they are using, to the idea of photojournalism telling stories with the camera, and to the concepts of truth and discovery. These various commitments must be based on honesty and integrity.

Photographers must understand their equipment. They must know its possibilities and limitations and keep up with the technical advances that would allow them to use their equipment to its best advantage. Photographers often end up using their own equipment even when they are on assignment because they do not feel comfortable working with equipment that others have used.

Good photographers believe in the importance and power of photojournalism. People want to see the world around them. Photographers give people an honest, unflinching view of that world, even though it may be disturbing. Photographers also understand how powerful their images can be. Like words, still images stick in our heads and sometimes become the filters through which we interpret our experiences. They evoke emotions that cannot be produced otherwise.

Finally, photographers must be committed to telling the truth. Their photographs should be accurate reflections of the actions and expressions of the people they cover. Photographers must resist the temptation to manipulate the photograph into one that they would like to have—or their audience would like for them to have—instead of the one they do have.

FIGURE 16.2   Expect the Unexpected Photojournalists should always be ready for the unexpected or candid shot when it is available, such as this moment when President Bill Clinton, meeting with Russian president Boris Yeltsin, picked up a saxophone and began playing. (Photo credit: White House)

The Photojournalist in Action

To be a photojournalist you have to take pictures. Too many beginning photographers act like they believe otherwise. They do not carry their cameras with them, and they are not ready when something happens in front of them that needs to be photographed. Photojournalism is something that photojournalists must be ready to do at all times, whether or not they are on the job or on an assignment.

With that in mind, the potential photojournalist should use these following rules of action.

Rules for the Beginning Photojournalist

All journalism students should learn the fundamentals of photojournalism. They should learn how to take pictures, and they should be given specific photo assignments. When completing those assignments, students should keep in mind the following rules.

PLAN.   Photojournalists and editors should talk about their photo assignments as thoroughly as possible. Editors should help plan what the photographers will shoot. Although some pictures happen spontaneously, most do not. They are shot because photographers planned to be there to shoot them.

Part of the planning process should be a diagram of the scene of a photo assignment, even if it is just a rough sketch. This helps photographers figure out where the action is and where they should be to take a good shot. Events such as speeches, parades, and sports events lend themselves to this kind of planning.

TAKE LOTS OF PICTURES.   Editors should probably expect a minimum number of pictures from an assignment, and that number should be high. For instance, if the photo is for a profile story in which the editor anticipates using only one shot, the photographer should come back with at least ten to fifteen shots. In fact, ten to fifteen shots for any assignment would be a good minimum.

Beginning photographers tend to not shoot enough pictures. They get one shot and one angle, and they don't think about doing anything else. Assigning a high minimum number of pictures makes them think about shooting different shots at different angles.

A PEN AND A NOTEBOOK ARE AS IMPORTANT AS A CAMERA.   Photographers have to write down what they are shooting. They will have to identify people for cutline information. They must have a pen and notebook with them at all times, and they must use it. They must also be accurate in getting their information, especially in spelling names correctly.

GET CLOSE.   Anybody can take wide-angle, establishing shots. Real photographers get as close to the action and the people as they can. They get expressions, hand movements, interactions, and so on. They literally get in people's faces.

If photographers show up at an event with a camera, people expect them to take pictures. Although they should try not to be intrusive, sometimes they have to be, and normally people will understand this.

SHOOT IN THE BEST LIGHT POSSIBLE. Photographers should shoot outside or near a window if possible. They may have to use a flash. Light is what makes pictures possible, and nothing makes up for an absence of light.

BE CREATIVE. Photographers should return from an assignment with shots from more than one angle. Situations such as sporting events will often dictate where photographers can be. In most other cases, they should always think about their physical proximity to the subject. A shot from a high or low angle can make a fairly standard shot much more interesting. Photographers should always move around, which will show them the options they have for each situation.

Newsworthy Photos

What makes a good photograph? Why is a particular photograph selected for publication and another not selected? What are the technical and aesthetic qualities editors look for in selecting photographs for a newspaper? Many divergent factors go into an editor's decision to use a photograph, and there are no definitive guidelines governing their selection. The three major purposes of publishing photographs are to capture the attention of the reader, to illustrate and supplement the editorial content, and to make pages look more presentable.

In the process of selection, an editor will be concerned with all three purposes, but at the beginning of the process of selection the first purpose (capturing the attention of the reader) will most likely be the major consideration. Following are some photographic elements editors consider in the selection process.

Drama.   Pictures that tell a story are most likely to be chosen by an editor for publication. Pictures that have high dramatic quality can clearly tell readers what is happening; in fact, there may be several things happening, as in an accident scene with someone standing nearby with an anguished expression.

Emotion.   Like dramatic pictures, those with emotional qualities often tell a story. An old journalistic proverb says that readers will always look at pictures of children and animals. These are the kinds of pictures that make the readers feel something.

Action.   Editors and readers are most likely to be drawn to pictures with action or movement in them. Pictures suggesting movement will be seen and studied by readers more readily than still-life pictures. Action pictures can serve as attention-capturing devices for the editor to use.

Artistic or technical quality.   Here we are talking about the photograph that has sharp, clear focus and good framing or that presents a subject in an unusual or pleasing manner. This kind of picture often appears in newspapers, especially with the change of seasons.

Bizarre or unusual subjects.   A picture of something unusual, something not likely to be seen by readers in their everyday lives, is a good candidate for publication. Unusual subjects may stem from the day's news events, such as a fire or wreck, or they may be simply something a photographer has happened upon or heard about, such as a twelve-pound tomato or an old man's wizened expression.

Prominence.   Prominence is a quality editors often consider in selecting pictures. Pictures of famous people are always likely candidates for publication, even when they do not contain any of the qualities mentioned previously. Readers will look at pictures of famous people, and editors will use such pictures for precisely that reason.

These elements are not a checklist of criteria for the selection of photographs; they are rather a list of things an editor may consider in deciding which pictures to publish. A good picture editor must have a "feel" for spotting the photograph that will capture the attention of the reader, illustrate the editorial content, and enhance the overall quality of the publication.

Photo Editing

Many news editors believe pictures to be the most important design element with which they have to work. On a printed page full of type, the picture stands out. Of all the elements, it is the one most likely to catch readers' eyes first and hold their attention the longest. A good picture can focus readers' eyes on the page and direct their attention to other parts of the page.

Because of these qualities, pictures can make a vital contribution to the overall quality and credibility of a newspaper. Pictures should not be treated as an afterthought or merely as material to go along with the stories and break up the type. Editors use pictures to help achieve the newspaper's goal of accuracy in telling the day's events.

The person who selects and directs pictures for publication is the picture editor. Only a few of the larger newspapers hire people solely for this purpose. More often, the picture editor's position may be combined with that of news editor, city editor, or chief photographer. A picture editor does not necessarily have to be a photographer. The skills required to be a good picture editor are quite different from those required to take a good photograph. The picture editor must be an expert in the three basic processes of putting photographs into a publication: selection, cropping, and scaling. Beyond that, however, the picture editor must demand high-quality photographs from photographers, and he or she must know how to reward their creativity and enterprise. Proper handling and display of good pictures can inspire photographers to increase the quality of their work.

The picture editor has a variety of types of pictures to work with, including the following.

News photos.   These pictures are most likely used to illustrate a news story (although occasionally news photos may be included without reference to stories). They illustrate the action, drama, and humor of the day's events and draw the reader's attention to a particular story.

Feature pictures.   These, too, may go with stories the paper prints, or they may stand by themselves. Those that go with stories are specifically tied to feature stories and may include staged or posed shots as well as action photos. Some feature pictures may stand alone; that is, they may not illustrate a story but may be used because the subject or photographic qualities brighten the page and catch the attention of the reader.

Head or "mug" shots.   These pictures are usually one column wide, though occasionally one-half or two columns, and they show only the face or head of the subject. These photos may be used because they contain an unusual facial expression or because an editor needs them to break up some body or headline type on a page.

Community art.   These pictures show groups of people either handing checks, awards, or papers to one another; looking at something in front of them; shaking hands; or staring at the camera. One of the pejorative terms for this kind of picture is "the grip 'n' grin shot." Community art also includes many "society" page pictures, such as engagement and wedding pictures and photos of club parties and teas. With a little forethought regarding angle and composition, they can become interesting additions to the paper.

Cropping

After the selection process has taken place, or along with it, comes the process of cropping. Cropping means taking out parts of a picture. It has two purposes: eliminating unnecessary parts of a picture and emphasizing or enhancing parts of a picture.

Eliminating Unnecessary Parts of a Picture

Some elements of a picture may simply be unnecessary to the subject and purpose of the photograph, and they should be eliminated. Often these parts are not only wasteful but also distracting. An editor must use the space in the paper efficiently, and proper cropping of a photograph is one way to do this. Good, tight cropping of pictures is just as important as editing to eliminate unnecessary parts of a story.

FIGURE 16.3   Cropping A photo editor's cropping takes away unnecessary parts of the photo and places emphasis on certain parts of the picture.

Emphasizing or Enhancing Parts of a Picture

One photograph may contain many pictures within it. A good picture editor must have an eye for these pictures within pictures and must be able to see and choose the picture that best fits the intended purpose. Cropping is a way of bringing out the particular picture the editor wants to use, of emphasizing the part of the picture that readers should notice. A picture that seems ordinary at first glance may be made dramatic by good cropping.

Pictures published in newspapers are generally rectangular, and cropping must be done with straight lines along the side. Occasionally, pictures are not rectangular but follow the lines of the subject. These are called dropouts or cutouts and may be used for dramatic effect.

Scaling

Scaling is the process of changing the size of a picture area by enlarging or reducing it while keeping the proportions of the original. Once an editor has selected and cropped a photograph for use in a publication, chances are the picture will not be the exact size needed. Enlargement or reduction will probably be needed to make the picture fit standard column widths. When that reduction or enlargement is made, the editor will have to find out how deep the reproduction of the picture will be.

The concept of proportionality must be understood by those who work with the scaling process. For our purposes, proportionality means that the width and depth of a picture must stay in the same proportion to each other whether the picture is enlarged or reduced. Let's say a cropped picture is 2 inches wide and 4 inches deep—that the depth is twice the width. Given these dimensions, it does not matter how much the picture is enlarged or reduced; the depth will always be twice the width. The proportion must remain the same. The only way it can be changed is to recrop the picture.

Two of the most common ways to scale a print are through use of arithmetic and through use of a mechanical device, such as a picture wheel or slide rule. The arithmetic method involves some simple multiplication and division, with substitution of the dimensions being used into the following formula.

$$\frac{\text{Original width}}{\text{Reproduction width}} = \frac{\text{Original depth}}{\text{Reproduction depth}}$$

Let's say an editor has a cropped picture that is 4 inches wide by 6 inches deep and wants that photo to run as a three-column picture, which means it should be about 6 inches wide. The editor will then have to find out how deep it is by using the foregoing formula. By substituting these dimensions into the formula, the editor will come up with the following.

$$\frac{4}{6} = \frac{6}{X}$$

The editor will then have to solve for the missing value by multiplying diagonally: $6 \times 6 = 36$ and $4 \times X = 4X$, then $4X = 36$. X would then equal 9. The reproduction depth of the picture is 9 inches.

The problem with this method of scaling is that frequently it is necessary to work with odd dimensions, such as $6\frac{5}{16}$ inches or $7\frac{3}{4}$ inches. Cross-multiplying these dimensions requires elaborate multiplication and allows more chance of error. One way of getting around this problem is to measure the picture in picas rather than in inches. By doing this, an editor is more likely to have whole numbers to work with than fractions.

The most popular method of scaling is by using some mechanical device, and by far the most popular of these devices is the picture wheel. The picture wheel is made up of two circular pieces of cardboard braided together to allow the two pieces to turn independently. The inside portions of the picture wheel represent the original (or cropped) dimensions of the photograph, and the outside wheel represents the reproduction dimensions.

You should note an additional thing about the picture wheel. On the inside portion of the original wheel is a window that gives the "percentage of the original size." For this problem the percentage is 150. This percentage is important because it is the only figure needed by the operator of the copy camera that will enlarge or reduce this print. The operator is never concerned with the original dimensions of the picture, and editors should always make a note of the desired percentage on the back of the photograph.

Digital Photography

Digital photography and electronic imaging have greatly simplified the process of handling pictures for editors and have made the chemical processing of photographs obsolete. This technology has cameras that record digital images on internal disks rather than on film. These images can then be downloaded into a publication's computer system and called up directly onto a computer screen. There, working with sophisticated software, photo editors can resize and retouch photographs to their liking. More and more newspapers are closing their darkrooms and using this technology.

An important part of this process is scanning. A scanner can digitize a photograph (or any piece of art or illustration) that has already been processed and printed so that it can be handled by a computer system. All of the photographs used for exercises in this book have been scanned into a computer system.

Digital technology was resisted by photojournalists and their editors in its first stages during the early 1990s. Digital cameras of any quality were expensive, difficult to handle and not nearly as flexible in terms of settings as the single-lens reflex that was standard for many photojournalists. There was also the problem of storing digital images, which took huge amounts of limited disk space. Photographers argued that digital cameras could not deliver the quality photograph that was necessary for the profession. Behind all of the protestations was the fear of change and the lack of desire to learn a new technology.

As the cost of cameras plummeted and the quality improved, newspaper publishers saw that their publications could realize great savings by switching from film to digital cameras. With digital cameras, publishers would not be faced with continually resupplying their departments with film, paper, and darkroom chemicals. They also realized that time could also be saved if a photo could go straight from a camera to a computer.

The profession today is gaining a new generation of photojournalists who have never handled a film camera and have never had firsthand experience in a darkroom. Instead, they have discovered and developed their skills with a variety of digital cameras, possibly even a camera-phone. Rather than the darkroom, they know Photoshop as the software that enables them to produce and edit quality pictures. The digital revolution is complete.

Ethics and Taste

- A local man who is nationally prominent dies. Many people from all parts of the country attend his funeral. The family has opened the funeral to the public, but it has said that no cameras should be used in the church or at the gravesite. Thousands of people attend the funeral and burial. Your photographer comes back to the office with some dramatic photographs of the family leaving the gravesite along with some highly prominent people.

- A woman is held hostage by a crazed killer for most of a day. She is made to take off all her clothes to prevent her from escaping. Somehow she manages to get away from the killer and out the front door of her house. Your photographer is there with other newsmen and shoots pictures of her escape. The pictures the photographer shows you do not reveal breasts or genital area, but it is clear that she does not have any clothes on.

- The president dozes off while listening to a visiting head of state speak to the White House press corps. The wire services send several photos of the president with his head down and eyes closed sitting behind the speaker.

- A movie star is decapitated in a car crash. The wire services send several pictures of the accident scene, including one of the actress's head placed on the car.

Pictures present editors with special problems of taste and ethics. These problems do not occur every day, fortunately, but they happen often enough that eventually every editor must make some decision for which he or she will be criticized. Some newspapers have tried to produce guidelines for handling certain kinds of pictures, but these guidelines do not cover all situations and sometimes do not provide the editor with sufficient guidance in making a decision. The following is not a set of guidelines but a list of things an editor should consider in deciding whether to run a photograph. None of these considerations is primary in every case; they should all be part of an editor's decision making.

Editors should remember that their business is to cover the news and inform their readers. A newspaper is supposed to give a full and accurate account of the day's news. Sometimes it takes a photograph to accomplish this mission. Generally, editors should avoid making agreements prior to covering an event that would restrict its photo coverage.

Editors should be sensitive to their readers. There are a number of subjects that will offend readers or that parents will want to keep from their children. An editor should be aware of these subjects and the sensibilities of the readers. He or she should try to avoid publishing pictures that are unnecessarily offensive.

Editors should be aware of the feelings of the people in the pictures. Even people who are photographed a great deal and who are highly visible have feelings that need consideration. Pictures can put people in a bad light or in embarrassing situations even when editors print those pictures with the most innocent of motives. One example may serve to illustrate this point. A newspaper in a medium-size town decided to publish a special section on home furnishings. In putting this section together, the editors looked in their files and found a picture of one of the town's prominent women in her living room. The picture was about a year old but fit perfectly with the theme of the section. The editors were all set to run the photo until they learned that in the year since the picture had been taken the woman had lost nearly 100 pounds. The editors decided not to run the picture.

Editors must remember that some photographs can get them into legal trouble. Even though a picture is taken in public and is coverage of a newsworthy event, it may constitute libel or an invasion of privacy. When there is any question about a photograph, editors should be extremely careful. The wrong decision in this regard could cost them and their newspaper thousands of dollars.

Decisions about pictures are often among the most difficult decisions an editor must make. Pictures are dramatic and powerful. They have an impact on readers, on their subjects, and on the newspaper itself. The watchwords for an editor in handling pictures are caution and sensitivity.

Cutlines

Cutlines are explanatory and descriptive copy that accompanies pictures. They range widely in style and length, from the one-line identifier called the "skel line" to the full "story" line. Cutlines are necessary to practically all pictures because of the functions they serve: identification, description, explanation, and elaboration.

A well-written cutline answers all of a reader's questions about a picture. What is this picture about? What is its relationship to the story it accompanies? Who are the people in it? Where are the events taking place and when? What does the picture mean? The cutline should answer these and other questions in such a manner that material found in the accompanying story is not repeated verbatim but is reinforced, amplified, or highlighted.

Every newspaper has its own particular standards for cutline writing and display. For example, a newspaper may use one typeface for "story cutlines" (cutlines for pictures without accompanying stories) and another for cutlines on pictures accompanied by a story. What is important is that each publication be consistent in its use of cutlines. An established style should exist for each particular type of cutline so that the reader will know what to expect from the publication and so that cutline writers experience a minimum of difficulty in deciding how to present information.

Cutlines are one of the most neglected parts of the newspaper. They are often written as an afterthought when all other parts of a story are finished. Sometimes reporters are assigned to write cutlines; other times it is the job of copy editors, and sometimes the photographers themselves have to write the cutlines. Whoever does the writing should remember that cutlines are as important as any other part of the paper and should be treated with care. The following are some general guidelines for writing cutlines.

- Use the present tense to describe what is in the picture.

- Always double-check identifications in a cutline. This rule cannot be stressed too much. Many newspapers have gotten into deep trouble through misidentification of people in a cutline, so cutline writers should take great care.

- Be as specific as possible in cutlines. Add to the reader's knowledge and go beyond what the reader can see in the picture. A cutline is useless if it simply tells the reader what can be seen already.

- Try to avoid cutline clichés. "Looking on," "is pictured," and other such expressions are trite and usually avoidable.

Because cutlines differ from other kinds of information the newspaper has to present, they should be displayed differently. Following are some commonly used guidelines that many newspapers use in displaying cutlines.

Cutlines should contrast with the publication's body type to make for easier reading. Using boldface or type one point larger than body type can accomplish this.

Cutlines should be set at different widths than most body type. For instance, if a picture is three or four columns wide, a cutline should be set in two stacks of type under the picture. Cutlines should also take up all or most of the allotted space.

Catchlines (headlines above the cutlines) look best in 18- or 24-point type and are generally centered above the cutline.

Two general principles should govern an editor's use of cutlines. One is that every picture should have a cutline. The words used in the cutline may be few, but they can add enormously to the reader's understanding of the picture and the story the editor is trying to tell. The second principle is that everyone in a picture should be identified. Nameless people are not very interesting, and their presence indicates a lack of interest on the part of the editor in doing a thorough job.

Cutlines are important because of the information they contain and because of the way they enhance the appearance of the paper. Cutlines should be simply and clearly written and displayed, and they should be given the same attention by the editors that other parts of the paper receive.

QUESTIONS FOR DISCUSSION

1. Some people who are not interested in taking pictures turn out to be good photo editors. What are some of the qualities of a good photo editor?
2. This chapter and Chapter 14 emphasize the heavy role that ethics plays in the work of the photojournalist. Why are ethical considerations so prevalent in this part of journalism?
3. A distorted photograph is an inaccurate photograph. Do you agree with that statement?

RELATED WEB SITES

American Photography: A Century of Images, www.pbs.org/ktca/americanphotography

Americanphotojournalist.com, www.americanphotojournalist.com

American Society of Media Photographers, www.asmp.org

American Society of Picture Professionals, www.aspp.com

Associated Press Photo Managers, www.apphotomanagers.org

Associated Press Photos of the Century, wire.ap.org/APpackages/centuryphotos

College Photographer of the Year, www.cpoy.org

The Digital Journalist, digitaljournalist.org

Digital Vision Network, www.dvnetwork.net

Editor & Publisher's **Photos of the Year Contest,** www.editorandpublisher.com/ editorandpublisher/features_columns/photo_contest.jsp

NPPA: National Press Photographers Association, www.nppa.org

Pictures of the Year International, www.poy.org/59/

Poynter Online's Photojournalism Tipsheets, http://poynteronline.org/content content_view.asp?id=31901

Pulitzer Prize Photos: Examples from the Newseum,
www.newseum.org/pulitzer/index.htm

Reportage: Online Magazine of Photojournalism, www.reportage.org

Sports Shooter, www.sportsshooter.com

Visual Edge, www.visualedge.org

White House News Photographers Association, www.whnpa.org

World Press Photo, www.worldpressphoto.nl/index.jsp

READINGS AND REFERENCES

Ang, T. (2000). *Picture editing* (2nd ed.). Oxford: Focal Press.
Giles, M. (Ed.). (2001). *Facing the world: Great moments in photojournalism.* New York:
    H. N. Abrams.
Kobre, K., & Brill, B. (2000). *Photojournalism, the professionals' approach* (4th ed.).
    Woburn, MA: Focal Press.
Newton, J. H. (2001). *The burden of visual truth: The role of photojournalism in mediating
    reality.* Hillsdale, NJ: Lawrence Erlbaum.
Parrish, F. S. (2001). *Photojournalism, an introduction.* Belmont, CA: Wadsworth/Thomson
    Learning.

Photography Exercises

EXERCISE 16.1

Planning a Photograph

Following are a number of possible photo assignments for a photojournalist. For each
of these assignments, you should prepare a photo plan that contains the following
information:

Photo Assignment Plan

General description of the event or assignment:

List of people who may be included in the photographs: (Be as specific as possible)

Location of the event: (Describe or diagram where this event will take place; also
describe or diagram the angles from which pictures might be taken.)

Actions

(Describe specific actions that might be included in the photographs.)

List at least five photographs that you would like to take on this assignment: (Be specific)

Assignments

- A day in the life of a teacher
- A portrait (think beyond the standard studio portraits)
- Speech story
- An event such as a pep rally, award ceremony, or sports event
- A public meeting such as a school board or city council meeting

EXERCISE 16.2

Crop the following picture.

Decide where you want to use it in your layouts; decide how many columns wide it should be.

Figure out what the dimensions and the percentage of reproduction should be for the picture. You will want to choose one of the following column widths as the reproduction width.

Column Widths

1 col. = 1.9 inches

2 col. = 4 inches

3 col. = 6.1 inches

4 col. = 8.3 inches

5 col. = 10.4 inches

Write a cutline for the picture based on the following information.

Cutline Information

Warm day in February yesterday; first time kids have been able to play outside in two months; temperature got up to 70, pretty unusual for this time of year; these kids go to school at Medford Elementary. Fourth grade teacher, Molly Evans: "We just couldn't keep them indoors."

Original width _____; Original depth _____

Reproduction width _____; Reproduction depth _____

Percentage of reproduction _____

FIGURE 16.4

Chapter Seventeen

Publication and Web Site Design

Key Concepts and Terms

1. Design is an important part of the journalistic process; without it, reporting and writing would have little effect.

2. Publication design is artificial; that is, everything about design results from a decision that someone has made; nothing occurs naturally.

3. Four modern principles of visual design are left to right, top to bottom, big to little, and dark to light.

4. Contrast: the relationship of the elements of design.

5. Type is an important but often ignored element of design.

6. The three major elements of design are type, illustration, and white space.

7. Graphic personality: the continuing elements of a publication's or web site's design that help distinguish it from other publications and web sites and that contribute to its content messages.

8. Good news judgment is necessary to execute good design in journalism.

9. Jump line: the line of type at the end of a column that tells the reader a story is continued on another page.

10. Load time: the time it takes to have a web site page appear on a computer screen; one of the goals of a designer is to have a page appear as quickly as possible.

This chapter is adapted from material in James Glen Stovall and Edward Mullins, *The Complete Editor*, 2000; and James Glen Stovall, *Web Journalism: Practice and Promise of a New Medium*, Allyn and Bacon, 2004.

Many people enjoy the news process but are not particularly interested in reporting, writing, photography, or editing. Instead, they feel their creative juices flow when they have the opportunity to take the products of others—the words and pictures—and put them together on a page or in a web site.

Design is a vital part of the journalistic process. It is how the information gets presented to the reader or viewer and in itself can send important messages to the audience. Design not only contributes to the day's information, but also it helps to establish the relationship of the news organization to the reader. Good design and presentation can enhance credibility. It can also lift the morale of those within the organization.

This chapter introduces some of the basic concepts of design and the process by which design is made to operate. The emphasis and many of the examples refer to newspapers, but the basic principles are the same whenever type and pictures are presented to a reader.

Design

Design is a visual process with content as the chief factor. Design is a way of presenting a reader with information and a way of communicating to the reader something about that information. The visual is an important way of communicating and, in fact, images predate text by many centuries.

All of us understand to some extent how important appearance is. Most people spend time grooming themselves and selecting what they wear because they know that their appearance sends a message to others about who they are. Publications are the same way. They communicate to their readers what they are and what they are about by their appearance.

Unlike our basic appearance, however, publications are not made by nature. They are the result of conscious decisions that designers and editors make. Everything on a web site or a newspaper page or a magazine layout is the product of a decision that someone has made.

Students learning design must understand this fact. They control everything that goes on their page. They may be following certain rules, edicts, or traditions when they put together a publication, but there is nothing about design that they cannot change. They must then understand why design for certain types of publications is done in certain ways.

Students must also become observant about design. Our educational systems do a woeful job in teaching us about design and visual logic. While we spend many hours learning to write or learning to do math, we spend practically no time at all learning why things look the way they do. Consequently, most of us grow up being completely unaware of design principles. We tend to believe that things "are the way they are" or that they "look the way they look" without any understanding of why this is so.

This chapter is designed to give you some tools to be a good observer of design as well as to teach you some of the principles of publication layout. When you look at a publication from now on, ask yourself why the editor chose to make it look that way; why did he or she put articles in certain places, use a specific style of type, or connect elements in particular ways?

Asking these questions will help you sharpen your visual sense and will make you more aware of what can be done with a publication. People who develop their skills to the point that they can control the look of a publication often come to enjoy knowing they can create something that readers pay attention to and that has an impact on the their publication. So be aware of design and layout. Give it your critical and analytical attention.

Design refers to the overall appearance of a publication. Layout is the day-to-day use of design rules and principles. Design takes in not only the way the elements are laid out on any one page but also how different sections of a publication relate to each other with body type, headline, the way pictures are cropped, the positioning of advertisements, and the types of designs and shapes used in standing heads and logos.

Editors must make many decisions in developing a design for their publications. These decisions provide the general rules of guidelines for the layout of the publication.

Visual Logic

Why do we look at things the way we do? The answer to that question is a combination of nature and training that results in what we call visual logic.

The eye, directed by the brain, tends to look at certain things first and other things next. Those directions are simple to observe and easy to catalog.

Big to small.   We see big things first, smaller things next. In publications, as in many other parts of life, size matters. We ascribe certain characteristics to "big" and other characteristics to "small."

Top to bottom.   For reasons that come from nature and from training, we tend to start at the top and go to the bottom. Reading material is certainly arranged in that fashion, but so are other things in life. Again, we think of the "top" as having certain characteristics, whereas "lower" or "bottom" has other characteristics.

Left to right.   With a few exceptions, we have learned to read from left to right. This training carries over into other aspects of our lives as we encounter the world. Left to right is not so much a natural tendency as it is one of training, but it is so much a part of our actions that we tend to think of it as a natural reaction to the visual world.

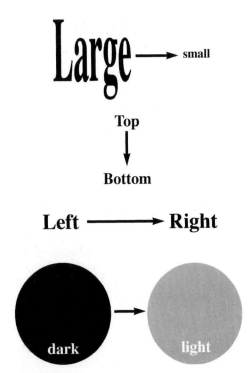

FIGURE 17.1   Visual Logic Principles of visual logic are simple but basic to the understanding of design.

Dark to light.   We tend to look at darker (or more colorful) items first and lighter (less colorful) items next. It is easier to "see" a darker item than it is a lighter one; our eyes have to work a bit harder on the lighter items.

These principles of visual logic are not immutable. There are exceptions, certainly, and the rules can be violated. A publication designer uses these principles to send messages to the reader. Sometimes the design can interrupt these principles to make a point.

With these principles in mind, a designer must understand some basic concepts in putting together elements on a page or on a web site. Like the principles of visual logic, these concepts are simple, and they are easy to observe if you are looking for them.

Balance.   This concept refers to putting the elements of design together so that all have the chance to be seen by the viewer. No element that is meant to be seen should be obscured. Big elements should not overwhelm small ones; dark elements should not obscure light ones. Many web site designers like to use black or dark backgrounds, demonstrating that they are not sensitive to the concept of balance. The dark background overwhelms the type and makes it unreadable.

Contrast and focus.   Contrast is the relationship of design elements as they are viewed by the eye; contrast specifically refers to the difference between these elements. Focus is the way a designer uses contrast to direct the eye of the reader.

Economy/simplicity.   The purpose of design is to present content. Every element used in a design should help the reader focus on the content of the publication. No element should be there to call attention to itself.

Repetition/variety.   Repeating elements gives strength and stability to a design. That is why designers generally choose one body type and size for their publication. Repeating that element allows the reader to focus on the content that is being presented.

But the reader needs variety as well as repetition. The reader should be shown what to look at first and should be directed to certain items on the page. In musical terms, repetition is the beat of the song whereas variety is its melody.

Despite all of these principles and concepts, a designer has only three basic design elements with which to work: type, illustration, and white space.

Type

One of the most important tools that an editor has to work with is type. Because it is a marvelously versatile tool, type is what we use the most, but we need to understand it from the ground up to be able to use it effectively. In this section, we will introduce some of the basics about type.

Families of Type

Typefaces are grouped into families, which means that they share similarities. Those similarities include the weight, or thickness, of the strokes making up the type and the width of the characters. Type families may have many different characteristics, such as bold, extra-bold, roman, italic, and so on.

Modern typefaces are characterized by "vertical stress," that is, emphasis on the vertical lines in the typeface, great contrast between thick and thin strokes, and hairline serifs. Old-style typefaces have small contrast between the thick and thin strokes, diagonal stress, and capitals shorter than ascenders.

Type families may be divided in other ways: display type for headlines designed to gain the attention of the reader and body type for large groups of characters, or body copy, that are not so intrusive in their design. Using a display type for body copy (and vice versa) can be a major mistake in page design.

Serif and Sans Serif

Another way of distinguishing type is by identifying it as serif or sans serif. Typefaces that have small extensions at the ends of strokes are called serif types; sans serif typefaces do not have these extensions. In serif faces, the strokes making up the various characters vary in thickness, whereas in sans serif faces they do not.

The Anatomy of Type

Designers must know the different parts of a typeface and its characters to be able to understand how it works. Type is measured in points; a point is a part of a measuring system that was developed by printers. There are 12 points to a pica; there are about 6 picas to an inch (and, thus, 72 points to an inch).

Another factor about type is its x-height. The x-height of a typeface is one of its most distinguishing features. X-heights can vary greatly from typeface to typeface, and the relationship of the x-height to the other parts of the typeface is important. In many typefaces, the larger the x-height, the more readable the type is at smaller point sizes. The ascender is the part of the type that extends above the x-height, and the descender is the part of the type that extends below the baseline.

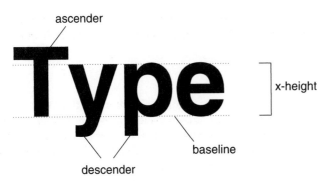

FIGURE 17.2   Anatomy of Type The illustration shows the various parts of type. Each has an important place in our understanding of how type works.

Type on the Page

In working with type on a page, we are most concerned with a type's size and leading. We may also be concerned with how closely the letters line up with each other. The following definitions will help you understand these concepts and the placement of type on a page.

Typesize.   The size of type is measured in points from the top of the tallest ascender to the bottom of the lowest descender.

Leading.   The amount of space measured from the baseline of one line of type to the baseline of another line of type. Leading should always be greater than typesize. For instance, 10-point type should have more than 10 points of leading to keep the lines from overlapping.

Kerning.   The amount of space between characters of type. When we talk about "kerning type," we are talking about changing the amount of space between the letters.

The chief concern for the page designer in using type is to make it easy to read. Following are a few of the guidelines that have been developed to aid in this process.

- Use serif type for body copy, sans serif for headlines.
- Avoid lines of all capitals; they are hard to read. Using small caps sometimes provides a good alternative to all caps. If you want to emphasize something, use boldface.
- Italics are harder to read then roman; avoid blocks of copy in italics.
- Don't overuse boldface particularly in body copy; bold fonts are used well in headlines.

■ A reverse (using white or light type on a dark background) is a good way to set off type, but don't overuse it. Generally, sans serif rather than serif should be used for reverses.

■ Mixing type fonts should be done carefully; too many type fonts on a page is distracting. Newspapers as a rule use three—one for body copy, one for headlines, cutlines, pullouts, and so on, and one for all other uses, such as refers, flags, and logos. Remember, when you have one font you really have three faces because of the ability to use each font in plain, bold, and italic forms. You can load up your computer with a wide variety of typefaces, but don't fool yourself into thinking that you are creative just because you use a lot of them.

Illustration

The second tool of design is illustration. Illustration can be considered anything on a page other than type that uses ink; on a web site, it is anything that is not type and not negative space or background.

We are talking about a variety of elements: pictures, illustrations, drawings, charts, graphs, maps, symbols, icons, logos, lines, dingbats, and so on. The major purpose of these elements is to aid in delivering the content of the publication. Sometimes they are heavily content-laden themselves (such as pictures), and other times they simply play a supporting role (such as lines that separate other elements).

Illustration can help draw the attention of the reader. It can separate elements or it can unify them. It can give the page visual variety or it can give the publication the repetition and consistency that we discussed earlier.

In working with illustration elements, designers should always remember that form follows function. That is, delivering the content, which is the first goal of a journalistic publication, is the primary function. The form that is created by the designer should help in achieving that goal.

White Space

White space (or negative space on web sites that use color backgrounds) is an extremely important but often ignored design tool. If it weren't for white space, we would not be able to see any of the other tools of design.

Yet many people who are learning design do not recognize the importance of white space and give little or no consideration to it. They butt headlines and body type against one another, or they put type next to a vertical line. They do not understand that the eye needs "breathing room" to help it separate visual elements.

Other beginners do not understand that too much white space is as bad as too little. They leave gaping holes of white space on their pages revealing that they have no idea about how elements fit together. These pages tend to look tattered and unfinished, and yet the creators cannot recognize what is wrong with them. They can't do that because they haven't been trained to use white space as a design element.

The key concept in using white space is proportion. There should be enough white space around an element that it can be seen. There shouldn't be so much that it becomes distracting. Larger items need more white space, smaller items less.

The idea of proportion is almost as elusive as the idea of good taste. Yet a sense of proportion can develop by careful observation and analysis. Students should look at well-designed pages and attempt to analyze what about them is good, particularly the way these pages use white space.

Newspaper Design

Newspaper design has three basic and interrelated purposes:

It should make the paper easy to read. A newspaper has a set design for the same reason it has a set style: consistency. Readers will be confused if they find several different spellings in the paper of the same word; so too will readers be confused if there are numerous styles of body type and headline faces, odd shapes and sizes, and various locations for the daily features of the paper. A good newspaper design sets the rules for reading the paper; these rules should be consistent and functional and should be changed only for specific purposes.

Newspaper design (the overall objective) and layout (the day-to-day execution) send messages to the reader. The layout of a newspaper is not content-free; that is, with the design and layout, an editor tells the reader what stories are the most important, what elements (pictures, headlines, and story) go together, and which groups of stories are related. A good newspaper design sets the rules for the editor (and the reader) but also allows for some flexibility in day-to-day work.

Design and layout establish a newspaper's "graphic personality." It is important for a newspaper to establish a particular appearance for the reader and to be consistent in that appearance. Many newspapers, such as the *New York Times,* the *Louisville Courier-Journal,* and the *Wall Street Journal,* have done just that. On appearance alone, there is no mistaking these newspapers. It is true that bad newspapers may be clothed in good design, but it is also true that good newspapers with bad or inconsistent designs put added strain on the loyalty of their readers. There is no reason for a newspaper to sacrifice form for function—the best papers have both. A newspaper with a pleasing and consistent design—a good "graphic personality"—builds faith and credibility with the reader.

Another important reason for a newspaper to have a clean, consistent graphic personality is that it shows craftsmanship and professionalism on the part of the editors and builds pride among the staff. Staff writers who know that their stories will be well displayed, easy to find, and easy to read will probably work harder to make sure the facts are straight, the stories are well written, and the deadlines are met.

Types of Newspaper Design

Since the advent of headlines, pictures, and other typographical devices, three types of newspaper design have evolved into general use: vertical, horizontal, and modu-

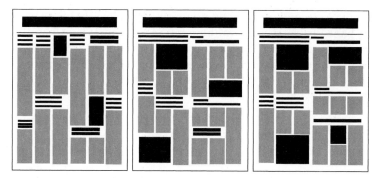

FIGURE 17.3   Types of Design These simulations show the differences among the three major types of design. The vertical design on the left is characterized by elements that run up and down on the page and by one- and two-column headlines. The horizontal design in the center has the elements running from left to right and has larger pictures and more multicolumn headlines. The modular design on the right has all story packages fitting into rectangles.

lar. Most other designs are variations on these general models, and the student of layout and design should be familiar with the characteristics of each.

Vertical

Vertical design demands an up-and-down movement of the reader's eye on the page. Pages using this design have a long, narrow look to them. They feature one- or two-column headlines with long strips of body type dropping down from them. The most prominent example of vertical design is seen in the *Wall Street Journal.*

Horizontal

In horizontal design, the elements on a page typically lie along horizontal rather than vertical lines. This effect is created by larger pictures, multicolumn headlines, wider columns of body type than normally found in vertical design, and generous but carefully controlled white space. The theory behind horizontal design is that natural eye movement is across a page rather than up and down. Horizontal design developed along with modern printing methods that allowed editors to break column rules (the lines between columns of type) or eliminate them altogether, including larger pictures and headlines and copy set in differing widths. Many newspapers have now adopted this design.

Modular

Modular design, which is the most popular design today, requires that story packages—headlines, photographs, illustrations, and body type—be shaped into rectangles on the page. These boxes create a unified and unmistakable space for all related items on a page. Such pages are laid out with these boxes in mind rather than the individual elements within each module. Modular design is an outgrowth of computerized layout and editors' tendency toward horizontal design and away from vertical design.

Principles of Layout

Once a consistent design, or graphic personality, has been developed, editors must attend to the daily production of the paper. In laying out each page according to the rules the publication has set, editors must consider the five major aspects of newspaper layout: proportion, balance, focus, dynamics, and unity.

Proportion

Proportion is concerned with two interrelated items: the shape of the elements on the page and the relationship of these elements to one another. The most pleasing shapes are those of the 3×4, 5×7, and 10×8 variety. Shapes in which the sides are wildly out of proportion to one another are distracting, confusing, or even boring (such as the square).

A newspaper should work to create pleasing shapes of proper proportions for its readers. Such shapes are simple, familiar, and easy on the eye and give the appearance of a neat, well-planned page.

This is not to say that every shape in the newspaper must be rectangular or modular. There is certainly room for variation. However, editors should avoid the jagged or ragged shapes caused by inattention to the bottom portions of a story unit or multiline headlines that do not fill out their assigned space. Proportion also refers to the relative size of the elements on the page. It means that the headline space should have the proper relationship to the body of the story and to other headlines on the page, that the pictures should be large enough to show the subject adequately, and that large blocks of type unbroken by other elements should not dominate the page. In fact, no typographical element should have accidental dominance over the page.

Balance

Balance refers to the relationship of all the elements on the page and the impression this relationship has on the reader. Pages with a lot of pictures or heavy typographical elements in any one particular part of the page are referred to as being heavy; except on rare occasions, editors should try to avoid heaviness. Instead, the page should have a good distribution of pictures and headlines.

The page should also have a mixture of headline styles; that is, there should be a mix of one-, two-, and three-column heads, as well as some single-line and multiline heads. A paper may also use devices such as kickers and hammerheads to create white space in the middle of the page and to offset the areas of heavy graphics. Inside pages can be balanced in part by placing pictures away from ads or other unrelated pictures.

Focus

It is natural that the reader's eye should be drawn to some typographical element on the page. The editors should control what that element is, and they should take care that other lines, shapes, and elements on the page do not distract from that focusing element.

A page should be built around a major element, usually a picture. Pictures should not be buried next to ads; nor should pictures or other elements be in competition with each other. The reason editors should pay close attention to the focus of their pages lies in another of the major considerations of newspaper layout: visual dynamics.

Visual Dynamics

Readers generally look at a page in a Z-like fashion, beginning with the upper left and moving down the page. It is important for an editor to select a focus above the fold to control the reader's beginning. If the upper left portion of the page is a jumble of heads, pictures, and other typographical elements, readers will be confused and easily distracted from what may be really important. Not knowing where to go on the page, they may miss something or may turn to another part of the paper entirely.

Another way of understanding dynamics is through the concept of rhythm. Rhythm refers to the logical flow of elements that readers are trained to expect when they see a newspaper. A page that has headlines or pictures bunched together may disrupt a reader's rhythm. Readers may then be unconsciously thrown off balance and not know what to expect or where to go in the paper to find the items they really want.

Unity

Newspaper pages should be thought of as a unit rather than as a set of typographical elements. These elements should relate well to one another on the page, just as the elements of a story package (story, headline, picture, cutline) should form a cohesive unit. The concept of unity takes into account all of the factors discussed previously. A page should look as if it were planned on one editor's desk, not on the desks of several people with differing ideas of how the final product should look.

News Judgment

On many newspapers the person who lays out the news pages is called the news editor. This person does not carry the title of layout editor because it would not be fully descriptive of the job. The news editor has a more important function than drawing the text and picture boxes for the different pages. The editor's function is one of selection and placement of stories, pictures, and other elements in the story.

To do the job correctly, a news editor not only must have a sense of what will look good on a page and how a page will fit together but must also have a keen sense of news judgment. News judgment is the ability to choose and position the stories, pictures, and other materials that are important to readers and that are expected from the paper.

The news editor's first job is to select the news of the day. In doing this, it is essential that the editor keep up with the day's events and be able to understand their relative importance. The editor must first read the paper in order to know what stories have been printed and what needs continuous coverage. A newspaper cannot afford to be episodic in its coverage of important, continuing news events. The news editor must also be aware of the content of other media, not only other newspapers but also radio and television. Many newspapers provide their newsrooms with television sets so that editors and reporters can watch the local news to make sure they have not missed any major items; they may also watch the national news to get an idea of what other journalists have deemed important for that day.

The news editor must also make sure that the paper carries the standard items readers have come to expect, such as weather reports, advice columns, and news briefs. Compiling and placing such items are tedious jobs, but they are necessary for providing continuity to the paper.

Not only must news editors select items for inclusion in the paper, but they also must decide where to place them. (It should be noted that on many newspapers these decisions are made at a daily meeting of editors, but often these decisions provide only guidelines for the news editor.) These decisions about placement are often difficult and sometimes delicate. A story may be "played up" or "played down," according to where it goes in the paper and what kind of headline the news editor assigns to it. To make these decisions, a news editor must have a definite idea of the kind of publication the editors and publishers want the newspaper to be and what the expectations of the readers are.

The news editor plays a critical role in the life of a newspaper. On a daily basis, this editor's decisions have more to do with the kind of publication that is presented to the reader than do the decisions of any other editor. It should be noted that different departments within the news and editorial division often have separate editors who function as news editors. For example, the sports, living, entertainment, national, and foreign desks may each have such an editor. On small and intermediate-sized papers, copy editors themselves may make many of the decisions on what stories and pictures to use and where to place them.

Laying Out a Page

When a news editor has assembled the elements to work with on any given day, the complex procedure of putting the pages together begins. The procedure is complex because numerous decisions have to be made at once, and almost every single decision has some effect on all other layout decisions. For instance, while deciding what to put at the top of a page, the news editor must also be considering what will go at the bottom of the page in order to create proper balance and contrast.

Because the procedure is so complex and because it will change daily due to the different elements to be used, there is no step-by-step guide on how to lay out a page.

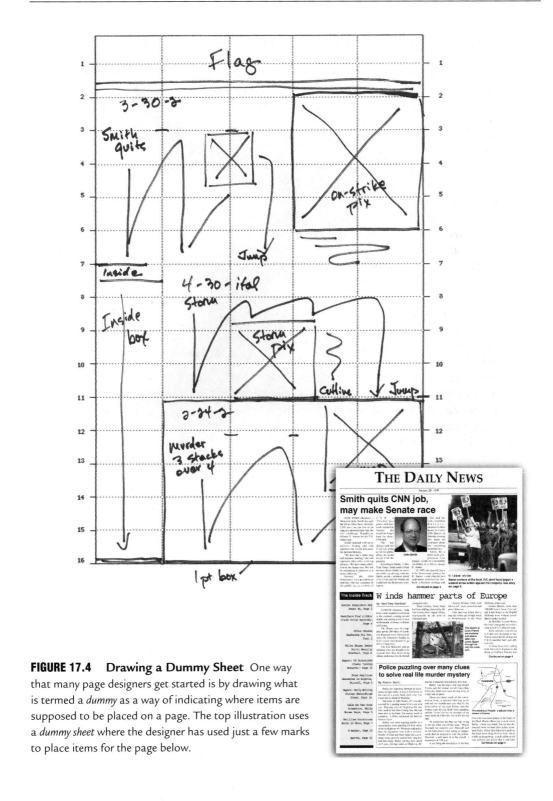

FIGURE 17.4   Drawing a Dummy Sheet One way that many page designers get started is by drawing what is termed a *dummy* as a way of indicating where items are supposed to be placed on a page. The top illustration uses a *dummy sheet* where the designer has used just a few marks to place items for the page below.

There are, however, some general guidelines or considerations that can be suggested to beginning students who are faced with various typographical elements and a blank computer screen. An editor needs to begin by considering all of the stories, pictures, illustrations, and any other elements available. Using these elements, the editor can form a general picture of the page in his or her imagination. At that point, the editor is ready to place elements on the page.

1. Begin at the top. If the flag is stationary (that is, always located at the top of the page), place it in the layout grid first. If the flag floats (can be moved to another position on the page), make some decision about where it should go on the page.

2. Make some preliminary decisions about where the photos and pictures will be placed on the page. Readers generally will begin looking at a page at the upper left (which is called the primary optical area, or POA). The editor should, therefore, select for this area the most important item or the one that will capture the attention of the reader. When a decision about the primary optical area has been made, the next logical decision is usually about what will go in the upper right corner of the page.

3. Decide what will be in the lower-right corner of the page. This decision needs to be made next, because the upper-left element will need some balancing element in the lower right. As with the top of the page, making this decision may also help the news editor decide what should be placed in the lower-left corner of the page.

4. When the corners of the page have been filled, the editor should go back to the top of the page and fill in toward the center. Here, of course, the decisions that have already been made on the page will determine what the editor can or cannot do with the rest of the page. Working from the corners to the center of the page is preferable to starting from the top and working down because this way the editor is less likely to leave small or odd holes at the bottom of the page. The center of the page offers the news editor more flexibility than the borders.

The following are some guidelines and suggestions for handling inside pages.

1. Each page should carry a dominant headline.

2. Each should have a good attention-getter, a focus around which other elements on the page revolve.

3. Each should have a good picture, especially at the top of the page and set away from the ads. This could be the attention-getter referred to earlier.

4. If a page is tight (that is, if there isn't much room for editorial matter on the page), one long story is preferable to several shorter ones.

5. If a page is open (that is, at least one-third is left for news), try to align a story with the highest ad and, thus, square off the rest of the page for editorial matter. Doing this can increase your flexibility in laying out the rest of the page.

Editors who deal with front and inside pages must also be concerned with jumps. A story beginning on one page and continuing onto another is known as a *jumped story.* The part of the story continued on the second page is called the *jump,* and the headline over that part of the story is called the *jump head. Jump lines* are those lines at the end of the first part of the story ("Continued on Page 2") and at the beginning of the jump ("Continued from Page 1").

A newspaper should have a consistent style in handling jumped stories, jump lines, and jump heads. Some newspapers, such as *USA Today,* try to avoid jumps almost entirely, but most papers find that this policy is not feasible. The best jump lines try to inform the reader of the jump head and the page number of the jump, such as "See PRESIDENT, Page 2." Jump heads may be just one word or rewrites of the first-page headline, or they may refer to an element in the jumped portion.

Twelve Rules

Following are twelve basic rules governing layout of newspaper pages. Not every newspaper follows every rule all the time, and there are cases when these rules can legitimately be broken. Most of the time, however, these rules should be observed as closely as possible.

1. Avoid "tombstoning" headlines. Tombstoning means running different headlines side-by-side on the page. When headlines are run together, they can be confusing to the reader and create an unattractive and cluttered appearance for the page. News editors should try to isolate major elements on a newspaper page. Headlines are more easily seen and break up gray areas better when they stand alone.

2. Avoid placing one headline directly under part of another without copy between (it's called "armpitting"). Again, the idea is to isolate the headline to help it be seen. If headlines run directly under one another, they lose isolation and create confusion.

3. Avoid splitting the page. A split occurs when the vertical space between two colums, called an alley in some layout programs and a gutter in others, is not crossed by a headline or a picture somewhere on the full length of the page. Modern design calls for a unified page. If an alley runs the length of the page, it splits the page in two, destroying both the unity of the page and the reader's eye flow.

4. Avoid large blocks of body type. Masses of gray type discourage even the most interested reader from becoming involved in the story. Make sure there is a good variety of body, headlines, pictures, and other typographical devices on every part of the page.

5. Place major stories on the primary focal point of the page, usually the upper left-hand corner. This should be the strongest part of the page where the editor places the strongest typographical elements.

6. Use contrasting but not conflicting headline typefaces and styles. The faces and styles should complement each other and be consistent. Wholesale use of serif and sans serif faces violates this principle. Simplicity of design and uniformity of page development are the objectives.

7. Use few typefaces and vary size and style (roman and italic, plain and bold). This guideline is again designed to isolate headlines and make them distinctive. Simplicity is also an abiding consideration. A reader should not have to wade through a great variety of typefaces but should have a page that presents enough variety to be interesting. Let the ad designer come up with new typefaces.

8. Follow the "step-down" rule. The step-down rule requires that larger headlines appear at the top of the page, with gradually smaller headlines appearing below them. This rule may be violated to maintain balance, especially at the bottom corners, but these violations should only occur to accomplish specific objectives.

9. Let pictures seem to stand on or hang from something. That is, the top of a picture could be aligned with the top of a headline. Photos are major attention-getters. They should always help lead the eye through the page.

10. Never run the copy of a story out from under its headline (except when using a side head) or related photo. Headlines should provide a kind of umbrella for the story. Running copy out from under that umbrella leads to confusion, especially if that copy moves below another headline.

11. Try to avoid running columns of type under a headline in such a way that it creates odd shapes. (See the illustration to the right in Figure 17.5.) The more regularly shaped a set of columns is (rectangular, square, etc.) the easier it is for a reader to isolate it visually.

12. Make sure the tops of story packages are level. Story packages include the headline, body type, pictures, and any other material related to the story grouped together on a page. The tops of these groups should form a straight line. Avoid, for instance, a three-column headline with a four-column related headline under it. Also avoid placing an adjacent, related photograph or illustration part of the way down a block of related type. It should square up evenly with the top of the headline.

Web Site Design

News web sites display a wide variety of design philosophies and approaches. These philosophies reflect views on what the news organization hopes to accomplish with its web site and how it views the audience that it is attempting to cultivate. No matter what the approach is, however, all web sites must deal with a fundamental set of design considerations.

Readability

Viewers must be able to see and read what is on the web site. Type must be clear and precise. Pictures and images must be recognizable. Elements must be clearly differentiated from one another.

Most professionally produced web sites have few problems with any of these standards, and yet, there are some that do not view readability as of primary importance.

Flag ——————

THE DAILY NEWS

January 20, 1998

Headline ——————

Evenson gets 20 years for role in bank robbery

Head shot ——————

A Brownsville woman received a 20-year prison sentence yesterday for her part in a robbery of the Trust National Bank last year.

Anne Evenson, who lived with her mother on Mine Road before the robbery, wept softly as Circuit Court Judge John Sloan read the verdict to a packed courtroom. The 20-year sentences means that she could be eligible for parole in seven years.

Gutter ——————

Evenson's attorney, Harriet Braden, said after the court recessed that she is planning to file an appeal.

Catchline ——————

"I think that we will be able to demonstrate that Miss

Evenson was an innocent victim and did not receive a fair trial," she said.

Braden said the appeal will be filed sometime next week.

District Attorney Ed Sims said, however, that he thought the trial had been a fair one and that Evenson received the sentence she deserved.

Evenson was convicted

Anne Evenson

last week of first degree robbery for driving the get-away car for her boyfriend, Reggie Holder, after he robbed the bank of almost $29,000. Holder was convicted last month for first-degree robbery and also received a 20-year sentence.

Evenson testified during

Continued on page 4

Wildcat strike

Some workers at the local JVC plant have begun a wildcat strike action against the company. See story on page 5.

Reverse type ——————

The Inside Track

Kenyan President Moi Sworn In, Page 2

Searchers Find SilkAir Crash Voice Recorder, Page 4

Gray screen ——————

China Denies Harboring Pol Pot, Page 2

White House Seeks Social Security Overhaul, Page 4

Cutline ——————

Report: US Scientists Create "Living Breasts," Page 16

Box ——————

Pope Deplores Massacres in Algeria, Burundi, Page 2

Report: Early Rolling Stones Recordings Found, Page 16

Calls for Tax Cuts Premature, White House Says, Page 5

Fertilizer Warehouse Burns in Ohio, Page 7

Winds hammer parts of Europe

By Geoffrey Cornford

LONDON (Reuters) - Gale force winds ripped across Europe at the weekend, causing several deaths, and cutting power to tens of thousands of homes in Britain and France.

The 10-man crew of a crippled trawler 200 miles off southern England were whisked to safety by helicopter Sunday as their vessel threatened to go down in huge seas.

The nine Spaniards and

an Irishman were not thought to be injured after their hours-long ordeal, spokesmen for the British coastguard said.

Their trawler, Sonia Naci,

had been drifting, battered by 60-foot waves, after engine failure, coastguards in the port of Falmouth said.

Across Britain, roofs were

The streets of Lyon, France are cluttered with debris after high winds ripped through the city this week-end.

blown off, trees uprooted and power lines cut.

One man was killed after a tree fell on his car in high winds in Wombourne in the West Midlands, police said.

Across Britain, more than 100,000 homes from Cornwall and South Wales to the English Midlands were without power, British media reported.

At Mumbles in south Wales, the local coastguard recorded a wind gust of 115 miles per hour.

Continued on page 4

Police puzzling over many clues to solve real life murder mystery

By Alexis Smith

Police are searching through an abundance of clues today, trying to find more in the case of a young bank clerk who was found shot to death on Thursday.

The body of John Bailey, 27, was discovered by a passing motorist in a car at 6 pm Thursday just off Highway 69, one mile north of the Hale County line. He had been shot in the head. The county medical examiner's office estimated the time of death at 5 pm.

Bailey was seen arguing earlier at a convenience store parking lot five miles north on Highway 69. Witnesses told police that the argument was with a woman. Neither of them had been inside the convenience store, and it is

unclear how long they had been there. Bailey left the store about 4:45 p.m., driving south on Highway 69, and the woman left immediately after him.

Bailey was driving a red, late model Toyota, and the woman was driving a blue Chevrolet. Both were seen driving away at a high rate of speed.

About two miles south of the convenience store, a motorist driving north noticed two southbound cars that fit the description of the cars Bailey and the woman were driving. Both were speeding, and the Toyota was on the shoulder of the road, while the Chevrolet was in the driving lane.

"It looked like the blue car was trying to run the other one off the road," Wayne Marshall, the motorist, said. Marshall said he felt both drivers were

Tuscaloosa

The remains of Fossett's balloon when it landed in Russia.

acting so dangerously that he stopped to call the police. Marshall's call came in to the sheriff's department at 5:05 p.m.

A car fitting the description of blue Chevrolet was found parked on the banks of the Black Warrior River

Continued on page 4

Jump line ——————

FIGURE 17.5   Design Terms The illustration shows some of the terms for items on a newspaper page.

One of the chief problems is having type that is too small to read. The size of type, to some extent, is in the hands of viewers in that they can set their browsers to view type at smaller or larger sizes than normal. Despite that, some web sites set their initial sizes so small that viewers are forced to increase the size on their own browsers.

Another problem in the realm of readability on web sites related to type size is that pages are too crowded. Some news web site editors believe that visitors should be given as many choices as possible as quickly as possible. Consequently, they crowd their home pages (sometimes referred to as "splash" pages) with as many words and links as possible.

Yet another problem that is found in less professionally produced sites is that of a background color that overwhelms the type. Black backgrounds, for example, make the type difficult to read. Professional designers understand that black type on a white background produces the greatest contrast and is, thus, the easiest type to read. The reverse (white type on a black background) does not produce the same contrast, however. Some designers make every attempt to get away from a white background by using colors with extremely soft tones or values. Even then, care should be taken that the strokes of the type are distinctive and that reading is not hindered.

Simplicity

The concept of simplicity is often undervalued in web site design. Some designers feel that animated graphics and flashy colors are necessary for a web site to gain and hold the attention of the reader. They are also seduced by the fact that it is so easy to do so many things on the Web. Sometimes the hardest thing to do in designing a web site is to keep it simple.

The idea of simplicity keeps the designer close to the content. The designer should ask: What does it take to present the content to the reader? What does it take for the reader to see and understand the content? What are the hierarchies (discussed earlier in this chapter) that are necessary for the design to carry its messages to the reader?

The concept of simplicity, as exemplified by the preceding questions, should be balanced with the natural and necessary tendency of the designer to develop a graphic personality for the site. A news web site that is simply type and pictures would probably not be very appealing to readers and would not offer reporters and editors an interesting environment in which to display their work.

Simplicity then should be a controlling but not a dominant concept in web site design. Designers should have specific reasons for doing everything they do, and those reasons should have both short-term and long-term goals. In the short term, they should help enhance the readability and usability of the site. In the long term, they should assist in developing a graphic personality that will make the look of the site distinctive and project an image that the news organization wants to build.

Consistency

Going hand in hand with simplicity is the concept of consistency. Some elements of design should be the same throughout the site. In most print publications, body copy has a consistent font and size throughout the publication. This standard has carried over to many news web sites. Most professional web sites maintain consistent elements such as top logos, navigation bars, and links with a consistent look throughout the site.

Consistency implies stability, which is an important concept to be associated with a news web site at several levels. A consistent design shows that the site is professional and confident in the design decisions that it has made. It also establishes a look and feel for the site that readers can count on. Once readers learn that a design will be maintained, they do not have to figure it out each time they visit the site, and they can concentrate on the content itself.

Credibility is associated with consistency, which is another reason for developing a design that readers can count on. Any news organization wants a readership that believes it will present accurate information. A consistent look helps to foster that feeling.

Consistency is not an easy thing to accomplish in a web design, however. It works at several levels. Not only should article pages look the same and have the same elements, but content—particularly links—should also be handled in the same way throughout the site. For instance, if text links are blue and underlined in one part of the site and red and bold in another, the result will be a mixed message to the reader and will be yet another vagary of the site that the reader has to deal with.

Web designers must also find ways of maintaining a consistent look while dealing with a variety of forms of information. Headlines, summaries, and stories can have a consistent graphic style, but what about video, audio, graphics, picture galleries, and the like? Each of these forms requires a different look. Yet, they must also maintain a visual relationship to other parts of the site. Some content itself will require variations on the consistent look of the site.

A graphics stylebook that lays out some of the basic design rules for the web site is a must for maintaining a consistent look. Not only will such a stylebook help editors understand what the style rules of the site are, but also it can be of great assistance when a new design challenge arises—that is, when the site wants to do something that it has not done before. A graphics stylebook can lay the groundwork for expanding the site and taking in new content forms.

Variety

Ralph Waldo Emerson, a nineteenth-century philosopher, wrote the much quoted line: "A foolish consistency is the hobgoblin of little minds adored by little statesmen and philosophers and divines." If designers only had to worry about consistency, their jobs would be relatively easy. Finding the proper balance between consistency and variety is possibly a designer's most difficult task, but the effort can save the site from becoming the hobgoblin of which Emerson wrote.

Designers should abide by a general principle: design should offer the readers consistency; content should offer variety. That is, it should be the content—packaged in a consistent design—that gives the site its flavor and uniqueness. Variety can be achieved by adding and subtracting elements such as pictures, pull quotes, graphics, and links.

Still, with the unpredictability of news, no design will be able to anticipate all of the content and situations that a news web site will encounter. Sometimes the design will have to change to fit the content, as it did on September 11, 2001.

Purpose

Why does the web site exist? What do the editors want visitors to do? These two questions should always be present in the minds of web site designers. The designs they form should advance the purposes of the site. The design should also make it easy for the visitors to do whatever the editors intend.

QUESTIONS FOR DISCUSSION

1. Having read this chapter, list some of the major differences between designing for a print publication and a web site.
2. Select a newspaper or news web site that you like. Try to find some of the design elements that give it a graphic personality. Is this personality well defined? What does it add to your feelings about the publication?
3. What skills are necessary for a person to become a good designer? What training is necessary?

RELATED WEB SITES

Design Management Institute, www.dmi.org/dmi/html/index.htm

Design with Reason, www.ronreason.com
The web site for newspaper designer and educator Ron Reason.

DeVigal Design, www.devigal.com
Andrew and Angelo DeVigal founded DeVigal Design in 1990.

News Page Designer, www.newspagedesigner.com
Visual journalism tips are shared at this web site.

Poynter Online's "Color, Contrast & Dimension in News Design," http://poynteronline.org/content/content_view.asp?id=2711

Poynter Online's "The Design Desk Column," http://poynteronline.org/column.asp?id=47

Poynter Online's Photojournalism Bibliography, http://poynteronline.org/content/content_view.asp?id=1214

Poynter Online's Stanford-Poynter EyeTrac Project, www.poynterextra.org/et/i.htm

Society for News Design, www.snd.org

Society of Publication Designers, www.spd.org

Typographic, www.rsub.com/typographic

READINGS AND REFERENCES

Ames, S. E. (1989). *Elements of newspaper design.* New York: Praeger.
Arnold, E. C. (1981). *Designing the total newspaper.* New York: Harper and Row.
Barnhurst, K. G. (1994). *Seeing the newspaper.* New York: St. Martin's Press.
Finberg, H., & Itule, B. D. (1990). *Visual editing: A graphic guide for journalists.* Belmont, CA: Wadsworth.

Garcia, M. R. (1993). *Contemporary newspaper design*. Englewood Cliffs, NJ: Prentice-Hall.

Garcia, M. R. (1996). *Newspaper evolutions*. St. Petersburg, FL: Poynter Institute.

Garcia, M. R. (1997). *Redesigning print for the Web*. Indianapolis, IN: Hayden Books.

Garcia, M. R. (2002). *Pure design*. St. Petersburg, FL: Miller Media.

Garcia, M. R., & Stark, P. (1991). *Eyes on the news*. St. Petersburg, FL: Poynter Institute.

Society for News Design. *Best of newspaper design*. Baltimore: SND, Annual.

Design and Layout Exercises

EXERCISE 17.1

Find a tabloid newspaper page and draw a dummy from that page. Refer to Figure 17.4 to complete this exercise.

EXERCISE 17.2

Find a full-size newspaper page and draw a dummy from that page. Refer to Figure 17.4 to complete this exercise.

EXERCISE 17.3

You are the news editor for a tabloid newspaper, and you have the following stories to work with on a particular day. Try drawing a dummy sheet that has at least three stories on the page. Which stories are you going to select to run? (Refer to Figure 17.4 to complete this exercise.)

- You do not have to fit all of the stories you select. They can be jumped.
- You can consider that you have head shots of any of the people mentioned in any of the stories, but you do not have to use them. Head shots normally are one column wide by 3 inches deep.
- You have at least one vertically shaped picture and one horizontally shaped picture to use on the page, much like the example in Figure 17.4.
- You may also draw an index box for your page, such as the one in Figure 17.4.

Stories

Cape Hatteras

CAPE HATTERAS, N.C. — The severed bridge that is the only link between Hatteras Island and the mainland could be repaired within 45 days, state officials say.

Previous estimates indicated repairs could take at least six months. A dredge battered the bridge during a Friday storm, causing a 370-foot section of the structure to collapse.

Residents of Hatteras and nearby Ocracoke Island are anxious to see the Herbert C. Bonner Bridge repaired. Hundreds of cars were waiting Monday morning for ferry service across Oregon Inlet to the mainland, officials said.

This story runs 12 column inches.

Chrysler negotiations

DETROIT — Top negotiators for Chrysler Corp. and the United Auto Workers bargained Monday night toward a midnight expiration of their extended contract, but the union urged workers to remain on the job until told otherwise.

Chrysler's 67,000 U.S. hourly employees have been working since Sept. 15 under extension of a contract negotiated in 1988. On Friday, however, frustrated by the slow pace of bargaining, the UAW told the No. 3 carmaker that pact would expire at 11:59 p.m. EST Monday.

This allows the UAW to authorize a company-wide walkout, or more likely, target specific Chrysler plants like its minivan plant in Fenton, Mo., if a tentative accord is not reached.

This story runs 10 column inches.

Chicago City Council

CHICAGO — The Chicago City Council considered a plan Tuesday that would allow city workers to take three days of paid leave if their "domestic partner" dies, which the sponsor acknowledged is the first step in extending health benefits to unmarried couples as well as gays.

The council's Finance Committee voted 8–3 to endorse the measure Monday but most of the 35 members found reasons to leave the room before the vote was taken.

Alderman William Beavers was one of those who argued against the measure that would grant three days of paid leave to city workers to mourn the death of a "sole domestic partner" who has been living with them at least six months.

This story runs 8 column inches.

Liver Transplant

PITTSBURGH — The liver of a baboon transplanted into a 62-year-old man was functioning satisfactorily Tuesday, surgeons at the University of Pittsburgh Medical Center said.

The man, whose identity was not released, remained in critical condition after the world's second such transplant at Presbyterian University Hospital in a 13-hour operation that ended early Monday. Surgeons said the man was dying from hepatitis B and did not have the option of a human-to-human liver transplant.

Surgeons said the man, who was awake Tuesday, may be weaned from his ventilator within a few days.

This story runs 10 column inches.

Explanation of a *column inch*: A column inch means that there is enough type to take up 1 inch of copy on a normal column. A story that is 10 column inches, for instance, would run 10 inches down one column of the page. Stories, of course, can run across several columns. A 10-inch story could run for 5 inches across two columns, or 3 1/3 inches across three columns.

EXERCISE 17.4

You are the news editor for a full-size newspaper, and you have the following stories to work with on a particular day. Try drawing a dummy sheet that has at least four stories on the page. Which stories are you going to select to run? (Refer to Figure 17.4 to complete this exercise.)

- You do not have to fit all of the stories you select. They can be jumped.

- You can consider that you have head shots of any of the people mentioned in any of the stories, but you do not have to use them. Head shots normally are one column wide by 3 inches deep.

- You have at least one vertically shaped picture and one horizontally shaped picture to use on the page, much like the example in Figure 17.4.

- You may also draw an index box for your page, such as the one in Figure 17.4.

Theater Revenues

HOLLYWOOD — The nation's movie theaters have grossed nearly $4 billion so far this year, only about 1 percent behind last year's record-setting pace, when box office sales reached $5 billion by year's end.

Despite a traditionally slow mid-fall performance, the year-to-date box office hit $3.99 billion over the weekend, compared with $4.05 billion for the same period last year, *Daily Variety* said Tuesday. In 1988, the total at the same juncture had reached $3.57 billion.

The top 10 movies of the weekend—led by Stephen King's *Graveyard Shift*—drew $30.8 million over the weekend, off 7 percent from the previous weekend's $33.1 million and 6 percent behind the $32.6 million scored by the top 10 a year ago.

This story runs 12 column inches.

Air Midwest

WICHITA, Kan. — Air Midwest Inc. said Monday it would sell certain assets and aircraft of its Trans World Express operations in St. Louis to Trans State Airlines Inc. of St. Louis for $16 million.

The purchase by Trans State—also a Trans World Express operator out of St. Louis—includes the assumption of about $7.4 million in Air Midwest's long-term debt obligations.

Air Midwest said the transaction covers eight EMB120 aircraft, fifteen J32 aircraft, spare parts, certain facilities, leases, and other obligations from its Trans World Express operations.

This story runs 10 column inches.

Rocket Launch

CAPE CANAVERAL, Fla. — A Delta rocket boosted a $90 million mobile communications satellite into orbit Tuesday in a spectacular night flight, marking the 200th launch of a workhorse Delta since the program's debut 30 years ago.

The $50 million 126-foot Delta 2's main engine and strap-on boosters ignited with a flash of fire and a thundering roar at 6:16 p.m. EST, instantly pushing the rocket away from the Cape Canaveral Air Force Station and into the darkening sky.

"We have ignition and we have liftoff. Liftoff of Delta number 200," said launch commentator Ray Adams as the slender rocket streaked away on a fiery flight visible for miles along Florida's "space coast." "This is the kind of flight we enjoy—watching that bird go up and do its job."

This story runs 15 column inches.

Record Low Temperatures

Record lows in the Midwest and cool weather elsewhere chilled much of the nation Monday with strong winds and storms in the extreme Northwest and Northeast and heavy fog in Southern California.

In New England, skiers hit the slopes as the season's first major snowfall blanketed northern mountains. At least one resort in northern Maine reported 15 inches of new snow.

On the West Coast, heavy rain and gusts topping 35 mph churned 18-foot seas near Cape Lookout on the Oregon coast.

This story runs 10 column inches.

Biltmore Hotel

CORAL GABLES, Fla. — Barnett Banks Inc. acquired the lease for the historic Biltmore Hotel Monday for $24 million in a bankruptcy proceeding and said it would move quickly to reopen the shuttered hotel.

Robert Stickler, a spokesman for Barnett in Jacksonville, Fla., said the purchase agreement was approved by a federal bankruptcy judge in Philadelphia presiding over the case of the previous leaseholder, Sovereign Group of Philadelphia.

The hotel closed its doors unexpectedly in July after Barnett, the major creditor, froze the hotel's operating funds.

This story runs 8 column inches.

Explanation of a *column inch:* A column inch means that there is enough type to take up 1 inch of copy on a normal column. A story that is 10 column inches, for instance, would run 10 inches down one column of the page. Stories, of course, can run across several columns. A 10-inch story could run for 5 inches across two columns, or 3 1/3 inches across three columns.

18

Broadcast Journalists

1. Broadcast journalism is governed by the concept of time. Deadlines are rigid because broadcast news shows are scheduled to air at certain times and cannot be delayed. Broadcast journalists must also be aware of how much time it takes to tell their stories.

2. Broadcast journalists always try to find audio or visual elements to include in their stories.

3. Copy: refers to the written form of broadcast news stories. Copy preparation is an important part of the broadcast news process.

4. Producer: someone who has production responsibilities either for a story or for an entire newscast; a producer is like an editor for a print publication, ensuring that stories are finished and put on the air and also maintaining the standards of journalism in the news organization.

5. Live shot: a broadcast news story that shows a reporter at the scene of the news presenting information or interviewing a source; these shots do not require scripts or broadcast copy but they do require preparation.

Vignette

Debbie Elliott knows that she has only one shot at her listeners.

"Print journalism offers the option to refer back or reread the information that might have been overlooked the first time around," the National Public Radio (NPR) correspondent says.

"Television can use pictures to get the point across. But in radio, every word has to count the first time."

Elliott is a regional correspondent, covering the South for the public radio network from her home in Orange Beach, Alabama. Her reports are regularly heard on NPR's daily national news broadcasts, Morning Edition *and* All Things Considered. *She has covered such diverse topics as hurricanes, politics, and the Olympic games. She is a specialist in the ongoing controversy over tobacco, and whenever there is a major legal dispute involving smokers and tobacco, Elliott is there.*

Elliott is a graduate of the University of Alabama where she got involved with the NPR station on campus and eventually became its news director. She worked in commercial radio for a time but has made her career in public radio.

Elliott says she enjoys the way radio lets her talk to her audience.

"The best way to connect with radio listeners is to have a conversation with them," she says. Elliott tries to think about how she would tell a story to a friend and the language she might use in doing that. "Your writing must be clear and engaging."

Elliott, like her colleagues in broadcasting, works in a unique part of journalism. Broadcast reporters do many of the same things that print reporters do (see Chapter 8). They receive assignments from their editors, producers, or news directors. They gather information by observing events and looking up facts in books, magazines, or on the Internet. They talk with people who know about an event or subject.

Their purpose, like that of print reporters, is to disseminate the news, but the demands and customs of broadcasting are quite different from print. This chapter seeks to give you an introduction to this part of journalism.

The World of Broadcasting

Broadcasting is the world's most pervasive medium of mass communication. It is not unusual for the American home to receive one hundred or more television channels from its cable system or satellite dish. A wide variety of radio stations has been available to anyone with a receiver since the early days of the medium. Underdeveloped areas that cannot get access to even a newspaper will usually have a transistor radio to link it with the rest of the world. Satellite broadcasting has drawn the world closer together by ensuring that we have instant, live coverage of major news events from almost anywhere in the world and even beyond. Consider the following:

- When an American first walked on the moon in 1969, a television camera was positioned outside the lunar lander to record the event.

- When Prince Charles of England married Princess Diana in 1981, television cameras were at every part of the event.

- In late 1992, when U.S. marines invaded Somalia, their landing was met not by hostile forces but by American, European, and Asian television crews who broadcast live pictures of the event all around the world. (The Marines, in fact, complained that the television lights made them more vulnerable to hostile fire, although they had made little secret of when and where they would land.)

- The automobile accident in Paris that took the life of Princess Diana in 1997 was not recorded, of course, but her funeral a week later was watched by people in almost every part of the world.

- On the morning of September 11, 2001, as word spread that something was happening in New York City, people across the nation turned on their television sets. Those who did so quickly saw a burning World Trade Center tower; then they were shocked to see an airplane slam into the second tower. Within two hours, both buildings had collapsed.

In America, broadcasting delivers information with immediacy and impact. Most Americans get their news from a variety of sources, and it would be a mistake to believe that broadcasting is always the dominant medium in this regard. Newspapers, newsmagazines, and web sites deliver a large amount of information to the American public and will continue to do so, but broadcasting is often perceived as dominant. More than 6,000 local radio and television stations in America (and thousands more shortwave radio operators) are broadcasting, as opposed to 1,500 daily newspapers.

A person who wants to succeed in the field of broadcasting needs to have intelligence, diligence, dependability, and the ability to write. Even though broadcasting is an audiovisual medium, almost everything you hear or see in the way of news or entertainment has been written down. The occasions for ad libbing before the cameras are certainly available, but even many of the "spontaneous" lines delivered by some broadcasters are written and rehearsed. Broadcasters consider airtime too valuable to leave to chance. Even reporters doing live news spots often work from notes and have a good understanding of the forms of writing for the medium.

Broadcasters look for the same qualities in writers that have been discussed in other parts of this book. They want people who know the language and its rules of usage, who are willing to research their subjects thoroughly and understand them well enough to report on them with clarity, who do not mind working hard, and who are willing to rewrite their work and have it rewritten by others. In addition, they are particularly interested in people who can write under pressure and can meet deadlines.

Writing for broadcasting is similar in many ways to writing for the print media, but there are some important differences. Those differences concern the way news is selected for broadcast, the characteristics of writing and story structure, and the style with which the information is presented.

FIGURE 18.1   The Importance of Visuals Television news covers many complicated and complex stories, but the strength of the medium is its ability to disseminate visual images with immediacy and impact. When something important happens, we are likely to turn to television first to see the pictures and hear the words. (Photo credit: Federal Emergency Management Agency)

Selection of News

How is broadcast journalism different from print? Most of the same news values that govern print journalism apply to news selection for broadcasting. Broadcast journalists are interested in events that have a wide impact, people in the news, current issues, events that happen close to home, and conflicts or unusual happenings. Because of the opportunities and limitations of their medium, however, broadcasters are likely to view such events in different ways than their counterparts in print or web journalism. The following are some of the factors that broadcasters use to select news.

Timeliness

Because of the nature of their medium, broadcasters often consider timeliness the most important news value. Broadcasters work on hourly, or less than hourly, cycles. A news broadcaster may go on the air several times a day. The news must be up-to-the-minute. News that is more than an hour or two old may be too stale for the broadcaster. It will need to be rewritten to include the latest information or to make it sound fresher. When you listen to a news report on a breaking news story, you expect to hear the very latest news—what happened just a few minutes before.

Information, Not Explanation

Broadcasters look for stories that do not need a lot of explanation in order for listeners or viewers to understand them. They prefer stories that are simple and can be told in a straightforward manner. The maximum length for almost any story on a television newscast is two minutes; the more normal length is twenty to thirty seconds. In some larger markets, radio reporters are being told to reduce their story lengths to ten seconds and actualities (using the actual voice of the source) to five seconds. That amount of time is not enough to explain a complex story. It is only enough time to give the listener or viewer a few pertinent facts. Of course, some stories are both complex and important, and explanation cannot be avoided. Still, even with complex and important stories, the broadcast writer must wrestle with condensing these stories to their essence. In the eyes of the broadcaster, even complex stories should not be complicated.

Audio or Visual Impact

Broadcasters want stories that their audience can hear or see. Playing a part of the president's state of the union address is more dramatic than a news reporter talking about it; pictures of a flood are more likely to be watched than an anchorman's description of it. Broadcasters often choose stories for their newscasts because they have sound or pictures, even though the stories themselves might not merit such attention otherwise. This is one of the major criticisms of broadcast news, but it remains one of the chief factors in news story selection.

These factors in news selection for broadcasters must carry a different set of considerations than print journalists as they approach news stories. Their equipment is different. Their methods and schedules fit the demands and deadlines of a newscast. Their facilities are different from those of a newspaper office, and their news process follows a different development.

News Department Organization

Broadcast news takes place on two levels: national and local. Although there are significant differences between organizations that are national and those that are local (see Chapter 6), the methods of reporting, editing, and broadcasting are much the same. So is the organization of the news operation. (We should note here that much of the descriptions in this chapter pertain to television news rather than radio news. Most radio stations, especially those in rural areas and small to medium-sized cities invest very little in local news production. They might have, at most, one or two people devoted to presenting the news and weather, but these people will have other duties that preclude them from practicing much journalism. These local radio stations do not generally believe news to be a wise investment. This picture changes somewhat, though not too much, in larger cities. With only a few exceptions, music is the overwhelming program of choice for radio.)

A news department is one of several divisions of a television station. Others include advertising or sales, programming, and administration. Television stations normally invest in news department to the extent that they believe local news will pay off for them in higher audience ratings. This investment may also be spurred by competition. Unlike most daily newspapers, television news departments often find themselves competing with other stations in their areas. Professional pride demands that they produce a newscast that people in their area will prefer to watch.

A news department is normally headed by a news director, who has the responsibility for hiring people and organizing the department in a way that fits the way the station hopes to cover news in the area. The news director is usually assisted by producers, assistant directors (such as sports director), and assignments editors. Producers act as editors, giving assignments to reporters and helping them put together their stories. A newscast will have a producer who is in charge of making sure that the show gets on the air and that various things happen at the right time. Other jobs at the station include producer assistants, newswriters, and video editors.

The most publicly visible people in the news department are the news anchors. These people, including the weather announcer and the sports anchor, are the public face of the station. They are usually physically attractive, though not necessarily young, and they are always poised and well-spoken. The newscast's audience gets to "know" them and counts on seeing them on the news broadcasts. Many in the television industry tie audience ratings directly to the personalities of the anchors. News and sports anchors do not report on news stories; that is, they rarely leave the newsroom to gather information to put together a story. That is the job of news reporters and camera operators. (Anchors and weather announcers are much more likely to leave the station to speak to school and civic groups and to participate in promotional activities for the station.)

News reporters and photographers (or videographers) usually make up the majority of people on the news staff. Reporters are the people who take assignments from the producers or assignment editors, put together stories, and appear on air. They are assisted by camera operators, who quickly become experts in the equipment they are handling and who learn what type of lighting and backgrounds will look best on their broadcasts. Most reporters place great value in a good camera operator because they know that he or she can make an enormous difference in how the story will appear on air.

How Reporters Work

News happens, and broadcast reporters never know how, when, or where it will happen. What they do know is that they must be ready to respond. One of the measures of a news department is how it can cover breaking news within its own community. Let's say a railroad car filled with a dangerous chemical overturns and spills near a populated area in the community. Broadcast newsrooms are usually equipped with a police scanner (or radio), and someone within the newsroom is assigned to listen to the scanner at least while they are writing copy or editing video. Police, fire, and rescue units will be notified by the police scanner, and someone in the newsroom will tell a reporter and photographer, who, if available, will be dispatched to the scene.

The reporter has two jobs. One is to find out what is going on, not an easy or simple task if the emergency is continuing. People who are working to alleviate the emergency—the chemical spill, in this case—are going to be too busy doing their jobs to spend much time with a reporter. A reporter who has contacts within these units will have an advantage. He or she will probably be able to find someone who knows enough to give a general outline of the situation. The reporter will have to assess the scene when he or she arrives and try to talk quickly to those people who know the most.

The second job of the reporter is to try, with the help of the photographer, to get into position to get good video shots of the situation. Again, this is neither an easy nor simple process. The emergency personnel at the scene have specific jobs to do, and they do not usually include ushering broadcast reporters around. A reporter and photographer will try to get as close to the action as possible but will try to stay out of danger and out of the way of the emergency workers.

If a station is equipped to do live, on-the-scene reporting, a reporter will have to put together a report very quickly. Usually, the reporter will talk with someone back in the newsroom about the situation and what he or she has been able to discover. An anchor may want to ask the reporter some questions during the live shot, and the reporter needs to be aware of these questions and have some information to provide the answers. Sometimes these kind of emergencies will happen during the station's news hour, and they can be integrated into the newscast. At other times, however, the station will have to break into the programming. A news director, and possibly the station manager, has to decide when breaking news is important enough to interrupt what people are watching. If having information about a situation, such as a chemical spill or a dangerous storm, would help save people from death or injury, the station will interrupt regular programs to give what information it has.

Not all reporting is breaking news, however. It does not involve getting to the scene of the action on short notice or doing live reports that interrupt normal programming. Rather, much of what television reporters do are assignments that they can give some thought to before they begin reporting. Reporters can consider what information they need and the people they will have to talk with in order to make the story complete. Reporters generally talk to several people before putting together an edited story, called a "news package," even though they may use only one or possibly two of those interviews in their story. A reporter may have all day to do a story or may have to work on several stories throughout the day.

At some point before a newscast, reporters will return to the newsroom to review what they have for a story. They will need to write the copy for the story and review the tape of the interviews and action they have. They will discuss with an editor or producer how the story will be handled. A newscast has a set amount of time for news, and the producer will make the ultimate call on which stories are used and how they are played. On some days, only the video that the reporter has gathered will be used with a voice-over summary by the anchor. On other days, the newscast may need the full package: introduction, interviews, voice-over tape, and conclusion, all done by the reporter.

Occasionally, a reporter will be fortunate enough to work up a series of stories about a topic that will be shown on successive nights. These types of stories allow reporters to take more of an in-depth look at a topic, and they are usually something that the station will promote to increase viewership. A series will not happen often, however, because of the episodic nature of television news. Rookie reporters find that broadcast journalism does not have much memory; that is, what is done on one day is quickly put away in the rush of the next day's events.

Time is the pervasive factor in putting together a newscast. Not only must stories be timely in themselves, but also they must be written to fill a certain amount of airtime. The producer or news director assigns the amount of time for a story to fill. The writer must then write a story that can be read in that amount of time. The producer, of course, must have enough copy to fill up the time allotted for the newscast. Sometimes, however, even with the most careful planning, a newscast producer will come up a few seconds short or long. The producer should always give the announcer one or two more stories than he or she will need in order to fill this time.

About half of all broadcast news stories shown in regular newscasts run for a minute or less. That is not much time for the reporter to tell the story. Clarity is an absolute necessity for broadcast journalists. They must have a clear, simple idea about their stories, and they must write so listeners and viewers will quickly understand their meaning.

Broadcast News Formats

A broadcast reporter has a variety of formats to use in putting together a newscast. The following is a brief description of some of those formats for radio. Generally, each of these formats, except the mini-documentary, runs for less than a minute.

Written copy/voicers.   This format is a story without actualities or sound bites.

Sound bite or actuality.   When possible and appropriate, a radio newswriter will want to include sound effects from an event. This actuality may be someone speaking or it may be some other identifiable sound, such as gunshots or crowd noise, that will give the listeners an added dimension to the story. News anchors introduce the sound bite with the copy they read.

Wraparound.   A news anchor briefly introduces a story and the reporter. The reporter then gives the story and includes a sound bite. The sound bite is followed by the reporter giving a conclusion or "tag line."

Mini-documentary.   This format allows a story to run for more than a minute, and some run for as much as fifteen minutes. They may include several sound bites with a variety of sources or sounds, such as interviews, noise from events, or even music. A reporter will weave in and out of the mini-documentary, guiding it along for the listener. A news anchor usually introduces a mini-documentary with

MAKE THE NEWS RELEVANT FOR PEOPLE'S LIVES

The following interview was conducted with Greg Screws, morning and midday news anchor for WAAY-TV in Huntsville, Alabama, by Jacy Douglas.

What advice would you give to students who want to get into broadcast news?

These days, local television news staffs are getting smaller and smaller . . . and reporters are making less and less money. Television stations need reporters who are experts in their field. Not only do reporters have to write stories and read the teleprompter, but also they must understand the news and have the ability to relate it to their audience.

My advice to students is to have a backup plan. This isn't the easiest way to do it, but it is much smarter. Students who plan to work in journalism should take classes in other subjects such as business, education, political science, and accounting.

What should you try to learn while you are in school?

Journalism classes can teach students to write a lead or do a standup, but it's very important for them to know how government works; how businesses work; how HMOs work. The key to being a good reporter is making news relevant to people's lives. The key to doing that is having a solid base of knowledge about how the world works. You may not get this kind of knowledge in a journalism class! Journalism classes are important, but this type of training should go hand in hand with real-life information.

And other advice?

If you insist on going into television news, be a weatherman. They make all the money.

Jacy Douglas was a graduate student at the University of Alabama when this interview was conducted.

a short lead-in that sets up what the listener is about to hear. This format is most commonly used on public radio news broadcasts.

Television newscasts can use any of the following formats:

Reader copy.   This format is a story read by an anchor or reporter without visual or audio aid. It may have a slide or graphic in the background.

Voice-overs.   A videotape of an event is shown with the sound of the event turned down. An anchor or reporter speaks over the tape to talk about what the viewer is seeing.

Voice-over to sound bite.   An anchor or reporter speaks over a videotape that includes someone talking. The news copy is timed so that when the reporter stops, the sound on the tape is turned up and the person on the tape is heard speaking.

Package stories.   An anchor, using what is called a "lead-in," introduces a story and the reporter. The prerecorded piece then includes a mix of video, sound bites, voice-overs, and a "stand-up" from the reporter who explains some element of the story or summarizes the entire story. These packages usually run from one minute fifteen seconds to one minute thirty seconds.

Live shots.   An anchor will introduce a reporter who is shown live at the scene of some news event. The reporter can then do one of several things: do a simple report, interview someone, introduce and voice-over a videotape, or answer questions

FIGURE 18.2	Television News Salaries			
	AVERAGE	MEDIAN	MINIMUM	MAXIMUM
News director	$73,800	$64,000	$18,000	$ 250,000
Assistant news director	62,300	57,000	19,000	150,000
Managing editor	56,900	50,000	19,000	200,000
Executive producer	48,900	47,000	18,000	115,000
Assignment editor	32,800	30,000	17,000	85,000
News producer	29,000	27,000	15,000	100,000
News anchor	69,800	50,000	17,000	1,000,000
Weathercaster	54,000	43,800	16,000	1,000,000
Sports anchor	50,600	35,000	16,000	1,000,000
News reporter	32,300	26,000	17,000	300,000
News writer	32,300	27,500	12,000	90,000
News assistant	22,000	21,000	8,000	55,000
Sports reporter	32,000	25,000	15,000	100,000
Photographer	27,600	25,000	8,000	110,000
Tape editor	26,600	23,000	8,000	80,000
Graphics specialist	28,700	25,000	13,000	60,000
Internet specialist	31,900	30,000	10,800	75,000

Source: Radio-Television News Directors Association/Ball State University annual salary survey, 2001 (http://rtnda.org/research/salaries02.shtml)

from the anchor. Satellite technology now allows even local news departments to use such live shots frequently.

Salaries in Broadcast Journalism

Some broadcast journalists make a lot of money. Anchors for the major national network news shows have multimillion-dollar contracts. A few news correspondents, especially those who have jumped from network to network, have been able to command large amounts of money. Those are the exceptions, however, and not the case for most people who work in broadcast journalism.

According to the annual salary survey of the Radio and Television News Directors Association, the median salary for a television news reporter in 2002 was $26,000, the median for a producer was $27,000, and the median for an anchor was $50,000. The survey put the median salary for a news director at $64,000. People in radio news generally made somewhat less than those in television.

FIGURE 18.3	Radio News Salaries			
	AVERAGE	MEDIAN	MINIMUM	MAXIMUM
News director	$31,400	$30,500	$10,000	$ 72,000
News anchor	30,500	27,500	10,000	150,000
News reporter	22,600	22,000	12,000	45,000
News producer	29,400	27,500	21,000	42,000
Sports anchor	28,000	29,500	14,000	50,000

Source: Radio-Television News Directors Association/Ball State University annual salary survey, 2001 (http://rtnda.org/research/salaries02.shtml)

Journalists who work in the larger markets usually make more money. In the top twenty-five markets, the median salary for a news reporter was $68,000; news anchor, $155,000; and news director, $140,000. Young people who get into broadcast journalism usually start at small market stations and try to move to the larger markets as opportunities become available. They are likely to increase their salaries as they do so, but they are also likely to find themselves in more competitive situations.

At any level, broadcast journalism is a competitive and often stressful occupation. Broadcast reporters are often frustrated because they do not get to cover meaningful assignments, they do not get the airtime they would like for the stories they do cover, and they sometimes see their stations doing more to increase audience ratings than to support good journalism.

But many people who enter the field find broadcast journalism to be exciting and rewarding. They enjoy the challenge of having to respond to story assignments quickly and the thought of having a large audience for their work. They like the excitement and fast pace of the newsroom as it readies itself for the evening newscasts. And they look forward to the opportunity to move to a larger market with its higher salaries and increased competition. If they work in front of the camera, they can become well known by many people in the community. Even if they are not on the air, people who work in broadcasting find that their jobs have a lot of prestige and that many people are very interested in what they do.

Getting into Broadcast Journalism

The first step toward a career in broadcast journalism is to gain an understanding of the field and to decide whether or not it is suitable for your personality. Many people watch news reporters on television or the anchors on ESPN and decide that would be a fun to do for a living. They do not realize how hard the job is, how much competition there is in the field, and what long hours and low pay they might have to endure.

Most young people determined to enter the field find a college or university that has a journalism program with a broadcasting component. Most professionals advise

FIGURE 18.4   Burden of Equipment Television reporters, despite advances in technology, must deal with some bulky pieces of equipment as they are covering their stories.

that students in these programs do more than take classes, however. They should seek out opportunities to gain professional experience while they are still on campus. Most campuses, even when they do not have journalism programs, will have campus radio or television stations, and these stations are always looking for hardworking and dependable volunteers.

A professional internship is the next step. Many people hoping to enter broadcast journalism spend at least one summer working at a television or radio station or at some broadcast organization. These internships may offer little in the way of compensation, and students have to pay their own housing and expenses. But the experience and contacts you can gain from these internships can be the route to a job after graduation.

Students who would like to work on the air can start in high school by joining forensics or debate teams. They should take any opportunity to learn and improve their public speaking skills. If students come out of childhood with a heavy or unusual accent, they will usually be advised to learn to speak with a more commonly accepted voice. While some are offended by this suggestion, there are good reasons for it. Broadcast journalists do not want their audience to pay more attention to their accent than to the information in their report.

Along the way to a career in broadcast journalism, students should learn to use the language in both spoken and written forms. Most professionals say the ability to write well—simply and clearly—is the number-one skill they look for when they interview young people. Dependability and a willingness to work hard are also much sought-after attributes.

QUESTIONS FOR DISCUSSION

1. Are you surprised by the amount of money that broadcast journalists make?
2. The author says little in this chapter about broadcasters being good looking or articulate. Do you think those qualities are important if a person wants to go into broadcasting?
3. What is your evaluation of the local television news in your area? Do you feel you are getting all of the information you should be getting? What about radio news?
4. Do you think the World Wide Web will have any effect on broadcast news in the near future? Why do you think this?

RELATED WEB SITES

BEA: The Broadcast Education Association, www.beaweb.org

Broadcasters: WWW Virtual Library, http://archive.museophile.sbu.ac.uk/broadcast

B Roll Online, www.b-roll.net

Current Online, www.current.org

Local TV News Project, www.journalism.org/resources/research/reports/localTV

MIBTB—Broadcasting Training Program, www.webcom.com/mibtp

NAB: National Association of Broadcasters, www.nab.org

National Association of Minorities in Cable, www.namic.com

NewsLab, www.NewsLab.org

Shoptalk, www.tvspy.com/shoptalk.cfm

TVnewz.com, www.tvnewz.com

READINGS AND REFERENCES

Allen, C. M. (2001). *News is people: The rise of local TV news and the fall of news from New York.* Ames, IA: Iowa State University Press.

Arya, B. (1999). *Thirty seconds to air.* Ames, IA: Iowa State University Press.

Beadle, M., & Murray, M. D. (2001). *Indelible images: Women of local television.* Ames, IA: Iowa State University Press.

Beaman, J. (2000). *Interviewing for radio.* New York: Routledge.

Bliss, E., & Hoyt, J. L. (1994). *Writing news for broadcast.* New York: Columbia University Press.

Block, M. (1994). *Broadcast newswriting: The RTNDA reference guide.* Chicago: Bonus Books.

Block, M., & Durso, J., Jr. (1999). *Writing news for TV and radio.* Chicago: Bonus Books.

Boyd, A. (2001). *Broadcast journalism: Techniques of radio and TV news* (5th ed.). Woburn, MA: Focal Press.

Carr, F., Huffman, S., & Tuggle, C. A. (2001). *Broadcast news handbook*. Boston: McGraw-Hill.

Carroll, V. (1997). *Writing news for television*. Ames, IA: Iowa State University Press.

Chantler, P., & Harris, S. (1997). *Local radio journalism*. Boston: Focal Press.

Cremer, C., et al. (1995). *ENG: Television news*. New York: McGraw-Hill.

Dotson, B., & Lauer, M. (2000). *Make it memorable: Writing and packaging TV news with style*. Chicago: Bonus Books.

Engelman, R. (1996). *Public radio and television in America: A political history*. Thousand Oaks, CA: Sage.

Foote, J. S. (Ed.). (1998). *Live from the trenches: The changing role of the television news correspondent*. Carbondale, IL: Southern Illinois University Press.

Gilbert, A. (Ed.). (2002). *Covering catastrophe: Broadcast journalists report September 11*. Chicago: Bonus Books.

Halper, D. L. (2001). *Invisible stars: A social history of women in American broadcasting*. Armonk, NY: M.E. Sharpe.

Hosley, D. H., & Yamada, G. K. (1987). *Hard news: Women in broadcast journalism*. New York: Greenwood Press.

Keith, M. C. (1995). *Signals in the air: Native broadcasting in America*. Westport, CT: Praeger Publishers.

Kerbel, N. (2000). *If it bleeds, it leads: An anatomy of television news*. Boulder, CO: Westview Press.

Marlane, J. (1999). *Women in television news revisited*. Austin, TX: The University of Texas Press.

Shook, F. (1994). *Television newswriting: Captivating an audience*. White Plains, NY: Longman.

Tompkins, A. (2002). *Write for the ear . . . shoot for the eye . . . aim for the heart*. Chicago: Bonus Books.

Utterback, A. S. (1997). *Broadcaster's survival guide*. Chicago: Bonus Books.

Yorke, I. (2000). *Television news* (4th ed.). Boston: Focal Press.

19

Writing for Broadcast

Key Concepts and Terms

1. Broadcast writing requires a different style of writing than print because both the medium and the expectations of the audience are different.

2. The commitment of broadcast writers to accuracy is just as strong as that of print journalists.

3. Broadcast writing is more conversational than print because it is written to be heard rather than read, but the writing has to be just as disciplined and precise.

4. Broadcast news stories emphasize the immediate and the most up-to-date information.

5. Broadcast news stories have to fit into a certain time period and cannot vary more than a few seconds.

6. Dramatic unity: the story structure used by most broadcast news writers; it consists of three parts: climax, cause, and effect.

7. *United Press International Stylebook:* the major source of style information for broadcast writing.

8. Broadcast writers attempt to simplify whenever possible, but simplification should not produce inaccuracy.

This chapter is adapted from material in James Glen Stovall, *Writing for the Mass Media,* 5/e. Published by Allyn and Bacon, Boston, MA. Copyright © 2002 by Pearson Education. Adapted by permission of the publisher.

All good media writing, as we have noted earlier in this book, shares the same four basic characteristics: accuracy, clarity, precision, and efficiency. Yet within journalism there are quite different styles of writing that have been developed as suitable for one medium but not another.

One of the great differences in writing styles exists between writing for print and writing for broadcast. Broadcasting is a different medium from print with differences in form and audience expectation. The customs and conventions of writing—and even many of the style rules—are different from those developed for print. This chapter will introduce the basics of writing for broadcast.

Characteristics of Writing

A 1960s edition of the *UPI Broadcast Stylebook* says that whereas print journalism has the five Ws, broadcast journalism has the four Cs—correctness, clarity, conciseness, and color. These four Cs still serve as the basis for broadcast writing and form a good framework for talking about broadcast writing styles.

The first commitment of the broadcast journalist is to correctness, or accuracy. Everything a broadcast journalist does must contribute to telling an accurate story. Even though the broadcast journalist must observe some strict rules about how stories are written, these rules should contribute to, not prevent, an accurate account of an event.

One of the most admirable characteristics of good broadcast writing is its clarity. Good broadcast writers employ clear, precise language that contains no ambiguity. Clarity is an absolute requirement for broadcast writing. Listeners and viewers cannot go back and rehear a news broadcast as they might be able to read a newspaper account more than once. They must understand what is said the first time. Broadcast writers achieve this kind of clarity by using simple sentences and familiar words, by avoiding the use of pronouns and repeating proper nouns if necessary and by keeping the subject close to the verb in their sentences. Most of all, however, they achieve clarity by thoroughly knowing and understanding their subject.

Another important characteristic of writing for broadcast is its conversational style. Even the clearest, simplest newspaper style tends to sound stilted when it is read aloud. Broadcast writing must sound more conversational because people will be reading it aloud. Broadcast news should be written for the ear, not the eye. The writer should keep in mind that someone is going to say the words and others will listen to them.

This casual or conversational style, however, does not give the writer freedom to break the rules of grammar, to use slang or off-color phrasing, or to use language that might be offensive to listeners. As with all writing, the broadcast writer should try to focus attention on the content of the writing and not the writing itself. Nor is casual-sounding prose particularly easy to produce. It takes a finely tuned ear for the language and a conciseness that we do not normally apply to writing.

Another characteristic of writing for broadcast is the emphasis on the immediate. Whereas past-tense verbs are preferred in the print media, broadcasters use the present tense as much as possible. A newspaper or web site story might begin like this:

> The president said Tuesday that he will support some limited tax increase proposals when Congress reconvenes this week. . . .

A broadcast news story might begin with this:

> The president says he's for higher taxes . . .

Another way of emphasizing the immediate is to omit the time element in the news story and assume that everything has happened close to the time of the broadcast. In the preceding example, the broadcast version has no time element because it would probably be heard on the day the president made that statement. The elimination of the time element cannot occur in every story. Sometimes the time element is important and must be mentioned.

The tight phrasing that characterizes broadcast writing is one of its chief assets and one of the most difficult qualities for a beginning writer to achieve. Because time is so short, the broadcaster cannot waste words. The broadcaster must work constantly to simplify and condense. There are a number of techniques for achieving this conciseness. One technique is the elimination of all but the most necessary adjectives and adverbs. Broadcasters know that their stories are built on nouns and verbs, the strongest words in the language. They avoid using the passive voice. Instead they rely on strong, active verbs that will allow the listener to form a picture of the story.

Another technique of broadcast writing is the use of short, simple sentences. Broadcasters do not need the variety of length and type of sentences that print journalists need to make their copy interesting. Broadcasters can more readily fire information at their readers like bullets in short, simple sentences.

The fourth C of the *UPI Stylebook*—color—refers to writing that allows the listener to paint a picture of the story or event. This picture can be achieved in a variety of ways, such as including pertinent and insightful details or allowing the personality of the writer or news reader to come through in a story. The nature of the broadcast medium allows for humor and human interest to be part of many stories.

A final characteristic of broadcast writing is its almost complete subjugation to deadlines. Broadcast copy is often written in an atmosphere in which a deadline is imminent. Broadcast writers have to learn to produce in a highly pressurized atmosphere. Unless broadcast writers are able to meet deadlines, their compact, understandable prose will never be heard.

Story Structure

The most common structure for broadcast news is called dramatic unity. This structure has three parts: climax, cause, and effect. The climax of the story gives the listener the point of the story in about the same way the lead of a print news story does; it tells the listener what happened. The cause portion of the story tells why it happened— the circumstances surrounding the event. The effect portion of the story gives the listener the context of the story and possibly some insight about what the story means. The following examples will show how dramatic unity works (note, too, some difference in style rules from print):

Climax
Taxpayers in the state will be paying an average of 15 dollars more in income taxes next year.

Cause
The state senate defeated several delaying amendments this afternoon and passed the governor's controversial revenue-raising bill by a 15 to 14 vote. The bill had been the subject of intense debate for more than a week.

Effect
The bill now goes to the governor for his signature. Estimates are that the measure will raise about 40 million dollars in new revenue for the state next year. Elementary and secondary education will get most of that money. Passage of the bill is a major victory for the governor and his education program.

Climax
Many children in the city school system will begin their classes at least a half hour later next year.

Cause
The City School Board last night voted to rearrange the school bus schedule for next year as a cost-cutting measure.

Effect
The new schedule will require most elementary school children to begin school one half hour later than they do now. Most high school students will begin one half hour earlier.

Broadcast journalists think of their stories as completed circles rather than inverted pyramids. Whereas the pyramid may be cut without losing the essential facts, the broadcast story, if written in this unified fashion, cannot be cut from the bottom or anywhere else. It stands as a unit. Broadcast journalists and their editors are not concerned with cutting stories after they have been written to make them fit into a news broadcast. Rather, stories should be written to fit into an amount of time designated by the editor or news director. For instance, an editor may allot twenty-five seconds for a story. The writer will know this and will write a story that can be read in twenty-five seconds. If the story is longer than it should be, the editor will ask that it be rewritten.

Because they are so brief, broadcast news stories must gain the attention of the listener from the beginning. The first words in the story are extremely important. Getting the attention of the listener is sometimes more important than summarizing the story or giving the most important facts of the story. The broadcast news lead may be short on facts, but if it captures the attention of the reader, it has served its purpose. Here is an example:

The lame duck keeps limping along.

Congress met for the third day of its lame-duck session today and again failed to act on the president's gas tax proposals.

The first sentence has very little in the way of facts, but it gets the listener into the story. This structure is only appropriate for certain stories, however. If the facts of the story are strong enough to gain the listener's attention, they should be used to open the story. For example:

The five-cents-a-gallon gas tax is law.

The president signed the bill authorizing the tax today while vacationing in Florida.

In both of these examples, the writer has not attempted to tell the whole story in the first sentence. Rather, the stories have attention-getting leads and are then supported by facts and details in subsequent sentences. This structure for broadcast news writing is a common one that should be mastered by the beginning student. Here are some more examples of newspaper stories and the attention-getting leads that could be written for broadcast:

Print
Americans overwhelmingly oppose the taxation of employee benefits, and congressmen who tamper with such tax-free worker benefits may face trouble at the polls, two Roper Organization surveys say.

Broadcast
Keep your hands off employee benefits.
   That's what Americans are willing to tell congressmen who want to tax things like retirement payments and educational allowances.

Print
The United States is turning out inferior products that are too costly for foreign customers and the problems go beyond a strong dollar, high wages, and high taxes, a presidential commission reports.

Broadcast
Many American products aren't worth what we are asking for them.

Print
A lone juror, a city sanitation department supervisor, forced a hung jury and a mistrial of Midville Mayor Reggie Holder's trial on perjury and conspiracy charges involving alleged illegal campaign contributions.

Broadcast
One man has made the difference in the perjury and conspiracy trial of Midville Mayor Reggie Holder.

Stories are measured in time—minutes and seconds. Whereas a newspaper can devote three hundred words to a story, a broadcaster may have only twenty to thirty

LOSE THE ACCENT

Henry Higgins, the professor in the play and musical *My Fair Lady,* spends a good bit of time in the story ridding Eliza Doolittle of her Cockney accent. The way she pronounced words marked her as someone that people in high London society looked down upon.

Higgins was right—maybe not morally or emotionally but certainly practically. And the thrust of his advice to Eliza Doolittle could be given to anyone interested in being on the air in broadcast news: Lose the accent.

The nation is filled with many distinctive regional variations in the way we speak. People recognize the Southern drawl, the Brooklyn "thirty" that becomes "toity," the Boston "ah" that turns "ask" to "ahh-sk," the Texas twang, and the Midwestern clip. In certain parts of life, these accents are interesting and fun.

But not in broadcasting, where the important thing is not how the broadcaster sounds but what he or she says. If a broadcaster's accent distracts from the information he or she is trying to present, the broadcaster is less effective as a journalist and, chances are, will not be able to advance from a region where the accent is not noticed.

Instead, broadcasters should learn standard American speech so that accent will not be an issue.

Losing an accent is no small task. We grow up speaking and hearing certain sounds and patterns, and most of us never think about them. In addition, the process of losing an accent can sometimes cause ill feelings among family and friends.

Many people entering the field of broadcast news hire speech coaches and spend many hours practicing new words and new patterns. Just like Eliza Doolittle.

seconds for it. The broadcast writer must keep this time factor in mind during every stage of the writing and editing process. Broadcast news stories cannot go into the detail and explanation that print or web stories can. The broadcast writer has to omit certain facts and explanations if the story is to fit into the time allowed.

Broadcast Writing Style

The style and customs of broadcast writing differ somewhat from the style you have learned for print and web journalism. Although the *AP Stylebook* is still consulted for many usage questions, broadcast writing has some conventions of its own. The following is an explanation of some of those conventions.

Titles usually come before names. Just as in print stories, most people mentioned in broadcast stories need to be identified. In broadcast newswriting, however, titles almost always precede a name. Consequently, whereas a print story might have "James Baker, former secretary of state," the broadcast journalist would say, "former Secretary of State James Baker."

Avoid abbreviations, even on second reference. Only the most commonly known abbreviations should be used in broadcast writing. The FBI and UN are two examples. FTC, however, should be spelled out as the Federal Trade Commission.

Avoid direct quotations if possible. Broadcast writers prefer paraphrasing rather than using direct quotations. Direct quotations are hard to handle in broadcast copy because signaling the listener that the statement is a direct quotation is difficult.

Sometimes a direct quotation is essential and should be used. When that is the case, the writer needs to tip the listener off to the fact that a direct quotation is being used. The use of the phrase "quote . . . unquote" is awkward and should be avoided. Instead, phrases such as "in the words of the speaker," "in his own words," "used these words," and "as she put it."

Attribution should come before a quotation, not after it. The sequence of direct quote–speaker–verb that is the standard in print journalism is not useful for the broadcast writer. Tagging an attribution onto the end of a direct or paraphrased quote is confusing to the listener. The listener should know where the quotation is coming from before hearing the quote.

Use as little punctuation as possible but enough to help the newscaster through the copy. Remember that broadcast news copy will be read by only one person, the news reader. That person should be able to read through the copy as easily as possible. The excessive use of commas, dashes, and semicolons will not help the newscaster.

Numbers and statistics should be rounded off. Whereas a print journalist will want to use an exact figure, a broadcast journalist will be satisfied with a more general figure. Consequently, $4,101,696 in print becomes "more than four million dollars" in broadcast copy.

Numbers themselves are handled somewhat differently than the *AP Stylebook* dictates for print journalists. Here are a few rules about handling numbers in broadcast copy: numbers one through nine should be spelled out; numbers 10 through 999 should be written as numerals; write out *hundred, thousand, million, billion,* and use a combination of numerals with these numbers where appropriate (for example, 15 hundred, 10 billion); don't write *a million* or *a billion,* but rather use the word *one* (*a* sounds like *eight*).

Personalize the news when possible and appropriate. In the example on page 345 the lead sentence could read, "Gas is going to cost you five cents more a gallon. . . ." When possible and appropriate, broadcast stories should draw the listeners into the story by telling how the story might affect them.

Avoid extended description. "President and chief executive officer of International Widgets John Smith said today . . . " would become "International Widgets President John Smith says . . . ."

Avoid using symbols when you write. The dollar sign should never be used. Nor should the percent sign be used. Spell these words out so there will be no mistake on the part of the news reader.

Use phonetic spelling for unfamiliar and hard to pronounce names and words. Again, you are trying to be helpful to the newscaster. Writing "California Governor George Duekmejian (Dook-MAY-gen) said today he will propose . . . " helps the newscaster get over a difficult name. Notice that the syllable that is emphasized in pronunciation is written in capital letters. Difficult place names also need phonetic spellings. "A car bomb exploded in downtown Caracas (ka-RAH-kus) today." Writers should also be knowledgeable about local pronunciations of place names. For instance, most people know that Louisville, Kentucky, is pronounced (LU-ee-vil), but most people do not know that residents of Louisville, Tennessee, pronounce the name of their community as (LU-iss-vil). Pronunciation to the broadcast writer is like spelling to the print journalist. It should always be checked if there is any doubt.

Avoid pronouns. When you have to use them, make sure the referents are clear to the listener. Putting too many pronouns in a story can be an obstacle to the kind of clarity a broadcaster must achieve. For instance, in the following sentences, it is unclear to whom the pronoun is referring: The president and the chief foreign affairs advisor met yesterday. They discussed his recent trip to the Mideast.

Avoid apposition. An apposition is a word or set of words that renames a noun. In "Tom Smith, mayor of Midville, said today . . . " the phrase "mayor of Midville" is an appositional phrase. These phrases are deadly in broadcast writing. They slow the newscaster down and confuse the listener. Appositions, when they are found in the middle of sentences, are surrounded by commas. Listeners to broadcast stories do not have the advantage of those commas, however. Consequently, they may hear the preceding example as " . . . Midville said today. . . ." Broadcast writers should keep subjects and verbs as close together as possible.

Use the present tense when it is appropriate. Using the present tense ("the president says" rather than "the president said") is one way broadcast writers have of bringing immediacy to their writing. Care should be taken, however, that using the present tense does not make the broadcaster sound foolish. For instance, if the president made a statement yesterday, a broadcast news story probably should not have the attribution in the present tense. The past tense would be more appropriate. The present tense should be used for action that is very recent or that is continuing.

Avoid dependent clauses at the beginning of sentences. Dependent clauses are troublesome to the broadcast writer because they are confusing and tend to hide the subject of the sentence. For instance, "Stopping on the first leg of his European tour today, the president said he . . . " gives the listener too much to digest before getting to the main point of the story. The broadcast writer should always remember that the simple sentence—subject, verb, object—is the best format to use.

Broadcast Copy Preparation

Copy is prepared for one person, the announcer. The copy should be presented in a way that makes the announcer's job as easy as possible. Different stations and news organizations will have rules about how to prepare copy. The list that follows should give you an idea of the kind of rules the station will employ:

- Type only one story on a page. A story should have some ending mark, such as "—30—", at the end.

- Use caps and lowercase. An old style of broadcast writing (and the one you see in some of the examples in this chapter) was to capitalize everything. That is changing. The all caps style is hard to read.

- Don't carry over a paragraph to another page. If a story is more than a page long, end the page at the end of a paragraph; begin the next page with a new paragraph.

- Don't hyphenate at the end of a line.

- Broadcasters often want to work tapes (either audio or video) of interviews into their stories. The following example shows you how to indicate this on your copy.

People who want to buy a Chevrolet next year are going to have to pay more. That's what company spokesman John Smith said today in Detroit. The new cars will cost about 7 percent more than last year's cars. Smith blamed the increase on the new contract recently negotiated with the United Auto Workers.

ROLL TAPE: The workers are getting more . . .

END TAPE: . . . really no way of avoiding this.

[:15]

Labor leaders disputed this reasoning, however. Local auto workers president Stanley Porter said Chevrolet was raising its prices just to make the union look bad. At a separate news conference in Detroit, he called on Chevrolet to roll back its prices.

ROLL TAPE: The union gave up a lot . . .

END TAPE: . . . without good reason.[:18]

The number in each of the sets of parentheses indicates the number of seconds of each tape.

THE HISSING SIBILANT

A broadcast news reporter's worst enemy is neither the Saffir-Simpson scale 5 hurricane from which the reporter is broadcasting or an important source who refuses to talk.

It's the letter *s*.

S produces a hissing sound that even the most trained voice cannot completely avoid, and any word that contains an *s* that must be sounded—called a *sibilant*—can cause some problems.

S cannot be avoided entirely, of course. We use too many words that contain the letter, and *s* is the most common way to form plurals. But writers will do their on-air broadcasters a big favor if they pay attention to the sibilants and avoid stories such as the following that once appeared on the United Press International newswire:

Nobel Prize winner Alexander Solzhenitsyn (sawl-zhehn-eet'-sihn) is in prison again. Dissident sources say Solzhenitsyn was jailed for disseminating slanders about the Soviet State system.

Putting Together a Newscast

Broadcast journalists work with and against time. They use time to measure their stories, but they are also always working against time in the form of tight deadlines. Their stories must be completed for the next newscast. People working in radio feel this pressure keenly because of the hourly news shows that many radio stations produce. Many local television stations are also producing such hourly newscasts. For the broadcast journalist, the clock is always ticking toward a deadline, and the deadline cannot be delayed.

Many broadcast journalists—even those who are fairly new in the business—must worry not only about writing their stories but also about putting together a newscast. Producing such a newscast, whether it is a forty-five-second news brief or a half-hour telecast, involves many of the skills learned as a newswriter.

The first such skill is that of exercising news judgment about what to include in the newscast. Writers must use traditional news values in deciding what events constitute news. Editors and producers use those same values in deciding what goes into a newscast. The key element in putting together newscasts is the timeliness of the stories. A newscast producer looks at the stories available and often decides which ones to run based on how recent the stories are. Because broadcasting is a medium that can emphasize the immediate, news producers often take advantage of this quality by telling listeners and viewers what happened only minutes before a newscast.

Timeliness is not the only news value used in these decisions. A story that is the most recent one available will not necessarily be the first one used in a newscast. Stories that have more impact or involve more prominent people may take precedence. All of the other news values come into play in putting together a newscast.

Another element that news producers use in deciding what to put into a newscast is the availability of audio tapes, slides, film, and videotapes. One of the criticisms of broadcast journalism is that decisions about what to run and what not to run are based on the availability of such aids. It is true that such decisions are often made, but broadcast journalists—especially television journalists—feel that they must take advantage of their medium to show a story rather than just tell it. Pictures compel viewers to watch, and the feeling of many in television is that the "talking head," the news announcer with no visual aid, is not as compelling to the viewer as the "talking head" with a picture or slide.

Time is the pervasive factor in putting together a newscast. Not only must stories be timely in themselves, but they must be written to fill a certain amount of airtime. The producer or news director is generally the one who assigns the amount of time for a story to fill. The writer must then write a story that can be read in that time. The producer, of course, must have enough copy to fill up the time allotted for the newscast. Sometimes, however, even with the most careful planning, a newscast producer will come up a few seconds short. The producer should always give the announcer one or two more stories than he or she will need in order to fill this time. (See Chapter 6 for some of the formats that broadcast journalists have available in putting together a newscast.)

Conclusion

The nature of broadcast news is changing dramatically, and the technology that is developing for broadcasters is placing new demands on them. Computer editing stations—allowing reporters to do all of the editing of both videotape and copy on a single workstation—will give reporters more direct control in producing their stories. These systems will also allow reporters to call up file footage—videotapes that may have run in previous stories—for use or reference. Those entering the field of broadcast news must be increasingly computer oriented.

Another development is the increased use of satellite technology to produce live shots from the scene of news events. This means that reporters will be called on to do more stand-ups and that they must develop the ability to think on their feet, outline stories quickly, and read unobtrusively from their notes. Reporters must understand the forms and formats of broadcast news to be able to put these shots together. Even though it may occur in a different form, the ability to write clearly and concisely will continue to be a must of the broadcast news reporter.

Still another development is the merging of broadcast and print news under a single roof. The *Chicago Tribune* has a broadcast news studio built into its newsroom; it owns CLTV, a twenty-four-hour news channel that is carried by many Chicago area cable companies, as well as WGN radio and television stations. News reporters for the *Tribune* often wear two hats. They write their copy for print, and then they do a stand-up spot for broadcast outlets. The *Tribune* is one of many newspaper/broadcast combinations that are developing throughout the nation. Increasingly, writers will have to know how to construct news in both print and broadcast form.

All of these characteristics of broadcast writing place a heavy burden on the writer of broadcast copy. Producing such copy is no easy task. The person who can do it consistently and well, however, is likely to have a large audience for his or her work.

QUESTIONS FOR DISCUSSION

1. Read a print or web news story about a subject after hearing or watching a broadcast news story about it. Note the differences. What kind of information do you get from the print or web story that you don't get from the broadcast story? What do you get from the broadcast story that you do not get from the print or web story?
2. Broadcast stories are very short because of the assumption that the audience does not want to listen to a long story. Do you think this assumption is correct?
3. Why is the use of the simple sentence so prevalent in broadcast writing? What qualities does it give to the writing that other types of sentences do not?
4. Watch a half-hour local news broadcast. Time each of the news stories to see how long they are. Does it surprise you about the number of stories there are? Do the reporters follow broadcast writing rules and structure outlined in this chapter?

RELATED WEB SITES

BBC News Styleguide, www.bbctraining.co.uk/pdfs/newsStyleGuide.pdf

Mervinblock.com, www.mervinblock.com/tips.html

MIBTB—Broadcasting Training Program, www.webcom.com/mibtp

NAB Information Resource Center, www.nab.org/irc

Poynter Online's TV/Radio Tipsheets, http://poynteronline.org/content/content_view.asp?id=31904

READINGS AND REFERENCES

Bliss, E. (1991). *Now the news: The story of broadcast journalism.* New York: Columbia University Press.

Hausman, C. (1992). *Crafting news for electronic media.* Belmont, CA: Wadsworth Publishing Co.

Hilliard, R. L. (2000). *Writing for television, radio and new media* (7th ed.). Belmont, CA: Wadsworth-Thomson Learning.

Keller, T., & Hawkins, S. (2002). *Television news: A handbook for writing, reporting, shooting and editing.* Scottsdale: Holcomb Hathaway.

Mayeux, P. E. (1994). *Writing for the broadcast media.* Madison: Brown and Benchmark.

Rosenbaum, M. D., & Dinges, J. (Eds.). (1992). *Sound reporting: The National Public Radio guide to radio journalism and production.* Dubuque, IA: Kendall-Hunt Publishing Co.

Shook, F., Lattimore, D., & Redmond, J. (2001). *The broadcast news process* (6th ed.). Englewood, CO: Morton Publishing Co.

Stephens, M. (1993). *Broadcast news* (3rd ed.). New York: Harcourt Brace Jovanovich.

Writing Exercises

EXERCISE 19.1

Writing Broadcast Stories

Write a thirty-second broadcast news story based on the following sets of information.

Faculty Death

Education prof. Elizabeth Billson, dead at age 58

had taught here for thirty-six years

estimated to have taught ten thousand future teachers during her years

awarded university's "Outstanding Professor" award last year

had suffered from cancer for ten years

Poll

Local polling firm, City Research Associates

poll of more than five hundred city residents

completed last week

showed 65 percent of citizens "satisfied" or "very satisfied" with the quality of life in the city; showed 75 percent of those with school-age children "satisfied" or "very satisfied" with city school system

poll sponsored by chamber of commerce

Wreck

Two trucks collided on I-59 last night

Caused a traffic jam because the road was blocked both ways for about forty-five minutes

Fuel from both trucks spilled onto the highway and caused a big oil slick

One truck was refrigerated and most of the contents thawed, causing a loss of an estimated $10,000 worth of goods.

Accident happened on a part of I-59 undergoing repairs, so it was two lanes at that point; the trucks met head on.

EXERCISE 19.2
Writing a Newscast

Construct a two-minute newscast based on the following items. You will need to select the stories that you want to use and decide how much time to give to each. Then you will have to write the stories so that they meet those time requirements. (*Note to instructors:* This exercise works well if you divide the class into teams and appoint a news director for each team.)

Capsize

A fifteen-foot boat capsized in rough waters off Point Lookout yesterday evening. Two men—Terry Reston, 23, and Will Bendix, 25—were in the boat. The men said offshore winds increased wave heights and capsized their boat. The men were picked up by a Coast Guard boat after an hour in the water. Both were hospitalized for observation, but the hospital lists their condition today as good. The men say they were hunting sharks about 200 yards offshore.

Basketball Death

A fifteen-year-old freshman basketball player died this morning during practice at Central High School. The freshman, Todd White, collapsed while running during a practice game. White had not had any known illness, according to trainer Mike Way. White was pronounced dead at Central Valley Memorial Hospital after all efforts to revive him failed. An autopsy will be performed by the county coroner today.

Energy Plan

The secretary of the interior announced a new $800 million energy plan while traveling through the western United States on a busy three-day tour. The secretary of the interior announced his plan at a Western Governor's Conference meeting in Salt Lake City. The plan calls for a five-year program to ease strains brought on by strip mining and other energy ventures.

Abuse Acquittal

A fourth-grade school teacher in Midville has been acquitted of child abuse for spanking a ten-year-old girl with a wooden paddle after the girl lied about having gum in her mouth. The District Court jury returned a verdict of not guilty after deliberating three hours. Lynda Kristle had been charged with child abuse after parents noted bruises on the child's buttocks.

Retirement

The speaker of the state House of Representatives, Milton Bradford, has announced that he will not seek reelection. He has served in the state house for twenty-seven years and has been speaker for the past ten years. He is a Democrat from Logansville. He has always been closely aligned with the state's education lobby and has recently worked for substantial pay raises for the state's elementary and secondary school teachers.

When

The history of journalism mirrors in many ways the history of humans. People need to share information about each other and their environment. Journalism was practiced long before the modern concept of journalism was formulated.

Professional practices, the development of an audience, and technological innovation form the basis for the study of journalism history. No matter what the age or era, these three factors have played vital roles in the field of journalism.

Journalism has helped spur some of the great inventions of mankind—the printing press, photography, the telegraph, and the harnessing of electromagnetic waves. Along the way, journalism history has been dotted with colorful and fascinating characters. All of this makes the study of journalism history vital to the understanding of the profession itself.

Chapter Twenty

Beginnings of Journalism

Key Concepts and Terms

1. Individuals and groups have always needed to communicate new information and the latest news to each other; consequently, journalism is a part of any society, ancient or modern.

2. Journalism in any age depends on the technology available to gather and disseminate information.

3. Writing makes information easier to convey than simply speaking; writing also creates a permanent record, something that establishes a history and a basis for a society.

4. *Acta Diurna:* a daily publication of political and society news begun during the reign of Julius Caesar in 59 B.C.

5. *Moveable type:* individual pieces of type that can be reused for different printing jobs. The concept of moveable type was the key to the invention of the printing press around 1450.

6. Printing was only one of the factors that brought Western civilization out of the Dark Ages. Other factors included an increase in literacy and easier means of dissemination (such as the development of safer travel routes).

7. *Censorship:* prevention by governmental or religious authorities of dissemination of information they believed threatening to their position.

8. Benjamin Franklin was the great journalistic innovator of the eighteenth century; he pioneered the development of newspapers throughout the American colonies by investing in start-up papers, creating news services among newspapers, and promoting a light and entertaining style of writing.

9. Modern journalism, with its emphasis on fair and accurate presentation of information, did not exist during the 1790s, the first decade of the American Constitutional republic. Instead, it was the age of partisanship when newspapers presented political points of view rather than information.

When we look back through the history of journalism, we see the same themes recurring.

Journalism is at the mercy of technology, for example. Certainly we no longer write on parchment with a quill, but rest assured that medieval scribes would have used electronic computers and photocopying machines had they the chance. Journalists use what's available to do the best job with the least effort.

Journalism is equally at the mercy of its financial base. The economics of publishing have changed over time, but journalism has never been free or cheap. Gathering, understanding, and distributing information takes enormous effort and usually substantial investment.

Journalists write for an audience. They keep a sharp eye on their readers, on who needs information, and on who is willing to pay for it. That audience has changed over the centuries, just like technology and the financial base of publishing have changed. But journalism is always a form of communication and, thus, requires people who write and people who read.

The history of journalism is also characterized by the steady development and acceptance of professional practices. Our medieval scribe took great pains to make his illuminated manuscript beautiful, and today the best journalists take equal pride in investigating an event and choosing just the right words to report it. Excellence never goes out of style.

These themes and others will be traced through the next four chapters.

Where Does Journalism Begin?

Most of our attention for the next two chapters will be on the written forms of communication that humans developed from the earliest known civilizations. But journalism itself is a prewriting concept. Oral and verbal communication was the first way in which humans communicated, and it continues to be an important means of communication today. As humans formed tribes and societies, they needed to exchange information about themselves and about the world around them. They did so orally.

But oral communication was inadequate for any society that grew more sophisticated. As hunting decreased and agriculture increased, societies grew more stable; workloads shifted and divisions of labor became more complex. Trading of goods and services meant that records had to be kept.

One of the earliest civilizations that we know about is that of the Sumerians, who populated the area of the Tigris and Euphrates rivers (present-day Iraq, Iran, Kuwait, and Saudi Arabia) about three thousand years before the birth of Christ. The Sumerians built a fascinating society in which writing played a vital role. The Sumerians developed a system of writing that used a standardized set of symbols and designs. This system did not evolve into a full alphabet as we think of it today, but it did allow Sumerians to scratch symbols into moistened clay so that they could keep records and know what others had written. (The Sumerians even developed some literature, stories about their people and past that included a tale about the world being flooded. This story appeared long before Jewish society was formed, and the story of Noah and the great flood was known.)

The remarkable thing about the Sumerians was not their system of writing but their system of printing. When multiple copies of an important mark were required, such as the designation of ownership, Sumerians first produced a stamp that they could press into soft clay. The stamp resembled the letters of a letterpress that came into use nearly five thousand years later.

But the Sumerians went beyond the stamp. At some point in their history, they developed cylinders that could be engraved with a number of symbols. These cylinders were small, about the size of an index finger. They could be easily transported and were used to spread information and ideas about the Sumerians beyond the immediate area. The idea of a rolling cylinder to "print" information was revived several thousand years later and is the way in which most of our printed information comes to us, but for the Sumerians (who did not have paper) cylinder "printing" was a simple idea that made life easier.

Writing, as crude as it was for the Sumerians, did for them what writing has always done for any individual or society that used it. It made information easier to convey, and it made the conveyance of that information more accurate. It also gave the information a permanence that extended the reach, and even the life, of the person who created it. Writing helped the individual Sumerians connect with each other and with those beyond their borders and their time. We know a great deal about the Sumerians today, five thousand years after their people dispersed and their buildings crumbled, because they wrote things down.

But was this journalism? Not in the modern sense possibly, but in the broadest sense, it was because the information was timely and what people needed and wanted. They needed information to operate their daily lives, and they needed the stories that helped them make sense of their world. These were basic needs, and journalism helped fulfill them.

Each civilization that succeeded the Sumerians developed their own means of communication and ways of exchanging information and making it permanent. The Chinese found ways to make paperlike substances on which to record their information; they also invented something very close to the nineteenth- and twentieth-century processes of printing. In addition, Chinese emperors instituted a postal system that enabled information to flow in from all parts of their vast holdings. Egyptians worked on a system of writing and, like the Sumerians, came close to creating a standardized alphabet. That achievement was finally accomplished by the Phoenicians (or so some historians believe); it was a system of symbols representing the sounds of speech. The Greeks took the alphabet from the Phoenicians or other peoples in the Orient and used it to articulate the information and ideas of a highly sophisticated society.

Greece, of course, had a far-flung empire that needed channels of communication to keep it together. Writing was a necessary but insufficient means for doing this. The Greeks had to send information quickly over long distances, and although sailing ships would do for this purpose in some instances, they did not always have the speed the times and situations demanded. Consequently, the Greeks put together a telegraph system with a series of signal fires and earthenware jars that would adjusted in a pre-arranged way to send messages quickly over great distances.* Several hundred years before the birth of Christ, Rome followed Greece in its role as the dominant world power. The Roman system of rule, both at home and outside of Italy, was more complex and sophisticated than any other the world had seen, and it depended on timely information. It is in Rome that we begin to see the first inklings of what we would recognize as journalism. Rome had inherited and developed its own system of writing that closely resembles the one we use today. A Roman citizen (and many within the empire who were not citizens) had a good chance of being literate. Citizenship required some degree of participation—at least to the extent that one was expected to understand the rights and responsibilities of citizenship—and that participation, to a greater or lesser degree, required current information.

FIGURE 20.1   Caesar Augustus A brilliant leader and organizer, Caesar Augustus understood the value of information and the importance of communicating with all parts of the Roman Empire. He built roads and established a postal system with regular deliveries. He also encouraged reading and the trading of books throughout the empire.

Rome, then, developed what many people believe is the first daily newspaper devoted to public and political affairs. The *Acta Diurna,* begun by Julius Caesar in 59 B.C., was an official daily account of political news and acts from the Senate. Its content went beyond governmental affairs, however. *Acta* contained information about events within the city of Rome, tidbits about famous people, news about executions, fires, and other calamities, and even news about the weather. The *Acta* was printed and posted around the city, read avidly, and remained a vital part of Roman life for many decades.

Augustus, who followed Julius as ruler of Rome, maintained and extended the system of roads and highways for which the Romans were justly famous. He put this system to good use by commissioning a postal system with a regular delivery schedule to make sure that Roman edicts and propaganda were spread to all parts of the empire.

Few of Augustus's successors could match his genius and innovation in governing the empire, and some were downright destructive. By the fifth century A.D., the empire was crumbling, beset by internal strife and by hoards of European tribes that the emperors had not been able to subdue. When the empire dissipated in 476 with the fall of Rome, Europe was plunged into several centuries when many of the progressive ideas the Romans had about communication and journalism were forgotten or abandoned. The Catholic Church became the dominant power, and for much of the next millennia it showed little inclination to encourage intellectual breakthroughs.

*For a detailed description of this system, see Jackson P. Hershell, "The Ancient Telegraph: War and Literacy," in *Communication Arts in the Ancient World,* Eric Havelock et. al., eds. (New York: Midpoint Trade Books, 1978) 82–87.

Most of the societies of Europe returned to reliance on an oral tradition. Writing was centered mainly in monasteries where book copying was a major activity. Books, which had replaced rolled manuscripts, were valued possessions, but any ideas about their mass production that might have followed from the Romans seem to have been lost. Instead, monks were put to the painstaking work of hand copying manuscripts.

The lack of development of Roman ideas of printing and mass communication was just one of several factors in the medieval environment that impeded intellectual progress. Travel was often dangerous, so commerce outside local areas was scarce. Literacy rates dropped, and people seemed to have little need for information. The Church maintained its position as the sole intermediary between the people and their Supreme Being. Despite all of these factors, some individuals, particularly monks and priests, continued to record events and develop ideas within their private journals and among select groups of contemporaries.

By A.D. 1400 this closed system was collapsing. Universities had sprung up around Europe, and students had taken over the tedious business of copying manuscripts. Order was returning to the major highways, and commerce was growing. A new spirit of inquiry about the world and humankind's place in it was forming. People wanted to know about themselves and about others. The time was right for a breakthrough, and that breakthrough occurred. It was technological, and it changed almost everything.

The Printing Press

No one knows who first had the combination of ideas that resulted in the modern printing process or who invented the first printing press. Some of those ideas had been around for a long time. The process of making a mold with raised or lowered letters or symbols had been developed by the Sumerians, as we have seen earlier in this chapter. The idea of a machine that could bring down a weight heavy enough to make an impression had also been around for a long time; such machines had been used for centuries to "press" the juice out of grapes to make wine. The idea of ink, a by-product of grapes and other natural substances, was also centuries old. Paper, too, had been developed by the Chinese and had been in use by Western civilizations for centuries.

But before the fifteenth century, none of these ideas or processes was enough to make printing as we know it feasible. The process was too cumbersome and expensive to make it worthwhile. Making the mold that would be used to print the page was the stumbling block. Unless the same mold could be used many times, it wasn't worth it.

The key idea that broke through this logjam was *moveable type*. Around 1450, someone thought about dividing the page mold into individual pieces. Each piece would contain one letter. Make enough of these pieces, organize them in different boxes, tie together the pieces you need to make a page, print however many copies you want, untie the pieces of type, and put them back in their boxes. The next day you could do the same thing but make a different page. And you could do the same thing the next day.

Suddenly, the winepress, the paper, and the ink made sense. You could print pages and do it efficiently. You could tell thousands of people what you knew or what you were thinking. You might even be able to make some money.

Johann Gutenberg is the name we generally associate with the invention of moveable type. Gutenberg was a printer in Mainz, Germany, around the middle part of the 1400s, and we know very little about him. He is connected with moveable type through some court documents (he was being sued by his partner), but it is not clear that he had the idea of moveable type first. About this time (around 1456), a set of Bibles—the first items that we know of printed with moveable type—appeared, and tradition has attached Gutenberg's name to them.

But who invented moveable type is not as important as what happened next. Everything began to change—including the way in which we saw the world.

Moveable type meant fast, efficient production of printed material. What had been very expensive was now very inexpensive and relatively easy to produce. It also ensured original duplication. That is, the last copy would be the same as the first. This was a problem with the hand copying of manuscripts that had gone on for centuries. You could never be sure what mistakes the hand copyist was making. With printing, no such mistakes occurred.

For printing to work—that is, for it to be effective in disseminating information—other things had to be in place, of course. For one, there needed to be supplies, particularly ink and paper. Paper was a problem because the process for making it cheaply was evolving. Yet, as any child who has ever owned a papermaking kit knows, there are lots of ways of making paper and lots of ingredients you can use.

Distribution was another problem. Getting what you had printed out of the printer's shop and into the hands of those you wanted to communicate with was no small chore. No post offices or delivery services existed at the time, so the distribution problem had to be solved by the individuals who had commissioned the printing. It was solved in a variety of ways, but it was expensive and cumbersome.

Finally, there needed to be a market for the printed material, and that required literacy, first, and then a need for information. Europe at this time was emerging from its medieval period. More people were taking part in commerce and learning to read. Universities were encouraging inquiry and the transmission of knowledge. Information was becoming more necessary for sustaining a good life. The world into which the modern printing process was born was changing.

Still, it was the solution to the technology problem—how to print quickly and efficiently—that was the engine that drove these other changes. With that problem solved, people could now concentrate on the message and the audience.

Dangerous Information

In 1517 Martin Luther, a German priest who had been questioning the teaching and practices of the Catholic Church for some years, nailed a piece of paper to the door of the university church in Wittenburg. The paper contained his "Ninety-five Theses," a bill of particulars that Luther had compiled against the Church. The door served as something of a public bulletin board, and Luther's paper resided there along with other notices that people had posted.

Luther's statement might have remained there, noticed only by those who passed by the door, but Luther took an additional step. He had copies printed and sent to all of the major cities in the country. Over the next three years, more copies were printed, and everyone who was anyone had read it and had an opinion about it. Through a combination of printing and word of mouth, Luther sparked the first great Reformation, and it changed the course of human history.

The advent of printing and the growth of literacy throughout Western Europe, as well as Luther's ideas about how the Church should operate, were part of a larger shift as to how human beings saw themselves. Before this period, the Scriptures were not considered terribly important in the development of a Christian life. Relatively few people read the Bible. It was not readily available even to those who might be literate. What was important in the religious life was what the priest and the Church said. How they interpreted the Scriptures was important; for individual laypeople to interpret for themselves was almost unheard of.

Luther, among many others at the time, had a different idea. He argued that individuals should read and interpret scripture for themselves, that God could speak to laypersons, and that they could choose a religious path that was correct for them.

And what was happening inside the Church was also happening in other aspects of people lives. Individuals were beginning to realize that they need not depend on others to make decisions about their lives. In their religious, political, and professional lives, they could decide things for themselves, based on their own acquisition of information. In addition, they could also speak for themselves if they felt that they had something to say.

These changes took root as more printed material appeared. Their effects were not always immediate, but they were profound. Religious, political, and social leaders could no longer rule with near absolute power because, try as they might they could not control the flow of information as they once had. They found they had to be more sensitive to something we know today as "public opinion."

Information, as well as being dangerous, became a valuable commodity. In the sixteenth century, as trade among cities and nations increased, merchants needed information on possible markets for their products. States were also developing identities and rivalries, and political news took on added importance. Those who produced information, from Bibles to gossipy tidbits, saw the possibility of making a profit on their product. They lacked a model, however, because there were no established newspapers or newsletters. Several forms of information dissemination sprang to life, including the broadside (a single sheet usually devoted to a single topic); the news pamphlet (a four-page booklet about a single subject); the newsletter (usually published by the government for disseminating an official version or interpretation of events); and the canto (a regularly published newsletter in Holland that was a precursor to what we now know as newspapers).

Possibly the first newspaper in the modern sense appeared in Oxford, England, in 1655. Published twice a week, the *Oxford Gazette* was produced by Henry Muddiman. Although it had news and information, it did little more than give the government's version of things. The paper was published in Oxford because much of the government had relocated there to avoid the plague. In 1666, with the government back in London, the paper moved to the capital city and became the *London Gazette* and continued its adherence to the government's point of view.

The first daily publication devoted to news and information came just after the turn of the century and may have had a woman, briefly, as its editor. The *Daily Courant* first appeared in 1702 under the editorship of "E. Mallett," probably Elizabeth Mallett. She lasted only a couple of weeks, however, and the paper was sold to Samuel Buckley, who continued with it for more than 30 years. The *Daily Courant* was real journalism, though in a crude form. It contained news and opinion, datelines, and an attempt at fair presentation of information.

Journalism was brand new to the people who were practicing it and the people who were consuming it. There were no rules and few precedents. People involved with publications were well aware that governments not long before then had executed heretics, many of whom had published information displeasing to the government and the established church. There was little to prevent an autocratic ruler from turning on some would-be journalist who stepped out of line. Various systems of licensing and censorship were put into place in every country in Europe, and printers often labored under the heavy yoke of government control.

Yet, ultimately these systems could not withstand the tendency of people to exchange information and opinions that did not meet with official approval. The European Enlightenment period of the 1680s put emphasis on the worth of the individuals, and philosopher John Locke argued eloquently that various opinions should be tolerated even when they did not conform to the government's interpretation. These ideas paved the way for believing that an independent press could exist and also be an asset to society.

The New World

The Reformation, Renaissance, and Enlightenment movements of the sixteenth and seventeenth centuries in Europe produced a feeling that people should look beyond themselves and their national borders. This feeling was enhanced by the possibility that profits could be made from the new worlds being "discovered" by European explorers. Consequently, the move by European governments to colonize various parts of the globe was economic. These lands, including America, might contain products that would appeal to domestic markets. They would also provide new markets for products produced domestically.

Beyond the economics, however, lay other ideas that drove colonization. The promise of land for land-starved Europe was one such idea. Being able to break out of the economic, social, and geographic confines of Europe appealed to many creative people as an opportunity not to be missed. America was especially rich in land, and as travelers returned, they brought fabulous tales of the abundance of soil and space.

The idea of refuge was another of the great appeals of the colonies. Groups who felt oppressed by governments or societies, who did not believe they could follow their religious and social beliefs in a corrupted Europe, and who simply wished to attempt living in a different way with different rules saw America as an ideal place.

Finally, the political idea of extending the reach and power of a nation by building colonies was a powerful one that appealed to many European monarchs. Colonies amounted to prestige, and every king or queen was tempted by that.

No nation was more aggressive or had more staying power in its colonization efforts than England. The English extended themselves to almost every part of the globe, and what became the British Empire dwarfed the ancient efforts of Rome and Greece to conquer the world. The jewel of that empire, however, was America. America's land, abundance, and accessibility offered golden economic opportunities to which the English freely availed themselves. Beginning in the early 1600s, groups and individuals poured across the Atlantic Ocean with the notion of making money and starting a new life.

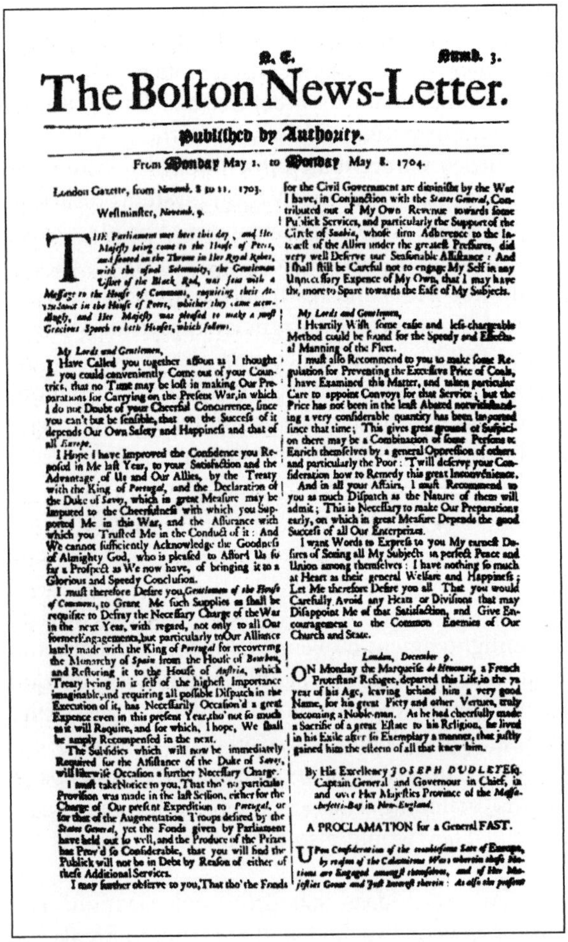

These people brought with them much of the world they left, including a civil and political society that was growing more mercantile and more convinced that a person's religious, political, and social beliefs were his own. This sense of tolerance was not mature—some things and people just were not allowed—but it was growing. In this society that these "Americans" were building, the free flow of information was necessary and natural. People had to know what was going on. They had to know about themselves and about the world outside their own experience. And they needed this information without interference from the government.

Journalism in this world grew, as it had in Europe, by fits and starts. Early colonists often did not bring with them the tools necessary for printing and did not manufacture it once they arrived. The technology had to be imported if it was to be put to use. The same systems of licensing that burdened printers in Europe also weighed down their American counterparts. At first, printing information was not especially necessary because colonies were so small. The church and

FIGURE 20.2   *Boston News-Letter* This first successful newspaper in America was about the size of a sheet of letterhead, but it contained news that was useful to its readers. John Campbell, its publisher, had the approval of the royal governor. Campbell was also Boston's postmaster, which gave his rather dull newspaper a decided edge.

the tavern, the two most prominent meeting places for people in the colonies, could suffice as the major channels of information. By the late 1600s with the colonies growing in population and sophistication, something more than public meetings was needed.

The first newspaper in America appeared in 1690 in Boston. It was published by Benjamin Harris, a man who had gained experience and jail time for his journalistic efforts in England. Harris's paper, *Public Occurrences Both Foreign and Domestic,* was planned as a weekly and had an official royal license, but it was closed down after just one issue. Two items in it were deemed offensive: one about native Americans that seemed to criticize the government and the other about the French king having an affair with his daughter-in-law that some thought salacious. It would be more than a decade before another newspaper with planned regularity appeared in the colonies.

That occurred when the *Boston News-Letter* was published by John Campbell in 1704. Campbell, the Boston postmaster, had been producing a handwritten newsletter for several years for distribution throughout the colonies. He found this burdensome, however, and turned to a printing press in 1704. The *Boston News-Letter* carried both news and advertising, something of an innovation for the time. Advertising, of course, has information that people consider newsworthy, and it also provides a source of revenue for the publication. Much of the news in Campbell's paper was foreign (people did not need to have local news in their papers since they were likely to know that anyway) and lifted from other newspapers (a common practice that continued long after this publication).

During the next two decades, several other men and women in Boston took an interest in starting a publication. Among them were James and Ann Franklin, who with backing from other prominent figures in the community, started the *New England Courant.* The paper was notable for its editorializing and particularly its anti-Puritan stance. Franklin eventually turned his editorial guns on the government itself and became so irritating that he was jailed at one point.

James Franklin was a notable figure in the early stages of American journalism because of his bold practices, but he is overshadowed by a far more prominent member of his family, his younger brother Benjamin, whose exploits in many fields, including science and politics, are well known. Benjamin, however, was first and foremost a printer, and his ideas and creativity made him the dominant figure in journalism in America in the 1700s.

Benjamin Franklin

No individual of the 1700s contributed more to the development of journalism than Benjamin Franklin. But Franklin did not consider himself a journalist. He was, rather, a printer. In those days printers could be editors and publishers of their own publications, but they might also print the publications of others. Franklin was proud of his vocation, so much so that it was the only one listed on his tombstone: "The Body of Benjamin Franklin, Printer (like the cover of an old Book, its contents worn out, and stript of its lettering and gildings) lies here, food for worms. Yet the work itself shall not be lost, for it will, as he believed, appear once more in a new and more beautiful edition, corrected and amended by its Author."

Franklin's self-composed epitaph shows the humor with which he approached both life and death. Fittingly, it was with humor that he entered journalism in 1722.

FIGURE 20.3   Benjamin Franklin No one had a more profound effect on life and politics in the eighteenth century than Benjamin Franklin. His journalistic accomplishments were many, including the beginning of American magazine journalism and the publishing of the first non-English newspaper in the colonies, the *Philadelphia Zeitung.* (Photo credit: United States Senate)

Franklin was apprenticed as a boy to his brother James's print shop, and there he learned the technical aspects of the trade. He also learned the power of words, being an avid reader, particularly of the works of English journalists Joseph Addison and Richard Steele, editors of the lively magazine the *Spectator.* The young Franklin could not help but notice the controversies in which his brother was involving himself, and at age 16 he decided to enter the fray. He wrote a series of articles under the pseudonym of "Silence Dogood," posing as a middle-aged woman and poking fun at the characters and controversies of the day. These weekly articles were lively and well written, showing a style and wit that Franklin had learned from reading Addison and Steele. Despite not knowing who the author was, his brother printed them. After about six months, Franklin confessed to his brother, who then stopped printing the articles.

Franklin never got along with his brother, and as soon as he could, he left his apprenticeship and left Boston for good. He went to Philadelphia where he set himself up as a printer and in 1728 took over the failing *Pennsylvania Gazette.* Franklin turned that publication into a lively and interesting newspaper, something that was informative and which people looked forward to reading. He brought to the newspaper business the same sense of spirit and innovation that he showed in his many other pursuits. He also made money. He was so successful that he was able to retire from the business at age 42 and devote himself to his many other interests, including invention, science, and politics. Franklin died in 1790 as one of the most famous people in the world, renowned for giving the world an understanding of electricity and a new nation called the United States of America.

As his epitaph indicates, Franklin always thought of himself as a printer and, along with that, a newspaperman. His contributions to the profession were enormous. They included a newspaper formula of news and advertising that satisfied and influenced readers. Franklin established a network of printers throughout the colonies by giving them the capital to begin their businesses and then sharing in their profits. These printers also shared some of the same editorial matter, thus creating a sense of unity among the scattered colonies. Franklin also pioneered a style of writing that broke away from the dull heavy-handedness that was normal for his time. His writing was short and lively, and one of the things we remember about him most today are his pithy sayings: "Early to bed, early to rise, makes a man healthy, wealthy and wise"; "A penny saved is a penny earned."

Most importantly, however, Franklin articulated the growing sense that people should be able to think, speak, and write freely. His famous editorial, "Apology for Printers," is still cited as an excellent defense for freedom of the press: "Printers are educated in the belief that when men differ in opinion, both sides ought equally to have the advantage of being heard by the public; and that when Truth and Error have fair play, the former is always an overmatch for the latter."

Due in part to Franklin but also to growing population and economic activity, the number of newspapers and circulation sizes grew during the 1700s. The growth was slow, hampered by governmental interference and lack of capital, equipment, and supplies, but the ideas and energy from which journalism springs were building. By the 1760s, American journalism was still toddling but was ready to fully participate in the political turmoils that lay ahead. Independence from England was an idea that some had advocated for decades. By 1765, it needed only a spark, and the king and Parliament in London obligingly provided one.

The Fire of Revolution

Taxes are necessary for the operation of a government, but few things spark more political opposition than taxes. This was true as much in the 1700s as it is today. And it was taxes—specifically the Stamp Act of 1765—that pushed many Americans from loyalty to the king to believing in independence.

The Stamp Act was imposed by Parliament at the end of a period of war when the British government needed money. Because part of the purpose of those wars was to secure the American colonies, the London lawmakers believed that Americans should foot at least part of the bill and that they might even be grateful to do so. They were wrong.

The provisions of the Stamp Act were particularly onerous. It required all legal papers, newspapers, and books to be printed on paper that carried a special stamp showing that a tax had been paid. Those who imposed the law not only misread the potential for opposition that the law would invoke but also aimed the law at those people who might be most dangerous in their opposition—lawyers, printers, and other members of the middle class who might deal with such documents. Printers were especially hard hit and, consequently, stridently vocal in their opposition.

London had handed radicals clamoring for revolution a nearly perfect issue. Even those sympathetic with the king found the Stamp Act difficult, if not impossible, to defend. The act was repealed in 1766, but the independence faction of America's political life never let it be forgotten. They did not need to. Every time Parliament attempted to impose another tax on the colonies, the perfidy of the Stamp Act could

WOMEN IN EIGHTEENTH-CENTURY JOURNALISM

No area of public or professional life in the eighteenth century offered women much of an opportunity. Journalism, unfortunately, was just as restrictive as any other area. Still, a few women managed to enter the profession and make significant contributions to it. Here are two examples:

Possibly the most prominent eighteenth-century female journalist was Elizabeth Timothy, publisher of the *South Carolina Gazette* in mid-century. Timothy was part of a French Huguenot family who immigrated to Philadelphia in 1731. Her husband, Louis, got to know Benjamin Franklin, who was looking for an editor of a German-language newspaper he wanted to start.

Louis Timothy published a couple of issues of the newspaper for Franklin, but then it turned out that Franklin needed an editor for a newspaper in Charleston that he had helped finance. He sent Timothy to take over the paper. Franklin's contract with publishers such as Timothy called for Franklin to finance the operation and receive a part of the profits for six years.

Timothy died in 1738, a year before his contract with Franklin was up. That's when Elizabeth Timothy took over. The publisher of the paper was listed as Peter Timothy, their son, but he was only 13

The first official printed copy of the Declaration of Independence. Mary Katherine Goddard's name appears at the bottom of the page.

years old at the time. It was Elizabeth who ran the operation, and she later received praise from Franklin for her good business practices. Timothy published the paper until her son turned 21 years old. She turned the paper over to him and opened a stationery shop next door to the newspaper printing office. She died in 1757.

Another prominent woman journalist was Mary Katherine Goddard, an experienced printer and publisher. Goddard had run printing operations in Rhode Island and Philadelphia. In 1774 she took charge of the *Maryland Journal* in Balti-more and ran it for her brother William until 1783. She supported the patriot cause, printed the first account of the Battle of Bunker Hill in Boston in 1775, and the next year was the printer chosen by Congress to print the first official copy of the Declaration of Independence.

In addition to her printing duties, she became Baltimore's postmistress in 1775 and remained in that job until 1789. After that she ran a bookstore in Baltimore for twenty years.

be recalled. By the 1770s, the argument over taxation had become more generalized with the radicals arguing that Parliament had no right to tax the colonies because America had no representation in Parliament. Because Parliament would never agree to having representatives from the colonies within its midst, the representation argument proved potent for the radicals.

All of these arguments were made in the newspapers of the nation by men such as Samuel Adams of Boston writing for the *Boston Gazette* and Thomas Paine, who wrote for various publications and often published his own works. Paine's simple style and short memorable sentences ("These are the times that try men's souls") lent power to his arguments. Once the fighting had begun, Paine was most effective in articulating the cause, and George Washington at one point ordered Paine's *American Crisis* pamphlet to be read to the men of his army as a boost to their morale.

Despite the drumbeating of the radicals and the fumbling of Parliament, Americans were not of one mind about independence. A number of prominent newspapers were published by men who did not believe that the colonies should separate themselves from the Crown. Most notable among them was James Rivington, editor of the *New York Gazetteer.* Rivington was an open, friendly man who became more conservative as others become more radical. At first, his newspaper printed opinions on all sides of the issue of independence, but he moved steadily to the king's side and eventually even changed the name of the paper to the *New York Royal Gazetteer.*

Neither side believed in freedom of the press, particularly for the opposition. Printers could find themselves in trouble with a mob if they said the wrong thing in their publications. Rivington, one of the few to call for tolerance in the early stages of the debate, was arrested and forced to sign a loyalty oath by the continental army. Once released he continued publishing Tory opinions, and his printing office was destroyed. The same type of thing happened to printers on the other side of the issue.

JAMES RIVINGTON AND THE TORY PRESS

Historians are still unsure of where the American public stood in the 1770s with regard to independence, but the public debate was dominated by those who favored separation from England. In the 1770s, it was hard to imagine a newspaper sympathetic to the colonies' remaining a part of Britain to stay in business. That was particularly so for the man who was the most prominent Tory-leaning editor, James Rivington.

Rivington was a charming, roguish bon vivant who had made a fortune in England as a bookseller and then had lost it gambling. He came to America and established a printing shop first in Philadelphia and later in New York. In 1773, seeing a good business opportunity for an informative, well-written newspaper, Rivington started the *New York Gazetteer.*

Rivington himself supported the British, but he opened his columns to those on the other side. The paper was hugely successful, reaching a circulation of 3,600 copies, but his editorial stands made many enemies during those fractious times. The separatists were not interested in a balanced debate. They demanded conversion to their point of view. Those who refused could be the objects of violence.

That's what happened to Rivington. In 1775 a mob destroyed his print shop and press. Rivington was apprehended and forced into signing a loyalty oath to the patriot cause. Once released, however, Rivington reverted to his old allegiance. Again, a mob attacked his offices, and Rivington fled to England. He returned a short time later to New York with the title of King's Printer for New York.

In truth, however, Rivington did not seem to have much enthusiasm for either side. In 1781, when the tide was turning toward the patriot cause, Rivington supplied George Washington with important information about the British. After New York was occupied by the American army, Rivington stayed in the city and took the British coat of arms off his door. His business, however, did not flourish, and he spent the rest of his life in relative poverty.

He became the object of much ridicule, including a sharp epigram from editor Phillip Freneau, who wrote "Rivington's Last Will and Testament." Part of it read:

Provided, however, and
  nevertheless,
That whatever estate I enjoy
  and possess
At the time of my death
  (if it be not then sold)
Shall remain to the Tories,
  to have and to hold.

News of the war effort spread fitfully throughout the colonies. The profession of journalism still had not progressed to the point of having reporters follow an army and write a summary of events. No system of news coverage had been developed that could supply information to printers or keep the public informed. Eyewitness accounts were used whenever they were available; second- and third-hand reports were more the norm. Each side touted its victories and downplayed its defeats. Many newspapers found the war difficult to deal with because of the shortage of equipment and supplies that it created, and some papers ceased publication altogether.

While the war itself was hard on the press, the debates that led up to it showed the power of newspapers to lead public opinion. Those lessons were learned and remembered as the new nation began to define itself.

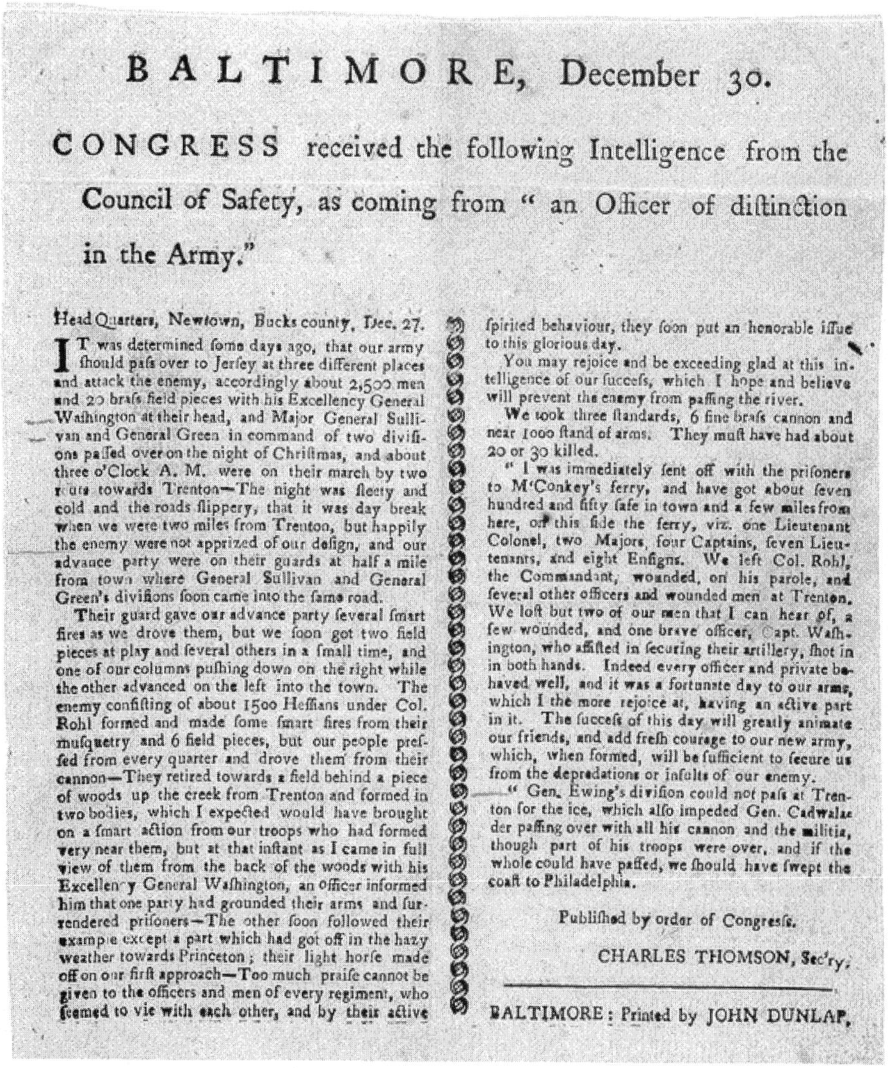

BALTIMORE, December 30.

CONGRESS received the following Intelligence from the Council of Safety, as coming from "an Officer of diſtinction in the Army."

Head Quarters, Newtown, Bucks county, Dec. 27.

IT was determined ſome days ago, that our army ſhould paſs over to Jerſey at three different places and attack the enemy, accordingly about 2,500 men and 20 braſs field pieces with his Excellency General Waſhington at their head, and Major General Sullivan and General Green in command of two diviſions paſſed over on the night of Chriſtmas, and about three o'Clock A. M. were on their march by two routs towards Trenton—The night was ſleety and cold and the roads ſlippery, that it was day break when we were two miles from Trenton, but happily the enemy were not apprized of our deſign, and our advance party were on their guards at half a mile from town where General Sullivan and General Green's diviſions ſoon came into the ſame road.

Their guard gave our advance party ſeveral ſmart fires as we drove them, but we ſoon got two field pieces at play and ſeveral others in a ſmall time, and one of our columns puſhing down on the right while the other advanced on the left into the town. The enemy conſiſting of about 1500 Heſſians under Col. Rohl formed and made ſome ſmart fires from their muſquetry and 6 field pieces, but our people preſſed from every quarter and drove them from their cannon—They retired towards a field behind a piece of woods up the creek from Trenton and formed in two bodies, which I expected would have brought on a ſmart action from our troops who had formed very near them, but at that inſtant as I came in full view of them from the back of the woods with his Excellency General Waſhington, an officer informed him that one party had grounded their arms and ſurrendered priſoners—The other ſoon followed their example except a part which had got off in the hazy weather towards Princeton; their light horſe made off on our firſt approach—Too much praiſe cannot be given to the officers and men of every regiment, who ſeemed to vie with each other, and by their active ſpirited behaviour, they ſoon put an honorable iſſue to this glorious day.

You may rejoice and be exceeding glad at this intelligence of our ſucceſs, which I hope and believe will prevent the enemy from paſſing the river.

We took three ſtandards, 6 fine braſs cannon and near 1000 ſtand of arms. They muſt have had about 20 or 30 killed.

"I was immediately ſent off with the priſoners to M'Conkey's ferry, and have got about ſeven hundred and fifty ſafe in town and a few miles from here, on this ſide the ferry, viz. one Lieutenant Colonel, two Majors, four Captains, ſeven Lieutenants, and eight Enſigns. We left Col. Rohl, the Commandant, wounded, on his parole, and ſeveral other officers and wounded men at Trenton. We loſt but two of our men that I can hear of, a few wounded, and one brave officer, Capt. Waſhington, who aſſiſted in ſecuring their artillery, ſhot in in both hands. Indeed every officer and private behaved well, and it was a fortunate day to our arms, which I the more rejoice at, having an active part in it. The ſucceſs of this day will greatly animate our friends, and add freſh courage to our new army, which, when formed, will be ſufficient to ſecure us from the depredations or inſults of our enemy.

"Gen. Ewing's diviſion could not paſs at Trenton for the ice, which alſo impeded Gen. Cadwalader paſſing over with all his cannon and the militia, though part of his troops were over, and if the whole could have paſſed, we ſhould have ſwept the coaſt to Philadelphia.

Publiſhed by order of Congreſs.

CHARLES THOMSON, Sec'ry.

BALTIMORE: Printed by JOHN DUNLAP.

FIGURE 20.4 **Baltimore Broadside** The broadside took on many forms, but it was usually a single sheet printed for a specific purpose. This broadside, printed in Baltimore on December 30, 1776, was the first announcement of the news of the American revolutionary forces' victory over the British at Trenton. The victory came after George Washington had ordered his men to cross the icy Delaware River on Christmas night. (Photo credit: Library of Congress)

Partisanship

With the war over in 1783 and independence won, the political landscape in America shifted. The major question that had occupied public discussion for more than two decades—whether or not the colonies would remain as part of the British

Empire—had been settled, but another one quickly took its place: Just what kind of a government and political system would the new nation have? The chief focus was on what kind of power the national and the state governments would exercise. The first government the states tried was the Articles of Confederation that left the federal government weak and the states with almost complete discretionary power. It did not work, and people on all sides knew that something else would have to be worked out.

Delegates from every state met in Philadelphia during the summer of 1787 to do just that. Under the leadership of people such as George Washington and James Madison, they worked out a Constitution that, while it did not answer every question, satisfied them enough to present it to the public. The delegates agreed that if nine of the thirteen states approved the Constitution, it would go into effect. Debates on the document occurred on a state-by-state basis, and for a time, the outcome was in some doubt. When the Constitution appeared to be failing, three of its chief proponents—James Madison, Alexander Hamilton, and John Jay—collaborated on a series of essays that was published in newspapers throughout the nation. These essays, later known as the *Federalist Papers,* were a high-minded articulation of the ideas the framers of the Constitution had about how it would work. (The *Federalist Papers* are still referred to regularly today when debates about the meaning of the Constitution come up.) Those essays represented the high point of journalism during this period.

What followed the institution of the new form of government and the election of Washington as president, however, was an era of partisanship and political infighting that would be shocking even to us today. Federalists were a loose coalition of those who felt the central government should be strong and should be able to enforce laws on the states. Nominally, they were led by George Washington, but Washington tried at all times to eschew partisanship. In reality, the Federalists were led by Alexander Hamilton and John Adams, the nation's first vice president. The Anti-Federalists (again, a very loose coalition) sought to preserve state prerogatives as much as possible; they were led by men such as Thomas Jefferson and James Madison.

More than at any other time in the nation's history, these coalitions (later to develop into political parties) exercised direct control over "their" newspapers. Newspaper editors saw themselves as the leading spokespersons for a political faction, and they did what they could to advance that faction's point of view. What these editors said about the opposing faction became increasingly bold and bitter. There were no rules and precedents for civil political debate. Opponents of a faction could be accused of all sorts of personal and social indiscretions and political highjinks. Even George Washington did not escape the battering ram of the opposition's newspapers.

Politicians even resorted to political appointments to keep "their" editors publishing. Accepting a government job, just as a postmastership or a clerk's appointment in a federal department, was nothing unusual for an editor or publisher. Each side used the power that it had to make sure that its point of view was heard, and editors had no scruples about any of this. John Fenno, editor of the *Gazette of the United States,* sided with the Federalists and got the printing contracts from the U.S.

Department of Treasury headed by Alexander Hamilton. Phillip Freneau, who published the *National Intelligencer* and spoke for the Anti-Federalists, received an appointment as a translator for the U.S. Department of State where Thomas Jefferson was in charge.

Vigorous debate is one thing, but the political discussions in the newspapers of the 1790s often degenerated into dialogues of disrespect and personal abuse. The new nation, through its newspapers, was learning to talk to itself, but the level and tone of discussion were as yet unsatisfactory. The low point of the period came not from the press but from the government. In 1798, with John Adams as president and Federalists in control of the legislature, Congress enacted the Alien and Sedition Acts. These laws made it a crime "to cause or procure to be written, printed, uttered or published . . . any false, scandalous, and malicious writing against the government of the United States or either house of Congress of the United States or the President of the United States. . . ." A number of prosecutions of Republican editors occurred under the law, but the danger of these laws to the political society that the nation was attempting to build was apparent. Though the Federalists were in power at the time, their hold on power was slipping, and the Alien and Sedition Acts have been viewed by some as a desperate attempt to maintain itself. The law expired after two years when Thomas Jefferson had assumed the presidency.

Newspapers experienced rapid growth through the 1790s. The decade began with about 91 newspapers and ended with about 234 in operation. Circulation sizes also grew. Equipment and supplies were somewhat easier to obtain. Literacy rates were high (as they had been all during the latter part of the century), and people were increasingly interested in what was happening with their new government.

Despite the extreme partisanship, some professional journalistic practices that were the precursors of what we would expect today began to emerge. Regular news coverage of the proceedings of Congress was a staple for many of these newspapers. While local news was still in short supply, newspapers shifted their outlook from foreign to domestic news. This change was helped by a law that allowed newspapers to send copies copies free to each other via the postal system. Newspapers would freely lift information from other papers for their own use.

But the major characteristic of any newspaper of the day was partisanship. A paper was expected to take sides in almost any dispute and to be a strong advocate for its faction. That partisanship would continue through the first two decades of the 1800s, but it abated because the Federalists had lost their leadership (John Adams had retired, and Alexander Hamilton had been killed in a duel) and their ability to attract a large number of adherents. No new faction or party had risen to take the place of the Federalists.

This era of partisanship ended on an important technological note for newspapers. The flatbed press, which had been a staple of printing since the days of Gutenberg, was replaced by the cylinder press. It required that single sheets be fed into it and pressed against a bed of type. The idea of the cylinder press had been around (as we saw earlier in this chapter) since the days of the Sumerians, but in the 1820s

R. Hoe and Company of New York introduced a press with large cylinders that greatly increased the speed with which the press could produce copies of the paper. That kind of speed would be necessary for what was ahead for American journalism.

QUESTIONS FOR DISCUSSION

1. The author makes the point that Roman rulers had to control their empire from the city of Rome. The federal government in Washington, DC, has to do the same thing. Can you see any parallels as to how this happens?

2. Many people have called the printing press the greatest invention of human beings. Do you agree? Can you think of any other invention that might rival it? (You might revisit this question after referring to Chapter 21.)

3. Why would people in authority have seen the printing press as a threat? What did they do about it?

4. Europeans began colonizing America in the early 1600s, but it was nearly a century before newspapers appeared. Why did it take so long? List and discuss all the reasons you can think of.

5. George Washington is a revered figure in American history today, but when he was president, he came in for blistering criticism from some of the newspapers of the day. Go to a book about Washington or a web site that might tell you some of the things these papers said. Compare them to some of the things that are said about politicians today.

RELATED WEB SITES

AEJMC History Division, www.utc.edu/~aejhist

American Journalism Historians Association, www.ajha.org

American Women's History: Journalism, www.mtsu.edu/~kmiddlet

Jhistory Home Page, www.h-net.msu.edu/~jhistory

Media History Project, http://mediahistory.umn.edu

United States Newspaper Project, www.neh.gov/projects/usnp.html

Women's History: Journalism, www.distinguishedwomen.com/subject/journ.html

READINGS AND REFERENCES

Blanchard, M. A. (Ed.). (1998). *History of the mass media in the United States, an encyclopedia.* Chicago: Fitzroy Dearborn Publishers.

Bliss, E. (1991). *Now the news: The story of broadcast journalism.* New York: Columbia University Press.

Briggs, A., & Burke, P. (2001). *A social history of the media from Gutenberg to the Internet.* Malden, MA: Blackwell.

Copeland, D. A. (2000). *Debating the issues in colonial newspapers.* Westport, CT: Greenwood Press.

Crowley, D. J., & Heyer, P. (2003). *Communication in history.* Boston: Allyn and Bacon.

Folkerts, J., & Teeter, D. L. Jr. (1997). *Voices of a nation: A history of mass media in the United States.* Boston: Allyn and Bacon.

Hartsock, J. C. (2000). *A history of American literary journalism: The emergence of a modern narrative form.* Amherst, MA: University of Massachusetts Press.

Hollis, D. W. (1995). *The media in America.* Santa Barbara, CA: ABC-CLIO, Inc.

Horan, J. D. (1955). *Mathew Brady: Historian with a camera.* New York: Bonanza.

Hudson, F. (2000). *Journalism in the United States from 1690–1872.* New York: Routledge.

Nord, D. P. (2001). *Communities of journalism: A history of American newspapers and their readers.* Urbana: University of Illinois Press.

Rafferty, A. M. (2000). *American journalism 1690–1904.* New York: Routledge.

Sloan, W. D. (1991). *Perspectives on mass communication history.* Hillsdale, NJ: Lawrence Erlbaum.

Sloan, W. D., & Parcell, L. M. (Eds.). (2002). *American journalism: History, principles, practices.* Jefferson, NC: McFarland & Company.

Sloan, W. D., Stovall, J. G., & Startt, J. D. (1999). *The media in America: A history* (4th ed.). Northport, AL: Vision.

Startt, J. D., & Sloan, W. D. (1994). *The significance of the media in American history.* Northport, AL: Vision Press.

Ward, H. H. (1997). *Mainsteams of American media history.* Boston: Allyn & Bacon.

Williams, J. H. (1999). *The significance of the printed word in early America: Colonists' thoughts on the role of the press.* Westport, CT: Greenwood Press.

21

Journalism Comes of Age

Key Concepts and Terms

1. The nineteenth century was a time of enormous change in the lives of Americans. One element of that change was the speed at which they were able to communicate. Another was the development of photography, which opened up a visual world of communication that had never before existed.

2. Journalism changed its very nature during the nineteenth century. Newspapers went from being organs of opinion to organs of information, and their audiences expanded to include more Americans than ever.

3. Journalism of the nineteenth century is often defined by the personalities who dominated the field—people such as James Gordon Bennett and Horace Greeley and, later in the century, Joseph Pulitzer and William Randolph Hearst.

4. Penny press: inexpensive newspapers (which often sold for a penny) that first appeared in the 1830s and that appealed to a large audience with stories of crime, human interest, and sports.

5. Abolition: the term used for the movement to abolish slavery; the fight over abolition was the great political issue of the first part of the nineteenth century affecting everything in political life, including journalism.

6. By the middle of the century, magazines had found their form and audience.

7. Photography was invented in 1839, and although it would be many years before photographs could be easily mass produced, photography began to change the way journalism was practiced by the mid-1800s.

8. The Civil War, 1861–1865, demonstrated profoundly the value of news to American news organizations and to their audiences.

Vignette

Many people who lived through a good part of the twentieth century have pronounced it the century of change. Certainly, knowledge expanded at an enormous rate during those years, and the technological changes were vast. We will be discussing some of those in Chapter 23. People who comment about all of the changes in the twentieth century sometimes imply that nothing like that had ever happened before.

Actually, it had. Profound changes in human activity and outlook occurred as well during the nineteenth century. Many of those changes set the stage for what we experienced in the twentieth century and will experience in the current century.

Imagine a young man born in 1815 in a mountainous county in western Virginia who lives until he is 80 years old. The president at the time he is born is James Madison, one of the founding fathers of the nation and the man chiefly responsible for the United States Constitution. The young man's father likely moved to that county years before and settled there to build a self-sufficient farm on which he could raise his family. He probably never traveled more than twenty miles from home after he settled there, and the young man did not travel outside the county either.

The young man could read, and books and newspapers were available to him. But the newspapers he read had news from faraway places, such as Washington, DC, New York, Boston, and even London, and the events the news stories referred to were weeks or even months old. Growing up, the boy would have no clear idea what these places looked like, how people in cities such as these lived, or how they dressed and spoke.

Closer to home, the boy wore clothes made for him by his mother, possibly from cloth purchased at a local store but just as likely from homespun wool made from sheep raised on the farm. Very little in the house was manufactured. Tools and household goods were handmade. Heat came from wood fireplaces, and oil lamps provided some light to pierce the darkness after sundown.

Once during the boy's childhood, a traveling artist came through the area and painted several small portraits of some of the people living there. The wealthier people had larger portraits. The artist was paid by some in cash and by others with what goods they made on their farms.

Travelers and occasionally relatives would come by, talking about the opportunities and the land—the unlimited quantities of land—that existed west of the mountains. The United States now owned most of the land west of the Mississippi River, a river so vast that the boy could not imagine it, and these travelers were headed there, convinced their future was there. Of course, they always talked politics. John Quincy Adams had stolen the election of 1824, they said; Andrew Jackson was a man of the people. Later they began to talk about how the federal government should leave the states alone to do as they pleased, especially on the question of slavery. Not many people owned slaves around the area where the boy grew up.

The young boy inherited his father's farm when he grew up. He married and had several children, some of whom survived their childhood and some of whom did not. He had once dreamed of moving west, but the family and the farm kept him there.

By the time he died at age 80 in 1895, the world had changed profoundly from his boyhood. The great public event of his life was the Civil War; two of his sons had fought for the Union, and one had been wounded. The area in which he lived was part of the state of Virginia at the beginning of the war but had seceded to form the state of West Virginia. Many people in the county now worked in the coal mines, which was difficult and dangerous work, and were thinking about joining a workers' organization called a union. When times were good, people had more cash than he had ever seen, but there also had been some bad times when some people just couldn't make ends meet.

The man had had his first picture taken by a traveling photographer sometime in the 1850s. It looked just like him; his wife kept it in the back of the family Bible. His picture was taken a couple of other times, too. Several years before his death, the man had traveled to Charleston, West Virginia, where some of his grandchildren and great-grandchildren lived. There he had seen electric lights, indoor plumbing, and large factories that manufactured all sorts of things. He had also read the newspaper published there; it contained news about local people and events that had occurred the day before. It even had news from Washington and Europe that did not seem very old. One of his great-grandchildren said that a friend of hers had a telephone in her house. She even took him by the house, a sprawling Victorian mansion that seemed larger than his farm. She said her friend's father was rich and had made his money in coal mines and railroads.

At the man's funeral, the men talked politics—something about reform and populism. People said one of these days, the rich would no longer be in control.

Change and More Change

The events of the life of the man just described intersect with many of the changes that occurred in communication and journalism in the nineteenth century. Those changes established the basis for the journalism that we know and practice today. In this chapter and the next, we will discuss how those changes occurred and the people who were responsible for them.

Here are some of the most important developments in journalism in the nineteenth century:

■ Journalists of the nineteenth century developed many of the modern customs and conventions of journalism. Particularly important is the definition of news and news events. Journalists began to give regular and systematic coverage to politics, which changed politics profoundly, and they began to cover other parts of society that had never received attention (such as business news) or simply had not existed (such as organized sporting events).

- Technical innovations occurred throughout the century that opened up new opportunities for journalism. The two most important were the speed at which information could be transmitted and the invention and development of photography.

- Audiences for journalism expanded. In the 1700s journalism consumers were intellectuals and those interested in politics, but in the next century, journalists discovered that people were interested in all parts of society. America was still a nation of newspaper readers, but in the nineteenth century there were many more people and many more readers.

- Journalism, and particularly newspapers, became big business. Money was to be made by those bright enough or lucky enough to satisfy an audience, and some people made huge fortunes. Advertising became a vital part of the journalism formula; merchants and manufacturers needed the nation's newspapers to sell their products and were willing to pay for space there.

- Newspapers changed from partisan voices to businesses with editorial opinions. Journalists were no longer always linked to a political faction. News coverage took on a neutral tone, and journalists developed a sense of being independent observers of an event. Some newspapers claimed to represent their readers rather than a set of politicians.

- Still, journalism in the nineteenth century was never very far from politics. The great issues of the era were sectionalism, slavery, and the government's activities in the business environment, and newspapers had plenty to say about all of these things.

- The nineteenth century was an era of great personalities in journalism. A few people exercised profound influence on the profession and its practices.

- The century also witnessed a new and expanded role for women in the profession. Women were certainly present in the journalistic world before the 1900s, but they were often anonymous. The 1900s saw women act as reporters and editors, proudly exhibiting their names and gender. By the end of the century, they were still restricted in what they could do within the profession, but the progress they had made to that point was extraordinary.

- Finally, the nineteenth century saw the rise of a new medium, the magazine. Its purpose and content were different from the newspaper, but its usefulness to an audience was unmistakable.

The Penny Press

The idea of a cheap newspaper, paid for at the time of purchase and not by subscription, was phenomenally successful and changed journalism profoundly in the 1830s, but it was no sure thing. A number of entrepreneurs had the idea—in fact, it had already been tried successfully in London—but getting the formula right was not simple. The idea was that in a large city such as New York with a population that most newspapers had ignored, a newspaper could be sold on the streets for a penny. A penny wasn't much. Heretofore, a newspaper's revenue came mainly through subscriptions and party contributions. Subscribers were notoriously unreliable about paying, and party officials kept the editor under their yoke.

An early failure was that of Horace Greeley, who later enjoyed great success with penny newspapers. He copublished the *Morning Post* with Horatio David Sheppard, but their planning was ill-starred. They produced their first issue on January 1, 1833, a holiday rather than a workday when the streets were likely to be full. In addition, a snowstorm had fallen on New York the night before, so what street traffic there might have been was blocked. The paper had not been advertised, so no one had been given an opportunity to subscribe. The paper never recovered from the initial setbacks and was soon out of business.

Benjamin Day, like Greeley, another struggling job printer, also wanted to produce a cheap paper, but he saw the failure that Greeley had experienced and was reluctant. He had financial backers willing to try, however, so in September 1833, he brought out the *New York Sun*. The paper was a combination of news, shipping notices, and police items, as well as poetry and short stories; a third of the four-page issue was advertising. For a penny, it was a bargain.

That was the verdict of the public. Newsboys sold enough copies of the paper each day to keep it going and to quickly turn a profit for its owners. The *Sun* deemphasized politics and concentrated on human interests and on stories about the people who bought it. By 1838, it was selling about 34,000 copies a day, enough for Day to sell it for about $38,000. The *Sun* had started a trend in newspapering, but it was left to another publisher to see how far that trend could be pushed.

James Gordon Bennett and the *New York Herald*

James Gordon Bennett had a big idea. He wanted to publish a newspaper that would change the world, a newspaper that would be "the great organ and pivot of government, society, commerce, finance, religion and all human civilization." While his *New York Herald* fell somewhat short of that lofty goal, it did change journalism in ways that are still being felt many decades later.

Bennett was another of the entrepreneurs who saw the possibilities of the cheap newspaper. But his vision went beyond just making money—though make money he did. Bennett sought to decalcify the language that journalists used. The *New York Herald,* begun in 1835, used words of the street rather than words of the parlor— "legs" rather than "limbs," "petticoats and pantaloons" rather than "inexpressibles." That was shocking to middle- and upper-class New York, but Bennett knew that his audience was elsewhere. He declared his political independence and freely criticized the government, financial institutions, and organized religion. His reporters covered crime news in detail, talking about battered women and shocking murders. His reporters and editors produced copy that was easy to read and understand by avoiding clichés and vague phrases.

Possibly Bennett's most important contribution to the definition of news was timeliness. Bennett realized that news was a perishable product. The faster it could be produced and distributed, the better it was. He also realized that people would prefer the newspaper that published information first, and he was determined for the *Herald* always to be first with the newspapers. Other editors had been willing to wait for two weeks for a report from Washington about what was happening in Congress. Bennett was not. He went to extraordinary lengths to get information into the *Herald* faster than other newspapers. Then he advertised the fact, making other papers seem like slackers. Who would buy the *Sun* when the *Herald* had the latest news?

Bennett's fellow publishers hated him. They hated him because of the *Herald*'s shocking content. They hated him because the *Herald* consistently beat them in news coverage. They hated him because he was so personally arrogant. In 1840, they organized what become known as the Moral War against him and his newspaper. They tried to persuade businesses to withdraw their advertising from the *Herald*. They tried to convince hotels to ban the *Herald,* and they called those who read the *Herald* immoral and antireligious. One editor even physically attacked Bennett in the street.

The Moral War did have some effect on curbing some of the rhetorical excesses in the *Herald*. The *Herald* lost circulation, and Bennett toned down some of the language to get it back, but his general journalistic fervor was unabated. He continued his quest always to have the news first. He tried to get news in every conceivable way, it seems. When steamships cut travel time to and from Europe from six weeks to less than three weeks, Bennett hired boats to meet the ships and get the news before the steamships came into port. Other newspapers did the same thing. Bennett at one time had people meeting ships in Boston and then sending him the news by carrier pigeon. Again other newspapers did the same thing. Then Bennett extended his carrier pigeon line to Halifax, Nova Scotia, to get news even faster. At that point, other papers hired sharpshooters to try to down the pigeons in flight. (Most of the pigeons survived.)

FIGURE 21.1   James Gordon Bennett James Gordon Bennett was ambitious and brilliant. He wanted to be remembered simply for his name, which he hoped would come to represent "one of the great benefactors of the human race." Bennett understood the essential nature of news—timeliness—and he always made every effort to get the latest news into his newspaper, the *New York Herald.*

These attempts to get news first were soon overcome by one of the nineteenth century's most important inventions, the telegraph. The first telegraph line was established between Washington and Baltimore. Bennett exploited the telegraph and tried to maintain a monopoly, but other newspapers banded together to form the precursor to today's Associated Press. Still, the competition among New York newspapers to get news first was fierce, and that aspect of journalism has remained to the present day.

Bennett introduced other basic concepts into the world of journalism. One of the most important was his attention to women and "women's news." In 1855 Bennett hired Jane Cunningham Croly, known to her readers as "Jennie June," who wrote about society, fashion, and beauty. She later left the *Herald* and wrote the first nationally syndicated column for women, founded the Women's Press Club of New York City, and in 1889 became the first woman appointed to teach journalism at the college level. Bennett demanded that advertising be as fresh as the paper's news. He stopped the practice of running the same ad again and again for months; he decreed that no advertisement could be run for more than two weeks and by 1848 was demanding that ads be changed every day.

By 1850 organized sporting clubs were forming in metropolitan areas in New York, and a new game—baseball—was becoming popular. Bennett's *Herald* produced some of the first sports writing in American journalism and gave regular coverage to the competition of these athletic clubs. He started a "personals" classified advertising column. When the occasion demanded it, he gave entire pages over to illustration rather than type, beginning the concept of visual journalism. Bennett also set up a series of foreign correspondents in most of the major cities in Europe, and he hired stringer correspondents throughout the nation and in Canada and Mexico. Those in Mexico became especially important when the Mexican War broke out in 1846.

The Mexican War freed the territory of Texas from the control of Mexico and ultimately gave the United States much of what is referred to as the Southwest today. Bennett and the *Herald* not only had their correspondents, but Bennett had also worked out an agreement with George W. Kendall, a cofounder of the *New Orleans Picayune,* to share information. Kendall was with General Zachary Taylor for much of the action and set up a series of riders to get the news back to Vera Cruz or another port in Mexico. From there ships would take the information to New Orleans. Then a set of 60 riders sped the information to Richmond, Virginia, which was then the southern tip of the telegraph system. Despite all these efforts, it still took about two weeks for northern readers to get news of the war. Still, covering the war taught reporters and editors much about getting information and this lesson would be useful for the next big conflict to come, the American Civil War.

Sectionalism, Slavery, and Abolition

The U.S. Constitution resolved many questions and conflicts about the American political system when it was adopted in 1789, but it did not solve the most fractious question: what powers would the federal government, and through it the people of a different region, have to impose their will on a state or region? The question specif-

FIGURE 21.2   Sports Coverage One of the great innovations that James Gordon Bennett made was an emphasis on sports coverage. Sports was becoming a more organized activity in social life in America, and the new game of baseball was taking hold. Some form of the game had been played since the 1820s, and many trace its origins back to the English game of rounders. Contrary to the image that many have of the beginnings of baseball, it was not a game that was played in bucolic fields. It was a city game, and the first real baseball was played by teams fielded by social clubs in the major cities, particularly New York and Boston. Even today, major league baseball teams have the word *club* in their official name as a connection to the beginnings of organized baseball.

ically revolved around the issue of slavery. As states were added to the Union in the early days of the republic, careful attention was paid to keep a numerical balance in Congress between those states that allowed slavery and those that did not. The hope was that the vexing question of slavery would somehow work itself out at some point in the near future.

It did not. Instead, by 1820 it seemed that slavery was as much entrenched in the South as it had been fifty years before. Many who had hoped for an end to slavery felt frustrated and betrayed. The South, they felt, had argued for years that it should be left alone to find its own solution to this problem. The solution it seemed to be finding was to grow more dependent on the slave economy.

SAMUEL F. B. MORSE: WHAT HATH GOD WROUGHT!

Samuel F. B. Morse was not a journalist, but he had as much to do with changing the profession in the nineteenth century as any American. Morse was a remarkable man, possessing a keen, inquiring, and inventive mind and the ability to inspire the same qualities in others.

Morse is most famous for the Morse code, a system of long and short clicks that enabled the telegraph to become a life-changing communication device in the 1840s. Morse did more than invent the code, however. He was instrumental in the invention of the telegraph itself.

Morse became fascinated by electricity while a student at Yale in the early part of the century, but he and others could see little practical use for it. Instead, Morse decided to become a painter and gained fame as one of the finest portrait artists in the country. He even studied for a time in Paris, where he met Louis Daguerre, the inventor of an early process that produced photographs called daguerreotypes.

When Morse returned to the United States, he advanced the cause of photography by encouraging others to pursue it. One of those he encouraged and trained was Matthew Brady.

What continued to fascinate Morse, however, was electricity and the idea that it could be used, somehow, to transmit messages over long distances. In 1837 Morse applied for a patent on a telegraph machine and sought financial backers to help him build a telegraph system. Few people could see the value of it, and Morse lived in poverty for several years trying to perfect his system and raise money.

Morse managed to secure some funds from Congress in the 1840s— enough to place telegraph poles from Baltimore to Washington, DC. In May 1844, he sat in the U.S. Capitol Building in Washington, DC, and tapped out a message that was received almost instantly in Baltimore. The message read, "What hath God wrought!"

What Morse had wrought was a revolution in communication. Never had people been able to send messages so far so fast. Within two years, telegraph lines stretched from Washington to Buffalo, New York, and Boston, Massachusetts. By 1853, every state east of the Mississippi except Florida was connected.

Morse became a wealthy man and remained an active businessman and public figure for many years. He died at the age of 80 in 1872. His home, Locus Grove, near Poughkeepsie, New York, is a national landmark (www.morse historicsite.org) and many of his papers are housed in the Library of Congress (http://memory.loc.gov/ammem/atthtml/mrshome.html).

Antislavery societies began to spring up in many parts of the North and upper South. These societies had as their goal the end of slavery in the United States. Some wanted it immediately; others gradually. Some wanted free Negroes sent back to Africa; others wanted them to have full citizenship. Occasionally, there was a call for slaves to rise up in violent revolt against their masters. More frequently, members of these societies sought to help slaves escape, often to Canada where they would not be deported.

No one in the South who owned slaves or who believed in a slave-based economy viewed these antislavery societies as benign. Even those societies and groups that called for a gradual end to slavery with compensation to slave owners for their losses were seen as a threat, not just to an economic system but also to a way of life and sometimes to life itself. What many slave owners feared most was a slave revolt, and they felt that any sentiments expressed about freeing the slaves might spark such a revolt. Even to discuss the possibility of abolition was to encourage such danger, and slaveholders and sympathizers could not abide that.

Abolitionist societies gained added potency when they began to publish their own newspapers. The first such paper was the *Manumission Intelligencer,* published by Elijah Embree in the east Tennessee mountain town of Jonesborough in 1819. His publication was followed by many others, a few of which became highly influential and gained fame for their editors. The best of these early publications was the *Genius of Universal Emancipation,* first published in 1821 by Benjamin Lundy. The paper was begun in Boston but later moved to Baltimore in search of more support. The *Genius of Universal Emancipation* suffered from the same ailments that plagued subsequent abolitionist papers—too few subscribers and too little money. And even among people who might be sympathetic to the abolitionist cause, there was a feeling that the moral certainty of the editors made discussion of the issue difficult and any compromise solution impossible.

Still, editors like Lundy were morally certain and said so many times in many ways. Lundy was an early voice for emancipation, but in the late 1820s, he took on a partner who would become the greatest abolitionist editor of them all, William Lloyd Garrison. His writing shockingly powerful, Garrison advocated immediate freedom for all slaves; he also thought black people were equal in every way to whites and wanted them to have full citizenship.

Such sentiments proved unpalatable for most citizens of the North and South. Garrison spent some time in jail because he could not pay a libel judgment against him. The article in question concerned the owner of a slave ship whom he equated with "highway robbers and murderers." When he was released, he left Lundy to begin his own newspaper. On January 1, 1831, *The Liberator* was born in Boston, and because of Garrison's commitment and style, the paper had a wide reach. Its circulation never passed 600, but Garrison's

FIGURE 21.3 William Lloyd Garrison
No one in the 1840s and 1850s possessed a stronger voice in favor of emancipation than William Lloyd Garrison, editor of *The Liberator.* He was considered the ultimate extremist on the issue because he argued that slaves were human beings, in no way inferior to whites. He not only wanted emancipation but also full rights of citizenship, including suffrage. Most strong proponents of emancipation were unwilling to go that far.

consistency in articulating his point of view made abolition a priority issue and framed many of the lines of the debate.

Garrison's advocacy did not include violence. He did not encourage slave revolts or white-led movements to free slaves. Still, his voice was so strong in favor of his cause that many felt he did not have to explicitly advocate revolution. The Georgia legislature offered $4,000 for the arrest of Garrison, and elsewhere in the South his newspaper was banned. He was attacked by a mob in Boston, and even fellow journalists often failed to protect his right to speak and write what he thought.

Garrison's fervor, though not his style and impact, were matched by others during the decades long debate over sectionalism and slavery. Being an abolitionist advocate could be dangerous. Elijah Lovejoy, an editor in St. Louis, Missouri, criticized a local judge for his leniency toward a mob that committed a racial murder, and he was told to get out of town. He moved his press across the Mississippi River to Alton, Illinois, and continued editorializing against slavery. Mobs twice charged his office and threw his printing press in the river. When he started again for the third time in 1837, the mob descended on his office and killed him.

Another powerful voice in the antislavery movement was that of Frederick Douglass, a former slave, who was editor of the *North Star* (later merged under the name *Frederick Douglass's Paper*). Douglass's paper spoke to a free black readership, urging them to improve themselves but also describing the restrictions they faced in a white-dominated society. Douglass was more than just an editor, however. He was a powerful speaker and a shrewd organizer and was easily the most famous black man of his time.

Among the mainstream press, the most ardent advocate of abolition was Horace Greeley, editor of the *New York Tribune*. Greeley held many radical political views. Not only was he staunchly antislavery, but also for a time he advocated socialism, and the *Tribune* carried a number of articles by the London-based Karl Marx. Greeley advocated prohibition (laws against selling alcohol), labor unions, and westward expansion. He was against capital punishment. Greeley was a powerful voice in favor of the election of Abraham Lincoln and was himself a losing presidential candidate in 1872.

Greeley's genius, however, was not the causes that he espoused but the personality that he imbued in the *Tribune*. He instituted many innova-

FIGURE 21.4   Horace Greeley One of the most interesting characters of the nineteenth century, Horace Greeley advocated abolition, socialism (for a time), Republicanism, and westward expansion. He had a great talent for making his newspaper, the *New York Tribune,* interesting to read—so much so that loyal subscribers came to consider it a necessity. Greeley refused to print accounts of sensational trials, theater, or reports from police courts, and the *Tribune* became known as the "Great Moral Organ."

tions to the journalistic world, including hiring the first woman to work regularly as a reporter and foreign correspondent. His weekly *Tribune* circulated throughout the nation, and one journalism historian of the period wrote that many people considered their Bible, Shakespeare, and the *Tribune* as the "three necessities of spiritual life."

Proslavery advocates generally did not establish newspapers specifically to advance their cause. They could count on the established press, particularly in the South. Newspapers there defended the institution in a variety of ways, and they had no trouble in pointing out the excesses of abolitionists or the damage they were doing to a way of life that many found comfortable and preferable to an increasingly industrialized North. As voices on both sides of the issue became increasingly shrill, a few southern editors were known as "fire-eaters," extremists who said that the South should secede from the union.

One such editor was Robert Barnwell Rhett of the *Charleston Mercury*. As early as 1837, he was writing that the South could no longer count on the federal government to protect its institutions or economy and that it might have to go its own way. Rhett came to believe in the future of an independent South so much that he envisioned a southern nation that would control its own economy and stretch from the Atlantic to the Pacific. When the South did secede in 1861, Rhett's was the first signature on the new constitution.

The Growth of Magazines

American readers wanted more than news and politics, however, and the nineteenth century saw the development of a different medium that would add to the culture that was American society. That medium was the magazine. Magazines had been in existence in some form since the early 1700s, but in these early years it was hard to distinguish between a magazine and a newspaper. Even then though, magazine editors sought to include in their publications poetry, literature, and commentary that readers would not necessarily find in newspapers. Magazines, though they might contain political content, were not part of the political environment in the same way that newspapers were. The high partisan years of the early republic (see the previous chapter) helped draw this distinction more clearly.

During the 1830s, with newspapers emphasizing news and politics—and, above all, speed—magazines became even more distinctive. They were published weekly or monthly, and their time frames for presenting information were much longer. Also distinguishing them from newspapers was the fact that many magazines appealed to special interests of the audience. There were publications that were solely concerned with fashion, literature, and scientific discovery.

In the early years of magazine publishing, editors struggled to find supplies and to find original editorial matter that was worth printing. They also had many problems with distribution because of the unreliability of the postal system. As the republic grew, these problems abated, and by the 1830s printing technology had advanced to make producing a magazine far easier. The postal system, too, had improved so that editors and readers could be confident that subscriptions would be filled.

Editorial content worthy of publication was still a problem, but the growing awareness of American writers of the country's assets and distinctiveness gave rise to an American genre of literature. Writers such as William Cullen Bryant, Nathaniel Hawthorne, James Fenimore Cooper, and Ralph Waldo Emerson were beginning to find their voices, and the magazine offered them the perfect outlet for their work. Edgar Allen Poe was another of America's foremost writers who worked to perfect the short story form, a form ideally suited to the periodical. Poe, whom many credit for inventing the mystery story, was editor for a short time of the *Southern Literary Messenger* published in Richmond, Virginia.

Many Americans, too, particularly in the middle and upper classes, were developing a reading habit, and they craved material that would satisfy this demand and help them pass the time. Americans also sought to educate themselves, developing a philosophy that the acquisition of knowledge could have not just moral benefits but economic benefits as well. Magazines offered them a chance to slow down lives that seemed to be accelerating at a dizzying pace. They could spend an evening reading a magazine to one another and discussing its contents.

Some of the most successful of the early genre magazines were those directed toward women. For more than eight years (1828–1836), Sara Josepha Hale published her *Ladies' Magazine* in Boston; it was a magazine filled with fashion news and helpful domestic advice. It was followed by the most successful of the early women's magazines, *Gody's Lady's Book,* published out of Philadelphia by Louis Gody. This magazine had huge appeal and gained a subscription list of an astonishing 40,000 by 1850.

The invention of photography indirectly affected magazines and helped make them more distinctive. The halftone process by which photographs could be integrated into the printing of publications had not been invented yet, so magazines and newspapers could not easily use photos. Photographs opened a world of possibilities for journalists, however. With photography, viewers for the first time could see faraway people and places, things they had never seen before. The technology of photography could bring these pictures into existence relatively quickly.

Photographs, which could not be used directly, gave rise to a realistic genre of illustration that had never been known before. Illustrators could look at photographs rather than having to go out and see the real-life objects. They could arrange those objects in various ways. Magazines soon developed several processes for using photographs to create illustrations that would be used in the printing of publication. One such process was to simply trace a photograph onto a smooth block of wood. Engravers would then chisel out the negative space of the photo—that is, the space where no ink should form. Once the chiseling was done, the block could be tied into the matrix along with the other type on a page so that a printing mold could be made. Wood engravers worked at this process mostly anonymously; they rarely received credit for their labors. Yet they produced thousands of extraordinarily detailed and beautiful illustrations that today are considered some of the period's best artwork.

General interest magaiznes, such as *Harper's Magazine* and *Frank Leslie's Illustrated Newspaper,* used large numbers of illustrations on their pages, and these and other publications were constantly working to improve the process. Because maga-

PHOTOGRAPHING THE RICH AND FAMOUS

Less than a decade after it was invented in Europe in 1839, photography became the rage in America. A number of Americans studied the process, and a few decided that money could be made from it. One of those was Matthew Brady.

Brady opened a photographic studio in New York City in 1844. He took advantage of the universal curiosity about the photographic process by inviting every famous person who came to the city to his studio to have his or her picture taken. The result of Brady's promotion is a remarkable collection of pictures of the glitterati of the mid-nineteenth century. It also made Brady the most famous photographer in America.

Brady's most important photograph was taken in 1860 when Abraham Lincoln came to town. Lincoln had been prominently mentioned as a presidential candidate of the young and growing Republican Party. He had left Illinois to complete a speaking tour in the Northeast, and

in February he was scheduled to address an audience at the Cooper Institute. On the day of the address, Lincoln went to Brady's studio at 359 Broadway. The photograph Brady took was widely used by engravers during the next few months, so that most of the nation knew what Lincoln looked like.

The speech that Lincoln gave that evening was his most famous to date. Speaking on the issue of slavery and its threat to the nation, Lincoln established himself as a serious presidential possibility in front of a Northeastern audience. Lincoln later said, "Brady and the Cooper Institute made me president."

Brady's name today is associated with the many photographs he and his associates took during the Civil War. But we would have known about him anyway because before 1861 he had already been photographing the rich and famous.

zines did not have to be produced on a daily basis, printers and engravers had more time than their counterparts on newspapers. The use of illustrations was another factor that made magazines distinctive.

Highly detailed illustrations had another effect on magazines and their readers, too. People did not have to read—or even know how to read—to view an illustration and to be entertained and informed about it. Most people in America at that time did know how to read, of course, but photography and illustration provided another means of presenting information that did not depend on type or literacy. It allowed people to form pictures in their heads about the world around them. That effect was one of the most important of the nineteenth century.

The Civil War

The period of war between the southern states and the rest of the country during 1861 to 1865 was the nation's most traumatic moment. It was also the nineteenth century's most dramatic and important news event. As all wars do, the Civil War called on every part of society to respond, sometimes in new and creative ways. American journalism did just that. Speed in gathering information and visual presentation of information—the two technical and content factors that had been developed before the war—had opportunities to develop more fully because of the demands of the conflict.

The war did not just suddenly happen, of course. The debates that led up to it had been going on for decades, and the discussions and events surrounding the issue of slavery in the 1850s had been particularly intense. Events such as the *Dred Scott* decision (in which the Supreme Court said that slaves could not be citizens and that Congress could not ban slavery from any territory); the fight over the Kansas territory; John Brown's raid on the military post at Harper's Ferry, Virginia; and Brown's subsequent trial and hanging were written about at length by the newspapers and magazines of the day and followed closely by the reading public. Abraham Lincoln's election as president in 1860 was the final blow for many proslavery advocates and secessionists. Although Lincoln denied that he had any plans to end slavery, Southerners could see that the rest of the country was demanding that the debate be put to rest, and the only means for doing that ultimately was abolition.

Among southern newspapers, there was little variance in opinion. Social pressures made almost all of them proslavery and eventually prosecessionist. A newspaper in the South simply could not survive—and, indeed, its editor and offices were in danger—if it took any other position. Northern newspaper opinion was more divided. Many newspapers said the Union could not be divided, and the South would have to be forced to return. Others, including the abolitionist Horace Greeley at one point, favored letting the South separate peacefully from the Union. Still others counseled both sides to continue negotiation so that conflict could be avoided.

It was too late for that. Early in 1861 the secessionist movement caught fire, and there seemed to be little anyone could do about that. South Carolinians demanded that the U.S. Army withdraw from its fortifications at Ft. Sumter in April, and when the commander refused, the Confederates of South Carolina opened fire. The war had begun.

In one sense, the nation was prepared for the demands that people would have for information about the conflict. The national telegraph system had grown from one line between Washington, DC, and Baltimore in the mid-1840s to more than 50,000 miles worth of lines in 1861. No war had ever been fought before during which information could be transmitted so quickly. That fact alone meant that this would be a profoundly different conflict, particularly for the news media.

In another sense, the newspapers—especially the larger newspapers in the larger northern cities—were prepared for the conflict. They had been refining their definition of news for three decades, and they had been honing their abilities to gather and process information quickly. This war promised to give them the opportunity to put all of their skills to use and also to gain readers and advertisers in the process. James Gordon Bennett's *New York Herald* claimed to have put sixty reporters into its war coverage, and other newspapers and magazines made similar commitments.

Despite these preparations, just about everything about the coverage of this war was new. There were few models or precedents to say how reporters should behave, where they should be, or even what they should be covering. The major battles, of course, were news items of greatest importance, but strategy and movement of armies turned out to be tremendously significant in this war. Some commanders welcomed reporters, hoping for favorable press reports to enhance their political standing in Washington and back home. Most generals, however, came to view reporters as a nuisance at best and even as a danger to their army. Reporters wrote about where the army was, what they were preparing for, and how many troops were available. Their newspapers sometimes printed maps tracing the army's movements—information that could be made readily available to the enemy. Reporters also pointed out flaws in command or strategy, sometimes relying on disgruntled junior officers or even more disgruntled enlisted men. Generals felt as though they had enough problems without having to deal with meddlesome reporters.

The tensions of this uneasy relationship produced the first modern methods of censorship of the news media by the armed forces. It is one of the many legacies of the Civil War to journalism that continues to this day. The war also proved how ineffective censorship could be in stopping a reporter determined to get information to his news organization. The war departments in Washington and Richmond, the Confederate capital, as well as the generals in the field, tried to limit what reporters saw and wrote. The simplest way to do this was to deny and limit their access to the telegraph lines; military censors would often read and delete information they felt put troops at risk. They also deleted material that made the army look bad, including on more than one occasion news of the army's defeat or retreat.

In one such instance, Henry Villard of the *New York Tribune* witnessed the battle of Fredericksburg in December 1863 and realized how badly the Union army had been beaten. He slipped off to Washington, DC, to try to scoop his fellow correspondents on a spectacular story only to be frustrated by Army censors who would not allow it to be transmitted. Villard then hired a special messenger to get his graphically told article to New York, but he ran up against another frustration. The *Tribune* would not print it; instead it ran a tepid account of the battle that did not inform readers of its true nature or conclusion. The pro-Republican *Tribune* was reluctant

FIGURE 21.5   Newspaper Vendors People back home were anxious to get news of the war, but so were the soldiers. They often had very little idea of where they were or where they were going. That's why newspaper carts such as the one pictured here were part of the entourage that followed the army, particularly in Virginia where Union forces were massed. (Photo credit: Library of Congress)

to tell its audience and the rest of the world that the Union forces had suffered yet another defeat. That year had not gone well for the Union or the Republicans, who had suffered a number of losses in the midterm elections in November. News of yet another defeat might tip public opinion against continuing the fight.

But the information Villard had was sought by at least one Republican— Abraham Lincoln. The president, desperate for details of the battle, asked Villard to come to the White House and describe to him what the reporter had seen. Villard, not wanting to be the one to give bad news to the president, tried to put the best face on what had happened, but he finally blurted out that this had been the Union's worst defeat of the war. Despite the efforts of Army censors and some Republican politicians and editors, word filtered out over the few days after the battle that the Union army had been completely repulsed, and Lincoln had yet another political crisis on his hands.

Such was the complex and conflicting nature of the work of correspondents who covered the war and those who tried to manage information about it. What correspondents saw and heard was important, but the way they interpreted this information was also important. Nor was it always easy to arrive at a conclusion. Sometimes the outcome of a battle was unclear. Even in the case of Fredericksburg, some correspondents had trouble in the early hours after the battle deciding if it was a victory or defeat for the Union. Few correspondents had any experience with the military or in covering a military campaign. Reporters for newspapers from the Confederacy faced all of the same difficulties of their northern counterparts but often with fewer resources. They too were subjected to censorship and to the difficulties of interpreting what they saw. Still, all of those involved realized that information had consequences whether it informed the enemy of troop movements or influenced public opinion.

And information was what the public demanded. The appetite for war news—even when the news was not good—was insatiable. One reason was that so many people were personally involved. Whenever word got out that a major battle was underway, crowds would gather at the newspaper office to get the latest information, even before it was in print. One of the things that people sought was the casualty list. They wanted to know who had been wounded or killed or who was missing. All too often, the name of a relative was on that list.

News correspondents were not the only ones who were providing up-to-the-minute information about the war. Americans were growing accustomed to seeing pictures of the places, people, and events that were in the news, and the Civil War accelerated the development of this form. Frank Leslie, publisher of *Frank Leslie's Illustrated Newspaper,* claimed to have put eighty artists to covering the war, and no one has been able to figure out how many others there were. (Some were actually members of the army who sent sketches to their favorite publications.) Illustrators who were in the war zone lived a lonely, dangerous, and nomadic existence. They traveled from place to place and army to army, hoping to find interesting subjects to depict. The most interesting subject, of course, was a battle, and the artist tried to position himself so he could see the action—something that took some skill and a good bit of luck.

Illustrators often did little more than outline sketches that they sent to the home office. There, in-house artists would fill in many of the details, based on their imaginations and on their own experiences. Once these illustrations were completed, they were given to engravers who cut these images into a block of wood. The process was speeded up by making a drawing on the wood's surface and then cutting the wood into two or three parts so that more than one engraver could work on the picture at the same time. When the engravers were finished, printers would tie the blocks back together so they could become part of the page mold. The final product of this multistep process was often inaccurate in many of its details, especially by today's standards, but they did give readers some visual idea of what the war was like.

One of the most famous illustrators was Alfred Waud, who worked for *Harper's Magazine* and who was a favorite of many of the Union soldiers. Not only did he produce excellent illustrations, but he was also good fun to be with. Many of his drawings, and those of his brother William, who worked for *Leslie's,* are now owned by the Library of Congress. The war also gave a start to two other artists who achieved later fame: Thomas Nast, the most prominent political cartoonist of the nineteenth century, and Winslow Homer, the pioneering turn-of-the-century watercolorist. Homer was a field artist who specialized in depicting camp life in the army.

FIGURE 21.6   Startling Pictures Matthew Brady and his assistants, including Alexander Gardner who took this picture, did not flinch at capturing the realities of battle. This photo of dead Union soldiers was taken just after the battle of Gettysburg in 1863 near the famous Little Round Top. These men were the ones that Abraham Lincoln referred to in his Gettysburg Address: "The brave men, living and dead, who struggled here have consecrated it far above our poor power to add or detract." (Photo credit: Library of Congress)

Photography is another medium that received a boost by the intense interest in the war. Photographs of the war could not be widely published in a timely manner, but those that were produced generated much attention and wide audiences. Matthew Brady is the name most often associated with Civil War photography, and his ideas and vision created an enduring legacy both for himself and for the nation's historical record. Brady had set up studios in New York and Washington, DC, in the 1840s, and by the time the war began, just about every famous person of the day had been to see him to have a photographic portrait taken. (Abraham Lincoln himself credited a Brady photograph with helping him win the presidency in 1860.)

Brady realized the opportunity that the war presented to enhance photography and also to make money. He received an official endorsement of his efforts from the war department (but not much else) and invested some $100,000 in equipment and people. He put numerous assistants into the field; they traveled in their "what-is-it" wagons, and their presence often sent a message to the common soldier that a battle was about to occur.

Despite the efforts of Brady and others, the technology that would allow newspapers and magazines to easily use their work had not developed yet. Printers still had to make woodcuts for the illustrations they used. Photographs were helpful certainly. A good photograph could be traced in detail, and the drawing would have a dramatic and lifelike appearance in a publication, but it was still missing many of the details that viewers could see in the photo. But even had the technology been available to reproduce photographs directly, they might have been rejected by both editors and readers. Many of the battlefield photos taken by Brady and his assistants were brutally honest, showing dead bodies and the awful physical destruction to landscapes and buildings that the war imposed. Illustrators were more likely to romanticize the war and sanitize its setting, thus making it more palatable for readers of the time.

The End of the War and Its Aftermath

The Union's vast resources and its willingness to pay a high price to preserve the United States finally overwhelmed the South, and General Robert E. Lee surrendered the Confederate Army at Appomattox Courthouse in central Virginia in April 1864. Most journalists believed the news would subside for a while, but there was one more great story of the period to be covered. Shortly after the surrender, Abraham Lincoln was assassinated while attending a production at Ford's Theater in Washington. He was the second president to die in office (William Henry Harrison had died in 1840, less than a month after being sworn in) and the first to be assassinated.

Celebrations of the war's end ceased and mourning for the slain president (at least in the northern states) began. The president's body was carried on a long, slow train back to Springfield, Illinois, and at every stop along the way newspapers did their best to outdo one another with their text and illustrations. The story continued as the assassin was captured and killed and as his conspirators were rounded up, tried, and executed.

By then, the great debate about how to deal with the southern states had begun in Congress, and the new president, Andrew Johnson, was having difficulty in exercising his influence. Those difficulties would eventually escalate into an impeachment of the president and a trial in the U.S. Senate, the first such trial in the history of the republic.

In other words, the fighting had stopped, but the news had not. Americans had become accustomed to news and to finding out about important events within a few days, if not a few hours, after they had occurred even in distant places. They expected their newspapers to give them that information, and they were far less interested in what the newspaper's editorial stance or party affiliation was. They were also accustomed to "seeing" the news, that is, to having pictures and illustrations that would give them visual information about those events.

In less than two generations Americans had gone from being citizens of localities to citizens of a vast nation. Part of that transition occurred because of the shared experience of the national debate over slavery and the war that concluded it. That transition continued, in great part, because of the shared information that newspapers and magazines were providing to all parts of the country. These trends would continue throughout the remainder of the century.

QUESTIONS FOR DISCUSSION

1. The chapter describes the invention of photography as making a profound change in the lives of people. Do you agree? What would it have been like before there was photography?
2. Of all the people mentioned in this and the previous chapter, who had the most effect on the history of journalism?
3. Why is speed so important in the practice of journalism?
4. Why do you think magazines came into their own in the middle of the 1800s? What need were they fulfilling that newspapers were not?

RELATED WEB SITES

American Journalism Historians Association, www.ajha.org

American Women's History: Journalism, www.mtsu.edu/~kmiddlet/history/women /wh-jour.html

Black Journalists History Project (Maynard Institute), www.maynardije.org/programs/ history/index

Center for History and New Media, http://chnm.gmu.edu

Encyclopaedia of USA History: Journalists, www.spartacus.schoolnet.co.uk/USA journalists.htm

Jhistory Home Page, www.h-net.msu.edu/~jhistory

Journalism: Antebellum and Civil War America, www.uncp.edu/home/canada/work/allam/ 17841865/history/journal.htm

Media History Monographs, www.scripps.ohiou.edu/mediahistory

Media History Project, http://mediahistory.umn.edu

Media on Stamps, www.spacetoday.org/Stamps/Stamps.html

Soldiers Without Swords: The Black Press, www.pbs.org/blackpress

United States Newspaper Project, www.neh.gov/projects/usnp.html

READINGS AND REFERENCES

Beasley, M. H., & Gibbons, S. (1993). *Taking their place: A documentary history of women and journalism.* Washington, DC: American University Press.

Blanchard, M. A. (Ed.). (1998). *History of the mass media in the United States, an encyclopedia.* Chicago: Fitzroy Dearborn Publishers.

Brennen, B., & Hardt, H. (Eds.). (1999). *Picturing the past: Media, history and photography.* Champaign, IL: University of Illinois Press.

Briggs, A., & Burke, P. (2001). *A social history of the media from Gutenberg to the Internet.* Malden, MA: Blackwell.

Danky, J. P., et al. (Eds.). (1999). *African-American newspapers and periodicals: A national bibliography.* Cambridge, MA: Harvard University Press.

Fedler, F. (2000). *Lessons from the past: Journalists' lives and work, 1850–1950.* Prospect Heights, IL: Waveland Press, Inc.

Folkerts, J., & Teeter, D. L. Jr. (1997). *Voices of a nation: A history of mass media in the United States.* Boston: Allyn and Bacon.

Hudson, F. (2000). *Journalism in the United States from 1690–1872.* New York: Routledge.

Hutton, F., & Reid, B. S. (Eds.). (1996). *Outsiders in 19th-century press history.* Bowling Green: Bowling Green State University Press.

Mindich, D. T. Z. (1998). *Just the facts: How objectivity came to define American journalism.* New York: New York University Press.

Perry, J. M. (2000). *A bohemian brigade: The Civil War correspondents.* New York: John Wiley & Sons, Inc.

Pride, A. S., & C. Wilson, C. C. (1997). *A history of the Black Press.* Washington, DC: Howard University Press.

Rable, G. (2002). *Fredericksburg! Fredericksburg!* Chapel Hill, NC: University of North Carolina Press.

Rafferty, A. M. (2000). *American journalism 1690–1904.* New York: Routledge.

Sachsman, D. B., et al. (Eds.). (2000). *The Civil War and the press.* New Brunswick, NJ: Transaction Publishers.

Sloan, W. D. (1991). *Perspectives on mass communication history.* Hillsdale, NJ: Lawrence Erlbaum.

Sloan, W. D., & Parcell, L. M. (Eds.). (2002). *American journalism: History, principles, practices.* Jefferson, NC: McFarland & Company.

Sloan, W. D., Stovall, J. G., & Startt, J. D. (1999). *The media in America: A history* (4th ed.). Northport, AL: Vision.

Streitmatter, R. (1997). *Mightier than the sword: How the news media have shaped American history.* Boulder, CO: Westview Press.

Wolseley, R. E. (1995). *Black achievers in American journalism.* Nashville: James C. Winston Publishing.

Woodhull, N. J., & Snyder, R. W. (Eds.). (1998). *Defining moments in journalism.* New Brunswick, NJ: Transaction Publishers.

Chapter Twenty-two

New Realities, New Journalism

Key Concepts and Terms

1. The Civil War began the consolidation of America into one nation, which continued with the industrialization that followed in the decades after the war. Journalism played a vital role in this consolidation and changed because of it.

2. During this period, newspapers as the major mass medium grew into corporate giants with high profitability.

3. Joseph Pulitzer: owner of the *New York World,* a newspaper known for its crusades and lively writing.

4. William Randolph Hearst: owner of the *New York Herald;* Hearst was a flamboyant personality who used the news columns of his newspapers to push his own issues, including war with Spain over Cuba.

5. Frank Leslie: published *Frank Leslie's Illustrated Newspaper,* which during the Civil War printed thousands of illustrations and drawings about news events of the day; when Frank Leslie died in 1880, his wife took over the publication (and changed her name to

"Frank Leslie") and ran it successfully for more than twenty years.

6. Mergenthaler: a typesetting machine that greatly speeded up the process of producing newspapers and magazines; named for Ottmar Mergenthaler, its developer.

7. Brand names: names given to products that were distributed nationally; newspapers offered an advertising venue that helped vault products from local to national sales and distribution.

8. Yellow journalism: a type of journalism that emphasizes sensationalism and distorts the accuracy and meaning of subjects and events that are covered; the major period of yellow journalism was the late 1890s and its chief practitioners were Joseph Pulitzer and William Randolph Hearst.

9. Watchdog press: the concept that journalism should be an independent observer of society, particularly government, and should point out its ills.

Vignette

The experience of the Civil War divided Americans, but in its aftermath, ironically, they found great unity. In fact, in 1865 for the first time in the nation's history, many people thought of themselves as Americans rather than Missourians, Pennsylvanians, or New Yorkers. (It took longer for most people in the South to accept this idea.) They had fought over a big idea—a nation, in the words of Abraham Lincoln, "conceived in liberty and dedicated to the proposition that all men are created equal." They had made enormous sacrifices. Lincoln himself, killed by an assassin just as the war ended in April 1865, had been lost to this idea.

During the fifty years after the war, America devoted itself to putting the nation back together and to building an enormous industrial engine. The nineteenth century had already seen enormous changes. Remember at the beginning of the previous chapter we described a young man born on a western Virginia farm in 1815. By 1865 he is 50 years old. Like his father, he is still a farmer, but he has experienced many changes in the world he inhabits. His farm is now in the state of West Virginia. Two of his sons fought in the Union Army during the Civil War; both saw action in battle and one was wounded. A third son, the youngest, has stayed with him on the farm and is likely to take over farming when his father gets too old to work. The other sons have come home from the war, but they show no interest in remaining on the farm. One wants to move to Charleston, the state capital, and get a job with the railroad. The other wants to head west, maybe California, he says.

Our farmer has seen all the changes he wants to see in his life. When he was growing up, an itinerant artist came into the area and painted small portraits of his parents. Just before the war, someone called a "photographer" came by and took a picture of him and his family. His newspaper now has news that is just a few days old, rather than three or four weeks old like when he was a boy. His wife subscribes to a "magazine," something he does not see much use for but she seems to enjoy it.

Change? He's seen enough of that. He would just as soon things stayed the way they are.

They won't, of course. By the time of his death in 1890, he will experience many more changes in his personal and economic life. The growing industries of America will demand a source of energy, and much of that energy will be found just below his farm in the coal mines. He will receive the sad news that his son—the one who migrated west—has died, and that news will come by telegraph. Almost despite himself, he will become more aware of the news of the nation and the world because there will be so much more news and information than he has ever experienced.

A Profession Matures

Journalism experienced many changes in its technology, economics, audience, and methods during the latter part of the nineteenth century, but the history of the profession can best be understood during this period with the concept of maturity. During the decades before the Civil War, journalism seemed to be finding itself, figuring out what it was. After 1865, many of these basic questions seemed to have been answered.

Growth, as much as change, is what we will be concentrating on in this chapter:

- Newspapers grew into giant, profit-making industries. The number of newspapers increased, as did circulation sizes. Advertising became a much more important part of the revenues of a newspaper.

- Journalists developed more sophisticated ideas about gathering and reporting the news. They obtained a better understanding of accuracy and accurately presenting information. The Civil War had taught them that the way they interpreted information could have great impact on their audiences, and they grew more sensitive as to how this power was used.

- Technological changes allowed presses to increase in size and capacity. Slowly newspapers developed a method of using photographs directly rather than converting them to woodcuts. The nation's telegraph and transportation system speeded up the flow of information to all parts of the nation. By the end of the century, journalists were using devices such as the telephone and the typewriter to help them gather and process information.

- The idea of the press as an independent voice, and as a watchdog over government and industry, developed during this period. That newspapers and magazines would speak "for" rather than "to" their audiences was a concept that grew slowly, but grow it did.

- As in the decades before the Civil War, journalism was dominated by a few outsized personalities. But these men were different. They had a broader outlook and understood many of the changes in society that were taking place. They were determined to have a hand in those changes through their newspapers and magazines. And they were determined to make money.

- Journalism opened its doors somewhat more widely to women than it had during the period before the Civil War. Women were still prevented from achieving their full potential as editors and publishers within the profession, but some were given opportunities as reporters that they had never had before, and a few women took full advantage of these opportunities.

The growth of journalism paralleled the growth and development of society during this Industrial Age. Indeed, journalism contributed to that growth, so that inside the home and inside the workplace, the world became very different during the two generations after the Civil War.

A Generation of Growth

Just as it had grown during the 1830s and 1840s, journalism experienced another spurt of growth in the decades after the Civil War. There was certainly room to grow. The western territories between Kansas and California presented Americans with some of the same opportunities that Europeans in the 1600s had seen in America itself. Indeed, descendents of those same Europeans who had looked but not immigrated looked again. This time many of them got on the boat. America's external borders, for the most part, were open. Internal borders did not exist. The land seemed to be limitless and the resources abundant.

As people moved west, they gathered into communities and demanded the benefits of nineteenth-century civilization. (The cowboy, the gunslinger, and the "wild West" existed but were only a small part of the movement that was taking place.) They wanted their own sources of information; they wanted newspapers. William Nelson moved to Kansas City, Missouri, in 1880 and founded the *Kansas City Star.* His was not the only newspaper in town, but his was the cheapest. It sold for two cents a copy, as opposed to the five cents that the others cost. Nelson made it a point to emphasize good news coverage and a dedication to making Kansas City a better place to live. Within three years, the *Star* had a circulation of 10,000, and by the end of the decade that figure had tripled.

Nelson's story was repeated in many places large and small. Charles Dana bought the *New York Sun,* the first of the penny newspapers, in 1868 when it lagged far behind many of the other newspapers in the city. Its circulation was less than 50,000, but in eight years he too had tripled the circulation. Nelson was a shrewd businessman; Dana was an editor who emphasized lively and interesting writing. Each found a different road to success.

These two examples are indicative of what was happening everywhere. The number of daily newspapers in the nation grew from fewer than 500 in 1860 to more than 2,000 in 1910. From 1860 to 1880, circulation of daily newspapers increased from 1.4 million copies to 3.5 million copies. The nation's population grew during this period but not at such an accelerated rate. People were simply demanding more newspapers.

One of the reasons for this demand was the increase in literacy that occurred during this time. Public school systems became more common, and the one thing that children did, even if they attended school for only a short time, was learn to read. By 1900, about three-fourths of all adults were fully literate. Another reason for the growth was that the price of newspapers generally decreased. Changes in technology made the newspaper less expensive to produce, and the increase in advertising that newspapers experienced lessened their dependence on circulation revenue.

A change had also occurred in the outlook of Americans. Service in the army during the Civil War had given a large number of Americans the opportunity to travel to a different part of America. This movement continued after the war, made possible by the growth of passenger railroads. Before the war, the West was populated by wagon trains and people traveled from place to place by stagecoach. Both were immensely difficult means of travel. The railroad, with its relative comfort and affordable prices,

FIGURE 22.1   Newspapers in the West Newspapers quickly found a ready audience of readers in western towns like Broken Bow, Nebraska, where this 1886 photograph of the *Nebraska Statesman* was taken. (Photo credit: Library of Congress)

made traveling long distances a reasonable idea. With that broader outlook came the demand for more information about more places, and newspapers and magazines stepped forward to meet that demand.

An Age of Personalities

More than any other time in the history of journalism, the Industrial Age was dominated by the great personalities who populated the field and by the work and the examples they produced. The pre–Civil War era had James Gordon Bennett, William Cullen Bryant, and Horace Greeley, but within a decade after the war's end, these men had died. (Horace Greeley, ever the most eccentric personality of the age, won the Democratic presidential nomination in 1872 and lost to Ulysses S. Grant in the general election; he died shortly after the votes were counted.) These men were replaced by a second generation of modern editors, who established their own tone of journalism and who set the stage for an even more forceful set of personalities that ended the century.

FIGURE 22.2   Charles Dana The editor of the *New York Sun*, Charles Dana grew up in the era of the penny press, but when he purchased the paper in 1868, he emphasized a clear, condensed form of writing that readers immediately took to. Dana tagged President Rutherford B. Hayes as "his fraudulency Mr. Hayes" because Hayes got into office after a dispute over how the votes were counted.

Chief among this second generation was Charles Dana, editor of the *New York Sun*. Dana's success in reviving the *Sun* and increasing its circulation was noted in the previous section. Dana emphasized good writing and hired people who could produce it. Possibly the most famous editorial ever to appear in a newspaper was written by Francis Church, one of the *Sun*'s editorial writers under Dana's direction. A young woman wrote to the paper one Christmas asking if there really was a Santa Claus, saying that she had heard from others that Santa Claus did not exist. Church gave her the famous answer: "Yes, Virginia, there is a Santa Claus. . . ."

Like his father, James Gordon Bennett Jr. was no paragon of virtue. In fact, he grew up spoiled and profligate. By one estimate, Bennett spent $30 million of the $50 million that the *New York Herald* was worth in his lifetime. Still, Bennett was like his father in that he understood the value of news and discerned what his readers wanted. One thing they wanted was adventure, and when the *Herald* had the opportunity to give it to them, it did.

The paper sent reporter Harold Stanley on a months-long search for the missionary David Livingstone—a search that ended with Stanley greeting Livingstone with the famous line: "Dr. Livingstone, I presume." All during the son's editorship, the *Herald* continued to produce high circulation figures and high profits.

E. L. Godkin's publications never achieved the circulation numbers of the *New York Sun* or the *Herald*, but no one could deny his influence. Editor of both the *Nation* magazine and the *New York Evening Post*, Godkin emphasized editorials and opinion over news. He had little interest in appealing to the masses of readers. Rather, he was interested in developing ideas that would improve and advance society. The opinions he formed and the editorials he wrote were closely reasoned and discomfiting to the comfortable. The story is told of Godkin that a subscriber to the *Evening Post* was once asked if she minded living alone in the country. No, she replied. When the newspaper carrier threw the *Evening Post* in her front lawn, "it just lay there and growled."

All of these editors, however, were overshadowed by two of journalism history's most dominant personalities: Joseph Pulitzer and William Randolph Hearst. Each appeared on the New York journalism scene after learning their trade elsewhere, Pulitzer

YES, VIRGINIA, THERE IS A SANTA CLAUS

The editorial that follows is one of the most famous in the history of journalism. It appeared in the *New York Sun* in 1897 and has been reprinted widely ever since. The editorial was written by Francis Church, a former reporter who had covered the Civil War for the *New York Times*.

We take pleasure in answering thus prominently the communication below, expressing at the same time our great gratification that its faithful author is numbered among the friends of *The Sun*:

Dear Editor—
I am 8 years old. Some of my little friends say there is no Santa Claus. Papa says, "If you see it in *The Sun*, it's so." Please tell me the truth, is there a Santa Claus?

Virginia O'Hanlon

Virginia, your little friends are wrong. They have been affected by the skepticism of a skeptical age. They do not believe except they see. They think that nothing can be which is not comprehensible by their little minds. All minds, Virginia, whether they be men's or children's, are little. In this great universe of ours, man is a mere insect, an ant, in his intellect as compared with the boundless world about him, as measured by the intelligence capable of grasping the whole of truth and knowledge.

Yes, Virginia, there is a Santa Claus. He exists as certainly as love and generosity and devotion exist, and you know that they abound and give to your life its highest beauty and joy. Alas! how dreary would be the world if there were no Santa Claus! It would be as dreary as if there were no Virginias. There would be no childlike faith then, no poetry, no romance to make tolerable this existence. We should have no enjoyment, except in sense and sight. The external light with which childhood fills the world would be extinguished.

Not believe in Santa Claus! You might as well not believe in fairies. You might get your papa to hire men to watch in all the chimneys on Christmas Eve to catch Santa Claus, but even if you did not see Santa Claus coming down, what would that prove? Nobody sees Santa Claus, but that is no sign that there is no Santa Claus. The most real things in the world are those that neither children nor men can see. Did you ever see fairies dancing on the lawn? Of course not, but that's no proof that they are not there. Nobody can conceive or imagine all the wonders there are unseen and unseeable in the world.

You tear apart the baby's rattle and see what makes the noise inside, but there is a veil covering the unseen world which not the strongest man, nor even the united strength of all the strongest men that ever lived could tear apart. Only faith, poetry, love, romance, can push aside that curtain and view and picture the supernal beauty and glory beyond. Is it all real? Ah, Virginia, in all this world there is nothing else real and abiding.

No Santa Claus! Thank God! he lives and lives forever. A thousand years from now, Virginia, nay 10 times 10,000 years from now, he will continue to make glad the heart of childhood.

in St. Louis and Hearst in San Francisco. Pulitzer came to New York in 1883, a dozen years before Hearst arrived, and he quickly established himself as a man with ideas, frenetic energy, and skill in selecting the very best people to work for him.

In St. Louis, Pulitzer had distinguished himself and his newspaper, the *Post-Dispatch*, by exposing and crusading against local corruption. His newspaper, he declared, would be an independent voice opposing "all frauds and shams wherever and whatever they are." He carried that same purpose to New York when he purchased the *New York World*. He promised more and better news coverage, and part of that coverage included massive and detailed illustrations. His newspaper gave people something to look at as well as something to read. A year after coming to New York, he installed a photoengraving plant in the newspaper to use the latest technology available in building illustrations. Within ten years every other newspaper in the city had done the same thing.

Pulitzer continued his crusades against corruption, particularly against prostitution, which became one of the newspaper's favorite topics. Pulitzer also engaged the *World* in a number of civic projects, including the raising of $200,000 from readers to pay for the base of the Statue of Liberty. An immigrant himself, Pulitzer was sympathetic to the growing immigrant population in New York City, and those people constituted a substantial part of the newspaper's readership. Within two years of his arrival in New York, the *World*'s circulation had passed 200,000 and led every other newspaper in the city. It was also producing huge profits for its owner.

Pulitzer himself, however, was becoming less able to enjoy those profits. He suffered from an increasing loss of sight and a nervous disorder that made him extremely sensitive to noise, and his condition was so bad that he was unable to work in the *World*'s building, even though the publisher's office was at the pinnacle of one of the tallest structures in New York at the time. By 1890 Pulitzer had to escape to his yacht and communicate with his editors by memo and messenger from there.

Despite his infirmities, no newspaper editor in New York could match Pulitzer's ideas and his drive until William Randolph Hearst showed up as the owner of the *New York Journal* in 1895. Hearst wanted to outdo Pulitzer by adopting Pulitzer's ideas and taking them beyond what Pulitzer had conceived.

Hearst was a flamboyant character who had grown up in California as the son of a rich mine owner. His father owned the *San Francisco Examiner,* and Hearst—after being kicked out of Harvard—asked his father to let him run it. His father refused, and Hearst went to New York and got a job on Pulitzer's *World*. There he got a close look at Pulitzer's methods of running a newspaper and increasing circulation. He was determined to do

FIGURE 22.3   Joseph Pulitzer Joseph Pulitzer was undoubtedly one of the leading editors of the day, but he managed to achieve journalistic immortality by endowing in his will a set of awards that became known as the Pulitzer prize, the highest award in journalism. Though a great editor himself, Pulitzer fell victim to the competition of the yellow journalism era.

the same in San Francisco. His chance came when his father was appointed to the U.S. Senate. The young Hearst (he was 24 at the time) took over the paper in 1887, spent boatloads of his father's money, engaged in Pulitzer-like editorial crusades, and increased circulation. By 1890 the newspaper was making a profit, and Hearst was ready to take on New York. He got his chance in 1895 when the *New York Journal*, a newspaper once owned by Pulitzer's brother, came up for sale. He bought it for $180,000.

Hearst did not have time to build a staff that would challenge Pulitzer, so he bought one—Pulitzer's. He hired away the entire staff of the *Sunday World*, including R. F. Outcault, the artist who drew the popular comic strip, "The Yellow Kid." (Pulitzer simply retained another artist to draw the comic strip, so both the *Journal* and the *World* had comic strips called "The Yellow Kid.") After that coup, Hearst made repeated attempts to hire individuals from the daily staff of the *World*. Often he was successful. His biggest catch was Arthur Brisbane, one of Pulitzer's top editors, who left to work for Hearst in 1897.

Hearst's raid on the *World*'s staff was an open declaration of war, and the two newspapers fought a journalistic hand-to-hand combat for several years after that. Each touted its own scoops and campaigns with huge pictures and illustrations and bold, blaring headlines. Each pointed out the misdeeds and mistakes of the other. Each declared itself the keeper of the public good and the voice of the people. They did so sometimes at the cost of perspective and even accuracy. Hearst had enormous personal resources inherited from his family. Pulitzer had made a fortune from his newspaper, but the war in which he was engaged eventually depleted that fortune.

The Hearst–Pulitzer competition pulled in many other newspapers to the conventions of using large illustrations and bold headlines to trumpet their own triumphs. But no two papers did it as well as the *Journal* and the *World*, and the late 1890s has been tabbed by historians as the age of yellow journalism (named after the comic strip "The Yellow Kid," as we will explain later). The apex of the yellow journalism period came in 1898 when, egged on particularly by Hearst's *Journal*, America declared war on Spain because of its treatment of Cuba. When tensions were building, Hearst, Pulitzer, and others sent an army of correspondents to Cuba to cover the conflict. One of those was artist Frederic Remington, who at one point wired Hearst: "Everything is quiet here. There is no trouble. There will be no war." Hearst replied in a return wire: "Please remain. You furnish the pictures and I'll furnish the war." Soon thereafter, the American battleship USS *Maine* was blown up in Havana harbor, and with very little evidence, the newspapers blamed the Spanish and beat the drums for war. Congress and President William McKinley eventually went along. Hearst even sailed his own yacht into the battle zone. Both Pulitzer and Hearst spent many thousands of dollars on war coverage, but it paid off at least temporarily. On its best day during the short conflict, the *Journal* sold slightly more than 1 million copies.

While Pulitzer and Hearst were shouting at each other, one other personality was making his presence felt in New York, and his work would continue to influence journalism long after his death. His name was Adolph Ochs. Ochs was born in Knoxville, Tennessee, and learned the printer's trade at a newspaper there. After failed attempts at running his own newspaper, he acquired the *Chattanooga Times* in 1878 and made

FIGURE 22.4   The War Hearst Wanted William Randolph Hearst had beat the drum steadily in his *New York Journal* for the United States to go to war with Spain over Cuba. The pretext for that war came when the USS *Maine* exploded in Havana harbor. With no real evidence, Hearst blamed Spain, and the United States soon declared war.

it a modest success. He had misread the possibilities of Chattanooga as a resort town, however, and accumulated massive debts over the next two decades. He left Chattanooga for New York in 1896 where he purchased the faltering *New York Times* for $75,000.

While Hearst continued to out-Pulitzer Pulitzer, Ochs was equally determined to be different from them both. He refused to engage the *New York Times* in the large headlines, bold illustrations, and thunder-and-lightning journalism of the *Journal* and the *World*. Ochs developed for the *Times* a calm, reasonable voice that gave the readers "All the News That's Fit to Print." Ochs appealed to the respectable and reasonable side of the readers. After two years, Ochs made another move that was a huge gamble in the circulation-dependent world of newspapers. He cut the price of his paper from two cents to one cent. (The *Journal* and *World* were also selling at two cents a copy at the time.) Circulation increased dramatically, and by 1900 Ochs had taken the paper from less than 10,000 copies a day to more than 80,000 copies.

The straightforward reporting of the *Times* won it a great deal of respect among an increasing number of New Yorkers who were tired of the sensationalism of the other newspapers in the city. The *Times* emerged from this era with a reputation for accuracy and objectivity, and Ochs made sure that reputation continued. His descendents continue to operate the vast publishing empire that is the *New York Times* while most other newspapers in New York City that were published at the beginning of the century have failed to survive.

Advancing Technology

Journalism's post–Civil War period witnessed a number of advances in technology that would aid its development and improvement. One such advance involved new techniques in making paper. Paper was an expensive product, and its cost and scarcity had frustrated publishers who were looking to increase the circulation of their newspapers and magazines. Paper was made of a combination of wood pulp and rags or cloth or other substantive material. New ways of making paper, using only wood pulp, promised to make the production of paper easier and cheaper, and by 1870 those techniques, perfected in Europe, had arrived in America. Paper production rose, and costs decreased, allowing newspapers to go all out in increasing their circulation.

Typesetting was another technology that improved greatly after the war, although in this area improvements were a long time in coming. Since the days of Gutenberg, type had been set by hand, letter by letter. Each metal letter would be picked up out of its own section of a giant case and placed into a matrix that formed the words and the lines of type. It was slow, laborious work and took a great deal of skill and practice. A machine that would automatically cast a line of type was finally developed by a German immigrant, Ottmar Mergenthaler, in 1890, greatly speeding the process of the newspaper's "backshop." Merganthaler Linotype machines were large units with the ability to melt and mold a line of type; they soon became a major part of a newspaper's operation and remained so until the 1970s.

Printing presses were also objects of the attention of inventors and innovators. Rotary presses were the great breakthrough in printing technology of the nineteenth century, but there were other innovations that allowed presses to run faster and more efficiently. The use of electricity for power became more widespread during the latter

FIGURE 22.5 **Newspaper Illustration** During the last two decades of the nineteenth century, technology made reproducing photos and illustrations much easier for newspapers, and the journalism of the age took full advantage of it. Newspapers hired excellent artists and gave them an extraordinary amount of space with which to work. The illustrations, such as those pictured here concerning the 1906 murder of a prominent New York architect, were not only meant to grab the attention of the reader but also to add a dimension of information that the reader could visualize.

part of the century. Presses grew bigger and faster in concert with the demand for more copies of the publication. Newspapers sought in every way they could to reduce the printing time so they could speed up getting the news to their readers. In addition to speed, these new presses allowed for the use of "spot" color. Spot color is use of a single color other than black on the page. One of the first uses of spot color was the placement of yellow inside a comic strip called "Hogan's Alley" in Pulitzer's *New York World*. The strip was dubbed "The Yellow Kid," which later became its official name and eventually became the nickname for the genre of journalism practiced by Pulitzer and Hearst.

Improvements in the process for reproducing pictures took place and typesetting and printing techniques advanced. The idea of converting a photograph to a series of dots that would serve as a code for where ink should and should not be had been around for some time, and by the 1870s, innovators were making strides to adapt it to the printing process. As they did this, the laborious process of making woodcuts was replaced, and the skill that went with this process gradually died out. By 1890 most of the major publications were using some type of photoengraving. Photos, of course, gave more accurate illustrations and in many ways could be more dramatic. Clear photographs of subjects in motion were rare, and color photography was yet to come, but journalistic publications in the 1890s looked far different than they did in the 1870s.

None of these technical advances represented the dramatic breakthrough that the invention of photography or the rotary press meant to journalism. Each played a part, however, in making journalism a little more professional and better able to serve the reader. They allowed newspapers to be larger and carry more content that would appeal to a broader readership and be produced more quickly. Taken together, new advances made the newspaper industry more accessible and efficient and increased the ability of owners to make a profit. As the industry grew and became more profitable, more people were involved at every level, especially as reporters and editors. Their world, too, was changing.

Reporters and Reporting

In the late nineteenth century prohibition, the idea of outlawing alcohol, had replaced abolition as the great moral issue of the day. Women's suffrage, which advocated giving women the right to vote, sprang from a sense that women could do many of the jobs that men did in the workplace and that women already had major responsibility for life at home. Many suffragettes, though by no means all, were prohibitionists, and some suffrage groups made prohibition a part of their state goals.

The prominence of women in these social movements was an indication that women were beginning to break away from the domestic roles that they had fulfilled for generations. Despite the prejudices and customs that continued to restrict them throughout the nineteenth century, women pushed the door ajar in many fields of endeavor. More were obtaining education, and women were becoming doctors, lawyers, and even politicians. They also became more prominent in the field of journalism.

YELLOW JOURNALISM

The competition for readers between Joseph Pulitzer's *New York World* and William Randolph Hearst's *New York Herald* spun out of control in the 1890s with each man trying to outdo the other on almost a daily basis. The type of journalism they practiced became known as *yellow journalism,* a term that still has meaning more than a century later.

The name actually comes from one of the first successful comic strips, the Yellow Kid. The strip was originated by R. F. Outcault, an illustrator for the *World,* who managed to capture working-class life in New York City with great sympathy and humor. Pulitzer used his advanced printing technology to shade the strip in yellow and, thus, the name.

Hearst knew how popular the comic strip was and eventually hired Outcault away to work for the *Herald,* where he continued to draw the strip. Pulitzer simply hired someone else to draw the strip for the *World,* and for a time both newspapers boasted of having a Yellow Kid comic strip.

But yellow journalism was not about comic strips. It came to symbolize sensationalism in presenting the news. Printing technology in the late 1800s allowed newspaper publishers to print large headlines and massive illustrations. Both Pulitzer and Hearst took full advantage to gain their readers' attention.

The result was blowing insignificant stories out of proportion, putting down articles and crusades mounted by the competition, and often turning the coverage of public policies into personal vendettas. The excesses of yellow journalism were intrusive journalists, inaccurate reporting, and even falsified stories and interviews.

More seriously, yellow journalism could result in bad public policy. Many believe that the United States would not have gone to war with Spain in 1898 had not the *World* and especially the *Herald* made such an issue out of what was occurring in Cuba.

And just as seriously, the period of yellow journalism taught journalism something about the importance of credibility. Eventually, many of the readers of both the *Herald* and the *World* turned to other newspapers—most notably the *New York Times*—because they simply did not trust what the papers were saying.

A good deal of journalism was being directed at women, not only in daily newspapers but particularly in magazines. Publications, such as *Woman's Home Journal* and *Ladies Home Journal,* tried to serve the domestic interests of women. This was where women journalists had the most natural entry. Among the most prominent women editors of the day was Mary Booth, who edited *Harper's Bazaar,* a fashion magazine, for more than twenty years. Others, such as suffragettes Susan B. Anthony and Elizabeth Cady Stanton, edited magazines devoted to their cause.

In daily journalism, the most notable woman of the age was Nellie Bly (née Elizabeth Cochrane), whom Pulitzer hired to work for the *New York World.* Bly was an adventuress and woman of uncommon courage; she feigned insanity so she could be committed to the notorious Blackwell Island insane asylum. There she found poor food, unhealthy conditions, and general abuse of patients, all of which she wrote about in a blistering exposé. Bly later gained more fame when she attempted to travel around the world in less than eighty days. Bly's feats have been dismissed as "stunt journalism," and there was certainly a sensational aspect to what she did. But she also proved that women could master the rigors of journalism just as men could.

"STUNT" JOURNALIST NELLIE BLY

The table reached the length of the room and was uncovered and uninviting. Long benches without backs were put for the patients to sit on, and over these they had to crawl in order to face the table. Placed close together all along the table were large dressing-bowls fixed with a pinkish looking stuff which the patients called tea. By each bowl was laid a piece of bread, cut thick and buttered. A small saucer containing five prunes accompanied the bread. One fat woman made a rush, and jerking up several saucers from those around her emptied their contents into her own saucer. Then while holding on to her own bowl she lifted up another and drained its contents at one gulp. This she did to a second bowl in shorter time than it takes to tell it. Indeed I was so amused at her successful grabbings that when I looked at my own share the woman opposite, without so much as by your leave, grabbed my bread and left me without any. Another patient, seeing this, kindly offered me hers, but I declined with thanks and turned to the nurse and asked for more. As she flung a thick piece down on the table she made some remark about the fact that if I forgot where my home was I had not forgotten how to eat. I tried the bread, but the butter was so horrible that I could not eat it.

Critics called it "stunt journalism," and some of it was, but the words that Elizabeth Cochrane, a.k.a. Nellie Bly, wrote for the *New York World* after spending ten days in New York's notorious insane asylum are still powerful today.

And they changed lives. Cochrane's exposé of the asylum sparked outrage and increased funding and needed reforms.

Cochrane was one of a number of "girl reporters" hired by the publishers of the time to pump up circulation and outdo one another. Unlike many of them, Cochrane took her job seriously and wrote about people, situations, and conditions that needed attention. In 1894 she went to Chicago to cover the Pullman railroad strike and was the only reporter to tell the side of the striking workers. Her writing, as always, was vivid, descriptive, and powerful.

Still, she was not above a stunt or two. In 1889, she circled the globe in seventy-two days (in a race against the mythical record of the Jules Verne novel, *Around the World in Eighty Days*), writing dispatches from every place she landed. The *World* gave her much space and ink (see the illustration).

Bly married an industrialist in the mid-1890s and lived quietly for about ten years. When her husband died, she resumed her public life and was writing for the *New York Journal* in 1922 when she died at the age of 58.

Another important woman journalist was Ida B. Wells, an African American who, against very long odds, edited the *Free Speech and Headlight* in Memphis, Tennessee. She put her life in danger with a campaign against lynching and a penchant for public oratory. After the turn of the century, a movement of reform journalism to expose ills in society so that they could be corrected was undertaken by a number of national magazines. One of the first of these "muckrakers," as President Theodore Roosevelt called them, was Ida Tarbell, who began a biographical series on John D. Rockefeller for *McClure's Magazine*. The series turned into an exposé of the corruption of Rockefeller's company, Standard Oil. It told how the company had systematically tried to destroy its competition and create a favorable environment for itself, even to the point of contracting with more than one hundred Ohio newspapers to run editorials and news favorable to the company.

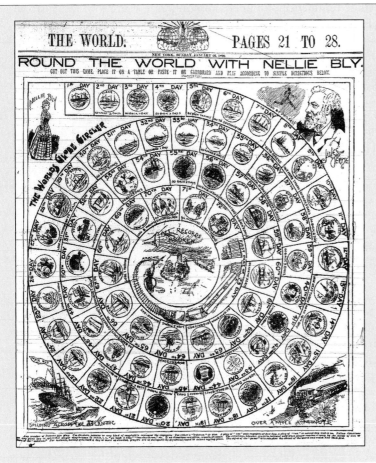

THE WORLD.   PAGES 21 TO 28.
NEW YORK, SUNDAY, JANUARY 26, 1890.
ROUND THE WORLD WITH NELLIE BLY.
CUT OUT THIS GAME, PLACE IT ON A TABLE OR PASTE IT ON CARDBOARD AND PLAY ACCORDING TO SIMPLE DIRECTIONS BELOW.

Nellie Bly's round-the-world trip was played for all it was worth by Joseph Pulitzer's *New York World.*

One of the highest-ranking women in the field was Mrs. Frank Leslie, whose husband had founded *Frank Leslie's Illustrated Newspaper,* one of the leading journals in reporting the Civil War. Frank Leslie died in 1880, and Mrs. Leslie took over the publication and ran it successfully for more than twenty years. She was a high-profile society character who changed her own name to Frank Leslie after her husband died.

Although women were more prominent in journalism than many have assumed, the accomplishments of Booth, Bly, Wells, Tarbell, and Leslie did not signal a general opening of the profession to women. Few women could count on building a career in journalism or advancing to an editorship. On most newspapers, if there were any women at all, they were restricted to clerical or proofreading duties or confined to writing for women's sections. Most of the journalistic work was done by men.

That work had changed with the times. Reporters and editors had achieved more status, and their assumed influence on public opinion made sources of information more cooperative. The "beat" system in which one reporter covered the same area day after day—something that had been in place to some extent since the days of the penny press—was now fully functional, and reporters were able to develop an expertise on their subjects. They were also becoming more dependent on their sources and, thus, making more efforts to be accurate in the information they presented. Journalism was still a long way from developing a full-fledged code of ethics, however. Hoaxes still occasionally appeared in print, and reporters used sly, deceptive, and unsavory methods to get information.

Journalists had new tools to use in their work. Possibly the most important was the advent of electric power to light the inside of buildings and to power machinery. Electricity was cheaper than oil-burning lamps and allowed journalists to extend their work well into the evening. Although much of the journalistic copy was written by hand, the typewriter was beginning to appear in a number of newspaper offices. Using a typewriter greatly increased how fast an article could be written. Telephones also aided reporters in obvious ways. A source could be called instead of seen personally. Reporters could call in a story rather than having to travel back to the newspaper office or find an intracity telegraph. And when traveling did occur, reporters had more choices than horse-drawn carriages. If they were nimble enough, they could hop on a bicycle and speed to the scene of the news. In some cities reporters could take streetcars, and if they had to travel any distance at all, they most often could take a train.

Journalism even developed something of a star system in this era. Reporters began getting bylines, often using their real names, for the first time, and many were free to display distinctive styles of writing. Reporters sometimes made themselves part of the story, as did Henry Stanley in his search for David Livingstone. A few notable reporters developed a style of humor and satire that made them famous. Samuel Clemens first used the name of Mark Twain in his dispatches from Carson City, Nevada, to the *Territorial Enterprise* in Virginia City in 1862. Twain went on to write for the *San Francisco Morning Call* and the *New York Tribune* and was editor for several years of the *Buffalo Express,* all experiences that contributed to his becoming America's chief man of letters late in the century.

The brightest light in the reportorial star system was Richard Harding Davis, whose drop-dead handsome looks were as charmed as his journalistic career. He paid a great deal of attention to his clothes and his demeanor, developing a devil-may-care swagger that many people, especially women, found irresistible. Davis sought adventure where he could find it and seemed to love covering war. He was the chief correspondent for William Randolph Hearst's *New York Journal* during the Spanish-American War (a war that Hearst had a great deal to do with). His writing was full of on-the-scene description, such as the following:

> They (the Americans) had no glittering bayonets, they were not massed in regular array. There were a few men in advance, bunched together, and creeping up a steep, sunny hill, the tops of which roared and flashed with flame. The men held their guns pressed across their breasts and stepped heavily as they climbed. Behind these first few, spreading out

FIGURE 22.6   Newspaper Humorists The latter part of the nineteenth century produced a number of outstanding and well-remembered newspaper humorists. Chief among them is Mark Twain (seated, second from right), but others (beginning at left) include David Ross Locke, whose pen name was Petroleum V. Nasby and was one of the era's great political satirists; Finley Peter Dunne, who often viewed the world as Martin Dooley, an Irish immigrant and saloonkeeper; Ambrose Bierce, a San Francisco journalist who was bitter and caustic in his observations; George Peck, a Wisconsin publisher who created the mischievous Peck's Bad Boy; and Edgar Wilson (Bill) Nye, a Westerner who came to New York and viewed what he saw with a simple but amazingly funny point of view.

like a fan, were single lines of men, slipping and scrambling in the smooth grass, moving forward with difficulty, as though they were wading waist-high through water, moving slowly, carefully, with strenuous effort. It was much more wonderful than any swinging charge could have been. They walked to greet death at every step, many of them, as they advanced, sinking suddenly or pitching forward and disappearing in the high grass, but the others waded on, stubbornly, forming a thin blue line that kept creeping higher and higher up the hill. It was as inevitable as the rising tide. (Lubow p. 186)

Davis' fellow journalist with the *Journal* in Cuba was artist Frederick Remington. His precise and economic drawings of the people participating in the war added immensely to the information that the readers of the *Journal* received. His work increased his fame and added to the value of the artwork that he later produced.

Change in Advertising

During the decades after the Civil War, America experienced a period of phenomenal economic growth. Although there were panics and depressions along the way, generally more people had more money and goods than ever before. The harnessing of electrical energy and the innovations in machinery turned life at home and in the workplace upside down. Mass production of goods meant that things were cheaper to buy and easier to acquire. America was becoming a consumer society.

A vital part of the consumer society is information. Manufacturers must know what goods and services people need; they must know where the markets are for those goods and services; and they must have a way of reaching those audiences and asking, or persuading, them to buy the products. Consumers also need information. They must learn what is available, how it can be obtained, and how much it will cost.

Before the Civil War, much of this economic activity took place on a local level. Goods were made locally and sold locally. After the war, however, manufacturers began to conceive of regional, national, and even international markets for their goods. Manufacturers developed "brand names" for the products they produced and began to foster brand loyalties. At the local level, one-product stores began to give way to "department" stories that carried a wide variety of goods produced locally and elsewhere. A transportation system in the form of trains was being built so that goods made in New York could be shipped to California and vice versa at a relatively low cost. But there needed to be an information system, and newspapers often provided the first step in that system.

Consequently, advertising became an increasingly important part of the newspaper after the Civil War. And as one manufacturer advertised, others who produced the same types of good had to advertise also in order to stay competitive. An established newspaper was assumed to have a ready audience that would be a good market for many products. Newspapers were in a perfect position to accept the money that advertisers were trying to give them. Advertising revenue became a growing part of a newspaper's revenue, often allowing newspapers to reduce their subscription prices and, thus, increase circulation. Increased circulation meant larger markets for advertisers and, consequently, higher advertising rates. It was a win-win-win situation for newspapers, and many newspaper owners and their families became fabulously wealthy during this time. By 1900, more than half of the revenue of the average newspaper was coming from advertising, a huge change from fifty years earlier.

There were side effects, however. One was that advertisers, because they spent so much money on the newspaper, sometimes believed they had the right to control the newspaper's editorial content. Honest publishers, editors, and reporters fought off these attempts and ultimately established in journalism a clear line between news and advertising.

Another effect of the increase in advertising was to help newspapers sever their last ties to political parties and organizations. At the beginning of the century, a newspaper's existence usually depended on the financial support of a political faction. If an editor fell out with the faction, that probably meant the newspaper would cease publication. By the end of the century, newspapers were big businesses. Editorially,

FIGURE 22.7   Bigger Newspapers, Bigger Buildings As newspapers grew in size and circulation, they needed bigger buildings to occupy. The age of "skyscrapers" was dawning. In the late 1800s, that meant multistoried buildings. Most major newspaper offices had a grand edifice to show off their prosperity.

they might (and probably did) support a political party or faction, but the politicians no longer controlled what they printed; nor could they wreak vengeance on them for straying from the party fold.

The Watchdog Press

Newspaper crusades against public corruption were nothing new to the nineteenth century. From the time newspapers have existed, they have carried on the fight for what editors considered the public good and have sought to expose those who were dishonest or who violated a trust.

Before the advent of the penny press in the 1830s, such campaigns were likely to be generated by political motives as much as a concern for the general welfare. One political faction sought to expose the nefarious dealings of its rival and did this through the newspapers that it published. As newspapers became more independent from their political ties, these campaigns became more credible and, in some cases, effective.

Newspaper publishers had more than the public good on their agendas when they undertook such campaigns, of course. These campaigns could provoke marvelous circulation gains for the newspaper. They could establish the credibility of the paper with

FIGURE 22.8   Thomas Nast, Cartoonist Thomas Nast began his
journalistic career as a field artist during the Civil War. He remained
with *Harper's Magazine* after the war and became American journalism's
best-known cartoonist. He aimed a sharp pen at the Boss Tweed ring in
New York City and was instrumental in drawing attention to the ring's
perfidy. (Photo credit: Library of Congress)

whole groups of people. Both Pulitzer and Hearst understood this perfectly and used
such campaigns to their great advantage. Other newspapers and magazines did the
same thing. The most famous public scandal of the age was that of the Tweed Ring
in New York City in the years just after the war. Political boss William Marcy Tweed

controlled the city government of New York and all of the contracts that it issued. In 1870, the *New York Times* received a series of documents that showed how many public officials were stealing money from the city by accepting bribes and payoffs. Along with *Harper's Weekly,* the *Times* campaigned against the ring's practices and finally got Tweed and many of his cronies thrown out of office and thrown into jail.

What made the newspaper campaigns of this age different was not only the lack of political ties of the newspaper but also the emphasis on reporting and bringing facts to light. Documentary evidence as well as eyewitness reports became the basis on which these campaigns were built. Editors could no longer assert or imply wrong-doing. They had to present specifics and the evidence to back it up.

By doing this again and again throughout the late nineteenth and early twentieth centuries, the press established itself as the watchdog of government—the independent voice the public could rely on to see that the public was well served. The press, of course, did not always live up to this role, but entering the twentieth century, it had taken on that responsibility as a new age of journalism approached.

QUESTIONS FOR DISCUSSION

1. Does the treatment that newspapers gave to news during the Yellow Journalism period sound different from the way news is treated today? Why or why not?
2. During the latter part of the nineteenth century, a large number of immigrants entered the United States. How would this have affected newspapers and the journalism of the time?
3. Which of the technologies mentioned in this chapter had the most effect on the practice of journalism during this period? Make a list of the technologies and put them in order of those that had the most effect.
4. The author mentions several women who were prominent in journalism during the nineteenth century. Find out more about them and find some of the other women who were pioneers in the field. What obstacles did women have to overcome generally in society at the time to have careers and professional lives?

RELATED WEB SITES

AEJMC History Division, www.utc.edu/~aejhist

American Journalism Historians Association, www.ajha.org

American Women's History: Journalism, www.mtsu.edu/~kmiddlet/history/women/wh-jour.html

Associated Press 150th Anniversary, www.ap.org/anniversary/nhistory/index.html

Black Journalists History Project (Maynard Institute), www.maynardije.org/programs/history/index

Center for History and New Media, chnm.gmu.edu

Encyclopaedia of USA History: Journalists, www.spartacus.schoolnet.co.uk/USAjournalists.htm

Jhistory Home Page, www.h-net.msu.edu/~jhistory

Media History Monographs, www.scripps.ohiou.edu/mediahistory

Media History Project, http://mediahistory.umn.edu

Newseum, www.newseum.org

New York Times Company History, www.nytco.com/company-timeline.html

Women's History: Journalism, www.distinguishedwomen.com/subject/journ.html

Yellow Journalism, www.pbs.org/crucible/journalism.html

Yellow Journalism and the Spanish American War, http://tnt.turner.com/movies/tntoriginals/roughriders/jour.home.html

READINGS AND REFERENCES

Beasley, M. H., & Gibbons, S. (1993). *Taking their place: A documentary history of women and journalism.* Washington, DC: American University Press.

Blanchard, M. A. (Ed.). (1998). *History of the mass media in the United States, an encyclopedia.* Chicago: Fitzroy Dearborn Publishers.

Brennen, B., & Hardt, H. (Eds.). (1999). *Picturing the past: Media, history and photography.* Champaign, IL: University of Illinois Press.

Briggs, A., & Burke, P. (2001). *A social history of the media from Gutenberg to the Internet.* Malden, MA: Blackwell.

Danky, J. P., et al. (Eds.). (1999). *African-American newspapers and periodicals: A national bibliography.* Cambridge, MA: Harvard University Press.

Fedler, F. (2000). *Lessons from the past: Journalists' lives and work, 1850–1950.* Prospect Heights, IL: Waveland Press.

Folkerts, J., & Teeter, D. L. Jr. (1997). *Voices of a nation: A history of mass media in the United States.* Boston: Allyn and Bacon.

Hudson, F. (2000). *Journalism in the United States from 1690–1872.* New York: Routledge.

Hutton, F., & Reid, B. S. (Eds.). (1996). *Outsiders in 19th-Century press history.* Bowling Green: Bowling Green State University Press.

Lubow, A. (1992). *The reporter who would be king: A biography of Richard Harding Davis.* New York: Charles Scribner's Sons.

Mindich, D. T. Z. (1998). *Just the facts: How objectivity came to define American journalism.* New York: New York University Press.

Pride, A. S., & Wilson, C. C. (1997). *A history of the Black Press.* Washington, DC: Howard University Press.

Rafferty, A. M. (2000). *American journalism 1690–1904.* New York: Routledge.

Sachsman, D. B., et al. (Eds.). (2000). *The Civil War and the press.* New Brunswick, NJ: Transaction Publishers.

Sloan, W. D. (1991). *Perspectives on mass communication history.* Hillsdale, NJ: Lawrence Erlbaum.

Sloan, W. D., & Parcell, L. M. (Eds.). (2002). *American journalism: History, principles, practices.* Jefferson, NC: McFarland & Company.

Sloan, W. D., Stovall, J. G., & Startt, J. D. (1999). *The media in America: A history* (4th ed.). Northport, AL: Vision.

Streitmatter, R. (1994). *Raising her voice: African-American women journalists who changed history.* Lexington, KY: University of Kentucky Press.

Streitmatter, R. (1997). *Mightier than the sword: How the news media have shaped American history.* Boulder, CO: Westview Press.

Suggs, H. L. (Ed.). (1996). *The Black Press in the Middle West, 1865–1985.* Westport, CT: Greenwood Press.

Tifft, S. E., & Jones, A. S. (1999). *The trust: The private and powerful family behind the New York Times.* New York: Little Brown and Company.

Wolseley, R. E. (1995). *Black achievers in American journalism.* Nashville: James C. Winston Publishing.

Woodhull, N. J., & Snyder, R. W. (Eds.). (1998). *Defining moments in journalism.* New Brunswick, NJ: Transaction Publishers.

Chapter Twenty-three

Twentieth Century and Beyond

Key Concepts and Terms

1. The most profound change in journalism in the twentieth century came with the development of broadcasting—first radio and then television.

2. At the end of the twentieth century, a new medium—the Web—promised to render additional profound changes in the profession.

3. Radio brought news events to its audience immediately, often as they were happening; consequently, audiences were able to share a single experience.

4. The twentieth century was the era of the Big News Event—from the Scopes Monkey Trial in 1925 in Dayton, Tennessee, to World War II.

5. Muckrakers: journalists who looked deeply into the ills of society, such as the abuses of child labor and governmental corruption, and wrote long exposés; the term was coined by President Theodore Roosevelt.

6. Radio Act of 1927: established that the electromagnetic spectrum belongs to the public, and the U.S. government has the power to regulate it.

7. Newsmagazine: a type of publication pioneered by Henry Luce and Brittan Hadden, founders of *Time*, that summarized and wrote entertainingly about the events of the week.

8. Edward R. Murrow: the chief European correspondent for CBS radio during World War II; Murrow set the standard for broadcast news.

9. Television came of age as a news medium in the 1960s with its coverage of three major stories: the assassination of President John F. Kennedy, the civil rights movement, and the war in Vietnam.

10. Watergate: the name given to the scandals of the Nixon administration in the 1970s that eventually resulted in the resignation of Richard Nixon in 1974; Watergate, a watershed in American journalism, was a story pursued by two young reporters for the *Washington Post*, Robert Woodward and Carl Bernstein.

Vignette

It was a moment of high drama.

The king of England sat in a room alone, a microphone in front of him. Weeks of negotiation with politicians, emotional exchanges with family and friends, rumors whispered in public and shouted in the press—all of it had come to this. Edward VIII, who had been king for less than a year, had decided to abdicate.

By all accounts, people not only in England but all around the world loved him. They thought he was handsome, debonair, and more than competent enough to be the symbol of the nation. But his romance with an American divorcée had put everything about his future in doubt. When he made it known that he wanted to marry Wallis Simpson, politicians and church leaders told him he could not. As these debates were taking place in the latter half of 1936, Edward could say nothing publicly.

Finally, on December 11, 1936, after he had made his decision, he had his chance. Around the world, millions of people bent their ears to their radios to hear his crackling voice. The king was speaking to more people at one time than any human being in history had ever addressed. In the middle of his short speech, he delivered these famous lines:

"But you must believe me when I tell you that I have found it impossible to carry the heavy burden of responsibility and to discharge my duties as King as I would wish to do without the help and support of the woman I love."

It was a quintessential moment of the twentieth century. The world had come together. Millions of people in many parts of the globe knew the same thing at the same moment. The king of England had sacrificed his throne for "the woman I love." That moment, and many after it, was made possible by radio.

Radio and its successor, television, changed the way the world got its news. The speed achieved by the telegraph in the nineteenth century seemed slow compared to the light-speed of radio waves that came straight into the home.

But broadcasting had introduced an even more profound change. It was exemplified by the king's speech. One person could talk directly to millions of people at the same time. The contact could be instantaneous and, to some extent, personal. The newsmaker didn't need to go through the media. He or she could go directly to the audience.

That kind of communication would define the century and many of the news events it produced.

A Century of Technology

The twentieth century saw the birth and development of two new technologies that changed the form and practice of journalism. One was broadcasting at the beginning

Quote 23.1

BOB TROUT

On radio in the 1930s

It's no exaggeration to say that radio brought the whole country together, all at the same instant, everyone listening to the same things. And the country liked being tied together that way. In the morning people would say, "Did you hear that last night? Did you hear Hitler speaking again? What was he talking about? Did you hear them all cheering, 'Sieg Heil'? What did you think?" It was on the tip of everybody's tongue. People didn't quite see, just yet, exactly how overseas events were ever going to intimately affect their daily lives. But it was the greatest show they'd ever been offered.

Bob Trout was a longtime radio broadcaster for CBS News. He introduced the radio broadcasts of President Franklin Roosevelt and first referred to them as "fireside chats."

of the century, and the other was the Internet toward the end of the century. Each technology began modestly with its original inventors and innovators not imagining the extraordinary implications of what they were doing.

The century also witnessed the maturation of the "old media," newspapers, both as news organizations and as businesses. The number of newspapers grew for a short time as the century began but then declined. The circulation and revenue of the newspapers that were left increased so that newspapers became healthy, stable institutions, destined to survive unchanged in many ways for many decades. Magazines continued on a less stable path (as they had in the nineteenth century), appearing and often dying as trends and styles faded. The print media, particularly newspapers, set the standard for journalism and journalistic practices, but that position was challenged and overtaken by broadcasting as the century wore on.

One of the most important phenomena of the twentieth century was the development of the audience as an important consideration in the practice and economics of journalism. Audiences, of course, had always been important to journalism, but in the nineteenth century, they seemed willing to accept what the "great men" of journalism—Pulitzer, Hearst, Greeley, and Bennett—decided to give them. In the twentieth century, the "great men" faded, and the needs and desires of the audience increased in importance. Many media organizations pursued the mass audience, trying to gain the attention and adherence of as many people as possible. Toward the end of the century, the concept of the specialized audience became more sophisticated. This changing view of the audience had a great deal to do with advertising, of course. Those people, companies, and organizations that had products to sell were beginning to discover the mass audience and mass marketing. They made demands on the news organizations to deliver large audiences for their advertising, and the news organizations responded. Later in the century, marketing to specialized or segmented audiences became more efficient for some products and manufacturers. Media systems matured so that they could also deliver these audiences for the advertiser.

Finally, the twentieth century was the century of the Big News Event. The two costliest wars in human history, World War I (1914–1918) and World War II (1939–1945), occurred during the first half of the century. World War II ended with the explosion of the atom bomb, an event that altered the course of human history. The century was dotted with Big Events—the Scopes Monkey Trial, the Lindbergh kidnapping, the civil rights movement, the Kennedy assassination, the first landing on the moon, the war in Vietnam, the resignation of Richard Nixon, the trial of O. J. Simpson, and so on. Some of these events were truly profound, some merely interesting. Either way, they captured the attention of the news media at the time and, thus, captured the attention of media consumers. Journalists and news organizations geared themselves to covering the Big Event of the moment and also to the ever-present charges that their very presence was creating the news.

Thus, journalism changed and developed throughout the century. The technical changes that occurred in the field were important, but they were only the beginning.

The Decline of Newspapers

Newspapers both prospered and declined during the twentieth century. Their size grew and their content became broader and more sophisticated. Circulation numbers increased, and they cemented their place as a major civic and social force in their communities. Financially, they developed into one of the most profitable of all businesses, by the end of the century often boasting of more than a 20 percent profit margin (huge by most business standards).

But newspapers also declined in the twentieth century, and that decline began in the first two decades. Newspapers entered the 1900s slightly hung over, as it were, from some of the excesses of the late nineteenth century. The yellow journalism period, fueled by the New York giants, the *Herald* and the *World*, revealed newspapers as more interested in gaining attention than in delivering a quality product. Publishers, exemplified by William Randolph Hearst and Joseph Pulitzer, acted imperiously and spent money lavishly and sometimes foolishly. Many blamed newspapers for the Spanish-American War and the costs associated with America's fit of imperialism.

The real problem for newspapers, however, was that they had overreached their business potential. Journalism historian Frank Luther Mott called newspapers "leviathans" at this point in their history. They were large and ponderous and could not adapt to a changing market or audience. They had grown faster than the population, and at the beginning of the century, there were simply too many of them. The number of newspapers continued to grow in the first decade until there were about 2,200 daily newspapers in the country, but by the beginning of World War I, that number had receded. Advertisers had begun putting their money into the newspapers that had the largest circulations because they wanted to attract the largest audience for their products. Those larger newspapers could then buy out the smaller ones and either close them down or merge their operations. This decreased the competition to the point that the surviving newspaper had a monopoly—that is, it was the only newspaper available for readers and advertisers in an area. By 1920, there were more cities in the nation with single newspapers than with competing newspapers.

Magazines rather than newspapers provided what sparks there were to the profession of journalism during this period. A few magazines employed journalists and editors who were willing to face up to the effects of industrialization and unwilling to accept the niceties of the Gilded Age. Notable among these was S. S. McClure, who launched *McClure's Magazine* in 1893. The magazine became popular with its readers because of its well-written feature stories and its excellent illustration. One of its best writers was Ida Tarbell, who in 1902 finished a ground-breaking series innocuously titled "A History of the Standard Oil Company." It had taken her four years to research and write the series, which detailed the way in which John D. Rockefeller had attempted to destroy the company's competition in the oil business. The series eventually led to an investigation of the company and a lawsuit that broke the giant corporation into smaller companies.

Tarbell's colleague at *McClure's* was Lincoln Steffens, one of the best investigative reporters in the history of journalism. In 1902 he began a series of articles that looked at how many of the major cities in the United States were run. He found example after example of waste, fraud, theft, and corruption, and often he was able to get those perpetrating the frauds to talk to him about it. The work of Tarbell and Steffens inspired other magazine journalists to take hard looks at the government and industries around them. They were called "muckrakers," and their work energized a reform movement that changed much about American life and society. Many reform measures, such as the Pure Food and Drug Act of 1907, were passed because of the work of the muckrakers.

The reformist movement played itself out by the time Europe went to war in 1914. World War I was the result of a series of mistakes and miscalculations by Europe's heads of state, but once it had begun, no one could find a way out. Nor could anyone figure out exactly how to fight it. Generals on both sides had modern weapons but fought with eighteenth-century tactics. The result was enormous casualties and stalemate. Americans were glad to be out of it, but the British–French side seemed determined to get America involved. They encouraged correspondents from American newspapers to visit, and they made sure that the American press had their side of the story. British officials in particular did everything they could to play upon the affinity that Americans had for Great Britain. After Germany had committed a number of acts of aggression against the United States and President Woodrow Wilson asked Congress for a declaration of war in 1917, the American mainstream was fully supportive of Wilson and the war effort.

The major postwar development for newspapers was the introduction of the tabloid newspaper to American readers. The tabloid newspaper was half the size of a full-size newspaper and easier to handle, particularly for urban readers. The first major tabloid was the *New York Daily News*, begun in 1919 by Joseph Medill, grandson and namesake of the founder of the *Chicago Tribune*. Whereas most newspapers presented their information in a graphically subdued fashion with small headlines and relatively small pictures, the tabloid used large pictures and headlines to attract readers to its sensational mix of news that often involved crime, sports, and sex. In the

FIGURE 23.1   Women in the Newsroom By 1910 when this photograph of the *Rocky Mountain News* newsroom in Denver, Colorado, was taken, women had, to some extent, taken their place beside men in journalism. Women writers and reporters were not plentiful, but they did exist and were showing that they could be every bit as effective as journalists as men. (Photo credit: Library of Congress)

1920s, Americans prospered economically and were distracted by new fashions and freedom for women, jazz, and sports, especially baseball, boxing, and horse racing. Tabloids fit perfectly into this era of "jazz journalism," as it came to be known, and by 1925 tabloid newspapers were found in most of the large cities in the country.

During these years, newspapers did not realize that their supremacy as the nation's major communication medium was about to end. Like the nation as a whole, they seemed prosperous and profitable. Despite the excesses of the tabloids, professional standards of reporting and writing had taken hold. Some of the great writers of the age—from Grantland Rice in the sports section to H. L. Mencken on the editorial page—could be found in the columns of the American press. But newspapers faced a challenge that they did not recognize—the advent of broadcasting.

The Development of Radio

The discovery of electromagnetic waves in the atmosphere and the harnessing of them for communication is one of the great achievements of mankind. The scientific and conceptual breakthroughs that were made in this area in the waning years of the nineteenth century laid the base for the structure of the life we live today.

Just who "invented" radio is a matter of some dispute among historians. Many people contributed to its development, beginning even before the Civil War with those who were interested in the properties of electronic telegraphy, or wireless telegraphs. Eventually those experiments and theories came to fruition with the work of Nathan Stubblefield, who broadcast speech and music from his home in Murray, Kentucky. Word of Stubblefield's success brought him great attention, and in 1904 he predicted that his invention would be used "for the general transmission of news of every description." At the same time, Italian Guglielmo Marconi was also figuring out how to get messages through the atmosphere. Marconi could see the commercial value of his work, and he conducted a number of public experiments in order to sell the idea to investors. In 1901 he sent wireless signals from England to Canada, demonstrating the possibility of transmitting messages across the ocean without cable.

But there were additional problems to be solved. Capturing and transmitting sound, not just telegraphic signals, was still difficult, and building devices that would receive those sounds conveniently had yet to be accomplished. Even before those problems had been overcome, radio proved its worth as a medium of news transmission during the *Titanic* disaster of 1912. The first reports of the disaster came from the radio signals of the ship *Carpathia,* which was about fifty miles from the *Titanic* when it sank. The enormous publicity given to the *Titanic*'s sinking helped focus attention on the value of wireless transmission, and later that year, Congress passed the Radio Act of 1912 that put the U.S. Department of Commerce in charge of licensing radio stations and assigning frequencies.

Experiments and innovations continued during the years of World War I, and by the end of the war, commercial companies were investing in this new technology. American Telephone and Telegraph manufactured and sold transmitters; General Electric and Westinghouse sold receiving sets. Radio Corporation of America (RCA) entered the fray as the sales agent collecting royalties on the patents that these devices used. The structure of broadcasting as we know it was beginning to form. In November 1920, radio station KDKA in Pittsburgh went on the air and broadcast the results of the presidential election that year. KDKA is widely acknowledged as the first radio station of the kind we listen to now, and it is still in operation today.

In the next few years, the popularity of radio exploded. In 1921, there were about 30 radio stations broadcasting with some regularity; by 1923 there were more than 600. Westinghouse had sold more than 600,000 receiving sets by that time. That number grew to 14 million by the end of the decade. Radio stations proliferated throughout the decade, with many entrepreneurs recognizing the value of radio as an advertising medium. A company could build a radio station simply to broadcast information about its products. Others conceived of the idea of selling time on their station to many companies that wanted to advertise. In just a few short years, radio was everywhere.

Even at this early stage, radio introduced a different kind of journalism to the world. Radio could take people to the scene of an event and could do so instantly. Audiences could hear the sounds of the event, rather than just reading about them. In 1925, the

FIGURE 23.2   Herbert Hoover and the Regulation of Radio As secretary of commerce under President Calvin Coolidge, Herbert Hoover recognized the importance and power of radio and was instrumental in overseeing some of the first regulations the U.S. government imposed. Hoover was elected president in 1928 but was defeated by Franklin Roosevelt in 1932. (Photo credit: Library of Congress)

small east Tennessee town of Dayton captured the world's attention by putting on trial a biology professor who had discussed the theory of evolution in his high school class. Such discussions were viewed as sacrilegious and were a violation of Tennessee law, and the trial was a clash of cultural forces represented by fundamentalist religion and science. The trial attracted two of the most famous figures of the day, defense lawyer Clarence Darrow and three-time presidential candidate William Jennings Bryant, who argued the case for the prosecution. The Scopes Monkey Trial, as it came to be known (after John Scopes, the biology teacher), also attracted the world's press. That press included WGN, a Chicago radio station that spent $1,000 to broadcast the weeklong trial. For the first time the entire nation could sit inside the courtroom of a sensational trial. Radio gave its audience an immediacy that it had never known before.

But there was a problem. The growth in the number of radio stations soon produced a babble rather than a coherent set of voices. The electromagnetic spectrum that can handle radio is limited. Radio signals travel for a limited geographic area, and within that area wavelengths can be used effectively by only one operator. The Radio Act of 1912 did not anticipate the problem of more than one operator in an area broadcasting over the same wavelength. That soon happened, and the result was interference on the part of the sounds and great irritation on the part of the listeners. The result of this babble and confusion was the Radio Act of 1927, an important piece of legislation that established a number of principles: that the electromagnetic spectrum belongs to the public; that the government has the power to regulate it; that broadcasting is an important service that should be equitably distributed; and that broadcasting is a form of speech that deserves First Amendment protection. The Radio Act of 1927 was followed by the Communication Act of 1934, which expanded the Federal Communications Commission (FCC) and gave it broad powers over the technical communication structure (telephone, telegraph, television, cables, etc.) in America.

With order imposed by the government, radio prospered. Even during the Depression years, radio audiences and advertising expanded. Networks used telephone lines to link local radio stations and provided programs and services that could be heard in every part of the nation. Music, drama, comedy, and variety show formats were developed to keep listeners entertained. Live performances were staged for the radio audience. Companies and products were identified with a show or a personality. Some politicians, the foremost being President Franklin Roosevelt, recognized the power of radio to communicate with the nation. Roosevelt used a series of radio broadcasts, called "fireside chats," to explain his ideas to America and rally support for his policies. Roosevelt's voice was clear, firm, and unmistakable. He spoke with assurance and with the power of radio installed a confidence in Americans when they desperately needed it.

Radio news was also developing its voice. One of the networks, the Columbia Broadcasting System, hired Lowell Thomas, a deep-throated writer and traveler, to be its news commentator in 1930. Many others followed, including personalities such as Dorothy Parker and Walter Winchell. Radio could use the ambient sounds of a news events to make listeners feel as if they were on the scene along with the correspondent. The style of writing and presentation was different. Correspondents used short, simple sentences to deliver the information and describe action. They could use their voices to be low-keyed or emphatic. They could interview news-makers and let their voices be heard.

Newspapers realized the threat that radio news was to their supremacy, and at first, most simply tried to ignore it, hoping it would go away. Radio did not go away, and newspapers became more aggressive. As cooperative owners of the Associated Press (AP), newspaper publishers refused to allow radio news departments to subscribe to the AP. An agreement in the mid-1930s between newspaper owners and radio networks designed a limit to the amount of "news" that radio stations could broadcast, but it did not limit "commentary." Radio continued to develop its news and information function through the guise of commentary. The power of radio as a news medium could not be suppressed, and after a few short years, all agreements with publishers had dissipated. By the end of the decade, with war raging in Europe, radio news was in full flower.

The brightest bloom of that flower was Edward R. Murrow. Born in North Carolina and raised in Washington state, Murrow was president of the National Student Federation when he graduated from college and convinced CBS to air a program called *A University of the Air*. Murrow joined

FIGURE 23.3   Edward R. Murrow
Edward R. Murrow became one of the most respected and revered of all news broadcasters because of the work he did in reporting the war in Europe in the 1930s and 1940s. He fostered a set of young correspondents, many of whom continued to have long careers in television and radio. (Photo credit: Library of Congress)

CBS in 1935 and two years later found himself in Europe covering the crisis that was enveloping the continent. When the Nazis marched into Vienna, Austria, in 1938, Murrow was there to describe Adolph Hitler's triumphal appearance: "Herr Hitler is now at the Imperial Hotel. Tomorrow, there is to be a big parade. . . . Please don't think that everyone in Vienna was out to greet Herr Hitler today. There is tragedy as well as rejoicing in this city tonight." The next year, Hitler invaded Poland, and Europe went to war. Murrow began his regular broadcasts with "This is London." Murrow had put together a team of reporters stationed in the major European capitals; many of them would achieve fame as writers and news reporters and commentators, but they would always be known as Murrow's Boys. CBS was not the only network to develop a news team, of course. The National Broadcasting Company had done the same thing, and other smaller networks had also put together news operations. As the world plunged into war, these teams went to work at home and abroad to bring the story of the world's biggest event into the offices and homes of radio listeners.

Time and Development of the Newsmagazine

Radio was not the only threat to the newspaper as the chief information medium for the nation. In 1923, college friends Henry Luce and Briton Hadden, graduates of Yale, produced an idea that had been stirring within them for some time. The nation was ready, they thought, for a weekly publication that would summarize news events. These summaries could be written in a livelier way than they appeared in newspapers. Because they were weekly, they could gather up events into a more coherent narrative. They could contain the point of the view of the writer, and they could be entertaining. The magazine that Luce and Hadden conceived was originally called *Facts;* that was soon changed to *Time.*

The first issue appeared on March 23, 1923. Hadden is credited with developing the peculiar writing style of *Time* (verbs before subjects, creative use of attribution, comments inserted straight into the news reports, etc.). Hadden and Luce gave their own twists to the news, and the magazine prospered. Hadden died in 1929, and Luce took over the business and built it into a publishing empire. In 1930 Luce began *Fortune* magazine, a publication aimed at covering the business world, a bold move at the beginning of the Depression.

But that was not Luce's boldest idea. That came six years later when the company published the first issue of *Life* magazine. *Life's* forte was pictures. Luce sensed that American journalism was ignoring an important dimension of its technology—photography. People wanted to see as well as read. *Life* gave them a chance to do just that. Its larger-than-average format and slick paper provided an ideal forum for the best photojournalism of the day. *Life* was an instant success, selling out the nearly 500,000 copies of the first issue it produced. It attracted millions of subscribers and the very best photojournalists available, including Margaret Bourke-White, Alfred Eisenstadt, and Robert Capa. The magazine spared no expense in putting photographers at the scene of an important story, and its editors were experts in selecting and cropping photos that emphasized all that was interesting and dramatic about the picture.

HENRY LUCE AND THE MARCH OF *TIME*

Henry Luce knew the value of news and information. And he knew how to give it to people in a way they wanted it.

Luce and his friend from Yale, Briton Hadden, had an idea in 1923 that people would like to get their news in a different form than the newspapers use. They wanted it brief, summed up and, if possible, entertaining. And rather than do it once a day, they would do it once a week. That would give the writers time to put information together and tell the story.

The original title of their magazine was *Facts;* it soon became *Time.*

The magazine was not an instant success, but it managed to survive and establish itself. The formula worked, and as more and more people learned about it, they signed up. Hadden died in 1929, and Luce took over the operation with expansion in mind. If *Time* worked for news, other magazines could work for other areas. His string of successes was phenomenal:

Fortune (1930)

Life (1936)

Sports Illustrated (1954)

And after Luce's death in 1967, Time, Inc. hit on yet another idea— *People* (1974), a celebration of celebrity.

No man has had such a successful magazine publishing career, and no company has been more influential than Time, Inc.

Luce's magazine empire produced its imitators. In 1933, two other newsmagazines came onto the scene that are still being published today: *Newsweek* and *U.S. News. Look* magazine was a more modest operation than *Life* but went after the same market. Magazines that combined news and pictures were the *Saturday Evening Post* and *Colliers.*

These publications were geared to bring Americans the biggest story of the century, World War II. By the time Pearl Harbor was bombed on December 7, 1941, Americans could hear the latest events on their radios, read the daily reports in their newspapers, catch up on the week's news in their newsmagazines and see the best and most dramatic pictures of the war in any of several national publications. They were inundated with information, and with their intimate involvement in the war, they could not get enough.

Television

The age of radio lasted less than three decades. Once World War II was finished, the world was about to get another medium that would go beyond radio. Television was coming, though its advent was delayed by first the war and then by the U.S. government. Those involved with radio were highly interested and gravitated to the new medium. Newspapers and magazines looked upon television with a mixture of fear and disdain. Nothing could ever replace print, they said. They were right, of course,

FIGURE 23.4   Attack on Pearl Harbor The Japanese attack on U.S. naval forces in Pearl Harbor, Hawaii (shown here is the USS *Shaw* exploding), plunged America into World War II, the greatest news story of the century. With radio, newsmagazines, and photomagazines, as well as newspapers, Americans had plenty of news sources at the beginning of the war. (Photo credit: National Archives)

but the electronic media of radio and television were destined to have a profound effect on print to revise, again, the whole concept of news.

Almost as soon as radio was formed, people began thinking in terms of pictures rather than just sound. The first demonstration of pictures being transmitted by electromagnetic waves occurred in 1927 in the laboratory of Philo Farnsworth in San Francisco. Farnsworth, an independent scientist, held many of the patents on the technology that would eventually produce television, and it was a dispute over these patents that delayed the introduction of television to the general public.

By the end of World War II there were six television stations in the United States. The number began to grow, but in 1948 the FCC stopped granting licenses in order to resolve some of the technical questions that various approaches to television had raised. Those questions were settled by 1952, and the prosperity of the times allowed television to boom. The FCC granted hundreds of new licenses over the next few years, and millions of television receivers were sold. The radio networks evolved into the television networks, and many of the stars and programs from radio became the stars and programs of early television. People who grew up imagining what the Lone Ranger and his faithful companion Tonto looked like when they heard the program on the radio could now see the pair as everyone else saw them.

Television news also brought many of its stars from radio, but the medium demanded something different, something that was much harder to acquire and edit—pictures, and moving pictures, at that. In 1948 CBS aired *Douglas Edwards and the News;* that was quickly followed by *John Cameron Swayze's Camel Caravan* on NBC. Both programs were fifteen minutes long, barely time enough to present a few short stories and pictures. But other news formats were developed. Edward R. Murrow and Fred Friendly produced an interview/documentary show called *See It Now.* Newsworthy interviews were often contained on entertainment shows such as the NBC's *Today Show,* hosted by Dave Garroway, and the late-night *Jack Paar Show.*

The network's nightly news programs spawned a generation of news superstars—the anchors. Among them were Chet Huntley and David Brinkley at NBC, who were first teamed to do the coverage of the national political conventions in 1952. Every night, one was in Washington and the other in New York, as they read the news and introduced reports from around the world. Networks became more sophisticated about the way they presented their reports, and the technology improved so they could obtain film and video faster and could do live, on-the-scene reports. In the summer of 1963, the networks expanded their fifteen-minute news shows to thirty minutes.

Nothing, however, had prepared the nation for the four traumatic days in November of that year when President John F. Kennedy was assassinated. Kennedy was riding in an open car in a motorcade in downtown Dallas, Texas, when he was hit by bullets from a long-range rifle. The time was 12:30 p.m. Central time on Friday, November 22, and the networks cut into their normal programming immediately to make the announcement. They stayed on the air, broadcasting what little information they had. About an hour later, Kennedy was pronounced dead at Parkland Hospital. The network news anchors stayed on the air all afternoon and evening following the story—the inauguration of Lyndon Johnson on *Air Force One,* the return of Kennedy's body to Washington, the arrest of Lee Harvey Oswald as the chief suspect in the shooting, and so on. On Saturday, the networks ceased their normal programs for the next seventy-two hours while America watched. The live cameras were there on Sunday morning when Lee Harvey Oswald was being moved from the Dallas City Jail and Jack Ruby stepped in front of him and shot him at close range. Oswald died later that day. On Monday, the world was transfixed by the images of Kennedy's funeral and procession to Arlington Cemetery. (See Chapter 6 for more on the television coverage of the Kennedy assassination.)

Those three days demonstrated the power of television to cover an event and hold an audience as never before. Newspapers, magazines, and radio played only supporting roles to television as Americans dealt with their shock, horror, and grief. Television proved itself able to provide both the pictures and the emotion of that tragic event.

FIGURE 23.5 **Television Tells the Civil Rights Story** Television news brought images such as this one—a 17-year-old civil rights demonstrator, defying an antiparade ordinance of Birmingham, Alabama, and being attacked by a police dog on May 3, 1963—into the living rooms of America. The civil rights movement was transformed from a local battle against segregation into a national moral issue. (Photo credit: AP Wide World Photos)

Newspapers: Clouded Stability and Prosperity

Despite the development of these new sources of information, newspapers continued to attract large audiences and to occupy the pinnacle of journalistic standards and integrity. Many of the people on television news programs had been former newspaper reporters. (Walter Cronkite, for instance, had once worked for the news service United Press International.)

By the 1960s, however, the strength of newspapers began to erode. Large cities were likely to have competing newspapers, but most newspapers operated as monopolies in their hometowns. Their profit margins remained high. But about 1960, overall newspaper circulation hit a plateau of slightly more than 60 million newspapers per day. That was disturbing because the population continued to grow. It meant that newspapers were being seen by a smaller and smaller percentage of the population.

That decrease was small and not life-threatening, but it has not abated during the past forty years.

Why the decline? In many ways newspapers had gotten better. During the 1960s, the technology of newspaper production changed, allowing them to be more innovative in their designs and freer to use pictures and illustrations. Newspaper writing improved as many editors allowed reporters more leeway in how they put together their stories. Journalism schools were coming into their own and graduating flocks of young journalists who were bringing a more sophisticated level of training into the newsroom. Computerization hit the newsroom in several waves, particularly in the 1970s and 1980s, allowing journalists more time and freedom to report and write their stories.

The slow demise of readership of newspapers has been attributed to many factors. Among them is the feeling that other media, especially television, are distracting people and taking away time that they would have once devoted to newspapers. Another reason that has been suggested for this decline is the content of newspapers themselves; that is, newspapers do not pay attention to events and subjects that many people are interested in, particularly young people. Some have even suggested that there is a general decline in literacy, or at least the value of literacy, and newspapers have suffered because of it. This suggestion is disputed by others who cite the fact that more books are being published, sold, and read than ever before. In surveys of how people spend their leisure time, respondents are likely to say "reading" more than any other activity.

Despite this decline in readership, newspapers remain a vital part of American life and the place where basic journalistic skills are most likely to be learned and practiced. Occasionally newspapers, because of their prominence and slower production schedules (compared to broadcasting and the Web), will lead the nation into news stories that other media avoid. One such instance was Watergate, the political scandal of the early 1970s that led to the resignation of Richard Nixon as president. In June 1972, five men broke into the Democratic Party headquarters in the Watergate building (thus, the name) in Washington, DC. They were found to have ties to the re-election campaign of Richard Nixon, and eventually it was discovered that Nixon himself had participated in a cover-up that kept investigators from properly investigating the crime. Two years after the break-in, Nixon had to resign as president.

The story had few visual angles so that its attraction for television journalists was not great. In the first months after the break-in, there were few major events associated with it because the Nixon administration had done such a good job in covering it up. The story was uncovered by two *Washington Post* reporters, Bob Woodward and Carl Bernstein, who spent months examining documents, interviewing people, and putting the story together. Their reporting eventually led to a Congressional investigation and the appointment of a special prosecutor by the U.S. Department of Justice. The actions of the *Washington Post* showed that newspapers could do what other media could not or would not; they could stay with an important story over a long period of time.

In addition to this strength, the continuing value of newspapers is their ability to report local news. No other news organization, including the largest television sta-

tions, can match the resources and effort that newspapers put into gathering and reporting local information. This kind of information is found nowhere else, and readers place great value on it. Consequently, despite declines in readership rates,
newspapers are likely to continue to have a strong place in their communities.

Expanding Television with Cable

The decades of the 1950s and 1960s saw television stabilize into a local system of
stations that was supported by three national networks. Those networks provided
thirty-minute newscasts each evening, whereas the local stations usually put together
an additional thirty minutes of news. Other news programs on both the national and
local levels might be aired (as we discussed earlier in this chapter), but news constituted a relatively small but important part of a station's offering to its viewers. Television stations and national networks were assured of large audiences because the
program offerings, both news and entertainment, were so limited.

Over-the-air broadcasting did not reach every area of the country, however. Even
the most powerful local stations could not send a very strong signal outside of a metropolitan area. The way television reached nonurban viewers was through cable. A
tall receiving tower would be set up in a small town to catch the television signals;
those signals would then be relayed through a cable that ran into the homes of the
residents. Local stations and networks were quite happy to have their audiences expanded in this way.

In the 1960s and 1970s, the United States launched a series of communication
satellites that would orbit the earth in a way that made them "stationary" above one
point on the earth. These satellites could send and receive signals and in many ways
revolutionized the global transmission of information. One of the things these satellites allowed was the direct transmission of television signals. That is, a local television station could transmit its programming directly to a satellite; that satellite could
then relay those signals to a receiving tower that could be a long way from the station itself.

One of the first people to understand the implications of this technology was Ted
Turner, owner of WTBS, a struggling, independent (non-network-affiliated) station
in Atlanta. Many people in Atlanta liked WTBS because it showed lots of old movies,
something they could not get on the network-affiliated channels. Turner had the idea
that viewers in other areas would also like to have that choice, and the availability
of satellites gave him the means of offering it to them. He began offering his station
to cable systems for a relatively small fee. WTBS became a "super-station," and Turner
made a huge profit on his idea.

Other entrepreneurs saw other opportunities and possibilities in the satellite–cable
technology. They realized that with cable, television sets were open to more channels
than just those provided by the local stations. Religious broadcasters, for instance,
found that people across the nation would view their programs. At the other end of
the technology, cable systems in the late 1970s and early 1980s began to grow. Urban
areas, which had heretofore never "needed" cable, became lucrative markets for cable

WATERGATE: A "THIRD-RATE BURGLARY" AND A PULITZER FOR TWO YOUNG REPORTERS

It was a story no one seemed to want to pursue.

Five burglars were caught breaking into the Democratic National Committee headquarters in the Watergate apartment building in Washington, DC, on June 17, 1972. Who were they? What were they doing there? Who sent them?

The questions begged for answers, but no one seemed to want to find them—no one except two young reporters for the *Washington Post*, Bob Woodward and Carl Bernstein. America was in the middle of a presidential election campaign. Republican Richard Nixon was seeking a second term and likely to swamp his Democratic opponent. Nixon's press secretary dismissed what happened at the Watergate as a "third-rate burglary."

But Woodward, Bernstein, and the *Post* would not be put off so easily. They began looking into the connections the burglars had with the White House and Nixon's reelection campaign organization. Their reporting took months. Some people would not talk; others gave them bits and pieces of infor-

Senator Sam Ervin of North Carolina, chairman of the Senate Watergate Committee, questions a witness during the televised hearings.

E. Howard Hunt, one of the Watergate burglars, demonstrates to the Senate committee the bugs that the burglars were trying to place in the Democratic National Committee headquarters.

systems because those viewers too wanted expanded choices. Between 1970 and 1985, the number of cable subscribers grew from about 5 million to more than 35 million.

Turner's success with marketing his superstation led him into another area—news. Turner realized that what the networks and the local stations offered in terms of news was relatively meager, particularly compared to what viewers wanted. His idea was to have a cable station that would broadcast news twenty-four hours a day and would be worldwide in its scope and coverage. Many people scoffed at the idea, saying that it would be too expensive and that the viewership would be small. Turner ignored those critics and in 1980 launched Cable News Network (CNN).

The critics were right about the first criticism. It was very expensive. But they were wrong about the second. CNN was immediately picked up by many cable systems, and its audience ratings were substantial. People had never been able to turn

President Richard Nixon (right) and his wife Pat prepare to board a helicopter on the south lawn of the White House just after Nixon had said farewell to his staff. Nixon was in the process of resigning as president. Gerald Ford (left) is about to be inaugurated as the new president.

The reporters still would not quit. Even after Nixon began his second term, their stories kept appearing in the *Post*. Finally, in 1973 the U.S. Senate appointed a special committee to investigate what had happened on the night of the burglary and who was responsible for it. That committee held public hearings and heard the testimony of current and former White House aides about how Nixon's reelection campaign had been run. Eventually, one aide revealed that most of the conversations in the Oval Office had been taped.

A long judicial battle ensued, with Nixon trying to keep the tapes from the public. When the U.S. Supreme Court ordered him to turn the tapes over to a special prosecutor in the summer of 1974, Nixon made public the fact that he had participated in covering up the scandal. Later that week, on August 8, 1974, he became the first president to resign from office.

Woodward and Bernstein were widely credited with bringing that resignation about. They won a Pulitzer prize for their efforts, and their book, *All the President's Men*, which described in detail their dogged reporting efforts, was made into a movie starring Robert Redford and Dustin Hoffman.

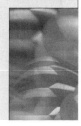

mation. While they were connecting these dots, Nixon was on his way to one of the biggest election victories in the history of the nation.

on their televisions and get news whenever they wanted it; they were always made to wait for scheduled newscasts. CNN had news any time they wanted it. And by gearing itself toward news and only news, CNN could cover live news events, from start to finish if necessary, without "breaking in" to normal programming. CNN paid top dollar to some of the most experienced television journalists in the business. When the Gulf War broke out in 1991, CNN had veteran war correspondent Peter Arnett in Baghdad, the capital city of Iraq, sending daily and sometimes hourly reports. Overall, it provided such thorough coverage of the war that when the fighting was over, most critics conceded that CNN had established itself as equal to the national news networks.

News has become a standard and substantial offering of cable television. A number of news operations have imitated CNN's twenty-four-hours-a-day, seven-days-a-week approach, so that cable viewers have many choices. In addition, news channels have been developed to deal with particular subjects, such as sports, and some large cities have their own twenty-four-hour news stations.

The Development of the Web

Just as the beginning of the twentieth century saw the development of the medium of radio, the end of the century saw the development of yet another medium—the World Wide Web. This medium, in the beginning, had little to do with journalism but a lot to do with news and information.

Two threads of creativity and problem solving—each as old as human intelligence—merged in the early 1990s to form the World Wide Web. Each thread had a tradition, a set of important personalities and contributors, and an approach. Each thread intersected and intertwined itself through the other in ways that ultimately helped to develop the communication system that we have today.

One thread was what we might call literary–scientific. The basic "problem" was the volume of human knowledge. The first half of the twentieth century witnessed a vast expansion of knowledge (information, ideas, technology), much of it wrought from a desire to win in warfare. At the end of World War II, Vannevar Bush, a scientist at the Massachusetts Institute of Technology, published a seminal article in the *Atlantic Monthly* on this problem.

> There is a growing mountain of research. But there is increased evidence that we are being bogged down today as specialization extends. The investigator is staggered by the findings and conclusions of thousands of other workers—conclusions which he cannot find time to grasp, much less to remember, as they appear. (Bush pp. 101–108)

Bush thought photography and compression might be the answer—taking pictures of documents and then reducing them so that a set of encyclopedias could fit into a matchbox. The cards on which these pictures would reside (microfiche) could then be read on some machine that would help the scientist in remembering the associations and threads of thinking. Bush's solution to the problem had some validity for a while, but it was his articulation of the problem itself and his ideas about sharing and linking that became important.

What Bush was beginning to envision was hypertext, a name later coined by Ted Nelson. In the 1960s Nelson conceived of a universe of documents, called a "docuverse," where documents would exist and be shared for a small fee. He called this docuverse Xanadu, the precursor of the World Wide Web that we know today.

The second thread was technological, and there were two "problems" that needed to be solved here. One was communicating over long distances, a problem that had existed from the time that individuals realized people lived beyond a day's walk. The other was a much more current problem. In the post–World War II nuclear age, the U.S. Department of Defense was fearful that a single, well-placed nuclear blast would eliminate the ability of the United States to communicate and defend itself. In the 1960s, the department's Advanced Research Project Agency (APRA) began developing an information distribution system that would not be knocked out with one blow.

The product of ARPA's work was a series of connected computers and computer networks called the Internet that was first instituted in 1969. Slowly and somewhat fitfully through the 1970s and 1980s, protocols for transferring information—email, online research tools and information, and even discussions groups—were formed.

In 1991, Tim Berners-Lee, a physicist working for a European research consortium in Switzerland, developed a hypertext system to allow people to share what they had through the Internet. It required a software program to be installed on an individual computer, and the information to be shared had to be formatted with a set of tags (hypertext markup language, or HTML). The browser that would allow all this to happen was called WorldWideWeb. More sophisticated browsers were later developed by others, but the name and the system that Berners-Lee donated to the world stuck (he has never made any money off his work).

The work of Berners-Lee and others took the Internet, previously confined to computer geeks and computer bulletin board users, and placed it into the hands of the general public. By the beginning of the twenty-first century, there were millions of web sites and web pages (collections of text and images) that represented individual people, organizations, companies, governments, and ideas. A survey by the U.S. Department of Commerce in September 2001 found that more than half the population was using the Internet, and the number of users was growing by about 2 million people per month. The Commerce Department report also said that 90 percent of children from ages 5 to 17 used computers, and 75 percent of 14- to 17-year-olds were on the Internet. In addition, 45 percent of the entire population used email (up from 35 percent in the previous year), and 36 percent used the Internet to search for product and service information, such as finding airline schedules and buying books online.

But after ten years, the Web has changed. The Web is certainly bigger, with more sites and more information. It is also technically easier to browse, or surf, and to find information. New design tools have made web sites easier to create and have allowed users increased ease in navigation. People who design and produce web sites have also become more sophisticated in presenting information and more adept at knowing why people visited a web site.

The web is now a "place," virtual though it may be, where people do things, and one of the chief web activities is getting information. People want airline schedules, recipes, Sunday school lessons, wedding registrations, the bestseller list, the latest prices on new computers—a wide variety of information that has one thing in common. It must be current.

That is why, above all else, the Web is a news medium.

People want news, and they want it immediately. Even when the information is not "breaking news," they expect the web sites they visit to be different whenever they show up. People rarely return to a web site if they keep seeing the same information. Web site producers quickly realized this, even though they may have begun their site with the idea that they could put it up and leave it alone. Web sites are not billboards. In order to maintain and increase their traffic, they must be changed often. The monster, as many webbies have found, must be fed.

This is, of course, what news organizations do, and this is one of the reasons the Web is so effective as a news medium. The development of Web journalism will allow, if not force, journalists to examine some basic questions about how we gather, process, and distribute information, and what our relationship with the audience is. The journalistic process itself is unlikely to shift dramatically as we enter this new medium. The culture of journalism is that we tell ourselves about ourselves; we try to do so with accuracy and grace and with the least harm, but we know that sometimes harm or discomfort will be the result.

How we do what we do is the question that is fascinating many web journalists in this era. The Web offers many possibilities and permutations on those possibilities, and anyone with energy, imagination, and a sense of adventure will enjoy the web environment for the next decade. New forms of storytelling and information presentation will be developed. Some will be discarded, and some will remain and mature. Watching and participating in this process will be fun.

The last question—the relationship of journalists with their audience—will probably be the most vexing and ultimately the most important one of all. How do we give the audience what it needs when there will be increased pressures to give the audience only what it wants? What kind of a dialogue should we develop with the audience, and when and how should the audience participate in the journalistic process? What standards of accountability will both journalists and the audience accept? Finally, how will web journalism achieve the ultimate goal of the journalist—to tell ourselves about ourselves in order to build a healthier community of people?

The journey of web journalism is just beginning.

QUESTIONS FOR DISCUSSION

1. What do you think are the three most important things that happened to journalism in the twentieth century? Be prepared to defend your answer with facts and logic.

2. Do you believe the World Wide Web will change journalism as much as the chapter predicts?

3. If you were going to publish a newspaper for your area (town, neighborhood, etc.), what would you do that is different from what your local newspaper is now doing? What kind of stories would you run that the local newspaper does not run?

4. Can you imagine a world without television? Some of your relatives may be old enough to remember what that was like. If so, it might be useful for you to have a discussion with them. What did people do with their time? Was radio a big deal? What kind of programs did they listen to?

RELATED WEB SITES

Center for History and New Media, http://chnm.gmu.edu

CNN 20th Anniversary Special Project, www.cnn.com/SPECIALS/2000/cnn20

Encyclopaedia of USA History: Journalists, www.spartacus.schoolnet.co.uk/USAjournalists.htm

Greensboro Sit-Ins: Media/Headlines, www.greensboro.com/sitins/media_headlines.htm

Image of the Journalist in Popular Culture, www.ijpc.org

Library of American Broadcasting, www.lib.umd.edu/UMCP/LAB

Media History Monographs, www.scripps.ohiou.edu/mediahistory

Media History Project, http://mediahistory.umn.edu

Media on Stamps, www.spacetoday.org/Stamps/Stamps.html

Milestones in Journalism Diversity (News Watch), http://newswatch.sfsu.edu/milestones

Museum of Broadcast Communications, www.museum.tv/index.shtml

Museum of Television and Radio, www.mtr.org

National Public Broadcasting Archives, www.lib.umd.edu/UMCP/NPBA/index.html

Newseum, www.newseum.org

New York Times Company History, www.nytco.com/company-timeline.html

Oral Histories Relating to Journalism History, www.elon.edu/dcopeland/ajha/oralhistory.htm

Poynter's "New Media Timeline," www.poynterextra.org/extra/Timeline/index.htm

Presstime: 20th Anniversary Issue, www.naa.org/presstime/9910/2019.html

Pulitzer Prize Photographs, www.newseum.org/pulitzer

Radio News, www.otr.com/news.html

Reporting Civil Rights, www.reportingcivilrights.org

Washington Post: 125th Anniversary, www.washingtonpost.com/wp-dyn/metro/specials/post125

What a Century! (CJR), www.cjr.org/year/99/1/century.asp

Women Come to the Front: Journalists, Photographers and Broadcasters During World War II, http://lcweb.loc.gov/exhibits/wcf/wcf0001.html

Women in Journalism Oral History Project, http://npc.press.org/wpforal/ohhome.htm

READINGS AND REFERENCES

Beasley, M. H., & Gibbons, S. (1993). *Taking their place: A documentary history of women and journalism.* Washington, DC: American University Press.

Blanchard, M. A. (Ed.). (1998). *History of the mass media in the United States, an encyclopedia.* Chicago: Fitzroy Dearborn Publishers.

Brennen, B., & Hardt, H. (Eds.). (1999). *Picturing the past: Media, history and photography.* Champaign, IL: University of Illinois Press.

Briggs, A., & Burke, P. (2001). *A social history of the media from Gutenberg to the Internet.* Malden, MA: Blackwell.

Bush, V. "As We May Think." Atlantic Monthly, July 1945, pp. 101–108.

Danky, J. P., et al. (Eds.). (1999). *African-American newspapers and periodicals: A national bibliography.* Cambridge, MA: Harvard University Press.

Fedler, F. (2000). *Lessons from the past: Journalists' lives and work, 1850–1950.* Prospect Heights, IL: Waveland Press.

Folkerts, J., & Teeter, D. L. Jr. (1997). *Voices of a nation: A history of mass media in the United States.* Boston: Allyn and Bacon.

Hudson, F. (2000). *Journalism in the United States from 1690–1872.* New York: Routledge.

Hutton, F., & Reid, B. S. (Eds.). (1996). *Outsiders in 19th-Century press history.* Bowling Green: Bowling Green State University Press.

Mindich, D. T. Z. (1998). *Just the facts: How objectivity came to define American journalism.* New York: New York University Press.

Pride, A. S., & Wilson, C. C. (1997). *A history of the Black Press.* Washington, DC: Howard University Press.

Rafferty, A. M. (2000). *American journalism 1690–1904.* New York: Routledge.

Sloan, W. D. (1991). *Perspectives on mass communication history.* Hillsdale, NJ: Lawrence Erlbaum.

Sloan, W. D., & Parcell, L. M. (Eds.). (2002) *American journalism: History, principles, practices.* Jefferson, NC: McFarland & Company.

Sloan, W. D., Stovall, J. G., & Startt, J. D. (1999). *The media in America: A history* (4th Ed.). Northport, AL: Vision.

Sorel, N. C. (1999). *The women who wrote the war.* New York: Arcade Publishing.

Streitmatter, R. (1994). *Raising her voice: African-American women journalists who changed history.* Lexington, KY: University of Kentucky Press.

Streitmatter, R. (1997). *Mightier than the sword: How the news media have shaped American history.* Boulder, CO: Westview Press.

Suggs, H. L. (Ed.). (1996). *The Black Press in the Middle West, 1865–1985.* Westport, CT: Greenwood Press.

Tifft, S. E., & Jones, A. S. (1999). *The trust: The private and powerful family behind the New York Times.* New York: Little Brown and Company.

Wolseley, R. E. (1995). *Black achievers in American journalism.* Nashville: James C. Winston Publishing.

Woodhull, N. J., & Snyder, R. W. (Eds.). (1998). *Defining moments in journalism.* New Brunswick, NJ: Transaction Publishers.

Why

Journalism is a field that constantly examines its place in society and constantly debates its role and its methods. In America, the basis of this role is the First Amendment to the United States Constitution, both as a legal and social document.

News as the product of journalism is free of many of the strictures that might be placed on the products of other businesses. News must satisfy its audience, but it cannot be compelled by the government to do so. In many ways, it serves as an independent force in society, a seemingly neutral voice, free to inform society about itself.

With this freedom comes a sense of responsibility among journalists and, consequently, the methods of journalism are under constant scrutiny. Journalists are concerned with serving the greater good, satisfying their own professional expectations, and protecting individuals. The conflicts among these loyalties produce some of its greatest internal debates.

Chapter Twenty-four

Law and the Journalist

Key Concepts and Terms

1. The First Amendment to the U.S. Constitution guarantees the nation a right to free speech and to a free press; it is the central legal element that allows journalism to operate and develop in this country.

2. Prior restraint: the power of the government to stop dissemination of information that the news media have acquired; except in a few rare instances, prior restraint does not occur in the United States.

3. American society generally operates as an open society; that is, we expect information to be available and we assume the right to distribute information.

4. One of the major legal restraints on news organizations is libel, the damage done to a person's reputation by the publication of false information.

5. *New York Times v. Sullivan:* this 1964 decision by the Supreme Court gave the news media an extra measure of protection from being sued for libel by public officials.

6. Actual malice: the standard of proof that was established by the *New York Times v. Sullivan* decision; a public official or public figure has to prove that a news organization showed "reckless disregard" for the truth to win a libel case.

7. Copyrights and trademarks protect intellectual property from unauthorized use.

8. The right of privacy is not guaranteed by the U.S. Constitution, but most courts recognize this right, and news organizations have to consider the right of privacy for individuals in making some editorial decisions.

9. News coverage of trials presents a problem for the news media and the legal system because of the feeling that too much publicity may prevent someone from getting a fair trial.

Vignette

When the Cherry Sisters decided to take their act on the road, they were simply trying to survive. They did not realize they would be making legal history.

The sisters—Addie, Effie, Jessie, and Lizzie—were left alone on the family farm near Marion, Iowa, in 1888 when their father died. A fifth sister, Ella, stayed on the farm, but the others decided to put together a vaudeville act that they hoped would get them at least to Chicago, where they planned to see the World's Fair and look for a long-lost brother.

Their act, consisting of songs and a variety of dramatic readings, was awful. It premiered before a local crowd that was apparently too polite to boo or express any displeasure. That did not stop other audiences, who booed and threw things. The sisters kept performing, apparently believing the crowd noise amounted to approval. Even when the crowds threw things on stage, the sisters seemed to think this was just part of what happened in the theater of the time.

Everywhere the Cherry Sisters went, the crowds got bigger and bigger. They were so awful that they had become a phenomenon. The sisters offered newspaper critics new opportunities to write vicious reviews, and the critics rarely passed up the opportunities. The sisters could not understand the reviewers. After all, they were drawing big crowds.

When the Cedar Rapids Gazette *wrote, "If some indefinable instinct of modesty could not have warned them that they were acting the part of monkeys, it does seem like the overshoes thrown at them would convey the idea," the sisters sued the city editor for libel. They dropped the suit, and showing a bit of humor agreed to perform before a mock court on stage. That stunt generated even more publicity, and the sisters were invited to New York to play on Broadway in 1896. This they did, performing before crowds of as many as four thousand people. The critics continued to blast away.*

Two years later, Billy Hamilton, editor of the Odebolt Chronicle *in Iowa, saw the act and described it for his readers in a particularly devastating way: "The mouths of their rancid features opened like caverns, and sounds like the wailing of damned souls issued therefrom." His review was reprinted in the* Des Moines Leader, *and this time the sisters sued for $15,000. The sisters lost their suit and appealed to the Iowa Supreme Court, which ruled against the sisters in a 1901 decision. The court wrote:*

> *One who goes upon the stage to exhibit himself to the public, or who gives any kind of a performance to which the public is invited, may be freely criticised. He may be held up to ridicule, and entire freedom of expression is guaranteed dramatic critics, provided they are not actuated by malice or evil purpose in what they write. Fitting strictures,*

sarcasm or ridicule, even, may be used, if based on facts, without liability, in the absence of malice or wicked purpose. The comments, however, must be based on truth, or on what in good faith and upon probable cause is believed to be true, and the matter must be pertinent to the conduct that is made the subject of criticism.

Without meaning to, the Cherry Sisters had established an important legal principle: the right to comment and criticize. That right is not unlimited, as we will see in this chapter, but the court's decision became a precedent that offers an important protection for journalists.

Corruption in Minneapolis

A quarter of a century later, in the middle of the Roaring Twenties, freedom of expression got another legal boost. Minneapolis today has a mild, even bland, reputation as a city. In 1927, however, as a major stopover for the route of illegal whiskey coming from Canada during the height of the Prohibition era, Minneapolis was a center for scandal and corruption. The mayor and much of the police force were on the take, bought by the bootleggers who were trying to get booze to Chicago, St. Louis, and points south.

Jay Near and his friend, Howard Guilford, did not like what they saw. Neither of them were paragons of virtue; they were opinionated and bigoted, openly disparaging ethnic groups they did not like. But they also felt they had a right to expose what public officials were doing to their city, so they started a publication called the *Saturday Press.* They told their readers that the city government was essentially mob

Quote 24.1

JAMES J. KILPATRICK

On individual liberty

The idea of individual liberty lies at the very heart of the American dream. In a very real sense, it is our national religion, and like other religions it is fearfully difficult to practice. It is not easy to be a good Christian, a good Jew. The tenets of faith are demanding. Many persons find it impossible to believe deeply—really, truly, to believe—in matters of doctrine. But as professing members of a church they have an obligation to try. So it is with freedom. Do we really believe in it? Really, deeply, believe in it? Do we believe in freedom sufficiently to tolerate the expression of political opinions we find intolerable? We must try.

James J. Kilpatrick is a columnist and former editor of the Richmond News-Leader.

THE SATURDAY PRESS
A WEEKLY "WHO'S WHO AND WHY"

The Northwest's Snappiest Newspaper
Business Office, 240 S. Fourth Street
Two Dollars per Year in Advance

On Sale on News Stands, Everywhere, Every Saturday

OUR MOTTO:
Laugh and the World Laughs With You
Grouch, and You Grouch Alone.

HOWARD A. GUILFORD
J. M. NEAR (The Old Man)
Editors and Owners

Application for Second Class Entry pending in the Post Office at Minneapolis, Minn.

Dealers and Subscription Agents wanted—Liberal Commissions

FACTS, NOT THEORIES

"I am a bosom friend of Mr. Olson," snorted a gentleman of Yiddish blood, "and I want to protest against your article," and blah, blah, blah, ad infinitum, ad nauseum.

I am not taking orders from men of Barnett faith, at least right now. There have been too many men in this city and especially those in official life, who HAVE been taking orders and suggestions from JEW GANGSTERS, therefore we HAVE Jew Gangsters, practically ruling Minneapolis.

It was buzzards of the Barnett stripe who shot down my buddy. It was Barnett gunmen who staged the assault on Samuel Shapiro. It is Jew thugs who have "pulled" practically every robbery in this city. It was a member of the Barnett gang who shot down George Rubenstein (Ruby) while he stood in the shelter of Mose Barnett's ham-cavern on Hennepin avenue. It was Mose Barnett himself who shot down Roy Rogers on Hennepin avenue. It was at Mose Barnett's place of "business" that the "13 dollar Jew" found a refuge while the police of New York were combing the country for him. It was a gang of Jew gunmen who boasted that for five hundred dollars they would kill any man in the city. It was Mose Barnett, a Jew, who boasted that he held the chief of police of Minneapolis in his hand—had bought and paid for him.

It is Jewish men and women — pliant tools of the Jew gangster, Mose Barnett, who stand charged with having falsified the election records and returns in the Third ward. And it is Mose Barnett himself, who, indicted for his part in the Shapiro assault, is a fugitive from justice today.

Practically every vendor of vile hooch, every owner of a moonshine still, every snake-faced gangster and embryonic yegg in the Twin Cities is a JEW.

Having these examples before me, I feel that I am justified in my refusal to take orders from a Jew who boasts that he is a "bosom friend" of Mr. Olson.

I find in the mail at least twice per week, letters from gentlemen of Jewish faith who advise me against "launching an attack on the Jewish people." These gentlemen have the cart before the horse. I am launching, nor is Mr. Guilford, no attack against any race, BUT:

When I find men of a certain race banding themselves together for the purpose of preying upon Gentile or Jew; gunmen, KILLERS, roaming our streets shooting down men against whom they have no personal grudge (or happen to have); defying OUR laws; corrupting OUR officials; assaulting business men; beating up unarmed citizens; spreading a reign of terror through every walk of life, then I say to you in all sincerity, that I refuse to back up a single step from that "issue" —if they choose to make it so.

If the people of Jewish faith in Minneapolis wish to avoid criticism of these vermin whom I rightly call "Jews" they can easily do so BY THEMSELVES CLEANING HOUSE.

I'm not out to cleanse Israel of the filth that clings to Israel's skirts. I'm out to "hew to the line, let the chips fly where they may."

I simply state a fact when I say that ninety per cent of the crimes committed against society in this city are committed by JEW gangsters.

It was a Jew who employed JEWS to shoot down Mr. Guilford. It was a Jew who employed a Jew to intimidate Mr. Shapiro and a Jew who employed JEWS to assault that gentleman when he refused to yield to their threats. It was a JEW who wheedled or employed Jews to manipulate the election records and returns in the Third ward in flagrant violation of law. It was a Jew who left two hundred dollars with another Jew to pay to our chief of police just before the last municipal election, and:

It is Jew, Jew, Jew, as long as one cares to comb over the records.

I am launching no attack against the Jewish people AS A RACE. I am merely calling attention to a FACT. And if the people of that race and faith wish to rid themselves of the odium and stigma THE RODENTS OF THEIR OWN RACE HAVE BROUGHT UPON THEM, they need only to step to the front and help the decent citizens of Minneapolis rid the city of these criminal Jews.

Either Mr Guilford or myself stand ready to do battle for a MAN, regardless of his race, color or creed, but neither of us will step one inch out of our chosen path to avoid a fight IF the Jews want the battle.

Both of us have some mighty loyal friends among the Jewish people but not one of them comes whining to ask that we "lay off" criticism of Jewish gangsters and none of them who comes carping to us of their "bosom friendship" for any public official now under our journalistic guns.

—o—
Weather forecast—Stormy, with lots of heat.
—o—

FOR FRANK'S PERUSAL

Frank Brunskill wants the heat pulled off his precious self. He demands that McCormick get things "fixed up," etc. Frank—get this through your dome. Nobody can fix anything except you. And here is what you will have to do:

1. See that every one of the thousands of dollars extorted by the Twin City Reporter is returned.

2. Return to every victim the thousands of dollars lost by them in the gambling house you fostered and protected at 208 11th avenue south, and 818 Hennepin.

3. Return the good name of those who stole money and lost it in your gambling hell, and went to prison for it.

4. Send out and arrest the many Yid thieves and gangsters of Big Mose's stable who were arrested by your department in the commission of crime, and were ordered released by you.

5. Get down to your proper station in life, and crawl out of the police department for once and for all time.

These, Frank Brunskill, are the terms on which everything can be "fixed up" and the heat taken off you. You state that you will stand for anything to pull the heat. Here's your tip.

The Half-Shot Editor.

A SECOND DEFI

It has been tipped off to the Press editors that an effort will be made to "knock off" Mr. Guilford before he has a chance to testify against the pair of babies now in the county jail, charged with his shooting on September 26th. "Gil" wants it strictly understood that two Irishmen can keep him in a house all day, but a thousand of the Big Mose crowd can't keep him from shooting marbles on the sidewalk, provided none of the Yids get behind him. So step right in, gangland, before the water gets frozen. You have stopped nothing and nobody. You have engendered hate where once was contempt. You have sowed the wind. Reap the whirlwind. Your type has failed miserably. Now see what printers' type will accomplish.

This little fight is not a private argument. It is open to any public official who wishes to hop in.

FIGURE 24.1 The Saturday Press Jay Near and Howard Guilford pulled no punches in fighting what they saw as corruption in Minneapolis, as this issue of the *Saturday Press* of 1927 demonstrates. Although many city officials of the time were corrupt, the two journalists went beyond exposing their corruption and disparaged their ethnicity. Despite this, the courts ruled that public officials could not use the city's nuisance laws to shut down the publication.

controlled, and they gave details. Just days after the first issue appeared (and was confiscated by city police), Guilford was shot and critically wounded by mobsters.

Near stepped up his crusade against the city as his friend recuperated. He targeted the mayor, the police chief, and even the county prosecutor. His weekly exposés increasingly irritated public officials for two months until they decided to use a Minnesota nuisance law against him. The law said that a "scandalous and defamatory" publication could be banned, and the publishers prevented from publishing.

Near and Guilford fought the banning order, and the case worked its way to the U.S. Supreme Court, which ruled in 1931 that no government at any level had the right to stop a publication before it was published. Writing for the majority in the case known as *Near v. Minnesota*, Chief Justice Charles Evans Hughes said:

> Public officers, whose character and conduct remain open to debate and free discussion in the press, find their remedies for false accusations in actions under libel laws providing for redress and punishment, and not in proceedings to restrain the publications of newspapers and periodicals. The fact that the liberty of the press may be abused by miscreant purveyors of scandal does not make any the less necessary the immunity of the press from previous restraint in dealing with official misconduct. Subsequent punishment for such abuses as may exist is the appropriate remedy, consistent with constitutional privilege.

Guilford recovered, but he and Near did not get to enjoy much of their legal victory. The *Saturday Press* continued for a couple of years but could not make enough money to sustain itself. Guilford quit in 1934 and ran for mayor but was killed by gangsters before his campaign got started. Near died two years later of natural causes.

The case they generated has had important implications. For the first time, the U.S. Supreme Court said that governments could not censor publications. They could not exercise "prior restraint."

Legal Precedents

The First Amendment to the U.S. Constitution gives people in America the legal right to speak and write what they think. It also gives citizens other important rights. It states:

> Congress shall make no law respecting an establishment of religion, or prohibiting the free exercise thereof; or abridging the freedom of speech, or of the press; or the right of the people peaceably to assemble, and to petition the government for a redress of grievances.

The amendment was added to the Constitution in 1791, four years after the republic was established and 140 years before the U.S. Supreme Court had issued its opinion in *Near v. Minnesota*. The First Amendment had been in place for more than one hundred years when the case of the Cherry Sisters, giving writers the right to comment and criticize on public affairs, was decided.

So what's going on here? Why did it take the courts more than a century to grant these rights? Did people have these rights before the Courts' decisions?

The answer to the last question is yes. From the nation's beginnings, people spoke and wrote freely, particularly about public subjects that merited comment and criticism. George Washington was treated very badly by his critics in the press, as has been every president since then. Throughout the nineteenth century, politicians and public corruption were the constant targets of newspapers and magazines. Unpopular causes such as abolition, women's suffrage, prohibition, unionism, anarchy, and the like were strongly advocated both by mainstream media and specialized publications devoted to a particular cause. Was prior restraint ever imposed on these publications by public officials?

Occasionally, it was, but the instances of prior restraint were relatively few and isolated. On the whole, however, the nineteenth century saw a free flow of information and ideas. Although those who participated in these public conversations may not have thought they were doing so as a First Amendment right, they certainly acted within the bounds and spirit of the First Amendment. The American public in the nineteenth century became used to an open and free conversation. They did not so much believe in it or advocate it as they practiced it. And that tells something important about legal cases and precedents.

A Court decision such as *Near v. Minnesota,* rather than granting new rights, will often confirm what has already become standard practice. In that particular case, the U.S. Supreme Court struck down a state law that got in the way of the commonly accepted exercise of First Amendment rights. In the case of the Cherry Sisters, the Iowa Supreme Court simply said that public criticism did not constitute libel, which is still an active and important legal concept, as we will see later in this chapter. The Court recognized that criticism of public figures and public officials was part of the way in which our social and political system works. Libel laws should not get in the way.

In these two cases, the Courts made the right decision in defending and expanding the freedoms granted by the First Amendment. Courts are not always so wise, however. Sometimes they hand down unwise or ill-considered decisions that restrict the liberties of the people to speak and to have access to information and ideas. State legislatures and the U.S. Congress also pass imprudent laws that they hope will fix a particular problem but that wind up attempting to restrict how people communicate with one another. Our system of laws and legal precedents is an imperfect one. Our hope is that all of us will be informed citizens who understand the value of the full freedoms granted by the First Amendment and who will actively oppose any restrictions on them.

The First Amendment

The First Amendment to the U.S. Constitution grants us five important rights:

- Freedom to hold religious beliefs and worship as we see fit; the government is prohibited from establishing an official religion.
- Freedom of speech.
- Freedom of the press; publications may generally publish what they wish without the permission of the government and without any prior restraint.
- Freedom to assemble peaceably; the government cannot prohibit people from getting together to talk about whatever is on their minds, as long as they are peaceful.

THE STATE OF THE FIRST AMENDMENT

The First Amendment Center, an arm of the Freedom Forum Foundation, conducts a national survey each year to see how Americans feel about the freedoms guaranteed by the First Amendment. The following are some of the key findings of the 2003 survey:

- About 60 percent of respondents indicated overall support for First Amendment freedoms, whereas 34 percent said the First Amendment goes too far.

- 52 percent said media ownership by fewer corporations has meant a decreased number of viewpoints available to the public; 53 percent said the quality of information also has suffered.

- Almost eight in ten respondents said owners exert substantial influence over news organizations' newsgathering and reporting decisions. Only 4 percent said they believed there is no tampering with story selection or play.

- 54 percent favored maintaining limits on how many radio, television, and newspaper outlets may be owned by a single company, but 50 percent opposed any increased regulation.

- 65 percent favored the policy of "embedding" U.S. journalists into individual combat units; 68 percent said the news media did an excellent or good job in covering the war in Iraq.

- 48 percent said they believe Americans have too little access to information about the federal government's efforts to combat terrorism—up from 40 percent last year.

- About 55 percent of those surveyed opposed a constitutional amendment to ban flag-burning, up from 51 percent in 2002.

■ Freedom to petition the government; that is, we can tell our lawmakers and public officials what we think, and we can ask them to change things if we disagree with what they are doing.

In the realms of journalism, the First Amendment is the most important legal document on the books. Its two parts about speech and the press constitute the basic tenet of journalism—that people can exchange information and ideas. The First Amendment provides the sturdiest protection that journalists have against assaults by those who disagree with what they are saying or reporting. Many subsequent laws and court decisions that have outlined the specific freedoms that journalists have are based on an interpretation of this section of the Constitution.

But the First Amendment is more than just a legal document. It essentially lays out the most important principles of public life in America and in some sense provides a description of how life in America is supposed to work. The man most responsible for the First Amendment was James Madison, a Virginia congressman when the Constitution was ratified. Madison had been a leader at the convention in Philadelphia that wrote the Constitution in 1787, and he argued forcefully and brilliantly for its ratification in the months afterward. He later became the fourth president of the United States.

The vision that Madison forms for America in the First Amendment and in his other writing is one based on the free flow of information. Madison, like many of his contemporaries among the Founding Fathers, believed in a "marketplace of ideas," a concept made popular at the time by philosophers John Milton, John Stuart Mill, and others. They felt that the best ideas for society could be found only through a system that allowed many voices to participate and contribute. In 1791, the year the First Amendment was added to the Constitution, Madison wrote, "Whatever facilitates a general intercourse of sentiments, as good roads, domestic commerce, a free press, and particularly a circulation of newspapers through the entire body of the people—is favorable to liberty."

But none of the framers of the Constitution, as far as we know, believed that speech and the press should be completely unfettered. Although there have been some absolutists—people who argued that no restrictions should be placed on these freedoms—in the history of America, most people have been convinced that reasonable restraints in limited areas of the law are good for society. Those areas that have the most to do with journalism are libel, copyright, and to some extent privacy.

Defamation

A person's reputation, his or her "good name," is not only socially important but legally valuable. To harm that reputation is to commit defamation. The concept of defamation comes from English common law with the idea that someone who damages the reputation of another person should be held responsible and should have to pay for those damages. There are two types of defamation: libel, or written defamation; and slander, spoken defamation. Some people use the term *libel* to cover both libel and defamation. Libel is one of the most important legal considerations for a journalist.

Legally, the concept of libel is limited. State laws have libel clauses, but they are rarely very specific about what constitutes libel. That has been left to courts and juries to decide. As we saw with the case of the Cherry Sisters at the beginning of this chapter, libel is not just negative comments or criticism. Saying something bad about a person is not necessarily to harm that person's reputation.

So what does constitute libel? Libel actions most often have been brought and won in four areas: comments about someone's political beliefs (such as calling someone a Nazi or a terrorist); saying that someone has a physical illness (such as AIDS) or a mental disease (calling somebody "crazy"); disparaging someone's business practices or professional conduct; saying that someone is a criminal. In any of these areas, libelous words will cause people to be shunned or thought less of and might endanger their ability to earn a living or advance in their profession. We should note here that libel laws protect not only individuals but also businesses and organizations. Saying that a bank cannot meet its obligations, for instance, might cause people to withdraw their money or keep people from doing business with the bank. The bank itself can sue for libel.

The person or organization that brings a libel suit has to prove five things for the court: publication, identification, defamation, fault, and damages. Libel has to involve at least three people: the person who is libeled, the person who says or prints the libel, and a third person who reads or sees it. A libelous statement in a newspaper has obviously been published, but a libelous statement about someone that you put into an email and send to a third person has also been published.

The person who brings a libel suit must also prove that he or she has been identified as the person who has been libeled. Using someone's name in a libelous context obviously identifies that person, but there are other ways to identify someone. For instance, to say that the Smyth County High School basketball team "is full of drug dealers" might be enough identification for a member of that team to bring a libel suit. Or let's say a story appears in the newspaper about a person being convicted of a crime, but mistakenly a picture along with the story is of the wrong person. Even though the person's name was not used, the person could claim that the picture identifies him as being a criminal. Identification is not always as straightforward as it appears.

Proving defamation is usually the key part of the libel suit. As mentioned earlier, a person must show that his or her reputation was harmed by the publication by making people hate or shun him or her or by diminishing that person's ability to make a living.

Fault is an important concept that will be discussed more fully momentarily. A libel plaintiff (the person bringing the libel suit) must prove that the defendant (the person being sued) was responsible for the publication and was, in legal terms, "negligent." For most potential plaintiffs who are private citizens, this means proving that a publisher was careless and did not take the proper precautions; that is, they did not exercise the proper reporting and editing procedures.

Finally, the plaintiff must prove that he or she has been damaged by the libelous statements. Sometimes libel plaintiffs can show actual dollar amounts in loss of business, but this is not always possible or necessary. Sometimes they must simply demonstrate that people think less of them because of what was published or broadcast. Interestingly, some people have reputations so heinous that they cannot be libeled. Take, for instance, a person who has been convicted of killing a child. It would be difficult to imagine that anyone could say or print anything that would damage that person's reputation further.

Defenses against Libel Suits

Libel is a civil, not a criminal, offense. English and American law once had provisions for criminal libel—and people could go to jail for committing such a libel—but those provisions have mostly been rescinded by state legislatures. In a civil action, the plaintiff must prove to a court (and often a jury) that he or she has been libeled, but the defendant can also use "affirmative defenses" against libel. That is, even if the plaintiff can prove all five things discussed in the previous section, a defendant still may not be guilty because of affirmative defenses. These defenses include statute of limitations, truth, qualified privilege, and constitutional privilege.

Many civil and some criminal laws have a statute of limitations; that is, a suit may not be filed after a certain time has passed. This time period varies from state to state but is usually one or two years. So, in many states, if a libelous statement is more than two years old, a plaintiff may not file a suit to recover damages.

Truth is one of the strongest defenses against libel. The nature of libel is that it is a false statement. To prove that a statement is true is to take away this essential ingredient. Truth, however, can sometimes be difficult to prove. A journalist using truth as a defense must have solid evidence such as documents or credible witnesses to back up a claim.

Journalists may also claim "qualified privilege" as a defense against libel. Journalists are charged with reporting and disseminating the news. Sometimes that can include information that is potentially libelous. For instance, a prosecutor may accuse an innocent person of a crime. The journalist has the right to report that accusation without fear of being open to a libel suit. Journalists, as always, need to be careful about what they report, particularly when it contains this kind of information, but they should not censor themselves for fear of being sued. Courts have tended to understand and be sympathetic to the reporting process.

The defense of constitutional privilege grows out of a case the United States Supreme Court decided in 1964 called *New York Times v. Sullivan*. L. B. Sullivan was the police commissioner in Montgomery and sued the *Times* for information it had printed about how he handled a civil rights demonstration. The Supreme Court used that case to give the news media a strong layer of protection against suits by public officials. The Court said that a public official had to prove "actual malice" on the part of the publisher of the libel. The Court defined actual malice as either knowing something was false or having "reckless disregard" of the truth in the way the information about a person was handled. In other words, a public official would have to prove that the journalist knew what the truth was and deliberately said or wrote something else or that the methods the journalist used were so shoddy that the journalist had reckless disregard for the truth. The Court's intent was to stop public officials from using libel suits to stifle criticism and debate on public issues. The actual malice standard made it almost impossible for a public official to win a libel suit. Later the Court took another case and expanded this burden of proof to people it labeled "public figures." These would be famous people who are not public officials, people such as movie stars and athletes. Again, the Court intended that discussion of issues and personalities not be burdened by the threat of libel suits. This is called the constitutional privilege defense because the Court used the First Amendment as the basis for formulating this defense.

Who is a public official? And who is a public figure? Courts have tended to say that anyone employed by any level of government in a position of responsibility is a public official. That would include everyone from the president of the United States

Quote 24.2

WILLIAM BRENNAN

On the principle underlying the First Amendment

If there is a bedrock principle underlying the First Amendment, it is that the government may not prohibit the expression of an idea simply because society finds the idea itself offensive or disagreeable.

William Brennan was a U.S. Supreme Court justice and author of the New York Times v. Sullivan *decision.*

to the local high school principal. Defining a public figure is an ongoing debate. Some people such as Michael Jordan and Jennifer Lopez are certainly public figures, but there are many questions about others. Courts have tended to look at whether or not someone voluntarily injects themselves into a public discussion or situation; those who do so are public figures.

DEVELOPING THE CONCEPT OF THE PUBLIC FIGURE

When the Supreme Court decided the *New York Times v. Sullivan* case in 1964, it gave extra protection to the media against libel suits by public officials. The Court was seeking to encourage vigorous debate and discussion on issues of the day. But vigorous debate often involves more than public officials. Three years after the *Sullivan* decision, the Court expanded the actual malice standard of proof to include public figures.

It took two major college football coaches and a retired Army general to make this happen. In the fall of 1962, Alabama's football team shellacked Georgia, 35–0. The next year, the *Saturday Evening Post* published an article about how the head coaches, Paul "Bear" Bryant of Alabama and Wally Butts of Georgia, colluded to fix the game. The article, "The Story of a College Football Fix," alleged that Butts had called Bryant during the week before the game and outlined the offensive and defensive plays the Bulldogs planned to run during the game. Butts sued the *Post* and won a $3 million judgment, which was reduced to $460,000 by an appeals court.

In a separate incident earlier in 1962, the Associated Press reported that retired Army Gen. Edwin Walker had encouraged people to riot when the first black student attempted to enroll at the University of Mississippi. Walker sued the AP in Texas and won a judgment of $800,000.

Both cases came to the Supreme Court at the same time, and as it occasionally does, the Court combined the cases into one decision.

University of Alabama football coach Paul "Bear" Bryant

The Court ruled that even though none of the plaintiffs in either of the cases held public office, they were "public figures"; that is, they were people involved in important issues of interest to the public. Therefore, if they were going to sue for libel, they had to prove actual malice, just as public officials had to prove it.

The Supreme Court did not define precisely who a "public figure" is, and courts have been struggling with the concept ever since. In 2003, for example, a U.S. Court of Appeals panel ruled that a former Navy lieutenant was a "limited purpose" public figure.

Cary Lohrenz was one of the first women trained to fly combat aircraft for the U.S. Navy in the early 1990s. In 1996 she sued the Center for Military Readiness, the *Washington Times,* and the *San Diego Union* for alleging that she was a substandard pilot. The appeals court said that her position as one of the first women to fly combat aircraft made her a public figure and that she had to prove actual malice.

You can read the full decisions in these cases on the Web at the following addresses: *Curtis v. Butts* (www.bc.edu/bc_org/avp/cas/comm/free_speech/curtis.html); *Lohrenz v. Donnelly* (http://fsnews.findlaw.com/cases/dc/025294a.html).

Copyright and Trademarks

Another area in which the freedom to write and publish is not unlimited is that of copyright and trademarks, which are part of a larger area of law known as intellectual property. People who create what we might term generally as *intellectual property*—books, musical works, art, sculpture, articles, poems, and so on—have some protection in the way that those works are used by others. If you write a poem, that poem is yours (at least for a limited amount of time), and no one else can reprint that poem without your permission.

Copyright protection does not extend to some things, however. Facts cannot be copyrighted. Let's say you are the only writer covering your high school basketball game, and you write a story about it for the high school paper. Another publication can take the facts that you have described (the details of the game, the score, etc.) and use them in its description of the game. That publication, however, cannot use your account of the game. The expression of facts can be copyrighted, but the facts themselves cannot. Ideas are the same way. Ideas cannot be copyrighted, but the expression of those ideas can. For instance, you can paint a picture of a tree, and that painting will be copyrighted. Others can paint a picture of the same tree. That's not against the law, as long as they do not use your painting.

Copyright protection is limited in two important ways. One is that it does not last forever. Currently, copyrights last for the life of the creator, plus seventy years. If the copyright is owned by a corporation, then copyright lasts longer, but it does not last forever. At some point, all creative works become part of the "public domain"; that is, everyone owns them. Consequently, the works of William Shakespeare, for instance, are in the public domain, and Shakespeare can be quoted at length without anyone's permission.

The other way in which copyright protection is limited is through the concept of fair use. This concept has been developed to encourage the dissemination of ideas and information without either putting a great burden on the user or infringing on the rights of the creator of the work. Fair use means that in certain limited circumstances, a copyrighted work—or more likely, some portion of it—may be used without the permission of the holder of the copyright. In considering what is fair use, courts have looked at four factors:

- the nature of the copyrighted material—how much effort it took to produce it;
- the nature of the use—for instance, material used in an educational setting for educational purposes is more likely to be thought of as fair use;
- the extent of the use—how much of the copyrighted material is used, whether just a few words or a whole passage;
- commercial infringement—most importantly, how much does the use hurt the commercial value of the work?

Unless material is being used in a very limited way, you should always get permission to use copyrighted material. Holders of copyright can be very aggressive about enforcing their copyrights, and the unauthorized user of a copyrighted work can be fined substantially. Many people in education believe that they can use any material in any way they wish, and it will be considered fair use. That is not the case. Educators are bound by copyright laws as much as anyone else.

A final important point: Material on the Internet has as much copyright protection as anything else. Some people believe that whatever is on a web site is in the public domain, but that is not the case. Just because material is easy to access does not mean that it does not have copyright protection.

Trademarks offer special protection for the commercial use of words, phrases, and symbols, and journalists need to be careful about how they use them. Many companies go to great lengths to protect their trademarks because that is how the public identifies their products. What if, for example, a shoe company named Nuke started using the Nike swoosh on its shoes? Consumers might become confused about what product to buy, and Nike, which holds a trademark on the swoosh, might be hurt by that.

Journalists generally do not run into much of a problem in using trademarks in what they right or print. If a newspaper used the Nike swoosh to illustrate a story about the company, that would probably be considered fair use because it would not be infringing on the commercial aspects of the swoosh or confusing consumers with it. But journalists should be careful about certain words they use that designate particular products. For example, *Xerox* is the name of a company, not a verb that means "photocopy." It should be capitalized and not used as a verb.

Privacy

Privacy is another area of the law that journalists need to be aware of, although it does not affect journalists as much as people think. The right of privacy is not a clearly established legal concept. In fact, some argue that because the U.S. Constitution says nothing about privacy, it should have no legal standing. Courts and some laws do protect certain aspects of a person's life, but these protections have more to do with advertising and commerce than they do with the publication of information about a person.

Essentially, the news media are allowed to publish almost anything about a person as long as it is true. They do not need a person's permission to publish anything about that person. How they get such information is often the important legal question. Journalists may not trespass on people's property, they may not steal information, and they may be in some trouble if they take information—particularly medical information—that state and federal laws try to protect. Otherwise, however, journalists are free to print and broadcast what they know. They are free to describe and photograph what they can see, even if what they see is on private property. For example, if someone is in a house but the window and curtains are open, a photographer standing in the street can take a picture of that person. No invasion of privacy has taken place.

Within the realm of journalism, privacy is more of a social and civil restraint than a legal one. Journalists may not choose to publish private facts about a person because they do not feel that it would be appropriate or necessary. Still, journalists should take some care in this area because in some situations the publication of private facts can be the basis for a legal action.

Legal Protections for Journalists

As we have noted throughout this chapter, very few laws restrict the work of journalists or the ability of news organizations to publish or broadcast what they know. In fact, there are a number of laws and legal precedents that protect journalists and assist them in their work. The most important, of course, is the First Amendment, which we discussed earlier in this chapter. Beyond that, courts and legislatures have recognized that the work of journalists is important enough that it needs some legal assistance.

One of the most important of these protections has been alluded to in our discussion of libel laws. That is the concept known as privilege, which means that a journalist should be given some leeway, that is sometimes not granted to others to do the job of reporting, writing, and editing. They are often able to go into areas from which the general public is restricted, such as crime scenes and disaster areas. Courtrooms reserve seats for reporters and make special accommodations for them to cover high-profile trials. Public officials plan for their presence because they are seen as agents of the public and disseminate valuable information.

Beyond these amenities, newsgathering itself is given some protection by the law and by courts. In some cases, journalists are protected from a lawsuit if they can demonstrate that they followed standard journalistic procedures or if they showed themselves to be "neutral reporters."

One of the most important areas in which journalists have received legal protection is that of confidential sources. Police investigators, prosecutors, and judges, in the course of their own duties, sometimes want to know what people journalists have talked with. There have been many instances in which they have tried to force journalists into revealing those sources. Journalists take seriously pledges they have given to sources to keep their identities confidential, and they usually resent others who try to intrude on their newsgathering procedures. To protect journalists from these intrusions, most states have laws that protect journalists from having to reveal anonymous sources. These laws have given journalists some, but not absolute, protection. As a result, legal officials usually try to avoid these confrontations with journalists.

Another area in which there are laws that help journalists has to do with meetings of public bodies, such as city councils and school boards, and with documents and records produced by all levels of government. Most states have laws that force governmental bodies to have public meetings and that mandate that most governmental records be open to the public. At the federal level, the U.S. government operates under the Freedom of Information Act, which allows citizens to make a formal request for records and documents. These laws are set up to help citizens, not just journalists, find out what their government is doing, but they are most often used by journalists in the reporting process. Unfortunately, many government officials at all levels spend a good deal of time ignoring or trying to get around these laws, believing they have no responsibility to the public for their actions or simply trying to cover up actions of which the public would not approve.

Free Press–Fair Trial

In 1954, the pregnant wife of Sam Sheppard, a prominent physician in Cleveland, Ohio, was murdered in her home in one of the city's better neighborhoods. The doctor was at home at the time and claimed that a one-armed intruder had broken in and injured him as well as killing his wife. Some evidence pointed to the doctor as the killer, but the police appeared slow to make an arrest. The *Cleveland Press* began an editorial campaign that criticized the police and called for the arrest of the doctor.

When Dr. Sheppard was arrested and charged, the newspaper's editors made no secret of their belief that he was guilty. Other news organizations in Cleveland joined in beating the editorial drums against the doctor. Sheppard's trial was conducted in a circus atmosphere that the judge did little to control. Sheppard was convicted, but he appealed, arguing that he did not receive a fair trial because of the negative comments in the city's newspapers. The Supreme Court agreed. It set aside Sheppard's conviction, criticized many aspects of how the investigation and trial were conducted, and had these words about the press coverage of the case:

> The massive, pervasive and prejudicial publicity attending petitioner's prosecution prevented him from receiving a fair trial consistent with the Due Process Clause of the 14th Amendment.

The U.S. Constitution guarantees citizens a speedy and fair trial if they are accused of a crime. That guarantee, some believe, is jeopardized by the First Amendment, the guarantee of a free press. Publicity about the accusation, the argument goes, will prejudice potential jurors and prevent the person accused from getting a fair trial.

The Sheppard trial was not an isolated incident, as we well know. (Dr. Sheppard, by the way, was tried again and found not guilty. His story inspired the television series *The Fugitive* and later the movie.) The news is constantly filled with stories about people accused of crimes. When the accused is famous or when the crime is unusual, news coverage can become massive, even overwhelming. People discuss the trial and even form opinions about the guilt or innocence of the accused.

Should the First Amendment be suspended whenever someone is accused of a crime? Should reporters not be allowed to write about anything connected with a trial until the courtroom proceedings begin? Although these ideas have been discussed, they are usually thought to be too radical or simply unworkable. In fact, they are dangerous. The judicial system is like any other part of government. People need to have confidence that it is working correctly, and the only way that confidence can be generated is if people are able to see how it works. The judicial system is also open to corruption, just as every other part of government is, and the press needs to serve its watchdog function in this area.

But what about the rights of the accused? In the glare of publicity, can the accused be assured of getting a fair trial? While the debate continues, all of those involved—prosecutors, defense attorneys, investigators, judges, and journalists—have generally tried to be sensitive to the legal fact that a person accused of a crime is innocent until proven guilty. Judges particularly have developed rules for judicial proceedings that reduce the circus atmosphere surrounding hearings and trials. They have used a number of standard legal options, such as gag orders for lawyers and witnesses and changing the location of a trial, to ensure that potential jurors will have an open mind about the charges against a person.

The free press–fair trial debate continues, however, and flares up every time a crime generates sustained coverage by the news media. Because both a "fair trial" and a "free press" are subjective concepts, there is unlikely to be any solution that will end this controversy.

Quote 24.3

KURT VONNEGUT

On the First Amendment

The First Amendment reads more like a dream than a law, and no other nation, so far as I know, has been crazy enough to include such a dream among its fundamental legal documents. I defend it because it has been so successful for two centuries in preserving our freedom and increasing our vitality, knowing that all arguments in support of it are certain to sound absurd.

Kurt Vonnegut is a novelist whose books include Cat's Cradle *and* Slaughterhouse Five.

Constant Vigilance

Journalists operate with great but not total legal freedom in the United States. Because of the way the First Amendment to the U.S. Constitution has been used by the public and the news media and reinforced by legislatures and interpreted by the courts, journalists are free to gather information and disseminate that information without the burden of prior restraint. This freedom is never completely secure. Journalists and the general public should always be on guard against efforts to restrict it, no matter how good the reasons are for wanting to do so.

QUESTIONS FOR DISCUSSION

1. Read the portion of this chapter that deals with how Americans feel about the First Amendment. What do you think about the responses to this survey? What would be your responses if you were asked questions like these?
2. Should privacy laws be stronger? If so, what should they protect?
3. What the reviewer said about the Cherry Sisters in the opening of this chapter was pretty vicious. Did the court make the right decision in this case? What if the sisters had been your relatives—how would you feel about the case then?
4. Do you feel that we should oppose all laws that might restrict First Amendment freedoms?

RELATED WEB SITES

First Amendment Center, www.fac.org

First Amendment Handbook, www.rcfp.org/handbook/viewpage.cgi

Media Watch, www.pbs.org/newshour/media

Minnesota News Council, www.mtn.org/~newscncl

Student Press Law Center, www.splc.org

READINGS AND REFERENCES

Bunker, M. (1996). *Justice and the media: Reconciling fair trials and a free press.* Mahwah, NJ: Lawrence Erlbaum and Associates.

Bunker, M. (2001) *Critiquing free speech: First amendment theory and the challenge of interdisciplinarity.* Mahwah, NJ: Lawrence Erlbaum and Associates.

Dennis, E., Gillmor, D. E., & Glasser, T. (Eds.). (1989). *Media freedom and accountability.* Westport, CT: Greenwood Press.

Gilmer, D., Barron, J. A., Simon, T., & Terry, H. (1996). *Fundamentals of communication law.* St. Paul, MN: West.

Middleton, K., Chamberlain, B., & Lee, W. E. (2003). *The law of public communication.* Boston: Allyn and Bacon.

Chapter Twenty-five

Ethical Practices

Key Concepts and Terms

1. As in most other professions, journalists find that there are few, if any, moral absolutes; even "tell the truth" is not something that can be strictly observed when telling the truth would do more harm than good.

2. Honesty is at the heart of the journalistic process; journalists should be honest not only about the information they present but also about their motivations.

3. Journalists should treat their audiences with respect.

4. The basic job of the journalist is to gather important and interesting information, put that information in a form acceptable to the medium for which the journalist works, and disseminate information to an audience.

5. One approach to journalistic ethics is to examine the loyalties that journalists have to their news organizations, their audiences, their professional colleagues, and themselves.

6. Plagiarism: using the work of another person and presenting it as your own without giving any credit.

7. Conflict of interest: a situation in which a journalist may have divided loyalties, a loyalty to the profession and a loyalty outside the profession; this conflict might prevent the journalist from presenting information honestly.

Vignette

On the afternoon of September 11, 2001, in the midst of a day of trauma, newspaper editors found that among the many pictures coming out of New York were shots of the World Trade Center before it collapsed with small black dots next to it. Those dots, while indistinct, were people who in desperation had jumped from the burning and falling towers. They were only a second or two away from death. The pictures were some of the most horrific of a horrific day. Editors across the country debated on where those pictures should be printed in the next day's edition of newspaper.

In order to investigate corruption in city and state government, the Chicago Sun-Times *secretly buys a downtown bar it names the Mirage. Reporters and editors run the bar and, thus, have to deal with inspectors and other officials governing such a business. They secretly record and photograph many of those officials taking bribes and payoffs rather than enforcing the legal regulations on the bar's owners. When the newspaper publishes a series detailing what has happened, a number of officials are indicted and eventually pay fines or go to jail.*

The committee that awards the Pulitzer prizes, the highest awards in journalism, decides not to give the award to the Sun-Times *because it used deception in getting the stories.*

A high school principal announces that students, when they leave campus in the afternoon, should not enter a convenience store just down the street from the school. He says the school has received complaints from the store's owners about all the students flooding in there in the afternoons. A couple of students on the school newspaper staff ask the owners of the store about these complaints, and they seem surprised. They say they have never complained to the principal about the school's students. In fact, they welcome the students in their store.

At the next meeting of the newspaper staff, the students debate whether or not they should write a story about this situation for the next edition of the newspaper.

Basketball star Kobe Bryant is accused of rape by a woman in Colorado. The accusation is shocking because Bryant has a reputation of quiet living and loyalty to his family. Bryant at first denies the accusation but later admits that he had sex with the woman. The sex, he says, was consensual. Most traditional news media organizations do not publish the names of rape victims or people who bring charges of rape. Because of Bryant's celebrity status, however, great attention is given to this charge, and the woman's name is broadcast over talk radio. She is identified on several non-news web sites, where details about her life can also be found. Every time a story about the case occurs, professional journalists have to decide whether or not to use her name and must face questions about what good they are doing by withholding her name.

An investigation by the St. Paul Pioneer-Press *finds that several members of the University of Minnesota basketball team have received too much academic help from one of their tutors. The tutor has regularly written English themes and other papers for the students. The newspaper's investigation has also shown that the university has been investigating this situation but has not made it public or reported it to the National Collegiate Athletic Association, the organization that enforces rules concerning athletics in colleges and universities.*

The newspaper publishes the story on the day before the team is to play its first game of the NCAA tournament. Four of the team members are suspended, and the team—even though heavily favored—loses the game and is out of the tournament. Many readers become angry with the newspaper, and some even cancel their subscriptions.

A pitcher for the hometown baseball team is having a good day. A great day, as a matter of fact. He has a no-hitter going into the bottom of the eighth inning. With two outs, the hitter hits a ground ball to the right of the first baseman. The infielder dives for the ball, knocks it down and keeps it close by, but he can't pick it up to throw the runner out. The play is officially scored an error, and the pitcher's no-hitter stays intact. He finishes the game without giving up any other hits and, thus, has a no-hitter to his credit. While he is cheered wildly, many of the discerning baseball fans believe that the hitter should have been given a hit in the eighth inning. They think the official scorer made a mistake. The official scorer is a sportswriter for the local newspaper, and he is covering the game for his newspaper, but his story the next day does not mention that he made a controversial call.

A police reporter for a small-town newspaper goes through arrest reports at the city police station. She is putting together a list that the newspaper publishes regularly. The list does not include names, only that arrests were made and what the charges are. On one of the reports is a name she recognizes. It's the minister at her church, who was arrested and charged with soliciting a male prostitute. Several other arrests were made that same night with the same charge. All of the arrests were made late at night in a downtown park that, during the day, is popular with many people, including mothers who bring their children to play on the park's extensive playground equipment. It is obvious to the reporter that the police have conducted a raid on the late-night activities in the park. This is a real story, she thinks.

Be good. Do right.

What mother has not admonished her children with these simple commands?

Most of us have learned about morality and moral behavior at a very early age. It was one of the big jobs of our parents or whoever was raising us to teach us what is acceptable behavior in a civil society. Many of the rules of moral behavior stem from religious training, but even if religion was not involved, we still learned that there were some basic tenants that we needed to follow to be good citizens and good people. We learned, we thought, the difference between right and wrong.

But did we?

As we grew up, we began to realize that maybe we did not know the difference between right and wrong as well as we thought. Life was complicated because people we knew to be good sometimes did things with which we disagreed. We learned that we could not be completely honest at all times. We were told to eat our aunt's cookies and tell her they were good, even though they tasted like cardboard, because if we did not, she would get her feelings hurt. We were told that when our friends did something wrong, we should not tell on them because nobody liked a "tattler." The moral absolutes that we began learning as small children were chipped away by life's real situations.

At some point, we learned that "being good" was not as easy as it sounds and "doing right" was no simple thing after all.

The Good Journalist

Life's many moral dilemmas, large and small, are reflected in the practice of journalism, as the situations described at the beginning of this chapter demonstrate. Journalists do not have an easy time in deciding what the right thing to do is. They have certain principles to which they try to adhere, but like the rest of us have discovered these principles are rarely absolute or applicable in every situation. The human condition demands that they be refined and sometimes shaped to the situation at hand.

So journalists, like the rest of us (we hope), strive to do the right thing. Quite often they are put in uncomfortable situations in which they have to choose between two or more good or moral principles that they will follow. Sometimes they have to choose between two bad things and have to decide which action would be worse. Most journalists try to make these decisions based on a commonly accepted set of practices and overlapping principles that includes the following.

Honesty

Being honest lies at the heart of journalistic attitudes and practices. Journalists attempt to present information based on facts to an audience. They are also obligated in many instances to tell the audience the source of these facts so the audience can have some basis on which to judge the facts. So, the outcome of what a journalist does should be an honest outcome.

That outcome, however, has an additional obligation. Journalists must be honest about who they are and what they are doing. Journalists should identify themselves and should make sure that people around them understand who they are and how they work. If someone is going to be quoted in a news article, the journalist is required to make it clear that this is the case before the person has said very much. If the journalist promises a person that he or she will not be quoted or that the person's name will not be used in a news article, the journalist is obligated to keep that promise. Many journalists have done this at great personal cost, including spending time in jail when a judge ordered them to reveal the name of an anonymous source.

Professional Practice

Journalists are expected to follow professional standards in practices. Some of those practices were referred to in the previous paragraphs, such as making sure that people know who they are and keeping confidences when they are given.

Professional practices also include trying to approach reporting, writing, and editing without an attitude that would limit or slant news coverage of a subject or event. A reporter who personally opposes abortion, for instance, is still obligated to seek out those who may favor abortion if that is at all relevant to the story. Political, personal, or religious feelings should be set aside, as much as possible, when journalists are pursuing a story.

Journalists are particularly obligated to allow people who may be disadvantaged by a story to have their say. If a source accuses someone of anything negative—from criminal acts to bad attitudes to incompetence—the person against whom the accusation is made should have ample opportunity to answer those accusations. Reporters are expected to take extra steps in the reporting process to be sure that this occurs.

Another part of professional practice expects journalists to take credit only for the original material they produce. Journalists should not copy the work of others without giving proper and appropriate credit to the source. In the same manner, journalists and news organizations are expected to acknowledge and correct errors quickly and appropriately. They should not try to cover up or explain away their mistakes.

Respect

Journalists should respect their audiences, the people with whom they deal, and each other.

The concept of respect is covered to some extent in some of the situations that we have just discussed. Journalists should be open not only to the information that people have but also their attitudes and points of view. They should be appropriately empathetic and sympathetic.

Journalists should understand how others see the news process and product. Many people regard journalists as intrusive, and they do not want to be in the news or subject to the attention of journalism. They are uncomfortable being in the limelight. For example, when Gerald Ford was president in the mid-1970s, his life was saved by a California man who saw that a woman was trying to shoot him. The man grabbed the gun from her. That act thrust the man onto the national spotlight and made him the subject of much investigation by reporters. Despite his pleas to be left alone, details about his life were found and published, including the facts that he was a homosexual and that he had a history of mental problems. After this information was made public, it was generally acknowledged that reporters had gone too far and should have respected the man's wishes.

Journalists are often accused of arrogance—essentially, of not having respect for others outside the profession. They are in a position to be arrogant for a number of reasons, the chief being that the First Amendment and other laws protect them from having to answer legally for most of what they do. For example, the fact that a person does not want his or her name published in the newspaper carries no legal weight. An editor can publish a name without consent, and the person has no recourse.

In addition to their legal position, the social and economic position of journalists can also spawn arrogance. Most daily newspapers in the country are monopolies; that is, they do not have any direct competition in their immediate area. Likewise,

FIGURE 25.1   Lunging into the Public Eye Oliver "Billy" Sipple (left) dives toward a woman who had just taken a shot at President Gerald Ford on September 22, 1975, outside a San Francisco hotel. Sipple grabbed the gun, wrestled it away from her, and was later regarded as a hero. When Ford took three days to thank Sipple, the *San Francisco Chronicle* ran a story speculating that it was because he was a homosexual. Sipple, an ex-Marine, had kept his homosexuality from his family, but once the story was out, his father in Detroit never spoke to him again. Sipple sued the newspaper but the case was dismissed. Sipple lapsed into obesity and alcoholism and died alone in 1989.

other media do not have to be directly responsive to individual complaints. Consequently, when people outside media organizations bring complaints or suggestions, they are not always satisfied with the response. Media professionals seem reluctant to admit mistakes or to acknowledge that there may be a point of view that is different from their own. For their part, media professionals often argue that theirs is a difficult job and that people outside the profession sometimes do not understand the procedures they must follow. Whatever the case, media people have a reputation of being unresponsive and disrespectful—a reputation that, justified or not, needs careful and constant attention.

An Approach to Ethical Behavior

Scholars and philosophers have attempted to outline many approaches to ethical behavior over the centuries, and some modern media scholars have tried to adapt these approaches to the profession of journalism. Such attempts have been occasionally interesting because the situations that journalists face involve substantive questions that many people find relevant. However, these approaches have often been ultimately dissatisfying. They are not easily applicable to the fast-paced world in which journalists work, where decisions to publish or not publish are made with few moments to spare and are often based on incomplete information.

In discussing ethical behavior, it is perhaps more productive to talk about the loyalties that journalists have to their audience, their organizations or employers, their profession, and themselves. These loyalties exert themselves simultaneously and usually harmoniously as the journalist works. Occasionally, however, these loyalties come into conflict, and the dilemma for journalists is choosing which loyalty is most important.

The basic job of journalists is to disseminate information to an audience. Journalists do not get paid, nor do news media organizations make money, by not gathering information or by withholding that information from the audience. Most journalists believe that their first duty is to their audience, and that duty is to give the audience as much information as possible. In most situations, the inclination of journalists will be to say as much as possible by finding an acceptable way to tell the audience what they know.

The information that journalists have should be properly vetted, of course. That is, it should be as full and as accurate as possible given proper journalistic procedures. The information should also be in a form that is appropriate for the medium and expected by the audience. Given that, however, disseminating information is the first duty of the journalist, and no journalist feels good about keeping information away from the audience.

Another strong loyalty that journalists feel is to their employer or news organization. Part of this loyalty stems from the fact that the news organization is providing their livelihood, and journalists—like anyone else—normally would not want to jeopardize the source of their income. But the sense of loyalty goes deeper than this. Journalists view their news organizations as the embodiment of the profession and understand the value of keeping it healthy. The news organization has rules and procedures that become the mode of practice for journalists who work there. Journalists who work for these organizations have accepted these procedures and are willing to abide by them at least for the term of their employment. Doing so is a way of preserving the stability of the profession and maintaining professional standards.

An additional element in the journalist's loyalty to the news organization is personal loyalty that develops among those who work together in an organization. Journalists who share their experiences (as well as work space, meals, and bits of information about their personal lives) often grow close to one another, help each other out, and defend each other against criticism from those outside the organization. Journalists may also develop personal loyalties to editors for whom they work. (None of this is unique to journalism, of course. Such personal loyalties can develop within any organization.)

What Do You Think?   25.1

LOYALTY TO WHAT?

The U.S. invasion of Iraq during the spring of 2003 provoked predictable reactions. Many people across the country favored the invasion and stood behind the Bush administration's decision to start the war. But many people opposed it just as strongly, and some even took to the streets. Almost every major city in the nation witnessed crowds in some prominent area, gathered to protest the war.

One of the largest demonstrations was in San Francisco. One of the people at that demonstration was Henry Norr, a technology columnist for the *San Francisco Chronicle*. He was there as a participant, not as a reporter. As a technology writer, Norr does not delve into many political issues.

Should he have been there?

The editors of the *Chronicle* did not think so, and they fired him. That set off a legal dispute that Norr and the *Chronicle* finally settled many months later. Details of the settlement were not disclosed, but Norr did not get his job back.

Should the newspaper's editors have fired him?

The paper's decision was defended by Dick Rogers, the *Chronicle*'s public editor, who argued that newspapers do not have a lot of credibility with the public and that they need to preserve what they have.

"If it were up to me, I'd take a cue from the Old West hotels that told gunslingers to check their weapons with the front desk clerk. Only the sign over the entrance to the *Chronicle* would read: 'Check your activism at the door.'"

But others argued that Norr had a First Amendment right to be a citizen, and the paper should encourage, not penalize, that. After all, the newspaper is produced under the auspices of the First Amendment. Beside, critics of the paper pointed out, Norr would have had the opinions he held whether or not he showed up at a public demonstration.

So what do you think? Should the newspaper have fired him?

And what about Norr? Should he have demonstrated knowing his newspaper's policies?

This description is not to say that all journalists are happy with their jobs or content with their organizations. Many journalists develop serious reservations about the approach their organizations take to covering the news and other journalistic methods. Even when that occurs, however, journalists understand the value of organizational loyalty and usually adhere to it in some form.

Loyalty to the profession is another means by which journalists work through ethical dilemmas. Most people who commit themselves to journalism believe that they are doing something good for society. They have accepted the norms and procedures that are the standard practice of journalism because these have been developed over a long period of time. Many of these procedures, customs, and expectations have been discussed earlier in this book (see Chapter 6) and exercise great influence on the thinking and behavior of journalists.

Finally, the profession of journalism allows a good deal of latitude for journalists to be loyal to themselves and their beliefs and attitudes and moral framework. Journalists are expected to bring to the profession a sense of honesty, integrity, and morality that will govern their actions both as they are working in the profession and as they are conducting their personal business. The profession generally does not expect them to act against personal moral precepts.

Again, none of this should lead to the impression that everyone in the profession is a paragon of moral virtue. Journalists have all of the personal failings that other people in society exhibit. But however they may fail in their personal standards, they are expected to have a good idea of what they should do in order to act humanely and morally. This sense also serves as a guide to making ethical decisions.

Ethical Difficulties

Modern journalists are most likely to confront ethical dilemmas in a number of areas described in this section. In some, the choices are fairly clear as to what the profession expects, and journalists who violate these expectations simply make the wrong choices. In other areas, however, the choices are not so clear, and the choices journalists make are open to debate.

Falsifying Information

Journalists should not make things up. They should not create "facts" that do not exist. They should not put words into the mouths of people who did not say them. They should not extend assumptions into information unless that information can be independently verified. The first duty of the journalist is to present true and accurate information. Nothing about the profession, it would seem, should be clearer.

Yet the journalism of this new century has been filled with stories of reporters who simply made up information. One of the most prominent of those stories is that of Jayson Blair, a young man of obvious talent, who was identified by editors of the *New York Times* as an excellent reporter and writer and for many month was given excellent and important assignments. (What happened to Blair's editors is described at the beginning of Chapter 8.) Blair, it seems, could always get information that other reporters could not discover. He could talk with people whom others could not find. Some editors did have doubts about his methods and abilities, but because he seemed to be favored by the top editors at the paper, these doubts were not explored.

Finally, in late April 2002, an editor of the *San Antonio Express-News* emailed the *Times* saying that information in one of Blair's stories was "disturbingly similar" to information that had appeared in his newspaper earlier in the month. That set off an investigation of Blair by the *Times* that resulted in his resignation and even the resignation of Howell Raines, the executive editor of the newspaper. Blair's deception and falsification might not be worth noting had it been an isolated incident, but the profession has been peppered with stories about reporters making up information or citing sources that turned out not to be verifiable. The fact is that violation of one of journalism's most basic tenants—presenting accurate information—is a continuing problem for the profession, and the reasons for it often mystify those who are steeped in professional principles.

Plagiarism

A related problem that haunts journalism is plagiarism— the copying of the work of another and presenting it as one's own. Jayson Blair had committed this sin against the profession, too, and that is how he was caught, but again, he is not the only one.

One of the fundamental procedures of journalism is that information is presented so that readers and viewers have an idea of its source. The basic assumption of this presentation is that the journalist has gathered the information, and what is not directly attributed is a product of the journalist's observation or experience. When journalists take the words and ideas of others and use them so they appear to be the creation of the journalist, that's plagiarism.

Plagiarism, like falsification, is a cardinal sin against the profession. Few people who get caught doing these deeds have much of a future in journalism. They cannot be trusted.

Conflicts of Interest

Less clear-cut for journalists than falsification or plagiarism is the area of conflict of interest. Journalists are supposed to be independent observers, working for a news organization and no one else. Some journalists take this sense of independence to extremes by not joining any social or civic organizations; a few even declare that they will not vote or participate in politics in any way.

Yet most journalists seek to balance their professional demands with the desire to be active and participating members of their communities. They join religious, social, civic, and even political organizations. Editors and publishers are actively sought after as members of civic and even commercial boards of directors. They have an expertise and community-wide view that few others have. Some editors have even been known to run for and hold public office (something that most in the profession would disapprove of).

So, how can journalists balance these conflicting loyalties—the loyalty to the profession and the loyalty to the desire to be a good citizen and a contributing part of the community?

Most journalists do this by trying to separate their personal activities from the organizations and events that they cover. For example, a journalist who is a member of a church that finds itself in the news would be expected not to have anything to do with the coverage of the story. Journalists are also expected to report (and get approval for) any employment they have outside of the news organization.

News organizations, of course, cannot monitor all of the activities of their reporters and editors, and they depend on their employees to be honest and forthright about what they do. Journalists are expected to inform their editors when situations arise in which there may be conflicts of interest. A journalist's loyalty to the news organization requires that he or she not put the organization in jeopardy or open the organization to criticism by allowing a conflict of interest to develop.

Another clear tenet of journalistic procedure is that reporters and editors should not accept compensation from any individual or organization for a news story other than the news organization they are working for. Journalists are rarely offered money to do a story, but they are offered many other types of gifts and gratuities. Theme parks and recreational destinations regularly give free travel and accommodations to travel writers. Movie theaters give tickets to reviewers. Promoters of sports events not only give sports writers tickets but also offer special accommodations during the event, such as certain rooms where food and drinks are free. Most news organizations have specific rules about what reporters can accept; sometimes it is an item or service that is less than $10 in value. That would preclude even being taken to lunch by someone with an interest in a story or the coverage of events. Even with the rules, however, news organizations have to rely on the honesty of the reporters to turn down such gifts or report them when they are made.

Privacy

Another area that creates ethical dilemmas for journalists is the privacy of individuals they cover. Although privacy does have some force as a legal concept (see Chapter 24), journalists generally do not get involved with the legalities of privacy. As long as journalists obtain information legally—that is, they do it without trespassing or stealing—they generally will suffer no legal consequences by publishing it.

But the human aspect of publishing information about people or even using their names does—and should—give journalists pause. As we mentioned earlier in this chapter, many people do not seek the limelight and are uncomfortable with having their names published or broadcast. They would prefer that they not be the objects of attention by journalists or the reading and viewing public. These people get caught up in news situations, and journalists, in order to do their jobs, must seek information from and about them.

When these situations are depicted in movies or television dramas, journalists are often depicted as rude, obnoxious, and unfeeling. The reality is usually quite different. Occasionally, journalists are persistent, but they often try to respect the wishes of those caught in news situations. They find there is little point in trying to persuade an unwilling source to talk or give information. Resourceful reporters know that there are many ways to get information, and harassing an individual is unnecessary and counterproductive.

Sometimes journalists face the decision of publishing very private or embarrassing information about an individual. The most publicized instances have concerned sexual activities of presidents or presidential candidates, but other instances of publishing private information pose dilemmas for journalists. Reporters and editors must decide if such information is relevant and necessary to present an accurate and fair picture of the people and events in a story. These decisions are easier when the people involved have thrust themselves before the public by running for public office or participating willingly in public debates.

Bias, Unfairness, Selective Reporting

When most people think about bias and the news media, they are likely thinking about some kind of political bias. For years the news media have been tagged as more "liberal" than their moderate or conservative audience, even though there is much evidence that conflicts with this perception. The more common and persistent problem with bias is not political, however, but what we might call "point-of-view" bias, and it does not have much to do with politics.

Every reporter approaches every story with a point of view, not necessarily political but one based on experience and inclinations. Journalistic procedure requires that reporters go through certain steps to gather information and talk to certain people. Usually these sources are experts or officials involved with the subject the reporter is covering. Which sources the reporter chooses or has the opportunity to interview will greatly influence the outcome of the story, more so than any political bias that the reporter has.

Reporters generally seek to include as many points of view about a controversial topic as they can in their stories. They try to get different versions of an event that they do not personally witness. They try to quote people as accurately as they can, even though most reporters do not have a good shorthand note-taking system. In doing all of these things, a reporter constantly exercises personal judgments about the information being gathered. The reporter has to make selections about what to use in a story and what to leave out. If an editor is particularly interested in a story, the editor's views about what is included will also come into play. Considerations of time and space—how close is the deadline, how much room is available for the story—are also influential in this selection process.

The outcome of this process is not always satisfactory to news consumers who are part of a story or vitally interested in it. They will complain that the story is biased, especially if it does not include their opinion or point of view. In a sense, they are correct. As reporters and editors select information—even as they select what stories and subjects they will cover—they are exhibiting a bias that leans toward their own inclinations about what is important and what their news organizations, given that they have limited resources, can do.

Journalists struggle with these dilemmas every day. The decisions they make are often ones of expediency given that they work under deadline pressure and in a competitive environment. Undoubtedly, they have their personal points of view about the events they cover, and sometimes those inclinations have a major influence on how stories are presented. But how could it be otherwise? Journalists are humans who attempt to achieve the status of objective observer but rarely succeed.

Persistent Problems

No matter how pure in heart or procedurally careful journalists are, they will never be able to avoid ethical dilemmas. The course of human events and activities makes conflicts and differing points of view inevitable. No system of moral behavior or ethical problem solving will provide the answers that journalists need to meet the day-to-day encounters with these conflicts.

Journalists must begin with a strong sense of personal honesty and integrity. They must understand the loyalties they are expected to exercise and must realize that sometimes journalistic procedures and conventions will bring those loyalties into conflict. They must be sensitive to their own points of view and try at every opportunity to rise above them, acting to advance not themselves but their profession and their audience.

In other words, as their mothers admonished them, they must be good and do right.

QUESTIONS FOR DISCUSSION

1. The chapter says that most journalists try to be ethical, but many people do not believe that. Some think that journalists have other agendas that they follow. What do you think? Do you have any experiences to relate in this regard?
2. Is plagiarism a problem for you or any of your colleagues? What is the nature of the problem? How is it different from the plagiarism difficulties that journalists face?
3. Select one of the situations described at the beginning of this chapter. What loyalties are involved? How do you think the situation should be resolved?
4. One fact of journalistic life that is hardly mentioned in this chapter is that of competition. Journalism is a highly competitive profession. How do you think this competition enters into ethical decision making?

RELATED WEB SITES

APME National Credibility Roundtables Project, www.apme-credibility.org

ASNE Ethics Codes Collection, www.asne.org/ideas/codes/codes.htm

Center for Religion, the Professions, and the Public, http://rpp.missouri.edu

Ethics Connection, www.scu.edu/SCU/Centers/Ethics

Ethics in Journalism, www.spj.org/ethics.asp

Ethics in Public Broadcasting, www.current.org/ethics

Ethics Matters, http://commfaculty.fullerton.edu/lester/writings/nppa.html

FAIR: Fairness and Accuracy in Reporting, www.fair.org

Global Journalism Ethics (World Press Institute), www.macalester.edu/~wpi/ethics.htm

Journal of Mass Media Ethics, http://jmme.byu.edu

Journalism Ethics Cases Online, www.journalism.indiana.edu/Ethics

OJR Section: Ethics, www.ojr.org/ojr/ethics

ONO: Organization of News Ombudsmen, www.newsombudsmen.org

Payne Awards for Ethics in Journalism, http://jcomm.uoregon.edu/departments/payneawards

Poynter Online's Ethics Journal, http://poynteronline.org/column.asp?id=53

Poynter Online's Ethics Resources, http://poynteronline.org/subject.asp?id=32

Poynter Online's Talk about Ethics, http://poynteronline.org/column.asp?id=36

RTNDA Code of Ethics, www.rtnda.org/ethics/coe.shtml

RTNDA Ethics Project and Coverage Guidelines, www.rtnda.org/ethics/fepcg.shtml

Web Resources for Studying Journalism Ethics, www2.hawaii.edu/~tbrislin/ethics/index.html

World Wide Codes of Conduct, www.presswise.org.uk/display_page.php?id=40

READINGS AND REFERENCES

Arant, D. (Ed.). (1999). *Perspectives: Ethics, issues and controversies in mass media.* St. Paul, MN: Coursewise Publishing.

Berkman, R. I., & Shumway, C. A. (2003). *Digital dilemmas: Ethical issues for online media professionals.* Ames, IA: Iowa State University Press.

Berry, D. (Ed.). (2000). *Ethics and media culture.* Woburn, MA: Focal Press.

Bertrand, C.-J. (2000). *Media ethics and accountability systems.* Piscataway, NJ: Transaction Publishers.

Bugeja, M. J. (1995). *Living ethics.* Boston: Allyn and Bacon.

Christians, C. G. (1993). *Good news.* New York: Oxford University Press.

Christians, C. G., et al. (2001). *Media ethics.* White Plains, NY: Longman Publishing Group.

Cohen, E. D., & Elliott, D. (Eds.). (1998). *Journalism ethics: A reference handbook.* Santa Barbara, CA: Abc-Clio.

Day, L. A. (2003). *Ethics in media communications* (4th ed.). Belmont, CA: Wadsworth.

Downie, L. Jr., & Kaiser, R. G. (2002). *The news about the news.* New York: Knopf.

Fallows, J. (1996). *Breaking the news: How the media undermine American democracy.* New York: Pantheon.

Fuller, J. (1996). *News values: Ideas for an information age.* Chicago: University of Chicago Press.

Goodwin, H. E., Smith, R. F., & Goodwin, G. (1999). *Groping for ethics in journalism.* Ames: Iowa State University Press.

Herbert, J. (2002). *Journalism and broadcast ethics.* Woburn, MA: Focal Press.

Iggers, J. (1998). *Good news, bad news: Journalism ethics and the public interest.* Boulder, CO: Westview Press.

Keeble, R. (2001). *Ethics for journalists.* New York: Routledge.

Knowlton, S. R. (1997). *Moral reasoning for journalists.* Westport, CT: Praeger.

Knowlton, S. R., & Parsons, P. R. (Eds.). (1995). *The journalist's moral compass.* Westport, CT: Praeger.

Kovach, B., & Rosenstiel, T. (2001). *The elements of journalism: What newspeople should know and the public should expect.* New York: Crown Publishers.

Leslie, L. Z. (2000). *Mass communication ethics: Decision making in postmodern culture.* Boston: Houghton Mifflin.

Lester, P. M. (1996). *Images that injure: Pictorial stereotypes in the media.* Westport, CT: Praeger.

Limburg, V. E. (1994). *Electronic media ethics.* Boston: Focal Press.

MacDonald, B., & Petheram, M. (1998). *Keyguide to information sources in media ethics.* London: Mansell Publishing.

Matelski, M. J. (1991). *TV news ethics.* Boston: Focal Press.

Patterson, P., & Wilkins, L. (2002). *Media ethics: Issues and cases.* Boston, MA: McGraw-Hill.

Pritchard, D. (Ed.). (2000). *Holding the media accountable: Citizens, ethics, and the law.* Bloomington: Indiana University Press.

Rosenstiel, T., & Mitchell, A. (2003). *Thinking clearly: Cases in journalistic decision-making.* New York: Columbia University Press.

Seib, P. (1994). *Campaigns and conscience: The ethics of political journalism.* Westport, CT: Praeger.

Seib, P., & Fitzpatrick, K. (1997). *Journalism ethics.* Fort Worth: Harcourt Brace.

Weaver, P. H. (1995). *News and the culture of lying: How journalism really works.* New York: The Free Press.

Chapter Twenty-six

Journalism: Present and Future

Key Concepts and Terms

1. Journalism is a profession in which even the most basic questions, such as the nature of news and the process of gathering and disseminating it, are being examined and debated continuously.

2. Journalism is an open profession; anyone can be a journalist without undergoing any training or gaining any credentials.

3. Media organizations are generally in good financial health.

4. One of the things that makes the future uncertain for journalism is the presence of the World Wide Web; no one can see clearly how it might change the practice or nature of journalism.

5. Journalists today struggle with the question of how to remain relevant to their audiences.

6. Attracting bright and thoughtful young people into journalism is one of the great challenges of today's profession.

Vignette

By the end of 2003, just about everybody in America knew the name Jessica Lynch. Most people also knew something about her, but just what they knew probably depended on how closely they had been paying attention to the news.

Jessica Lynch—19 years old, West Virginian, blond, small (some described her as "waif-like"), photogenic—had been a private in the U.S. Army. Her unit had been assigned to Iraq for combat support. Less than two weeks into the war, her unit was ambushed in central Iraq, with some soldiers killed and others captured. During that time, British and American forces had been making steady progress toward the capital city of Baghdad, but Iraqi forces were not collapsing at the sight of the Westerners as some in the Bush administration had rosily predicted.

In the midst of the not-so-good news came the word on April 1, from the U.S. Army command, that Lynch had been rescued. Anonymous sources within the Army command leaked details of Lynch's ordeal: she had fought bravely when her unit was ambushed; she had been wounded, including a stab wound that indicated hand-to-hand combat; she had "not wanted to be taken alive." Here is what the Washington Post *wrote about her on April 3, two days after her rescue:*

> *Lynch, a 19-year-old supply clerk, continued firing at the Iraqis even after she sustained multiple gunshot wounds and watched several other soldiers in her unit die around her in fighting March 23, one official said. The ambush took place after a 507th convoy, supporting the advancing 3rd Infantry Division, took a wrong turn near the southern city of Nasiriyah.*
>
> *"She was fighting to the death," the official said.*

The details of her rescue seemed equally heroic. Under cover of darkness, a Special Operations unit of the Army entered the hospital where she was being treated and whisked her away on a stretcher. The unit did not meet any resistance, but it was under constant threat, according to the Army, and it was the skill and courage of the soldiers in the unit that got her out.

In the few days after her rescue, the story of her ambush, capture, and rescue grew. Fed by Army sources, newspapers described—or, in some cases, speculated—on her actions and circumstances. Her wounds, gunshot and stabbing, were described in more detail. Her fighting determination turned her into a Rambo-like warrior. Some stories said she had been mistreated and even tortured while in captivity. In stories about her rescue, Navy Seals (a Special Operations unit of the U.S. Navy) joined the Army unit that helped get her out.

Overnight Lynch became the new American hero—a silent symbol (Lynch had not spoken to anyone in the news media about what had happened to her) that America's newest generation of young people could produce soldiers worthy of American history.

But just as this was happening, information began to emerge that did not fit into the story that had been constructed. Prompted by questioning, reporters from the

British Broadcasting Company, the Washington Post *and other news organizations began to reexamine the whole Jessica Lynch story. Ultimately, they found that:*

- *Lynch had not been engaged in a gunfight with Iraqi forces. Her unit had gotten lost when it was ambushed, and her injuries occurred because the vehicle in which she was riding had overturned. She did not shoot her gun or kill any enemy soldiers.*
- *She had not been wounded or stabbed. She had suffered numerous broken bones and other injuries because of the accident.*
- *She had not been mistreated while in captivity. Quite the opposite, she had received good treatment.*
- *Some evidence emerged that indicated some Iraqis had tried to return her to American forces but were unsuccessful. Whatever the case, her rescue was considerably less dramatic and dangerous than had first been described. All Iraqi forces had left the hospital by the time U.S. forces came to get her.*

In late May, in its reprise of the Jessica Lynch story, the Chicago Tribune *concluded that it was "the story of how a modern war icon is made and perhaps how easily journalists with different agendas accepted contradictory self-serving versions of what happened to her." (Read a more detailed assessment of the Jessica Lynch story at Journalism.Org, www.journalism.org.) The* Tribune *was one of several news organizations that revisited the whole story.*

Even though they did, however, Jessica Lynch—whatever her heroine status—had become a celebrity. She returned to her West Virginia hometown in the summer, still recovering from her injuries, with a parade, massive media coverage, and television networks vying to sign her up for news exclusive interview shows. The cycles of her story had been rapid and confounding.

The profession of journalism remains in a state of constant flux, always seemingly confused about its present and unsure about its future. What does the Jessica Lynch episode tell us about the profession and how it is practiced? Maybe not much. The circumstances of combat are highly unusual. The United States was in full combat mode, and yet information was sparse and sometimes unreliable. The war was not going as predicted, and the frustration of armed forces and administration officials with what they perceived as the "mood swings" of the media were widely known. Their claims were that the war was going better than the new media were reporting. When the Jessica Lynch story first appeared, it may have sounded too good to be true, but it gave some relief to all involved, including a concerned public.

FIGURE 26.1   Jessica Lynch Tells Her Story Jessica Lynch, second from left, and author Rick Bragg, a former reporter for the *New York Times,* sign a copy of their book *I Am a Soldier Too, The Jessica Lynch Story* at the Wirt County High School in Elizabeth, West Virginia, Saturday, December 20, 2003. Jessica's father Greg Lynch, center rear, organizes and readies books to be autographed. Lynch was always careful not to take credit for actions in battle that were attributed to her in the early reports of capture. For a time, the book was on national bestseller lists. (Photo credit: AP Wide World Photos)

But maybe Jessica Lynch's story tells us a great deal about the news media. It was a good tale with appealing characters and interesting details. Many reporters gravitated to it. As they did, they fed off of each other's reports. They also placed themselves at the mercy of sources who were not willing to be identified. The information from these sources should have been treated with more suspicion, but the pressure to report something—sometimes anything at all—in the pressurized and competitive atmosphere of today's journalism tempts reporters to set aside those suspicions.

The state of the profession and where it is headed is far more complex a topic than can be exemplified for a single incident, even one with the twists and turns of the Jessica Lynch story. To get a handle on this topic, we need to examine a variety of aspects about the news media.

An Open Profession

Almost every generation of journalists in the twentieth century spent a good deal of time and effort debating the question of whether or not journalism is a profession.

Professions are occupations that require some level of education, testing, and even governmental licensing on the part of those who enter them. In addition, the profession itself may require some additional training throughout one's career. Professionals that we are likely to know most about are attorneys, medical doctors, accountants, and clergy. One aspect of a profession that some people find particularly appealing is that they usually have a structure to police themselves; that is, when a professional violates a rule or practice of the profession, other members of the profession may judge whether or not that person should answer for that behavior.

Should journalists also be part of a profession?

Some parts of becoming a professional have great appeal, particularly the aspects of education and training. Most believe that journalists should have a college education—if not a journalism degree then a liberal arts degree of some kind. They should also be trained in the rudiments of reporting, writing, and editing. This requirement would certainly relieve employers of the responsibilities of basic on-the-job training.

Another aspect of professionalism that appeals to many people is the self-policing of professionals. Good journalists are very aware of those who do not abide by professional standards and often feel embarrassed or tarnished by them. They are often frustrated because they would like to have some way of telling the public that journalism has its own way of separating good journalism from that which does not live up to the commonly accepted standards of the field. A formal policing mechanism would also offer members of the public a way to ask questions or make complaints about those in the field. Many who argue for such a process believe that it would enhance the credibility of journalists with the public.

Finally, making journalism into a profession would likely raise the pay for those who achieve professional status. Compensation, especially entry-level pay, is a continuing problem for journalists who feel that many news organizations do not pay them what they are worth or in relation to the profits the organization makes. Status as a professional, some feel, would help alleviate this situation.

Not everyone believes that making journalism into a profession is a good idea, however. In fact, there are many who are vehemently opposed to it. Most of those people oppose it on the grounds of the First Amendment and what it is supposed to guarantee to all citizens, not just journalists. The U.S. Constitution does not guarantee all citizens the right to practice law or medicine. The opportunity to do that may be available to most of us, but it is not a fundamental right. States grant that privilege to certain people only after they have done certain things (obtain a degree, pass a test, etc.).

The First Amendment, however, does grant to all citizens the right to speak and to write (see Chapter 24). No one has to go to school or pass a test. A person can simply do it whenever he or she chooses. In the same vein, a person who makes a living doing something else can research and write an article for a newsletter, newspaper, magazine, or web site. No formal training or certification from the government is required for that activity. Nor should there be. It is a right guaranteed by the First Amendment.

The rights guaranteed by the First Amendment (freedom of religion, speech, press, and assembly and the right to petition the government) continue to be in force no matter what a person does or how that person uses or misuses those rights. (Even people in jail convicted of vicious crimes still have First Amendment rights, even though they may be limited because of incarceration.) Although the government or some professional agency can tell lawyers that they can no longer practice law or doctors that they cannot practice medicine, no government or agency can tell people they can no longer write or speak. Consequently, a self-policing journalism profession would mean a fundamental alteration of the way that we exercise basic rights.

So, probably the best that journalism can do is to call itself an "open profession," available to anyone who wishes to join it. Although journalism has no formal and enforceable policing process, it does what few other fields of endeavor do: conduct open investigations of itself and discuss vigorously its failures and shortcomings. The progress of the Jessica Lynch story shows that news organizations are often willing to examine what they do, correct their errors, and attempt to revise procedures. (Another example of this is the *New York Times*–Jayson Blair fiasco, described at the beginning of Chapter 11.) These critiques and revisions are not always satisfactory to those involved or to outside critics, but the fact that they take place at all speaks well for the field.

Financial State of the Profession

Journalism is no simple matter, and assessing its health is a complex task. An overview of various aspects of journalism shows that the profession in the early twenty-first century is thriving in many ways. Still, there are many great questions about the future and some dark clouds looming on the horizon.

Economically, most news organizations report themselves to be in good shape as the century begins. The latter half of the twentieth century witnessed the death of a great many newspapers. The number of daily newspapers in the United States declined from nearly 2,000 in 1910 to less than 1,500 in 2001. Many of the newspapers that have gone out of existence were the weaker or smaller newspaper of a two-newspaper city and had been owned by the larger paper. Eventually, they were swallowed up by the larger paper, leaving the surviving newspaper in a monopoly position.

For most newspapers, being in such a position has been extremely profitable. Many newspapers have profit margins far above other businesses, and even with the advent of new technology, the likelihood of this monopoly position being challenged is small. A one-newspaper town will probably remain a one-newspaper town for the foreseeable future. The greatest possibility for those who would like to start a new newspaper is in suburban enclaves of growing cities. As a city grows, the ability of the large newspaper located in the downtown area to cover suburbs and neighborhoods diminishes. It is also less able to serve local retail advertisers efficiently. This situation gives an opening to those who might attempt to begin a newspaper based on local readership and local advertising. Still, start-up costs are high for such ventures, and success is not guaranteed.

Despite their high profits, established newspapers do not face a cloudless future. The number of newspaper readers has been flat for many years and has begun in the last years of the twentieth century to decline slightly. Young people particularly are not growing up as newspaper readers, and although in previous generations newspapers could count on them becoming readers as they became adults, it is no longer safe to make that assumption. Many young readers get their news from the Web, and experts expect that trend to continue and grow. Newspapers are beginning to wake up to this trend and to respond by investing in their web sites and gearing them to younger readers. That response, however, has been slow and has met mighty resistance from print-loving traditionalists within the industry. The financial health of newspapers in the next generation, then, is very much in question.

Television stations have also been high-profit organizations, but they too face serious questions about their audience. A local television station can no long guarantee a local and passive audience for an advertiser. Individual viewers have many choices, a clicker that allows them to switch channels quickly, and a recording system that enables viewers to watch programs at any time and to skip the commercials if they so choose. Local cable systems are also selling advertising that can be slotted into popular national cable networks (such as CNN, MSNBC, and ESPN). In addition, the Web is eroding the monopoly that television has had in delivering breaking news immediately.

The one thing local television stations can offer viewers is local news in a timely fashion. That news, including weather and traffic information, is difficult and expensive to gather. Many television journalists are discouraged about the willingness of local stations to invest in quality news coverage. Pay scales at many stations continue to be low in an effort to save money, and many people in television journalism fear that good people will be discouraged from entering the field.

Magazines also face an uncertain future, but individual magazines have always lived more precariously than other traditional media. Magazines that have a solid readership and advertising base and that continue to deliver useful and interesting content to their readers are likely to survive. The magazine format, despite the invasion of the Web, is still an easy format for readers to use and for advertisers to understand. Magazines, however, will have to find some way of coexisting with and using the Web to maintain their print products. They need to have their web sites and print edition complement and promote one another.

News web sites, by contrast, are beginning to find a means of operation that will generate profitable revenue. Audiences for such sites are growing, and web journalists are finding new ways to use the technology to market their news and the products of their advertisers. As the economy improves from its slump at the beginning of the century, the financial outlook for news sites has brightened, and many predict that they will be highly profitable in the future.

Areas of Concern, Optimism

As journalism enters a new century, it faces a number of challenges and opportunities. The major challenge of journalism is to improve both its practices and its product in an environment of increasing speed and competition. Specifically, the profession needs to address the following issues:

FIGURE 26.2	25 Leading Media Companies

RANK U.S.	MEDIA COMPANY	HEADQUARTERS	MEDIA REVENUE 2002*
1	AOL Time Warner	New York	$28,629
2	Viacom	New York	16,326
3	Comcast Corp.	Philadelphia	16,043
4	Walt Disney Co.	New York/Burbank	9,763
5	NBC-TV (General Electric Co.)	Fairfield, CT	7,390
6	Cox Enterprises	Atlanta	7,349
7	News Corp.	Sydney	6,645
8	DirecTV (General Motors Corp.)	El Segundo, CA	6,445
9	Clear Channel Communications	San Antonio, TX	5,851
10	Gannett Co.	McLean, VA	5,617
11	Advance Publications	Newark, NJ	5,420
12	Tribune Co.	Chicago	5,162
13	Charter Communications	St. Louis	4,566
14	EchoStar Communications Corp.	Littleton, CO	4,430
15	Hearst Corp.	New York	4,231
16	Adelphia Communications Corp.	Coudersport, PA	3,426
17	Cablevision Systems Corp.	Bethpage, NY	3,292
18	The New York Times Co.	New York	3,092
19	Knight Ridder	San Jose, CA	2,841
20	Bloomberg	New York	2,240
21	The Washington Post Co.	Washington	1,963
22	Primedia	New York	1,684
23	Dow Jones & Co.	New York	1,559
24	Belo	Dallas	1,428
25	E. W. Scripps Co.	Cincinnati	1,402

*Numbers represent millions of dollars.

Source: Advertising Age, Top Media Companies, 2002.

Bias

Journalists need to continue efforts to include more points of view in their reporting. The society they cover is increasingly diverse, not just ethnically but also in attitude and spirit. Journalists who continue to reflect the information and attitudes of traditional sources will miss a great deal of the stories they are asked to cover, and more seriously, they will lose touch with their audience. Journalists should learn to reach beyond their own attitudes and experience.

Errors/Credibility

Most journalists try to gather accurate information and present it in an accurate context. Even so, they make many mistakes—mistakes that could be avoided with greater care and experience. Consequently, publishers and managers should invest more in quality people and should do more to retain people who are experienced. They also need to encourage reporters and editors to take more time in gathering and producing their reports. Although competition will always be part of the journalistic culture, competitive attitudes should be dampened when it endangers accuracy and completeness.

Sensationalism/Relevance

In its "Statement of Shared Purpose," the Committee of Concerned Journalists and the Project for Excellence in Journalism (both can be found at the Journalism.org web site) have addressed this issue elegantly:

> Keeping news in proportion and not leaving important things out are also cornerstones of truthfulness. Journalism is a form of cartography: it creates a map for citizens to navigate society. Inflating events for sensation, neglecting others, stereotyping or being disproportionately negative all make a less reliable map. The map also should include news of all our communities, not just those with attractive demographics. This is best achieved by newsrooms with a diversity of backgrounds and perspectives. The map is only an analogy; proportion and comprehensiveness are subjective, yet their elusiveness does not lessen their significance.

Intrusiveness

Journalists should recognize and constantly remind themselves that what they do has real and sometimes lasting effects on people's lives. Journalists should approach their jobs not just with a sense of purpose but also with a sense of humanity. Although most working journalists are rarely as insensitive as they are portrayed in movies and television dramas, they do need to remind themselves that their work can disrupt the lives of people. News organizations should develop a culture that allows questions to arise about the effects of their reports on the people involved.

Recruitment, Training, and Retention

One of the ongoing problems of journalism is attracting and keeping good people. Journalism training is not usually a part of high school curriculum, in part because local media do not get involved with the schools and do not insist that it be included. Where high school journalism does exist, local news organizations often are not supportive of the efforts of teachers and students. In addition, many professional journalists are openly dismissive of collegiate journalistic training. They argue, with little evidence, that such training is not valuable and not worth supporting. Finally, journalism is known as a profession that wears people out. Young people who enter the field often leave after just a few years because of the difficulty of the work, the long hours, and the low compensation. The profession needs the benefits of more people with long-term experience, and news organizations should renew their commitment to keeping their best people, paying them generously, and offering them expanding opportunities.

Changing Technology, Changing Audience

In 2003 the A. C. Nielsen company, the most prominent of the television audience measurement services, reported that young men were spending less time watching television and more time going online or playing video games. In the November sweeps period, Nielsen said, young men (ages 18–34) watched 6 percent less television than previous sweeps periods; primetime watching among this group was down nearly 8 percent. Because advertising rates that television networks and stations charge are based on such ratings, the new figures were likely to cost television a lot of money. Young men are a prime audience for advertisers because they have a lot of money to spend.

Some television executives reacted with fury—against Nielsen. They blamed Nielsen for doing shoddy research and tried to poke holes in the findings, hoping to convince advertisers that DVDs, TiVo, video games, and the Web were not drawing this audience away from the traditional media. Their fury has been indicative of the way in which traditional media (newspapers and television) have reacted to the new technology that is available to the audience and how the audience is using it.

The fact is that we have become an online society. Media Audit, another audience analysis company, reported early in 2004 that the number of "heavy users" of the Internet had surpassed that of television and newspapers and was growing. More adults spent an hour a day online rather than with a newspaper, but more significantly, online time seems also to be drawing away from time spent with television.

Still another survey organization, The Harris Poll, found in late 2003 that two-thirds of adults were online at home, work, school, the library, or some other location. The increasing availability of fast broadband connections is making online information and activities available to more people.

All of these studies indicate that the audience for the mass media is shifting. These shifts are going to change the way journalists operate and the relationship that journalists have with their readers and viewers. Just what those changes will mean is by no means clear. Journalists will continue gathering information, processing it, and disseminating it to an audience. But finding that audience and interacting with it will be a challenge that no other generation of journalists has ever had to face.

Despite these problems and challenges, the future of journalism has many bright spots. Journalism is well on its way to developing a new medium, the Web, which has myriad possibilities for innovative and creative people. Journalism remains a vital

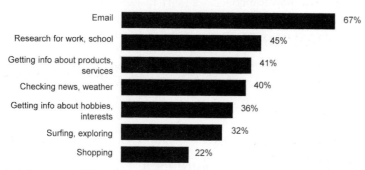

Most common online activies

Based on a survey of 729 adults in the United States
conducted by The Harris Poll, Dec. 10-16, 2003.
www.harrisinteractive.com

FIGURE 26.3   Going Online—What People Do Study after study has
shown the number of people using the Web is growing. This graph, based
on research conducted by The Harris Poll, shows what people say are their
most common activities when they go online. The number of people who
seek news, weather, and other information is significant for journalists and
for the profession of journalism.

area of endeavor, one in which individuals and organizations can make a real difference in their communities and in society as a whole. Journalism can help improve the
lives of the people it serves. As long as it does that, it will remain a field that attracts
the best and brightest people of any generation.

QUESTIONS FOR DISCUSSION

1. The chapter lists several areas to which the field of journalism needs to pay attention. Can you think of others where the field might be having problems?
2. One area of concern for the future of journalism is the concentration of ownership. Many news organizations that were once independently owned are now part
   of conglomerate companies. What effect will that have on the profession?
3. How can journalists and news organizations connect more effectively with young
   people so that they become a reliable part of the news organization's audience?
4. Is journalism an attractive profession for you? Why or why not?

RELATED WEB SITES

Cyberjournalist, www.cyberjournalist.net

New Directions for News, www.newdirectionsfornews.com

NewsLab, www.newslab.org

Online Journalism Review, www.ojr.org

Poynter Institute, www.poynter.org

READINGS AND REFERENCES

Downie, L., & Kaiser, R. (2003). *The news about the news.* New York: Vintage Books.

Fallows, J. (1996). *Breaking the news: How the media undermine American democracy.* New York: Pantheon.

Fuller, J. (1997). *News values: Ideas for an information age.* Chicago: University of Chicago Press.

Kovach, B., & Rosenstiel, T. (2001). *The elements of journalism: What newspeople should know and the public should expect.* New York: Crown.

Jamieson, K. H., & Waldman, P. (2002). *The press effect: Politicians, journalists and the stories that shape the political world.* New York: Oxford Press.

Serrin, W. (Ed.). (2000). *The business of journalism.* New York: New Press.

Index